Microsoft® Office 2010

FUNDAMENTALS

Laura Story
Dawna Walls

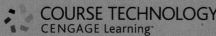
COURSE TECHNOLOGY
CENGAGE Learning™

Australia • Brazil • Japan • Korea • Mexico • Singapore • Spain • United Kingdom • United States

COURSE TECHNOLOGY
CENGAGE Learning

Microsoft® Office 2010 Fundamentals
Laura Story and Dawna Walls

Executive Editor: Donna Gridley

Freelance Product Manager: Tricia Coia

Development Editors: Jeanne Herring, Karen Porter

Associate Product Manager: Amanda Lyons

Editorial Assistant: Kimberly Klasner

Content Project Manager: Lisa Weidenfeld

Marketing Manager: Julie Schuster

Director of Manufacturing: Denise Powers

Text Designer: Shawn Girsberger

Manuscript Quality Assurance Lead: Jeff Schwartz

Manuscript Quality Assurance Reviewers: Green Pen
    Quality Assurance, John Freitas, Serge Palladino,
    Danielle Shaw, Marianne Snow, Susan Whalen

Copy Editor: Mark Goodin

Proofreader: Vicki Zimmer

Indexer: Rich Carlson

Art Director: Faith Brosnan

Cover Designer: Robert Pehlke

Cover Image: © Digital Vision Photography / Veer

Compositor: GEX Publishing Services

Library of Congress Control Number: 2010932617

ISBN-13: 978-0-538-47246-3
ISBN-10: 0-538-47246-4

Course Technology
20 Channel Center Street
Boston, Massachusetts 02210
USA

Cengage Learning is a leading provider of customized learning solutions with office locations around the globe, including Singapore, the United Kingdom, Australia, Mexico, Brazil, and Japan. Locate your local office at: **international.cengage.com/region**

Cengage Learning products are represented in Canada by Nelson Education, Ltd.

To learn more about Course Technology, visit **www.cengage.com/coursetechnology**

To learn more about Cengage Learning, visit **www.cengage.com**

Any fictional data related to persons or companies or URLs used throughout this book is intended for instructional purposes only. At the time this book was printed, any such data was fictional and not belonging to any real persons or companies.

Printed in the United States of America
1 2 3 4 5 6 7 12 11 10

ABOUT THIS BOOK

Microsoft Office 2010 Fundamentals introduces students to the programs included in the Microsoft Office 2010 suite of software. By following the lessons presented in this text, students will quickly and efficiently learn to use Word, Excel, PowerPoint, Access, and Publisher to create professional-looking documents, spreadsheets, presentations, databases, and publications. *Microsoft Office 2010 Fundamentals* presents the basic features and commands for each of these programs in an easy-to-follow, hands-on approach.

It is very important that students watch their screens carefully as they work through the exercises in this book. If a student clicks the mouse or presses keys without understanding what is happening, they will miss a great deal. It is also important to work through each lesson within a unit in the order presented. Each lesson builds on what was learned in previous lessons, so it is vital to complete lessons thoroughly and in order. Instructors may choose to work through the units in a different order; for example, it does not matter whether the instructor approaches the Access unit before completing the Word unit.

Every effort is made throughout this book to use Microsoft terminology when working with the programs. The first few times a student uses a tool within a program, the student might need to refer to this book or the Help system to refresh their memory about the steps involved.

Some keyboards do not have the full range of keys; however, students should be able to access a needed keystroke with alternate combination keys, which are described in the lessons.

Instructors can assign as many or as few of the projects at the end of the lesson as they like. The projects concentrate on the main concepts covered in the lesson and provide valuable opportunities to apply or extend the skills learned in the lesson.

About the Authors

Laura Story and Dawna Walls, both graduates of Texas Tech University, have co-authored six books for Course Technology and have collaborated on dozens of other writing and editing projects during the past two decades, including software textbooks, user's guides, tutorials, i-manuals, site documentation, training material, and supplements. With similar backgrounds in technical writing, Web development, computer education, and the IT industry, they bring a breadth of experience and expertise to the teaching process.

Start-up Checklist

Hardware

- Computer and processor: 500 megahertz (MHz) processor or higher
- Memory: 256 megabyte (MB) RAM or higher
- Hard disk: 3.5 gigabyte (GB) available disk space
- Display: 1024 × 768 or higher resolution monitor

Software

- Operating system: Windows XP with Service Pack (SP) 3, Windows Vista with SP1, or Windows 7

Features of This Book

Microsoft Office 2010 Fundamentals covers the primary features and commands of each program in self-contained units. Units can comprise multiple lessons. Units with multiple lessons include unit review sections that present a summary of exercise and practice activities and serve as an additional learning tool. Within each lesson, the program's various features and tools are first presented in a conceptual discussion, as well as the skills required to understand these features. Appendices on the Windows 7 operating system and Microsoft Outlook extend students' understanding of the Office suite.

Microsoft Office 2010 Fundamentals emphasizes learning by going through the hands-on application of concepts. Each conceptual discussion is followed by a Step-by-Step exercise that allows students to apply the concepts just covered. Commands and buttons students should click during the exercises, and text the students should type, are all shown in boldface text. Figures showing students what their screen should look like at certain points in the Step-by-Step help them stay on track.

The figures in this book show the Office program windows as they appear at a screen resolution of 1024 × 768; modifying screen settings might cause the buttons, Ribbons, and other Office features to look slightly different on students' screens. Regardless of any visual discrepancy, students will be able to follow the steps and complete the exercises by referring to the figures in each lesson. Each lesson has been through Course Technology's rigorous quality assurance testing program to ensure the validity of the steps and data files provided with the book.

Many lessons require students to use data files. Data files are available on the Review Pack and Instructor Resources CD, and online behind the Cengage Learning-wide platform SSO (Single Sign On). Depending on security settings, data files may initially open with a yellow Protected View bar near the top of the program window. In that event, students should click Enable Editing to begin working with the file.

Students can expand their mastery of the text content by referring to text in the Extra for Experts boxes, which provides advanced information related to conceptual information. Warning boxes address potential issues students might encounter and offer solutions to those problem scenarios. Key vocabulary terms appear in boldface and italic type in the text where they are defined. Key vocabulary terms are also compiled in a glossary at the end of the text for easy reference.

Each lesson concludes with a lesson summary, a vocabulary list of terms defined in the lesson, multiple-choice exercises, and fill-in-the-blank exercises. Individual projects, Teamwork or Web projects, and Critical Thinking activities are designed to help students practice the skills covered in the lesson. Some projects have optional On Your Own activities that provide open-ended challenges for students to go a step further using select commands. The instructor might assign a combination of exercises and projects.

To complete all lessons, this book will require approximately 30.5 hours of classroom contact time. Hours required for end-of-lesson activities and reviews vary depending on the number and type of activities selected.

INSIDE FUNDAMENTALS

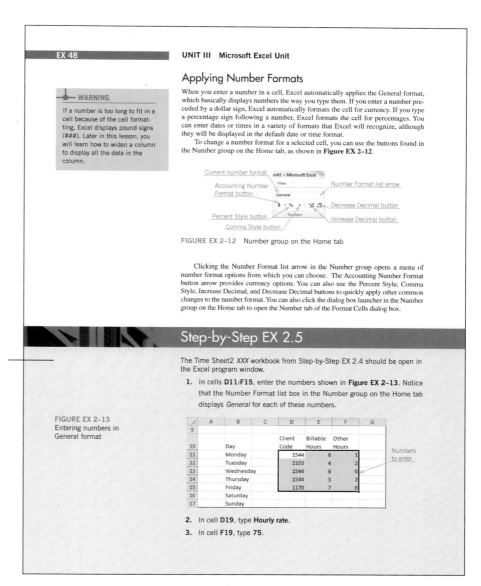

Step-by-Step Exercises offer "hands-on practice" of the material just learned. Each exercise uses a data file or requires you to create a file from scratch.

Lesson opener elements include the **Objectives** and **Suggested Completion Time**.

End of Lesson elements include the **Summary**, **Vocabulary Review**, **Review Questions**, **Lesson Projects**, and **Critical Thinking Activities**.

Instructor Resources Disk

ISBN-13: 978-0-538-47247-0
ISBN-10: 0-538-47247-2

The Instructor Resources disk contains the following teaching resources:

The Data and Solution files for this course

ExamView® tests for each lesson

Instructor's Manual that includes lecture notes for each lesson and references to the end-of-lesson activities and Unit Review projects

Answer Keys that include solutions to the lesson and unit review questions

Copies of the figures that appear in the student text

Suggested Syllabus with block, two quarter, and 18-week schedule

Annotated Solutions and Grading Rubrics

PowerPoint presentations for each lesson

Spanish glossary

ExamView®

This textbook is accompanied by ExamView, a powerful testing software package that allows instructors to create and administer printed, computer (LAN-based), and Internet exams. ExamView includes hundreds of questions that correspond to the topics covered in this text, enabling students to generate detailed study guides that include page references for further review. The computer-based and Internet testing components allow students to take exams at their computers, and save the instructor time by grading each exam automatically.

SAM 2010 SAM

SAM 2010 Assessment, Projects, and Training version 1.0 offers a real-world approach to applying Microsoft Office 2010 skills. The Assessment portion of this powerful and easy-to-use software simulates Office 2010 applications, allowing users to demonstrate their computer knowledge in a hands-on environment. The Projects portion allows students to work live-in-the-application on project-based assignments. The Training portion helps students learn in the way that works best for them by reading, watching, or receiving guided help.

- SAM 2010 captures the key features of the actual Office 2010 software, allowing students to work in high-fidelity, multi-pathway simulation exercises for a real-world experience.

- SAM 2010 includes realistic and explorable simulations of Office 2010, Windows 7 coverage, and a new user interface.

- Easy, web-based deployment means SAM is more accessible than ever to both you and your students.

- Direct correlation to the skills covered on a chapter-by-chapter basis in your Course Technology textbooks allows you to create a detailed lesson plan.

- SAM Projects offers live-in-the-application project-based assignments. Student work is automatically graded, providing instant feedback. A unique cheating detection feature identifies students who may have shared files.

- Because SAM Training is tied to textbook exams and study guides, instructors can spend more time teaching and let SAM Training help those who need additional time to grasp concepts.

ACKNOWLEDGMENTS

Many thanks to Donna Gridley for this opportunity; to Jeanne Herring and Karen Porter for the vital role they played in shaping this book with their editorial expertise; to Tricia Coia for her skillful management of this project; and to Lisa Weidenfeld and the GEX team for their excellent production work.

Laura Story: Thanks to Dawna who has unfailingly kept me laughing and sane one project after another and to Karen, whose exceptional helicopter skills kept me on track for this one.

Dawna Walls: Thanks to Laura for being a competent and congenial co-author, to Jeanne for always improving my work, and to my family and friends for their continued love and support.

THE FUNDAMENTALS ARE KEY

Integrate extra hands-on practice for your students with the *Microsoft® Office 2010 Fundamentals Projects Binder*. This binder has 150 step-by-step projects that allow students to expand their Microsoft Office 2010 skills within a variety of scenarios. The variety of real-world business, personal, school, community, and cross-curricular projects give students the hands-on practice they need with the Microsoft Office 2010 versions of Word, Excel, PowerPoint, Access, and Publisher, as well as Integrated projects. In addition, open-ended and critical thinking projects provide extended learning opportunities for more advanced students. This learning-by-doing approach helps prepare students to use these skills in their personal and professional lives.

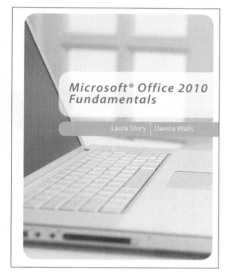

ISBN-13: 978-0-538-47989-9
ISBN-10: 0-538-47989-2

CONTENTS

UNIT I GETTING STARTED

UNIT II MICROSOFT WORD

UNIT III MICROSOFT EXCEL

UNIT IV   MICROSOFT POWERPOINT

UNIT V   MICROSOFT ACCESS

UNIT VI MICROSOFT PUBLISHER

UNIT VII INTEGRATION BASICS

UNIT I

GETTING STARTED

LESSON 1   1.5 HRS.

Working with Microsoft Office 2010

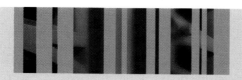

LESSON 1

Working with Microsoft Office 2010

■ OBJECTIVES

Upon completion of this lesson, you should be able to:

■ Describe Microsoft Office 2010 and its programs.

■ Start an Office program.

■ Identify the parts of an Office window.

■ Access contextual tools.

■ Customize Office programs.

■ Get help with Office.

■ Close an Office program.

■ DATA FILES

You do not need data files to complete this lesson.

■ VOCABULARY

Backstage view

badge

contextual tabs

dialog box launcher

gallery

groups

integrate

interface

KeyTip

launch

Live Preview

Microsoft Office 2010

Mini toolbar

Office

Quick Access Toolbar

Ribbon

ScreenTip

suite

tabs

Introduction to Microsoft Office 2010

Microsoft Office 2010

Office

interface

suite

integrate

Microsoft Office 2010, or *Office*, is a group of computer programs that provides different tools for completing certain tasks. For example, you can create documents, analyze data, organize information, and prepare presentations. Even though the Office programs help you to accomplish different tasks, they all use the same basic *interface*, or way of interacting with you, the user. This means the programs have a similar appearance; they share common elements and commands, and many tasks are performed the same way in each program. Once you learn how to work with one program, you know the fundamentals of the other programs as well.

Office comes in different suites. Each *suite* is a package that combines some or all of the Office programs. The Office programs on your computer will vary depending on which Office suite is installed, but at a minimum you will have Word, Excel, and PowerPoint. **Table GS 1–1** describes the Office programs that you will learn about in this book. You can also visit the Microsoft Office Web site at *http://www.microsoft.com/office/2010* to learn more about the various Office suites available or to get more information about individual Office programs.

Each Office program is also designed to work well together, or *integrate*, with the other programs in the suite by easily sharing or transferring information. You will learn more about how to integrate Office programs later in this book.

In this lesson, you will learn some basic skills for using Office programs. Because Word is probably the most widely used Office program, this lesson uses Word to demonstrate these skills, but you can use the same procedures for other programs.

TABLE GS 1–1   Office 2010 programs

ICON	PROGRAM	DESCRIPTION
	Word	Word-processing program used to create documents such as letters, research papers, memos, and reports
	Excel	Spreadsheet program used to enter, calculate, analyze, and visually represent numerical data
	PowerPoint	Presentation program used to create a collection of slides containing text, pictures, charts, and other visual items for slide shows, meetings, or Web pages
	Access	Database program used to compile, track, report, and manage related information
	Publisher	Publication program used to create and edit publications such as newsletters, brochures, flyers, or business cards
	Outlook	Personal information management program used to send and receive e-mail, set up a calendar, manage tasks, and record contacts

Starting an Office Program

To begin using an Office program, you first need to start, or *launch* it. You can do this by clicking the Start button on the Windows taskbar, and then clicking the program name (or the folder name and then the program name) on the All Programs menu, or by double-clicking a program icon on the desktop. When the program has launched, you can use it to create a new document or file, or you can open an existing file. Once you begin using an Office program frequently, it will be listed in the left pane of the Start menu, and you can click the program name from that list to open the program.

Throughout this book, it is assumed that your computer is turned on and the Windows 7 desktop is displayed on your computer screen. You can learn more about working in the Windows 7 operating system in Appendix A.

▶ **VOCABULARY**
launch

⊞ EXTRA FOR EXPERTS

To create a desktop shortcut to an Office program, right-click the name of the program on the All Programs menu, point to Send to, and then click Desktop (create shortcut) to place a program icon on the desktop. Then you can double-click the program icon on the desktop to open the program.

Step-by-Step GS 1.1

1. Click the **Start** button 🌐 on the Windows taskbar. The Start menu opens.

2. Click **All Programs**. A list of programs and program folders opens in the left pane of the Start menu. This list varies depending on the programs that are installed on your computer.

3. Click the **Microsoft Office** program folder (scroll if necessary). A list of available Microsoft Office programs opens, as shown in **Figure GS 1–1**.

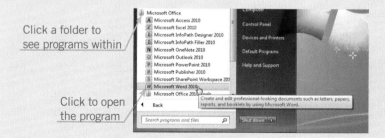

Click a folder to see programs within

Click to open the program

FIGURE GS 1–1
All Programs pane

4. Click **Microsoft Word 2010**. Microsoft Word 2010 starts, and its program window opens on the desktop with a new, blank document displayed.

Identifying the Parts of an Office Window

When you start Word, you will see a program window similar to the one in **Figure GS 1–2**. Many parts of this window are the same for other programs in the Office 2010 suite. Use this figure and **Table GS 1–2** to become familiar with these common elements.

TABLE GS 1–2   Common program window elements in Office 2010

ELEMENT	FUNCTION
Ribbon	Provides access to a collection of commands organized by tabs and groups
File tab	Displays Backstage view, which contains common file-related commands, such as Save, Open, and Close, as well as other document management tasks and information
Program icon	Visually identifies the program that is open; when clicked it displays a menu with options for sizing, moving, or closing the open window
Quick Access Toolbar	Keeps icons for frequently used commands, such as Save, Undo, and Redo, in a convenient location
Title bar	Shows the name of the active program and the file name
Windows sizing buttons	Adjusts the size of the program window
Help button	Provides assistance with the program
Insertion point	Blinking vertical bar indicates where the next character you type will appear
Scroll bar	Adjusts the view in the document window to access another part of the document
Status bar	Displays information about current position and settings
View buttons	Changes the way the document, worksheet, or presentation is displayed on the screen
Zoom controls	Magnifies or decreases the content currently displayed on the screen

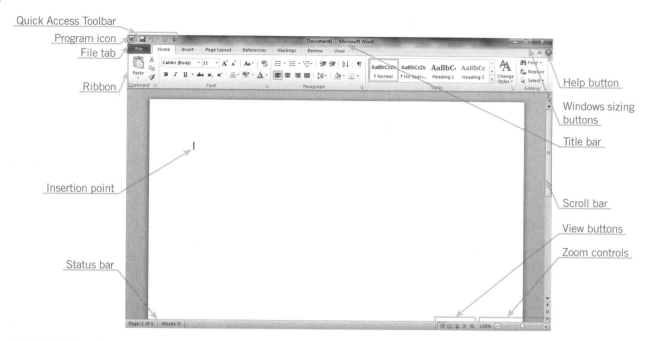

FIGURE GS 1–2 Word program window

Using the Ribbon

The *Ribbon*, shown in **Figure GS 1–3**, is an element of the program window that displays and organizes the commands and tools of the program for easy access.

FIGURE GS 1–3 The Ribbon

Commands on the Ribbon are organized into categories, called *tabs,* and each one relates to a particular type of activity in that program. You can click a tab to activate it and display related commands. On a tab, commands are organized into *groups*, or logical sets of related commands. For example, the Home tab includes the Font group of commands, with options for selecting font faces, changing font size, and applying font styles and effects. The set of tabs available on the Ribbon can also change depending on the task you are working on. The Table Tools tabs in Word are displayed only when a table is selected, for instance. The tabs that appear only under certain conditions are called *contextual tabs*.

Some groups have a *dialog box launcher* in the lower-right corner—a small arrow that you click to open a dialog box or task pane with more options for executing related commands. Dialog boxes appear on top of the program window, and task panes appear to the side.

To choose a command, you click a button on the Ribbon. Some buttons have arrows that are part of the button, like the Change Styles button in the Styles group

▶ **VOCABULARY**

Ribbon

tabs

groups

contextual tabs

dialog box launcher

▶ **VOCABULARY**

gallery

Live Preview

 EXTRA FOR EXPERTS

You can personalize the Ribbon by creating a custom tab to keep all the features you need easily accessible in one place. Click the File tab and then click Options to open the Options dialog box. Click Customize Ribbon, and in the lower-right corner of the dialog box click the New Tab button, and then choose the commands you want.

on the Home tab. When you click a button with an arrow, a menu opens and you can choose from a list of options. Some buttons have a list arrow that you can click separately from the button, like the Paste button in the Clipboard group on the Home tab. When you click the icon part of the button, a command is executed, and when you click the list arrow on the button, a menu opens with a list of options.

Some tabs on the Ribbon include galleries. A *gallery* is a set of options that shows you a sample end result, which simplifies the process of making choices. If a gallery has more options than those shown on the Ribbon, you can click the More button to see the full gallery. When using galleries, you can take advantage of *Live Preview*, a feature that previews the editing or formatting change to your document as you point to a gallery option. This allows you to experiment with the end result before actually making a selection.

To increase available window space, you can hide the Ribbon by clicking the Minimize the Ribbon button next to the Help button on the right. The Minimize the Ribbon button changes to the Expand the Ribbon button, which you can then click to display the entire Ribbon again. You can also show or hide the Ribbon by double-clicking the name of the active tab. When the Ribbon is hidden, only the tab names are shown.

Step-by-Step GS 1.2

A new, blank document from Step-by-Step GS 1.1 should be open in the Word program window.

1. Click the **Insert** tab and notice the commands available.

2. Click each tab on the Ribbon and notice how the commands are organized in groups.

3. Click the **Home** tab to display the commands available on this tab.

4. In the Clipboard group, click the **Clipboard dialog box launcher** to open the Clipboard task pane.

5. In the Font group, click the **Font dialog box launcher** to open the Font dialog box. Your screen should look similar to **Figure GS 1–4**.

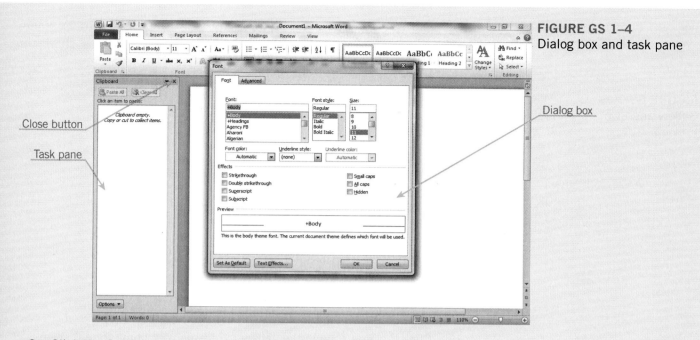

6. Click the **Cancel** button to close the Font dialog box.

7. Click the **Close** button in the upper-right corner of the Clipboard task pane to close it.

8. In the Clipboard group, click the **Paste** button arrow to open the menu shown in **Figure GS 1–5**. Notice that the arrow can be clicked separately from the button.

9. In the Styles group, click the **Change Styles** button to open the menu. Notice that the arrow is part of the button and cannot be clicked separately.

10. Click a blank area of the document window to close the menu, and then type your **first name** and **last name**.

11. On the Home tab, in the Styles group, click the **More** button to display the full Styles gallery.

12. Point to the **Intense Quote** style and notice how Live Preview shows what that change would look like in your document, as shown in **Figure GS 1–6**.

FIGURE GS 1–6
Gallery and Live
Preview

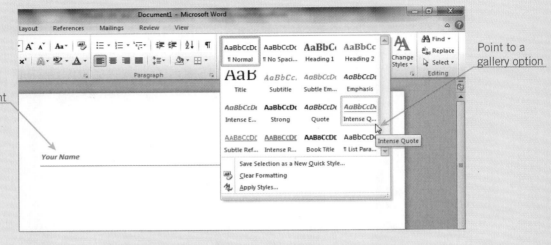

13. Click the **Title** style in the gallery to change your name to that style.

14. Leave the document open for use in the next Step-by-Step.

Using Backstage View

Backstage view allows you to access file-related commands, such as those used to open, save, and close documents. You can also view information about your document and perform document management tasks such as attaching the document to an e-mail or restricting what types of changes other people can make to the document. To display Backstage view, you click the File tab to the left of the other Ribbon tabs. In Backstage view, when you click an option on the menu in the left pane, a list of related options opens on the right.

Customizing the Quick Access Toolbar

EXTRA FOR EXPERTS

You can add a command to the Quick Access Toolbar directly from the Ribbon. Right-click the command on the Ribbon that you want to add, and then click Add to Quick Access Toolbar on the shortcut menu.

The *Quick Access Toolbar* is a toolbar located on the left side of the title bar that contains regularly used tools, making them easy to find. The Save, Undo, and Redo (or Repeat) commands are available by default, but you can add others by clicking the Customize Quick Access Toolbar button to open a menu of common commands that you can select to add. You can also click More Commands for additional options.

The Quick Access Toolbar can be positioned in two places in the program window—in its default location on the title bar or just below the Ribbon. To move the Quick Access Toolbar below the Ribbon, click Show Below the Ribbon on the Customize Quick Access Toolbar menu. To move it back to its default position, click Show Above the Ribbon on the same menu.

Step-by-Step GS 1.3

The document from Step-by-Step GS 1.2 should be open in the Word program window.

1. Click the **File** tab on the Ribbon to access the file-related commands.

2. Click **Info** if necessary, and then click the **Check for Issues** button to open a list of related commands, as shown in **Figure GS 1–7**.

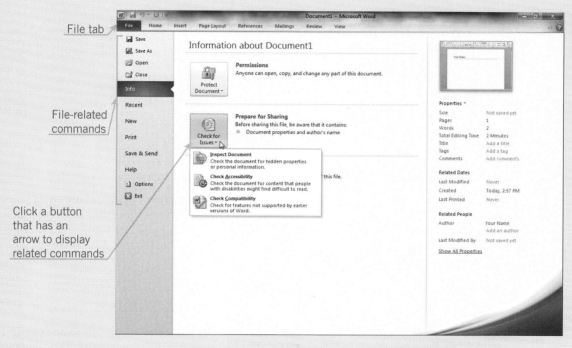

FIGURE GS 1–7
File commands in Backstage view

3. Click the **File** tab again to return to your document.

4. Click the **Customize Quick Access Toolbar** button ⏷ on the Quick Access Toolbar to open the menu shown in **Figure GS 1–8**.

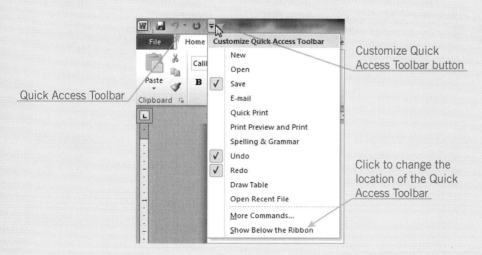

FIGURE GS 1–8
Quick Access Toolbar and menu

5. Click **Show Below the Ribbon** to move the Quick Access Toolbar below the Ribbon, as shown in **Figure GS 1–9**.

FIGURE GS 1–9
Quick Access Toolbar positioned below the Ribbon

Quick Access Toolbar

6. Click the **Customize Quick Access Toolbar** button again, and click **Show Above the Ribbon** to move the Quick Access Toolbar back to its original location.

7. Leave the document open for use in the next Step-by-Step.

Accessing Contextual Tools

Some tools in Office are visible all the time, and others are displayed only when you need them. Just as contextual tabs on the Ribbon become available when you are working with certain items, there are also contextual tools that are displayed only when needed. These contextual tools provide shortcuts to help you access commands more quickly when you are working with selected items.

Using the Mini Toolbar and Shortcut Menus

VOCABULARY
Mini toolbar

The *Mini toolbar* is a small toolbar of common formatting commands that becomes available when you select text. The Mini toolbar opens above the selected text and is transparent, becoming active only after you point to a command on it. When you move the mouse pointer away from the selected text, the Mini toolbar closes. You cannot customize the Mini toolbar.

The active Mini toolbar also opens at the top of the shortcut menu that opens when you right-click selected text or a selected object, as shown in **Figure GS 1–10**. Shortcut menus provide a quick way to access relevant commands. To close the Mini toolbar and shortcut menu, press Esc or click elsewhere in the document.

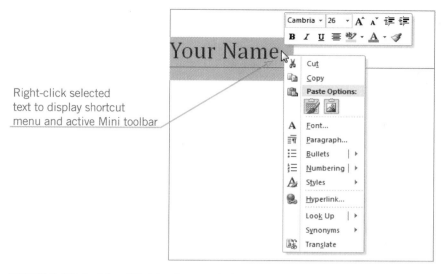

FIGURE GS 1–10   Mini toolbar and shortcut menu

Using KeyTips

If you prefer using the keyboard instead of the mouse, you can access all the options on the Ribbon using KeyTips. A *KeyTip* is a small label with a letter or number, called a *badge*, that appears on each button, menu, or command on the Ribbon when you press Alt, as shown in **Figure GS 1–11**. You can execute a command by pressing the KeyTip or a sequence of KeyTips. The KeyTips disappear when you have executed a command, or you can press Alt again to remove the KeyTips without executing a command.

▶ **VOCABULARY**
KeyTip
badge

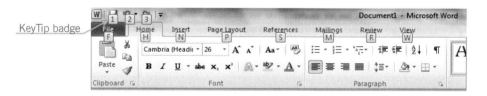

FIGURE GS 1–11   KeyTips

Step-by-Step GS 1.4

The document from Step-by-Step GS 1.3 should be open in the Word program window.

1. Select **Your Name** in the document. The transparent Mini toolbar opens, as shown in **Figure GS 1–12**.

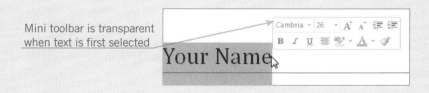

FIGURE GS 1–12
Mini toolbar

2. Point to any button on the Mini toolbar to activate the toolbar.

3. Move the mouse pointer away from the Mini toolbar until it closes.

4. Right-click **Your Name** to display the shortcut menu and active Mini toolbar.

5. Click **Cut** on the shortcut menu to remove your name. The Mini toolbar and shortcut menu also close. Notice the line that is part of the Title style remains.

6. Press **Alt** to display the KeyTips on the Ribbon.

7. Press the **W** key, which is the KeyTip for the View tab. The View tab becomes the active tab and each command displays a KeyTip, as shown in **Figure GS 1–13**.

FIGURE GS 1–13
KeyTips on View tab

8. Press the **J** key to zoom your document to 100% of its normal size, if it is not already. Notice that the KeyTips disappear after you have executed a command.

9. Leave the document open for use in the next Step-by-Step.

Customizing Office Programs

The default Office program settings are not always ideal for everyone. It is easy to customize various aspects of the Office programs to suit the way you work.

Changing Program Options

You can customize program settings in any Office program. For example, in Word, you can click the File tab to display Backstage view and then click Options to open the Word Options dialog box. In this dialog box, you can customize settings for various Word tools. You customize program settings in the other Office programs following a similar procedure.

Using Zoom Controls

You can control the size of your document on the screen using the Zoom controls, shown in **Figure GS 1–14**, located on the right side of the status bar. To zoom out and see more of your document, click the Zoom Out button. To zoom in and see a closer view of your document, click the Zoom In button. Or you can move the Zoom slider to the percentage zoom setting you want. To access more zoom options, click the Zoom level button to open the Zoom dialog box.

EXTRA FOR EXPERTS

In the programs that have Zoom controls, you can also access zoom settings in the Zoom group on the View tab of the Ribbon.

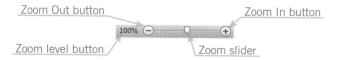

FIGURE GS 1–14   Zoom controls

Resizing Program Windows

At any given time, there are three sizing buttons on the right side of the title bar that you can use to adjust the size of the program window—the Minimize button, the Restore Down or Maximize button, and the Close button. See **Figure GS 1–15**. Click the Minimize button to reduce the window to a program button on the Windows taskbar. When you want to redisplay the program window, click the program button on the taskbar. If you want to make the program window smaller so you can see some of the desktop, click the Restore Down button. The Restore Down button changes to the Maximize button, which you can then click to make the window full size again. To close the open document and the program, click the Close button.

FIGURE GS 1–15   Windows resizing buttons

You can also manually resize the program window by pointing to a corner or border of a window that has been restored down until the mouse pointer changes to a two-headed arrow. Then you can click and drag the border or corner to resize the window as desired.

EXTRA FOR EXPERTS

When you right-click the Windows taskbar, a shortcut menu opens with options to cascade all open program windows, show windows stacked, show windows side by side, or show the desktop by minimizing all windows at once.

EXTRA FOR EXPERTS

You can also move, resize, or close a document by clicking the program icon in the upper-left corner and then clicking a command from the menu.

Step-by-Step GS 1.5

The document from Step-by-Step GS 1.4 should be open in the Word program window.

1. Click the **File** tab on the Ribbon to access the file-related commands.

2. Click **Options** to open the Word Options dialog box, shown in **Figure GS 1–16**.

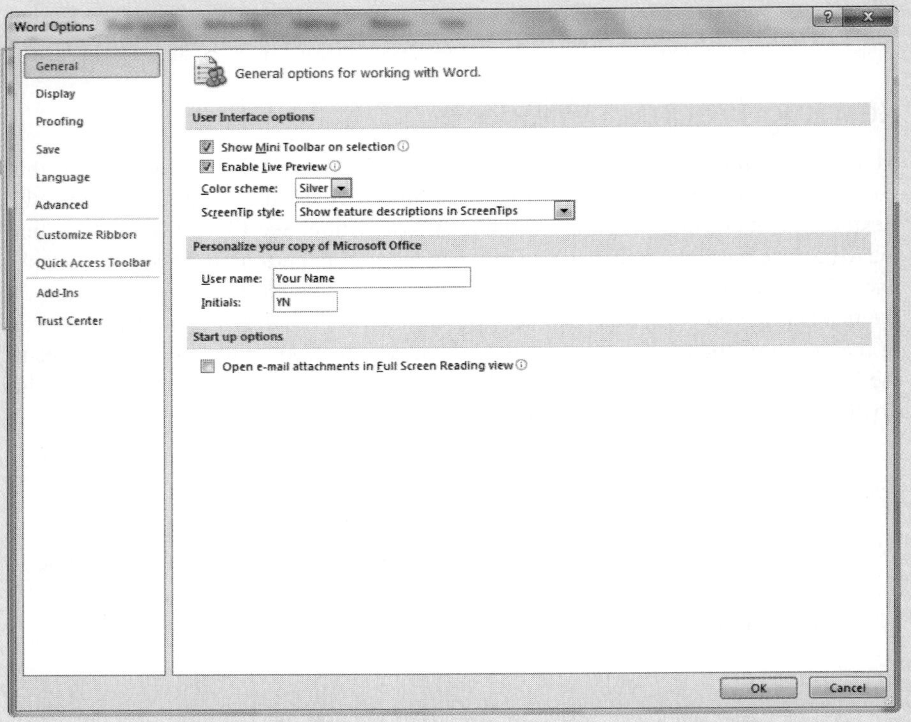

FIGURE GS 1–16
General settings in
the Word Options
dialog box

Click an option
to see additional
settings to customize

3. Click each of the options in the left pane to view the related settings in the right pane that you can customize, and then click the **Cancel** button to close the Word Options dialog box.

4. Click the **Zoom Out** button ⊖ on the status bar to zoom your document to 90%.

5. Click the **Zoom In** button ⊕ twice to zoom your document to 110%.

6. Drag the **Zoom** slider to the left until your document zooms to approximately 75%.

7. Click the **Zoom level** button to open the Zoom dialog box. See **Figure GS 1–17**.

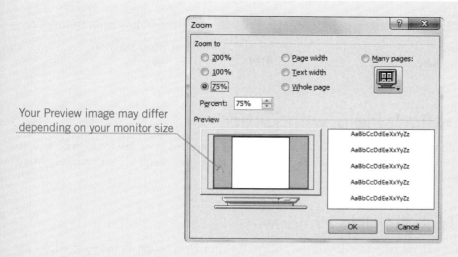

FIGURE GS 1–17
Zoom dialog box

Your Preview image may differ depending on your monitor size

8. In the Zoom to section, click the **100%** option button, and then click the **OK** button to close the Zoom dialog box.

9. Click the **Minimize** button ⬜ on the title bar to reduce the window to a button on the taskbar.

10. Click the **Word** program button on the taskbar to display the Word program window again.

11. Click the **Restore Down** button ⬜. The window is resized.

12. Position the mouse pointer on the lower-right corner until it changes to a two-headed arrow, as shown in **Figure GS 1–18**, and then click and drag up to the left to make the window smaller.

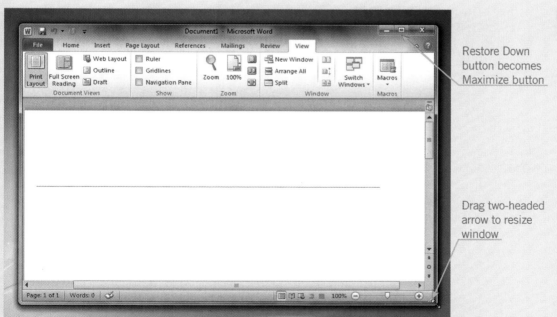

FIGURE GS 1–18
Resized window

Restore Down button becomes Maximize button

Drag two-headed arrow to resize window

13. Click the **Maximize** button 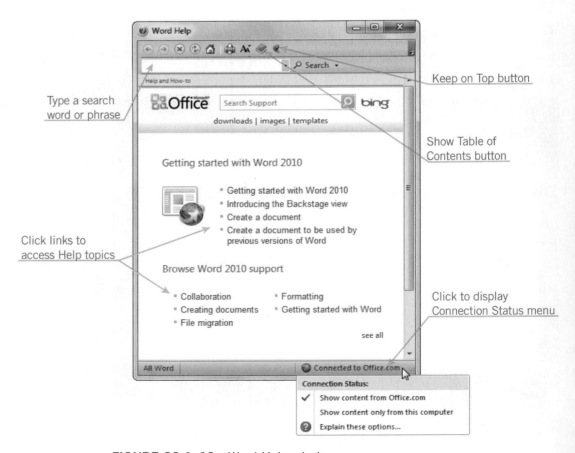 to change the window back to full size.

14. Leave the document open for use in the next Step-by-Step.

Getting Help with Office

You will learn many skills in this book, but if you need more information on how to use the tools in Office to accomplish a task, there are several ways to get help using the Office Help system.

Using the Help Window

You can get help by clicking the Microsoft Office Help button on the right side of the Ribbon, or you can press F1 to open a Help window. **Figure GS 1–19** shows the Word Help window. You can use the Help window to browse topics or search for a specific word or phrase. You can also view a complete table of contents for the Help system by clicking the Show Table of Contents button in the Help window. When working with Help, you can choose to display the Help window on top of the open program window, or you can choose to leave Help open behind your program window, and access it from the Help window button on the Windows taskbar. You select these options for displaying the Help window by toggling the Keep On Top and Not On Top buttons.

FIGURE GS 1–19   Word Help window

At the bottom of the Help window, there is the Connected to Office.com button that you can click to display the Connection Status menu. You can use this menu to choose whether you want to access online or offline content in the Help window.

Using ScreenTips

Another way to get more information is to rest the mouse pointer on a button to display a box with descriptive text, called a *ScreenTip*. As shown in **Figure GS 1–20**, a ScreenTip includes the button name, a keyboard shortcut if there is one, and a description of the button's function. If a Help icon is displayed, you can press F1 to open a Help window with more information about that topic.

EXTRA FOR EXPERTS

Keyboard shortcuts can be used to navigate through a document or work more efficiently by pressing certain keys or key combinations. You can use the Help system to learn more about the keyboard shortcuts available in each program.

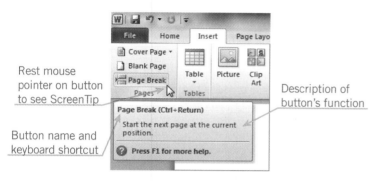

Rest mouse pointer on button to see ScreenTip

Button name and keyboard shortcut

Description of button's function

FIGURE GS 1–20   ScreenTip

Step-by-Step GS 1.6

The document from Step-by-Step GS 1.5 should be open in the Word program window.

1. Click the **Microsoft Word Help** button on the right side of the Ribbon. The Word Help window opens with a list of links to various Help topics.

2. Click the **Introducing the Backstage view** link, and then read the information displayed.

3. In the Search text box on the dialog box toolbar, type **ScreenTip**, and then click the **Search** button to search all of the Word Help files.

4. In the list of search results, click the **Show or hide ScreenTips** link, and read the information displayed.

5. Click the **Show Table of Contents** button . Your Help window should look similar to **Figure GS 1–21**.

FIGURE GS 1–21
Word Help window displaying table
of contents

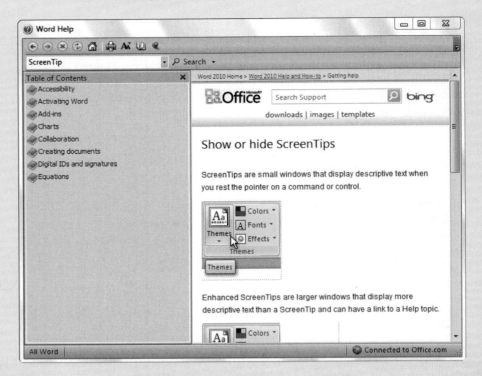

6. Click the **Connected to Office.com** button in the lower-right corner of the Word Help window to open the Connection Status menu. Click a blank space in the dialog box to close the menu.

7. Point to each button on the Word Help toolbar to display the button's ScreenTip, and then click the **Hide Table of Contents** button .

8. If necessary, click the **Keep On Top** button to toggle to the Not On Top setting. Click your Word document. Notice that the program window is now displayed in front of the Help window.

9. Click the **Word Help** button on the taskbar to display the Word Help window again.

10. Click the **Not On Top** button to toggle to the Keep On Top setting. Click the Word document. Notice that the Word Help window stays on top of the document.

11. Click the **Close** button on the Word Help window's title bar to close the Word Help window and return to the document.

12. Click the **Home** tab, and in the Paragraph group, point to each button to display the ScreenTip and read the descriptive text.

13. Leave the document open for use in the next Step-by-Step.

ETHICS IN TECHNOLOGY

Some schools and businesses have an Acceptable Use Policy (AUP) that must be signed by those using the organization's computers. These statements provide a code of ethics that details what kinds of computer-related activities are appropriate and what kinds are not acceptable. Students and/or employees agree to act responsibly and agree not to use the computers for inappropriate or illegal activities. If you are asked to sign an Acceptable Use Policy, be sure to read it carefully so you can abide by the established guidelines.

Closing an Office Program

When you have only one document open in a program, you can click the Close button on the title bar to close the document and exit the program at the same time. If any changes to your work have not been saved, a message box will open asking if you want to save the document before closing. If more than one document is open in a program, you can close all open documents by right-clicking a document button on the taskbar and then clicking Close all windows on the menu.

Step-by-Step GS 1.7

The document from Step-by-Step GS 1.6 should be open in the Word program window.

1. Click the **Close** button on the Word title bar.

2. When a message box opens asking if you want to save the changes to the document, click the **Don't Save** button. The Word program window closes, and you return to the desktop.

SUMMARY

In this lesson, you learned:

- About Microsoft Office 2010 and its programs.
- How to start an Office program using the Start menu.
- The parts of an Office program window, including the Ribbon, Quick Access Toolbar, title bar, Help button, insertion point, scroll bar, and status bar.
- To access contextual tools, including the Mini toolbar, shortcut menus, and KeyTips.

- Ways to customize various aspects of Office programs to suit your work style, such as changing program options, using Zoom controls, and resizing the program windows.
- To get help with Office using the Help window and ScreenTips.
- How to close an Office program.

▪ VOCABULARY REVIEW

Define the following terms:

Backstage view
badge
contextual tabs
dialog box launcher
gallery
groups
integrate

interface
KeyTip
launch
Live Preview
Microsoft Office 2010
Mini toolbar
Office

Quick Access Toolbar
Ribbon
ScreenTip
suite
tabs

▪ REVIEW QUESTIONS

MULTIPLE CHOICE

Select the best response for the following statements.

1. To begin using an Office program, you first need to open or ___*launch*___ it.

   A. integrate
   C. launch
   B. customize
   D. resize

2. If a gallery has more options than those shown on the Ribbon, you can click the ___*More*___ button to see the full gallery.

   A. Help
   C. More
   B. All
   D. Options

3. To open a list of installed programs from the Start menu, click ___*all programs*___.

   A. All Programs
   C. List Programs
   B. Open Programs
   D. Show Programs

4. The _____ displays information about current position and settings.

   A. title bar
   C. taskbar
   B. scroll bar
   D. status bar

5. If a button on the Ribbon has an arrow, you can click the arrow to open a ___*dialog box*___.

   A. dialog box
   C. task pane
   B. menu
   D. toolbar

6. You can use ___*backstage*___ view to open, save, print, and close your documents and perform other file-related tasks.

   A. Backstage
   C. Preview
   B. Outline
   D. Office

7. Which of the following commands is *not* available by default on the Quick Access Toolbar?

   A. Save
   C. Undo
   B. Print
   D. Redo

8. To display KeyTips on the Ribbon, press ___*alt*___.

   A. Shift
   C. Alt
   B. Ctrl
   D. F1

9. When you click the Restore Down button on the title bar, it changes to the _Maximize_ button.

    A.   Restore Back   C.   Minimize

    B.   Close   (D.) Maximize

10. To display a ScreenTip, _point to_ a button.

    A.   click   (C.) point to

    B.   right-click   D.   double-click

FILL IN THE BLANK

Complete the following sentences by writing the correct word or words in the blanks provided.

1. The Office programs on your computer will vary depending on which Office _____ is installed.

2. The _____ button is a common Office program window element that provides assistance with a program.

3. _____ on the Ribbon only appear when the commands on it are needed for the task you are doing.

4. _____ is a feature that previews the editing or formatting change to your document as you point to a gallery option.

5. The _____ opens when you select text and is transparent, becoming active only after you point to a command on it.

6. A(n) _____ opens when you right-click selected text.

7. You can customize Word settings by clicking the _____ tab to display Backstage view and then clicking Options.

8. You can control the size of your document in the document window using the _____ controls on the right side of the status bar.

9. You can use the _____ menu to choose whether you want to access online or offline content in the Help window.

10. When you have only one document open in a program, you can click the Close button on the _____ to close the document and exit the program at the same time.

■ PROJECTS

PROJECT GS 1–1

1. Use the Start menu to open Word 2010.
2. Click the **Page Layout** tab on the Ribbon.
3. Click the **Page Setup dialog box launcher** to open the Page Setup dialog box.
4. Close the Page Setup dialog box.
5. Activate KeyTips, use them to display Backstage view, and then open the Word Options dialog box.
6. Open the Advanced options.
7. Close the Word Options dialog box.
8. Right-click the blank document to open the Mini toolbar and shortcut menu.
9. Press **Esc** to close the Mini toolbar and shortcut menu.
10. Minimize the program window to a button on the taskbar.
11. Click the **Word program** button on the taskbar to restore the window.
12. Close Word.

PROJECT GS 1–2

1. Open Word 2010.
2. In the first line of the blank document, enter **Getting Started Lesson** and then select the text you just entered.
3. In the Styles group on the Home tab on the Ribbon, click the **More** button to open the Styles gallery.
4. Point to the different gallery options to see the text styles change using Live Preview, and click one you like.
5. Use the **Zoom** slider to zoom the document to 110%.
6. Click the **Zoom Out** button to zoom the document to 90%.
7. Click the **Zoom level** button to open the Zoom dialog box.
8. Zoom the document to 100%, and click the **OK** button to close the Zoom dialog box.
9. Click the **Restore Down** button to make the window smaller.
10. Click and drag to resize the window and make it half its current size.
11. Maximize the window to make it full size again.
12. Leave Word and the document open for use in Project GS 1–3.

PROJECT GS 1–3

The document from Project GS 1–2 should be open in the Word program window.

1. Open the Word Help window.
2. Open the Connection Status menu, and click **Show content from Office.com**, if it is not already selected.
3. In the Browse Word 2010 support section, click **see all**, and then click the **Training courses** link.
4. In the Topics section, click the **Use the Navigation Pane to search and move around in your document** link.
5. Read the course overview.
6. Close the browser window.
7. In the Word Help window, click the **Keep On Top** button.
8. Display the Help table of contents.
9. Close the Word Help window.
10. Leave Word and the document open for use in Project GS 1–4.

ON YOUR OWN

Complete the lesson and practice session in the Use the Navigation Pane to search and move around in your document online training course that you accessed in Step 4.

PROJECT GS 1–4

The document from Project GS 1–3 should be open in the Word program window.

1. Move the Quick Access Toolbar below the Ribbon.
2. Open the Word Help window.
3. Search for *Quick Access Toolbar* and click the **Customize the Quick Access Toolbar** link.
4. Scroll down to the Show me how to add commands to the Quick Access Toolbar section, click the **Video: Add commands to the Quick Access Toolbar** link, and watch the video. Close the browser window.
5. In the Word Help window, click the **Not On Top** button.
6. Hide the Table of Contents.
7. Close the Word Help window.
8. Move the Quick Access Toolbar above the Ribbon.
9. Close the document without saving changes.

ON YOUR OWN

Open each program included in your Office suite. Explore all the Ribbon tabs and see what commands are available. Open the program options, and view the various settings available for customizing the program.

CRITICAL THINKING

ACTIVITY GS 1–1

When using Office programs, it will be helpful to be able to locate any information that you need. Practice using the Help system to find out how to customize the Ribbon or customize keyboard short-cuts. Are there any other questions you have as you prepare to work with Office 2010? Use Help to find the answers!

ACTIVITY GS 1–2

In this lesson, you learned briefly about Microsoft Office Backstage view. This is where you can manage your files and data about them. Use the Help system to locate the video titled "What and where is the Backstage view" and watch it to learn more about creating and saving files, viewing properties, and setting options.

Estimated Time for Unit:
9 hours

UNIT II

MICROSOFT WORD

LESSON 1   **1.5 HRS.**
Understanding Word Fundamentals

LESSON 2   **2 HRS.**
Editing and Formatting Text

LESSON 3   **2 HRS.**
Formatting Documents

LESSON 4   **2 HRS.**
Working with Graphic Objects

Estimated Time: 1.5 hours

LESSON 1

Understanding Word Fundamentals

OBJECTIVES

Upon completion of this lesson, you should be able to:

- Open an existing Word document.
- Navigate a document.
- Select text.
- Enter text.
- Save a document.
- Change document views and page formatting.
- Preview and print a document.
- Close a document.

DATA FILES

To complete this lesson, you will need these data files:

Step WD 1-1.docx
Project WD 1-1.docx
Project WD 1-2.docx
Project WD 1-3.docx
Project WD 1-4.docx

VOCABULARY

collate
document
drag
I-beam
insertion point
landscape
margins
portrait
select
word-processing software
word wrap

Introduction

Microsoft Word 2010 is the word-processing program included in the Microsoft Office 2010 suite of software. ***Word-processing software*** lets you insert and manipulate text and graphics to create all kinds of professional-looking documents. A ***document*** is written information that can be printed on paper or distributed electronically. Examples of documents include lists, letters, reports, flyers, brochures, and any other types of written information. As in other Office programs, the various writing and editing tools in Word are organized on the Ribbon tabs. Word includes predefined styles, formats, and effects to help you create documents that are attractive, well-organized, and make an impact. Before you start creating documents, you need to learn basic skills such as opening, saving, and printing documents. In this lesson, you will learn techniques for performing fundamental skills using Word.

Examining the Word Program Window

A Word file is called a document. When you start Word, a blank document opens, as shown in **Figure WD 1–1**. Use this figure to become familiar with the parts of the Word program window. The default file name of a new document is *Document1,* and it is displayed at the top of the screen in the title bar. You can begin typing text in the document at the insertion point.

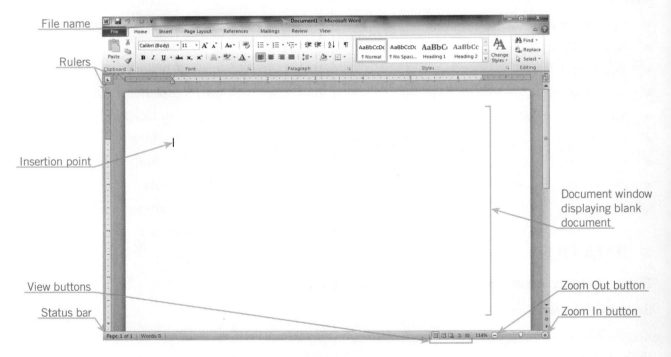

FIGURE WD 1–1   Word program window

Starting Word and Opening an Existing Document

To begin using Word, you first need to open it. You can do this by clicking the Start button on the Windows taskbar, and then clicking the program name in the Microsoft Office folder on the All Programs menu, or by double-clicking a Word program icon on the desktop. Once Word is started, you can begin using it to create a new document or open an existing document.

To open an existing document, you can search for and then open Word files using the Open dialog box, as shown in **Figure WD 1–2**. Word provides three methods for displaying the Open dialog box. The most common method is through the Open command found on the File tab in Backstage view. You can also add an Open command to your Quick Access Toolbar, or use the Ctrl+O keyboard shortcut.

You can use the Open dialog box to find and open existing files on your hard drive, CD, or other removable media; on a network drive to which you are connected; on your organization's intranet; or on the Internet.

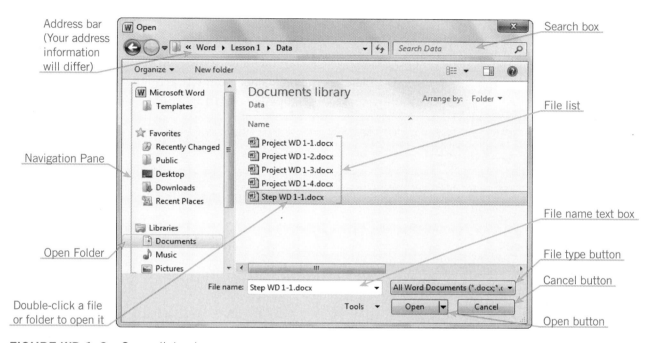

FIGURE WD 1–2   Open dialog box

The following are parts of the Open dialog box:

- The Navigation Pane displays links to folders and libraries that contain files. You can view a folder's contents or open a folder from the Navigation Pane.

- The Address bar at the top of the dialog box shows the folder path.

- The File type button lists other file types you can choose to open.

- The Open button provides options for opening files, including opening the original file, opening a read-only version (when you want to open a file but keep the original file intact), or opening a copy of the original. If you open a copy or read-only version and edit or change the file, you cannot save changes to the original file. You can, however, use the Save As command to save your revisions with a new filename.

- The Search box allows you to find a file by name, file type, or location.

- The Cancel button closes the dialog box without opening a file.

EXTRA FOR EXPERTS

By default, the names of the most recent files you opened in Word are listed in the Recent Documents list, which you can access by choosing Recent on the File tab. You can click a file in the list to open it. You can customize the number of files displayed in the list using the Advanced section of the Word Options dialog box.

Step-by-Step WD 1.1

1. Click the **Start** button 🪟 on the Windows taskbar. The Start menu opens.

2. Click **All Programs**. A list of programs and program folders opens.

3. Click the **Microsoft Office** folder. A list of Office programs opens.

4. Click **Microsoft Word 2010**. Word starts and its program window opens on the desktop with a new, blank document displayed.

5. Click the **File** tab on the Ribbon to access the file-related commands.

6. Click **Open** to display the Open dialog box.

7. If necessary, navigate to the folder containing the data files for this lesson. Double-click the file named **Step WD 1-1** in the File list. The document opens, as shown in **Figure WD 1–3**.

FIGURE WD 1–3
Step WD 1-1 document

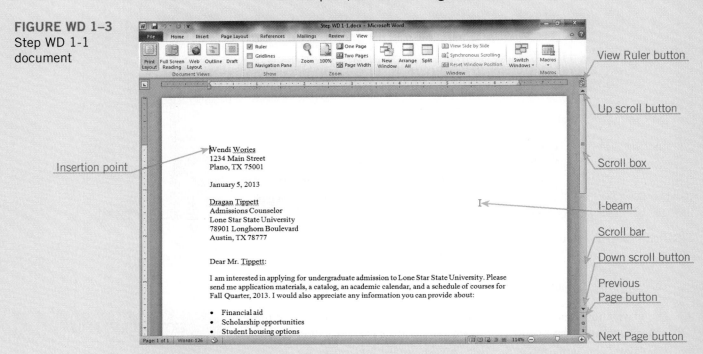

8. Leave the document open for use in the next Step-by-Step.

Navigating the Word Document

One of the most useful aspects of word-processing software is the freedom it gives you to move around the page, which you do by moving the insertion point from place to place within the document. The *insertion point* is the blinking vertical bar that signals where any text you type will appear.

You can move the insertion point several ways: with the mouse; with the arrow, Home, Page Up, Page Down, End, and Tab keys; and with the Go To command.

▶ **VOCABULARY**
insertion point

Using the Mouse

The mouse pointer looks like an *I-beam* (the letter *I*) when you slide it over text. The easiest way to move the insertion point in existing text is to position the I-beam pointer where you want to work, and then click. When you move the mouse pointer beyond the text area in the left margin, it becomes a selection arrow pointer that you can click to select lines, paragraphs, or the entire document. When you click in the right margin, the insertion point moves to the end of the line closest to where you clicked.

If you want to move the mouse pointer to a position not displayed in the document window, use the scroll bars or the mouse wheel to change the document's visible area. To move up or down the document quickly, you can *drag* the scroll box by moving the mouse pointer over it, pressing and holding the mouse button, and then moving the scroll box up or down the scroll bar. To enter text in a new area, you must place the insertion point where you want to make a change. **Table WD 1–1** contains directions for using the scroll bars.

▶ **VOCABULARY**

I-beam

drag

TABLE WD 1–1   Using scroll bars

DO THIS	TO
Click the up or down scroll button	Scroll up or down one line
Click above or below the scroll box in the vertical bar	Scroll up or down one screen
Drag the scroll box	Move up or down in the document
Click the left or right scroll button	Scroll left or right
Click Previous Page or Next Page button	Move to the previous or next page
Right-click the scroll bar	Select a scroll location from the shortcut menu

Your mouse might have a scroll wheel that is located between the left and right mouse buttons. You can roll the wheel with your finger to scroll up and down, and, depending on the type of mouse, horizontally as well.

Using the Keyboard Shortcuts

Table WD 1–2 contains some of the keys and key combinations you can use to move the insertion point.

TABLE WD 1–2   Using keystrokes to navigate

PRESS KEY(S)	TO MOVE
Left arrow ←	One character to the left
Right arrow →	One character to the right
Up arrow ↑	One line up
Down arrow ↓	One line down
End	To the end of a line
Home	To the beginning of a line
Page Up	Up one screen
Page Down	Down one screen
Ctrl+End	To the end of the document
Ctrl+Home	To the beginning of the document

Using the Go To Command

The Go To command lets you move the insertion point to various locations in your document. You could use Go To to jump to a specific page, section, line, comment, or other element within a document. To use Go To, you open the Find and Replace dialog box, which is accessed using the Go To command on the Find menu in the Editing group (located on the Home tab on the Ribbon). You can also click the page number on the status bar to display the Go To tab in the Find and Replace dialog box.

EXTRA FOR EXPERTS

You can also use the Bookmark button on the Insert tab to move around a document. For example, you can place a bookmark at a position in your document to where you often return for editing. Whenever you want to locate that position, simply use either the Bookmark or Go To command.

Step-by-Step WD 1.2

The document from Step-by-Step WD 1.1 should be open in the Word program window.

1. Point to the **down scroll** button ▼, and click and hold the mouse button until you scroll to the end of the document. Click to the right of the last word of the document.

2. Press **Home** to move the insertion point to the beginning of the line.

3. Press **Ctrl+Home**. The insertion point moves to the beginning of the document.

4. On the Home tab, in the Editing group, click the **Find** button arrow and then click **Go To.** The Find and Replace dialog box opens with the Go To tab selected, as shown in **Figure WD 1–4**.

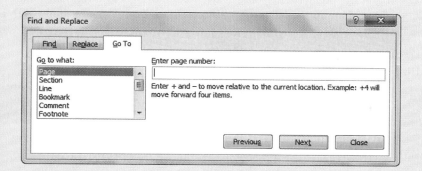

5. In the Go to what list box, click **Line**.

6. Type **20** in the Enter line number text box, and then click the **Go To** button. The insertion point moves to line 20. Click the **Close** button to close the Find and Replace dialog box.

7. Press **Ctrl+End**. The insertion point moves to the end of the document.

8. Drag the scroll box to the top of the scroll bar.

9. Click anywhere in the right margin. The insertion point moves to the end of the line closest to where you clicked.

10. Click to the left of the *J* in *January* to move the insertion point.

11. Leave the document open for use in the next Step-by-Step.

Selecting Text

Before you can format text or move or delete text or graphics, you must *select*, or highlight, the text or object you want to change. You can select text with the mouse or the keyboard. When you select text and then start typing, the selected text is deleted and replaced with the first character you type.

You can cancel a selection by pressing an arrow key or clicking in white space outside the selection.

Selecting with the Mouse

You are probably already familiar with selecting text with the mouse by dragging across the text. When the mouse pointer is moved to the left margin, it changes to

▶ **VOCABULARY**
select

a selection arrow pointer that you can click or drag to select various amounts of text. Triple-clicking in the left margin selects an entire document. **Table WD 1–3** describes some additional techniques for selecting text.

TABLE WD 1–3   Selecting with the mouse

DO THIS	TO SELECT
Drag across the text you want to select or Place the insertion point at the beginning of the selection, then press and hold Shift and click at the end of the selection	Any item or amount of text
Double-click the word	Word
Click the left margin to the left of the line	Line of text
Drag in the left margin to the left of the lines	Multiple lines of text
Press and hold Ctrl, and then click anywhere in the sentence	Sentence
Double-click the left margin of the paragraph, or triple-click the paragraph	Paragraph
Triple-click the left margin	Entire document
Press and hold Alt, and then drag vertically over the text	Vertical block of text
Select the first item, press and hold Ctrl, and select additional items	Multiple items that aren't side by side

Step-by-Step WD 1.3

The document from Step-by-Step WD 1.2 should be open in the Word program window.

1. Click to the left of the *J* in *January,* and then drag across the date **January 5, 2013** to select it, as shown in **Figure WD 1–5**.

FIGURE WD 1–5
Dragging to select text

Wendi Wories
1234 Main Street
Plano, TX 75001

January 5, 2013

Dragan Tippett
Admissions Counselor
Lone Star State University
78901 Longhorn Boulevard
Austin, TX 78777

Drag the I-beam
across text to
select it

2. Click a blank area on the right side of the document window to cancel the selection.

3. Point to an area in the margin to the left of the date, ensure that the pointer changes to a right-pointing arrow, and then click to select the date again.

4. Click a blank area on the right side of the document window to cancel the selection.

5. Double-click the margin to the left of the paragraph to select the first three-line paragraph.

6. Triple-click somewhere in the paragraph below the bulleted list to select the entire paragraph, as shown in **Figure WD 1–6**. You might have to try triple-clicking a few times before you are successful.

January 5, 2013

Dragan Tippett
Admissions Counselor
Lone Star State University
78901 Longhorn Boulevard
Austin, TX 78777

Dear Mr. Tippett:

I am interested in applying for undergraduate admission to Lone Star State University. Please send me application materials, a catalog, an academic calendar, and a schedule of courses for Fall Quarter, 2013. I would also appreciate any information you can provide about:

- Financial aid
- Scholarship opportunities
- Student housing options
- On-campus, part-time work opportunities

Please send this information to me at the address listed above. If you have questions about my request, please contact me by phone at 555-469-0123 or by e-mail at Wendi_Wories@example.com.

Thank you for your assistance. I look forward to receiving this information.

Sincerely,

Triple-click within a paragraph to select it

FIGURE WD 1–6
Selecting a paragraph

7. Double-click the word **January** in the date line. Press and hold **Ctrl**, and double-click the year **2013** in the date to select multiple items that are not side by side.

8. Click a blank area on the right side of the document window to cancel the selections.

9. Leave the document open for use in the next Step-by-Step.

EXTRA FOR EXPERTS

You can select all the text in a document with the same formatting by selecting a portion of the text, clicking the Home tab on the Ribbon, clicking the Select button in the Editing group, and then clicking Select Text with Similar Formatting.

Selecting with the Keyboard

Table WD 1–4 describes the keystrokes you use to select text and graphics with the keyboard.

TABLE WD 1–4   Keyboard commands

PRESS KEYS	TO SELECT
Shift+right arrow →	One character to the right
Shift+left arrow ←	One character to the left
Ctrl+Shift+right arrow →	To the end of a word
Ctrl+Shift+left arrow ←	To the beginning of a word
Shift+End	To the end of a line
Shift+Home	To the beginning of a line
Ctrl+Shift+down arrow ↓	To the end of a paragraph
Ctrl+Shift+End	To the end of a document
Ctrl+Shift+Home	To the beginning of a document
Ctrl+A	The entire document

Step-by-Step WD 1.4

The document from Step-by-Step WD 1.3 should be open in the Word program window.

1. Click at the beginning of the document.
2. Press **Shift+End**. The line is selected.
3. Press the **down arrow** key to cancel the selection. Position the insertion point at the end of the second line.
4. Press and hold **Shift** and press the **left arrow** key to select the **t** in *Street*.
5. Continue pressing and holding **Shift** while pressing the **left arrow** key until the word **Street** is selected, as shown in **Figure WD 1–7**.

FIGURE WD 1–7
Selecting one character at a time

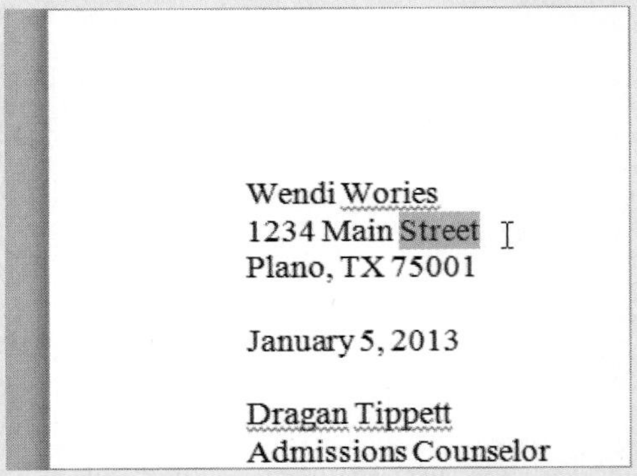

Wendi Wories
1234 Main Street
Plano, TX 75001

January 5, 2013

Dragan Tippett
Admissions Counselor

6. Press and hold **Ctrl** and press the **A** key to select the entire document.

7. Press the **up arrow** key to cancel the selection.

8. Leave the document open for use in the next Step-by-Step.

Entering Text

To add new text, position the insertion point where you want to insert text and then type the text. Word enters text at the insertion point—to the left of anything that may be there already.

When you see a wavy red or green line underneath text, it means that Word has detected a possible spelling or grammatical error. Ignore the wavy lines for now; you will learn how to check the underlined text in Lesson 2.

When you enter text, Word uses a feature called **_word wrap_** to automatically continue text to the next line within a paragraph. When you finish a paragraph, press Enter to create the first line of a new paragraph.

▶ **VOCABULARY**
word wrap

Step-by-Step WD 1.5

The document from Step-by-Step WD 1.4 should be open in the Word program window.

1. Click at the beginning of the line that begins *I am interested.*

2. Type **I am a senior at Cougar Hill High School.** Press the **spacebar** to create a space between sentences, as shown in **Figure WD 1–8**. Notice that the text at the end of the line wrapped to the next line.

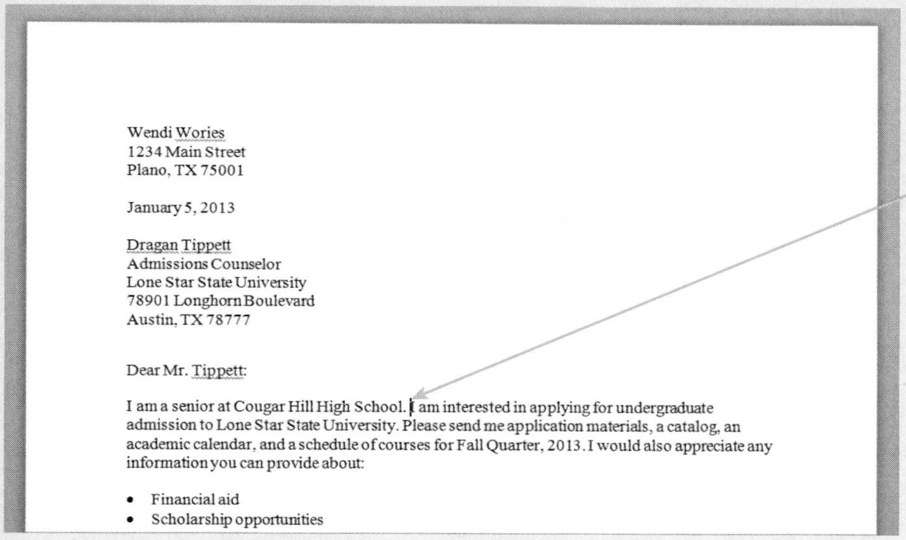

FIGURE WD 1–8
Entering new text

Insertion point now follows new sentence and space

Wendi Wories
1234 Main Street
Plano, TX 75001

January 5, 2013

Dragan Tippett
Admissions Counselor
Lone Star State University
78901 Longhorn Boulevard
Austin, TX 78777

Dear Mr. Tippett:

I am a senior at Cougar Hill High School. I am interested in applying for undergraduate admission to Lone Star State University. Please send me application materials, a catalog, an academic calendar, and a schedule of courses for Fall Quarter, 2013. I would also appreciate any information you can provide about:

• Financial aid
• Scholarship opportunities

3. Select the word **work** in the fourth bulleted list item.

4. Type **employment**. Notice that the word *work* was deleted after you typed the *e* in *employment*.

5. Leave the document open for use in the next Step-by-Step.

Saving a Document

The first time you save a document, the options for saving include the Save command on the File tab, the Save As command on the File tab, or the Save button on the Quick Access Toolbar. Each of these methods displays the Save As dialog box (see **Figure WD 1–9**).

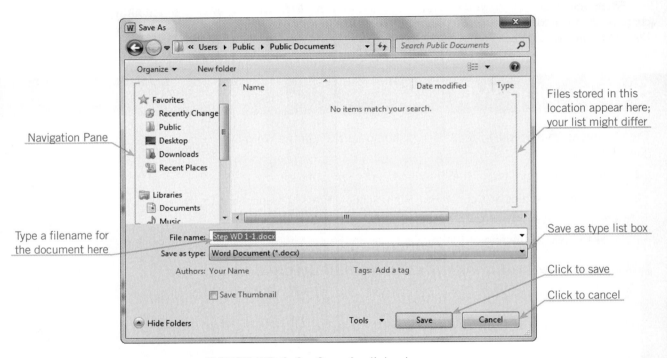

FIGURE WD 1–9   Save As dialog box

After you save a file for the first time, the Save command saves your file with the previously specified name in the location you specified. The Save As command opens the Save As dialog box, in which you can make a copy of the file with a new name, location, or file type. The Save as type list box lets you save a document in another format or as a template. You might need to change the file format or program and version if you share files with others who use different software. You will learn more about templates later in this book. To save a document in a specific location, you use the Navigation Pane in the Save As dialog box to navigate to the folder in which you want to save the document.

Once you have saved the file, you can use the Save button on the Quick Access Toolbar or the Save command on the File tab to update it.

You can use the Save & Send option on the File tab to save a document online in two ways. You can save to Windows Live SkyDrive, which is a free online storage

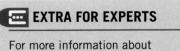
EXTRA FOR EXPERTS

For more information about Microsoft Office Web Apps, visit http://www.microsoft.com/office/2010.

service from Microsoft, to make the document accessible from any computer with Internet access. You can also save to an organization's SharePoint site, which provides additional opportunities for collaboration, such as editing documents with multiple people at the same time. Saving online allows you to share and access documents through an Internet connection and to view and edit them in a Web browser using Microsoft Office Web Apps, which are free online companion programs to Word, Excel, and PowerPoint.

Word's AutoRecover feature automatically saves your document at regular intervals so that you can recover at least some of your work in case of a power outage or other unexpected shutdown. You can turn this feature on or off and change the setting to save more or less often by opening the Word Options dialog box from the File tab. In the Save section of the dialog box, specify a number in the Save AutoRecover information every *x* minutes box. However, you should not rely on this automatic saving feature. Remember to save your work often.

EXTRA FOR EXPERTS

Word 2010 files and Word 2007 files have a .docx extension that cannot be opened with previous versions of Word. If you need to share files with someone using an earlier version, select Word 97-2003 Document on the Save as type list in the Save As dialog box to save files with the .doc extension.

Step-by-Step WD 1.6

The document from Step-by-Step WD 1.5 should be open in the Word program window.

1. Click the **File** tab and then click **Save As** to open the Save As dialog box.

2. Navigate to the location where you save your files.

3. Click the **File name** text box. Type **Admissions Letter XXX** (replace *XXX* with your initials) in the box. See **Figure WD 1–10**.

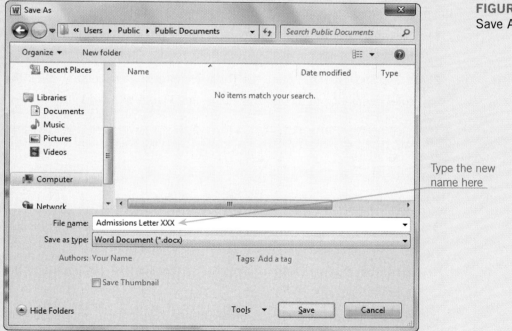

FIGURE WD 1–10
Save As dialog box

4. Click the **Save** button to save a copy of the document with the new name in the specified location.

5. Leave the document open for use in the next Step-by-Step.

Changing Document Views

You might find it useful to preview how your document would look as a printout, as a Web page, or in an outline. Word provides five different views using the buttons in the Document Views group on the View tab on the Ribbon. You can also use the View buttons on the right side of the status bar to switch easily from view to view. The five document views are:

■ Print Layout view, which displays the page as it will print, including headers, footers, footnotes, and graphics. It is the most common view.

■ Full Screen Reading view, which maximizes the space available for reading documents on the screen.

■ Web Layout view, which shows you how your document would look as a Web page.

■ Outline view, which displays the structure of your document in classic outline format.

■ Draft view, which displays the document for editing purposes. Elements such as headers and footers are not shown.

You can display a ruler to help you position text and graphics on your pages. For the ruler to be visible, a check mark must appear next to the Ruler command in the Show group, which appears on the View tab on the Ribbon. Or, you can click the View Ruler button, found at the top of the vertical scroll bar.

Step-by-Step WD 1.7

The document Admissions Letter *XXX* from Step-by-Step WD 1.6 should be open in the Word program window.

1. Click the **View** tab on the Ribbon. In the Document Views group, notice that the document is displayed in Print Layout view.

2. In the Show group, notice the Ruler check box. If necessary, click the **Ruler** check box to display the Ruler. See **Figure WD 1–11**.

FIGURE WD 1–11
View tab

Ruler check box

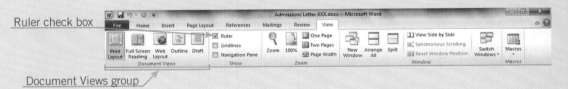

Document Views group

3. In the Document Views group, click the **Web Layout** button to display the letter as it would appear as a Web page in a browser.

4. Click the **Outline** button. Notice the commands available on the Outlining tab.

5. In the Close group, click the **Close Outline View** button. Your document should once again be in Print Layout View.

6. Click the **View** tab. In the Document Views group, click the **Draft** button.

7. In the Document Views group, click the **Full Screen Reading** button to open the document in Full Screen Reading view. Notice the commands available on the toolbar, as shown in **Figure WD 1–12**.

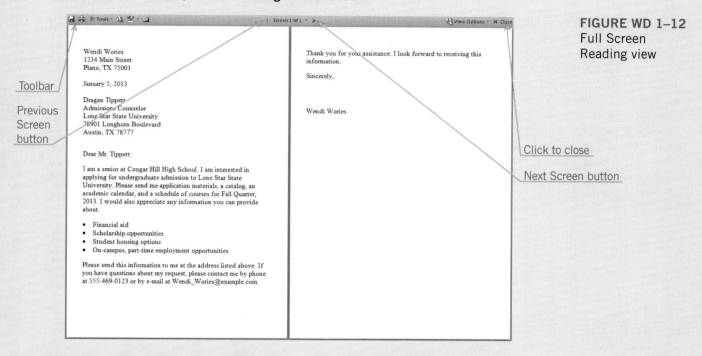

FIGURE WD 1–12
Full Screen
Reading view

8. Click the **Close** button or press **Esc** to return to Print Layout view.

9. Leave the document open for use in the next Step-by-Step.

Changing Page Formatting

One of the first things you do when working with a new document is to format the page. Formatting the page involves setting margins, establishing the size of the paper you will be using for printouts, and determining whether your document will be horizontally or vertically oriented.

You can use the Page Setup group of commands on the Page Layout tab, shown in **Figure WD 1–13**, to change how you set up a document's pages. Use the dialog box launcher to open the Page Setup dialog box for access to more options.

EXTRA FOR EXPERTS

You can change margins for the whole document, from the insertion point forward, or for a selected section of text. Word inserts a section break if you choose to change margins from the insertion point forward or for a selection.

Page Setup group   Dialog box launcher

FIGURE WD 1–13   Page Layout tab

Setting Margins

Margins are the areas of white space that border the text on the edges of a page. Word sets default margins for new documents, but you can change them to fit your document requirements. Most printers cannot print all the way to the edge of the paper, and therefore, printers have rules for minimum margin settings.

You set margins using the Margins button in the Page Setup group, found on the Page Layout tab on the Ribbon. Word provides commands for common margin settings, as shown in **Figure WD 1–14**. The Custom Margins command lets you insert custom measurements for the top, bottom, left, and right margins.

Choosing Page Size

You can use the Size button and menu, also found in the Page Setup group, to choose from a list of page sizes available for your printer. **Figure WD 1–15** shows a list of available page sizes; your list may be different. The More Paper Sizes command lets you create a custom page size.

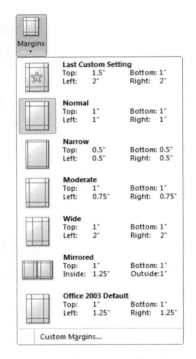

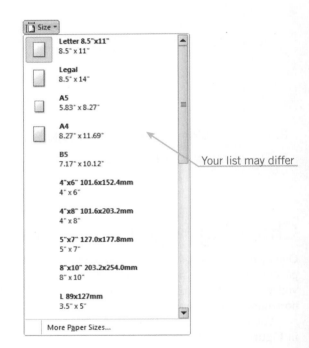

Your list may differ

FIGURE WD 1–14   Margins menu   **FIGURE WD 1–15**   Page Size menu

Changing Orientation

While most documents are set up in a vertical orientation, called *portrait*, sometimes you might need to use a horizontal setup, called *landscape*, shown in **Figure WD 1–16**. Word's default page orientation is portrait, but you can change to landscape using the Orientation button found in the Page Setup group.

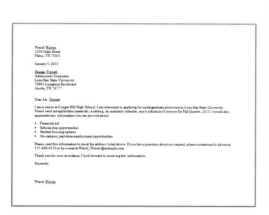

Landscape orientation   Portrait orientation

FIGURE WD 1–16   Portrait and landscape orientation

Step-by-Step WD 1.8

The document Admissions Letter *XXX* from Step-by-Step WD 1.7 should be open in the Word program window.

1. Click the **Page Layout** tab on the Ribbon. In the Page Setup group, click the **Margins** button to open the Margins menu.

2. Click **Wide** to apply left and right margins that are 2-inches wide.

3. Click the **Margins** button again, and then click **Custom Margins**. The Page Setup dialog box opens, as shown in **Figure WD 1–17**.

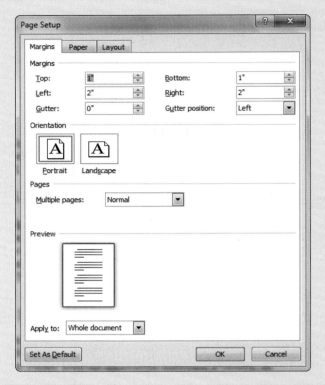

4. Type **1.5** in the Top text box, and then click the **OK** button.

5. Click the **Size** button in the Page Setup group on the Page Layout tab.

6. Click **Legal** to change the page height to 14 inches. Scroll down the document and notice the new, longer page.

7. Click the **Size** button and then click **Letter 8.5"×11"** to return to the original page size setting.

8. Click the **Orientation** button in the Page Setup group and click **Landscape**. Scroll down and notice that the new layout caused the letter to go to two pages.

9. Click the **Orientation** button and click **Portrait** to return to the original page orientation.

10. Save the document and leave it open for use in the next Step-by-Step.

Previewing and Printing a Document

You will need to print many of the documents that you create. Whether you are working with a letter, a fax, or other type of document, you will likely send it to another user, distribute printouts in a meeting, post a flyer, or have some other need for a printed version. You can preview a document and change formatting and printing options on the File tab in Backstage view before you click the Print button.

When you choose Print on the File tab, Backstage view displays the Print button and default print settings in the center pane of the window and a preview of the current page in the right pane, as shown in **Figure WD 1-18**. To change a print setting in the center pane, click the setting you want to change, and then select a new option from the gallery that opens.

You can preview any page in a multi-page document using the scroll bars or the Next Page and Previous Page buttons at the bottom of the right pane. You can zoom in and out to see different magnifications of a document using the Zoom In and Zoom Out buttons or by moving the Zoom slider. The Zoom to Page button displays the entire page within the preview pane.

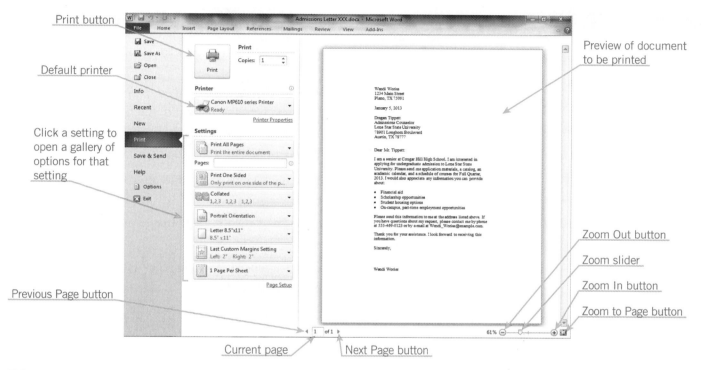

FIGURE WD 1–18 Printing and previewing options in Backstage view

The following printing and previewing options are available in Backstage view:

- The Print button prints the document with current settings.
- Use the Copies box up and down arrows to choose the number of copies to print.
- The Printer area displays the default printer. Click the default printer to select a different printer from the gallery of available printers. The Printer Properties link lets you choose paper type, print quality, and other printer options.
- The Settings area lists the current print settings. Clicking the settings opens galleries of options that let you indicate whether to print:
    - All pages, the current page, or specified pages of a document
    - One sided, on both sides, or manually on both sides
    - Multiple copies of a document with pages in order, called **collated**, or uncollated
    - Portrait or landscape orientation
    - Letter 8.5"×11" size or another page size
    - Current margin settings or other margin settings
    - 1 page per sheet or 2, 4, 6, 8, or 16 pages per sheet

▶ **VOCABULARY**
collate

UNIT II   Microsoft Word

- The Page Setup link opens the Page Setup dialog box where you can make changes to the margins, orientation, page size, and page layout.
- The preview pane shows a preview of the document and allows you to zoom in and out to check for errors. As you make changes to the print settings, the preview is updated to reflect the changes so that you can be sure you are happy with the document settings before printing.

Step-by-Step WD 1.9

The document Admissions Letter *XXX* from Step-by-Step WD 1.8 should be open in the Word program window.

1. Click the **File** tab to display Backstage view, and then click **Print**.
2. Click the **Zoom In** button ⊕ at the bottom of the right pane two times.
3. Click the **Zoom to Page** button 🔲 to view the entire page.
4. In the center pane under Settings, click **Letter** to open a gallery of page size options, and then click **Legal** to change the page size. Notice that the preview reflects this change.
5. Click the **Legal** setting, and then click **Letter** to change the page size back to the original.
6. Notice the other settings available, and then click the **Print** button. If you have been instructed not to print, click the File tab to close Backstage view.
7. Save the document and leave it open for use in the next Step-by-Step.

Closing a Document

When you are finished with a document, you can close it without closing Word using the Close command on the File tab. When you have only one document open, you can click the Close button on the title bar to close the document and exit the program at the same time. If you have more than one document open, you can close all documents and exit the program using the Exit command on the File tab. The software prompts you to save your work if you made any changes since you last saved.

Step-by-Step WD 1.10

The document Admissions Letter *XXX* from Step-by-Step WD 1.9 should be open in the Word program window.

1. Click the **File** tab and then click **Close**. The document closes and the Word program window remains open.
2. Click the **Close** button 　✕　 on the title bar to close Word.

TECHNOLOGY CAREERS

Computer support technicians, or help-desk personnel, provide assistance and advice to computer users. Help technicians must be able to communicate effectively to interpret the user's problem. They must also be knowledgeable about the hardware, software (such as Microsoft Word), or system for which they are providing support so they can help to solve the problem. Help technicians receive constant training and certification to stay current with the latest technology developments.

SUMMARY

In this lesson, you learned:

- To open an existing document using the Open dialog box.
- Ways to move the insertion point in the Word document using the mouse, keyboard shortcuts, and the Go To command.
- To select text using the mouse and the keyboard.
- That when you enter text, Word automatically wraps it to the next line.
- How to save a document using the Save As dialog box.

- The five different ways to view a document.
- Ways to change margins, page size, and orientation.
- To preview and print a document using Backstage view on the File tab.
- To close a file.

▪ VOCABULARY REVIEW

Define the following terms:

collate	insertion point	select
document	landscape	word-processing software
drag	margins	word wrap
I-beam	portrait	

■ REVIEW QUESTIONS

MULTIPLE CHOICE

Select the best response for the following statements.

1. To open a file as read-only means _____ .

   A. to open the original file
   C. to open a copy of the original file

   B. to open a file but keep the original intact
   D. to open a file in Full Screen Reading view

2. If you click the mouse one time when the pointer is in the left margin, you select the ___*line*___ .

   (A.) line
   C. paragraph

   B. word
   D. entire document

3. The Find and Replace dialog box contains the _____ command.

   A. Orientation
   C. Print

   B. Go To
   D. Print Preview

4. The mouse pointer looks like a(n) ___*I-beam*___ when you move it over text.

   A. arrow pointer
   (C.) I-beam

   B. insertion point
   D. scroll bar

5. When you enter text, Word uses a feature called ___*word wrap*___ to automatically wrap text to the next line.

   A. navigation
   C. multiselection

   B. mirrored margins
   (D.) word wrap

6. After you save a file for the first time, the _____ command saves your file to the previously specified name and location.

   A. Save As
   C. Save

   B. Open
   D. File

7. You can use the _____ option on the File tab in Backstage view to save a document online.

   A. Open
   C. Save

   B. Print
   D. Save & Send

8. Legal is a common _____ .

   A. orientation
   C. margin setting

   B. page size
   D. print option

9. _____ view maximizes the space available for reading documents on the screen.

   A. Web Layout
   C. Full Screen Reading

   B. Outline
   D. Print Layout

10. You can preview a document and adjust print settings in ___*Backstage view*___

   (A.) Backstage view
   C. the Print menu

   B. Full Screen Reading view
   D. the Open dialog box

FILL IN THE BLANK

Complete the following sentences by writing the correct word or words in the blanks provided.

1. You can cancel a selection by pressing a(n) _____ key.

2. _____ _____ _____ lets you insert and manipulate text and graphics to create all kinds of professional-looking documents.

3. You can hold _____ and press _____ to move to the beginning of a document.

4. You can _____-click a word to select it.

5. You can click a paragraph _____ times to select it.

6. When you select text and then start typing, the selected text is _____ and replaced with the first character you type.

7. _____ are the areas of white space separating the text on a page from the edges of the paper.

8. Vertical orientation is called _____ .

9. When you choose Print on the File tab, the _____ print settings are displayed in the center pane of the screen.

10. Click the _____ button to close a document.

■ PROJECTS

PROJECT WD 1–1

1. Open **Project WD 1-1** from the folder containing the data files for this lesson.

2. Use the Save As command on the File tab to save the document with the filename **Lone Star Fax XXX** (replace *XXX* with your initials).

3. Click to the right of the Comments section of the fax and type the following text:

   Thank you for your application. However, I need some additional information. Please fill out the attached form and return it to me as soon as possible.

4. Press **Ctrl+Home** to move the insertion point to the beginning of the document.

5. Type **Lone Star State University** and press **Enter**.

6. Save, print, and close the document.

PROJECT WD 1–2

1. Open **Project WD 1-2** from the folder containing the data files for this lesson.

2. Save the document with the filename **Graduation Postcard XXX** (replace *XXX* with your initials).

3. Change the page orientation to landscape.

4. Use the Size menu to change the page size to **4" × 6"**.

5. Change the Margins to Narrow.

6. Click below the last line of text, and type **RSVP to (469) 555-0155**.

7. Save the document.

8. Preview the document in Backstage view.

9. Print the document. (If you do not have 4" × 6" paper in your printer, most printers will let you print on letter-size paper. You can trim it later if you wish.)

10. Close the document.

ON YOUR OWN

Open **Graduation Postcard XXX** and change the look of this document by setting custom margins and a custom page size of your choice. Save and close the document.

PROJECT WD 1–3

1. Open **Project WD 1-3** from the folder containing the data files for this lesson.

2. Save the document with the filename **Computer Care *XXX*** (replace *XXX* with your initials).

3. Use the Go To command to move the insertion point to page 3.

4. Select the word newspaper on the first line of page 3, and type **Internet**.

5. Drag the scroll box to the top of the scroll bar, and click at the beginning of the document.

6. Preview the document in Backstage view.

7. Use the Next Page and Previous Page buttons to preview each page.

8. Return to the document window.

9. View the document using Full Screen Reading view.

10. Use the Next Screen and Previous Screen buttons to scroll through the pages.

11. Close Full Screen Reading view.

12. Save and close the document.

ON YOUR OWN

Open **Computer Care *XXX*,** change the margins to Mirrored, and experiment with the gutter measurement in the Page Setup dialog box. Preview the results in Backstage view. Save and close the document.

PROJECT WD 1–4

1. Open **Project WD 1-4** from the folder containing the data files for this lesson.

2. Save the document with the filename **Florida Admissions *XXX*** (replace *XXX* with your initials).

3. Select *January 5* and type **February 23**.

4. In the letter address, select *Dragan Tippett,* and then type **Marc Zimprich.**

5. Select *Lone Star State University* and the two address lines below it and type the following:

Florida Park University

9876 Palm Tree Road

Orlando, FL 32868

6. In the greeting line, select *Tippett* and type **Zimprich**.

7. In the first paragraph, select *Lone Star State University,* and then type **Florida Park University**.

8. Change the margins to Normal.

9. Preview the document in Backstage view.

10. Close Backstage view and add four blank lines at the beginning to center the letter on the page.

11. Save, print, and close the document.

ON YOUR OWN

Open **Florida Admissions *XXX*,** delete the four blank lines at the beginning of the document, and use the Vertical alignment option on the Layout tab of the Page Setup dialog box to center the letter attractively on the page. Save and close the document.

WEB PROJECT

1. Open **Florida Admissions** *XXX* from the folder containing the data files you created for this lesson.

2. Save the document with the filename **Florida Address** *XXX* (replace *XXX* with your initials).

3. Assume you are planning on attending college in Florida. Search the Web for the names of three colleges in the greater Miami area.

4. In the document, replace the existing university name and address information with the name and address of one of the colleges you looked up on the Web.

5. Save, print, and close the document.

CRITICAL THINKING

ACTIVITY WD 1–1

You will inevitably encounter a situation in which you change your mind about printing a document—after you have sent it to the printer. How do you cancel printing? Use Help to find out. Try it by printing one of the documents from this lesson and then canceling it.

ACTIVITY WD 1–2

A power outage, low battery level, or other problem can cause your Word document to shut down before you have a chance to save it. What happens to the document you are working on if Word suddenly closes or the power goes out? Use Help to learn about document recovery and the AutoRecover command. Locate and evaluate your AutoRecover settings.

LESSON 2

Editing and Formatting Text

■ OBJECTIVES

Upon completion of this lesson, you should be able to:

- Create a new document.
- Format text.
- Set tabs.
- Format paragraphs.
- Delete, move, and copy text.
- Use Undo, Redo, and Repeat.
- Find and replace text.
- Proof a document.

■ DATA FILES

To complete this lesson, you will need these data files:

Step WD 2-2.docx

Step WD 2-7.docx

Step WD 2-8.docx

Step WD 2-10.docx

Project WD 2-1.docx

Project WD 2-2.docx

Project WD 2-3.docx

Project WD 2-4.docx

Project WD 2-5.docx

■ VOCABULARY

characters

Clipboard

copy

cut

drag-and-drop

first-line indent

font

hanging indent

indent

leader

negative indent

nonprinting symbols

paragraph

paste

point size

tab

Introduction

After you have created a document, you will likely need to fine-tune it using Word tools for formatting and editing. Formatting refers to how your documents look, whereas editing refers to revising, changing, and correcting the wording of your documents. The word *formatting* is also used to describe the visual text characteristics. The ongoing processes of formatting and editing add interest, clarity, and emphasis to the documents you create. You can easily format and edit text as you write, or format and edit after you have organized your thoughts within the document. Formatting and editing can occur in either order, and most people find that they go back and forth interchangeably between the two tasks.

Creating a New Document

You can create a new blank document by choosing New on the File tab, and then clicking the Create button with the Blank document icon selected in Backstage view, as shown in **Figure WD 2–1**.

Step-by-Step WD 2.1

1. Start Word, if necessary.

2. Click the **File** tab on the Ribbon and then click **New**. Options are displayed for creating a new document based on available templates, as shown in Figure WD 2–1. Under Available Templates, the Blank document icon is selected, and a preview of the blank document appears on the right.

FIGURE WD 2–1
Options for creating a new document

Blank document icon

Click to create a new document based on the selected template

3. Click the **Create** button. A new, blank document opens, as shown in **Figure WD 2–2**.

Insertion point

4. Type **June 11, 2013** and press **Enter** twice to move the insertion point down two lines.

5. Type **Dear Professor Reynolds,** and then press **Enter**.

6. Type **I am enjoying your course on South American cultures and would like to learn more about the Yanomamo tribe. Can you recommend some books or research papers? Thank you**, and then press **Enter** twice.

7. Type **Sincerely,** and then press **Enter**. Type **Chris Smith** to sign the note.

8. Your document should look similar to **Figure WD 2–3**. Save the document as **Reynolds Note *XXX*** (replace *XXX* with your initials) and close the document.

FIGURE WD 2–3
Reynolds Note *XXX* file

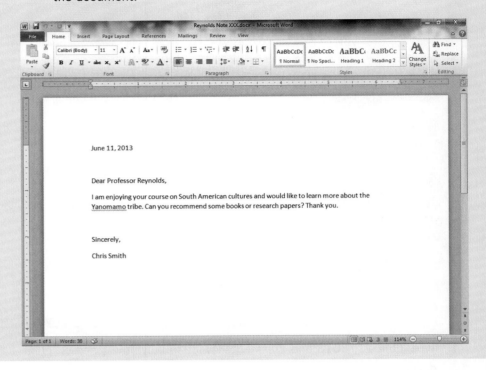

Formatting Text

▶ **VOCABULARY**
characters

Characters are individual letters, numbers, symbols, punctuation marks, and spaces. You can apply one or more formats to a single character or multiple characters. The character formats you can apply are font and font size; font style such as italic and bold; font effects such as strikethrough or superscript; and text effects such as shadow, glow, or reflection. The Font group is on the Home tab of the Ribbon, shown in **Figure WD 2–4**, and contains buttons for formatting text. Later in this lesson you will learn to copy formats using the Format Painter button in the Clipboard group.

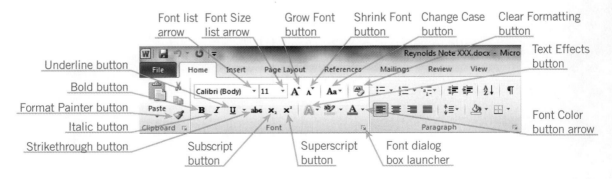

FIGURE WD 2–4   Font group on the Home tab

You can make several changes at once and see a preview of your choices in the Font dialog box, which you can display using the dialog box launcher in the Font group.

Changing Fonts and Font Sizes

The *font* is the design of a set of letters and numbers. Each set has a name. Below are some examples:

Times New Roman   Arial   **Impact**

Clicking the Font list arrow in the Font group on the Home tab displays each font's design on the Font menu. The Font menu is divided into three sections to make it easier for you to choose the appropriate font: Theme Fonts, Recently Used Fonts, and All Fonts. You can also access the Font menu on the Mini toolbar. By default, Word uses the Calibri 11-point font. You change to a different font by selecting text and choosing one of the fonts listed on the Font menu or in the Font dialog box. You can also choose to begin typing text with a new font by selecting the font before typing at the insertion point.

Font sizes are measured in points. *Point size* refers to a measurement for the height of characters. A point is equal to approximately 1/72 inch. A 10-point font is approximately 10/72 inch high. The examples below show what different point sizes look like in the Times New Roman font.

8 Point   12 Point   24 Point   36 Point

To change the font size for existing text, you first select the text and then choose a new size by clicking the Font Size list arrow and clicking a size on the Font Size menu, or by choosing a new size in the Size list in the Font dialog box. You can change the size of text you are about to enter by choosing a new size before typing at the insertion point.

The Grow Font button increases font size one increment on the Font Size menu, which may be one point, two points, or eight points in the larger sizes, and the Shrink Font button decreases the size one increment.

Applying Font Styles and Effects

Font styles are variations in the shape or weight of a font's characters. Bold, italic, and underline are common font styles that you can access easily in the Font group.

In the Font dialog box, the Effects area contains seven different formatting effects, from Strikethrough to Hidden. You can apply more than one effect at a time. The Strikethrough, Subscript, Superscript, and Change Case buttons are also available in the Font group.

Use the Change Case button to change the case, or capitalization, of text quickly. The Change Case menu has five options:

- Sentence case: Capitalizes the first word in each sentence.
- lowercase: Changes all characters to lowercase.
- UPPERCASE: Changes all characters to capitals.
- Capitalize Each Word: Capitalizes the first character of each word.
- tOGGLE cASE: Changes each character to the opposite of how it was originally typed.

To change the color of text, you apply one of the color choices available through the Font Color button arrow.

The Text Effects button in the Font group contains options for changing the outline color of text characters and for applying shadow, reflection, and glow effects. You can choose predefined text effects from the galleries or use each effect's Options command to create custom effects.

Step-by-Step WD 2.2

1. Open **Step WD 2-2** from the folder containing the data files for this lesson.

2. Save the document as **Zare Resume XXX** (replace *XXX* with your initials).

3. On the Home tab, in the Editing group, click the **Select** button, and then click **Select All** to select all the text in the document.

4. On the Home tab, in the Font group, click the **Font list arrow** `Calibri (Body) ▼` and click **Baskerville Old Face**, as shown in **Figure WD 2–5**. All of the document text changes from the default font, Calibri, to the new font. If your computer does not have Baskerville Old Face available, click another font of your choice.

FIGURE WD 2–5
Font menu

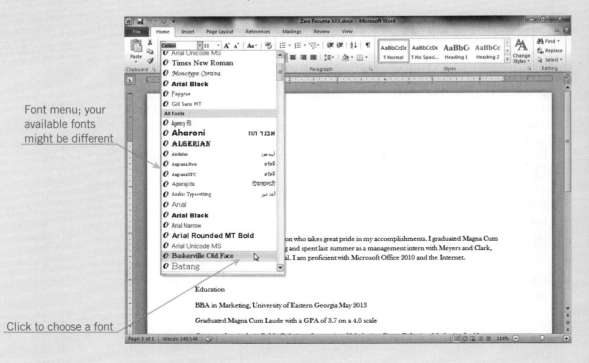

Font menu; your available fonts might be different

Click to choose a font

5. With the text still selected, in the Font group, click the **Font Size list arrow** `11 ▾`, and click **12** to increase the point size of the text.

6. In the Font group, click the **Shrink Font** button `A˅` one time to change the point size back to 11.

7. Select **MANDY ZARE**. In the Font group, click the **Underline** button `U` to underline the selected text.

8. Make sure MANDY ZARE is still selected. In the Font group, click the **Bold** button `B` to change the selected text to bold.

9. Make sure MANDY ZARE is still selected. In the Font group, click the **Change Case** button `Aa▾` and click **Capitalize Each Word**, as shown in **Figure WD 2–6**.

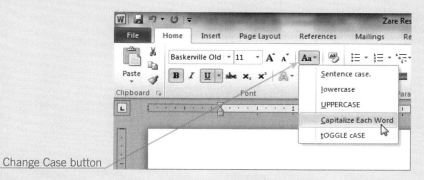

10. Click the **Text Effects** button `A˅` and click **Gradient Fill – Orange, Accent 6, Inner Shadow**, as shown in **Figure WD 2-7**.

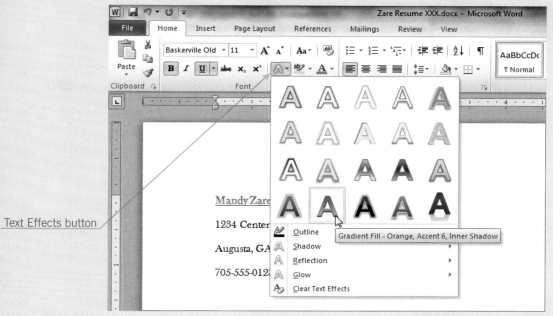

11. Make sure Mandy Zare is still selected. In the Font group, click the **dialog box launcher** to open the Font dialog box.

12. In the Font list in the Font dialog box, click **Arial Rounded MT Bold** or another font of your choice. In the Size list, click **14**. Click the **Underline style** list arrow, and then click **(none)**. In the Effects section, click the **Small caps** check box. See **Figure WD 2–8**. Click the **OK** button to close the dialog box.

FIGURE WD 2–8
Font dialog box

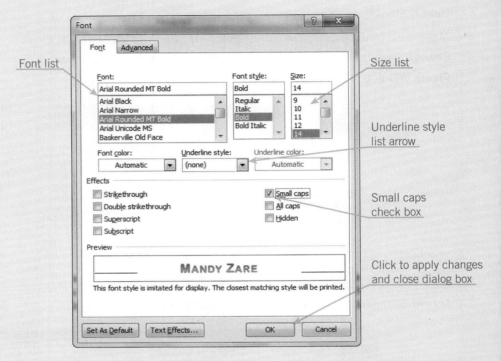

13. Make sure Mandy Zare is still selected. On the Home tab, in the Font group, click the **Font Color** button arrow and click **Blue** from the Standard Colors section of the gallery, as shown in **Figure WD 2–9**.

FIGURE WD 2–9
Font Color gallery

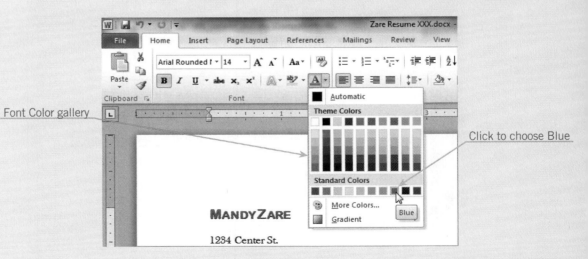

14. Save the document and leave it open for use in the next Step-by-Step.

Clearing Formatting

To remove formatting from selected text, you perform the same steps you took to apply the formatting, which effectively reverses the formatting. For example, if you want to remove bold formatting that you added to a word, you would click the Bold button again to remove the bold formatting from selected text. Or, use the Clear Formatting button to remove all formatting from selected text. Reversing a font change does not work in the same way; if you want to restore text to a font you had previously used, you must select the text and use the Font list arrow to change the text back to the original font.

Using the Format Painter

The Format Painter button can save you time and provide consistency by allowing you to copy multiple formatting characteristics from a section of text and then apply the same formatting to other parts of the document.

To copy the formatting of a section of text, you first select the text or paragraph that contains the formatting you want to copy and then click the Format Painter button in the Clipboard group on the Home tab. When you click the Format Painter button, the mouse pointer changes to an I-beam with a paintbrush "loaded" with the copied format. Next, you can select the text to which you want to apply the formatting.

Double-clicking the Format Painter button allows you to "paint" the copied formatting to more than one selection. When you finish painting formats, click the Format Painter button or press Esc to turn off the Format Painter.

Step-by-Step WD 2.3

The document Zare Resume *XXX* from Step-by-Step WD 2.2 should be open in the Word program window.

1. Select the word **Summary** in the document.

2. On the Home tab, in the Font group, click the **Bold** button **B**, the **Italic** button *I*, and the **Underline** button **U** to modify the selected text.

3. With Summary still selected, in the Font group, click the **Clear Formatting** button to change the text back to the default style of Calibri, 11 point.

4. In the Font group, click the **Bold** button to apply bold formatting.

5. In the Font group, click the **Grow Font** button **A** twice to increase the size to 14 point.

6. Make sure Summary is still selected. On the Home tab, in the Clipboard group, click the **Format Painter** button 🖌. The pointer changes to an I-beam with a paintbrush beside it.

7. Drag across Education, as shown in **Figure WD 2–10**. When the entire word is selected, release the mouse button to apply the new formatting.

FIGURE WD 2–10
Format Painter

Format Painter button

Drag across text with Format Painter pointer

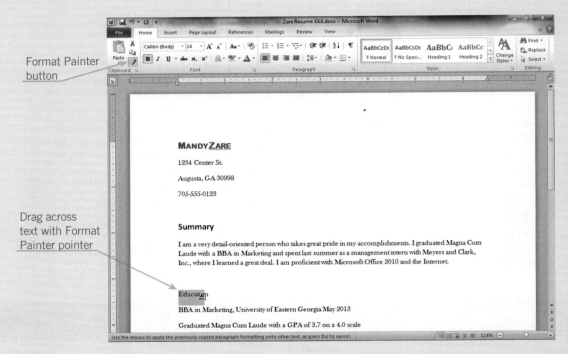

8. Make sure Education is still selected. In the Clipboard group, double-click the **Format Painter** button. The pointer changes again to an I-beam with a paintbrush beside it.

9. Select **Experience** to apply the new formatting.

10. Select **Activities**. The new formatting is applied.

11. Click the **Format Painter** button again to turn it off.

12. Save and leave the document open for use in the next Step-by-Step.

Setting Tabs

A *tab* is used to align or position text in a document. Word has default tab stops set at one-half-inch intervals from the left margin. If no other tabs are set, pressing the Tab key moves the insertion point to each default tab stop. However, you may need to set your own tab stops to align text at different locations. Word offers five types of tab stops, as described in **Table WD 2–1**.

TABLE WD 2–1   Tab stops

TAB STOP	TYPE	DESCRIPTION
⌞	Left	Aligns text flush left at the tab stop
⌟	Right	Aligns text flush right at the tab stop
⊥	Center	Centers text at the tab stop
⊥	Decimal	Aligns characters on the decimal point at the tab stop
│	Bar	Displays a vertical line at the tab stop

Setting Tabs Using the Ruler

The Tab Selector, which is located below the Ribbon in the left portion of the horizontal ruler, is used to pick the type of tab you want to set. Clicking the Tab Selector changes the type of tab. When you click on the ruler, a tab stop is inserted. To remove a tab stop, drag it off the ruler. To move a tab stop, drag it to another location on the ruler. When setting tab stops in existing text, first be sure to select the paragraph or paragraphs in which you want to set or change tab stops.

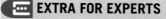

EXTRA FOR EXPERTS

You can clear all the tabs by clicking the Clear All button in the Tabs dialog box.

Setting Tabs Using the Tabs Dialog Box

The Tabs dialog box contains options for setting precise tabs, changing tab alignment, and choosing a *leader*, which is a dotted, dashed, or solid line used to fill the empty space before a tab stop. You access the Tabs dialog box through the Tabs button in the Paragraph dialog box or by double-clicking a tab on the ruler.

Step-by-Step WD 2.4

The document Zare Resume *XXX* from Step-by-Step WD 2.3 should be open in the Word program window.

1. Click the **View Ruler** button at the top of the vertical scroll bar, if necessary, to display the ruler.

2. Click to the left of *Mandy Zare*.

3. Press **Tab**. Notice that the text moves over to the default one-half inch tab stop.

4. Press **Backspace**. The text returns to the left margin.

5. Notice that a Left Tab is displayed in the Tab Selector. Click the ruler at approximately 4.25", as shown in **Figure WD 2–11**. A left tab is inserted.

FIGURE WD 2–11
Tab stop set on the ruler

Tab Selector displays a left tab

Select the paragraph or position the insertion point within the paragraph where you want to insert a tab

Click the ruler to set a left tab

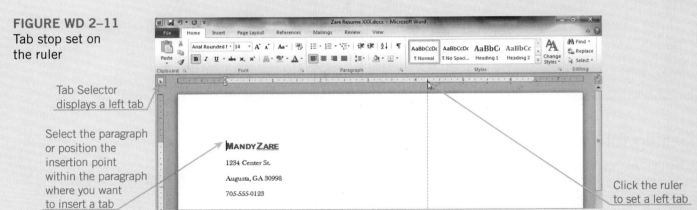

6. Press **Tab**. The text moves to the tab stop.

7. In the Education section, select the line that begins *BBA in Marketing*.

8. Press and hold **Ctrl**, and select the first line in the Experience section, which begins *Internship with Meyers and Clark.*

9. On the Home tab, in the Paragraph group, click the **dialog box launcher** to open the Paragraph dialog box.

10. Click the **Tabs** button to open the Tabs dialog box.

11. Type **6.25** in the Tab stop position box. In the Alignment section, click the **Right** option button, and in the Leader section, click the **2** option button, as shown in **Figure WD 2–12**. Click the **OK** button to close the Tabs dialog box.

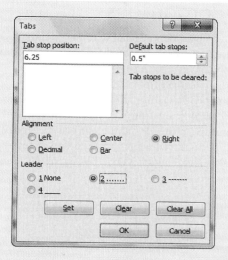

FIGURE WD 2–12
Tabs dialog box

12. In the first line of the Education section, click to the left of the date, *May 2013*, and press **Tab**. The date moves to the right tab stop and a leader is inserted.

13. In the Experience section, click to the left of the date, *Summer 2013*, and press **Tab**. The text moves to the right tab stop and a leader is inserted, as shown in **Figure WD 2–13**.

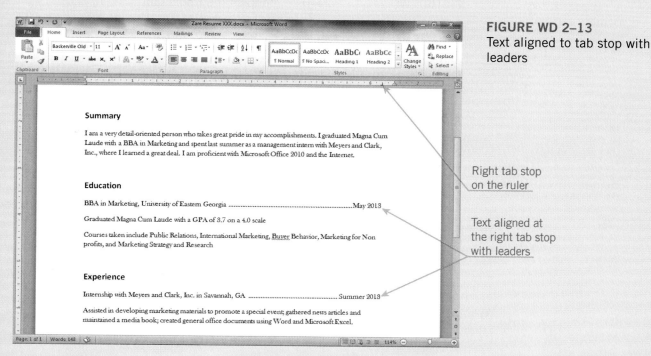

FIGURE WD 2–13
Text aligned to tab stop with leaders

Right tab stop on the ruler

Text aligned at the right tab stop with leaders

14. Save the document and leave it open for use in the next Step-by-Step.

Formatting Paragraphs

The alignment, spacing, and indentation of text in a document depend on the formatting you apply to paragraphs. Word refers to any amount of text or other items followed by a paragraph mark as a ***paragraph***.

To apply paragraph formatting, position your insertion point anywhere in a paragraph. Word will apply the paragraph formats you select to the entire paragraph. You cannot apply paragraph formatting to only a selection of the paragraph.

The Paragraph group on the Home tab, shown in **Figure WD 2–14**, contains buttons for changing paragraph formatting. You can access additional commands in the Paragraph dialog box, which you can display by clicking the dialog box launcher.

▶ **VOCABULARY**
paragraph

nonprinting symbols

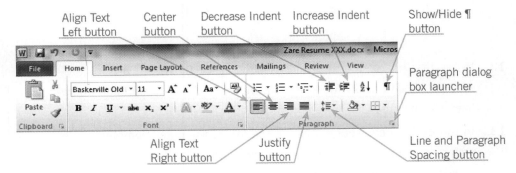

FIGURE WD 2–14   Paragraph group on the Home tab

Showing Nonprinting Symbols

It can be difficult to tell how many spaces, paragraph marks, tabs, and other ***nonprinting symbols*** exist within a document, especially if your document contains various font styles and sizes. Although they are not printed, these characters affect the appearance of your document, and it is often helpful to have the nonprinting symbols displayed when editing text. The Show/Hide ¶ button in the Paragraph group on the Home tab displays or hides paragraph marks, spaces, tabs, and other nonprinting symbols. See **Figure WD 2–15**.

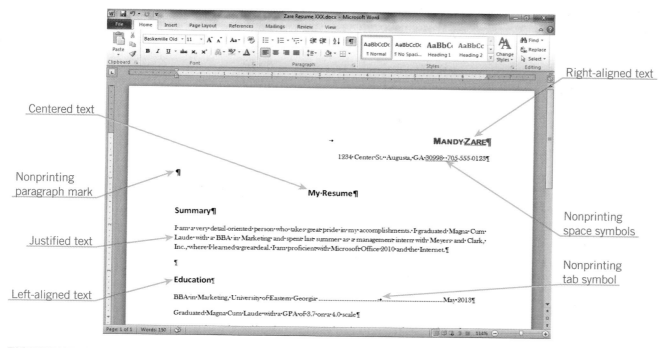

FIGURE WD 2–15   Nonprinting symbols and aligned text

Aligning Text

You can left-align, center, right-align, or justify text in Word, as shown in Figure WD 2–15. The easiest way to align text is to use the alignment buttons in the Paragraph group on the Home tab. **Table WD 2–2** describes the alignment options.

TABLE WD 2–2   Alignment options

OPTION	BUTTON	SHORTCUT KEYS	DESCRIPTION
Align Text Left		Ctrl+L	Lines up text flush with the left margin and leaves a ragged right edge
Align Text Right		Ctrl+R	Lines up text flush with the right margin and leaves a ragged left edge
Center		Ctrl+E	Centers the text between the margins
Justify		Ctrl+J	Aligns text flush with the left margin and flush with the right margin

Step-by-Step WD 2.5

The document Zare Resume *XXX* from Step-by-Step WD 2.4 should be open in the Word program window.

1. On the Home tab, in the Paragraph group, click the **Show/Hide ¶** button ¶ to display the nonprinting symbols.

2. Select the paragraph mark after *Center St.*

3. Press **Delete** to delete the paragraph mark and move up the line below.

4. Press the **spacebar** twice to add extra spaces.

5. Select the paragraph mark after the zip code *30998* and press **Delete**. The paragraph mark is deleted and the line below moves up.

6. Press the **spacebar** twice to add extra spaces.

7. Select **Mandy Zare** and the line containing the address and telephone number. On the Home tab, in the Paragraph group, click the **Align Text Right** button ▤ to align text at the right margin.

8. Click to the left of the *S* in the *Summary* heading. Type **My Resume** and press **Enter**.

9. Select **My Resume**. On the Home tab, in the Paragraph group, click the **Center** button ▤ to center the paragraph.

10. Select the paragraph under the Summary heading. In the Paragraph group, click the **Justify** button ▤ to justify the paragraph.

11. Select the paragraph under the Education heading that begins *Courses taken include,* and click the **Justify** button to justify the paragraph.

12. Select the paragraph under the Experience heading that begins *Assisted in developing,* and click the **Justify** button to justify the paragraph.

13. On the Home tab, in the Paragraph group, click the **Show/Hide ¶** button to hide the nonprinting symbols.

14. Save the document and leave it open for use in the next Step-by-Step.

Setting Line and Paragraph Spacing

Line spacing determines the vertical distance between lines of text in a paragraph. The space allocated for single-spacing is just a little taller than the point size used for the largest font size on the line. When you choose double-spacing, the line is approximately twice the point size of the characters. If a line contains a large character, graphic, or formula, Word increases the spacing for that line.

The Line and Paragraph Spacing button on the Home tab in the Paragraph group lets you choose a common line spacing option, such as 1.0 (single-spacing) or 2.0 (double-spacing). You can also display the Paragraph dialog box, which contains options for creating custom line spacing.

You can add space before (above) or after (below) a paragraph without pressing Enter by entering measurements in the Before and After boxes in the Spacing section of the Paragraph dialog box or in the Paragraph group on the Page Layout tab of the Ribbon. You can also click the Line and Spacing Paragraph button in the Paragraph group on the Home tab, and then choose the Remove Space Before Paragraph option to remove all spacing before the paragraph. Likewise, the Remove Space After Paragraph command removes space following the paragraph. When the selected paragraph does not have preceding or following line spaces, these commands change to Add Space Before Paragraph and Add Space After Paragraph. These commands add 12 pts of spacing before or after a paragraph.

EXTRA FOR EXPERTS

If you choose At least, Exactly, or Multiple on the Line Spacing menu in the Spacing section of the Paragraph dialog box, you enter a value for the line size, and Word no longer adjusts for font sizes used on the line.

Step-by-Step WD 2.6

The document Zare Resume *XXX* from Step-by-Step WD 2.5 should be open in the Word program window.

1. Select **Mandy Zare** and the address and telephone number below it.

2. On the Home tab, in the Paragraph group, click the **Line and Paragraph Spacing** button and click **2.0**. The line spacing is increased to 2.0, or double-spacing. See **Figure WD 2–16**.

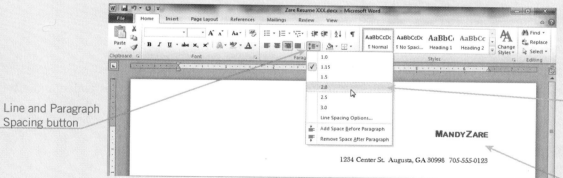

Line and Paragraph Spacing button

FIGURE WD 2–16
Line and Paragraph Spacing button and menu

Click to choose double spacing

Word's Live Preview feature shows the text with double spacing before you click 2.0

3. In the Paragraph group, click the **Line and Paragraph Spacing** button and click **1.0**. The line spacing is decreased to 1.0, or single-spacing.

4. In the Paragraph group, click the **Line and Paragraph Spacing** button and click **Remove Space After Paragraph** to change the spacing.

5. In the Paragraph group, click the **Line and Paragraph Spacing** button and click **Add Space Before Paragraph** to change the spacing.

6. Select **My Resume**.

7. On the Home tab, in the Paragraph group, click the **dialog box launcher** to open the Paragraph dialog box.

8. On the Indents and Spacing tab, in the Spacing area, click the **up arrow** on the Before menu three times or until it reads 18 pt, and then click the **Line spacing** list arrow and click **Double**, as shown in **Figure WD 2–17**.

FIGURE WD 2–17
Paragraph dialog box

Click arrow to increase space before (above) a paragraph

Line spacing list arrow

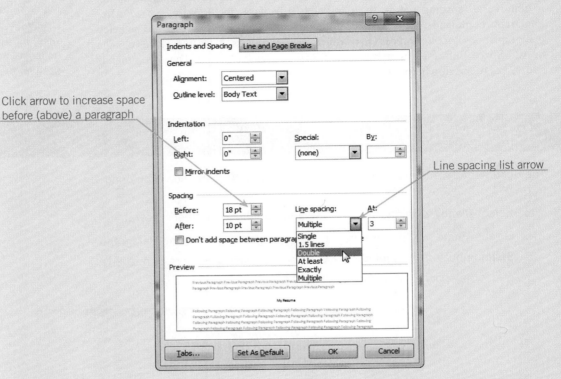

9. Click the **OK** button to accept the settings. Spacing is added above the paragraph and line spacing is changed to double.

10. Save and close the document.

Setting Indents

An *indent* is the space between text and the margin. You can indent text on the left, right, or on both sides. When you indent only the first line of a paragraph, it is called a *first-line indent*. A *negative indent*, also called an outdent, extends into the left margin. A *hanging indent* occurs when you indent all the lines from the left except the first one.

Figure WD 2–18 shows several ways you can use indentation to set paragraphs off from other text in your documents.

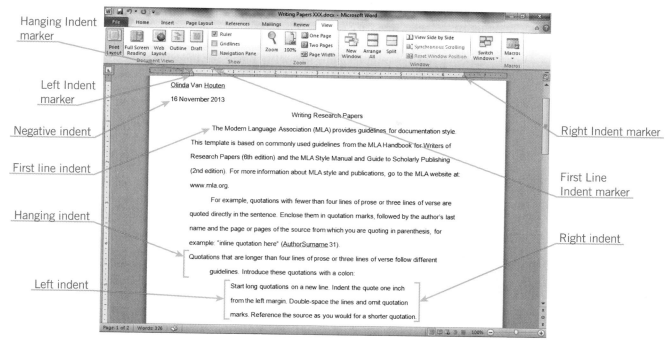

FIGURE WD 2–18   Indents

Do not use Tab or the spacebar to create indents. Also, do not attempt to control indentation by pressing Enter at the end of each line. These methods make editing a Word document or converting a document to another file format very difficult. Instead, set precise measurements for paragraph indents in the Paragraph dialog box, as shown in **Figure WD 2–19**.

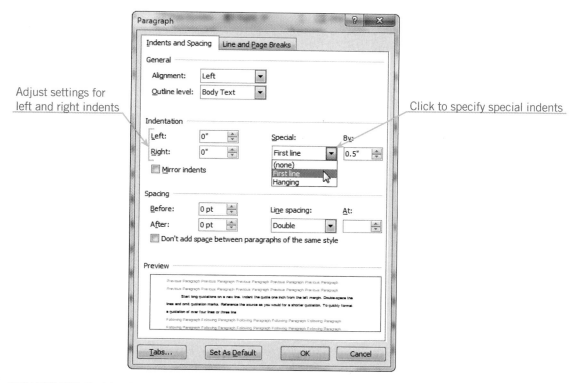

FIGURE WD 2–19   Paragraph dialog box

You can also specify left and right indents in the Paragraph group on the Page Layout tab of the Ribbon. In addition, you can control paragraph indents by dragging the indent markers on the horizontal ruler. The ruler contains three left indent markers and one right indent marker. The First Line Indent marker controls the indentation of the first line of a paragraph. The Hanging Indent marker indents all lines except the first one.

The Left Indent marker box beneath the Hanging Indent marker indents the entire paragraph from the left. The Right Indent marker indents a selected paragraph from the right. To use these markers, make sure the insertion point is in the paragraph you want to indent and then simply drag the appropriate marker to the desired position on the ruler.

Use the Increase Indent and Decrease Indent buttons in the Paragraph group to set and remove indents quickly. Each time you use one of these buttons, you increase or decrease the indent by one-half inch.

Step-by-Step WD 2.7

1. Open **Step WD 2-7** from the folder containing the data files for this lesson. Save the document as **Writing Papers _XXX_** (replace _XXX_ with your initials).

2. Select the name and date on the first two lines of the document.

3. On the ruler, click and drag the **Left Indent marker** ⬜ one-half inch to the left to create a negative indent, as shown in **Figure WD 2–20**.

FIGURE WD 2–20
Negative indent

Drag Left Indent marker into the left margin

Negative indent

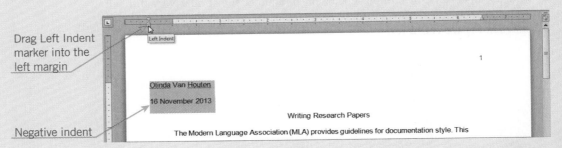

4. Click in the paragraph that begins _The Modern Language_. Click and drag the **First Line Indent** marker ▽ to the right one-half inch, as shown in **Figure WD 2–21**.

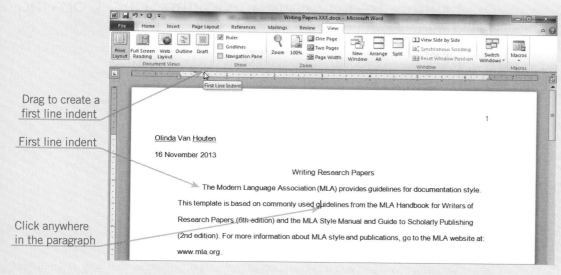

FIGURE WD 2–21
First line indent

5. Triple-click the first paragraph to select it.

6. On the Home tab, in the Clipboard group, click the **Format Painter** button.

7. Drag across the second and third paragraphs with the Format Painter pointer to apply the same formatting.

8. Click the fourth paragraph, which begins with *Start long quotations*. Click the **Increase Indent** button to indent the paragraph one-half inch.

9. On the Page Layout tab, in the Paragraph group, click the **Indent Right** up arrow five times, or until the text box reads 0.5", as shown in **Figure WD 2–22**. The paragraph is indented one-half inch from the right margin.

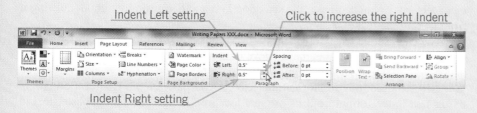

FIGURE WD 2–22
Left Indent and Right Indent settings

10. Scroll to the second page of the document and select the five lines below the *Works Cited* title.

11. On the Page Layout tab, in the Paragraph group, click the **dialog box launcher** to open the Paragraph dialog box.

12. In the Indentation area, click the **Special** list arrow and then click **Hanging**. The 0.5" measurement automatically appears in the By box.

13. Click the **OK** button to close the Paragraph dialog box. Now the five lines are formatted to have a hanging indent if they wrap to another line.

14. Save and close the document.

Editing Text: Deleting, Moving, and Copying

During the writing process, you will often find that you need to remove, rearrange, and revise text. The Cut, Paste, and Copy commands in the Clipboard group on the Home tab of the Ribbon, shown in **Figure WD 2-23**, can help.

FIGURE WD 2-23   Clipboard group

Deleting Text

Deleting text is just about as common as typing text, and the easiest way to delete text you just typed is to use the Backspace and Delete keys on the keyboard. Backspace removes characters to the left of the insertion point, whereas Delete removes characters to the right of the insertion point. You can also delete a section of text by selecting it and then pressing either Delete or Backspace.

Cutting, Copying, and Pasting Text

The Clipboard is a convenient way to move or copy text not only within a document but also to other Word documents, Office files, and other files such as PDF documents and e-mail messages. The *Clipboard* is an area of memory that temporarily stores a cut or copied selection. The cut or copied selection remains in the Clipboard until you cut or copy another selection from Word or another program, or until you shut down the computer.

To move a selection, you *cut* or remove the selection from one position and *paste* the selection into another position. When you *copy* a selection, you duplicate the selection so you can paste the selection into another position without deleting it from its original location.

You can use the Cut, Copy, and Paste buttons in the Clipboard group or use the commands on the shortcut menu to move or copy data from one location to another. When you click the Paste button arrow, the Paste Options area on the Paste menu provides three options for formatting text as you paste: Keep Source Formatting pastes text in the format from its original location; Merge Formatting pastes text in the format of the paragraph in the new location; and Keep Text Only pastes unformatted text. Use the Paste Special command on the Paste menu to open the Paste Special dialog box, which you can use to paste links or embed Clipboard contents in the format you specify. The Set Default Paste command on the Paste menu opens the Word Options dialog box where you can change default paste options for various paste operations such as pasting between documents or pasting from other programs.

You can also right-click a selection and use the commands on the shortcut menu to move or copy text or graphics from one location to another.

Using Drag-and-Drop Editing

You can use the ***drag-and-drop*** feature to move or copy a selection to a new location on your screen. To move text, you select text with the mouse, drag the selection until the dotted line insertion point is located where you want to position the new text, and then release the mouse button to "drop" the text in its new location.

To copy text, you select, drag, and drop text while holding the Ctrl key. When you copy a selection, you will see a plus sign (+) on the pointer. When you move or copy a selection using the drag-and-drop method, the selection is not stored in the Clipboard.

▶ **VOCABULARY**
drag-and-drop

Step-by-Step WD 2.8

1. Open **Step WD 2-8** from the folder containing the data files for this lesson. Save the document as **Zare Resume Edit XXX** (replace *XXX* with your initials).

2. In the Summary section, click after the *y* in *very*.

3. Press **Backspace** until the word is deleted and there is one blank space between words.

4. In the last paragraph of the Education section, select **Public Relations** (include the comma and the blank space in the selection).

5. On the Home tab, in the Clipboard group, click the **Cut** button ✄. The words are removed from the screen, leaving the insertion point at the beginning of the word *International*.

6. Click before the letter *a* in *and Marketing Strategy* at the end of the line. In the Clipboard group, click the **Paste** button 📋 to insert the text you cut in Step 5. Notice the Paste Options button appears next to the insertion point after the text is pasted, making it convenient to change the formatting of pasted text.

7. In the Education section, click before the *G* in *Graduated* and press **Delete** until the word *Graduated* and the space after it is deleted, as shown in **Figure WD 2–24**.

Insertion point after deletion of *Graduated*

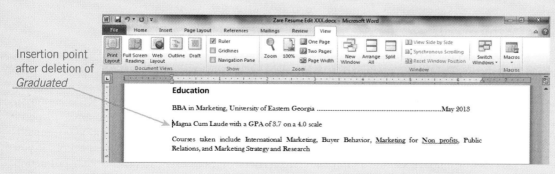

FIGURE WD 2–24
Word deleted from resume

8. In the Education section, select the words **Strategy and Research** on the last line. In the Clipboard group, click the **Copy** button 📋.

9. Click after the *s* in *Public Relations* (before the comma), and then click the **Paste** button to paste a copy of the words in a new location.

10. In the last line of the Experience section, select the word **Microsoft,** drag the selection until the dotted line insertion point precedes the word *Word*, as shown in **Figure WD 2–25**, and then release the mouse button to "drop" the word in its new location. Adjust spacing between words if necessary.

FIGURE WD 2–25
Drag-and-drop editing

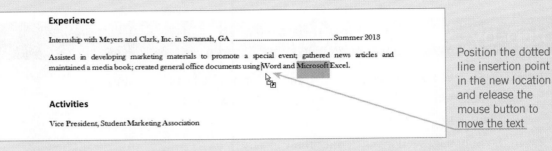

Experience

Internship with Meyers and Clark, Inc. in Savannah, GA .... Summer 2013

Assisted in developing marketing materials to promote a special event; gathered news articles and maintained a media book; created general office documents using Word and Microsoft Excel.

Activities

Vice President, Student Marketing Association

Position the dotted line insertion point in the new location and release the mouse button to move the text

11. Save the document and leave it open for use in the next Step-by-Step.

Using Undo, Redo, and Repeat

Sometimes you will need to reverse, or undo, your most recent action. The Undo button on the Quick Access Toolbar, shown in **Figure WD 2–26**, undoes the last action; clicking the Undo button a second time undoes the prior action, and so on. If you click the Undo button arrow, you see a list of actions you can undo. The Undo ScreenTip changes to reflect the last action that can be undone. For example, if you just pasted text, the screen tip would say Undo Paste, because Paste was the last action you performed, and you can undo it with one click of the Undo button. Some actions cannot be undone; if you cannot undo an action, such as saving a file, the Undo button is dimmed, and its ScreenTip changes to Can't Undo.

Quick Access Toolbar

Undo button

Repeat button

FIGURE WD 2–26   Quick Access Toolbar

If you undo an action but then decide against the undo, use the Redo button on the Quick Access Toolbar to reverse an Undo action. The Redo button arrow displays a list of actions you can redo. When you cannot redo an action, the button is dimmed.

The Repeat button on the Quick Access Toolbar repeats your last action. If you cannot repeat the action, the ScreenTip changes to Can't Repeat. If your last action was an Undo, the Repeat button changes to the Redo button.

Step-by-Step WD 2.9

The document Zare Resume Edit *XXX* from Step-by-Step WD 2.8 should be open in the Word program window.

1. In the Education section, select **Buyer Behavior.**

2. On the Home tab, in the Clipboard group, click the **Cut** button. The selected words are removed from the screen.

3. On the Quick Access Toolbar, click the **Undo** button arrow. Click **Cut** at the top of the list, as shown in **Figure WD 2–27.** (Your list might look different.) The words *Buyer Behavior* reappear in their previous location.

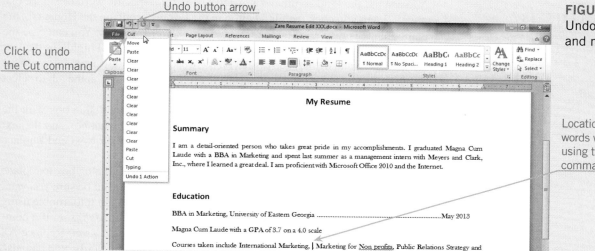

FIGURE WD 2–27
Undo button and menu

4. On the Quick Access Toolbar, click the **Redo** button to remove the words from the document.

5. Click the **Undo** button to return the words to the document.

6. Click after *Public Relations Strategy and Research* (before the comma), press the **spacebar**, and then type **Topics.**

7. On the Quick Access Toolbar, click the **Repeat** button. The inserted text is repeated.

8. Click the **Undo** button. The repeated word is removed from the screen.

9. Save and close the document.

Finding and Replacing Text

The Find and Replace commands are two separate commands that are often used together to find and replace text, formats, and other items. The Find and Replace buttons are located in the Editing group on the Home tab, as shown in **Figure WD 2–28**.

FIGURE WD 2–28   Editing group on the Home tab

EXTRA FOR EXPERTS

You can also use the Navigation Pane to navigate a document by heading or by page, as you will learn in Lesson 3.

You can use the Find command alone to search for a specific word or phrase in a document. When you click the Find button in the Editing group on the Home tab, the Navigation Pane is displayed on the left side of the Word window. You can type the text you want to find in the Search Document box, and Word will highlight the text in your document and display the results on the Browse the results from your current search tab in the Navigation Pane. You can click one of the results on the tab to select that occurrence of the text in the document.

Clicking the Replace button displays the Find and Replace dialog box with the Replace tab active. Type the text you want to find in the Find what box and the text you want to replace it with in the Replace with box. Use the Find Next and Replace buttons to make just one replacement at a time.

You can use the Replace All button in the Find and Replace dialog box to replace all occurrences of a word at once without confirming each one. But be sure you want to replace every occurrence of the word. For instance, you can run into trouble using Replace All when changing a person's name, such as *Jackson* to *Johnson*. If a company name or city name in the document contains the name *Jackson*, Replace All changes it to *Johnson* as well. Since Word also replaces partial words, you can also run into trouble when changing the word *and* to *or* because it would change the word *sand* to *sor*.

Use the More button to expand the Find and Replace dialog box and then refine your find-and-replace operations by matching case, finding only specific formats, and using special characters. You can limit the Replace search by selecting all or part of a document, or by selecting Up or Down in the Search menu.

Step-by-Step WD 2.10

1. Open **Step WD 2-10** from the folder containing the data files for this lesson and save it as **Research Letter *XXX*** (replace *XXX* with your initials).

2. On the Home tab, in the Editing group, click the **Find** button. The Navigation Pane is displayed on the left side of the window.

3. Type **Trey Research Company** in the Search Document box. All occurrences of *Trey Research Company* are highlighted in the document, and the search results are displayed in the Navigation Pane, as shown in **Figure WD 2–29**.

Type the text you want to find in the Search Document box

Browse the results from your search tab

Search results; click one of the results to select that occurrence in the document

Searched-for text is highlighted in the document

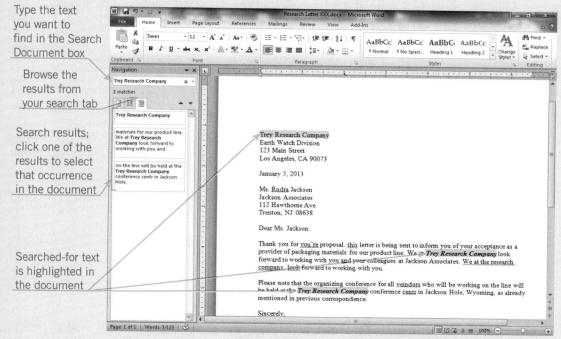

FIGURE WD 2–29
Navigation Pane

4. On the Home tab, in the Editing group, click the **Replace** button to display the Find and Replace dialog box. The text you entered in the Search Document box in the Navigation Pane already appears in the Find what text box in the dialog box.

5. Type **Trey-Davis Research Corporation** in the Replace with box, as shown in **Figure WD 2–30**.

FIGURE WD 2–30
Find and Replace dialog box

6. Click the **Replace All** button to replace all occurrences of *Trey Research Company*.

7. A message box is displayed telling you that three replacements were made. Click the **OK** button to close the message box. Leave the Find and Replace dialog box open.

8. Click a blank area on the letter. Press **Ctrl+Home** to position the insertion point at the beginning of the document with nothing selected.

9. Type **Jackson** in the Find what box in the Find and Replace dialog box, and then press **Tab** to move to the Replace with box. Type **Johnson** and click the **Find Next** button. Notice that clicking the Find Next button only selects the name Jackson; it does not perform a replacement operation yet, even though you have entered a replacement term in the Replace with box.

10. The first occurrence of Rudra Jackson's last name is highlighted. Click the **Replace** button to replace it with Johnson.

11. The name of Rudra Jackson's company is highlighted. Click the **Find Next** button to leave the company name unchanged.

12. The second occurrence of Rudra Jackson's last name is highlighted. Click the **Replace** button to change the name.

13. Click the **Find Next** button to skip the company name and then click the **Find Next** button again to skip Jackson Hole.

14. Click the **OK** button to close the dialog box telling you the search is finished. Click the **Close** button ![X] to close the Find and Replace dialog box click the **Close** button ![X] on the Navigation Pane to close it.

15. Save the document and leave it open for use in the next Step-by-Step.

Proofing a Document

One of the last steps in creating a document is refining the text and checking for mistakes. The Proofing group on the Review tab of the Ribbon, shown in **Figure WD 2–31**, contains commands to help you look up words in a dictionary or thesaurus, check spelling and grammar, and count the words in the document.

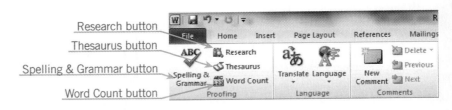

FIGURE WD 2–31   Proofing group on the Review tab

Checking Spelling and Grammar

Word automatically checks spelling and grammar as you type by comparing a document's language to Word's built-in dictionary and grammar rules. Word flags words that might be misspelled with a wavy red underline. If Word detects a grammatical construction that does not conform to rules of grammar, it adds a wavy green underline to the language in question. If Word suspects you have used a word incorrectly, such as typing *there* instead of *their*, it adds a blue wavy line. You can right-click a word that has a red, green, or blue wavy line and see a shortcut menu with suggestions for corrections. If you don't want to use one of the suggested corrections, you can change the text manually.

You can also check all spelling and grammar in a document with a single action using the Spelling & Grammar button in the Proofing group on the Review tab. This approach is useful when you have finished editing a document but you want to check it one more time to make sure you didn't miss any mistakes or introduce errors while editing. When a possible error is detected, Word displays the Spelling and Grammar dialog box to show you the error and suggest a correction. Use the Change button in the Spelling and Grammar dialog box to correct an error, or use the Change All button to correct all instances of the same error.

When you use the Spelling & Grammar button, Word checks the entire document from the insertion point forward and then works from the beginning of the document to the insertion point. To check only a portion of a document, select the area before starting the check.

The spell checker will flag many proper nouns and other words as being incorrect. Ignore the word or phrase, or ignore all occurrences of the word or phrase, using the Ignore Once or Ignore All buttons as you spell check documents.

Remember, the Spelling and Grammar feature does not eliminate the need to proofread a document. Likewise, the grammar feature is not foolproof. Although it finds many common errors, the Spelling and Grammar feature does not always understand the context of the text and may suggest inappropriate corrections. Be sure to look at suggestions carefully before you decide to accept them.

EXTRA FOR EXPERTS

Word's main dictionary contains most common words, including country names, names of many U.S. cities, some company names, and many proper names. However, you probably use words that are not in Word's main dictionary. You can add those words to a custom dictionary so Word does not flag them each time you type them.

Step-by-Step WD 2.11

The document Research Letter *XXX* from Step-by-Step WD 2.10 should be open in the Word program window.

1. In the first paragraph of the letter, right-click the blue underlined word *you're* to display the shortcut menu.

2. Click the suggested word **your** at the top of the menu, as shown in **Figure WD 2–32**. The word *you're* is changed to *your*.

FIGURE WD 2–32
Using the shortcut menu to correct errors

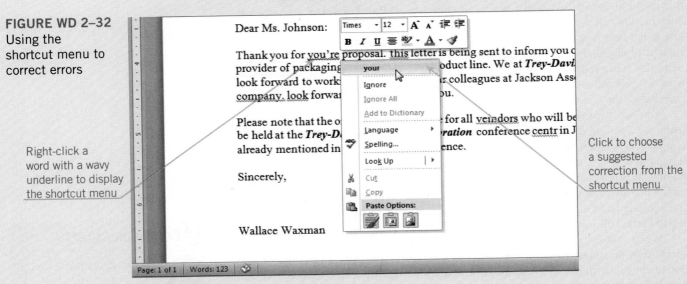

Right-click a word with a wavy underline to display the shortcut menu

Click to choose a suggested correction from the shortcut menu

3. On the Review tab, in the Proofing group, click the **Spelling & Grammar** button to open the Spelling and Grammar dialog box.

4. Click the **Change** button to accept the suggestion to capitalize the *t* in *This*.

5. Click in the Fragment box if necessary, delete the period after *company*, and click the **Change** button, as shown in **Figure WD 2–33**, to remove the period and combine two incomplete sentences into one.

FIGURE WD 2–33
Spelling and Grammar dialog box

Fragment box

Change button

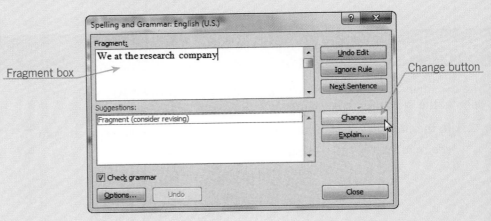

6. Click the **Change** button to accept the correct spelling of *vendors*.

7. Click **center** in the Suggestions list and click **Change** to accept the correct spelling.

8. Click the **Ignore Once** button to ignore the suggestions for changing the name.

9. To respond to the prompt that the spelling and grammar check is complete, click the **OK** button.

10. Save the document and leave it open for use in the next Step-by-Step.

Looking up a Word in the Dictionary

If you need to look up the definition of a word, you can do so by using the Research command in the Proofing group on the Review tab. The Reference Books list contains a list of references that are searchable with Word's Research tool. Another way to look up a word's definition is to right-click a word and choose Look Up from the shortcut menu.

Step-by-Step WD 2.12

The document Research Letter *XXX* from Step-by-Step WD 2.11 should be open in the Word program window.

1. In the first paragraph, second sentence of the letter, right-click the word **provider**, point to **Look Up** on the shortcut menu, and click **Encarta Dictionary: English (North America)**. The Research pane opens displaying results, as shown in **Figure WD 2–34**.

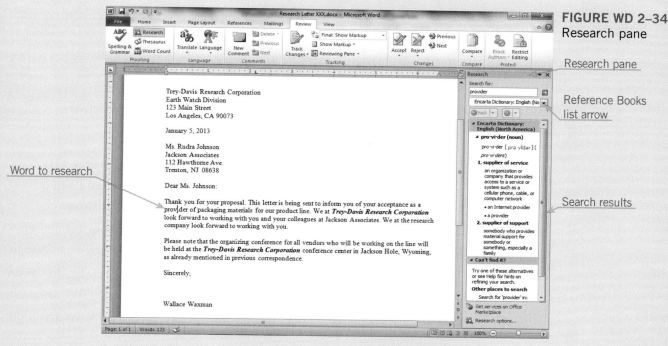

FIGURE WD 2–34
Research pane

Research pane

Reference Books list arrow

Word to research

Search results

2. Save the document and leave it open for use in the next Step-by-Step.

Using the Thesaurus

Make your documents even more interesting and effective using the Thesaurus to replace a word or phrase with a synonym, an antonym, or a related word. The Thesaurus button in the Proofing group opens the Research pane with a list of suggested replacement terms. View more results by selecting a new reference book or search site.

Step-by-Step WD 2.13

The document Research Letter *XXX* from Step-by-Step WD 2.12 should be open in the Word program window.

1. In the first paragraph, second sentence, right-click the word **inform** to open the shortcut menu.

2. Point to **Synonyms** on the shortcut menu, and then click **notify** on the submenu to replace *inform* with *notify*, as shown in **Figure WD 2–35**.

FIGURE WD 2–35
Synonyms on submenu

Click to replace word with this synonym

Point to Synonyms

3. In the second paragraph, first sentence, press and hold **ALT** while clicking **conference**. The word *conference* is looked up in the Research pane.

4. In the Research pane, click the **Reference Books** list arrow and click **Thesaurus: English (U.S.)** to display the list of synonyms for *conference*.

5. Point to the word *meeting* in the list of synonyms, click the **list arrow** to the right of *meeting*, and then click **Insert** on the menu, as shown in **Figure WD 2–36**. The word *meeting* replaces the word *conference* in the document.

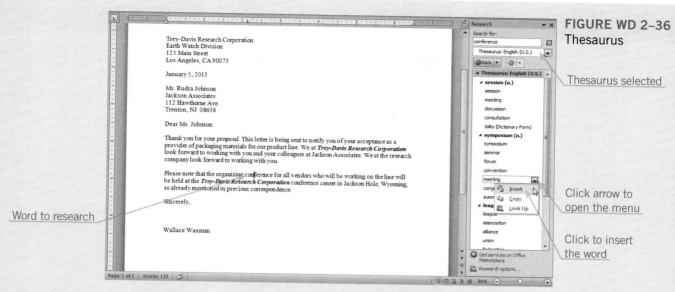

FIGURE WD 2–36
Thesaurus

Thesaurus selected

Word to research

Click arrow to
open the menu

Click to insert
the word

6. Click the **Close** button ☒ on the Research pane to close it.

7. Save the document and leave it open for use in the next Step-by-Step.

Using Word Count

The Word Count command in the Proofing group counts the number of pages, words, characters (with or without spaces), paragraphs, and lines in a document or selection. The count can include text in text boxes, footnotes, and endnotes. To perform a word count for the entire document, no text can be selected in the document.

TECHNOLOGY CAREERS

With the rapid expansion of computer technology, there comes an increased demand for people who can write clear and concise hardware and software documentation. Technical writers are specially trained for this purpose. The information they communicate must be accurate and understandable. In the computer industry, technical writers may use Microsoft Word to write software instructions, reference manuals, or installation guides.

Step-by-Step WD 2.14

The document Research Letter *XXX* from Step-by-Step WD 2.13 should be open in the Word program window.

1. Be sure nothing is selected in the document. On the Review tab, in the Proofing group, click the **Word Count** button. The Word Count dialog box opens with the results, as shown in **Figure WD 2–37**.

FIGURE WD 2–37
Word Count dialog box

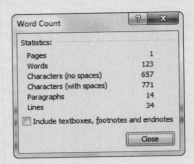

2. Click the **Close** button to close the dialog box.

3. Save and close the document, and then exit Word.

SUMMARY

In this lesson, you learned:

■ That you create a new document using the New command on the File tab.

■ Formatting text changes fonts, font sizes, font styles, and font effects.

■ Clearing formatting removes all new formats.

■ The Format Painter copies formatting characteristics from selected text and applies it to other text.

■ How to set tabs using the ruler and the Tabs dialog box.

■ How to format paragraphs by aligning text and setting line spacing and indents.

■ How to move, delete, cut, copy, and paste text and use drag-and-drop editing.

■ That editing tasks typically involve the Undo, Redo, and Repeat commands.

■ How to use Find and Replace commands to find and replace text, formats, and other items.

■ That documents are corrected and improved by using the Spelling & Grammar checker, looking up words in Word's dictionary, finding synonyms with the Thesaurus, and using Word Count.

◼ VOCABULARY REVIEW

Define the following terms:

characters
Clipboard
copy
cut
drag-and-drop
first-line indent

font
hanging indent
indent
leader
negative indent

nonprinting symbols
paragraph
paste
point size
tab

◼ REVIEW QUESTIONS

MULTIPLE CHOICE

Select the best response for the following statements.

1. _____ measures the height of characters.

   A. Point size   C. Toggle case

   B. Font   D. Drag-and-drop

2. You can use the _____ button to change the capitalization of text quickly.

   A. Underline   C. Change Case

   B. Bold   D. Grow Font

3. The mouse pointer looks like a(n) _____ when you use the Format Painter.

   A. arrow pointer   C. rectangle

   B. insertion point   D. I-beam with a paintbrush

4. The _____ button duplicates a selection so you can paste it into another position.

   A. Format Painter   C. Cut

   B. Paste   D. Copy

5. _____ can be added in the Tabs dialog box.

   A. Indents   C. Line Spacing

   B. Leaders   D. Justification

6. _____ is the alignment option that aligns text flush with the left and right margins.

   A. Align Text Left   C. Justify

   B. Align Text Right   D. Center

7. A _____ indent occurs when you indent all the lines from the left except the first one.

   A. negative   C. right

   B. first-line   D. hanging

8. Use the _____ button when you want to reverse an Undo action.

   A. Redo   C. Repeat

   B. Undo   D. Change Case

9. The _____ button replaces all occurrences of a selection at once without confirming each one.

   A. Format Painter   C. Replace

   B. Replace All   D. Find

10. The _____ command analyzes a document and displays statistics on the number of pages, words, characters, paragraphs, and lines in a document.

    A. Thesaurus   C. Spelling & Grammar

    B. Research   D. Word Count

FILL IN THE BLANK

Complete the following sentences by writing the correct word or words in the blanks provided.

1. _____ are letters, numbers, symbols, punctuation marks, and spaces.

2. A(n) _____ is the design of a set of letters and numbers.

3. When you use the Cut or the Copy buttons, a copy of the cut or copied text is placed on the _____.

4. Use the _____ buttons to display nonprinting symbols when editing.

5. Any amount of text followed by a paragraph mark is considered to be a(n) _____.

6. A(n) _____ is the space between the text and the margin.

7. When you delete something by mistake, immediately click the _____ button.

8. An easy way to find every occurrence of a word in a document is to use the _____ command to open the Navigation Pane.

9. Word automatically checks _____ and _____ as you type.

10. You can use the _____ to replace a word with a synonym, an antonym, or a related word.

■ PROJECTS

PROJECT WD 2–1

1. Open the file **Project WD 2–1** from the folder containing your data files and save it as **Spelling&Grammar XXX** (replace XXX with your initials).

2. Run the Spelling and Grammar checker and correct the mistakes.

3. Save and close the document.

ON YOUR OWN

The Spelling & Grammar checker missed at least one mistake. Can you find it? Open the **Spelling&Grammar XXX** file, correct the error, then save and close the document.

PROJECT WD 2–2

1. Open the file **Project WD 2–2** from the folder containing your data files and save it as **ABC Computers XXX** (replace XXX with your initials).

2. Change all the text to Calibri 12 point.

3. Center *ABC Computers* and its address.

4. Apply bold to *ABC Computers* and its address and change the point size to 14.

5. Change the font color of *ABC Computers* to Orange.

6. Add the Gradient Fill – Blue, Accent 1 text effect to *ABC Computers*.

7. Create half-inch first-line indents on the three paragraphs that make up the body of the letter.

8. In the first paragraph, look up a synonym for the word *company* and insert it.

9. Save and close the document.

ON YOUR OWN

Open the **ABC Computers XXX** file and change the letterhead for *ABC Computers* by applying different fonts, sizes, styles, effects, alignment, and spacing. Save and close the document.

PROJECT WD 2–3

1. Open **Project WD 2–3** from the folder containing your data files and save it as **Appointment Policy** *XXX* (replace the *XXX* with your initials).

2. Right-align the heading *Yasinski Family Practice*. Change the line spacing to double with 18-point spacing before the paragraph and 10 point after the paragraph.

3. Left-align the date, *September 2013*.

4. Center the *Appointment Policy* title.

5. Justify the paragraph that begins *To remain on schedule*. Change the line spacing of the paragraph to 2.0, and remove the space after the paragraph.

6. Select the four-line address and telephone number. Use the Tabs dialog box to insert a left tab at tab stop position 3.8", and then move the text to the tab stop.

7. Save and close the document.

ON YOUR OWN

Open the **Appointment Policy** *XXX* file and use the Thesaurus to replace two words with synonyms. Save and close the document.

PROJECT WD 2–5

1. Open the file **Project WD 2-5** from the folder containing your data files and save it as **Computers** *XXX* (replace the *XXX* with your initials).

2. Center the title, change it to 18 point, and change the case to uppercase.

3. Correct the spelling error in the first paragraph.

4. Select the heading *Prepare for Power Surges*, and change the format to bold, 14-point Arial.

5. With the heading still selected, add 12-point spacing before the paragraph and 6 pt after the paragraph.

6. Use the Format Painter to apply the format to the remaining six headings.

7. Justify, double-space, and add a one half-inch first-line indent to all the paragraphs in the document (not the headings or the title).

8. Use Word Count.

9. Use Find and Replace to find the word *Computer* and replace all occurrences with **PC**.

10. Save and close the document.

ON YOUR OWN

Open the **Computers** *XXX* file. Use the More options in the Find and Replace dialog box to find all occurrences of *PC* that have bold formatting and replace them with *PC* with a blue font color and bold formatting. Save and close the document.

PROJECT WD 2–4

1. Open the file **Project WD 2-4** from the folder containing your data files and save it as **Travel Destinations** *XXX* (replace *XXX* with your initials).

2. Show nonprinting symbols.

3. Select the list of countries and center it.

4. Select *Austria* (be sure to select the paragraph mark, too) and move it above Turkey.

5. Select *United Kingdom* and move it above *China*.

6. Select *Italy* and move it above *United States*.

7. Delete *Mexico*.

8. Undo the deletion.

9. Change the line spacing of the list to 1.5, and remove the space after the paragraphs.

10. Hide nonprinting symbols.

11. Save and close the document.

WEB PROJECT

Search the Web for a digital camera (or other item) to purchase. Decide on the particular camera you would like to purchase, then comparison shop at two different sites. Copy relevant data from the Web sites such as price, shipping costs, availability, and service, and paste it into a new blank document. Create a neatly organized report using text formatting such as fonts, font styles, and sizes as well as page formatting commands like tabs, indents, and spacing to compare the data from each site. Decide from which site you would purchase and why. Name and save the document. Be prepared to share your information and decision with the class.

CRITICAL THINKING

ACTIVITY WD 2–1

Open the Zare Resume document and save it with a new name. Use this document to create your own resume, applying what you've learned about editing and formatting text. Be creative, and be prepared to share your resume with the class, noting the changes or additions you made to the original document.

ACTIVITY WD 2–2

Play "Stump the Spelling & Grammar Checker" by writing one or two sentences containing at least three mistakes that Word's spelling and grammar checker cannot detect. Compare sentences with classmates. Are you surprised at the results? Explore the settings available for adding functionality to the Spelling & Grammar checker. Is there a setting that you can change that will allow Word to detect one or more of the mistakes in your sentences? If so, is this an option you should turn on? Why or why not?

ACTIVITY WD 2–3

What are wildcards? Use Word Help to find out what they are and how to use them when searching Word documents. Be prepared to give two examples of how to use wildcards to find certain words in a document.

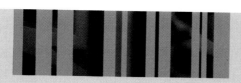

**Estimated Time:
2 hours**

LESSON 3

Formatting Documents

■ OBJECTIVES

Upon completion of this lesson, you should be able to:

- Use templates to create new documents.
- Change document themes.
- Apply styles.
- Navigate long documents.
- Work with lists.
- Add page backgrounds.
- Create columns.
- Use built-in headers or footers.
- Insert and break pages.

■ DATA FILES

To complete this lesson, you will need these data files:

Step WD 3-3.docx
Project WD 3-2.docx
Project WD 3-3.docx
Project WD 3-4.docx
Activity WD 3-3.docx

■ VOCABULARY

bullets

columns

content control

cover page

footer

header

list

orphan

page borders

page break

placeholder

sort

style

template

themes

thumbnails

watermark

widow

Introduction

You learned in the previous lesson that formatting text makes it more attractive and easier to read. Formatting an entire document has the same result. Adding formatting elements such as styles, themes, columns, headers, footers, and page numbers enhances the appearance of a document and helps guide the reader through it.

Creating New Documents Using Templates

One method of quickly and attractively formatting documents is to use templates. A *template* is a master copy, or model, for a certain type of document. Word includes templates for many common types of documents, including memos, letters, fax cover sheets, and reports.

Templates contain settings for margins, page size and orientation, and text and/ or graphics that are standard for a particular type of document. For instance, instead of having to create a layout each time you want to type a memo, you can use one of the memo templates included in Word.

When you create a new blank document using the Blank document icon in Backstage view, the blank document that opens is actually a copy of the Normal template, which serves as a starting point for creating a new document. It is possible to change the settings in the Normal document template, named Normal.dotm, but this should be avoided because any changes made to the template are applied to all future blank documents.

Some templates come already installed with Word, and you can access them by clicking the File tab, clicking New, and then clicking the Sample templates category in the Available Templates section of Backstage view shown in **Figure WD 3–1**. Many more templates are available online, which you can access by clicking a category in the Office.com Templates section of Backstage view. You can also use the Search Office.com for templates box in the Office.com Templates section to look for an online template using keywords.

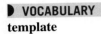

▶ **VOCABULARY**
template

EXTRA FOR EXPERTS

Word templates are saved as the Word Template type with the extension .dotx. If you want to save a document as a template, click the File tab on the Ribbon, click Save As, and then choose Word Template from the Save as type menu in the Save As dialog box.

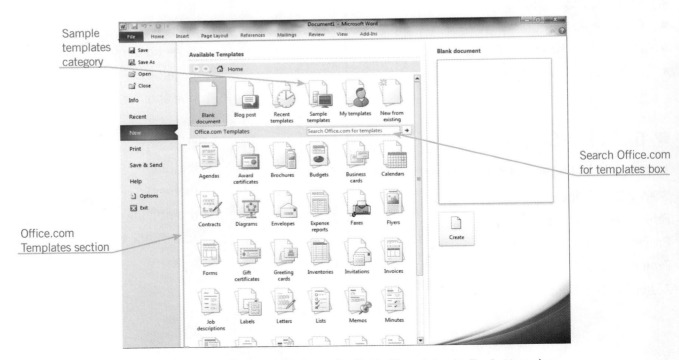

Sample templates category

Office.com Templates section

Search Office.com for templates box

FIGURE WD 3–1   Available Templates in Backstage view

When you have selected the template you want, as shown in **Figure WD 3–2**, you can click the Create button (if it is an installed template) or the Download button (if it is an online template) to open the template. When you select a template file, you can choose to open it in one of two formats—as a document or as a template—using the option buttons below the preview. When you open a template as a document, which is the default option, you are actually opening a copy of the template in the .docx document format, so as you make changes to it, the original template is not altered. When you choose the template option, a copy of the template opens in .dotx format, and you can make changes to it and save it as a new template without altering the original.

You add your own text to a document based on a template by clicking a *placeholder*, such as [Type your text here], which tells you where to insert text, and then beginning to type. To name and save the new document, use the Save or Save As command.

▶ **VOCABULARY**
placeholder

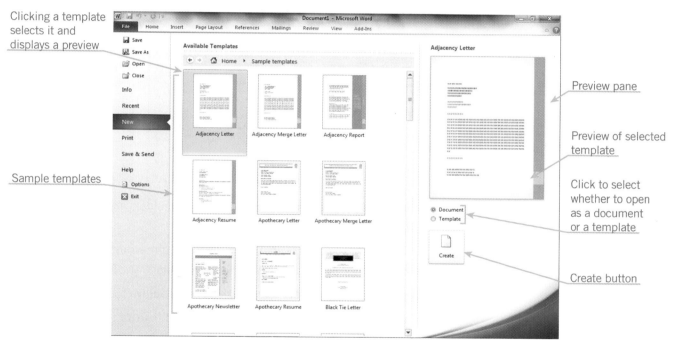

Clicking a template selects it and displays a preview

Sample templates

Preview pane

Preview of selected template

Click to select whether to open as a document or a template

Create button

FIGURE WD 3–2 Template selected in Sample templates category

Step-by-Step WD 3.1

1. Start Word.

2. Click the **File** tab on the Ribbon, and then click **New**. On the right, options are displayed for creating a new document based on available templates.

3. Click **Sample templates** to display sample templates in the center pane.

4. In the Sample templates section, scroll down and click **Oriel Letter**. Notice the preview in the right pane.

5. Confirm that the Document option button is selected under the template preview in the right pane, and then click the **Create** button. The template opens on your screen as a document containing placeholders.

6. Click the **[Pick the date]** placeholder, and then click the placeholder list arrow that is displayed to its right. Click the **Today** button on the calendar, as shown in **Figure WD 3–3**.

FIGURE WD 3–3
Placeholders in document

Placeholders

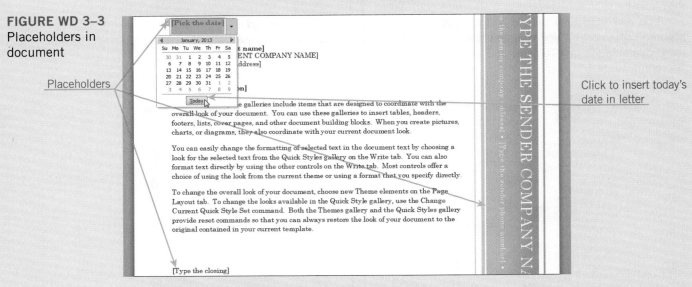

Click to insert today's date in letter

7. Click the **[Type the recipient name]** placeholder, and then type **Ridge Nixon** to overwrite the placeholder.

8. Click the placeholders in the document (some might require double-clicking to select all the text in the placeholder), and type the text below:

    [Type the recipient company name]: **Nixon Sullivan**

    [Type the recipient address]: **54321 Sun Cliff Drive**

    Colorado Springs, CO 80956

    [Type the salutation]: **Dear Mr. Nixon:**

9. Click the body of the letter to display the [Type the body of the letter] placeholder:

    Thank you for enrolling in our class. All classes begin at 9 a.m. and end at 4 p.m. We look forward to seeing you in the Word Fundamentals class on January 25.

    [Type the closing]: **Sincerely,**

    [Your Name]: Type your first and last name. (Your name may already appear here if you have personalized your copy of Microsoft Office with a user name.)

    [Type the sender company name]: **Super Computer Services, Inc.** (Notice that the company name is automatically inserted in the [Type the sender company name] placeholder in the orange sidebar.)

10. Click the placeholders in the orange sidebar (don't worry about the placeholders being turned sideways; you can type as usual) and replace with the following text:

[Type the sender company address]: **10001 Nations Drive, Colorado Springs, CO 80955**

[Type the sender phone number]: **719-555-1000**

[Type the sender e-mail address]: **info@supercomputerservicesinc.com**

11. Save the file as **Class Confirmation *XXX*** (replace *XXX* with your initials), and leave it open for use in the next Step-by-Step.

Changing Document Themes

Modern word-processing software such as Word provides so many different fonts, sizes, colors, font styles, and effects that it can be difficult to figure out which formatting options you should use together to create a professional-looking document. Unless you have an eye for design, choosing one font for headings and a coordinating font for text can be tricky. To make these decisions easier, Word includes built-in *themes*, which are sets of formatting choices that include colors, fonts, and effects that were predesigned to work well together. The themes are available in other Office programs as well, so you can apply the same theme to an Excel spreadsheet, a Word report, and a PowerPoint presentation, resulting in a professionally coordinated package of files.

Each document you create is associated with one of Word's document themes. Even a new blank document is based on a theme. When you change the theme, you change the entire document's color scheme, fonts, and effects to the new design theme. Word provides several different built-in themes, or you can customize a theme using the buttons in the Themes group on the Page Layout tab on the Ribbon. See **Figure WD 3–4**.

> **VOCABULARY**
> **themes**

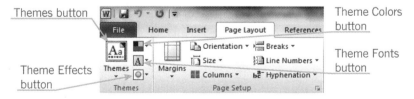

FIGURE WD 3–4   Themes group on the Page Layout tab

The Themes button displays a gallery of built-in theme choices and several menu commands. You can use the Theme Colors button to change the established colors of a theme. The Theme Fonts button displays multiple options for applying a new set of fonts, and the Theme Effects button lets you choose new line and fill effects.

If you change the theme of a document and decide you liked the original look better, you can use the Reset to Theme from Template command on the Themes menu to revert to the document's original theme. Use the Browse for Themes command on the menu to locate a document that contains a theme you want to apply to the current document. After you have customized a theme, you can use the Save Current Theme command to name and save it to the Document Themes folder.

Step-by-Step WD 3.2

The document Class Confirmation *XXX* from Step-by-Step WD 3.1 should be open in the Word program window.

1. On the Page Layout tab, in the Themes group, click the **Themes** button and point to **Opulent**. Notice that Live Preview allows you to see the document as it would look with the theme applied, as shown in **Figure WD 3–5**.

FIGURE WD 3–5
Themes button
and gallery

Themes button

Opulent theme

Menu commands

Live Preview of
theme applied
to document

2. In the Themes gallery, click **Concourse**. The new theme is applied.

3. In the Themes group, click the **Theme Colors** button ![icon], and then scroll down and click **Slipstream**, as shown in **Figure WD 3–6**. The new color is applied.

Theme Colors button

Slipstream option

FIGURE WD 3–6
Theme Colors button and menu

4. In the Themes group, click the **Theme Fonts** button ![icon], and then scroll down and click **Grid**, as shown in **Figure WD 3–7**. The new fonts are applied. Notice how the applied theme changes have altered the appearance of the document.

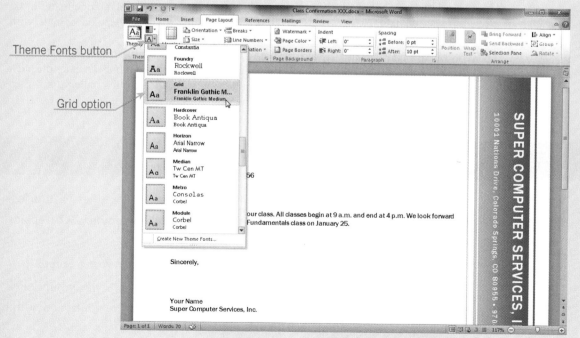

Theme Fonts button

Grid option

FIGURE WD 3–7
Theme Fonts button and menu

5. In the Themes group, click the **Themes** button, and then click **Reset to Theme from OrielLetter Template**. The original theme is applied.

6. Save and close the document.

Applying Styles

▶ **VOCABULARY**
style

When you are formatting documents, it is important to maintain consistency among page elements. For example, each level of headings should be formatted with the same font, font style, size, and color. However, it could take some time to format each heading by manually applying the font, style, size, and color separately. Instead, you can save all those formatting specifications into a style, name it, and then apply it to each heading at once. A *style* is a set of character or paragraph formats stored with a name. Word provides predefined styles you can use, or you can create your own. The Quick Styles gallery in the Styles group on the Home tab displays a few of the styles that are available, as shown in **Figure WD 3–8**. Clicking the More button displays the entire gallery of styles.

FIGURE WD 3–8   Styles group on the Home tab

To apply a style, select the text that you want to change, and then click a style in the Quick Styles gallery.

The styles available in the Quick Styles gallery coordinate with the Word theme that has been applied to a document. Remember, even a new blank document has a theme applied, so the styles available in the Quick Styles gallery coordinate with that theme.

You can format a paragraph with any font, font size, alignment, and other formats you want and then create a new style using that paragraph as an example. Just select the paragraph, click the More button on the Quick Styles gallery, and then click Save Selection as a New Quick Style.

Step-by-Step WD 3.3

1. Open **Step WD 3-3** from the folder containing the data files for this lesson, and save the document as **Caring for Your Computer *XXX*** (replace *XXX* with your initials).

2. Scroll down and select the first heading, **Prepare for Power Surges**.

3. On the Home tab, in the Quick Styles gallery in the Styles group, click the **Heading 1** style. (If you need to display the entire gallery, click the More button.) The new style is applied.

4. Select the heading **Keep Your Computer Clean**.

5. Press and hold **CTRL** while selecting the remaining five headings in the document.

6. In the Quick Styles gallery, click the **Heading 1** style to apply the style to all of the selected headings at once.

7. Select the title **CARING FOR YOUR COMPUTER**.

8. On the Quick Styles gallery, click the **More** button ⬇ to display the entire gallery.

9. Click the **Title** style, as shown in **Figure WD 3–9**. The new style is applied.

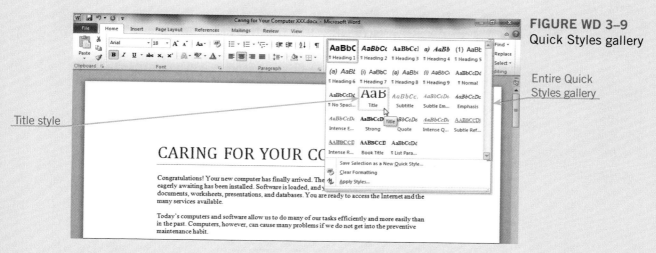

FIGURE WD 3–9
Quick Styles gallery

Entire Quick Styles gallery

Title style

10. Save the file and leave it open for use in the next Step-by-Step.

Navigating Long Documents

As you learned in Lesson 2, you can use the Navigation pane to find specific words in a document. The Navigation pane can also be a useful tool for formatting and editing long documents by helping you quickly navigate to a specific heading or page. When your document contains text formatted with heading styles, the headings are shown in the Browse the headings in your document tab of the Navigation pane. You can click a heading to display that section of the document on the right side of the screen. When you click the Browse the pages in your document tab in the Navigation pane, small pictures of each document page, called *thumbnails*, appear in the pane; click a thumbnail to move the insertion point to that page. To display the Navigation pane, click the Navigation Pane check box in the Show group on the View tab.

▶ **VOCABULARY**
thumbnails

Step-by-Step WD 3.4

The document Caring for Your Computer *XXX* from Step-by-Step WD 3.3 should be open in the Word program window.

1. On the View tab, in the Show group, click the **Navigation Pane** check box to insert a check mark. The Navigation Pane is displayed on the left side of the screen, and the headings are displayed in the Browse the headings in your document tab, as shown in **Figure WD 3–10**.

FIGURE WD 3–10
Navigation Pane

Browse the pages in your document tab

Browse the headings in your document tab

Document headings formatted with styles

Close button

Navigation Pane check box

Navigation Pane

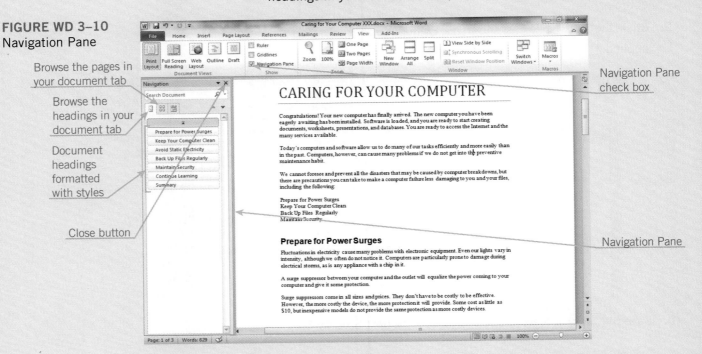

2. In the Navigation Pane, click the **Back Up Files Regularly** heading. The section of the document with the *Back up Files Regularly* heading is displayed on the right side of the screen. The insertion point appears at the beginning of the heading.

3. In the Navigation Pane, click the **Browse the pages in your document** tab to display the document pages as thumbnails.

4. In the Navigation Pane, click page **3** to move the insertion point to the top of the last page in the document, as shown in **Figure WD 3–11**.

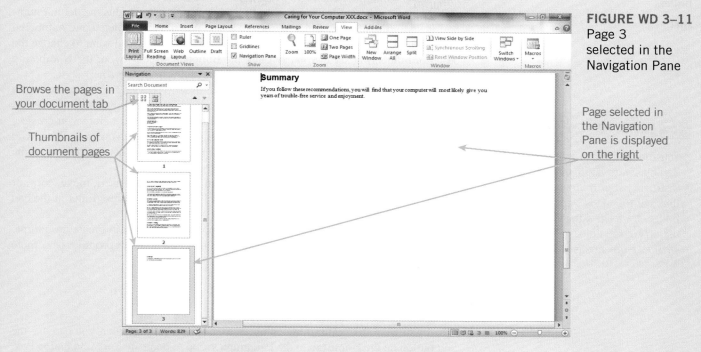

Browse the pages in your document tab

Thumbnails of document pages

FIGURE WD 3–11
Page 3
selected in the
Navigation Pane

Page selected in the Navigation Pane is displayed on the right

5. In the Navigation Pane, click page **1** to move the insertion point to the top of the first page of the document.

6. Click the **Close** button ⊠ on the Navigation pane to close it.

7. Save the file and leave it open for use in the next Step-by-Step.

Working with Lists

A *list* is a series of related words, numbers, or phrases. As you go about your day, you probably make lists of things to do, grocery items to pick up, or assignments that are due. You can create lists with bullets or numbers and sort them using the buttons in the Paragraph group of the Home tab on the Ribbon, shown in **Figure WD 3–12**.

▶ **VOCABULARY**
list

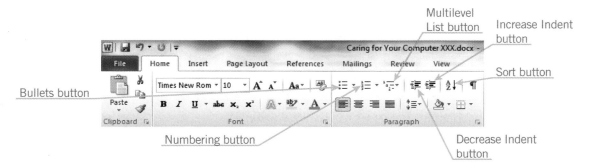

Multilevel List button

Increase Indent button

Sort button

Bullets button

Numbering button

Decrease Indent button

FIGURE WD 3–12   Paragraph group on the Home tab

Adding Bullets and Numbering to Lists

Bullets and numbers help organize items arranged in a list. *Bullets* are symbols that mark the beginning of each entry in a list. The Bullets button adds the default bullet style (a small solid circle) to a list, and the Numbering button adds the default numbering style (the number and a period) to a list. When using bulleted and numbered lists, each list item begins on its own line of the document. If you want to change the bullet or numbering style, you can click the Bullets button arrow or the Numbering button arrow and then choose from the available styles or define a new style.

The Bullets and Numbering buttons can be used in two ways. You can select an existing list and then click the Bullets button or the Numbering button to add bullets or numbers, or you can click the Bullets or Numbering button before you create a list to have Word automatically add the bullets or numbers as you type. When you use the second method, press Enter after you finish typing the list and then click the Bullets or Numbering button again to turn off the feature.

Word automatically renumbers a numbered list when you insert, move, copy, or delete items. A new bullet is added on a blank line when you press Enter at the end of a bulleted item.

The Multilevel list button in the Paragraph group is used to create an outline. You can use the Increase Indent and Decrease Indent buttons to promote or demote items to different outline levels.

Sorting Lists

When you want to organize data in ascending or descending order, you can use the Sort button on the Home tab in the Paragraph group to open the Sort Text dialog box. When you *sort* text, Word rearranges selected text, numbers, or dates alphabetically, numerically, or chronologically.

When you choose ascending order, text is sorted from A to Z, numbers are sorted from 1 to 9, and dates are sorted from earliest to latest. Descending order sorts text from Z to A, numbers from 9 to 1, and dates from latest to earliest.

The Sort Text dialog box, as shown in **Figure WD 3–13**, allows you to sort by up to three levels and choose other sort options.

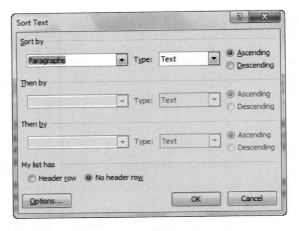

FIGURE WD 3–13   Sort Text dialog box

Step-by-Step WD 3.5

The document Caring for Your Computer *XXX* from Step-by-Step WD 3.4 should be open in the Word program window.

1. In the first section of the document, select the four-line list that begins with *Prepare for Power Surges*.

2. On the Home tab, in the Paragraph group, click the **Numbering** button arrow, and then click the **numbers with parentheses** format from the Numbering Library, as shown in **Figure WD 3–14**. The format is applied.

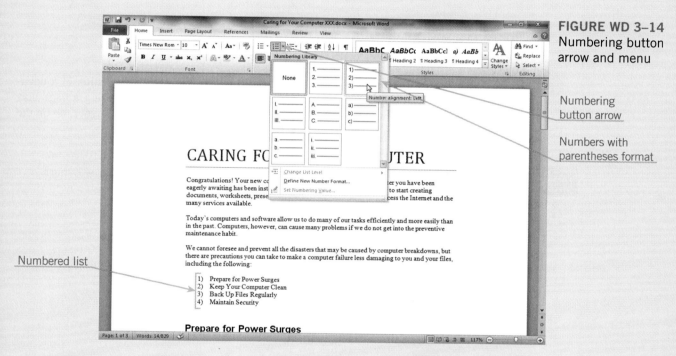

FIGURE WD 3–14
Numbering button arrow and menu

Numbering button arrow

Numbers with parentheses format

Numbered list

3. Click at the end of the list item *Keep Your Computer Clean*, and press **Enter**. The number *3)* is inserted, and the remaining items are renumbered.

4. Type **Avoid Static Electricity** to add a new list item.

5. Select the entire list and click the **Numbering** button to remove the numbering.

6. With the list still selected, click the **Bullets** button. The default bullet format is applied.

7. With the list still selected, click the **Bullets** button arrow, and then click the **square bullet** format from the Bullet Library. The format is applied.

8. Click at the end of the list item *Maintain Security*, and then press **Enter**. A new bullet is inserted.

9. Type **Continue Learning**.

10. Select the entire list. On the Home tab, in the Paragraph group, click the **Sort** button  to display the Sort Text dialog box.

11. Click **OK** to sort the list in ascending order using the default settings in the dialog box.

12. On the Quick Access Toolbar, click the **Undo** button to remove the sort, because this list needs to be in the same order as the headings in the document.

13. Save the file and leave it open for use in the next Step-by-Step.

Adding Page Backgrounds

You can add interest, emphasize text, or include important information in a document by inserting a watermark, changing the page color, or inserting a page border using the buttons in the Page Background group on the Page Layout tab on the Ribbon, shown in **Figure WD 3–15.**

FIGURE WD 3–15   Page Background group on the Page Layout tab

Inserting a Watermark

A *watermark* is text or a graphic that appears behind text in a document. A watermark can display a company logo or text, such as the word *Draft* or *Confidential*, in the background of each printed page, as shown in **Figure WD 3–16**. Word provides built-in watermarks, or you can create a custom watermark.

▶ **VOCABULARY**
watermark
page borders

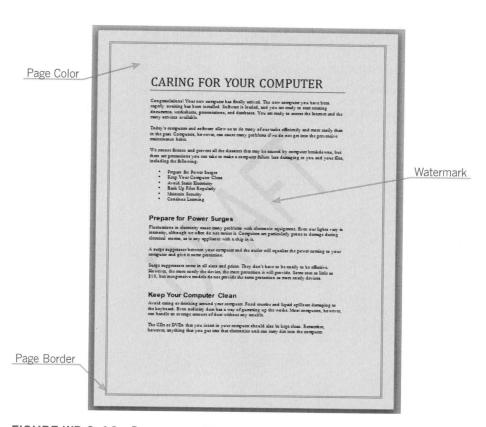

FIGURE WD 3–16 Document with watermark

Changing the Page Color

While adding colors to pages can look attractive on the computer screen, you should use color sparingly if you intend to print a document, because it can make the text difficult to read and it requires a lot of printer ink. Consider using light colors or shades of color for best results, or plan to add a background color only to a document that you know will be viewed on a computer and not printed.

You use the Page Color button to add a background color. The Page Color menu offers a gallery of color choices, including Theme Colors, Standard Colors, and the No Color option. The More Colors command on the menu allows you to create a custom color, and the Fill Effects command lets you add a gradient, texture, pattern, or picture after selecting a background color.

Adding a Page Border

Documents such as flyers and invitations often have decorative borders that outline the contents of the page. You can add *page borders*, or lines that frame the page, using the Page Borders button, which displays the Borders and Shading dialog box. Page borders can be solid, dashed, dotted, or multiple lines, or small repeated pictures or designs. You can add page borders to the whole document or to sections of a document.

Step-by-Step WD 3.6

The document Caring for Your Computer *XXX* from Step-by-Step WD 3.5 should be open in the Word program window.

1. On the Page Layout tab, in the Page Background group, click the **Watermark** button. The gallery is displayed.

2. Scroll down to the Disclaimers section and click the **DRAFT 1** watermark, as shown in **Figure WD 3–17**. The word *DRAFT* now appears behind the existing text in the document.

FIGURE WD 3–17
Watermark button and gallery

Click to choose
Draft 1 watermark

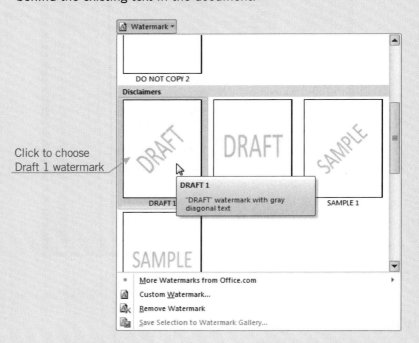

3. In the Page Background group, click the **Page Color** button.

4. In the Theme Colors section of the color gallery, click the **Aqua, Accent 5, Lighter 80%** color, as shown in **Figure WD 3–18**, to apply a light aqua background to the document.

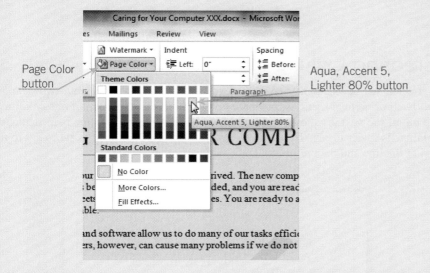

FIGURE WD 3–18
Page Color button and color gallery

5. In the Page Background group, click the **Page Borders** button. The Borders and Shading dialog box opens.

6. On the Page Border tab, in the Setting area, click **Box**, and in the Style list, scroll down and click the **double line** style.

7. Click the **Color** list arrow to display the color gallery. In the Theme Colors section, click **Aqua, Accent 5** in the top row. Click the **Width** list arrow, and then click **1½ pt**. Your dialog box should look similar to the one shown in **Figure WD 3–19**.

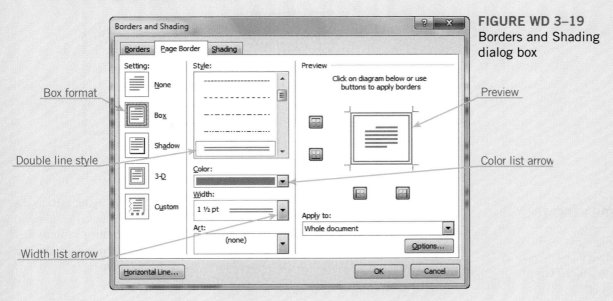

FIGURE WD 3–19
Borders and Shading dialog box

8. Click the **OK** button. The border is applied.

9. Click the **Page Color** button again, and click **No Color** in the gallery to remove the page color.

10. Save the document and leave it open for use in the next Step-by-Step.

Creating Columns

▶ **VOCABULARY**
columns

You often see newspapers, newsletters, and brochures formatted into two or more *columns*, or vertical sections, in which text flows from the bottom of one column to the top of the next, as shown in **Figure WD 3–20**. Usually, text that is formatted in columns is easier to read because your eye doesn't have to travel as far to get to the end of the line and then return to the beginning of the next line.

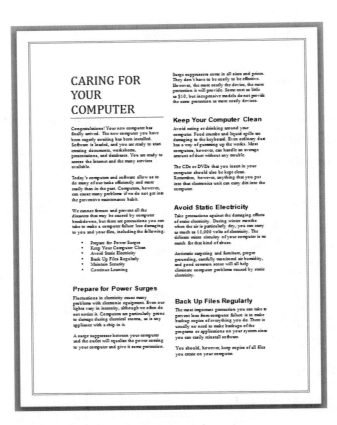

FIGURE WD 3–20   Two-column document layout

📇 **EXTRA FOR EXPERTS**

You can add a line between columns by inserting a check mark in the Line between check box in the Columns dialog box.

The Columns button in the Page Setup group on the Page Layout tab on the Ribbon lets you format all or part of a document in columns of equal or unequal width. The More Columns command on the Columns menu opens the Columns dialog box, which allows you to create custom column formats by choosing the number of columns you want and specifying the width of individual columns.

Step-by-Step WD 3.7

The document Caring for Your Computer *XXX* from Step-by-Step WD 3.6 should be open in the Word program window.

1. Click at the top of the page to make sure no text is selected.

2. On the Page Layout tab on the Ribbon, in the Page Setup group, click the **Columns** button.

3. Click **Three** on the menu, as shown in **Figure WD 3–21**. The document text, including the title, is formatted into three columns.

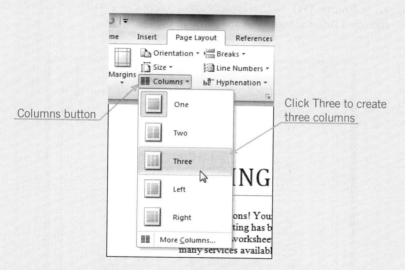

Columns button

Click Three to create three columns

FIGURE WD 3–21
Columns button and menu

4. In the Page Setup group, click the **Columns** button again, and then click **More Columns**. The Columns dialog box opens.

5. In the Presets area, click **Two**. In the Width and spacing area, click the **up arrow** in the Width box until *2.6"* is displayed, as shown in **Figure WD 3–22**. The Spacing measurement automatically adjusts to .3".

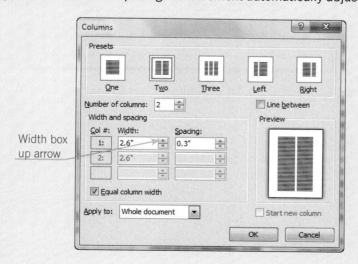

Width box up arrow

FIGURE WD 3–22
Columns dialog box

6. Click the **OK** button. The text is formatted into two columns.

7. Save the file and leave it open for use in the next Step-by-Step.

Adding Headers and Footers

▶ **VOCABULARY**

header

footer

A *header* is content (text or graphics) that appears in the top margin of each page in a document. A *footer* refers to content that appears in the bottom margin of each page in a document. You can use headers and footers to include useful information that you would not include as document text, such as document titles and page numbers, as shown in **Figure WD 3–23**. Headers and footers can also include dates, times, logos, and other information.

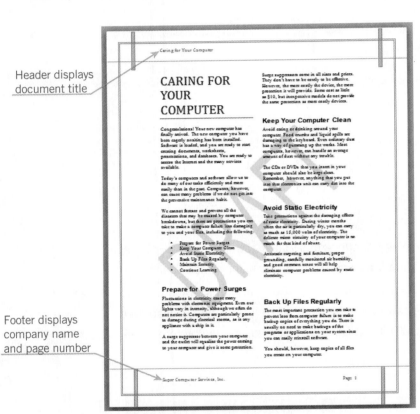

Header displays document title

Footer displays company name and page number

FIGURE WD 3–23   Document with header and footer

To create a header or footer, you use the Header, Footer, and Page Number buttons located in the Header & Footer group on the Insert tab on the Ribbon. See **Figure WD 3–24**. These buttons provide galleries of predesigned, built-in headers, footers, and page number formats that you can use for your documents. The Header and Footer buttons also contain menu commands for seeing more predesigned formats from Office.com and provide Blank styles you can use to create your own headers and footers.

FIGURE WD 3–24   Header & Footer group on the Insert tab

Inserting Headers and Footers

When you insert a header or footer, it is placed on each page of the document, and Word displays the Header & Footer Tools Design contextual tab on the Ribbon with more options for formatting and displaying the header or footer. You can opt not to print a header or footer on the first page of a document, and you can specify a different header or footer for odd and even pages.

When the header and footer are open, each is set off from the body of the document by a nonprinting dashed line and text and graphics in the document are visible, but dimmed. You can type and format text in the header or footer area the same way you do in the document.

When the insertion point is in the body of the document, you can double-click the top or bottom margin to open and edit the header or footer, or you can choose the Edit Header or Edit Footer command on the Header menu or Footer menu. The menus also contain options for editing and removing headers and footers.

Step-by-Step WD 3.8

The document Caring for Your Computer *XXX* from Step-by-Step WD 3.7 should be open in the Word program window.

1. On the Insert tab on the Ribbon, in the Header & Footer group, click the **Header** button. Scroll down and click the **Pinstripes** header, as shown in **Figure WD 3–25**.

FIGURE WD 3–25
Header button and gallery

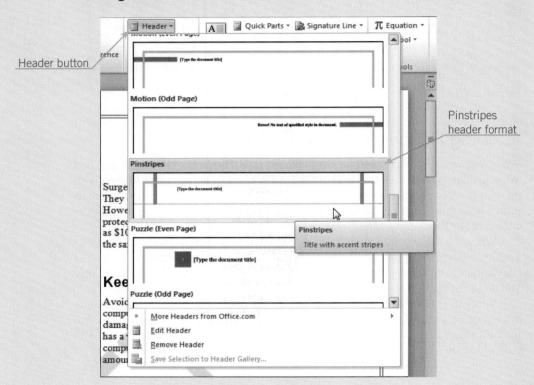

2. The header is inserted and the Header & Footer Tools Design contextual tab is displayed on the Ribbon, as shown in **Figure WD 3–26**. Select the **[Type the document title]** placeholder, if necessary.

FIGURE WD 3–26
Header

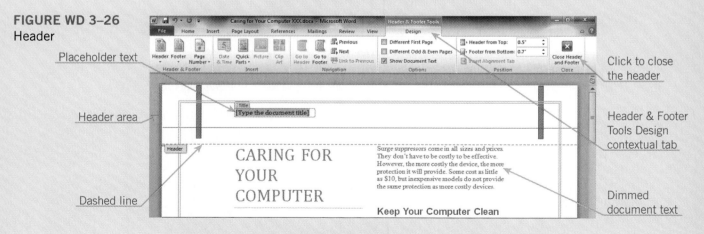

3. Type **Caring for Your Computer** as the document title.

4. On the Header & Footer Tools Design contextual tab, in the Close group, click the **Close Header and Footer** button. The header area is closed, along with the Header & Footer Tools Design tab.

5. On the Insert tab on the Ribbon, in the Header & Footer group, click the **Footer** button. Scroll down and click the **Pinstripes** footer, as shown in **Figure WD 3–27**. The footer is inserted and the Header & Footer Tools Design contextual tab is displayed on the Ribbon.

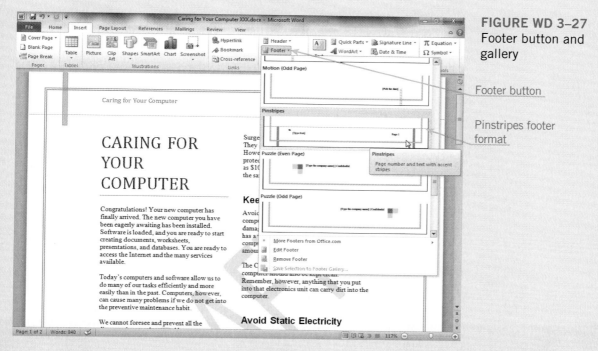

FIGURE WD 3–27
Footer button and gallery

Footer button

Pinstripes footer format

6. In the footer, click the **[Type text]** placeholder and type **Super Computer Services, Inc.**, as shown in **Figure WD 3–28**.

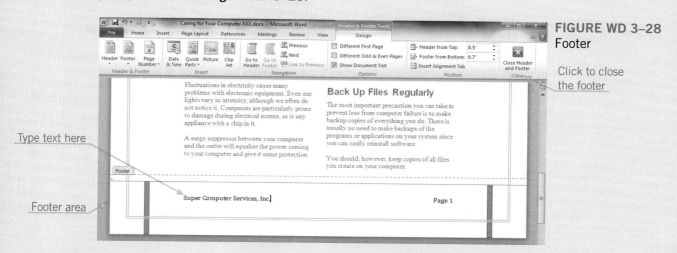

FIGURE WD 3–28
Footer

Click to close the footer

Type text here

Footer area

7. Press **Tab**. On the Header & Footer Tools Design contextual tab, in the Insert group, click the **Date & Time** button to display the Date and Time dialog box. Click the **OK** button to accept the default date format and insert the current date in the center of the footer.

8. On the Header & Footer Tools Design contextual tab, in the Header & Footer group, click the **Footer** button, and then click **Remove Footer**. The footer is removed.

9. On the Header & Footer Tools Design contextual tab, in the Close group, click the **Close Header and Footer** button.

10. Save the file and leave it open for use in the next Step-by-Step.

Inserting Page Numbers

There may be times when you want to display only a page number, and no other text, in a header or footer. The Page Number button in the Header & Footer group inserts a page number with no additional content. From the Page Number menu, you can choose from a variety of built-in formats for inserting page numbers at the top or bottom of the page, in the margin, or at the current position of the insertion point. You can also change the format of a page number or remove the page number.

After you insert a page number, the Header & Footer Tools Design contextual tab is displayed on the Ribbon, allowing you to choose additional options for page numbers. You can specify a position and opt to not display the number on the first page of a document.

Step-by-Step WD 3.9

The document Caring for Your Computer *XXX* from Step-by-Step WD 3.8 should be open in the Word program window.

1. On the Insert tab, in the Header & Footer group, click the **Page Number** button and point to **Bottom of Page**. A gallery of page number options is displayed.

2. Scroll down to the With Shapes section, and then click **Outline Circle 2**, as shown in **Figure WD 3–29**. A new footer with a page number is inserted, and the Header & Footer Tools Design contextual tab is displayed on the Ribbon.

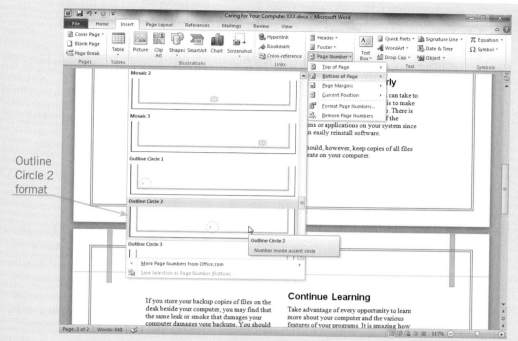

FIGURE WD 3–29
Page Number menu and
Bottom of Page gallery

3. In the Header & Footer group on the Header & Footer Tools Design contextual tab, click the **Page Number** button, and then click **Format Page Numbers**. The Page Number Format dialog box opens.

4. Click the **Number format list** arrow, and then click the **i, ii, iii,...** format. Click the **OK** button to apply the new numbering format.

5. On the Header & Footer Tools Design contextual tab, in the Close group, click the **Close Header and Foote**r button.

6. Save the document and leave it open for use in the next Step-by-Step.

Inserting and Breaking Pages

A *page break* ends a page and starts a new one. At the end of a page, Word inserts an automatic page break and starts a new page. As you reformat or edit, Word adjusts these page breaks. There may be times when you need to insert a manual page break in a different location, such as when you need to create a blank page for a graphic or block of text you intend to insert. Word will always break the page at a manual page break, no matter where on a page it is inserted.

When you create reports or other documents that need cover sheets, you can insert a cover page at the beginning of the document. The Cover Page, Blank Page,

▶ **VOCABULARY**
page break

and Page Break buttons in the Pages group on the Insert tab on the Ribbon let you add or break pages. These buttons are shown in **Figure WD 3–30.**

FIGURE WD 3–30   Pages group on the Insert tab

Inserting a Page Break

When you use the Page Break button, a manual page break is inserted at the location of the insertion point. Word inserts a dotted line with the words *Page Break,* as shown in **Figure WD 3–31**, that you can see when you display nonprinting symbols with the Show/Hide ¶ button. If you need to delete a manual page break, first display nonprinting symbols, and then select and delete the page break. You can also delete a page break by clicking at the left (the beginning) of the page break and pressing Delete, or by clicking at the end (at the right) of the page break and pressing Backspace.

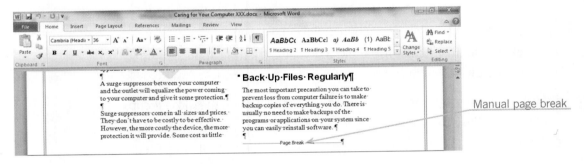

FIGURE WD 3–31   Manual page break

You cannot delete an automatic page break, but you can change the way Word inserts them using the Line and Page Breaks tab in the Paragraph dialog box, which you can open using the dialog box launcher in the Paragraph group on the Home tab on the Ribbon. The Widow/Orphan check box on the Line and Page Breaks tab is selected by default, so Word does not allow single lines or words to be displayed at the top (*widow*) or bottom (*orphan*) of an otherwise empty page. You can use the Keep with next check box to specify that selected paragraphs aren't separated by page breaks but instead are kept together on a page. The Keep lines together check box specifies that lines in a paragraph be kept together on a page, and the Page break before check box specifies that a paragraph will always be at the top of a page.

Word provides other types of page breaks to help you format complex documents. Tools for column breaks and text-wrapping breaks can be found on the Breaks menu in the Page Setup group on the Page Layout tab, as shown in **Figure WD 3–32.**

> **VOCABULARY**
> **widow**
>
> **orphan**

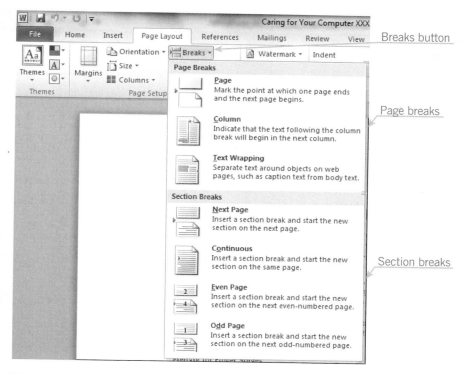

FIGURE WD 3–32   Breaks button and menu

Inserting a Section Break

Section breaks are used to control a document's layout. A section can be as small as a single paragraph or as long as an entire document. When you break a document into sections, you can format each section differently. A Continuous section break starts a new section on the current page, and a Next Page section break starts a new section on the next page. You can also specify that the new section start on an odd or even page. Use the Breaks button and menu in the Page Setup group of the Page Layout tab to insert a section break, as shown in Figure WD 3–32.

After you insert a section break, the words *Section Break* and the kind of break (for example, *Next Page*) appear on a dotted line in the document when nonprinting symbols are showing, similar to a page break. To remove a section break, select it or click to the left of it and press Delete.

Inserting a Blank Page

When you need to insert a blank page anywhere in a document, place the insertion point where you want to add the page, and then click the Blank Page button in the Pages group on the Insert tab. Word will insert a page break and a new blank page in the document. You can delete the added page by displaying nonprinting symbols and deleting the page break.

Step-by-Step WD 3.10

The document Caring for Your Computer *XXX* from Step-by-Step WD 3.9 should be open in the Word program window.

1. On the Home tab, in the Paragraph group, click the **Show/Hide ¶** button ¶, if necessary, to display the nonprinting symbols.

2. At the bottom of the second column on page 1, click at the beginning of the last paragraph, which begins *You should, however.*

3. On the Insert tab, in the Pages group, click the **Page Break** button. A manual page break is inserted, and the paragraph moves to the next page, as shown in **Figure WD 3–33**.

FIGURE WD 3–33
Manual page break inserted

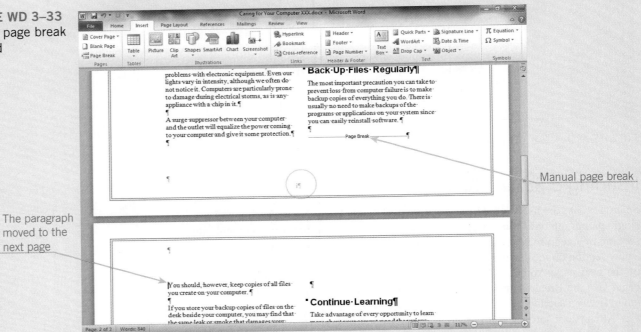

Manual page break

The paragraph moved to the next page

4. In the Pages group, click the **Blank Page** button. A new blank page is inserted.

5. Scroll up if necessary, and then select the paragraph mark and the page break on the blank page, as shown in **Figure WD 3–34**.

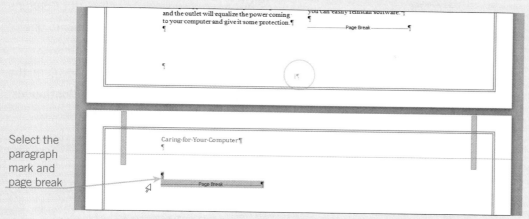

FIGURE WD 3–34
Selected paragraph mark and page break

Select the paragraph mark and page break

6. Press **Delete**. The page break and the blank page are removed.

7. On page 2, select the last two paragraphs in the first column, beginning with *You can use a screen saver.*

8. On the Page Layout tab, in the Paragraph group, click the **dialog box launcher** . The Paragraph dialog box opens.

9. Click the **Line and Page Breaks** tab if necessary. In the Pagination area, click the **Keep with next** check box, as shown in **Figure WD 3–35**.

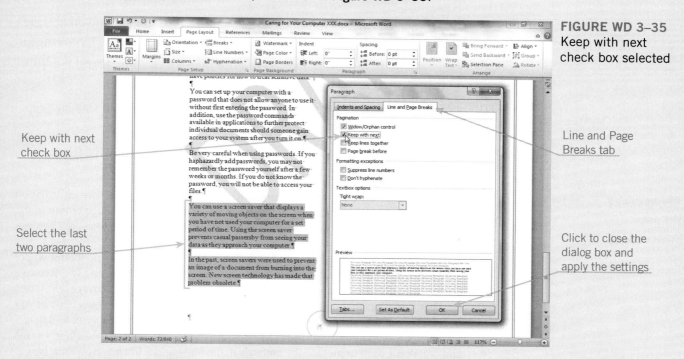

FIGURE WD 3–35
Keep with next check box selected

Keep with next check box

Line and Page Breaks tab

Select the last two paragraphs

Click to close the dialog box and apply the settings

10. Click the **OK** button. The paragraphs are moved to the top of the next column, keeping them with the next paragraph and making the columns more even.

11. Click to the left of the title on the first page of the document to make sure no text is selected.

12. On the Page Layout tab, in the Page Setup group, click the **Columns** button, and click **One** to change the format from two columns to one.

13. Click at the end of the title, and press **Enter** to add a blank line.

14. In the first paragraph, click before the *C* in *Congratulations!*. In the Page Setup group, click the **Breaks** button and then click **Continuous**, as shown in **Figure WD 3–36**, to insert a continuous section break.

FIGURE WD 3–36
Inserting a section break

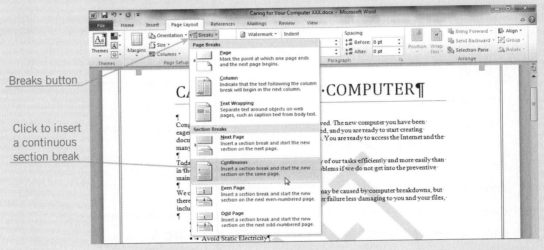

15. If necessary, click in the first paragraph. In the Page Setup group, click the **Columns** button, and then click **Two** to change the format in the section to a two-column layout. The first section containing the document title remains as one column.

16. Save the document and leave it open for use in the next Step-by-Step.

Adding a Cover Page

A ***cover page*** is the first page of a document that provides introductory information about the document, such as the title, author, and date. The Cover Page button in the Pages group on the Insert tab provides a gallery of built-in cover pages you can use in your documents.

A cover page is always inserted at the beginning of a document, no matter where the insertion point is located when you click the Cover Page button. The Remove Current Cover Page command on the Cover Page menu removes a cover page.

You can replace the placeholder text in a cover page with your own text, as you do when using a template or a header or footer. Sometimes you may want to delete a placeholder, such as when a cover page contains a placeholder for the author's name and you don't want to include the author's name on your document. However, before you delete a placeholder, consider whether the same placeholder appears in other areas of the document. Each placeholder contains a small program called a ***content control***; the content control saves the content entered in the placeholder and displays it automatically in all locations in the document using that same placeholder.

For example, if you enter the current date in a footer placeholder, that date will appear automatically on a cover page that also contains the date placeholder.

Step-by-Step WD 3.11

The document Caring for Your Computer *XXX* from Step-by-Step WD 3.10 should be open in the Word program window.

1. On the Insert tab on the Ribbon, in the Pages group, click the **Cover Page** button, and then scroll down and click the **Pinstripes** cover page, as shown in **Figure WD 3–37**. A cover page is inserted at the beginning of the document, and the title is included automatically exactly as you entered it in the document title placeholder in the header.

Click the Pinstripes cover page

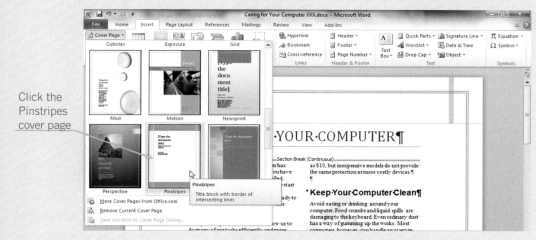

FIGURE WD 3–37
Cover Page button and gallery

2. Right-click the **[Type the document subtitle]** placeholder to display the shortcut menu, and then click **Remove Content Control**, as shown in **Figure WD 3–38**, to delete the placeholder.

FIGURE WD 3–38
Remove Content
Control command

Right-click the
Subtitle placeholder

Remove Content
Control command

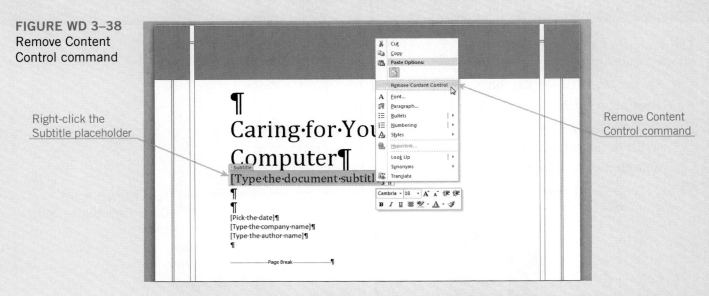

3. Click the remaining placeholders and replace them with the following:

   [Pick the date]: *Today's date*

   [Type the company name]: **Super Computer Services, Inc.**

   [Type the author name]: Your *first* and *last name*

4. Right-click **Super Computer Services, Inc.** and click **Remove Content Control** to remove the content control without removing the text. The text becomes part of the document.

5. Right-click your name and click **Remove Content Control** to remove the content control without removing the text.

6. Click the **Home** tab on the Ribbon if necessary. In the Paragraph group, click the **Show/Hide ¶** button ¶ to hide nonprinting symbols.

7. Save and close the document and then close Word.

ETHICS IN TECHNOLOGY

Software Piracy

The unauthorized use of copyrighted software is considered software piracy. The software industry estimates that it loses billions of dollars each year when people copy, distribute, or use software in an illegal manner. The penalties for using or distributing a pirated copy of Microsoft Word could include large fines or even imprisonment.

SUMMARY

In this lesson, you learned:

- How to create new documents using templates and placeholders.
- That you can use themes to change the design scheme of a document.
- That applying styles is a convenient way to maintain consistent formatting.
- How to navigate long documents using the Navigation pane.
- How to add bullets and numbering to lists.

- How to add page backgrounds such as watermarks, page color, and page borders.
- That you can format documents in columns.
- Ways to format documents using built-in headers or footers.
- How to insert blank pages and cover pages and how to insert and delete page breaks.

VOCABULARY REVIEW

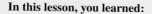

Define the following terms:

bullets	list	style
columns	orphan	template
content control	page borders	themes
cover page	page break	thumbnails
footer	placeholder	watermark
header	sort	widow

■ REVIEW QUESTIONS

MULTIPLE CHOICE

Select the best response for the following statements.

1. You can replace the text in a template by clicking a(n) _____ and typing.

   A. italicized phrase
   B. placeholder
   C. Theme
   D. preview

2. _____ are sets of formatting choices that include colors, fonts, and effects that were predesigned to work well together.

   A. Themes
   B. Templates
   C. Watermarks
   D. Placeholders

3. The _____ button displays the entire Quick Styles gallery.

   A. Styles
   B. Home
   C. More
   D. Heading 1

4. _____ are symbols that mark the beginning of each entry in a list.

   A. Numbers
   B. Watermarks
   C. Placeholders
   D. Bullets

5. A _____ is text or a graphic that appears behind text in a document.

   A. page border
   B. bullet
   C. watermark
   D. placeholder

6. You can use the _____ button to add gradient, texture, pattern, or a picture to the background of a page.

   A. Page Color
   B. Page Border
   C. Header
   D. Cover Page

7. Newspapers, newsletters, and brochures are often formatted into two or more _____.

   A. watermarks
   B. placeholders
   C. columns
   D. nonprinting symbols

8. A _____ is text or graphics that is displayed in the top margin of each page in a document.

   A. footer
   B. header
   C. placeholder
   D. page border

9. You can see a manual page break if you click the _____ button.

   A. Cover Page
   B. Columns
   C. Page Number
   D. Show/Hide ¶

10. A _____ provides introductory information about a document, such as the title, author, and date.

    A. page break
    B. cover page
    C. blank page
    D. placeholder

FILL IN THE BLANK

Complete the following sentences by writing the correct word or words in the blanks provided.

1. A(n) _____ is a master copy for a certain type of document.

2. The Theme _____ button lets you choose new line and fill effects.

3. A(n) _____ is a set of character or paragraph formats stored with a name.

4. Word _____ a numbered list when you insert, move, copy, or delete items.

5. The Multilevel list button is used to create a(n) _____.

6. Clicking the _____ _____ button displays the Borders and Shading dialog box.

7. Text formatted in _____ is easier to read.

8. A(n) _____ is text or graphics that is displayed in the bottom margin of each page in a document.

9. A(n) _____ _____ ends a page and starts a new one.

10. A(n) _____ page is always inserted at the beginning of a document, no matter where the insertion point is located.

■ PROJECTS

PROJECT WD 3–1

1. Create a new document using the Median Resume template, which you can access by clicking Sample templates in the Available Templates section of Backstage view. Save the document as **Verhoff Resume XXX** *(replace XXX with your initials).*

2. Replace the placeholders with the following information:

   [Type your name]: **Karin Verhoff**

   [Select the Date]: **Today's date**

   [Type your address]: **5555 Shady Oak Drive, Ashland, OR 97590**

   [Type your phone number]: **541-555-1023**

   [Type your e-mail address] : **KV@karinverhoff.com**

   [Type your website address]: **karinverhoff.com**

   [Type your objectives]: **I am an accomplished accountant, but I would love to leave my office job to pursue a career in the outdoor industry as an adventure guide for a tourism company.**

   [Type the school name]: **Florida Park University**

   [Type the completion date]: **2000**

   [Type list of degrees, awards and accomplishments]: **B.S. in Accounting and Finance**

   [Type the job title]: **Staff Property Accountant**

   [Type the company name]: **Vande Associates**

   [Type the start date]: **September 2000**

   [Type the end date]: **Present**

   [Type list of job responsibilities]: **Prepared monthly, quarterly, and annual financial statements**

   Provided balance sheet account analysis

   Analyzed escrow and reconciliation of all escrow accounts

   [Type list of skills]: **Wilderness First Aid**

   Mountain Biking

   Rock Climbing

   Fly Fishing

3. Remove the content control from the name at the top of the resume, *Karin Verhoff*.

4. Save and close the document.

ON YOUR OWN

Open the **Verhoff Resume XXX** file, and change the document theme and experiment with the styles to change the look of the resume. Save and close the document.

PROJECT WD 3–2

1. Open the file **Project WD 3-2** from the folder containing the data files for this lesson and save it as **Reappointment Letter** *XXX* *(replace XXX with your initials).*

2. Add the Confidential 1 watermark to the page background.

3. Insert the Stacks footer with the following company information:

   Lone Star State University / 78901 Longhorn Boulevard / Austin, TX 78777

4. Insert the Stacks header with the following document title information:

   Office of the President

5. Apply the Strong style to *FY 2013* and *FY 2014* in the document.

6. Apply the Strong style to the entire *TOTAL*: line.

7. Change the document theme to Paper.

8. Save and close the document.

ON YOUR OWN

Open the **Reappointment Letter** *XXX* file, and add a background color with a fill effect, such as a gradient, texture, pattern, or picture. Save and close the document.

PROJECT WD 3–4

1. Open the file **Project WD 3-4** from the folder containing the data files for this lesson and save it as **Pizza Menu** *XXX* (replace *XXX* with your initials).

2. Change the theme to Verve.

3. Change the Theme Colors to Opulent.

4. Change the style of the quote and quote source at the bottom of the document to Intense Quote.

5. Insert the Tiles cover page.

6. Delete the Author placeholder by selecting and deleting it, delete the Subtitle placeholder using the Remove Content Control command, and then replace the remaining placeholders with the following text:

   Home: **Purple Street Pizza**

   [Type the document title]: **Menu**

PROJECT WD 3–3

1. Open the file **Project WD 3-3** from the folder containing the data files for this lesson and save it as **MLA Guidelines** *XXX* (replace *XXX* with your initials).

2. Change the numbered list to the default bullet style.

3. Sort the list in ascending order.

4. Apply the Title style to the *Writing Research Papers* title and to the *Works Cited* heading.

5. Change the theme to Metro.

6. Click to the left of the *Works Cited* heading, and then insert a continuous section break. (Display nonprinting symbols, if necessary, to view the section break.)

7. At the start of the first paragraph (before the *T* in *The Modern Language*) in the top section of the document, insert a continuous section break.

8. Format the top section of the document (excluding the title) in two columns. Adjust the width of the columns to 4.4" and the spacing between columns to .2".

9. Remove the header.

10. Insert a page border formatted as Box style, a dotted line (the second format in the Style list), ½ pt, and Green, Accent 1 color.

11. Save and close the document.

ON YOUR OWN

Open the **MLA Guidelines** *XXX* file and change the font, size, alignment, color, and/or font style of the *Writing Research Papers* heading. Save the new format as a style with a new name, add it to the Quick Style gallery, and apply it to the *Works Cited* heading. Save and close the document.

[Year]: **Current Year**

[Type the company address]: **7765 Purple Street, New Orleans, LA 70198**

7. Apply **Lavender, Background 2** as the background page color.

8. Open the Navigation Pane and navigate to the last page of the document.

9. Close the Navigation Pane.

10. Save and close the document.

ON YOUR OWN

Open the **Pizza Menu** *XXX* file and insert a custom text watermark. You choose the text, font, size, color, and layout. Save and close the document.

WEB PROJECT

Explore the templates available in the Office.com Templates section of Backstage view. This project will require you to access templates from the Microsoft Web site, so you must be connected to the Internet and have permission to download a document. Choose a favorite template to download as a document and modify to your specifications.

 TEAMWORK PROJECT

In small groups, invent a business with a name, address, and slogan. Create a letterhead, business cards, and fax cover sheet using one of Word's document themes. Assign each person in the team one of the documents to create. Use templates and styles. Work together to make sure the documents coordinate. Elect a team leader to present the documents to the class.

CRITICAL THINKING

ACTIVITY WD 3–1

Create a new document using the Median Report template from the Sample templates category in the Available Templates section of Backstage view. Save it with a new name. View the picture in the document. Think about the various reasons for including such an image in a document. How you would feel to visit a place like the scene included in the template? Perhaps you have been somewhere like it in the past, you are planning to go somewhere similar in the future, or you would not be interested in being in such a place at all. Create a report as if you have been there and are reporting your experience to the class. Write your observations and experiences in a one-page report, replacing the placeholders with new text. Be sure to use styles to format headings and other text elements. Include a quote. Be prepared to share your report with the class.

ACTIVITY WD 3–2

Type a list of careers that interest you. Use the Define New Bullet command to create your own bulleted list style. Copy the list and paste it below the first list. Now arrange the items in the copied list, ranking them in order of interest to you. Create your own numbering style using the Define New Number Format command on the Numbering menu, and then apply the style to the copied list.

ACTIVITY WD 3–3

Open the file **Activity WD 3–3** from the folder containing the data files for this lesson and save it as **Green News** *XXX* (replace *XXX* with your initials). Use what you have learned in this lesson about styles, headers, footers, columns, numbering, and section breaks, and do your best to format the document to look like the one in **Figure WD 3–39**.

FIGURE WD 3–39   Green News *XXX*

LESSON 4

Working with Graphic Objects

■ OBJECTIVES

Upon completion of this lesson, you should be able to:

- Insert and modify illustrations.
- Insert and modify objects.
- Create and modify tables.

■ DATA FILES

To complete this lesson, you will need these data files:

Step WD 4-1.docx
Step WD 4-9.docx
Project WD 4-1.docx
Project WD 4-2.docx

■ VOCABULARY

building blocks
cell
chart
clip art
crop
drawing objects
drop cap
floating object
inline object
picture
Quick Part
screenshot
selection handles
SmartArt graphic
table
text box
text wrapping
WordArt

Introduction

Graphics are visual components that add impact to documents and help explain the meaning of the text. Pictures, shapes, clip art, SmartArt, charts, screenshots, WordArt, text boxes, Quick Parts, and drop caps are all types of graphics that you can add to and customize in your Word documents. Tables provide another way to illustrate, explain, or supplement text. In this lesson, you will learn to insert and modify these graphic elements. You use buttons on the Insert tab on the Ribbon, shown in **Figure WD 4–1**, to insert various types of graphic objects and tables.

FIGURE WD 4–1   Insert tab

Inserting and Modifying Illustrations

Pictures, shapes, clip art, SmartArt, charts, and screenshots are all types of illustrations you can add to your Word documents. The Illustrations group on the Insert tab on the Ribbon provides a range of options for working with these various types of graphics. When you click a button in the Illustrations group, you will be able to choose the graphic you want to insert using a dialog box, task pane, or menu, depending on the type of illustration. After you insert an illustration, you have many options for modifying it, most of which are the same for each type of illustration.

Inserting and Modifying Pictures

The Insert Picture from File button in the Illustrations group on the Insert tab can be used to insert a *picture*, or digital photograph or image, that is stored on your computer or network. You can insert pictures of various formats, including .tif, .gif, and .jpeg. The Picture button opens the Insert Picture dialog box, which you can use to navigate to and insert a picture file from your computer or network.

Before you can modify or resize a picture or other graphic object, you must select it. To select a graphic within a document, click the graphic once. The small circles and squares that are displayed at the sides and corners of the selected graphic are called *selection handles.* You drag these handles to change the graphic's size. When you want to resize a graphic proportionally, that is, to maintain the original height:width ratio, you must drag a corner handle. Some types of graphics require that you hold the Shift key while dragging a corner handle to resize proportionally. If you want to distort a graphic horizontally or vertically, drag a middle handle.

You can click the green rotate circle at the top of a graphic to rotate the graphic on its central axis left or right to any position.

When a graphic is selected, you can copy, paste, and delete it the same as you would text using the Cut, Copy, and Paste commands. A copy of a graphic is the same size and contains the same formatting as the original graphic. When you paste a copy of a graphic, the new copy might appear on top of or next to the original. Simply drag it to the desired position.

After you insert a picture and any time the picture is selected, the Picture Tools Format contextual tab is displayed on the Ribbon. This tab contains commands for

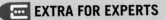

VOCABULARY

picture

selection handles

EXTRA FOR EXPERTS

Hold the Shift key when using rectangular or oval drawing shapes or tools to draw squares or circles (shapes with the same height and width). To create a straight line, hold the Shift key while using line tools.

adjusting the picture, modifying the picture style, arranging the picture on the page, and sizing the picture precisely.

Common commands on this tab include the Color and Artistic Effects commands in the Adjust group, which allow you to change the color of a picture or add interesting effects such as paint strokes or blurring. The Picture Styles gallery in the Pictures group contains predesigned styles for altering a picture's shape, adding a frame, or changing the perspective. Often you may want to insert a picture within or near a paragraph of text to help illustrate a point. You can use the Wrap Text button in the Arrange group to adjust **text wrapping**, which is the flow of text around the edges of an object. When a picture is inserted at the insertion point, it is an **inline object** that appears on the same line as text and moves with the text around it. Text does not wrap around inline objects. On the Wrap Text button menu, shown in **Figure WD 4–2**, you can use several of the options, such as Behind Text or Square, to change a picture from an inline object into a floating object. A **floating object** is not connected to the text in a document; text can wrap around a floating object several different ways or flow in front of or behind it.

> **VOCABULARY**
> **text wrapping**
> **inline object**
> **floating object**
> **crop**

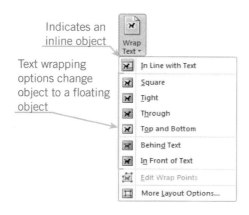

FIGURE WD 4–2   Wrap Text button and menu

> **EXTRA FOR EXPERTS**
>
> Large files can take longer to download, and some may be rejected by e-mail servers. Including pictures in documents increases file size, but you can use the Compress Pictures button in the Adjust group on the Picture Tools Format tab to decrease a picture's file size by reducing the resolution, or the number of pixels, in a picture.

You can also use the Position button in the Arrange group to change an object's position on the page and apply text wrapping at the same time. The Crop button in the Size group lets you **crop**, or remove, unwanted parts of a picture by dragging cropping handles on the sides and corners of the picture.

Step-by-Step WD 4.1

1. Start Word.

2. Open **Step WD 4-1** from the folder containing the data files for this lesson, and save the document as **Go Green Newsletter XXX** (replace **XXX** with your initials).

3. On the Insert tab, in the Illustrations group, click the **Insert Picture from File** button to open the Insert Picture dialog box.

4. Navigate to the **Sample Pictures** folder in the Pictures library, and then double-click to open it.

5. Click **Tulips** (or another picture of your choice) to select the image, and then click the **Insert** button. The picture is inserted on the page as an inline graphic, as shown in **Figure WD 4–3**, and the words are moved down the page.

FIGURE WD 4–3
Inserted inline image

Rotation handle

Selection handles

6. On the Picture Tools Format contextual tab, in the Arrange group, click the **Wrap Text** button, and then click **Behind Text** to change the picture to a floating object and position it behind the text.

7. Display the ruler, if necessary.

8. In the Size group, click the **Crop** button to display the cropping handles at the sides and corners of the picture.

9. Click the top-center cropping handle and drag it down to the 1" mark on the vertical ruler. Notice that the parts of the picture to be removed are shaded in gray.

10. Click the bottom-center cropping handle (scroll down, if necessary), drag it up until you reach approximately the 3.5" mark on the vertical ruler, and then release the mouse button. Your screen should look similar to **Figure WD 4–4**.

FIGURE WD 4–4
Cropped picture

Crop button

Cropping handles

Shaded areas indicate parts of the picture that will be removed

Drag to crop picture

11. Click the **Crop** button to remove the shaded portions of the picture.

12. Position the mouse pointer on the picture until the pointer changes to a move pointer with a selection pointer and then drag the picture up about half an inch to position it just below the header.

13. On the Picture Tools Format tab, in the Adjust group, click the **Artistic Effects** button, and then click the **Paint Brush** option, as shown in **Figure WD 4–5**.

Artistic Effects button

Paint Brush option

FIGURE WD 4–5
Artistic Effects button and gallery

14. In the Picture Styles group, click the **More** button  to open the Picture Styles gallery.

15. Click the **Center Shadow Rectangle** option to apply a shadow around the picture.

16. Save the document and leave it open for use in the next Step-by-Step.

Inserting and Modifying Shapes

Word provides a set of common shapes that you can add to documents with one click and drag of the mouse. The Shapes button in the Illustrations group on the Insert tab displays a gallery containing lines, rectangles, basic shapes, block arrows, equation shapes, flowchart elements, stars and banners, and callouts that you can insert anywhere in your document.

After inserting a shape, you can delete it by pressing Delete while the shape is selected, or by clicking the Undo button immediately after creating the shape.

Shapes, curves, and lines are considered ***drawing objects***, which are created with Word and become part of your document, rather than being a separate file. After you insert a shape into a document, the Drawing Tools Format contextual tab is displayed on the Ribbon with commands for modifying drawing objects.

▶ **VOCABULARY**
drawing objects

▦ EXTRA FOR EXPERTS

You might want to combine shapes to create a single drawing object. To do this, select more than one object at a time by pressing and holding Shift while you click each of the objects, click the Group button in the Arrange group on the Drawing Tools Format tab, and then click Group.

Step-by-Step WD 4.2

The document Go Green Newsletter *XXX* from Step-by-Step WD 4.1 should be open in the Word program window.

1. On the Insert menu, in the Illustrations group, click the **Shapes** button to display the Shapes gallery.

2. In the Rectangles category, click the **Rectangle**, as shown in **Figure WD 4–6**. The mouse pointer changes to a crosshair ✛.

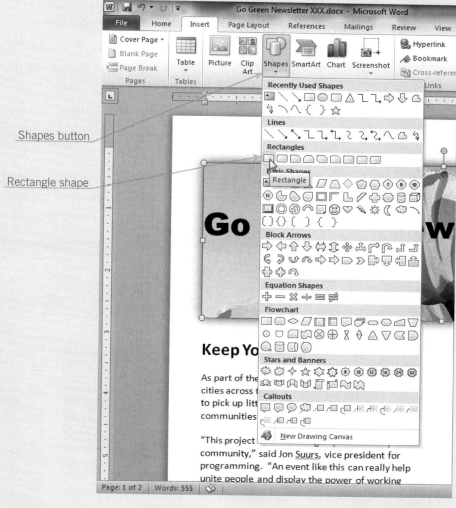

FIGURE WD 4–6
Shapes button and gallery

3. With the crosshair pointer, click above the upper-left corner of the *G* in *Go*, drag down and to the right diagonally across the words to create an outline similar to the one in **Figure WD 4–7**. After you release the mouse button, a blue rectangle shape is inserted, covering the text.

Drag crosshair pointer here to complete the rectangle drawing

Click here to start drawing the rectangle

FIGURE WD 4–7
Drawing a shape

4. On the Drawing Tools Format tab, in the Shape Styles group, click the **More** button ⊽ to display the entire Shape Styles gallery.

5. In the Shape Styles gallery, click the green **Light 1 Outline, Colored Fill – Olive Green, Accent 3** option (fourth from the left in the third row).

6. In the Shape Styles group, click the **Shape Outline** button to display the menu, and click the **No Outline** command to remove the line around the rectangle.

7. In the Shape Styles group, click the **Shape Effects** button, point to **Shadow**, and then in the Outer section of the effects gallery, click **Offset Diagonal Bottom Right**.

8. On the Drawing Tools Format tab, in the Arrange group, click the **Send Backward** button arrow, and then click **Send Behind Text** to move the rectangle behind the text. Your screen should look similar to **Figure WD 4–8**.

FIGURE WD 4–8
Go Green Newsletter

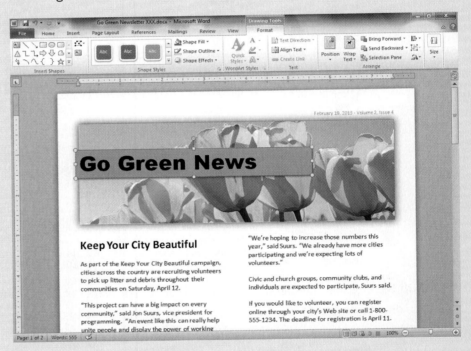

9. Save the document and leave it open for use in the next Step-by-Step.

Inserting and Modifying Clip Art

▶ **VOCABULARY**
clip art

Clip art is ready-made artwork, usually created with a computer, that is used to illustrate documents. Clip art files may be in formats like .gif, .wmf, or .bmp. Sometimes the term *clip art* refers to any piece of artwork, including pictures, that has been made available on a Web site, on a CD, or with a software program for the purpose of illustrating documents. The Clip Art button in the Illustrations group displays the Clip Art task pane, shown in **Figure WD 4–9**, which you can use to search for and insert clip art located on your computer, network, or on the Internet. The task pane contains a Search for text box where you can enter a keyword to find related clip art. The Results should be menu lets you choose the types of media files to search for, including illustrations, photos, videos, and audio files.

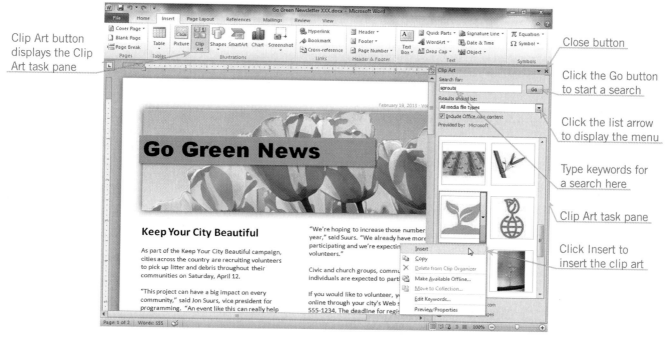

FIGURE WD 4–9   Clip Art task pane

You can insert clip art simply by clicking an image in the Clip Art task pane. In addition, when you point to a graphic in the Clip Art task pane, an arrow appears next to the graphic that, when clicked, displays a menu containing the Insert command as well as other commands for copying, moving, and previewing the file properties of clip art. Just like with pictures, once you've inserted clip art into a document, contextual tabs on the Ribbon enable you to modify the clip art.

> **⊸— WARNING**
>
> You can use the images, sounds, and movies Microsoft provides with Word, or for free on its Web site, in any advertising, promotional, and marketing materials, or product or service created with Word, provided the material, product, or service is for noncommercial purposes. You may not sell any promotional and marketing materials or any products or services containing the images.

Step-by-Step WD 4.3

The document Go Green Newsletter *XXX* from Step-by-Step WD 4.2 should be open in the Word program window.

1. Click to the left of the *G* in *Go Green News*.

2. On the Insert tab, in the Illustrations group, click the **Clip Art** button to display the Clip Art task pane.

3. In the Search for box, type **sprouts**. If necessary, click the **Results should be** list arrow, and then click the **All media file types** check box to insert a check mark, and then click the **Include Office.com content** check box to insert a check mark. Click the **Go** button to start the search.

4. In the Clip Art task pane, scroll down, if necessary, and point to the picture of the sprout, shown in **Figure WD 4–10**, in the results pane. (The sprout clip art might appear in a different location in your Clip Art task pane.)

FIGURE WD 4–10
Resized clip art

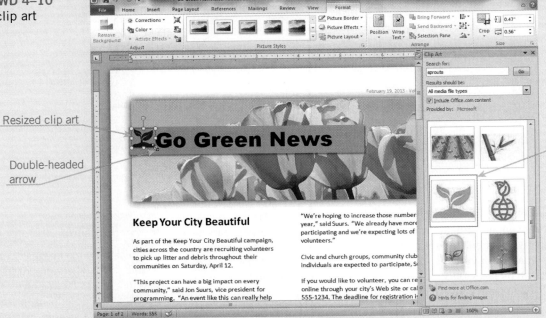

5. Click the **arrow** on the right side of the image to display a menu.

6. Click **Insert** to insert the clip art at the location of the insertion point.

7. On the Picture Tools Format tab, in the Adjust group, click the **Color** button.

8. Click the **Olive Green, Accent color 3 Dark** option (fourth from the left in the second row) to change the color of the clip art.

9. In the Adjust group, click the **Corrections** button, and then click the **Brightness: –40% Contrast: 0% (Normal)** option (first one in the third row) to adjust the brightness and contrast of the image.

10. Point to the lower-right corner selection handle on the sprout image. The pointer changes to a double-headed arrow ⬁. With the double-headed arrow pointer, click the corner handle and drag it toward the center of the clip art to resize the image to be approximately ½" square, as shown in Figure WD 4–10.

11. Click the **Close** button 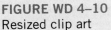 on the Clip Art task pane to close it.

12. Save the document and leave it open for use in the next Step-by-Step.

Inserting and Modifying SmartArt

Sometimes the best way to convey information is to use a chart or diagram. For example, an organization chart can clearly show the hierarchy of who reports to whom, while a flowchart can depict a series of actions. A *SmartArt graphic* is a predesigned diagram made up of shapes containing text that illustrates a concept or idea. The hierarchy chart for an organization shown in **Figure WD 4–11** is an example of one type of SmartArt graphic you can create easily in Word. Other types of SmartArt graphics include lists, processes, cycles, relationships, matrices, and pyramids.

▶ VOCABULARY
SmartArt graphic

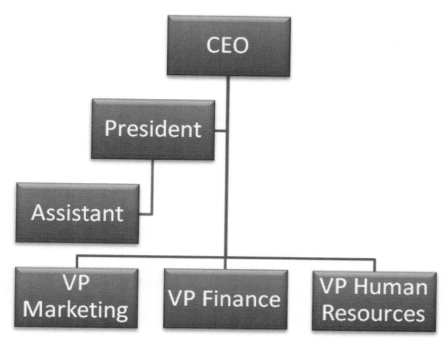

FIGURE WD 4–11   Hierarchy chart SmartArt graphic

You insert a SmartArt graphic using the Insert SmartArt Graphic button in the Illustrations group on the Insert tab. SmartArt graphics are inserted with placeholder text, much like the placeholders used in templates. You can replace the placeholder text with your own text.

After you insert a SmartArt graphic, the SmartArt Tools Design and Format contextual tabs are displayed on the Ribbon and provide access to a range of tools for customizing the graphic.

When you insert a SmartArt graphic, a Text pane is also displayed next to the graphic to help simplify the process of entering text. You can click a [Text] placeholder beside a bullet in the Text pane to enter text in a shape. The Text pane can be hidden or displayed by clicking the Text Pane button on the SmartArt Tools Design tab in the Create Graphic group.

Step-by-Step WD 4.4

The document Go Green Newsletter *XXX* from Step-by-Step WD 4.3 should be open in the Word program window.

1. Scroll to page 2 and click a blank line at the top of the right column.

2. On the Insert tab, in the Illustrations group, click the **Insert SmartArt Graphic** button to open the Choose a SmartArt Graphic dialog box.

3. Click the **Cycle** category, click the **Block Cycle** layout, as shown in **Figure WD 4–12**, and then click the **OK** button to insert the graphic into the document. Notice the Text pane is also displayed. (If the Text pane is not displayed, click the Text Pane button on the SmartArt Tools Design tab to display it.)

FIGURE WD 4–12
Choose a SmartArt
Graphic dialog box

Click a category

Select a layout

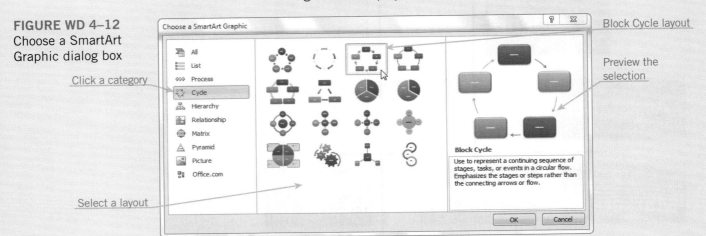

Block Cycle layout

Preview the selection

4. Click the top shape within the block cycle graphic to select it, if necessary, and press **Delete** to remove it.

5. Press **Delete** again to delete a second shape.

6. On the top shape, click the **[Text]** placeholder and type **Reduce**. Notice that the text automatically adjusts to fit in the shape.

7. In the lower-right shape, click the **[Text]** placeholder and type **Reuse**.

8. In the Text pane, click the remaining **[Text]** placeholder and type **Recycle** beside the third bullet.

9. On the SmartArt Tools Design tab, in the Layouts group, click the **More** button ⌄ to display the Layouts gallery, and then click the **Multidirectional Cycle** layout, as shown in **Figure WD 4–13**.

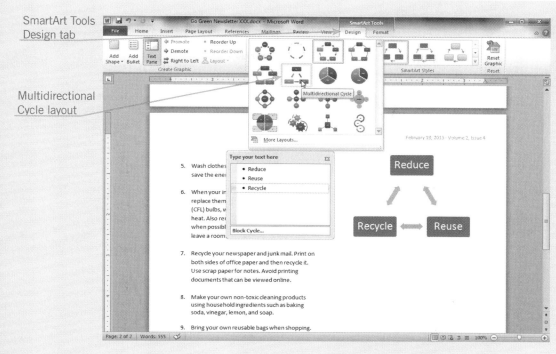

SmartArt Tools
Design tab

Multidirectional
Cycle layout

FIGURE WD 4–13
Layouts gallery on the
Design tab

10. In the Create Graphic group, click the **Text Pane** button to hide the Text Pane.

11. In the SmartArt Styles group, click the **More** button to display the SmartArt Styles gallery. In the Best Match for Document category, click the **Moderate Effect** option.

12. In the SmartArt Styles group, click the **Change Colors** button. In the Accent 3 category, click the **Colored Fill – Accent 3** option, the second choice in the row.

13. Select the **Reuse** shape on the SmartArt graphic. In the Create Graphic group, click the **Right to Left** button to switch the direction of the layout.

14. Point to the bottom-center resize handle on the SmartArt diagram until you see the double-headed arrow shown in **Figure WD 4–14**. Click and drag down about an inch to increase the size of the graphic.

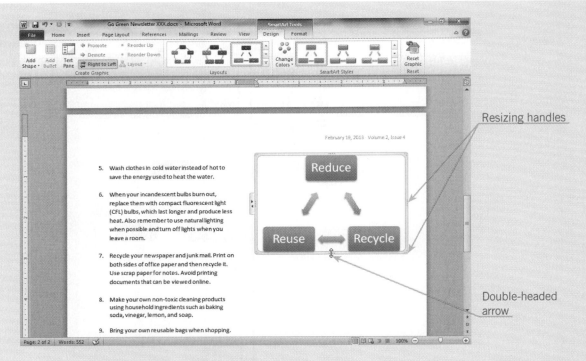

15. Save the document and leave it open for use in the next Step-by-Step.

Inserting and Modifying Charts

When you need to illustrate or compare numbers (instead of text) such as sales figures, it is helpful to use a chart. A *chart* is a graphical representation of numeric data that can be inserted into Word. Charts allow users to see at a glance patterns or relationships in the data, such as whether sales are rising or falling.

The Chart button in the Illustrations group on the Insert tab provides access to different types of charts, such as bar, line, or pie charts. Using a chart in a Word document differs slightly from using other types of graphics because charts are based on numeric data. The data that makes up the chart is stored in an Excel worksheet that is included in the Word file. (*Note*: When you initially create the chart, you enter data in the Excel worksheet; however, you do not need to be familiar with Excel to create a chart.)

As with other types of graphics, after you insert a chart within a document, Word displays the Chart Tools Design, Layout, and Format contextual tabs for customizing the chart.

Step-by-Step WD 4.5

The document Go Green Newsletter *XXX* from Step-by-Step WD 4.4 should be open in the Word program window.

1. On page 1 of the document, click to the left of the *K* in *Keep Your City Beautiful*.

2. On the **Insert** tab, in the Illustrations group, click the **Insert Chart** button to display the Insert Chart dialog box.

3. Click the **Pie** category, as shown in **Figure WD 4–15**, and click the **OK** button to accept the default Pie chart type. An Excel spreadsheet opens with sample data that you will replace.

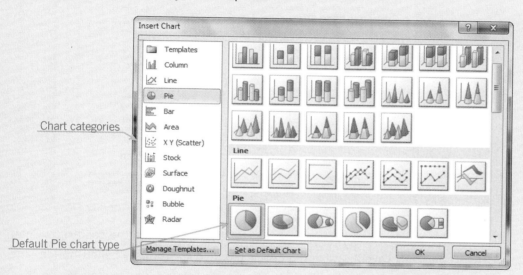

Chart categories

Default Pie chart type

FIGURE WD 4–15
Insert Chart dialog box

4. In the Excel spreadsheet, click cell **B1**, which contains the word *Sales*, and type **Where does our trash go?**

5. Click cell **A2** and type **Incinerator**. Press **Tab** to move to cell B2. Type **13%** and press **Tab** to move to the next active cell.

6. In cell A3, type **Recycling Center**. Press **Tab** to move to cell B3. Type **30%** and press **Tab**.

7. In cell A4, type **Landfill**. Press **Tab** to move to cell B4. Type **55%** and press **Tab**.

8. In cell A5, type **Other**. Press **Tab** to move to cell B5. Type **2%** and press **Enter**.

9. Click the **Close** button [X] on the Excel window to close the spreadsheet and view the chart in the document.

10. If necessary, click the chart to select it. On the contextual Chart Tools Format tab, in the Arrange group, click the **Position** button, and then click the **Position in Bottom Left with Square Text Wrapping** option, as shown in **Figure WD 4–16**. The chart is now positioned in the lower-left corner of the first page.

FIGURE WD 4–16
Position button
and gallery

Position button

Click to position chart in lower-left corner

Chart in lower-left corner

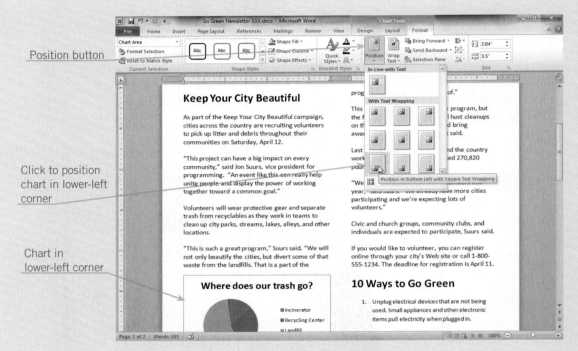

11. Scroll down, if necessary, and select the chart. On the contextual Chart Tools Layout tab, in the Labels group, click the **Data Labels** button, and then click the **Inside End** option. Data labels are added to each piece of the pie chart.

12. On the contextual Chart Tools Design tab, in the Chart Styles group, click the **More** button ⯆ to display the Chart Styles gallery. Click **Style 29**, as shown in **Figure WD 4–17**.

Chart Tools
Design tab

Click Style 29
to change the
chart style

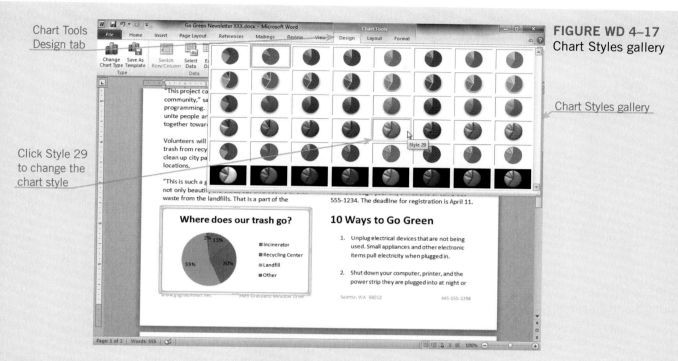

Chart Styles gallery

13. In the Type group, click the **Change Chart Type** button to display the Change Chart Type dialog box. Click the **Column** category and the **Stacked Column** chart type (second from the left in the top row), and then click the **OK** button to replace the pie chart with a stacked column chart.

14. Click the **Undo** button 🔄 on the Quick Access Toolbar to revert back to the pie chart.

15. Move the chart up about ¼" until there are two lines of text above it.

16. Save the document and leave it open for use in the next Step-by-Step.

Inserting and Modifying Screenshots

Textbooks such as this one contain illustrations that show you what a tab on the Ribbon looks like or what your screen should look like at a certain point in an activity. These visuals provide you with details that would be difficult to describe using words. You can easily include these types of pictures in your own documents using the Screenshot button in the Illustrations group on the Insert tab. A *screenshot* is a picture of a computer screen or part of a screen, such as a window or button. The Insert Screenshot button enables you to insert a picture of a nonminimized window on your computer (other than the currently open document window) into your document. The Screen Clipping command on the Screenshot menu lets you use the mouse to cut out and insert any part of a screen into your document. After you insert a screenshot or clipping, you can modify it using the contextual Picture Tools Format tab.

▶ **VOCABULARY**
screenshot

Step-by-Step WD 4.6

The document Go Green Newsletter *XXX* from Step-by-Step WD 4.5 should be open in the Word program window.

1. Position the insertion point at the bottom of page 1 in the right column before the *S* in *Shut down your computer.*

2. On the Insert tab, in the Illustrations group, click the **Screenshot** button to display the Screenshot menu, and then click **Screen Clipping**. The current document window is minimized, and the pointer changes to a crosshair +.

3. Use the crosshair pointer to draw a square around the Start button on the Windows taskbar, as shown in **Figure WD 4–18**.

FIGURE WD 4–18
Creating a screen clipping

Crosshair pointer

Start button on
Windows taskbar

4. Release the mouse button to insert the clipping into the document at the insertion point.

5. Resize the picture to approximately .3" square. (To track the size of the image, refer to the Shape Height and Shape Width boxes in the Size group on the Picture Tools Format tab.)

6. On the Picture Tools Format tab, in the Picture Styles group, click the **Picture Effects** button, point to **Glow**, and then in the Glow Variations section, click the **Olive Green, 5 pt glow, Accent color 3** option (the third one in the first row).

7. Save the document and leave it open for use in the next Step-by-Step.

Inserting and Modifying Objects

You just learned to add interest to documents by inserting graphic objects that are mainly made up of pictures, drawings, and shapes. In addition to these eye-catching images, you can also use objects that are largely made up of text as graphic elements in documents. Text boxes, WordArt, drop caps, and Quick Parts are examples of objects you can insert using the buttons in the Text group on the Insert tab, shown in **Figure WD 4–19**.

Text group

FIGURE WD 4–19   Text group on the Insert tab

Inserting a Text Box

A *text box* is a container for text that can be positioned and modified like a graphic in a document. Text boxes can be especially useful for adding enlarged quotations (called pull quotes) to documents, but also for keeping paragraphs and graphics together and for making text flow around other text or graphics.

The Text Box button is located in the Text group on the Insert tab. The Text Box gallery contains predesigned text boxes you can insert into documents, or you can draw a new blank text box. Text boxes can be moved and resized; options are available for modifying borders, fills, and effects. You can apply custom formatting to text within a text box the same way you would any text in the document.

The Drawing Tools Format contextual tab is displayed on the Ribbon when you insert or select a text box. This tab contains tools for modifying and moving text boxes.

▶ **VOCABULARY**
text box

Step-by-Step WD 4.7

The document Go Green Newsletter *XXX* from Step-by-Step WD 4.6 should be open in the Word program window.

1. On page 1 of the document, position the insertion point before the *K* in *Keep Your City Beautiful*.

2. On the Insert tab, in the Text group, click the **Text Box** button to display the Text Box gallery.

3. Scroll down and click the **Stacks Quote** option.

4. With the placeholder text in the inserted text box already selected, type **"An event like this can really help unite people and display the power of working together toward a common goal."**.

5. Select the text you just typed. On the Home tab, in the Font group, click the **Font** list arrow, and then click **Cambria** to change the font.

6. Select the text box, position the pointer over one of its edges until you see the move pointer with the selection pointer 🔩, and then drag the text box to the top of the second column.

7. Select the text box if necessary. On the Drawing Tools Format tab, in the Arrange group, click the **Wrap Text** button, and then click **Top and Bottom** so that text will not wrap around the sides of the text box.

8. Click away from the text box to deselect it. Your screen should look similar to **Figure WD 4–20**.

9. Save the document and leave it open for use in the next Step-by-Step.

Inserting and Modifying WordArt

WordArt is a drawing tool that turns text characters into graphic images. You can use the WordArt feature to create interesting text effects to enhance documents. WordArt lets you fit text into a variety of shapes, use unusual alignments, and add three-dimensional effects. The bright colors and unusual alignments can be fun to combine, but you must make sure the graphic you create is appropriate for the document. For example, a rainbow-colored, curvy design would not be appropriate for a report in an attorney's office, but it might be suitable for a newsletter from a child care center. The WordArt button is located in the Text group on the Insert tab.

You edit and format a WordArt drawing object using the WordArt Styles group on the Drawing Tools Format contextual tab on the Ribbon. You can change its WordArt style, change its fill or outline colors, or add a text effect. Like other Word graphics, you can also resize and reposition WordArt objects.

Step-by-Step WD 4.8

The document Go Green Newsletter *XXX* from Step-by-Step WD 4.7 should be open in the Word program window.

1. Scroll to page 2 and select the heading *Did You Know?*.

2. On the Insert tab on the Ribbon, in the Text group, click the **WordArt** button and click **Fill – Red, Accent 2, Matte Bevel**, as shown in **Figure WD 4–21**.

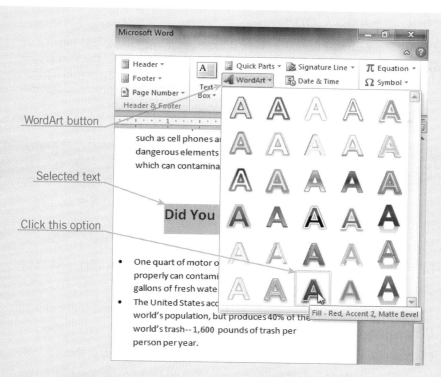

3. On the Drawing Tools Format tab, in the WordArt Styles group, click the
Text Effects button ![icon], point to **Transform**, and then in the Warp section, click **Chevron Up** (first option in the second row).

4. In the WordArt Styles group, click the **Text Fill** button arrow ![icon], and
then click **Olive Green, Accent 3, Darker 25%** to change the color to
match the other colors in the document, as shown in **Figure WD 4–22**.

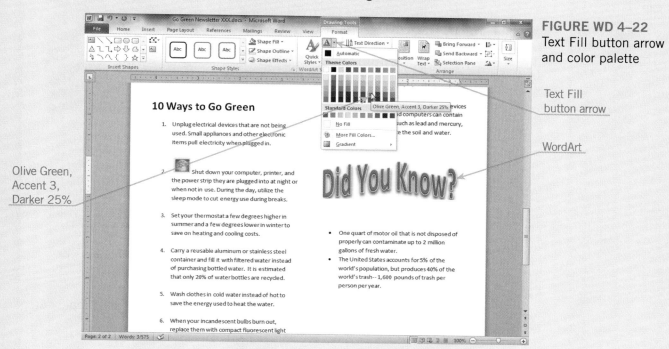

FIGURE WD 4–22
Text Fill button arrow
and color palette

5. Save the document and leave it open for use in the next Step-by-Step.

Inserting a Drop Cap

A *drop cap* is a large initial capital letter or a large first word used to add interest to text, such as at the beginning of a document. The Drop Cap button in the Text group on the Insert tab displays a menu with options for inserting a drop cap within a paragraph or in the margin. The Drop Cap Options command lets you specify additional options for positioning and formatting a drop cap.

Step-by-Step WD 4.9

The document Go Green Newsletter *XXX* from Step-by-Step WD 4.8 should be open in the Word program window.

1. Select the *A* in *As* in the first paragraph of text on page 1.

2. On the Insert tab, in the Text group, click the **Drop Cap** button, and then click the **Dropped** option.

3. Using the tools on the Home tab on the Ribbon, change the font color to **Olive Green, Accent 3, Darker 25%**, and apply bold to the drop cap.

4. Click away from the drop cap to deselect it. Your drop cap should look similar to **Figure WD 4–23**. Take a moment to review the page. If a few lines of text from the *Keep Your City Beautiful* article have moved to the next page, adjust the placement of the chart if necessary, and reduce the size of the text box and/or move it slightly higher in the column so that all the text for that article fits on one page.

FIGURE WD 4–23
Drop cap

5. Save the document and leave it open for use in the next Step-by-Step.

Creating and Inserting Quick Parts

In previous activities, you have inserted predesigned document parts, such as headers, text boxes, and cover pages called *building blocks*. These reusable parts are accessible in galleries and are stored in the Building Blocks Organizer. A *Quick Part* is a type of building block made up of an image and/or text that you can create, save, and reuse, such as a company logo or address.

The Quick Parts button is located in the Text group on the Insert tab. To save a selected set of graphics and/or text as a Quick Part, click the Quick Parts button, and then click the Save Selection to Quick Parts Gallery command on the Quick Parts menu. The selection is saved as a Quick Part in the Building Blocks Organizer and becomes available in the Quick Parts gallery, which is displayed at the top of the Quick Parts menu when you click the Quick Parts button. To open the Building Blocks Organizer, where you can insert, delete, edit, and preview building blocks, click the Building Blocks Organizer command on the Quick Parts menu.

> **VOCABULARY**
> **building blocks**
> **Quick Part**

> **EXTRA FOR EXPERTS**
>
> To insert a Quick Part, you can type the name you saved it with and then press F3.

Step-by-Step WD 4.10

The document Go Green Newsletter *XXX* from Step-by-Step WD 4.9 should be open in the Word program window.

1. In the document title, click after the *s* in *Go Green News.*

2. Drag to the left to select *Go Green News,* the sprout clip art, and the green rectangle. (Make sure you select only the sprout clip art, text, and rectangle, because these will become your Quick Part.)

3. On the Insert tab on the Ribbon, in the Text group, click the **Quick Parts** button, and then click **Save Selection to Quick Part Gallery**, as shown in **Figure WD 4–24**. The Create New Building Block dialog box opens.

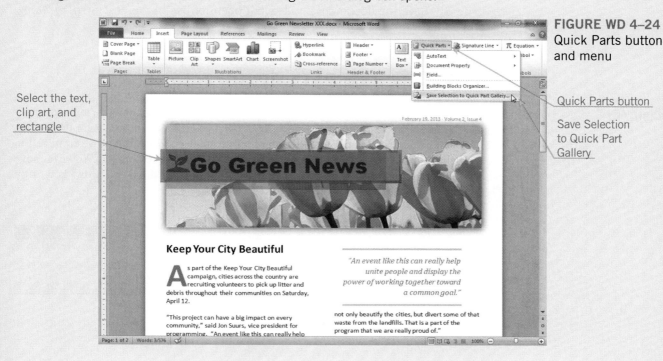

FIGURE WD 4–24
Quick Parts button and menu

Quick Parts button

Save Selection to Quick Part Gallery

Select the text, clip art, and rectangle

4. Notice that Word has inserted a name for this building block and that it will be stored in the Quick Parts gallery. Click the **OK** button to save it to the Building Blocks Organizer.

5. Save the Go Green Newsletter *XXX* document and then close it.

6. Open **Step WD 4-9** from the folder containing the data files for this lesson, and save it as **Go Green Sales Letter *XXX*** (replace the *XXX* with your initials).

7. On the Insert tab, in the Text group, click the **Quick Parts** button, and then click the ***Go Green News** Quick Part from the gallery, as shown in **Figure WD 4–25**, to insert it into the document.

FIGURE WD 4–25
Quick Parts button, gallery, and menu

8. Save the document and leave it open for use in the next Step-by-Step.

Creating and Modifying Tables

> **VOCABULARY**
> **table**
> **cell**

A *table* is a grid of horizontal rows and vertical columns of numbers, text, or graphics, as shown in **Figure WD 4–26**. It is often easier to align text using tables than using tabs. A *cell* is the intersection of a row and a column. You move from cell to cell from left to right and then down to the next row by pressing Tab. You can move out of a table when you reach the last cell by pressing the down arrow key or by clicking outside of the table.

2013 Sales				
	Qtr1	Qtr2	Qtr3	Qtr4
Collins, J.	$38,456	$56,934	$34,457	$36,421
Jenkins, S.	$31,213	$29,456	$37,432	$32,534
Wong, Y.	$25,421	$32,365	$44,343	$33,893
Haig, H.	$32,238	$28,452	$26,476	$46,222

FIGURE WD 4–26   Table

Word offers several ways to create a table using the Table button in the Tables group on the Insert tab. You can use the Insert Table grid, the Insert Table dialog box, the Draw Table command, or the Quick Tables command.

Creating a Table

To insert a new blank table, you use the Table button in the Tables group on the Insert tab. To specify the number of columns and rows in the table, you can either drag across the Insert Table grid and click the appropriate square, or click Insert Table on the Table menu and then edit the number of columns and rows in the Insert Table dialog box. To modify the table design with an added row, you can press Tab with the insertion point in the last cell to create a new row and move the insertion point into it.

> **EXTRA FOR EXPERTS**
>
> Quick Tables are predesigned tables, such as calendars, that you can insert in your documents. Word comes with several built-in table formats that are stored in the Quick Tables gallery on the Table menu, and you can add your own table to the gallery using the Save Selection to Quick Tables Gallery command.

Step-by-Step WD 4.11

The document Go Green Sales Letter *XXX* from Step-by-Step WD 4.10 should be open in the Word program window.

1. Click the second blank line below the second paragraph that begins *We recently conducted.*

2. On the Insert tab, in the Tables group, click the **Table** button to display the Insert Table grid and Table menu.

3. Click the **Insert Table** command on the Table menu to open the Insert Table dialog box.

4. In the Number of columns box, type **2** and press **Tab**.

5. In the Number of rows box, type **12**, as shown in **Figure WD 4–27**.

FIGURE WD 4–27
Insert Table dialog box

6. Click the **OK** button to insert the blank table.

7. Type the following data in the table as shown, pressing **Tab** to move to the next cell and to the next row.

Reader Survey Responses	
Characteristic	Percentage
Recycle regularly	94%
Purchase "green" products often	44%
Are concerned about the environment	86%
Have an income above $60,000	57%
Have a college degree	66%
Are under the age of 40	38%
Are above the age of 40	62%
Are female	65%
Are male	35%

8. Save the document and leave it open for use in the next Step-by-Step.

Modifying a Table

You can apply different fonts, font styles, and font sizes to table text the same way you apply them to other text in a document. To apply a style or other formatting to a table, you first need to select the table by clicking the Table Move handle outside the upper-left corner of the table.

When you insert a table, the contextual Table Tools Design and Layout tabs are displayed with options for modifying a table. The Table Styles group on the Table Tools Design tab includes the Table Styles gallery, which you can use to apply pre-designed formats to a table. On the Table Tools Layout tab, you can use the buttons in the Rows & Columns group to insert columns and rows and delete cells, columns, rows, and tables. The Merge group contains buttons for merging (combining multiple cells into one) or splitting (dividing one cell into multiple) cells. The Cell Size group contains the AutoFit button, which automatically resizes selected columns to fit their contents.

EXTRA FOR EXPERTS

When you want to insert more than one row or column in a table, select that number of rows or columns before choosing an Insert command from the Table Tools Layout tab. Word inserts that many rows or columns.

EXTRA FOR EXPERTS

You can use the Convert Text to Table command on the Table menu to convert text separated by paragraph marks, commas, tabs, or other characters to cells in a table. You can also reverse the process to convert a table to paragraphs or tabbed text.

Step-by-Step WD 4.12

The document Go Green Sales Letter *XXX* from Step-by-Step WD 4.11 should be open in the Word program window.

1. If necessary, click the table to display the Table Move handle by the upper-left corner of the table.

2. Click the **Table Move handle** ⊞ to select the entire table.

3. On the contextual Table Tools Design tab, in the Table Styles group, click the **More** button ⊡ to display the Table Styles gallery.

4. Scroll down in the gallery if necessary, point to the **Medium Grid 1 – Accent 3** table style, shown in **Figure WD 4–28**, and then click to apply the style.

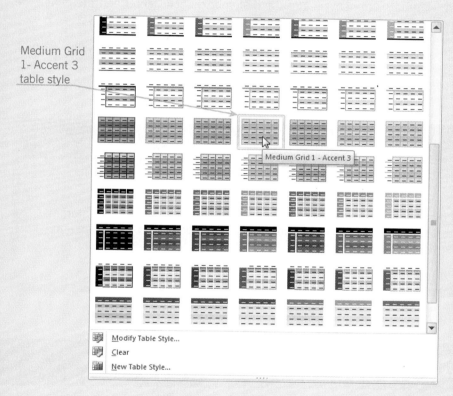

Medium Grid 1- Accent 3 table style

FIGURE WD 4–28
Table Styles gallery

5. On the contextual Table Tools Design tab, in the Table Style Options group, click the **First Column** check box to remove the check mark indicating that special formatting should be applied to the first column.

6. Click to the left of the first row to select it. On the contextual Table Tools Layout tab, in the Merge group, click the **Merge Cells** button to combine the two cells into one.

7. In the Alignment group, click the **Align Center** button ▤ to center the title.

8. Click to the left of the blank second row to select it. In the Rows & Columns group, click the **Delete** button, and then click **Delete Rows** to delete the row.

9. Select the second row and bold the headings.

10. Select the row that contains *Have a college degree*. In the Rows & Columns group, click the **Insert Below** button to insert a new row.

11. In the blank row, type **Vote regularly**. Press **Tab** and type **71%**.

12. In the Cell Size group, click the **AutoFit** button, and then click **AutoFit Contents** to resize the columns to fit the contents.

13. In the Table group, click the **Properties** button to display the Table Properties dialog box.

14. In the Alignment area of the dialog box, click **Center** and then click the **OK** button to center the table horizontally in the document.

15. Save and close the document, and then close Word. If you get a warning message about saving the building blocks file, click **Save**.

ETHICS IN TECHNOLOGY

Copyrighted Images

There are many colorful graphics and beautiful pictures displayed on the Web. But as you surf the Internet, remember that copyright laws apply online also. You cannot just download an image from a Web page and use it in your Word documents or other files without permission. Some images are freely available, but always check an image's copyright before taking it for your own purposes.

SUMMARY

In this lesson, you learned:

- To insert and modify pictures, shapes, clip art, SmartArt, charts, and screenshots to add visual impact to documents.

- That text objects such as text boxes, WordArt, drop caps, and Quick Parts can be used to add interest to documents.

- Text can be efficiently aligned and presented in rows and columns using tables.

■ VOCABULARY REVIEW

Define the following terms:

building blocks
cell
chart
clip art
crop
drawing objects

drop cap
floating object
inline object
picture
Quick Part
screenshot

selection handles
SmartArt graphic
table
text box
text wrapping
WordArt

■ REVIEW QUESTIONS

MULTIPLE CHOICE

Select the best response for the following statements.

1. The green circle at the top of a graphic is used to _____ a graphic.

   A. insert

   B. crop

   C. resize

   D. rotate

2. Small circles and squares at the sides and corners of a graphic are called _____.

   A. SmartArt

   B. pictures

   C. selection handles

   D. rotate circles

3. Text cannot wrap around _____ objects.

   A. floating

   B. drawing

   C. graphic

   D. inline

4. Enter a _____ to search for related clip art in the Clip Art task pane.

   A. keyword

   B. formula

   C. picture

   D. placeholder

5. A hierarchy chart is an example of a _____.

   A. table

   B. WordArt graphic

   C. picture

   D. SmartArt graphic

6. The data that makes up a chart is stored in a(n) _____.

   A. table

   B. Excel worksheet

   C. Quick Part

   D. Word document

7. A _____ is a container for text that can be positioned like a graphic in a document.

   A. chart

   B. placeholder

   C. table

   D. text box

8. A _____ is a large initial capital letter or a large first word used to add interest to text.

   A. chart

   B. WordArt style

   C. drop cap

   D. Quick Part

9. Predesigned document parts, such as headers and cover pages, are called _____.

   A. text boxes   C. drop caps

   B. building blocks   D. placeholders

10. The _____ command combines cells so you can center a heading over an entire table.

   A. Merge Cells   C. Insert Table

   B. Properties   D. Group

FILL IN THE BLANK

Complete the following sentences by writing the correct word or words in the blanks provided.

1. _____ are digital photographs or images.

2. Shapes, curves, and lines are considered _____ objects.

3. You can search for photos, videos, and audio files in the _____ _____ task pane.

4. SmartArt graphics are inserted with _____ that you can replace with your own text.

5. A(n) _____ is used to illustrate or compare numeric data.

6. A pull quote is an example of a(n) _____ _____.

7. _____ turns text characters into graphic images.

8. A(n) _____ _____ is a type of building block that you can create, save, and reuse.

9. A(n) _____ is the intersection of a row and a column.

10. You can add a new row to a table by pressing _____ with the insertion point in the last cell.

■ PROJECTS

PROJECT WD 4–1

1. Open the **Project WD 4-1** document from the folder containing the data files for this lesson, and save it as **Earth Day Award XXX** (replace *XXX* with your initials).

2. Use the keywords **Earth Day** to search the Clip Art task pane (include Office.com content) for the photo shown in **Figure WD 4–29** (or another photo of your choice). Change it to a floating object, resize it, crop it, and position it as shown.

3. Insert the 24-Point star shape as shown. Apply the Intense Effect – Olive Green, Accent 3 shape style.

4. Position the insertion point before the *E* in *Earth Day* at the bottom of the page. Search the Clip Art task pane using the keywords **planet Earth** (include Office.com content), and insert the Earth clip art shown in Figure WD 4–29 (or a similar one of your choice) as an inline object. Resize it and change the color to Blue, Accent color 1 Dark.

5. Select the clip art and the Earth Day 2013 text, and save it to the Quick Parts gallery.

6. Insert a line approximately 4" long above *Committee Chair*. Apply the Subtle Line - Dark 1 shape style.

7. Save and close the document.

ON YOUR OWN

Open the **Earth Day Award XXX** document, compress the photo in the document, and then add an Artistic Effect or Picture Style to the photo. Save and close the document.

PROJECT WD 4–2

1. Open the **Project WD 4-2** document from the folder containing the data files for this lesson, and save it as **Sales Memo XXX** (replace *XXX* with your initials).

2. In the table, merge the cells in the first row and center the title.

3. Insert a blank row above the second row.

4. Add the following data in the new row:

	Qtr1	Qtr2	Qtr3	Qtr4

5. Select the table and apply the blue Medium Shading 2 – Accent 4 table style.

6. Insert the Transcend Sidebar from the Text Box gallery (it should appear at the top of the document). In the placeholder, type **Connerton Manufacturing**. **Specializing in eco-friendly business solutions**.

7. Insert the *Earth Day 2013 Quick Part created in Project WD 4–1 (or, if you have not completed Project WD 4–1, type **Earth Day 2013**) at the bottom of the page, and then type **Award Winner** after it.

8. Save and close the document.

ON YOUR OWN

Open the **Sales Memo XXX** document, and then sort the rows using the first column. Save and close the document.

ON YOUR OWN

Delete the *Earth Day 2013 Quick Part (created in Step-by-Step WD 4.10) and the *Go Green News Quick Part from the Building Blocks Organizer.

FIGURE WD 4–29   Earth Day Award *XXX*.docx

PROJECT WD 4–3

1. Create a new blank document and save it as **Profits** *XXX* (replace *XXX* with your initials).

2. Create a Line with Markers chart using the following data:

	Product 1	Product 2	Product 3
Northeast	23,456	53,547	59,034
Midwest	41,703	29,048	46,900
Pacific	63,345	99,331	33,987
Atlantic	53,806	107,853	52,357

3. Change the chart to a Clustered Column chart.

4. Add data labels using the Outside End option.

5. Format the chart using Style 27 from the Chart Styles gallery.

6. Save and close the document.

ON YOUR OWN

Open the **Profits** *XXX*.docx file, and edit the Product 1 data for the Northeast to 41,987. Add a chart title above the chart, and change the title to **Profits**. Save and close the document.

PROJECT WD 4–4

1. Create a new blank document, and save it as **Organization Chart** *XXX* (replace *XXX* with your initials).

2. Type **Organization Chart** at the top of the page using 18-point Calibri, and then bold and center the text.

3. Create the SmartArt graphic shown in **Figure WD 4–30**. (*Hint*: Select the President shape, and use the Add Shape button arrow to add an assistant. Apply the Intense Effect Smart Art style to the SmartArt graphic, and change its color to Colored Fill – Accent 2.)

4. Save and close the document.

ON YOUR OWN

Open the **Organization Chart** *XXX* file and create WordArt using the Organization Chart title. Save and close the document.

FIGURE WD 4–30　Organization Chart *XXX*

WEB PROJECT

Create a logo for the Sandy Beach Resort using one or more pieces of clip art, WordArt, pictures, SmartArt, or shapes. Use the *Find more at Office.com* link at the bottom of the Clip Art task pane to search for free images on the Microsoft Web site that you can use in your logo. Browse the site for additional hints and tips on how to use clip art effectively. Save the logo as a Quick Part.

 TEAMWORK PROJECT

With a partner, create a two-page newsletter on the topic of your choice, such as your favorite sport, a place you would like to visit, or your favorite hobby. Work together to plan and write the articles and format the document. Include appropriate graphic objects, such as drop caps, text boxes, and clip art.

CRITICAL THINKING

ACTIVITY WD 4–1

Search the Clip Art task pane for an advertising character to promote a favorite product. Insert the clip art and create an advertisement using the picture. Crop, resize, rotate, and adjust color and effects to change the graphic. Use shapes and other objects such as WordArt to display the product's name and/or slogan. Be prepared to share your advertisement with the class.

ACTIVITY WD 4–2

Did you know that text boxes can be linked? Use Word Help to learn how to link text boxes. Create a text box and type a paragraph of text in the text box. Insert a second text box, add some text, and link it to the first. Experiment with the size of the text boxes so that your text fits within both text boxes. How many text boxes can be linked? Can text boxes be linked across pages? How could text box linking be helpful in a document?

UNIT II REVIEW

Word

■ REVIEW QUESTIONS

MULTIPLE CHOICE

Select the best response for the following statements.

1. A(n) _____ is written information that can be printed on paper or distributed electronically.

   A. margin   C. insertion point

   B. document   D. I-beam

2. Which feature automatically saves your document at regular intervals so that you can recover at least some of your work in case of a power outage or other unexpected shutdown?

   A. Quick Access Toolbar   C. AutoRecover

   B. Print Preview   D. word wrap

3. When you click the _____ button, the software prompts you to save your work if you made any changes since you last saved.

   A. Margins   C. Help

   B. Save   D. Close

4. The _____ button allows you to copy multiple text formatting characteristics and then apply the same formatting to other parts of the document.

   A. Paste   C. Redo

   B. Copy   D. Format Painter

5. _____ is the vertical distance between lines of text in a paragraph.

   A. Line spacing   C. Alignment

   B. Indentation   D. Point size

6. A _____ is a series of related words, numbers, or phrases.

   A. theme   C. style

   B. list   D. bullet

7. When you break a document into _____, you can control a document's layout by formatting each differently.

    A. paragraphs   C. sections

    B. lists   D. styles

8. _____ are vertical sections in which text flows from the bottom of one section to the top of the next.

    A. Pages   C. Lists

    B. Columns   D. Styles

9. A(n) _____ object moves with the text around it.

    A. recolored   C. inline

    B. cropped   D. floating

10. _____ lets you fit text into a variety of shapes, use unusual alignments, and add three-dimensional effects.

    A. WordArt   C. A table

    B. Clip art   D. A drop cap

FILL IN THE BLANK

Complete the following sentences by writing the correct word or words in the blanks provided.

1. The _____ _____ is the blinking vertical bar that signals where any text you type will appear.

2. Before you can format text or move or delete text or graphics, you must _____, or highlight, the text or object you want to change.

3. Click the _____ tab to access the New command.

4. Word flags words that might be misspelled with a wavy _____ underline.

5. A(n) _____ contains settings for margins, page size and orientation, and text and/or graphics that are standard for a particular type of document.

6. When you _____ text, Word rearranges selected text, numbers, or dates alphabetically, numerically, or chronologically.

7. A(n) _____ is text or graphics that appears in the top margin of each page in a document.

8. _____ are digital photographs or images.

9. A(n) _____ _____ is a large initial capital letter or a large first word used to add interest to text.

10. A(n) _____ is an arrangement of rows and columns of numbers, text, or graphics.

■ PROJECTS

PROJECT WD 1

1. Open a new blank document, and save it as **Postcard *XXX*** (replace *XXX* with your initials).

2. Change the paper size to A5 or 5.83" × 8.27".

3. Set the orientation to Landscape.

4. Change the margins to Narrow.

5. Change the page layout to two even columns.

6. Type the word **checkmates** in the Search for text box in the Clip Art task pane and insert the black-and-white picture of the multiple chess pieces. (Include Office.com content when searching for clip art.)

7. Click to the right of the lower-right corner of the inserted image, press Enter to position the insertion point at the top of the second column, and then type the following text:

    We Moved! (Press Enter three times.)

    Visit us at our new location:

    Games, Gifts & Gadgets Galore

    1900 Newberry Street

    Providence, RI 02987

    401-555-3456

8. Center all the text and change the point size to 12.

9. Select *Games, Gifts & Gadgets Galore* and apply bold.

10. Select the bold line and the three lines below it. Change the line spacing to 1.0 with no space after the paragraph.

11. Select *We Moved!* and create WordArt using Gradient Fill - Orange, Accent 6, Inner Shadow and change the font to Impact, size 48 point.

12. Apply the text effect Transform, Deflate to the WordArt.

13. Change the document theme to Verve.

14. Save and close the document.

    ON YOUR OWN

    Open the **Postcard *XXX*** file. Add a page border and add an artistic effect to the picture. Save and close the document.

PROJECT WD 2

1. Open the file **Project WD 2** from the folder containing the data files for this lesson, and save it as **Thank You *XXX*** (replace *XXX* with your initials).

2. Change the page size to 5 inches wide x 8 inches high.

3. Create custom margins of .75 inches on top, bottom, left, and right.

4. Select all the text in the document, then change the font to Gil Sans MT, 12 point.

5. Select the *W* at the beginning of the first paragraph, and insert a Dropped style drop cap.

6. Select the three sentences after the paragraph ending with …*following perks*:, and create a bulleted list using square bullets.

7. Use the Thesaurus to change the word *customers* in the second sentence of the first paragraph to the synonym *clients*.

8. Select all the text in the document and justify it.

9. Show nonprinting symbols.

10. Select the words *Thank You* at the bottom of the document, and insert WordArt using Gradient Fill - Gray, Outline - Gray.

11. Change the case of the WordArt to uppercase.

12. Change the text fill of the WordArt to Blue, Accent 1, Darker 50%. Add a gradient to the text fill using the From Center option under Dark Variations on the Gradient submenu.

13. Select the WordArt and rotate it 180 degrees so it is upside down. (*Hint*: Use the Rotate button in the Arrange group on the Drawing Tools Format contextual tab.) When you print this document on both sides and fold it in the middle, the words Thank You will be on the front and the other text inside.

14. Save the document and leave it open for use in the next project.

PROJECT WD 3

The document Thank You *XXX* from Project WD 2 should be open in the Word program window.

1. Save the document as **Thank You 2 *XXX*** (replace *XXX* with your initials).

2. Open the Clip Art task pane, and search for clip art with the keywords **coffee cup**. (Include Office.com content.)

3. Insert the picture of the coffee cup shown (upside down) in **Figure WD 1** or a similar one of your choice.

4. If necessary, apply the text wrapping option In Front of Text to change the clip art to a floating object.

5. Resize the picture to approximately 1.18" high and 1" wide, and then position it centered below the WordArt.

6. Flip the picture vertically, as shown in **Figure WD 1**.

7. Hide nonprinting symbols.

8. Draw a text box at the bottom of the first page, as shown in **Figure WD 1**, and type and format the text shown.

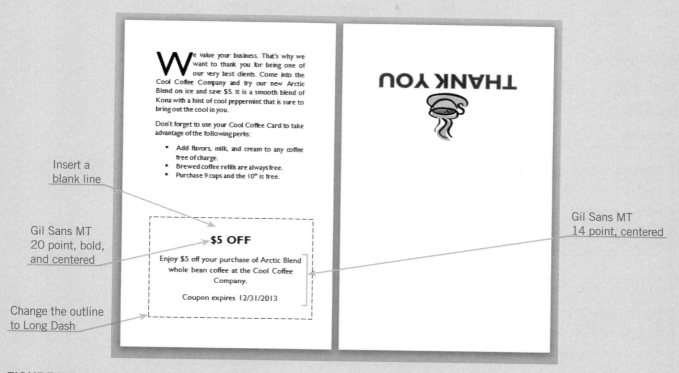

FIGURE WD 1   Thank You 2 *XXX*

9. Save and close the document.

ON YOUR OWN

Open the **Thank You 2 *XXX*** file. Change the color of the drop cap, and add a color fill to the text box. Save and close the document.

PROJECT WD 4

1. Open the file **Project WD 4** from the folder containing the data files for this lesson, and save it as **Proposal Letter *XXX*** (replace *XXX* with your initials).

2. Select *ABC Computers* and apply the Title style from the Quick Styles gallery.

3. Select the two-line address and apply the Subtitle style.

4. Select the remaining text in the letter and apply the Normal style.

5. Click the blank line after the paragraph that begins *Please look over the following table*. Insert a table with four columns and seven rows.

6. Enter text in the table as shown.

Hardware/Software Solutions			
Item	**Description**	**Availability**	**Price**
Color printer	ColorJet Pro	2-day delivery	$450.00
Computer	ComQuest 2	In stock	$2599.99
Scanner	ScanMaster PE	2-day delivery	$529.99
Software	FileMaster 7	In stock	$899.00

7. Select the numbers in the Price column, and then insert a decimal tab at the 5.25" mark to align the numbers at the decimal point.

8. Merge the cells in the first row and center the title horizontally and vertically.

9. Apply the Medium Shading 2 - Accent 1 table style, in the fifth row in the gallery, to the entire table.

10. Deselect the First Column table style option.

11. Save the document and leave it open for use in the next project.

PROJECT WD 5

The Proposal Letter *XXX* document from Project WD 4 should be open in the Word program window.

1. Save the document as **Proposal Letter 2 *XXX*** (replace *XXX* with your initials).

2. Insert a blank row below the first row of the table.

3. Change the document's theme to Austin.

4. Check the spelling and grammar. Ignore the company, product, and personal names, and correct the misspelled words and grammar mistakes.

5. Use Find and Replace to change all occurrences of *Chung* to **Baldwin**.

6. Insert a diagonal confidential watermark.

7. Insert the Alphabet footer and replace the placeholder text with the company telephone number, **214-555-1234**.

8. Delete the word *Page* and the page number in the footer.

9. Create a Quick Part using the ABC Computers title at the top of the page.

10. Insert the Conservative cover page.

11. Delete the Company content control (and the words Thompson Steele), and insert the ABC Computers quick part.

12. Type **Equipment Proposal** as the document's title, and remove the subtitle and abstract content controls.

13. Type **Cathan Baldwin** as the author of the document, and insert the current date as indicated.

14. Save and close the document and exit Word.

ON YOUR OWN

Open the **Proposal Letter 2 *XXX*** file. Sort the bottom four rows in the table in ascending order by the Price column. Save and close the document.

WEB PROJECT

Visit a job search Web site and conduct a search for jobs that require the use of Microsoft Word. What job titles require experience with Word? What level of experience is required? What are the other job requirements? What are the salary ranges? Choose a job in which you would be interested and read the entire job description. Choose a letter template and write a letter of application for the job. Explain the reasons why you believe you are qualified for the job as well as why you believe the job is right for you.

TEAMWORK PROJECT

With a partner, research the history of your school. Find out when it was established, who or what it was named after, how many students attend, and other relevant information. Create a brochure detailing this information that will be given to new students. Collaborate on the planning, writing, and design. With your instructor's permission, access the Office.com brochure templates for ideas. If you wish, you may download and use one of the templates. Include appropriate clip art, WordArt, or other graphic elements. When your project is complete, present it to the class.

■ CRITICAL THINKING

ACTIVITY WD 1

Create a one-page flyer announcing an upcoming school event. Assume the flyer will be posted in approved areas around the school. Use appropriate wording and graphics to convey the necessary information.

ACTIVITY WD 2

Create a table that displays your schedule of classes. Include columns for the class name, room number, time, day, instructor, and any other relevant information. Apply your choice of formatting and table styles.

ACTIVITY WD 3

Refer to Project WD 3. Design and create a business-card-sized Cool Coffee Rewards card for the company.

■ PORTFOLIO CHECKLIST

_____	Lesson 1	Florida Admissions *XXX*.docx
_____	Lesson 1	Graduation Postcard *XXX*.docx
_____	Lesson 1	Lone Star Fax *XXX*.docx
_____	Lesson 2	Appointment Policy *XXX*.docx
_____	Lesson 2	Spelling&Grammar *XXX*.docx
_____	Lesson 2	Zare Resume Edit *XXX*.docx
_____	Lesson 3	Caring for Your Computer *XXX*.docx
_____	Lesson 3	Verhoff Resume *XXX*.docx
_____	Lesson 4	Go Green Newsletter *XXX*.docx
_____	Lesson 4	Sales Memo *XXX*.docx
_____	Unit Review	Postcard *XXX*.docx

UNIT III

MICROSOFT EXCEL

LESSON 1

Understanding Excel Fundamentals

■ OBJECTIVES

Upon completion of this lesson, you should be able to:

■ Start Excel, open an existing workbook, and navigate a worksheet.

■ Save a workbook.

■ Select cells, enter data, and edit cell contents.

■ Manage worksheets in the workbook.

■ Change workbook views.

■ Add headers and footers.

■ Preview and print worksheets.

■ Close a workbook.

■ DATA FILES

To complete this lesson, you will need these data files:

Step EX 1-1.xlsx
Project EX 1-1.xlsx
Project EX 1-3.xlsx
Project EX 1-4.xlsx
Project EX 1-5.xlsx
Activity EX 1-1.xlsx

■ VOCABULARY

active cell

cell

cell reference

collated

columns

footer

formula bar

freeze panes

header

Name box

range

rows

select

sheet

sheet tab

spreadsheet software

workbook

workbook window

worksheet

VOCABULARY

spreadsheet software

workbook

worksheet

sheet

workbook window

sheet tab

Introduction

Microsoft Excel 2010 is the spreadsheet program included in the Microsoft Office 2010 suite of software. *Spreadsheet software* is used to calculate, analyze, and visually represent numerical data. You can perform a variety of tasks, from creating budgets to tracking inventory to totaling sales figures.

As in other Office programs, the various tools for entering and editing data in Excel are organized on the Ribbon tabs. Excel includes predefined formulas, functions, and charts that allow you to quickly and accurately perform calculations from the most basic to the most complex. With Excel you can create worksheets that are attractive and well organized, and that help you manage data effectively. Before you discover Excel's power to calculate and represent data quickly and easily, you need to learn basic skills such as opening, saving, and printing. In this lesson, you will learn techniques for performing fundamental skills using Excel.

Examining the Excel Program Window

An Excel file is called a *workbook*. Each workbook contains a collection of related worksheets. A *worksheet* (also commonly called a spreadsheet or just a *sheet*) is the grid with columns and rows where you enter and summarize data.

When you start Excel, a blank workbook opens, as shown in **Figure EX 1–1**. Use this figure to become familiar with the parts of the Excel program window.

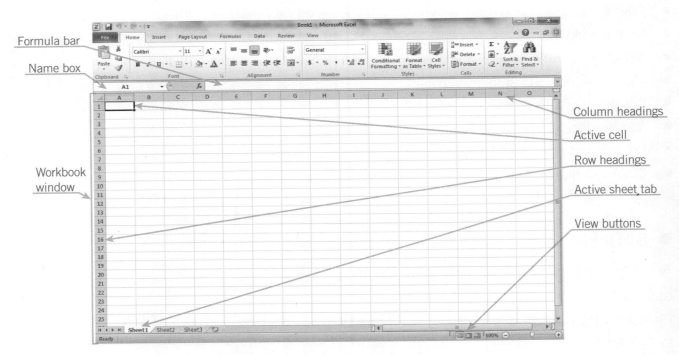

FIGURE EX 1–1   Excel program window

The portion of the program window displaying the worksheets is the *workbook window*, and the name of each sheet is displayed on a sheet tab at the bottom of the workbook window. In Figure EX 1–1, Sheet1 is the active sheet, as shown by the *sheet tab*. By default, a new workbook contains three worksheets. You can add as many sheets as you need to a workbook, up to 255 worksheets.

Columns in the worksheet are displayed vertically and are labeled with column headings from left to right beginning with A through Z, then AA through AZ, and so on. *Rows* are displayed horizontally and have numbered row headings running consecutively down the left side of the worksheet.

The rectangle where a column and row intersect is called a *cell*. Each cell is identified by a *cell reference*—the column letter heading followed by the row number heading, such as B5. The cell that is selected is called the *active cell*, which means it is ready for data entry. Clicking a cell makes it active, as indicated by a thick black border around it. The column letter and row number headings of the active cell are also shaded for easy identification.

The *Name box* below the Ribbon displays the cell reference of the active cell. The *formula bar* next to the Name box displays the value or formula of the active cell.

Starting Excel and Opening an Existing Workbook

To begin using Excel, you first need to start the program. You can do this by clicking the Start button on the Windows taskbar, and then clicking the program name on the All Programs menu, or by double-clicking an Excel program icon on the desktop. Once Excel starts, you can begin using it to create a new workbook or to open an existing workbook.

To open an existing workbook, you can search for and then open the workbook file using the Open dialog box shown in **Figure EX 1–2**. Excel provides three methods for displaying the Open dialog box. The most common method is through the Open command found on the File tab. You can also add an Open command to your Quick Access Toolbar or use the keyboard shortcut Ctrl+O.

> **VOCABULARY**
>
> **columns**
>
> **rows**
>
> **cell**
>
> **cell reference**
>
> **active cell**
>
> **Name box**
>
> **formula bar**

> **EXTRA FOR EXPERTS**
>
> You can access the General options in the Excel Options dialog box to change the number of sheets that are included by default in a new workbook. Click the File tab and then click Options to open the Excel Options dialog box.

> **EXTRA FOR EXPERTS**
>
> The names of the most recent workbooks you opened in Excel are displayed when you click Recent on the File tab. You can click a file in the list to open it. You can customize the number of files displayed in the list using the Advanced section of the Excel Options dialog box.

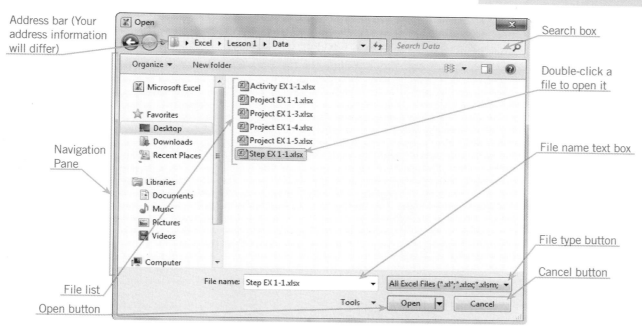

FIGURE EX 1–2   Open dialog box

You can use the Open dialog box to find and open existing files on your hard drive, CD, or other removable media; on a network drive to which you are connected; on your organization's intranet; or on the Internet. Double-clicking a file in the File list will open the file.

The following are parts of the Open dialog box:

- The Navigation Pane displays favorite links to folders that contain workbooks. You can open and view a folder's contents from the Navigation Pane.
- The Address bar at the top of the dialog box shows the folder path.
- The Search box allows you to find a file by name, file type, or location.
- The File type button lists other file types you can choose to open.
- The Open button arrow provides options for opening files, including opening the original file, opening a read-only version (when you want to open a file but keep the original file intact), or opening a copy of the original. If you open a copy or read-only version and edit or change the file, you cannot save changes to the original file. You can, however, use the Save As command to save your revisions with a new filename.
- The Cancel button closes the dialog box without opening a file.

Step-by-Step EX 1.1

1. Click the **Start** button 🌐 on the Windows taskbar. The Start menu opens.
2. Click **All Programs**. A list of programs and program folders opens.
3. Click the **Microsoft Office** program folder. A list of Microsoft Office programs opens.
4. Click **Microsoft Excel 2010**. Excel 2010 starts and its program window opens a new, blank workbook.
5. Click the **File** tab on the Ribbon, and then click **Open** to open the Open dialog box.
6. If necessary, navigate to the folder containing the data files for this lesson. Double-click the file **Step EX 1-1.xlsx** in the File list. The workbook opens, as shown in **Figure EX 1–3**.

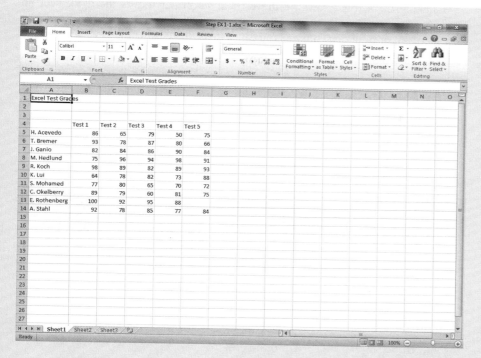

FIGURE EX 1–3
Step EX 1-1.xlsx workbook

7. Leave the workbook open for use in the next Step-by-Step.

Navigating in a Worksheet

A worksheet can, and often does, contain more data than can be displayed within the workbook window. You can use the scroll bars, scroll boxes, and scroll arrows to move through a worksheet. When you drag the vertical scroll box, a ScreenTip displays the number of the topmost row that is visible in the workbook window. When you drag the horizontal scroll box, the ScreenTip displays the letter of the leftmost column that is visible in the workbook window, as shown in **Figure EX 1–4**.

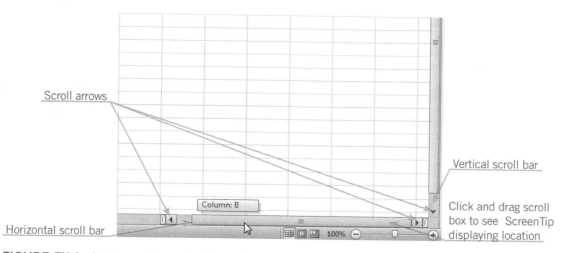

FIGURE EX 1–4   ScreenTip on horizontal scroll box

Clicking the scroll arrows on the vertical scroll bar moves the worksheet up or down one row. Clicking the scroll arrows on the horizontal scroll bar moves the worksheet left or right one column. You can also navigate using the keyboard and the Go To command.

Using the Keyboard

Table EX 1–1 contains some of the keys and key combinations you can use to move around a worksheet. When you use these keystrokes, you change the active cell.

TABLE EX 1–1   Using keystrokes to navigate the worksheet

PRESS KEY(S)	TO MOVE
Left arrow ←	One cell to the left
Right arrow →	One cell to the right
Up arrow ↑	One cell up
Down arrow ↓	One cell down
Page Up	Up one screen
Page Down	Down one screen
Home	To the first cell of a row
Ctrl+Home	To cell A1 at the beginning of the worksheet
Ctrl+End	To last cell of the worksheet containing data or formatting

EXTRA FOR EXPERTS

You can also navigate to cells that meet certain conditions or contain specific data. Click the Find & Select button, then click Go To Special to open the Go To Special dialog box and then select an option, such as Comments, Blanks, or Last cell.

Using the Go To Command

You can use the Go To dialog box to navigate to a particular location in the worksheet. The Go To dialog box is opened by clicking the Find & Select button in the Editing group on the Home tab and then clicking Go To. When you enter the cell name or range name in the Reference text box and click OK, the active cell moves to that specific location. This command is especially helpful when you want to move to a part of the worksheet that is not visible in the workbook window.

Step-by-Step EX 1.2

The Step EX 1-1 workbook from Step-by-Step EX 1.1 should be open in the Excel program window.

1. Press **Ctrl+Home** to move to cell A1 in the worksheet, if necessary.

2. Press the **right arrow** key to move one cell to the right, to cell B1.

3. Press the **down arrow** key to move down one cell, to cell B2.

4. Click and drag the **scroll box** on the horizontal scroll bar to the right and notice the ScreenTip displays the letter of the leftmost column that is visible on the screen, column B.

5. In the Editing group on the Home tab on the Ribbon, click the **Find & Select** button, and then click **Go To** on the menu to open the Go To dialog box.

6. In the Reference text box, type **A7**, as shown in **Figure EX 1–5**, and then click the **OK** button to close the dialog box and move to cell A7.

FIGURE EX 1–5
Go To dialog box

7. Press **Ctrl+End** to move to the last cell of the worksheet containing data or formatting, cell F14.

8. Press **Home** to move to the first cell of the row, cell A14.

9. Click cell **D7** to move to that cell.

10. Click the **down scroll arrow** on the vertical scroll bar to move the worksheet down one row, so row 2 becomes the top row displayed in the workbook window.

11. Press **Page Down** to move down one page. Because it is not a long worksheet, no data is visible in the worksheet grid.

12. Press **Ctrl+Home** to move to cell A1.

13. Leave the workbook open for use in the next Step-by-Step.

Saving Workbooks

The first time you save a workbook, the options for saving include the Save command on the File tab, the Save As command on the File tab, or the Save button on the Quick Access Toolbar. Each of these methods opens the Save As dialog box shown in **Figure EX 1–6**.

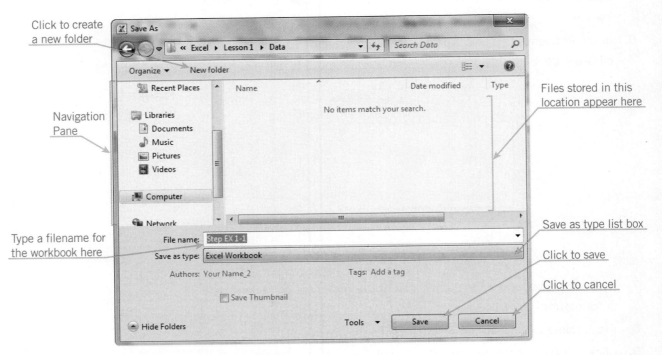

FIGURE EX 1–6   Save As dialog box

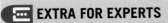

Excel 2010 files and Excel 2007 files have an .xlsx extension that cannot be opened with previous versions of Excel. If you need to share a file with someone using an earlier version, you can use the Save As command located on the File tab to save files as an Excel 97-2003 Workbook with the .xls extension.

EXTRA FOR EXPERTS

For more information about Microsoft Office Web Apps, visit http://www.microsoft.com/office/2010.

After you save a file for the first time, the Save command saves your file with the previously specified name in the location you specified. The Save As command opens the Save As dialog box, in which you can make a copy of the file with a new name, location, or file type. The Save as type list box lets you save a document in another format or as a template. You might need to change the file format or program and version if you share files with others who use different software. To save a worksheet in a specific location, you use the Navigation Pane of the Save As dialog box to navigate to the folder in which you want to save the workbook.

Excel's AutoRecover feature automatically saves your workbook at regular intervals so that you can recover at least some of your work in case of a power outage or other unexpected shutdown. You can turn the AutoRecover feature off or change the frequency of saving by opening the Save page in the Excel Options dialog box from the File tab. However, you should still save your work often and not rely on this automatic saving feature.

You can use the Save & Send command on the File tab to save a document online in two ways. You can click the Save to Web button to make the file accessible from any computer using Windows Live SkyDrive, a free online storage service from Microsoft. You can also save to an organization's SharePoint site, which provides additional opportunities for collaboration, such as editing documents with multiple people at the same time. Saving online allows you to share and access documents through an Internet connection and to view and edit them in a Web browser using Microsoft Office Web Apps, which are free online companions to Word, Excel, and PowerPoint.

Step-by-Step EX 1.3

The Step EX 1-1 workbook from Step-by-Step EX 1.2 should be open in the Excel program window.

1. Click the **File** tab and then click **Save As** to open the Save As dialog box.

2. Navigate to the location where you save your files.

3. Click the **File name** text box, and type **Test Grades *XXX*** (replace *XXX* with your initials).

4. Click the **Save** button to save a copy of the workbook with the new name in the specified location.

5. Leave the workbook open for use in the next Step-by-Step.

Selecting Cells

Before you can enter data or use Excel commands, you must *select*, or highlight, a cell or range. You can select a single cell by clicking it. A *range* is a group of cells. It can be a column, a row, or a group of cells forming a rectangle. A range is identified by the name of the cell in the upper-left corner of the range and the cell in the lower-right corner of the range, separated by a colon (:). For example, a range that includes all the cells between cells A1 and D5 is identified as A1:D5. To select a range, you can click the first cell and then drag to the last cell in the range.

Excel identifies a selected range by using a different background color for the cells included in the range (except for the first cell, which does not change color), as shown in **Figure EX 1–7**. The row number and column letter of any cells in the range are also shaded a different color. You can deselect a cell or range by pressing an arrow key or clicking any cell in the worksheet.

▶ **VOCABULARY**
select

range

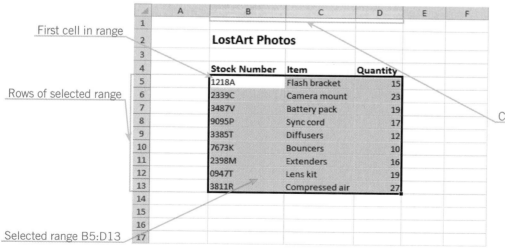

FIGURE EX 1–7   Selected range

You can select ranges or cells that are nonadjacent, meaning not side by side, by pressing and holding Ctrl while you click. You can select a column and a row at the same time using the same method. **Table EX 1–2** shows how to select cells using the mouse. You can also select cells using the keyboard by pressing and holding Shift and using the arrow keys to extend the selection. Another way to select a range is to type the range reference (for example, A1:C5) in the Name box and then press Enter.

TABLE EX 1–2   Selecting cells using the mouse

TO SELECT	DO THIS
A single cell	Click the cell
A range of cells	Click the first cell in the range (in the upper-left corner) and drag to the last cell in the range (in the lower-right corner) or Click the first cell in the range and then press and hold Shift and click the last cell in the range
Nonadjacent cells or ranges	Press and hold Ctrl as you click to select additional cells or click and drag to select additional ranges
An entire row	Click the row heading
An entire column	Click the column heading
All cells on the worksheet	Click the Select All button in the upper-left corner of the workbook window

Step-by-Step EX 1.4

The Test Grades *XXX* workbook from Step-by-Step EX 1.3 should be open in the Excel program window.

1. Click cell **C8** to select it, as shown in **Figure EX 1–8**.

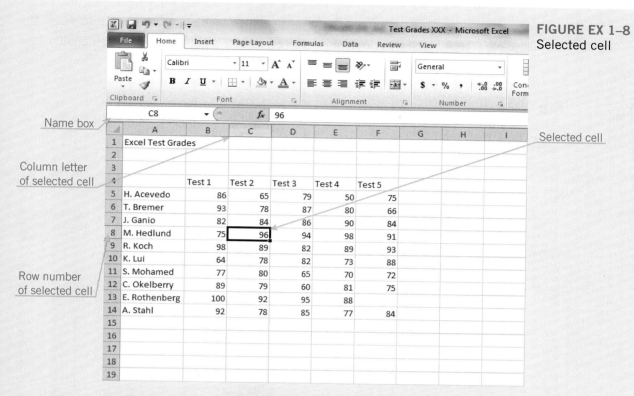

FIGURE EX 1–8
Selected cell

2. Click cell **B5** and, holding the mouse button down, drag to cell **F14** to select the range B5:F14. Notice the selected range is shaded, except for the first cell, which does not change color.

3. Click the **row heading 10** to select the entire row. Notice the whole row is shaded (except for the first cell), including the row number.

4. Press and hold **Ctrl** and then click the **column heading E** to select the entire column while row 10 is still selected. Your screen should look similar to **Figure EX 1–9**.

FIGURE EX 1–9
Selected column and row

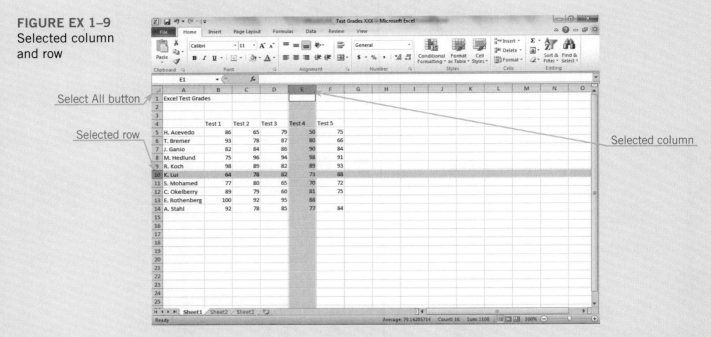

5. Click the **Name** box, type **A5:A14**, and then press **Enter** to select that range.

6. Click the **Select All** button ⬜ to select the entire worksheet.

7. Click cell **A1** to select it. Notice all the other cells on the worksheet are deselected.

8. Leave the workbook open for use in the next Step-by-Step.

Entering Data

You can enter data in Excel by typing numbers or text in the active cell and then pressing Enter or clicking the Enter button on the formula bar. The cell below then becomes the active cell. Entering data and then pressing Tab selects the cell to the right, making it the active cell. You can also press an arrow key after typing data to enter it, and then move to the cell above or below or to the right or left.

As you enter data in a cell, the data is displayed in the active cell and in the formula bar, as shown in **Figure EX 1–10**. As you begin entering data, the message in the status bar changes from *Ready* to *Enter*. You can click the Cancel button on the formula bar or press Esc to cancel the entry you started to type.

Active cell reference displayed in Name box

Cancel button

Active cell

Data in active cell displayed in formula bar

Enter button

FIGURE EX 1–10   Formula bar

Understanding Data Types

Data in a cell can be text, such as letters, symbols, and other characters; or numbers, such as values, dates, and times. Generally speaking, numeric data can be used in calculations, whereas text cannot. Excel automatically determines whether data is text or numeric as you enter it.

By default, text is left-aligned in a cell and numbers are right-aligned, as shown in **Figure EX 1–11**. If you want to enter a number (such as a postal code) as text, you can type an apostrophe before the number to signal that it is not to be used in calculations. Otherwise, a postal code such as 07458 would be displayed without the leading zero and would be right-aligned. If a cell contains a combination of text and numbers, the contents are left-aligned.

> **WARNING**
>
> The alignment of data in a cell is not an accurate indicator of the data type. For example, do not assume data in a cell is numeric just because it is right-aligned. Cell alignment can be changed without affecting the data type.

Number preceded by an apostrophe is formatted as text

	B13		f_x '3811			
	A	B	C	D	E	F	G

LostArt Photos

Stock Numl	Item	Quantity
1218A	Flash bracket	15
2339C	Camera mount	23
3487V	Battery pack	19
9095P	Sync cord	17
3385T	Diffusers	12
7673K	Bouncers	10
2398M	Extenders	16
0947T	Lens kit	19
3811	Compressed air	27

The number in this cell is formatted as text or preceded by an apostrophe.

Text display cut off

Numbers and text together treated as text

Text spills over if next cell is empty

Numbers right-aligned

Text left-aligned

FIGURE EX 1–11   Data types

Text entries are often used as labels or headings that identify the numeric data you enter in a worksheet. If you enter text in a cell that is longer than the cell can display, it may spill over into empty cells to the right. The entire entry is still stored in the one cell, even though some of it is visible in adjacent cells. If the cell to the right already contains data, the text displayed in the cell in which it was entered is truncated, or cut off. The entire entry is still stored in the cell even though you cannot see all of it.

Step-by-Step EX 1.5

The Test Grades *XXX* workbook from Step-by-Step EX 1.4 should be open in the Excel program window.

1. Click cell **F13** to make it the active cell, and then type **87**. Notice that the number is displayed in the cell and in the formula bar, and the *Ready* message on the left of the status bar changes to *Enter*, as shown in **Figure EX 1–12**.

FIGURE EX 1–12
Entering data

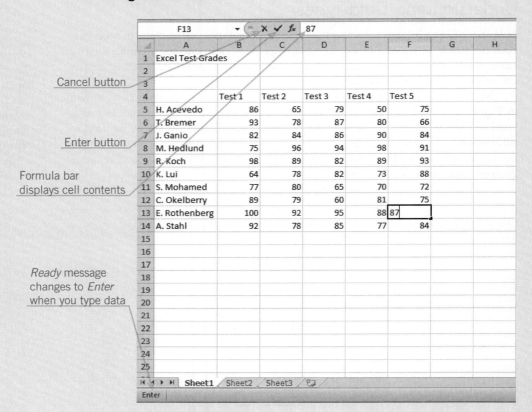

2. Press **Esc** to cancel the entry.

3. In cell F13, type **89** and then press **Enter** to enter the number. Notice the number is right-aligned in the cell.

4. Press **Ctrl+Home** and then press the **down arrow** to navigate to cell A2. Type **Winter Term,** and press the **right arrow** key to enter the text and move the active cell to the right. Notice the text is left-aligned in the cell.

5. Click cell **A4**, and then type **Name**.

6. Click the **Cancel** button ☒ on the formula bar to cancel the entry.

7. In cell A4, type **Student** and then click the **Enter** button ☑ on the formula bar. Your screen should look similar to **Figure EX 1–13**.

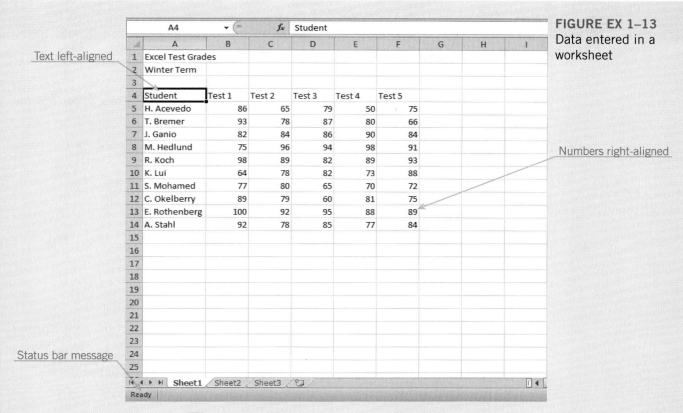

FIGURE EX 1–13
Data entered in a worksheet

Text left-aligned

Numbers right-aligned

Status bar message

	A	B	C	D	E	F	G	H	I
1	Excel Test Grades								
2	Winter Term								
3									
4	Student	Test 1	Test 2	Test 3	Test 4	Test 5			
5	H. Acevedo	86	65	79	50	75			
6	T. Bremer	93	78	87	80	66			
7	J. Ganio	82	84	86	90	84			
8	M. Hedlund	75	96	94	98	91			
9	R. Koch	98	89	82	89	93			
10	K. Lui	64	78	82	73	88			
11	S. Mohamed	77	80	65	70	72			
12	C. Okelberry	89	79	60	81	75			
13	E. Rothenberg	100	92	95	88	89			
14	A. Stahl	92	78	85	77	84			

A4 — Student

Sheet1 / Sheet2 / Sheet3

Ready

8. Click the **Save** button 💾 on the Quick Access Toolbar to save the changes to the workbook.

9. Leave the workbook open for use in the next Step-by-Step.

Editing Cell Contents

When you need to make changes to the data in your worksheet, you can overwrite the existing contents using the same methods you use to enter data in a blank cell. When you select a cell, type new data, and press Enter, the new data replaces the original cell contents.

You can also edit data directly in the cell by double-clicking the cell or by selecting the cell and pressing F2. Or, you can select the cell and click in the formula bar. In the cell or the formula bar, you can click and drag to select the data or position the insertion point using arrow keys. Then you can use the Backspace or Delete keys to remove data or type new data.

If you want to remove all the data from a cell, you can clear it by right-clicking a cell and clicking Clear Contents or by using the Clear button located in the Editing group on the Home tab. When you click the Clear button, a menu is displayed with options to clear the cell's formats, the cell's contents, the cell's comments, or the cell's hyperlinks. You can also choose to clear the cell of all formatting, contents, comments, and links at once.

Step-by-Step EX 1.6

The Test Grades *XXX* workbook from Step-by-Step EX 1.5 should be open in the Excel program window.

1. Click cell **E5** to select it, type **65**, and then press **Enter** to replace the cell contents.

2. Double-click cell **A14** to activate it, and then double-click the name **Stahl** to select it, as shown in **Figure EX 1–14**.

FIGURE EX 1–14
Editing contents in a cell

Select cell contents to be edited

11	S. Mohamed	77	80	65	70	72
12	C. Okelberry	89	79	60	81	75
13	E. Rothenberg	100	92	95	88	89
14	A. Stahl		92	78	85	77	84
15						
16						
17						

3. Type **Teal** to edit the cell contents, and then press **Enter**.

4. Click cell **A4** to select it, and then click at the end of the word *Student* in the formula bar to position the insertion point.

5. Press the **spacebar** to insert a space, and then type **Name** in the formula bar after the word *Student*, as shown in **Figure EX 1–15**.

FIGURE EX 1–15
Editing contents in the formula bar

Click to enter changes

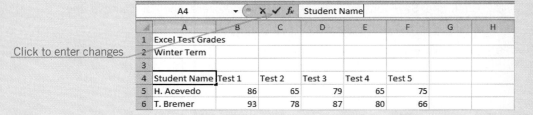

6. Click the **Enter** button on the formula bar to enter the changes in the cell.

7. Select the range **A5:F5**.

8. On the Home tab on the Ribbon, in the Editing group, click the **Clear** button, and then click **Clear All** on the menu to clear the contents and formatting from the cells in that range.

9. Save the workbook and leave it open for use in the next Step-by-Step.

Using Undo and Redo

You will often find it necessary to reverse, or undo, your most recent action. The Undo button on the Quick Access Toolbar, shown in **Figure EX 1–16**, undoes the last action; clicking the Undo button a second time undoes the prior action, and so on. If you click the Undo button arrow, you see a list of actions you can undo. Not all actions can be undone. The Undo ScreenTip changes to reflect the last action that can be undone. For example, if you just entered the value of 65 in cell E5, the screen tip would read *Undo Typing '65' in E5*, because this was the last action you performed, and you can undo it with one click of the Undo button. Some actions cannot be undone; if you cannot undo an action, such as saving a file, then the button is dimmed and the ScreenTip reads *Can't Undo*.

Undo button

Redo button

FIGURE EX 1–16   Undo and Redo buttons on the Quick Access Toolbar

If you perform and undo an action but then decide against the undo, you can use the Redo button on the Quick Access Toolbar to reverse an Undo action. The Redo button arrow displays a list of actions you can redo. When you cannot redo an action, the button is dimmed, and the ScreenTip reads *Can't Redo*.

Step-by-Step EX 1.7

The Test Grades *XXX* workbook from Step-by-Step EX 1.6 should be open in the Excel program window.

1. Click cell **G4**, type **Test 6**, and then press **Enter** twice.

2. In cell G6, type **76**, and then press **Enter**.

3. Click the **Undo** button arrow ![undo arrow] on the Quick Access Toolbar. Click the second item from the top of the menu, **Typing 'Test 6' in G4**, as shown in **Figure EX 1–17**. The last two actions are undone in the worksheet.

Click to display Undo menu
(Your menu might differ)

Click to undo two actions

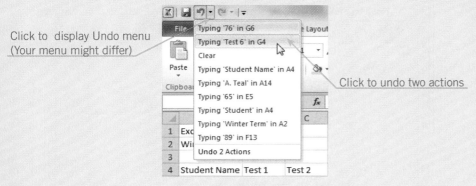

FIGURE EX 1–17
Undo button menu

4. In cell G4, type **Quiz 1**, and then press **Tab**.

5. Click the **Undo** button ![undo] on the Quick Access Toolbar to undo the action.

6. Click the **Redo** button ![redo] on the Quick Access Toolbar to redo the action.

7. Save the workbook and leave it open for use in the next Step-by-Step.

Managing Worksheets

You can customize a workbook by renaming, inserting, or deleting the worksheets as needed. You can move from worksheet to worksheet by clicking a sheet tab to make a different worksheet active.

EXTRA FOR EXPERTS

Another way to help identify a worksheet is to change the tab color by right-clicking a sheet tab, pointing to Tab Color on the shortcut menu, and then clicking a color in the palette.

Renaming a Worksheet

By default, the worksheets contained in a new workbook are labeled Sheet1, Sheet2, and Sheet3. You can rename them with descriptive names to better identify the data they contain. When you double-click the sheet tab, the sheet name is selected and you can type a new name, as shown in **Figure EX 1–18**. You can also right-click a sheet tab and then click Rename on the shortcut menu.

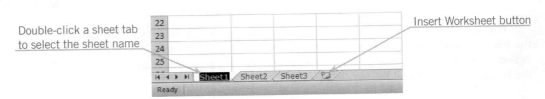

FIGURE EX 1–18   Rename a worksheet

Inserting a Worksheet

When you want to add another worksheet to your workbook, you can do so quickly by clicking the Insert Worksheet button to the right of the sheet tabs. You can also insert a worksheet by clicking the Insert Cells button arrow in the Cells group on the Home tab, and then clicking Insert Sheet or by right-clicking a sheet tab and then clicking Insert on the shortcut menu to open the Insert dialog box, shown in **Figure EX 1–19**.

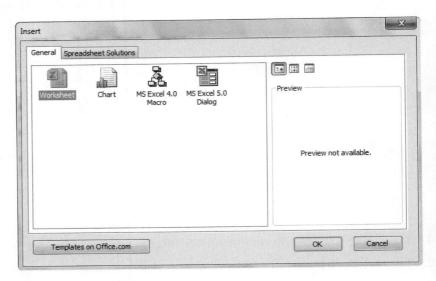

FIGURE EX 1–19   Insert dialog box

Deleting a Worksheet

If you don't need a worksheet, you can delete it from the workbook by right-clicking the sheet tab to open the shortcut menu and then clicking Delete; or, on the Home tab on the Ribbon, in the Cells group, click the Delete Cells button arrow and then click Delete Sheet.

Moving or Copying Worksheets within a Workbook

If you need to order worksheets in a more logical way within a workbook, it is easy to rearrange them by clicking a sheet tab and dragging it to a new position. A page icon is displayed beneath the mouse pointer, and a black arrow helps you choose the position as you drag. You can copy a worksheet by pressing and holding Ctrl while you drag. The page icon displays a plus sign when you are copying a worksheet.

You can also open the Move or Copy dialog box, shown in **Figure EX 1–20**, by right-clicking a sheet tab and clicking Move or Copy on the shortcut menu. You can select where to position the worksheet in the Before sheet list box and select the Create a copy check box if you want to copy the worksheet.

> **⊣— WARNING**
>
> If there is any data in the worksheet you are deleting, a message box opens asking you to confirm that you want to delete the sheet. Deleting a sheet permanently deletes the data it contains. You cannot undo this command, so be sure you want to take this action.

> **⊞ EXTRA FOR EXPERTS**
>
> You can move or copy worksheets to another workbook by right-clicking the sheet tab and clicking Move or Copy to open the Move or Copy dialog box, and then selecting a different workbook from the To book list box.

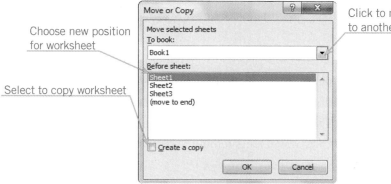

Choose new position for worksheet

Select to copy worksheet

Click to move or copy to another workbook

FIGURE EX 1–20   Move or Copy dialog box

Step-by-Step EX 1.8

The Test Grades *XXX* workbook from Step-by-Step EX 1.7 should be open in the Excel program window.

1. Right-click the **Sheet1** sheet tab, and click **Rename** on the shortcut menu to select the name.

2. Type **Winter** and press **Enter** to rename the worksheet.

3. Double-click the **Sheet2** sheet tab to select the name.

4. Type **Fall** and press **Enter** to rename the worksheet.

5. Click the **Fall** sheet tab and drag it to the left. When the black arrow is positioned before the *Winter* sheet tab, as shown in **Figure EX 1–21**, release the mouse button to move the worksheet.

FIGURE EX 1–21
Move a worksheet

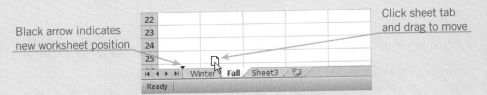

6. Click the **Insert Worksheet** button 🗓 to the right of the Sheet3 sheet tab to insert a new worksheet named *Sheet1*.

7. Right-click the **Sheet1** sheet tab, and click **Insert** on the shortcut menu to open the Insert dialog box.

8. Click the **OK** button to insert a new worksheet named *Sheet2*.

9. On the Home tab on the Ribbon, in the Cells group, click the **Insert Cells** button arrow, and then click **Insert Sheet** to insert a new worksheet named *Sheet4*.

10. Click the **Sheet3** sheet tab, press and hold **Shift**, and then click the **Sheet1** tab to select four sheet tabs—*Sheet3*, *Sheet4*, *Sheet2*, and *Sheet1*.

11. On the Home tab, in the Cells group, click the **Delete Cells** button arrow, and then click **Delete Sheet** to delete all four selected sheet tabs so only the *Fall* and *Winter* worksheets remain in the workbook.

12. Save the workbook and leave it open for use in the next Step-by-Step.

Changing Workbook Views

You might find it useful to preview how your worksheet would look as a printout, see where the pages would break when the worksheet is printed, create a custom view, or view more data on the screen. Excel provides five different views using the buttons in the Workbook Views group on the View tab on the Ribbon, as shown in **Figure EX 1–22**. You can also switch easily between the first three of these views by using the View buttons located on the right side of the status bar.

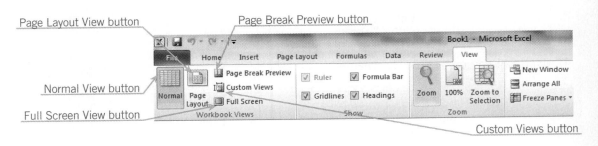

FIGURE EX 1–22   Workbook views

The five workbook view buttons are:

- Normal View, which displays the view most commonly used.
- Page Layout View, which displays the worksheet as it will print so you can make any necessary changes.
- Page Break Preview, which you can use to view and adjust page breaks before printing a worksheet.
- Custom Views, which you can use to create, apply, or delete a view you have created with specific display or print settings.
- Full Screen View, which maximizes the space available for viewing data on the screen by hiding the Ribbon, the formula bar, and the status bar.

Freezing and Unfreezing Panes

The Freeze Panes button, located on the View tab in the Window group, as shown in **Figure EX 1–23**, is useful when you want to keep some parts of a large worksheet visible while you scroll to another. When you *freeze panes*, you lock specified rows or columns into place.

▶ **VOCABULARY**
freeze panes

Click Freeze Panes button to open menu

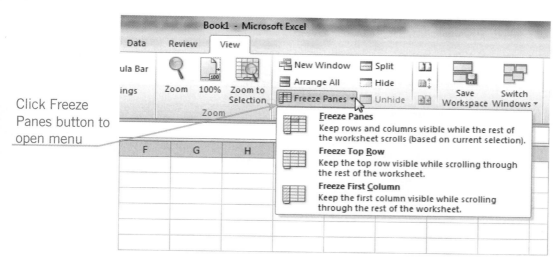

FIGURE EX 1–23   Freeze Panes menu on the View tab

You can use the Freeze Panes menu to freeze the top row, the first column, or an area that you select. You select an area to freeze in one of the following ways:

- To freeze a row or rows, select the row below the row(s) you want to freeze.
- To freeze a column or columns, select the column to the right of the column(s) you want to freeze.
- To freeze both, select the cell below and to the right of the row(s) and column(s) you want to freeze.

A solid line on the worksheet indicates that the area above and/or to the left is frozen. When you want to unfreeze panes, click the Freeze Panes button on the View tab in the Window group, and then click Unfreeze Panes.

EXTRA FOR EXPERTS

The buttons on the View tab in the Window group offer more ways to change how worksheets and workbooks are displayed on the screen. For example, you can split a worksheet into multiple panes, open a new window, tile all open program windows, or hide the current window.

Step-by-Step EX 1.9

The Test Grades *XXX* workbook from Step-by-Step EX 1.8 should be open in the Excel program window.

1. Click the **View** tab on the Ribbon. In the Workbook Views group, notice that the Normal View button is selected, as this is the default view.

2. On the View tab, in the Workbook Views group, click the **Page Layout View** button to display the worksheet as it would appear when printed.

3. On the View tab, in the Workbook Views group, click the **Page Break Preview** button to preview where pages will break when the worksheet is printed, as shown in **Figure EX 1–24**. If a Welcome to Page Break Preview dialog box opens, click the **OK** button to close it.

FIGURE EX 1–24
Page Break Preview

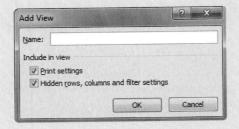

4. On the View tab, in the Workbook Views group, click the **Custom Views** button to open the Custom Views dialog box.

5. In the Custom Views dialog box, click the **Add** button to open the Add View dialog box, as shown in **Figure EX 1–25**.

FIGURE EX 1–25
Add View dialog box

6. Click the **Cancel** button to close the Add View dialog box without creating a custom view.

7. On the View tab, in the Workbook Views group, click the **Full Screen View** button to display the worksheet in full screen mode.

8. Press **Esc** to return to the previous view.

9. On the View tab, in the Workbook Views group, click the **Normal View** button to display the worksheet in Normal view.

10. Click cell **B5** to select the cell below and to the right of where you want to freeze panes.

11. On the View tab, in the Window group, click the **Freeze Panes** button, and then click **Freeze Panes** to freeze the panes, as indicated by the solid line (see **Figure EX 1–26**).

Select cell below and to the right of where you want to freeze panes

	A	B	C	D	E	F	G	H	I
1	Excel Test Grades								
2	Winter Term								
3									
4	Student Name	Test 1	Test 2	Test 3	Test 4	Test 5	Quiz 1		
5									
6	T. Bremer	93	78	87	80	66			
7	J. Ganjo	82	84	86	90	84			
8	M. Hedlund	75	96	94	98	91			
9	R. Koch	98	89	82	89	93			
10	K. Lui	64	78	82	73	88			
11	S. Mohamed	77	80	65	70	72			
12	C. Okelberry	89	79	60	81	75			
13	E. Rothenberg	100	92	95	88	89			
14	A. Teal	92	78	85	77	84			
15									
16									
17									
18									

FIGURE EX 1–26
Freeze panes

Solid lines indicate frozen panes

12. Scroll down and to the right to see that the panes are frozen.

13. Save the workbook and leave it open for use in the next Step-by-Step.

Printing Workbooks

Often you will want to print the worksheets from a workbook that you create to distribute or keep. You can add headers and footers so you can include useful information on a printed worksheet, such as the filename or date. If you only want to print part of a worksheet, you can set the print area. You can preview a worksheet and change formatting and printing options in Backstage view before you click the Print button.

Adding Headers and Footers

A **header** is text that appears in the top margin of a worksheet when printed, and a **footer** refers to text that appears in the bottom margin of a worksheet when printed. You can use headers and footers to include useful information that you would not include in the worksheet grid, such as page numbers, titles, the date, or a logo. To create a header or footer, you click the Header & Footer button, located in the Text group on the Insert tab on the Ribbon. The Header & Footer Tools contextual tab opens on the Ribbon, and header text boxes appear at the top of the worksheet, and footer text boxes appear at the bottom of the worksheet.

There are three header and footer text boxes—left, center, and right. You can either type the text you want to appear in each text box, or you can click an element on the Header & Footer Elements group of the Header and Footer Tools Design contextual tab on the Ribbon, shown in **Figure EX 1–27**. For example, if you wanted to include the current date in the right text box of a worksheet's header, you would click the right header text box, and then click the Current Date button in the Header & Footer Elements group. The code *&[Date]* appears in the right text box, and when you click outside the right header text box, the actual date is displayed in the header.

When you work with headers and footers, you are in Page Layout view. To close the Header & Footer Tools contextual tab, simply click somewhere on the worksheet. If you want to return to Normal view, you can then click the Normal View button in the Workbook Views group on the View tab.

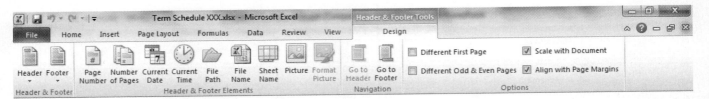

FIGURE EX 1–27   Header & Footer Tools Design tab

Setting the Print Area

Unless you specify otherwise, Excel prints all the data on the active worksheet. If you only want to print part of the worksheet, you can set the print area by selecting the range(s) you want to include and then clicking the Print Area button in the Page Setup group of the Page Layout tab. The menu that opens contains options for setting the print area and clearing the print area. The defined print area will be saved with the worksheet, so you need to clear it if you want to print the entire worksheet or workbook again.

Step-by-Step EX 1.10

The Test Grades *XXX* workbook from Step-by-Step EX 1.9 should be open in the Excel program window.

1. Click the **Insert** tab on the Ribbon, and then, in the Text group, click the **Header & Footer** button. When a message is displayed, click the **OK** button to unfreeze panes.

2. On the Header & Footer Tools Design tab, in the Header & Footer Elements group, click the **Current Date** button to add a code for the current date to the center header text box, as shown in **Figure EX 1–28**.

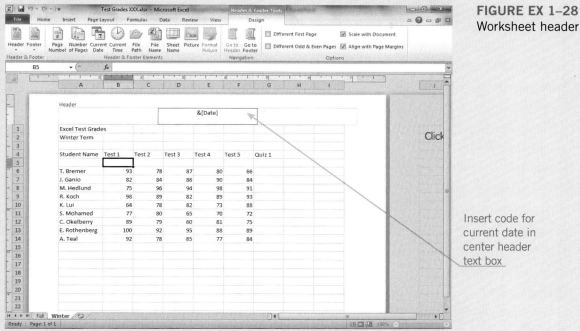

FIGURE EX 1–28
Worksheet header

Insert code for current date in center header text box

3. Click the right text box of the header. Notice that the code you inserted in the center text box now displays the current date.

4. On the Header & Footer Tools Design tab, in the Navigation group, click the **Go to Footer** button to switch to the footer.

5. Click the **left text box** of the footer and type your first and last name, as shown in **Figure EX 1–29**.

FIGURE EX 1–29
Worksheet footer

FIGURE EX 1–29
Worksheet footer

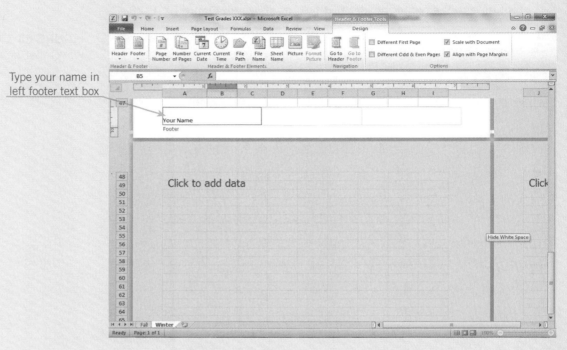

Type your name in left footer text box

6. Click any blank cell in the worksheet to close the Header & Footer Tools Design tab.

7. Click the **View** tab on the Ribbon, and in the Workbook Views group, click the **Normal View** button.

8. Scroll up, if necessary, and select the range **A4:F14** in preparation for setting the print area.

9. Click the **Page Layout** tab, and in the Page Setup group, click the **Print Area** button. Click **Set Print Area** to define the range you want to print. The print area is outlined with a dotted border, as shown in **Figure EX 1–30**.

FIGURE EX 1–30
Print area

	A	B	C	D	E	F	G	H	I
1	Excel Test Grades								
2	Winter Term								
3									
4	Student Name	Test 1	Test 2	Test 3	Test 4	Test 5	Quiz 1		
5									
6	T. Bremer	93	78	87	80	66			
7	J. Ganio	82	84	86	90	84			
8	M. Hedlund	75	96	94	98	91			
9	R. Koch	98	89	82	89	93			
10	K. Lui	64	78	82	73	88			
11	S. Mohamed	77	80	65	70	72			
12	C. Okelberry	89	79	60	81	75			
13	E. Rothenberg	100	92	95	88	89			
14	A. Teal	92	78	85	77	84			
15									
16									
17									
18									

Print area indicated by dotted border around range

10. On the Page Layout tab on the Ribbon, in the Page Setup group, click the **Print Area** button and then click **Clear Print Area** to clear the print area.

11. Save the workbook and leave it open for use in the next Step-by-Step.

Previewing and Printing a Worksheet

When you choose Print on the File tab, Backstage view displays the Print button and default print settings in the center pane of the window and a preview of the worksheet in the right pane, as shown in **Figure EX 1–31**. To change a print setting in the center pane, click the setting that you want to change, and then select a new option from the gallery that opens.

You can click the Show Margins button in the lower-right corner of the right pane to show or hide the margins on the worksheet preview pane. You can click the Zoom to Page button in the lower-right corner of the right pane to zoom in on the worksheet and then click it again to return the preview to the original magnification.

EXTRA FOR EXPERTS

If you do not want the worksheet gridlines to print, or be displayed in the workbook window, you can click the Gridlines check box on the View tab in the Show group to remove the check mark.

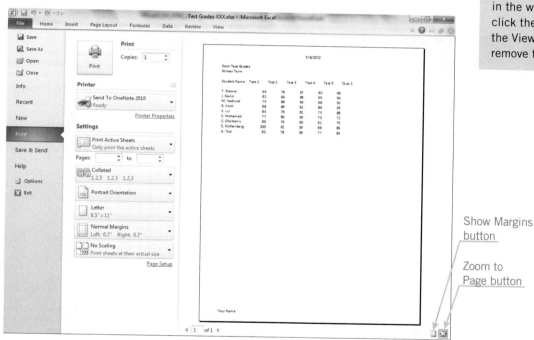

FIGURE EX 1–31 Previewing and printing options in Backstage view

The following printing and previewing options are available in Backstage view:

- The Print button prints the worksheet with current settings.
- Use the up and down arrows in the Copies box to indicate the quantity of copies to print.
- The Printer area displays the default printer. Click the default printer to select a different printer from the gallery of available printers. The Printer Properties link lets you choose paper type, print quality, color, or to specify other options for your printer.

- The Settings area lists the current print settings. Clicking the settings opens galleries of options that let you indicate whether to print:
    - The active sheets, the entire workbook, or the current selection.
    - One sided, on both sides, or manually on both sides.
    - Multiple copies of a workbook or worksheet with pages in order, called *collated*, or uncollated.
    - Portrait or landscape orientation.
    - Letter 8.5"×11" size or another paper size.
    - Current margin settings or other margin settings.
    - Sheets at their actual size, or shrunk to fit on one page, one page wide, or one page high.
- The Page Setup link opens the Page Setup dialog box where you can make changes to the orientation, page or paper size, margins, header and footer, and gridlines.
- The preview pane shows a preview of the worksheet and allows you to check margins and zoom in and out to check for errors. As you make changes to the print settings, the preview is updated to reflect the changes so that you can be sure you are satisfied with the settings before printing.

▶ **VOCABULARY**
collated

▦ **EXTRA FOR EXPERTS**

You can add the Quick Print command to the Quick Access Toolbar to print to the default printer with the default settings without opening Backstage view.

Step-by-Step EX 1.11

The Test Grades *XXX* workbook from Step-by-Step EX 1.10 should be open in the Excel program window.

1. Click the **File** tab to display Backstage view, and then click **Print**.
2. Click the **Show Margins** button ▦ in the lower-right corner of the right pane to preview the worksheet margins.
3. Click the **Show Margins** button again to hide the margins on the worksheet preview.
4. Click the **Zoom to Page** button ▦ in the lower-right corner of the right pane to zoom in on the worksheet.
5. Click the **Zoom to Page** button again to return to the original magnification.
6. At the bottom of the center pane, click the **Page Setup** link to open the Page Setup dialog box.
7. Click the **Cancel** button to close the Page Setup dialog box without making changes.
8. Click each of the buttons in the center pane under Settings to see the printing options available.
9. Click the **Print** button to print the worksheet. If you have been instructed not to print, click the File tab to close Backstage view.
10. Leave the workbook open for use in the next Step-by-Step.

Closing a Workbook

When you are finished with a workbook, you can remove it from your screen using the Close command. To close a workbook without closing Excel, choose the Close command on the File tab. When you have only one workbook open, you can click the Close button on the title bar to close the document and exit the program at the same time. If you have more than one workbook open, you can close all workbooks and exit the program using the Exit command on the File tab. The software prompts you to save your work if you made any changes since you last saved.

Step-by-Step EX 1.12

The Test Grades *XXX* workbook from Step-by-Step EX 1.11 should be open in the Excel program window.

1. Click the **File** tab and then click **Close**. The workbook closes, and the Excel program window remains open.

2. Click the **Close** button [X] on the title bar to close Excel.

SUMMARY

In this lesson, you learned:

- How to open an existing workbook.

- Methods of navigating in a worksheet using the mouse, keyboard, and Go To command.

- How to save a workbook.

- The processes for selecting cells, entering data, and editing data.

- To use the Undo and Redo commands to undo or reverse previous actions.

- Ways to manage worksheets by renaming, inserting, deleting, moving, or copying worksheets.

- How to change worksheet views.

- How to add headers and footers.

- To preview and print a workbook using Backstage view.

- To close a workbook.

■ VOCABULARY REVIEW

Define the following terms:

active cell	freeze panes	sheet
cell	header	sheet tab
cell reference	Name box	spreadsheet software
collated	range	workbook
columns	rows	workbook window
footer	select	worksheet
formula bar		

■ REVIEW QUESTIONS

MULTIPLE CHOICE

Select the best response for the following statements.

1. The _____ below the Ribbon displays the cell reference of the active cell.

   A. formula bar   C. Name box

   B. Navigation Pane   D. Address bar

2. To move to the first cell of a row, press the _____ key(s).

   A. Page Up   C. Ctrl+Home

   B. Home   D. Ctrl+End

3. The Go To dialog box is opened by clicking the Go To command on the Find & Select menu in the Editing group on the _____ tab on the Ribbon.

   A. Home   C. Page Layout

   B. Insert   D. View

4. To select nonadjacent cells or ranges, press and hold the _____ key as you click or drag to select additional cells or ranges.

   A. Shift   C. Alt

   B. Ctrl   D. Enter

5. By default, numbers are _____ in a cell.

   A. left-aligned   C. centered

   B. right-aligned   D. justified

6. If you want to remove all the data from a cell, you can clear it using the _____ button in the Editing group on the Home tab.

   A. Delete   C. Replace

   B. Remove   D. Clear

7. To add another worksheet to your workbook, you can click the Insert Worksheet button to the right of the _____.

   A. File tab   C. Quick Access Toolbar

   B. sheet tabs   D. View buttons

8. If you don't need a worksheet, you can delete it by _____ on the sheet tab to open the shortcut menu and then clicking Delete.

   A. clicking   C. right-clicking

   B. double-clicking   D. none of the above

9. Which workbook view is the most commonly used?

   A. Normal   C. Page Break Preview

   B. Page Layout   D. Full Screen

10. When you are finished with a file, you can remove it from your screen using the _____ command on the File tab.

   A. Remove   C. Exit

   B. Clear   D. Close

FILL IN THE BLANK

Complete the following sentences by writing the correct word or words in the blanks provided.

1. A(n) _____ contains a collection of related worksheets.

2. The rectangle where a column and row intersect is called a(n) _____.

3. The _____ command lets you make a copy of the file with a new name, location, or file type.

4. Excel's _____ feature automatically saves your workbook at regular intervals so that you can recover at least some of your work in case of a power outage or other unexpected shutdown.

5. The _____ tab on the Ribbon has many options to help you create a header or footer.

6. Use the _____ button on the Quick Access Toolbar when you want to reverse an Undo action.

7. You can copy a worksheet by holding down the _____ key while you drag the sheet tab.

8. The _____ workbook view displays the worksheet as it will be printed so you can make any necessary changes.

9. The _____ button in the Windows group on the View tab is useful for large worksheets when you want to keep some parts of the worksheet visible while you scroll to another part of the worksheet.

10. When you click _____ on the File tab, Backstage view displays the default print settings in the center pane of the window and a preview of the worksheet in the right pane.

■ PROJECTS

PROJECT EX 1–1

1. Open the file **Project EX 1-1** from the folder containing the data files for this lesson.

2. Use the Save As command on the File tab to save the workbook with the filename **LostArt XXX** (replace *XXX* with your initials).

3. Rename the Sheet1 tab **Items to Reorder**.

4. Create a header with the filename in the center section.

5. Switch to Normal view and freeze column A.

6. Scroll to the right to see that the first column is frozen.

7. In cell A15, enter **9085D**.

8. In cell B15, enter **Camera bag**.

9. In cell C15, enter **4**.

10. Edit cell A3 to **Stock #**.

11. Edit cell B12 so the letter **A** in *Air* is lowercase.

12. Undo the change you made in Step 11, then redo the action.

13. Save the workbook, and leave it open for use in Project EX 1–2.

PROJECT EX 1–2

The LostArt *XXX* workbook from Project EX 1–1 should be open in the Excel program window.

1. Save the workbook as **LostArt2 XXX** (replace *XXX* with your initials).

2. Navigate to the last cell in the worksheet containing data or formatting and change the contents of that cell to 5.

3. Create a copy of the *Items to Reorder* worksheet.

4. Rename the new worksheet **Items on Backorder**.

5. Select the range C4:C15 on the Items on Backorder worksheet.

6. Clear all contents and formatting from the selected range.

7. Edit cell C3 to display **Backordered**.

8. Edit cells C7 and C13 to display an **X**.

9. Unfreeze column A, and freeze the rows above row 4.

10. Scroll down to see that the pane is frozen.

11. Move the *Items to Reorder* worksheet so it is the first worksheet in the workbook.

12. Select the Sheet2 and Sheet3 sheet tabs and delete the worksheets.

13. Save and close the workbook.

PROJECT EX 1–3

1. Open the file **Project EX 1-3** from the folder containing the data files for this lesson.

2. Save the workbook with the filename **Term Schedule** *XXX* (replace *XXX* with your initials).

3. In cell A1, replace *School Name* with the name of your school.

4. In cell A2, replace *Term* with **Spring**.

5. View the worksheet in Full Screen view.

6. Return to Normal view.

7. Create a header with your name in the center section.

8. Create a footer with the current date in the center section.

9. Return to Normal view.

10. Freeze the rows above row 5 and to the left of column B. Scroll down and to the right to see that the panes are frozen.

11. Select the range B4:F10 and set the print area.

12. Preview the worksheet in Backstage view.

13. Zoom in on the worksheet preview.

14. Save, print, and close the workbook.

ON YOUR OWN

Open the **Term Schedule** *XXX* workbook, and customize the header and footer by adding other elements from the Header & Footer Elements group on the Header & Footer Tools Design tab on the Ribbon. Experiment with placing elements in the left and right sections of the header or footer. Save and close the workbook.

PROJECT EX 1–4

1. Open the file **Project EX 1-4** from the folder containing the data files for this lesson.

2. Save the workbook with the filename **Chess Club** *XXX* (replace *XXX* with your initials).

3. In cell A4, type your first and last name.

4. In cell B4, type today's date.

5. In cells C4:H4, enter your contact information in the appropriate columns. (*Note*: Remember that for postal codes, you can type an apostrophe before the number to signal that it is not to be used in calculations.)

6. Use the skills you have learned in this lesson to enter data for at least six more members in the appropriate cells. Use your classmates' names and contact information, or create some fictitious data.

7. Use the Go To command to move to cell I4 and enter **Elected president for next year**.

8. Rename the worksheet **Member Info**.

9. Insert a new worksheet and name it **Tournament Dates**.

10. Switch to the Member Info sheet, and use Page Break Preview to see where the pages will break when the worksheet is printed.

11. Switch to Page Layout view.

12. Return to Normal view.

13. Select the range A3:C10, and set the print area.

14. Save, print, and close the workbook.

ON YOUR OWN

Open the **Chess Club** *XXX* workbook, and then create a custom view for the worksheet that includes the print settings, and name the custom view **Custom** *XXX* (replace *XXX* with your initials). Save and close the workbook.

WEB PROJECT

1. Open the file **Project EX 1-5** from the folder containing the data files for this lesson.

2. Save the workbook with the filename **Hotels *XXX*** (replace *XXX* with your initials).

3. Rename the first worksheet **Dallas**.

4. Assume you are going on a trip to Dallas this coming weekend. Search the Web for information on hotels in that city. In the range B4:C8, list the names of five hotels where you would like to stay and the price per night.

5. Delete Sheet2 and Sheet3.

6. Save and close the workbook.

ON YOUR OWN

Open the **Hotels *XXX*** workbook, then copy the *Dallas* worksheet, and rename it **Chicago** (or another city where you would like to stay). Search for five hotels and the price per night in that city, and record them in the new worksheet, replacing and editing data as needed. Save and close the workbook.

TEAMWORK PROJECT

Open a workbook that you used in this lesson. Have a partner call out cell references to move to or ranges to select (for example, "move to cell Z155" or "select range D10:H25"). See how quickly you can navigate to the cells or select ranges. Use different methods and see which one you prefer. For an extra challenge, try navigating to cells that meet certain conditions or contain specific data using the Go To Special dialog box (for example, blank cells).

■ CRITICAL THINKING

ACTIVITY EX 1–1

Open the file **Activity EX 1–1** from the folder containing the data files for this lesson, and then perform the following tasks, using Excel Help if necessary:

■ Save the workbook as an Excel 97-2003 Workbook with the filename **All About Me *XXX***.

■ Add data about yourself in cells C3:C8.

■ Continue the list, adding at least five more facts about yourself.

■ Create a header and insert a picture of yourself (or another picture that you like) and resize as needed.

■ Hide the gridlines on the worksheet.

■ Rename Sheet1 with your name, and change the color of the sheet tab.

■ Save, print, and close the workbook.

ACTIVITY EX 1–2

Search for the video in Excel Help titled *Backstage view in Excel 2010* and watch it. What options are available on the Info tab? Open a workbook you used in this lesson and check to see what properties are listed for that file. Click each of the other tabs in Backstage view to see the options available. Close the workbook without saving any changes.

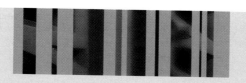

LESSON 2

Formatting and Editing Worksheets

■ OBJECTIVES

Upon completion of this lesson, you should be able to:

- Create a new workbook.
- Format cells.
- Apply themes and styles and use conditional formatting.
- Adjust column widths and row heights.
- Insert and delete rows and columns.
- Find and replace data.
- Copy and move worksheet data.
- Check spelling.

■ DATA FILES

To complete this lesson, you will need these data files:

Step EX 2-4.xlsx

Step EX 2-9.xlsx

Project EX 2-1.xlsx

Project EX 2-3.xlsx

Project EX 2-6.xlsx

■ VOCABULARY

cell style

Clipboard

conditional formatting

copy

cut

drag-and-drop method

fill

font

font styles

paste

point size

theme

Introduction

Now that you know the fundamentals of working with Excel, you will learn more about how to use Excel's editing and formatting features to enhance the appearance of a worksheet. In this lesson, you will learn how to create a new workbook, how to format a workbook, and how to organize data to get the information you need.

Creating a New Workbook

As you already learned, a new blank workbook is displayed in the program window when you open Excel. You can also create a new workbook at any time from Backstage view. Click the File tab to display Backstage view, and then click New. Click the Blank workbook icon in the center pane, as shown in **Figure EX 2–1**, and then click the Create button.

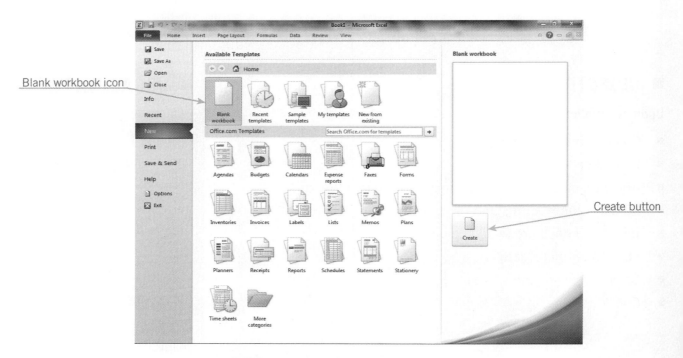

FIGURE EX 2–1   Creating a new workbook in Backstage view

 **EXTRA FOR EXPERTS**

When you do not want to create a workbook from scratch, you can choose one of the many templates available. Excel templates are pre-designed workbooks—such as billing statements, monthly budgets, or sales reports—that can save you time. You can access installed and online templates using the New command in Backstage view.

When creating a new workbook, spend some time planning it first. Think about what you want the worksheet to accomplish, what information needs to be included, and possible ways to organize the data. You can even sketch out a design with the basic format of the rows and columns. It will always be possible to make adjustments to the worksheet later, but it is helpful to have a well-designed beginning.

Step-by-Step EX 2.1

1. Start Excel.

2. Click the **File** tab on the Ribbon to open Backstage view, and then click **New**.

3. Select the **Blank workbook** icon in the center pane, if necessary, and then click the **Create** button in the right pane to open a new blank workbook.

4. Click cell **B2**, type **ZPM Courier Service**, and then press **Enter**.

5. Click cell **F1**, type **Weekly Time Sheet**, and then press **Enter**.

6. Save the workbook as **Time Sheet XXX** (replace *XXX* with your initials).

7. Continue creating the worksheet by entering the data for rows 4 through 17 of the worksheet, as shown in **Figure EX 2–2**.

	A	B	C	D	E	F	G	H
1						Weekly Time Sheet		
2		ZPM Courier Service						
3								
4		4001 East Millerton Road						
5		Suite 400						
6		Portland, OR 97214						
7								
8		Week ending:						
9								
10		Day	Client	Billable	Other	Total		
11		Monday						
12		Tuesday						
13		Wednesday						
14		Thursday						
15		Friday						
16		Saturday						
17		Sunday						

Enter data in these rows

FIGURE EX 2–2
Creating a worksheet

8. Save the workbook and leave it open for the next Step-by-Step.

Formatting Cells

There are numerous ways that you can format cells. You can format the contents of the cell by specifying a number format, setting the alignment of the text or numbers in the cell, and selecting a font and font style and color. You can also format the cell itself by choosing to show the borders of the cell and setting a border style, and you can add a background color or pattern, referred to as a *fill*. The most common cell formatting options are located on the Home tab on the Ribbon in the Font, Alignment, and Number groups. You can also click the dialog box launcher in any of

> **VOCABULARY**
> **fill**

these groups to open the Format Cells dialog box, shown in **Figure EX 2–3**, and then click the tabs in the dialog box to access additional cell-formatting options. Once you have applied a cell format to a cell, it is easy to copy the formatting to other cells using the Format Painter button, located in the Clipboard group on the Home tab.

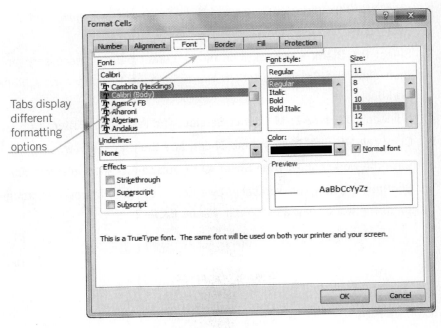

FIGURE EX 2–3   Format Cells dialog box

Setting Font Formats

A *font* is the design of a set of letters and numbers. Each font set has a name. The Font group on the Home tab on the Ribbon, shown in **Figure EX 2–4**, includes options for selecting fonts, font size, font style, underline, and font color. You can also click the dialog box launcher in the Font group to open the Font tab of the Format Cells dialog box to access additional font options such as special font effects.

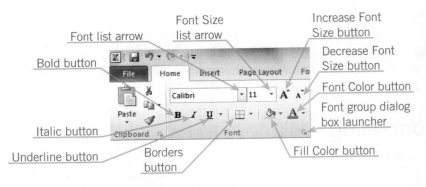

FIGURE EX 2–4   Font group on the Home tab

The default font used in all Excel workbooks is Calibri. You can choose a different font by selecting a cell, a range of cells, or a whole sheet, clicking the Font list arrow in the Font group on the Home tab, and then choosing one of the fonts listed. The Font list displays each font's design and is divided into two sections: Theme Fonts and All Fonts. You can also select a font from the Font list box on the Font tab of the Format Cells dialog box, and preview the selected font in the Preview box.

Font sizes are measured in points. *Point size* refers to a measurement for the height of characters. A point is equal to approximately 1/72 inch. A 10-point font is approximately 10/72 inch high. You can change the font size by selecting the cell or range of cells, clicking the Font Size list arrow in the Font group on the Home tab, and then selecting a size from the Font Size list. You can also select a new font size from the Size list box on the Font tab of the Format Cells dialog box.

You can use the Increase Font Size button to increase the font size or the Decrease Font Size button to decrease the font size. These buttons are located in the Font group on the Home tab. You can also select a specific font size from the Size list box on the Font tab of the Format Cells dialog box.

Font styles are variations in the shape or weight of a font's characters, such as **bold** and *italic*. You can change the font style by clicking the Bold and Italic buttons in the Font group on the Home tab, or by selecting a font style from the Font style list box on the Font tab of the Format Cells dialog box. The Underline button in the Font group on the Home tab has a menu with two options. More underline options are available on the Font tab of the Format Cells dialog box.

You can select the font color by clicking the Font Color button in the Font group on the Home tab on the Ribbon. If you click the Font Color button, the most recently used font color is applied to the selected cell. If you click the Font Color button arrow, a menu opens with theme colors and standard colors, as shown in **Figure EX 2–5**. Or, you can click More Colors on the menu to select a custom color. The Font tab of the Format Cells dialog box also includes more font color choices.

▶ **VOCABULARY**

point size

font styles

📟 **EXTRA FOR EXPERTS**

You can change the default Excel font and font size for new workbooks by opening the Excel Options dialog box from the File menu, and selecting a new default font from the Use this font list box on the General page of the dialog box.

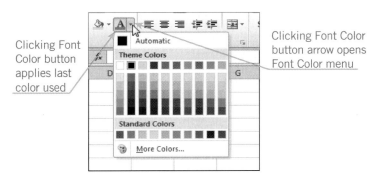

Clicking Font Color button applies last color used

Clicking Font Color button arrow opens Font Color menu

FIGURE EX 2–5   Font Color menu

Step-by-Step EX 2.2

The Time Sheet *XXX* workbook from Step-by-Step EX 2.1 should be open in the Excel program window.

1. Select cell **B2**. On the Home tab, in the Font group, click the **Font** list arrow to open the Font menu.

2. In the Theme Fonts section of the Font menu, click **Cambria**, as shown in **Figure EX 2–6**, to change the font to the theme font for headings.

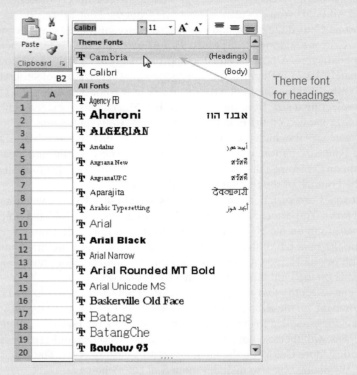

3. With cell B2 still selected, click the **Font Size** list arrow in the Font group to open the Font Size menu, and then click **20** to change the font size of the text. Notice that the row height automatically adjusts to accommodate the larger font size.

4. With cell B2 still selected, click the **Decrease Font Size** button A in the Font group to change the font size of the text to 18.

5. With cell B2 still selected, click the **Bold** button B in the Font group to bold the text.

6. With cell B2 still selected, click the **Underline** button arrow U in the Font group to open the Underline menu, and then click **Double Underline**.

7. With cell B2 still selected, click the **Font Color** button arrow A in the Font group to open the Font Color menu, and then click the **Red, Accent 2** theme color (first row, sixth from left).

8. Save the workbook and leave it open for use in the next Step-by-Step.

Using the Format Painter

Once you have applied formatting to cells, you can use the Format Painter button in the Clipboard group on the Home tab to add the same formatting to other cells. This is useful because you can copy multiple formatting characteristics at once, such as font, font size, effects, and color.

To copy formatting of a cell, you first select the cell that contains the formatting you want to apply to other cells, and then click the Format Painter button. Your mouse pointer changes to a plus sign with a paintbrush. Then, you select the cells to which you want to apply the formatting.

If you want to add the formatting to more than one cell, you can double-click the Format Painter button so that it stays active. When you finish painting formats, click the Format Painter button again or press Esc to turn off Format Painter.

Adding and Removing Cell Borders

Borders can be applied to any side of a cell using predefined styles or by creating custom borders. If you click the Borders button in the Font group on the Home tab, the most recently used border style is applied. You can apply a different predefined style by clicking the Borders button arrow and selecting an option on the menu. The Borders menu is divided into two sections: Borders, with preset border styles; and Draw Borders, with options for drawing your own border. Clicking More Borders opens the Border tab of the Format Cells dialog box, where you can create a custom border by choosing a line style and color.

Changing Fill Color

You can change a cell's background color using the Fill Color button in the Font group on the Home tab. If you click the Fill Color button, the most recently used color is applied. If you click the Fill Color button arrow, a menu of colors opens. You can choose theme colors, standard colors, no fill color, or click More Colors to select a custom color. The Fill tab of the Format Cells dialog box also includes options for filling a cell with patterns or gradients.

Step-by-Step EX 2.3

The Time Sheet *XXX* workbook from Step-by-Step EX 2.2 should be open in the Excel program window.

1. Select cell **B2**, if necessary. On the Home tab, in the Clipboard group, click the **Format Painter** button to activate it. Notice the rotating border around cell B2, indicating this cell's formatting is ready to be copied.

2. Click cell **F1** to apply the same formats as cell B2.

3. Select cells **B4:D6**. On the Home tab, in the Font group, click the **Borders** button arrow to open the Borders menu, as shown in **Figure EX 2–7**.

FIGURE EX 2–7
Borders menu

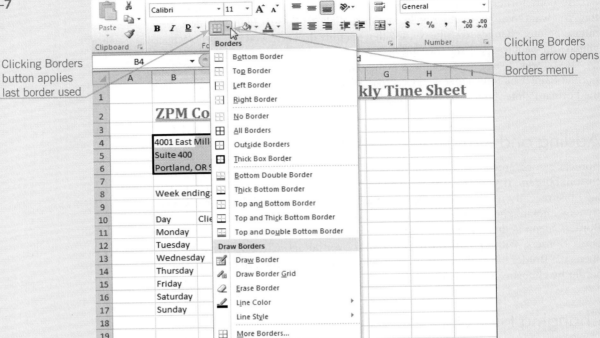

4. Click **Thick Box Border** to apply that border style to the selected range.

5. With cells B4:D6 still selected, click the **Fill Color** button arrow in the Font group on the Home tab to open the Fill Color menu.

6. Click the **Red, Accent 2, Lighter 80%** option, as shown in **Figure EX 2–8**. Click a blank area of the worksheet to view the newly applied cell formatting.

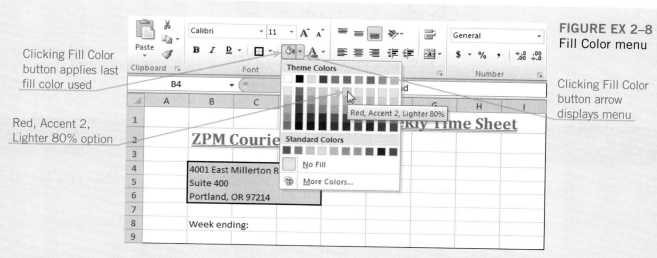

FIGURE EX 2–8
Fill Color menu

Clicking Fill Color button applies last fill color used

Red, Accent 2, Lighter 80% option

Clicking Fill Color button arrow displays menu

7. Save and close the workbook.

Changing Cell Alignment

Using the buttons in the Alignment group on the Home tab, shown in **Figure EX 2–9**, you can left-align, center, or right-align cell contents. You can also align the contents to the top, middle, or bottom of a cell. The Orientation button allows you to rotate text. Using the Decrease Indent and Increase Indent buttons, you can change the margins between the border and the cell contents.

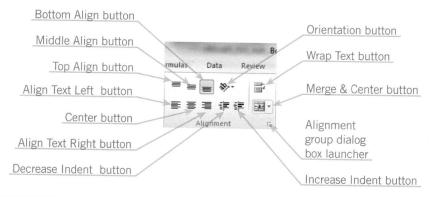

FIGURE EX 2–9   Alignment group on the Home tab

You can use the Wrap Text button to display text in a cell on multiple lines so it is all visible. To align text over several columns or rows, you can use the Merge & Center button to join selected cells together into one larger cell, which is useful for creating labels. Once cells are merged, the content from the upper-left cell in the range is preserved, and the upper-left cell becomes the cell reference for the merged cells. More options for positioning data within a cell are located on the Alignment tab of the Format Cells dialog box.

Clearing Cell Formats

Sometimes you might want to remove all the formatting from a cell or range of cells. On the Home tab, in the Editing group, you can click the Clear button and select Clear Formats to remove all of the formatting that has been applied to the cell or range that you have selected. The contents will not be affected.

Step-by-Step EX 2.4

1. Open **Step EX 2-4** from the folder containing the data files for this lesson.

2. Save the workbook as **Time Sheet2 XXX** (replace *XXX* with your initials).

3. Select cells **A2:I2**. On the Home tab, in the Alignment group, click the **Merge & Center** button arrow to open the Merge & Center menu, shown in **Figure EX 2–10**.

FIGURE EX 2–10
Merge & Center menu

4. Click **Merge & Center** to join the cells in the range together and center the contents. Notice that the row height reverts back to its original size.

5. Select cells **F4:G4**. On the Home tab, in the Alignment group, click the **Merge & Center** button to join the cells together and center the contents.

6. With cells **F4:G4** still selected, click the **Align Text Right** button 🔲 in the Alignment group on the Home tab to right-align the cell contents.

7. With cells **F4:G4** still selected, click the **Increase Indent** button 🔲 in the Alignment group on the Home tab to increase the space between the cell border and the cell contents.

8. With cells **F4:G4** still selected, click the **Format Painter** button in the Clipboard group of the Home tab to activate it, and then select the range **F5:G7** to copy the cell formats from F4:G4.

9. Select cells **D10:F10**. On the Home tab, in the Alignment group, click the **Wrap Text** button ▦ to make the text in each cell visible by displaying it over two lines.

10. Select cell **H10**. On the Home tab, in the Alignment group, click the **Middle Align** button ▤ to center the text between the top and bottom of the cell.

11. With cell **H10** still selected, click the **Center** button ▤ in the Alignment group to center the text in the cell.

12. Select cell **F1**. On the Home tab, in the Editing group, click the **Clear** button to open the Clear menu.

13. Click **Clear Formats** to clear all the formatting from the cell. Your workbook window should look similar to **Figure EX 2–11**.

	A	B	C	D	E	F	G	H	I	J
1						Weekly Time Sheet				
2				ZPM Courier Service						
3										
4		4001 East Millerton Road				Contractor:				
5		Suite 400				Client:				
6		Portland, OR 97214				Contractor phone:				
7						Contractor e-mail:				
8		Week ending:								
9										
10		Day		Client Code	Billable Hours	Other Hours		Total		
11		Monday								
12		Tuesday								
13		Wednesday								
14		Thursday								
15		Friday								
16		Saturday								
17		Sunday								
18				Total hours						
19										
20										
21				Contractor signature				Date		
22										
23				Client signature				Date		
24										

Weekly Time Sheet

FIGURE EX 2–11
Time Sheet2 *XXX* worksheet

14. Save the workbook and leave it open for use in the next Step-by-Step.

Applying Number Formats

When you enter a number in a cell, Excel automatically applies the General format, which basically displays numbers the way you type them. If you enter a number preceded by a dollar sign, Excel automatically formats the cell for currency. If you type a percentage sign following a number, Excel formats the cell for percentages. You can enter dates or times in a variety of formats that Excel will recognize, although they will be displayed in the default date or time format.

To change a number format for a selected cell, you can use the buttons found in the Number group on the Home tab, as shown in **Figure EX 2–12**.

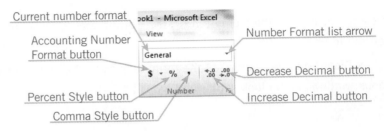

FIGURE EX 2–12   Number group on the Home tab

Clicking the Number Format list arrow in the Number group opens a menu of number format options from which you can choose. The Accounting Number Format button arrow provides currency options. You can also use the Percent Style, Comma Style, Increase Decimal, and Decrease Decimal buttons to quickly apply other common changes to the number format. You can also click the dialog box launcher in the Number group on the Home tab to open the Number tab of the Format Cells dialog box.

Step-by-Step EX 2.5

The Time Sheet2 *XXX* workbook from Step-by-Step EX 2.4 should be open in the Excel program window.

1. In cells **D11:F15**, enter the numbers shown in **Figure EX 2–13**. Notice that the Number Format list box in the Number group on the Home tab displays *General* for each of these numbers.

FIGURE EX 2–13
Entering numbers in
General format

	A	B	C	D	E	F	G
9							
10		Day		Client Code	Billable Hours	Other Hours	
11		Monday		1544	6	1	
12		Tuesday		2103	4	2	
13		Wednesday		1544	6	0	
14		Thursday		1544	3	2	
15		Friday		1170	7	0	
16		Saturday					
17		Sunday					

Numbers to enter

2. In cell **D19**, type **Hourly rate**.

3. In cell **F19**, type **75**.

4. Select cell **F19**, if necessary. On the Home tab, in the Number group, click the **Number Format** list arrow to open the Number Format menu, as shown in **Figure EX 2–14**.

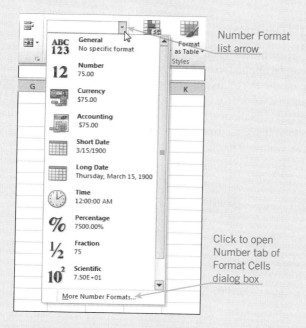

FIGURE EX 2–14
Number Format menu

5. On the Number Format menu, click **Currency** to change the number format of the cell.

6. With cell **F19** still selected, click the **Decrease Decimal** button in the Number group to show one fewer decimal place. Click the **Decrease Decimal** button again to remove the decimal place from the number.

7. In cell **I21**, type **July 22**, and then press **Enter**. Notice how Excel automatically changes the format to the default date format when you enter the contents.

8. Select cell **I21**, if necessary. On the Home tab, in the Number group, click the **Number Format** list arrow to display the Number Format menu, and click **Short Date** to format the cell with a short date format. Notice the column width automatically adjusts to accommodate the new format.

9. Save the workbook and leave it open for use in the next Step-by-Step.

Applying Themes and Styles

If you want to quickly change the look of individual cells or an entire workbook, you can use predefined formatting options that Excel provides, such as themes and styles. Using themes and styles allows you to apply multiple formats at one time and helps keep formatting in the workbook consistent. Excel provides a variety of built-in themes and styles from which to choose, or you can create your own custom ones. Some of the options are displayed in galleries, so you can use Live Preview to see what the formatting changes would look like before applying them to your workbook.

Applying Themes

▶ **VOCABULARY**
theme

A *theme* is a set of predesigned formatting elements—including colors, fonts, and effects—that can be applied to an entire workbook. You can use the commands in the Themes group on the Page Layout tab on the Ribbon, as shown in **Figure EX 2–15**, to apply themes to a workbook. Clicking the Themes button opens a gallery of theme options, organized alphabetically, so you can choose a theme and change the color, font, and effects at the same time. If you want to change only one element, you can click the Theme Colors, Theme Fonts, or Theme Effects button.

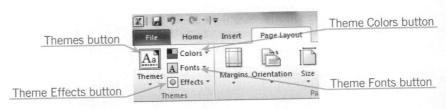

FIGURE EX 2–15   Themes group on the Page Layout tab

In the Themes gallery, you can click the Browse for Themes command to locate a workbook that contains a theme you want to apply to the current workbook. After you have customized a theme, you can use the Save Current Theme command to name and save it to the Document Themes folder.

Working with Table Styles

You can select a range of related data in a worksheet and format it as an Excel table using table styles. Excel automatically converts the data to a table and places sort and filter arrows on the column headers to help you manage and analyze the table data. You can also specify formats for the individual table elements, such as the header row containing titles for the columns, and a totals row that uses predefined formulas to total the values in the table.

When you select a range of cells and then click the Format as Table button in the Styles group on the Home tab, a gallery of Light, Medium, and Dark table style options opens, as shown in **Figure EX 2–16**. Notice that many of these styles include alternating bands of color, which makes text in a table easier to read. Once you click a table style, the Format As Table dialog box opens, in which you can verify or adjust the range of data for the table and specify whether it includes headers.

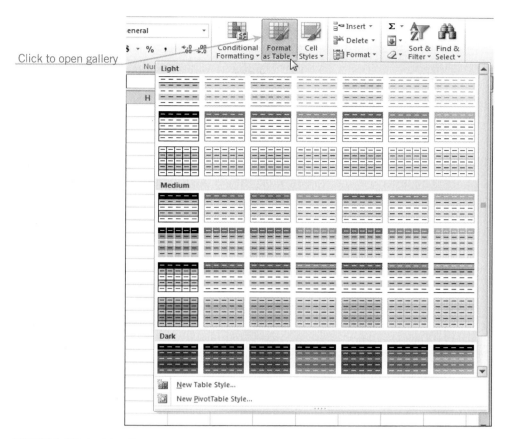

FIGURE EX 2–16   Table Styles gallery

When the data is formatted as a table, a contextual Table Tools Design tab is displayed on the Ribbon providing advanced tools designed for sorting the table data, filtering the table data, and transferring the data to another file for interpretation. If you do not want to work with the data as a table, you can convert the table to a regular range and still keep the table formatting by selecting the range and then clicking the Convert to Range button in the Tools group on the Table Tools Design tab or by right-clicking the table, pointing to Table, and clicking Convert to Range.

Applying Cell Styles

A defined combination of formatting characteristics—such as number, alignment, font, border, and fill—is called a *cell style*. Cell styles can save time because you can apply multiple formatting characteristics in one step. They also help you format a worksheet consistently because you can apply the same cell style to common elements, such as headings, and know that they will be formatted the same way. Excel has a variety of built-in styles that can be accessed by clicking the Cell Styles button in the Styles group on the Home tab to open a gallery of cell style options. The cell styles available are determined by which theme has been applied to the workbook. If you switch themes, the available cell styles change to match.

▶ **VOCABULARY**
cell style

Step-by-Step EX 2.6

The Time Sheet2 *XXX* workbook from Step-by-Step EX 2.5 should be open in the Excel program window.

1. Click the **Page Layout** tab on the Ribbon, and in the **Themes** group, click the **Themes** button to open the Themes gallery.

2. In the Themes gallery, point to the **Foundry** theme, as shown in **Figure EX 2–17**, to see what the applied theme would look like using Live Preview.

FIGURE EX 2–17
Applying a theme

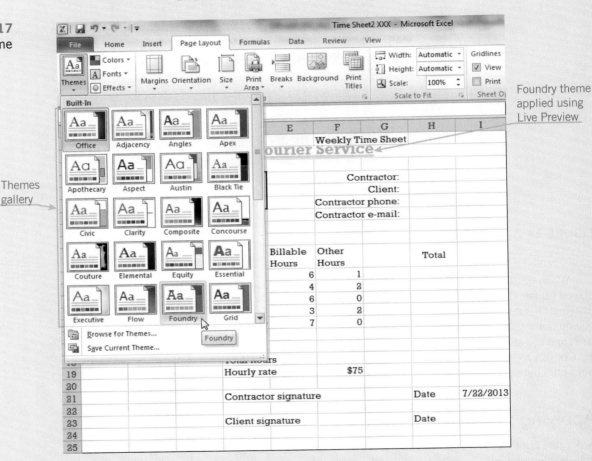

Themes gallery

Foundry theme applied using Live Preview

3. Click the **Foundry** theme. Notice that some of the cell formats you previously applied are changed to match the new theme.

4. Select cells **B10:H17**.

5. Click the Home tab, and in the Styles group click the **Format as Table** button to open a gallery of table style options.

6. Click the **Table Style Light 9** table style (second row, second option from the left) to open the Format As Table dialog box, as shown in **Figure EX 2–18**.

FIGURE EX 2–18
Format As Table dialog box

Selected range

7. In the Format As Table dialog box, click the **My table has headers** check box to select this option, and click the **OK** button to close the dialog box. The range is formatted as a table, with filter arrows on the column headers. Notice that the Table Tools Design contextual tab is displayed on the Ribbon.

8. With the table selected, click the **Convert to Range** button in the Tools group on the Table Tools Design tab. When a message box opens, click the **Yes** button to convert the table to a normal range and remove the filter arrows from the headings.

9. Select the **A2:I2** merged cell.

10. Click the **Cell Styles** button in the Styles group to open a gallery of cell style options.

11. Point to the **Title** cell style to see what the cell style would look like using Live Preview, as shown in **Figure EX 2–19**.

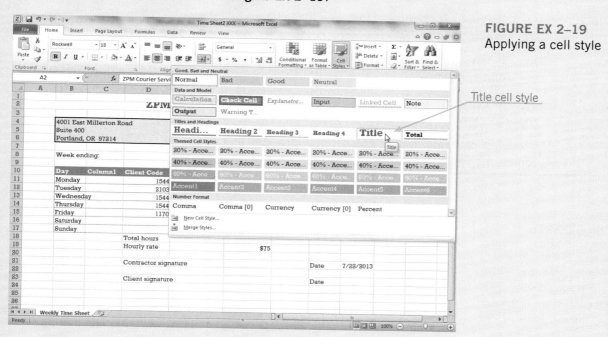

FIGURE EX 2–19
Applying a cell style

Title cell style

12. Click the **Title** cell style to apply that cell style. Notice the row height does not allow for the text to be displayed fully. You will learn how to correct this later in this lesson.

13. Select cell **B8**. On the Home tab, in the Styles group, click the **Cell Styles** button, and then click the **Heading 4** cell style in the gallery.

14. Save the workbook and leave it open for use in the next Step-by-Step.

Using Conditional Formatting

You can also use formatting techniques to analyze data by visually identifying key data or trends in data. *Conditional formatting* is a feature of Excel that enables you to apply specific formatting to cells that meet specific conditions. This can be useful if, for example, you want sales above or below a certain amount to stand out. When you click the Conditional Formatting button on the Home tab in the Styles group, a menu of built-in conditional formatting options opens. For example, you could choose to highlight all the cells containing duplicate values or to highlight the top 10 items in a range.

Table EX 2–1 lists the specific conditional formats that you can apply.

TABLE EX 2–1   Conditional formats

FORMAT	DESCRIPTION	OPTION EXAMPLE
Highlight Cells Rules	Formats cells containing text, numbers, or date/time values based on criteria that you specify	Greater Than
Top/Bottom Rules	Formats the top or bottom values in a range based on criteria you provide	Top 10%
Data Bars	Indicates relative values of cells; data bar length represents the value in the cell	Blue Data Bar
Color Scales	Visually compares data using shades of two or three colors that represent higher or lower values	Green–Yellow–Red Color Scale
Icon Sets	Classifies data into three to five categories where an icon represents a range of values	3 Arrows (Colored)

If you want to clear the conditional formatting, you can click the Conditional Formatting button on the Home tab in the Styles group, point to Clear Rules, and then choose whether to clear rules from the selected cells, the entire sheet, or from the table.

Step-by-Step EX 2.7

The Time Sheet2 *XXX* workbook from Step-by-Step EX 2.6 should be open in the Excel program window.

1. Select cells **E11:E15**.

2. On the Home tab, in the Styles group, click the **Conditional Formatting** button to open the Conditional Formatting menu.

3. On the Conditional Formatting menu, point to **Data Bars**, and then point to the **Green Data Bar** option on the submenu to see what the data would look like with the conditional formatting applied, as shown in **Figure EX 2–20**.

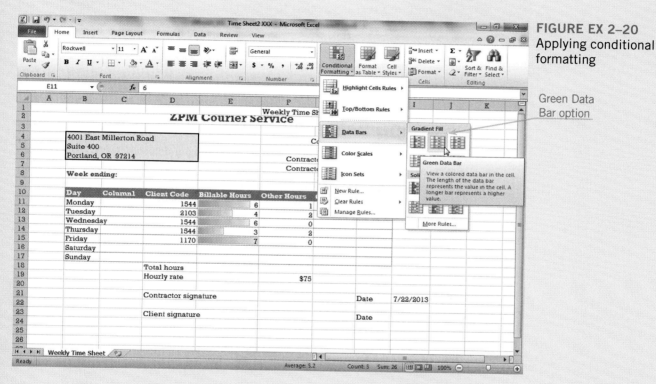

FIGURE EX 2–20
Applying conditional formatting

Green Data Bar option

4. Click the **Green Data Bar** option to apply colored data bars that represent the values in the cells.

5. Select cells **F11:F15**.

6. Click the **Conditional Formatting** button, point to **Highlight Cells Rules**, and then click **Equal To** to open the Equal To dialog box, shown in **Figure EX 2–21**.

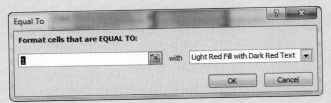

7. In the Format cells that are EQUAL TO box, type **0** (the number zero), and then click the **OK** button to close the dialog box. A light red fill with dark red text is applied to all numbers in the selected range that are equal to zero.

8. Save the workbook and leave it open for use in the next Step-by-Step.

Working with Rows and Columns

You can alter the structure of a worksheet by making changes to the rows and columns. When you create a new workbook, columns are set to a default width of 8.43 characters, and rows are set to a default height of 12.75 points. These default sizes may not accommodate the data in your worksheet. For example, some cell contents might get truncated, or cut off, because the column width is too narrow. Or the font size may be taller than the default row height when you merge and center cells. To correct these types of problems, you can adjust the size of the columns and rows in the worksheet. You can change these settings for all columns and rows in a worksheet by clicking the Select All button before making adjustments, or you can just select the individual column(s) or row(s) that you want to adjust.

You can also insert and delete rows and columns in a worksheet. Other cells, rows, or columns shift to make a place for the insertion. The commands for working with rows and columns are located in the Cells group on the Home tab, as shown in **Figure EX 2–22**.

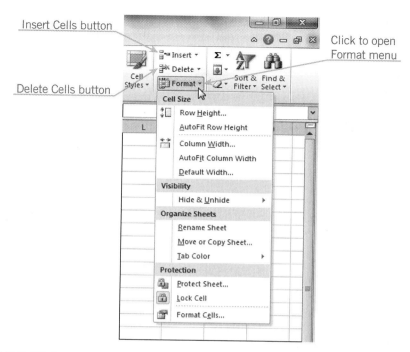

FIGURE EX 2–22   Cells group on Home tab

Adjusting Column Width

An easy way to adjust column width is by using the mouse to drag the right border of the column heading to the width you want. A ScreenTip is displayed showing the new width as you drag. If you double-click the right border of the column heading, the column automatically resizes to fit the data currently in the column. You can also resize a column to fit its widest entry by clicking the Format button in the Cells group on the Home tab, and then clicking AutoFit Column Width.

If you want to specify an exact width, you can click the Format button and then click Column Width on the menu, or right-click a column heading letter and then click Column Width on the shortcut menu. These actions open the Column Width dialog box, shown in **Figure EX 2–23**, where you can enter a new width.

FIGURE EX 2–23   Column Width dialog box

Adjusting Row Height

You will not typically need to use the Row Height commands, because Excel changes the row height automatically to accommodate the data and font size. But when necessary, you can adjust row height using the same methods as for adjusting column width.

Using the mouse, you can click the row heading lower border and drag it up or down to a new height, as shown in **Figure EX 2–24**. If you double-click on the lower border of the row heading, the row automatically resizes to fit the current data in the row.

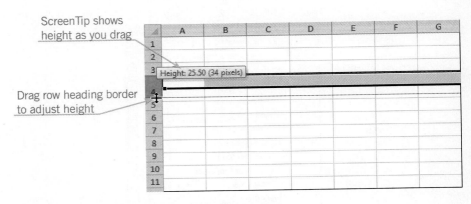

ScreenTip shows height as you drag

Height: 25.50 (34 pixels)

Drag row heading border to adjust height

FIGURE EX 2–24   Drag to change row height

You can also resize a row to fit its tallest entry by clicking the Format button in the Cells group on the Home tab, and then clicking AutoFit Row Height. You can open the Row Height dialog box to specify a row height by clicking the Format button and then clicking Row Height, or by right-clicking the row heading number and then clicking Row Height.

Inserting a Row or Column

When you click the Insert Cells button arrow in the Cells group on the Home tab, a menu opens with options for inserting cells, rows, columns, or a sheet. If you click Insert Sheet Rows, a new row will be inserted above the current selection. If you click Insert Sheet Columns, a new column will be inserted to the left of the current selection. The same number of columns or rows that you have selected will be inserted, so to insert multiple columns or rows at a time, you select the same number of columns or rows that you want to insert before clicking the command.

If you click the Insert Cells command, the Insert dialog box shown in **Figure EX 2–25** opens, where you can insert cells, as well as an entire row or an entire column.

FIGURE EX 2–25   Insert dialog box

Deleting a Row or Column

When you delete rows or columns, the rows beneath the deleted row and the columns to the right of the deleted column automatically shift up or left to fill in the space. Clicking the Delete Cells button arrow in the Cells group on the Home tab will open a menu with the option to delete rows or columns. If you click Delete Cells, the Delete dialog box opens, in which you can delete cells, as well as an entire row or an entire column.

Step-by-Step EX 2.8

The Time Sheet2 *XXX* workbook from Step-by-Step EX 2.7 should be open in the Excel program window.

1. Select cell **B13**.

2. On the Home tab, in the Cells group, click the **Format** button, and then click **AutoFit Column Width**. The column widens to accommodate the data in the cell.

3. Click the **column A heading** to select column A.

4. Drag the **right column A heading border** to the left until the ScreenTip reads *Width: 3.25 (31 pixels)*, as shown in **Figure EX 2–26**.

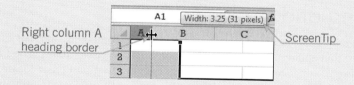

FIGURE EX 2–26
Dragging to adjust column width

5. Click the **row 2 heading** to select row 2.

6. Click the **Format** button, and then click **Row Height** to open the Row Height dialog box.

7. In the Row height text box, type **25** and then click the **OK** button to close the dialog box and increase the height of the row.

8. Select cell **A1**.

9. On the Home tab, in the Cells group, click the **Delete Cells** button arrow, and then click **Delete Sheet Rows** to delete row 1 and shift the other cells up.

10. Select cell **A17**.

11. On the Home tab, in the Cells group, click the **Insert Cells** button arrow, and then click **Insert Sheet Rows** to insert a row above the selected cell.

12. Select **column C**. Note that even though column C displays data that spills over from column B, it does not contain any data. Click the **Delete Cells** button to delete the column and shift the other cells left.

13. Delete **column F**. Note that even though column F contains data from cells that you merged and centered, no data is deleted when you delete this column. Your worksheet should look similar to **Figure EX 2–27**.

FIGURE EX 2–27
Formatted worksheet

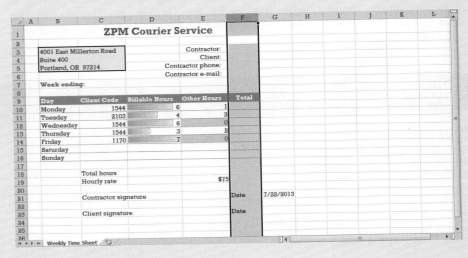

14. Save and close the workbook.

Finding and Replacing Data

The Find and Replace commands are two separate commands that are often used together to find and replace data, formats, formulas, and other items. The Find command is useful for locating specific data or moving to a particular location in the worksheet. The Replace command is useful for changing data or formatting in a worksheet. You click the Find & Select button in the Editing group on the Home tab to access the Find and Replace commands.

When you click the Find command, the Find tab of the Find and Replace dialog box opens, as shown in **Figure EX 2–28**. In this dialog box, you can type data in the Find what list box and click the Find Next button to search for each occurrence. The Options button shows or hides additional Find options, such as searching for a specific format. If you click the Find All button, each occurrence is listed in the Find and Replace dialog box and you can move to a specific occurrence by clicking it to make the cell active.

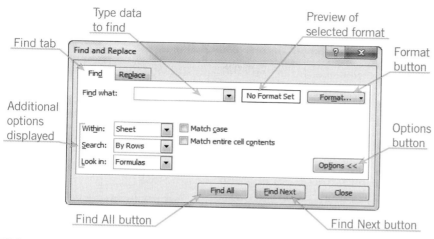

FIGURE EX 2–28   Find tab of the Find and Replace dialog box with options displayed

The Replace command opens the Find and Replace dialog box with the Replace tab active, as shown in **Figure EX 2–29**. Type the data you want to find in the Find what list box and the data you want to replace it with in the Replace with list box. The Options button shows or hides additional options. Use the Find Next and Replace buttons to make just one replacement at a time. You can use the Replace All button to replace all occurrences of data at once without confirming each instance.

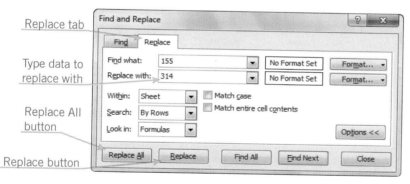

FIGURE EX 2–29   Replace tab of the Find and Replace dialog box with options displayed

Step-by-Step EX 2.9

1. Open **Step EX 2-9** from the folder containing the data files for this lesson.

2. Save the workbook as **Team Stats XXX** (replace XXX with your initials).

3. On the Home tab, in the Editing group, click the **Find & Select** button 🔍 to open the menu, and then click **Find** to open the Find tab of the Find and Replace dialog box.

4. In the Find what list box, type **2B,** and then click the **Find Next** button to move to the first occurrence of the text *2B* in the worksheet, cell F3.

5. Click the **Find All** button to display all occurrences of the text in a list at the bottom of the Find and Replace dialog box.

6. Click the **Replace** tab in the Find and Replace dialog box to make the Replace tab active.

7. In the Replace with list box, type **Doubles**. Your workbook window should look similar to **Figure EX 2–30**.

FIGURE EX 2–30
Replacing data

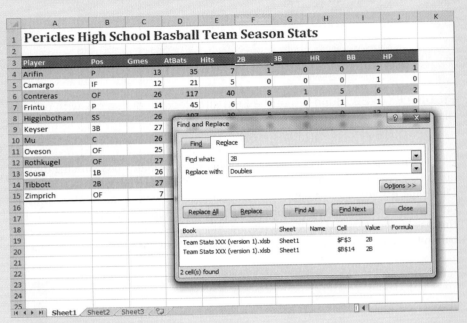

8. Click the **Replace** button to replace the first occurrence of *2B* with *Doubles*.

9. Click the **Options** button to see all the options available when finding and replacing data.

10. Click the **Close** button to close the Find and Replace dialog box.

11. Save the workbook and leave it open for use in the next Step-by-Step.

Copying and Moving Worksheet Data

▶ **VOCABULARY**
Clipboard

Excel offers different ways to move or copy data. You can use the *Clipboard*—an area of memory that temporarily stores up to 24 cut or copied selections—or you can use the drag-and-drop method.

Cutting, Copying, and Pasting to the Clipboard

The Clipboard is a convenient way to move or copy text not only within a workbook but also to other Excel workbooks, Office files, and other files such as PDF documents and e-mail messages. The cut or copied selections remain on the Clipboard until you delete them or exit all Office programs.

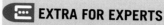
To move a selection, you *cut*, or remove, the contents (data and formatting) from a cell or range and *paste*, or insert, it into another cell or range. When you *copy* a selection, you duplicate the contents so you can paste it into another cell or range without deleting it from its original location. You need only select the upper-left cell of the paste area because Excel will set the paste area to match the same size and range as the cells you are pasting.

After selecting the cell or range you want to move or copy (indicated by a rotating border around the cells), you can use the Cut, Copy, and Paste buttons in the Clipboard group on the Home tab, as shown in **Figure EX 2–31**. Clicking the Clipboard task pane launcher opens the Clipboard task pane so you can view, paste, or delete items.

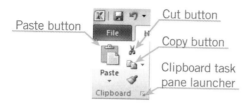

FIGURE EX 2–31   Clipboard group on Home tab

The Paste button menu offers a variety of ways to paste copied data, such as pasting only formulas, pasting only values, or pasting all contents except the borders. When you use the Paste Special command, additional options are available in the Paste Special dialog box. When you paste data in a cell or range, Excel replaces any existing data.

You can also right-click a selection and use the commands on the shortcut menu to move or copy data from one location to another.

Using the Drag-and-Drop Method

You can use the *drag-and-drop method* to move or copy a selection to a new location in your worksheet. If you position the mouse pointer on the border of a selected cell or range, it will change to a cross with an arrow. Then you can press and hold the mouse button while dragging the cell or range to its new position. You release the mouse button to drop the selection in its new location.

To copy a selection, press and hold Ctrl while you drag and drop the selection. When you copy a selection, you will see a plus sign (+) with the pointer.

When you move or copy a selection using the drag-and-drop method, the selection is not stored on the Clipboard. Therefore, you should use the Clipboard group buttons if you plan to paste an item repeatedly.

Step-by-Step EX 2.10

The Team Stats *XXX* workbook from Step-by-Step EX 2.9 should be open in the Excel program window.

1. Click cell **C4**. On the Home tab, in the Clipboard group, click the **Copy** button 📋 to display a rotating border around the cell.

2. Select cell **C11**. On the Home tab, in the Clipboard group, click the **Paste** button arrow to open the Paste menu, as shown in **Figure 2–32**.

FIGURE EX 2–32
Paste menu

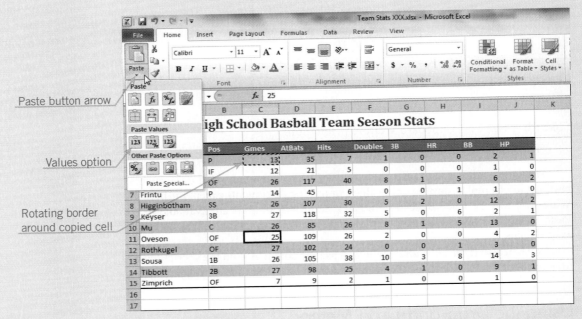

Paste button arrow

Values option

Rotating border
around copied cell

3. Click the **Values** option, the first option in the Paste Values section, to paste just the value of the copied cell.

4. Press **Esc** to remove the rotating border from the copied cell.

5. On the Home tab, in the Clipboard group, click the **Clipboard task pane launcher** to open the Clipboard task pane.

6. Select cell **D7**, and in the Clipboard group, click **Copy**. The value from cell D7 now appears at the top of the Clipboard task pane, as shown in **Figure EX 2–33**.

Close button

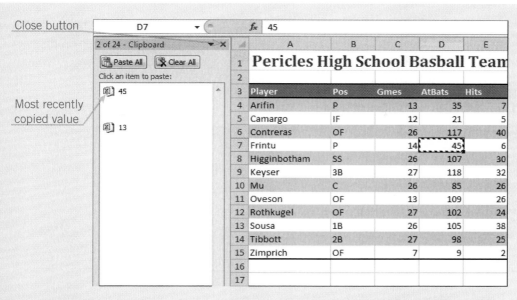

Most recently copied value

FIGURE EX 2–33
Clipboard task pane

7. Select cell **D4**, and then click **45** in the Clipboard task pane to paste the data.

8. Click the **Paste Options** button 📋 to the lower right of the pasted data, and then click the **Match Destination Formatting** button on the menu, as shown in **Figure EX 2–34**.

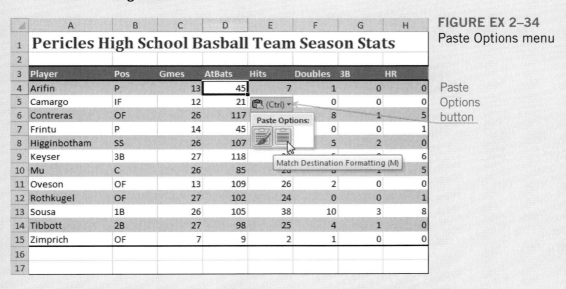

FIGURE EX 2–34
Paste Options menu

Paste Options button

9. Press **Esc** to remove the Paste Options button. Click the **Close** button in the Clipboard task pane to close the Clipboard task pane.

10. Select cell **G8** and point to the bottom border until the pointer changes to a four-headed arrow ✥.

11. Press and hold **Ctrl** to display a small plus sign, and then click and drag to cell **G11**, as shown in **Figure EX 2–35**. Notice the ScreenTip displaying the new location.

FIGURE EX 2–35
Drag-and-drop
copied data

	A	B	C	D	E	F	G	H	I	J	K
1	Pericles High School Basball Team Season Stats										
2											
3	Player	Pos	Gmes	AtBats	Hits	Doubles	3B	HR	BB	HP	
4	Arifin	P	13	45	7	1	0	0	2	1	
5	Camargo	IF	12	21	5	0	0	0	1	0	
6	Contreras	OF	26	117	40	8	1	5	6	2	
7	Frintu	P	14	45	6	0	0	1	1	0	
8	Higginbotham	SS	26	107	30	5	2	0	12	2	
9	Keyser	3B	27	118	32	5	0	6	2	1	
10	Mu	C	26	85	26	8	1	5	13	0	
11	Oveson	OF	13	109	26	2	+ 0	0	4	2	
12	Rothkugel	OF	27	102	24	0	0	1	3	0	
13	Sousa	1B	26	105	38	10	3	8	14	3	
14	Tibbott	2B	27	98	25	4	1	0	9	1	
15	Zimprich	OF	7	9	2	1	0	0	1	0	
16											
17											
18											

Pointer with plus
sign indicating
copied data

ScreenTip for
new location

12. Release the mouse button and the Ctrl key to paste the copied data.

13. Click cell **G9**, and in the Clipboard group, click the **Format Painter** button, and then click cell **G11** to copy the formatting from cell G9 to cell G11.

14. Save the workbook and leave it open for use in the next Step-by-Step.

Checking Spelling

When you are finished creating a workbook, it is a good idea to check it for any spelling mistakes. Clicking the Spelling button in the Proofing group on the Review tab opens the Spelling dialog box where you can correct any errors. In this dialog box, the Not in the Dictionary text box displays the possible misspelling and the Suggestions list box offers possible fixes for the word. You can select a suggestion or type your own correction and then use the Change button to correct an error, or use the Change All button to correct all instances of the same error. The spelling checker will flag many proper nouns as being incorrect. You can choose to ignore a specific instance of a word or you can choose to have Excel ignore all occurrences of the word. If it is a mistake that you make frequently, you can set Excel to automatically correct the word any time you misspell it.

Step-by-Step EX 2.11

The Team Stats *XXX* workbook from Step-by-Step EX 2.10 should be open in the Excel program window.

1. Select cell **A1**.

2. Click the **Review** tab on the Ribbon. In the Proofing group, click the **Spelling** button to open the Spelling dialog box, as shown in **Figure EX 2–36**.

Potential misspelling

Suggested corrections

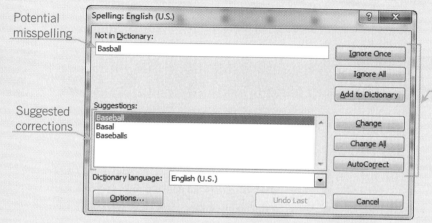

Options for correcting errors

FIGURE EX 2–36
Spelling dialog box

3. In the Spelling dialog box, click the **Change** button to change *Basball* to Excel's suggested spelling and move to the next possible spelling error.

4. In the Not in Dictionary text box, edit *Pos* to read *Position,* and then click the **Change** button to accept this correction and move to the next possible spelling error.

5. In the Suggestions text box, select **Games**. Then click the **Change** button to accept this correction and move to the next possible spelling error.

6. Click the **Ignore Once** button to ignore *AtBats* and move to the next possible spelling error.

7. Since the remaining words on the worksheet that are not in the dictionary are proper names, click the **Close** button to close the Spelling dialog box.

8. Click the **OK** button to close the message that the spelling check is complete for selected objects.

9. Save and close the workbook and then close Excel.

NET BUSINESS

Excel has numerous templates that can help you get started creating workbooks for a small business—including agendas, budgets, calendars, expense reports, invoices, and memos. You can apply the same theme to all your documents or create your own customized theme that reflects the style of your business. Then if you save each type of worksheet as a template, you will have a set of professional-looking forms and documents that are coordinated. You can upload them to your company intranet, so they can be easily accessed and used as many times as needed.

SUMMARY

In this lesson, you learned:

- How to create new workbooks.
- Various ways to format cells.
- How to apply themes and styles.
- Conditional formatting can help highlight and interpret data.

- The processes for adjusting column widths and row heights.
- Methods of inserting and deleting rows and columns.
- How to find, replace, copy, and move worksheet data.
- It is a good idea to check spelling.

 VOCABULARY REVIEW

Define the following terms:

cell style	cut	font styles
Clipboard	drag-and-drop method	paste
conditional formatting	fill	point size
copy	font	theme

REVIEW QUESTIONS

MULTIPLE CHOICE

Select the best response for the following statements.

1. Many of the most common cell formatting options are located on the _____ tab on the Ribbon.

    A. Home   C. Page Layout

    B. Insert   D. Review

2. Font _____ are variations in the shape or weight of a font's characters.

    A. sizes   C. styles

    B effects   D. colors

3. Which button can be used to change the margin between the border and the text in a cell?

    A. Orientation   C. Text Wrap

    B. Increase Indent   D. Merge & Center

4. The cell styles available are determined by the _____ that has been applied to the workbook.

   A. conditional formatting   C. number format

   B. table style   D. theme

5. When you create a new workbook, columns are set to a default width of _____ characters.

   A. 8   C. 12

   B. 8.43   D. 12.75

6. Excel changes the _____ automatically to accommodate the data and font size.

   A. row height   C. cell style

   B. column width   D. cell alignment

7. When you insert a new column, it is inserted _____.

   A. to the right of the   C. at the beginning
       current selection   of the worksheet

   B. to the left of the   D. at the end of
       current selection   the worksheet

8. If you wanted to highlight the top 10 items in a range, which feature would you most likely use?

   A. Cell styles   C. Conditional formatting

   B. Table styles   D. Format Painter

9. To copy a selection, press and hold the _____ key while you drag and drop the selection.

   A. Shift   C. Enter

   B. Alt   D. Ctrl

10. In the Spelling dialog box, you can click the _____ button to correct all instances of the same error.

   A. AutoCorrect   C. Change All

   B. Change   D. Ignore All

FILL IN THE BLANK

Complete the following sentences by writing the correct word or words in the blanks provided.

1. A(n) _____ is a master copy of a certain type of worksheet that has predesigned layout, style, and formatting.

2. You can use the _____ button to copy formatting from one cell to other cells.

3. You can use the _____ button to display text in a cell on multiple lines so it is all visible.

4. When you enter a number in a cell, Excel automatically applies the _____ format.

5. A(n) _____ is a set of predesigned formatting elements—including colors, fonts, and effects—that can be applied to an entire workbook.

6. When data is formatted as a table, a contextual _____ tab is displayed on the Ribbon.

7. _____ is a feature of Excel that enables you to apply specific formatting to cells that meet specific conditions.

8. The _____ command is useful for locating specific data or moving to a particular location in the worksheet.

9. The _____ is an area of memory that temporarily stores up to 24 cut or copied selections.

10. When you _____ a selection, you duplicate the contents so you can paste it into another cell or range without deleting it from its original location.

■ PROJECTS

PROJECT EX 2–1

1. Open the **Project EX 2-1** workbook from the folder containing the data files for this lesson.

2. Save the workbook as **Bus Parts** *XXX* (replace *XXX* with your initials).

3. Select cell **A1**. Change the font to **Cambria**, the font size to **18**, the font style to **bold**, and the font color to **Blue, Accent 1**.

4. Select cell **A2**. Change the font to **Cambria**, the font size to **12**, the font style to **italic**, and the font color to **Blue, Accent 1**.

5. Merge and center **A1:D1**.

6. Merge and center **A2:D2**.

7. Change the width of columns **A, C**, and **D** to **11.00 (82 pixels)**.

8. Change the width of column **B** to **36.00 (257 pixels)**.

9. Select cell **A4**. Center and bold the text.

10. Use the Format Painter to copy the formatting from cell A4 to cells **B4:D4**.

11. Select cells **C5:D12**. Change the number format to **Currency**.

12. Save the workbook and leave it open for use in the next project.

PROJECT EX 2–3

1. Open the **Project EX 2-3** workbook from the folder containing the data files for this lesson.

2. Save the workbook as **Employee List** *XXX* (replace *XXX* with your initials).

3. Change the theme to **Urban**.

4. Select cell **A1**, and change the cell style to **Title**.

5. Select cells **A2:C2**, and change the cell style to **Heading 2**.

6. Insert a row above row 3.

7. Select cells **A3:C3**, and clear the formatting.

8. Select cells **A4:G4**. Center the text, bold the text, and change the cell style to **20% - Accent1**.

9. Delete column D.

10. Insert a column before column A, and change the width to **2.00 (25 pixels)**.

11. Use AutoFit to change the width of column E.

12. Save the workbook and leave it open for use in the next project.

PROJECT EX 2–2

The Bus Parts *XXX* workbook from Project EX 2–1 should be open in the Excel program window.

1. Save the workbook as **Bus Parts2** *XXX* (replace XXX with your initials).

2. Select cells **A1:D2**, and add a **Thick Box Border**.

3. With cells A1:D2 still selected, fill the cells with a **Blue, Accent 1, Lighter 80%** color.

4. Select cell **A4**, and change the text to **Item Number**.

5. Select cell **A4**, if necessary, and wrap the text.

6. Select cells **B4:D4**, and middle-align the text in the cells.

7. Select **A4:D4**, and add a **Bottom Double Border**.

8. Delete row 3.

9. Check the spelling of the worksheet, and change each error to the first suggested option.

10. Save and close the workbook.

PROJECT EX 2–4

The Employee List *XXX* workbook from Project EX 2–3 should be open in the Excel program window.

1. Save the workbook as **Employee List2** *XXX* (replace *XXX* with your initials).

2. Select cells **B6:B26**. Center the data, and change the number format to **Number** with zero (0) decimal places.

3. Select cells **G6:G26**, and change the number format to **Currency** with zero (0) decimal places.

4. Delete row 5.

5. In column G, highlight the **Top 10 Items** with **Light Red Fill with Dark Red Text**. (*Hint*: Use conditional formatting Top/Bottom Rules.)

6. Select cell **A1**. Search for **Edwards**, and replace the second occurrence with **Evans**.

7. Select cell **E7**. Copy and paste the text to cell **E19**.

8. Select cells **B4:G25**, and format them as a table with **Table Style Medium 2**. (*Note*: Your table has headers.)

9. Convert the table to a normal range.

10. Save and close the workbook.

Open the **Employee List2** *XXX* file. Reformat the range B4:G25 as a table. Explore the options on the Table Tools Design tab in the Table Style Options group, and experiment with changing them. For example, remove the header row, add a total row, emphasize the first column or the last column, or change from banded rows to banded columns. Save and close the workbook.

 WEB PROJECT

When you want to reinforce what you have already learned or learn more about a new skill, Microsoft has online training courses available that can be a great resource. Search Excel Help for the online training session titled *Get to know Excel 2010: Create your first spreadsheet*. Complete the lessons and practice sessions.

Open the **Employee List2** *XXX* file. In column G, clear the conditional formatting, and then apply different conditional formatting options. For example, highlight cells between two values; highlight values in the bottom 10%; or use color scales, data bars, or icon sets to represent values in the cells. Save and close the workbook.

 TEAMWORK PROJECT

Open the workbook **Team Project EX 2** from the folder containing the data files for this lesson, and save it as **Open Water Sports** *XXX* (replace *XXX* with your initials). With a partner, use the skills you have learned in this lesson to format the worksheet attractively. When you are finished, compare your results with others in your class, and discuss which commands you used and why. Vote on which team's worksheet formatting you like the best.

 CRITICAL THINKING

ACTIVITY EX 2–1

Think of a worksheet you would like to create. Perhaps you want a personal budget, an expense report, a schedule, or a receipt. Spend some time deciding what type of information it will contain and how it will be designed, then sketch a rough draft on paper. After planning your worksheet, use Excel to create it. Compare it to your original design. Did you need to make any adjustments? Now search through the Excel templates for the same type you created (e.g., agenda, planner, time sheet) and download it. Compare the template to yours. How is it similar or different? Are there any changes you want to make to your worksheet based on the template?

ACTIVITY EX 2–2

Search for the video in Excel Help titled *Apply conditional formatting* and watch it. What are the benefits of conditional formatting? How can conditional formatting help you answer specific questions about your data? What is the difference between color scales, data bars, and icon sets—and when would you format cells using each one?

LESSON 3

Using Formulas and Functions

■ OBJECTIVES

Upon completion of this lesson, you should be able to:

- Enter formulas in a worksheet.
- Understand cell references.
- Copy formulas.
- Use functions.
- Review and edit formulas.

■ DATA FILES

To complete this lesson, you will need these data files:

Step EX 3-1.xlsx

Project EX 3-1.xlsx

Project EX 3-3.xlsx

Activity EX 3-3.xlsx

■ VOCABULARY

absolute reference

argument

arithmetic operators

Auto Fill

comparison operators

constants

error value

fill handle

formula

functions

mixed reference

operator

order of operations

relative reference

syntax

Introduction

The real power of a spreadsheet program such as Excel is its ability to perform simple and complex calculations on worksheet data. In this lesson, you will learn how to enter formulas to perform calculations. You will also be introduced to Excel's functions—those predefined formulas that allow you to construct complex mathematical, statistical, financial, and other formulas. The commands for working with formulas and functions are located on the Formulas tab on the Ribbon.

Entering Formulas

A *formula* is a set of instructions used to perform calculations on values in a worksheet. Formulas can set up a relationship between two or more cells. You might, for instance, want Excel to total the numbers in a range of cells. An Excel formula must begin with the equal sign (=) and is followed by the set of instructions for completing a calculation.

A formula's instructions contain operators and the values you want calculated. An *operator* is a sign or symbol that indicates what calculation is to be performed. The most commonly used operators are the *arithmetic operators* used for addition, subtraction, multiplication, division, and exponentiation.

For example, the formula =3+2 entered in a cell will return a resulting value of 5 in the cell in which the formula is entered. In this case, the values are *constants*, which are numbers entered directly into a formula that do not change. More commonly, formulas in Excel use cell references to identify the cells containing the values you want to use in the formula. If cell C1 contains the value of 3 and cell D1 contains the value of 2, you could use the formula =C1+D1 to return a value of 5. The benefit to using cell references in a formula is that the results automatically update if the values in those cells change.

You can also use a combination of constants and cell references in a formula. For example, in the formula =C9+5, the equal sign (=) indicates that it is a formula, C9 is a cell reference, the plus sign (+) is an operator, and the number 5 is a constant. Excel calculates the formula's result by adding five to the value in cell C9. If the value in C9 changes, the formula result would also be updated.

Table EX 3–1 lists the arithmetic operators and examples of how they are used in formulas.

> ▶ **VOCABULARY**
> formula
> operator
> arithmetic operators
> constants

> 📟 **EXTRA FOR EXPERTS**
>
> When entering a formula, you can minimize typing errors by using the Formula AutoComplete feature. When you enter an equal sign (=) and then begin typing, a drop-down list of functions, arguments, and names beginning with those letters are displayed. Click to select from the list and enter it into the formula.

TABLE EX 3–1   Arithmetic operators

OPERATOR	OPERATION	EXAMPLE	DESCRIPTION
+ (plus sign)	Addition	A7+D9	Adds the values in cells A7 and D9
– (minus sign)	Subtraction	A7–D9	Subtracts the value in D9 from the value in A7
* (asterisk)	Multiplication	A7*D9	Multiplies the values in cells A7 and D9
/ (forward slash)	Division	A7/D9	Divides the value in A7 by the value in D9
% (percent sign)	Percent	A7*25%	Calculates 25% of the value in A7
^ (caret)	Exponentiation	A7^4	Raises the value in A7 to the fourth power

One way to enter a formula in a cell is to type it. For example, if you want to add the values in cells B5 through B8 and enter the result in cell B9, you can enter the formula =B5+B6+B7+B8 in cell B9 and press Enter. The result is displayed in the cell, but the cell actually contains the formula. You can see the formula in the formula bar when the cell is active, as shown in **Figure EX 3–1**.

Formula displayed in formula bar

Result of formula displayed in cell

FIGURE EX 3–1   Entering formulas

You get the same result by using the mouse: Click to activate cell B9, type =, click cell B5, type +, click B6, type +, click B7, type +, click B8, and press Enter. This method of pointing and clicking to enter cell references eliminates the need to look up cell references and avoids potential typing errors.

If you see a problem in your results after you enter a formula, you can view the formula by selecting the cell and reviewing the formula in the formula bar. Often it is the cell references that contain an error. Excel uses a simple color-coding method to identify the cell references used in the formula. You can display the color-coded cells by double-clicking a cell containing a formula. Excel displays each cell reference in the formula and the border of the corresponding cell in the worksheet with a distinct color, as shown in **Figure EX 3–2**.

Cell reference color matches corresponding cell border color

FIGURE EX 3–2   Color-coded cells

▶ **VOCABULARY**
order of operations

comparison operators

Some formulas will contain more than one arithmetic operator. Excel follows the *order of operations*, a specific sequence used to calculate the value of a formula. When you use operators, Excel performs calculations in the normal algebraic precedence. That means the calculations are executed from left to right in the following order:

1. Exponentiation (^)
2. Multiplication (*) or division (/)
3. Addition (+) or subtraction (−)

If you want to change the order of operations, you use parentheses to group expressions in your formula. The expression inside the parentheses gets calculated first. The example below shows how the order of operations can affect the resulting value of a formula.

$$3 + 7 * 2 = 17$$

Multiplication calculation is done first, then addition: $7 \times 2 = 14 + 3 = 17$

$$(3 + 7) * 2 = 20$$

Parentheses calculation is done first: $3 + 7 = 10 \times 2 = 20$

Using *comparison operators*, shown in **Table EX 3–2**, you can compare two values to obtain a logical value, either TRUE or FALSE.

TABLE EX 3–2   Comparison operators

OPERATOR	MEANING	EXAMPLE	DESCRIPTION
=	Equal to	A7=D9	Displays the value TRUE if the values in cell A7 and D9 are equal; displays the value FALSE if the two values are not equal
>	Greater than	A7>D9	Displays the value TRUE if the value in cell A7 is greater than the value in cell D9; displays the value FALSE if the value in cell A7 is less than or equal to the value in cell D9
<	Less than	A7<D9	Displays the value TRUE if the value in cell A7 is less than the value in cell D9; displays the value FALSE if the value in cell A7 is greater than or equal to the value in cell D9
>=	Greater than or equal to	A7>=D9	Displays the value TRUE if the value in cell A7 is greater than or equal to the value in cell D9; displays the value FALSE if the value in cell A7 is less than the value in cell D9
<=	Less than or equal to	A7<=D9	Displays the value TRUE if the value in cell A7 is less than or equal to the value in cell D9; displays the value FALSE if the value in cell A7 is greater than the value in cell D9
<>	Not equal to	A7<>D9	Displays the value TRUE if the value in cell A7 is not equal to the value in cell D9; displays the value FALSE if the value in cell A7 is equal to the value in cell D9

Step-by-Step EX 3.1

1. Start Excel.

2. Open **Step EX 3-1** from the folder containing the data files for this lesson.

3. Save the workbook as **Trip Budget XXX** (replace *XXX* with your initials).

4. In cell **B12**, type **=B8+B9+B10+B11**. Your worksheet window should look similar to **Figure EX 3–3**.

	A	B	C	D
	SUM	✗ ✓ *fx* =B8+B9+B10+B11		
1	**Business Trip Budget**			
2				
3	*Target Trip Budget*			
4	*Over/Under Amount*			
5				
6	Seattle			
7		Projected	Actual	
8	Airfare	$625	$575	
9	Hotel	$750	$795	
10	Food	$175	$148	
11	Car rental/gas	$560	$540	
12	Total	=B8+B9+B10+B11		
13				
14				

Type formula

FIGURE EX 3–3
Typing a formula

5. Click the **Enter** button ✔ on the formula bar to enter the formula. Notice the formula is displayed in the formula bar, and the resulting value, $2,110, is displayed in cell B12.

6. In cell **C12**, type **=**, click cell **C8**, type **+**, click cell **C9**, type **+**, click cell **C10**, type **+**, and then click cell **C11**.

7. Press **Enter** to enter the formula in cell C12 and display the resulting value, $2,058.

8. Save the workbook and leave it open for use in the next Step-by-Step.

Understanding Cell References and Copying Formulas

Excel uses relative, absolute, and mixed cell references. These are especially important to understand when you are copying formulas. You can copy formulas the same way you copy data, using the Cut, Copy, and Paste commands, or you can use the Auto Fill feature.

Auto Fill is a feature that you can use to automatically fill in worksheet data in any direction. You can use it to copy data or formatting. You can also use it to quickly copy a formula down a column or across a row by dragging the fill handle of the cell containing the formula. The *fill handle* is a little black square in the lower-right corner of the

VOCABULARY
Auto Fill
fill handle

EXTRA FOR EXPERTS

The fill handle can also be used to fill in a series. For example, you can click a cell containing the word *June* and then drag the fill handle to automatically fill in the previous or following months in adjacent cells.

VOCABULARY

relative reference

absolute reference

selected cell. When you point to the fill handle, the pointer turns to a black cross that you can click and drag over adjacent cells as far as you want to copy the formula. When you release the mouse button, the range is filled with the results of the copied formulas.

When you finish using the fill handle, the Auto Fill Options button is displayed next to the fill handle. You can click it to open a menu to choose to fill only the formatting or to fill without formatting.

Copying formulas is not as straightforward as copying formatting or text entries. When you copy, or move, a formula to another location in the worksheet, it can change depending on what type of cell references it contains.

A ***relative reference*** means the reference to a cell changes in relation to the location of the formula. For example, if you enter the formula =B9+B10 in cell B11, you are indicating Excel needs to add the contents in cells B9 and B10, the two cells immediately above cell B11. If you copy that same formula to C11, Excel adjusts the formula to add the values in the two cells immediately above cell C11 (cells C9 and C10). This saves you the time of typing a new formula each time. **Figure EX 3–4** shows a formula with relative references that has been copied.

Original formula with relative cell references

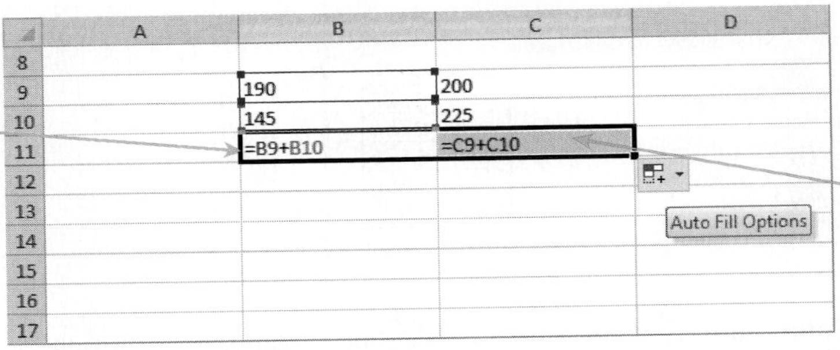

Relative cell references change when formula is copied

FIGURE EX 3–4 Using relative cell references in a formula

An ***absolute reference*** is a permanent reference to a cell and does not change in relation to the location of the formula. You create an absolute reference by typing a dollar sign before the column letter and before the row number ($B$9). If you copy a formula with absolute references ($B$9+$B$10) from one cell to another cell, it stays exactly the same, as shown in **Figure EX 3–5**. Absolute references can be useful when you want to reference the same cell repeatedly in different formulas or use the same formula in a different location in the workbook.

Original formula with absolute cell references

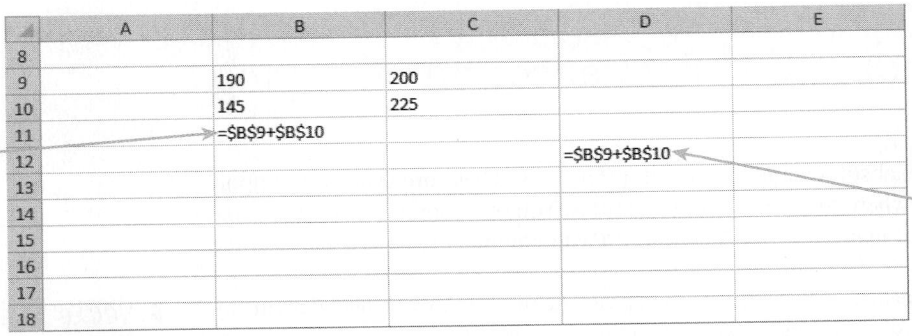

Absolute cell references do not change when formula is copied

FIGURE EX 3–5 Using absolute cell references in a formula

LESSON 3   Using Formulas and Functions

Sometimes you may only want one part of the formula to change when it is copied, and another part of the formula to stay the same. A *mixed reference* contains both relative and absolute cell references. For example, the cell reference $B9 has an absolute column and a relative row; B$10 has a relative column and an absolute row. When you copy a formula with a mixed cell reference, the relative reference changes based on the new location, but the absolute reference does not. **Figure EX 3–6** shows a formula with relative column references and absolute row references and how it changes when copied.

Original formula with mixed cell references → =B$9+B$10

Relative column references change when formula is copied; absolute row references do not → =C$9+C$10

	A	B	C	D
8				
9		190	200	
10		145	225	
11		=B$9+B$10		
12				
13			=C$9+C$10	
14				
15				
16				
17				
18				

FIGURE EX 3–6   Using mixed cell references in a formula

Step-by-Step EX 3.2

The Trip Budget *XXX* workbook from Step-by-Step EX 3.1 should be open in the Excel program window.

1. Click cell **D8**, type **=B8-C8**, and then press **Enter** to enter a formula with relative references and display the value $50 in the cell.

2. Click cell **D8** and point to the fill handle. The pointer changes to a black cross **+**.

3. Click and drag the **fill handle** to cell **D11**, as shown in **Figure EX 3–7**. When you release the mouse button, the formula in cell D8 is copied and the cells are filled with formula results.

FIGURE EX 3–7
Copying a formula using Auto Fill

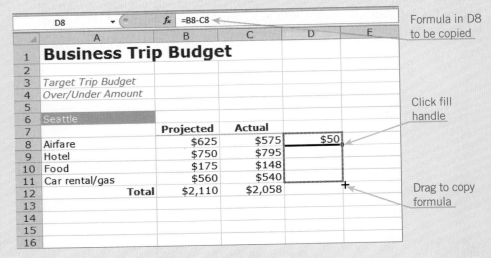

4. In cell **D7**, type **Difference** and press **Enter**.

5. Click cell **C7** and then click and drag the fill handle to cell **D7**. When you release the mouse button, the data is copied and the Auto Fill Options button is displayed.

6. Click the **Auto Fill Options** button, and click **Fill Formatting Only**, as shown in **Figure EX 3–8**, to copy the formatting, but not the data.

FIGURE EX 3–8
Copying formatting using Auto Fill

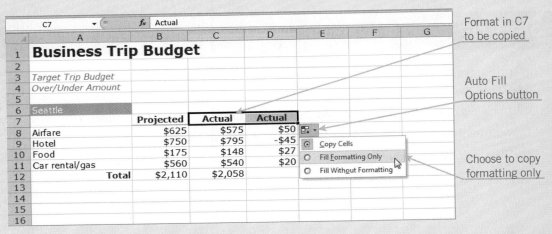

7. Click a blank cell in the worksheet, and notice that the formatting in cell D7 is now the same as the formatting in cell C7.

8. In cell **B3**, type **=$B$12*110%** and press **Enter** to enter a formula with absolute references and display the value of $2,321 in the cell.

9. In cell **B4**, type **=$B$3-C12** and press **Enter** to enter a formula with mixed references and display the value of $263 in the cell.

10. Save the workbook and leave it open for use in the next Step-by-Step.

Using Functions

Excel provides the user with built-in formulas, called *functions*, that enable you to perform complex calculations easily. Instead of entering all the cell references and operators as you have done in previous exercises, you can use a function in a formula to tell Excel to perform a calculation. For example, the SUM function totals the values in a range of cells, which is easier than typing each cell reference separately.

A function must follow a set of established rules, called *syntax*, that specifies how the function must be entered. The standard syntax for Excel functions is:

=*Function name (argument1, argument2...)*

Most functions require an argument. An *argument*, which follows the function name and is enclosed in parentheses, refers to the text, numbers, or cell references on which the function is to be performed. For example, in the function =SUM(B8:B11), the range B8:B11 is the argument. If you use more than one argument in a function, separate them with a comma.

Hundreds of functions are available in Excel, and they are organized into categories based upon their general purpose, such as Financial, Date and Time, and Statistical. **Table 3–3** lists examples of some functions from the various categories.

> ▶ **VOCABULARY**
> **functions**
> **syntax**
> **argument**

TABLE EX 3–3   Examples of functions

FUNCTION	CATEGORY	RETURNS	EXAMPLE
OR	Logical	TRUE if any of the arguments are true; FALSE if none of the arguments are true	=OR(A8<100) returns TRUE if the value in A8 is less than 100 and FALSE if the value in A8 is greater than or equal to 100
LOWER	Text	All letters in the cell as lowercase	=LOWER(A15) converts all the letters in A15 to lowercase
DATE	Date & Time	The number that represents the date	=DATE(2013,6,12) returns 6/12/2013 (when cell is formatted with General or Date format)
SQRT	Math & Trig	The square root of the number in the argument	=SQRT(A6) calculates the square root of the value in A6
COUNT	Statistical	The number of cells in a range that contain numbers	=COUNT(A2:A7) counts all the cells in the range that contain numbers
TBILLYIELD	Financial	The yield for a Treasury bill	=TBILLYIELD(A2,B2,C2) calculates the yield on a Treasury bill with a settlement date in A2, a maturity date in B2, and the price per $100 face value of C2

To quickly total a range of cells without manually typing the formula, you can use the Sum function. When you click the Sum button on the Home tab in the Editing group, or on the Formulas tab in the Function Library group, you usually do not need to even select a range. If you select a cell to the right or below a range of numbers, Excel automatically includes that range in the formula, as shown in **Figure EX 3–9**.

Excel selects the range to total

Formula is automatically entered

Syntax of function appears as ScreenTip

Sweet Time Tea Company
Sales Projections

Region	Jan-Feb	Mar-Apr	May-Jun	Jul-Aug	Sep-Oct	Nov-Dec
East	$35,000	$38,000	$41,000	$44,000	$47,000	$50,000
West	$36,000	$39,000	$42,000	$45,000	$48,000	$51,000
North	$40,000	$43,000	$46,000	$49,000	$52,000	$55,000
South	$30,000	$33,000	$36,000	$39,000	$42,000	$45,000
	=SUM(B5:B8)					
	SUM(**number1**, [number2], ...)					

FIGURE EX 3–9   Using the Sum function

When you click the Sum button arrow in the Function Library group on the Formulas tab, or the Sum button arrow in the Editing group on the Home tab, a menu of the most common statistical functions is displayed, as shown in **Figure EX 3–10**. The Average function returns the average of a set of values; the Count Numbers function counts the number of cells in a range that contain numbers; the Max function returns the largest value in a set of values; and the Min function returns the smallest value in a set of values. You can also use the buttons in the Function Library group on the Formulas tab to choose functions from other categories.

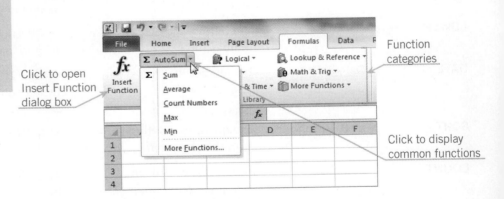

FIGURE EX 3–10   Sum menu options

Another way to choose a function is to click the Insert Function button in the Function Library group on the Formulas tab to open the Insert Function dialog box, shown in **Figure EX 3–11**.

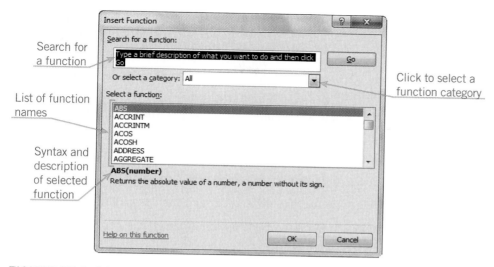

FIGURE EX 3-11   Insert Function dialog box

Once you select a function in the Insert Function dialog box or on the Ribbon, Excel opens the Function Arguments dialog box, shown in **Figure EX 3-12**. The Function Arguments dialog box displays the name of the function, each of its arguments, the current result of a function, and the current result of the entire formula. The Function Arguments dialog box makes it easy to enter arguments for functions. You can either type the arguments into this dialog box, or click the Collapse button to reduce the size of the Function Arguments dialog box temporarily, and click the cells to be used as cell references in the argument. When you finish selecting cells for the argument, click the Expand button to redisplay the dialog box at full size. If no arguments are required, the Function Arguments dialog box displays a message, and you can simply click the OK button to close the dialog box and enter the function.

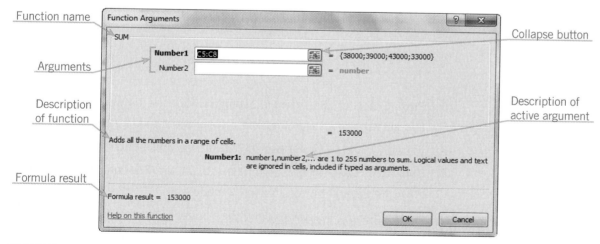

FIGURE EX 3-12   Function Arguments dialog box

Step-by-Step EX 3.3

The Trip Budget *XXX* workbook from Step-by-Step EX 3.2 should be open in the Excel program window.

1. Click cell **D12**. Click the **Formulas** tab on the Ribbon, and then click the **Sum** button in the Function Library group to enter the SUM function in cell D12. Notice that Excel automatically selects the range D8:D11.

2. Press **Enter** to enter the formula and display a value of $52 in cell D12.

3. In cell C15, type **Average difference**, and then press **Enter**.

4. Select cell **E15**. Click the **Sum** button arrow on the Formulas tab in the Function Library group to open a menu.

5. On the menu, click **Average** to enter the AVERAGE function in cell E15. Notice the blinking insertion point appears between the argument parentheses. With the blinking insertion point between the parentheses, type **D8:D11**. Your worksheet should look similar to **Figure EX 3–13**.

FIGURE EX 3–13
Insert AVERAGE function

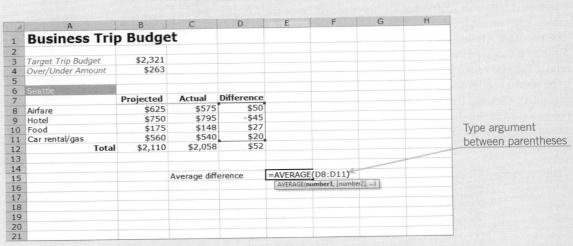

6. Press **Enter** to calculate the average difference between the projected and actual budget amounts and display the value of $13 in cell E15.

7. In cell C16, type **Under budget?**, and then press **Enter**.

8. Click cell **E16**. On the Formulas tab, in the Function Library group, click the **Logical** button to open a menu.

9. On the menu, click **OR** to open the Function Arguments dialog box.

10. In the Function Arguments dialog box, click the **Collapse** button 🖳 in the Logical1 box to collapse the dialog box.

11. Click cell **B4** to add an argument to the function in cell E16, as shown in **Figure EX 3–14**, and then click the **Expand** button 🖳 to expand the Function Arguments dialog box. Notice the cell reference *B4* is displayed in the Logical1 text box in the Function Arguments dialog box.

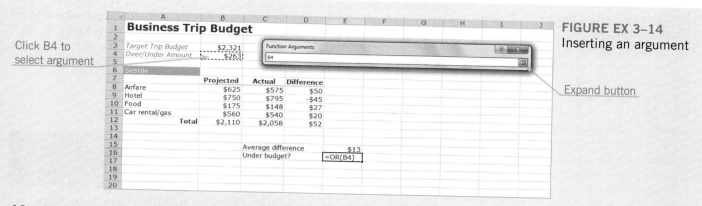

FIGURE EX 3–14
Inserting an argument

Click B4 to select argument

Expand button

12. In the Logical1 text box, after B4, type **>0**. This argument indicates to Excel that if the value in cell B4 is greater than 0, then the value TRUE should be displayed in cell E16.

13. Click the **OK** button to enter the formula and display TRUE in cell E16, since the current value in B4 is greater than zero.

14. Save the workbook and leave it open for use in the next Step-by-Step.

Reviewing and Editing Formulas

You can choose to display the formulas in a worksheet instead of the resulting values. This can be helpful if you want to print a copy of your worksheet showing all the formulas for documentation, or if you want to review the formulas for accuracy. To display the formulas, click the Show Formulas button in the Formula Auditing group on the Formulas tab. Or you can quickly switch between displaying values and formulas by using the keyboard shortcut Ctrl+`.

Sometimes you may need to check the formulas in your worksheet for accuracy. The buttons in the Formula Auditing group on the Formulas tab can help you check for errors and troubleshoot your formulas. When you click the Error Checking button, Excel checks for common errors in your worksheet and opens the Error Checking dialog box with options for resolving the error, as shown in **Figure EX 3–15**.

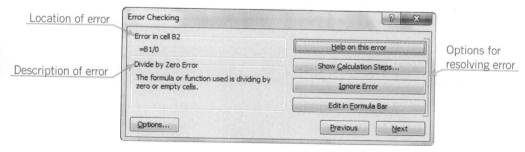

Location of error

Description of error

Options for resolving error

FIGURE EX 3–15   Error Checking dialog box

Excel indicates when a formula you have entered results in an error by displaying an *error value*. For example, when the cell containing a formula result displays *#DIV/0!*, Excel is indicating that a number in the formula is divided by zero, or the

▶ **VOCABULARY**
error value

formula references a cell that contains no value. A cell with an error also displays a triangle in the upper-left corner. When you click the cell, a button is displayed next to the cell and you can point to it to display a ScreenTip describing the type of error. If a cell contains a series of number symbols, ######, the cell is not wide enough to display the results of the formula. In this case, you can display the value by widening the column.

Table EX 3–4 lists common error values and what they indicate.

EXTRA FOR EXPERTS

A circular reference is a type of error that occurs when a formula refers to its own cell reference. In this case, a warning box is displayed to identify the problem and prompt you to correct it. If the formula containing the error is complex, you can click the OK button in this warning box to open a Help window with information on how to locate and correct the circular reference.

TABLE EX 3–4 Error values

ERROR VALUE	DESCRIPTION OF ERROR
#DIV/0!	Formula contains a number divided by zero or by a cell containing no value
#NA	A value in the formula is not available in the worksheet
#NAME?	Formula contains incorrect text; this often occurs when a function name is misspelled
#NULL!	Formula specifies an intersection of two ranges which do not intersect
#NUM!	Invalid use of a number in the formula, or when text is used in a formula or function's argument when a number is required
#REF!	Formula or function uses a cell reference that is no longer valid, which can occur if a cell or range of cells was deleted from the worksheet
#VALUE!	Incorrect data type used in the function or formula
#####	Cell is not wide enough to display formula results

If you want to change or edit a formula, you can activate the cell containing the formula, type your changes in the formula bar, and then press Enter. You can also double-click the cell containing the formula, or activate the cell and then press F2, which highlights each cell or range of cells with a different color so you can easily edit the formula in the cell.

Step-by-Step EX 3.4

The Trip Budget *XXX* workbook from Step-by-Step EX 3.3 should be open in the Excel program window.

1. Double-click cell **B3** to display the formula in the cell.
2. In the formula bar, delete 110, type **105**, and then press **Enter** to edit the formula and calculate the new results. The new value of $2,216 is displayed in cell B3. (If necessary, format cell B3 for zero decimal places.) Notice the value in cell B4 also changes (to $158).

3. If necessary, click the **Formulas** tab on the Ribbon, and then click the **Show Formulas** button in the Formula Auditing group. The formulas are displayed in the worksheet, as shown in **Figure EX 3–16**.

Formulas are displayed instead of values

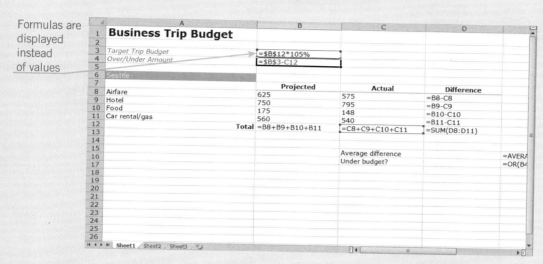

FIGURE EX 3–16
Displaying formulas

4. On the Formulas tab, in the Formula Auditing group, click the **Show Formulas** button again to display the values.

5. Delete rows 3 and 4. Notice that cell E14 now contains the error value #REF!, and a green triangle appears in the upper-left corner of the cell, because the formula in this cell references one of the cells you just deleted.

6. Click cell **E14** and point to the Error Checking button to the left of the cell to display the ScreenTip explaining the type of error, as shown in **Figure EX 3–17**.

Triangle in upper-left corner and error value in cell

Point to icon to display ScreenTip describing error

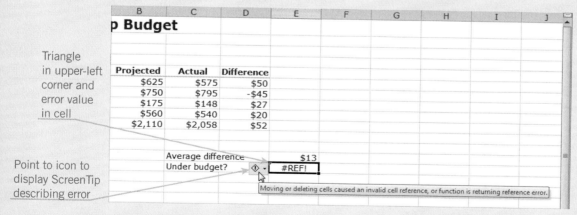

FIGURE EX 3–17
Cell with an error

7. Double-click cell **E14** to display the formula in the cell.

8. In the formula in cell E14, delete **#REF!**, and click **D10** to correct the formula, as shown in **Figure EX 3–18**.

FIGURE EX 3–18
Correcting a formula

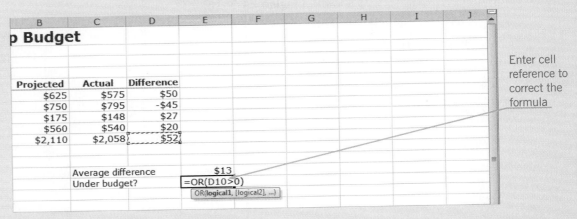

Enter cell reference to correct the formula

9. Press **Enter** to edit the formula and resolve the error. The value TRUE appears in cell E14.

10. Save and close the workbook and then close Excel.

SUMMARY

In this lesson, you learned:

- Ways to enter a formula.
- The different types of cell references.
- How to copy a formula.

- Functions are easy-to-use predefined formulas that can be used in worksheets to perform various calculations.
- Various ways to review and edit formulas.

 VOCABULARY REVIEW

Define the following terms:

absolute reference	constants	mixed reference
argument	error value	operator
arithmetic operators	fill handle	order of operations
Auto Fill	formula	relative reference
comparison operators	functions	syntax

■ REVIEW QUESTIONS

MULTIPLE CHOICE

Select the best response for the following statements.

1. All formulas must begin with _____.

   A. parentheses ( )

   B. the equal sign (=)

   C. a caret (^)

   D. the greater than sign (>)

2. Each cell reference in the formula is coded with a different _____.

   A. font

   B. point size

   C. border

   D. color

3. A forward slash (/) is an example of a(n) _____.

   A. arithmetic operator

   B. cell reference

   C. argument

   D. order of operations

4. What is the result of the following formula: =C6+D6*3, where cell C6 contains the value of 4 and cell D6 contains the value of 5?

   A. 17

   B. 19

   C. 23

   D. 27

5. Which of the following is a relative reference?

   A. B4

   B. $B4

   C. B$4

   D. $B$4

6. Which is *not* an option on the Auto Fill Options menu?

   A. Copy Cells

   B. Clear Cells

   C. Fill Formatting Only

   D. Fill Without Formatting

7. To edit a formula, double-click the cell containing the formula or select the cell and press the _____ key.

   A. Ctrl

   B. Alt

   C. F2

   D. F4

8. Excel indicates when a formula you have entered results in an error by displaying _____ in the cell.

   A. a ScreenTip

   B. an error value

   C. a fill handle

   D. nothing

9. A(n) _____ refers to the values or cell references on which a function is to be performed.

   A. operator

   B. mixed reference

   C. constant

   D. argument

10. A function must follow a set of established rules, called _____, which specifies how the function must be entered.

   A. syntax

   B. order of operations

   C. relative reference

   D. calculation

FILL IN THE BLANK

Complete the following sentences by writing the correct word or words in the blanks provided.

1. The commands for working with formulas and functions are located on the _____ tab on the Ribbon.

2. A(n) _____ is a set of instructions used to perform calculations on values in a worksheet.

3. Numbers entered directly into a formula that do not change are called _____.

4. A(n) _____ is a sign or symbol that indicates what calculation is to be performed.

5. A(n) _____ reference is a permanent reference to a cell and does not change in relation to the location of the formula.

6. _____ is a feature that you can use to automatically fill in worksheet data in any direction.

7. The _____ is a little black square in the lower-right corner of the selected cell used to copy formulas or cell formatting.

8. A(n) _____ is a built-in formula.

9. To enter cell references as an argument, click the Collapse button to reduce the size of the _____ dialog box temporarily so it is not in your way.

10. A cell with an error has a(n) _____ in the upper-left corner.

■ PROJECTS

PROJECT EX 3–1

1. Open the file **Project EX 3-1** from the folder containing the data files for this lesson.

2. Save the workbook as **Open Water** *XXX* (replace *XXX* with your initials).

3. In cell A23, enter the row heading **Total**. Apply bold formatting to cell A23.

4. Click cell **B23**. Use the Sum function to get a total for the range B5:B22.

5. Copy the formula in cell B23 to the range C23:M23.

6. In cell N4, enter the column heading **Total**.

7. Click cell **N5**. Use the Sum function to get a total for the range B5:M5.

8. Copy the formula in cell N5 to the range N6:N23.

9. Use the AutoFit feature to widen column N so the value in cell N23 is displayed instead of ######.

10. Save the workbook and leave it open for use in the next project.

PROJECT EX 3–2

The Open Water *XXX* workbook from Project EX 3-1 should be open in the Excel program window.

1. Save the workbook as **Open Water2** *XXX* (replace *XXX* with your initials).

2. In cell A25, type **Highest Sales**.

3. In cell B25, enter a function to determine the highest amount of sales in the range B5:B22. (*Hint*: Use the Max function on the Sum menu, and edit the range in the formula bar as necessary.)

4. Use the Auto Fill feature to copy the function in cell B25 to the range C25:M25.

5. In cell A26, type **Lowest Sales**.

6. In cell B26, enter a function to determine the lowest amount of sales in the range B5:B22. (*Hint*: Use the Min function on the Sum menu and edit the range in the formula bar as necessary.)

7. Use the Auto Fill feature to copy the function in cell B26 to the range C26:M26.

8. In cell A27, type **Average Sales**.

9. In cell B27, enter a function to determine the average amount of sales in the range B5:B22. (*Hint*: Use the AVERAGE function, and edit the range in the formula bar as necessary.)

10. Use the Auto Fill feature to copy the function in cell B27 to the range C27:M27.

11. Save and close the workbook.

ON YOUR OWN

Open the **Open Water2** *XXX* workbook, and create a formula that determines which employee had the highest total sales for the year. Save and close the workbook.

PROJECT EX 3–3

1. Open the file **Project EX 3-3** from the folder containing the data files for this lesson.

2. Save the workbook as **Tea Invoice XXX** (replace *XXX* with your initials).

3. In cell E10, enter **Total**.

4. In cell E11, enter a formula to multiply the value in cell C11 by the value in cell D11.

5. Use the Auto Fill feature to copy the formula in cell E11 to the range E12:E15.

6. In the range E11:E15, change the number format to **Currency** with two decimal places.

7. In cell E18, use the Sum command to get a total for the range E11:E17.

8. In cell E19, create a formula that calculates a 7% sales tax on the value in cell E18. (*Hint*: Use the formula =7%*E18.)

9. In cell E20, type **7.95**, and change the number format to **Currency** with two decimal places.

10. In cell E21, enter a formula with absolute references that totals of the values of the cells in the range E18:E20.

11. Save the workbook and leave it open for use in the next project.

WEB PROJECT

Visit Web sites of companies that sell cell phone plans. Create a worksheet containing information about at least three different options—including the price of the cell phone, cost of the cell plan per month, how many minutes are included, cost of features such as text messaging, and any additional charges. Use a formula to determine the best plan for your budget. Use functions to determine the highest price plan, the lowest price plan, and the average price of the plans.

PROJECT EX 3–4

The Tea Invoice *XXX* workbook from Project EX 3-3 should be open in the Excel program window.

1. Save the workbook as **Tea Invoice2 XXX** (replace *XXX* with your initials).

2. In cell E19, edit the formula from a 7% sales tax to 6% sales tax.

3. Display the formulas in the worksheet.

4. Check the worksheet for errors.

5. Display the values in the worksheet.

6. Only sales totals over $300 qualify for a discount. In cell B23, enter **Qualifies for discount?**.

7. In cell C23, create a formula using the OR function with E21>300 as the argument. (*Hint*: Use the Function Arguments dialog box.)

8. Save and close the workbook.

ON YOUR OWN

Open the **Tea Invoice2 XXX** workbook, and then in cell A8 create a function that inserts the current date and time. (*Hint*: Use the NOW function.) Adjust the column widths as necessary. Save and close the workbook.

 ## TEAMWORK PROJECT

With a partner, open the Insert Function dialog box. Browse through all the various categories, and familiarize yourselves with the various functions available in each one. Click a function to see the description displayed below it. Choose one that you want to know more about, and click the Help on this function link to get more information. Learn as much as possible about it. Present your findings to the class, and include a worksheet you have created that demonstrates the use of the function.

■ CRITICAL THINKING

ACTIVITY EX 3–1

In Excel, you can create a defined name that you assign to a cell or range of cells and then use the defined name as a reference in formulas. Use Excel Help to learn the different ways you can define a name for a range, how to use defined names in a formula, and how to use the Name Manager to create, edit, delete, or find names in a workbook. Open an existing workbook, and then create at least one defined name for a range of cells and use the defined name in a formula.

ACTIVITY EX 3–3

You can also use the fill handle to complete a series, which can be useful. Use Excel Help to find out how this Auto Fill feature works. Then open the file **Activity EX 3-3** from the folder containing the data files for this lesson and save it as **Auto Fill *XXX*** (replace *XXX* with your initials). Using the existing data, create a vertical Auto Fill series for each of the items listed below:

- A series of months from March through August
- A series of days from Monday through Friday
- A series of times from 2:00 through 9:00
- A series of labels from Employee1 through Employee5
- A series of years from 2013 through 2021 (*Hint*: You have to select two entries before filling the rest.)

Save and close the workbook and then close Excel.

ACTIVITY EX 3–2

Search for the video in Excel Help titled *Fix broken formulas* and watch it. List at least three ways to avoid common error messages when creating formulas.

LESSON 4

Working with Charts and Graphics

Estimated Time: 1.5 hours

■ OBJECTIVES

Upon completion of this lesson, you should be able to:

- Describe the elements of a chart.
- Create a chart.
- Modify a chart.
- Create and customize a sparkline.
- Insert and modify illustrations.

■ DATA FILES

To complete this lesson, you will need these data files:

- Step EX 4-1.xlsx
- Project EX 4-1.xlsx
- Project EX 4-4.xlsx
- Activity EX 4-1.xlsx

■ VOCABULARY

chart

chart area

chart sheet

clip art

data marker

data series

data source

drawing objects

embedded chart

gridlines

horizontal axis

legend

pictures

plot area

screenshot

SmartArt graphic

sparklines

title

vertical axis

WordArt

Introduction

Charts and graphics add visual impact to worksheets and help convey the meaning of the worksheet data. Excel includes chart tools that can help make data clearer, more visually interesting, and easier to read and understand. Charts allow users to see at a glance patterns or relationships in the worksheet data, as in whether sales are rising or falling. Another way to see data trends is to use sparklines, which are tiny charts that you can insert into a single cell. Excel also includes graphics, or illustration, tools that let you add visual interest to your workbooks. You can add and manipulate pictures, clip art, shapes, and SmartArt. In this lesson, you will learn to insert and modify charts and graphic elements. You will use buttons in the Illustrations, Charts, and Sparklines groups on the Insert tab, shown in **Figure EX 4–1**, to insert various types of illustrations, charts, and sparklines.

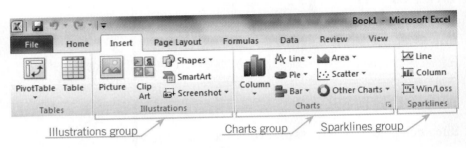

FIGURE EX 4–1   Insert tab on the Ribbon

Understanding Charts

When you need to illustrate or compare data, it is helpful to use a chart. A *chart* is a graphical representation of worksheet data. There are a variety of different chart types you can use to represent your data, depending on what you want to convey to your audience. **Table EX 4–1** shows some of the types of charts available in Excel. Buttons for the most common chart types are located in the Charts group on the Insert tab on the Ribbon.

TABLE EX 4–1   Common chart types

TYPE	BUTTON	USEFUL FOR
Column		Displaying changes in data over time; comparing data
Line		Displaying continuous data over time; showing trends
Pie		Plotting data from one row or column; showing values as a percentage of a whole
Bar		Comparing individual items
Area		Showing changes over time
Scatter		Plotting many data points; comparing data without representing time lapse

Charts are made up of different parts, or elements. Depending on the type of chart, not every element will be included. Some elements are displayed by default, and others can be displayed if needed. If you do not want a chart element displayed, you can hide it. Use **Figure EX 4–2** and **Table EX 4–2** to become familiar with some of the basic elements of a chart.

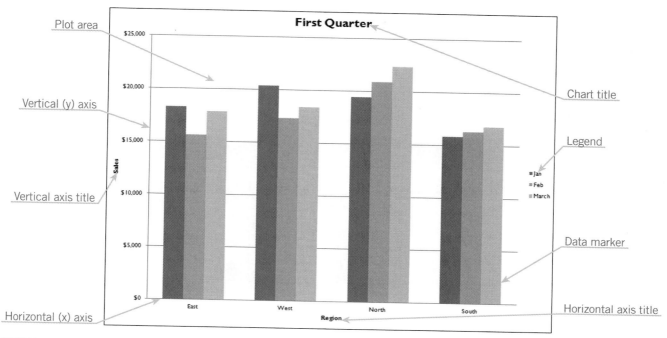

FIGURE EX 4–2   Elements of a chart

TABLE EX 4–2   Chart elements

ELEMENT	DESCRIPTION
Chart area	The complete chart and all its elements, which includes the plot area, titles, axes, legend, and any other objects
Plot area	The area in the chart where the values from the data series are displayed graphically; this includes the axes and data series
Axes (vertical and horizontal)	The lines on a chart that are used to measure and represent data series values; the *horizontal axis* (x) is used for showing categories, and the *vertical axis* (y) is used for plotting values
Data marker	A dot, a bar, or a symbol used to represent one number from the worksheet; related data markers in a chart constitute a data series
Data series	A series of related values from the worksheet graphically represented by a unique color or pattern; the data series is represented in the legend; for example, in Figure 4–2, the lime green bars representing March sales are a data series
Legend	A list that identifies the patterns or colors of the data series or categories in a chart
Title	Descriptive name that identifies a chart or axis
Gridlines	Lines extending from the vertical or horizontal axes across the plot area of a chart

Creating Charts

▶ VOCABULARY

data source

The first step in creating a chart is to select the *data source*, which is the range of cells that contains the data you want to display in the chart. You can use column and row labels as axes titles or data marker labels in the chart by including them in your range selection.

▣ **EXTRA FOR EXPERTS**

If you frequently create the same type of chart, you can set it as the default chart type to be used when creating a new chart by clicking the Set as Default Chart button in the Insert Chart dialog box.

Next, you need to decide what type of chart you want to use. When you click a button in the Charts group on the Insert tab, the subtypes available for that type of chart are displayed. You can point to a subtype to display a ScreenTip with its description and then click to insert the type of chart you want. When you click the Charts group dialog box launcher, the Insert Chart dialog box, shown in **Figure EX 4–3**, where you can also choose from categories of different types of charts, opens.

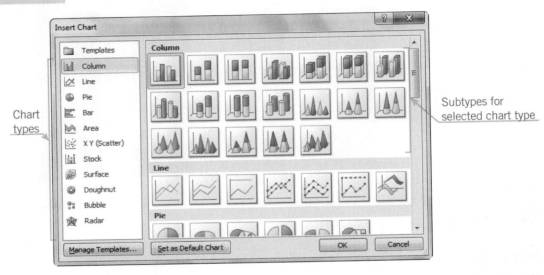

FIGURE EX 4–3   Insert Chart dialog box

After the chart is created, the Chart Tools Design, Layout, and Format contextual tabs are available on the Ribbon so that you can modify the chart. These tabs are displayed on the Ribbon only when a chart or one of its elements is selected. When you select a chart, the corresponding data on the worksheet is color coded so you can easily identify it.

When you create a chart, Excel links the chart to its related data on the worksheet. If the worksheet data is changed, Excel automatically updates the chart.

Step-by-Step EX 4.1

1. Start Excel.
2. Open the **Step EX 4-1** workbook from the folder containing the data files for this lesson.
3. Save the workbook as **First Quarter *XXX*** (replace *XXX* with your initials).
4. Select range **A4:D8**.

5. Click the **Insert** tab on the Ribbon, and in the Charts group, click the **Bar** button, and then point to the **Clustered Bar** subtype in the 2-D Bar section, as shown in **Figure EX 4-4**.

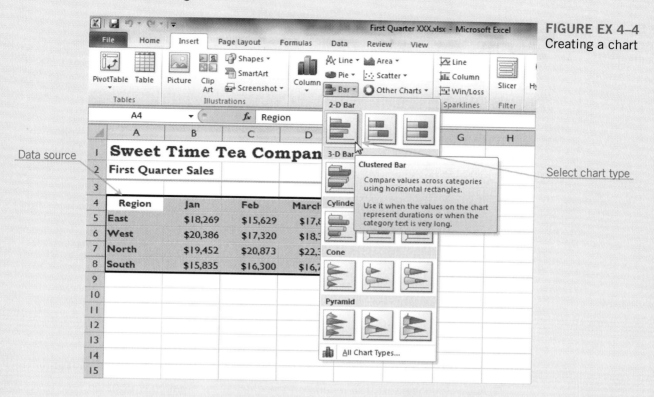

FIGURE EX 4-4
Creating a chart

6. Click the **Clustered Bar** chart type to create a chart in the worksheet. Your worksheet window should look similar to **Figure EX 4–5**. Notice the color-coded data in the worksheet and the Chart Tools contextual tabs.

Corresponding
color-coded data

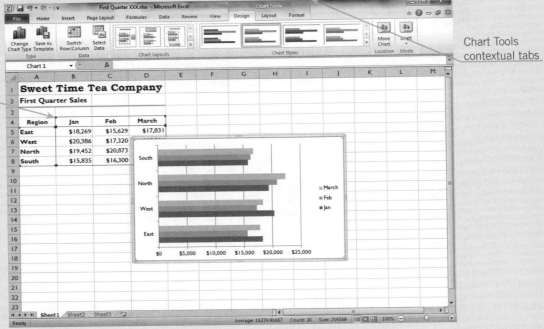

7. Edit the contents of cell **B4** to read **January**. Notice when you enter the new text, the legend on the chart is automatically updated.

8. Edit the contents of cell **C4** to read **February**.

9. Save the workbook and leave it open for use in the next Step-by-Step.

Modifying Charts

Once you have created a chart, you may want to make changes to it. You can change the design of your chart, for example, by using a different chart type to depict the worksheet data. Sometimes the design of the chart is ideal, but the chart elements need to be adjusted. You can also enhance charts by adding special formatting options such as shapes or WordArt to chart elements.

Changing Chart Design

The Chart Tools Design tab, shown in **Figure EX 4–6**, includes commands for changing the chart type, saving the formatting and layout as a template that can be used with other charts, applying a Quick Layout, changing the chart's style, moving the chart to another worksheet, and applying a draft mode.

FIGURE EX 4–6   Chart Tools Design tab

If the chart that you created does not visually represent the data the way you intended, you can easily change it to another type of chart. When you click the Change Chart Type button in the Type group on the Chart Tools Design tab, the Change Chart Type dialog box opens, allowing you to select a different chart type.

It is easy to change the look of your chart by choosing a layout that has different chart elements or by applying a style to change the formatting. Excel has a variety of predefined options to help you quickly customize your chart. The layouts and styles available depend on the type of chart you are working with. To change the overall layout of the chart, you can choose a chart layout in the Chart Layouts group on the Chart Tools Design tab or click the More button for additional layouts. You can change the overall visual look of the chart by choosing a chart style in the Chart Styles group on the Chart Tools Design tab. The colors available for the chart styles depend on which theme is applied to the workbook. To see the full gallery of chart styles, click the More button.

Moving and Sizing Charts

By default, a newly created chart is placed in the worksheet as an ***embedded chart*** that is a graphic object and is saved as part of the worksheet. This allows you to view or print the chart along with its source data. You can also choose to place the chart on a ***chart sheet***, which is a separate sheet in the workbook. To change the location of a chart, click the Move Chart button in the Location group of the Chart Tools Design tab to open the Move Chart dialog box and then select where you want the chart to be placed.

▶ VOCABULARY
embedded chart
chart sheet

To move a selected chart within the worksheet, you can click its border and drag it to a new location. You can resize the chart by selecting it and then dragging one of the dotted sizing handles, as shown in **Figure EX 4–7**. To resize a chart proportionally, press and hold Shift while dragging a corner handle. Or you can resize a chart precisely using the Shape Height and Shape Width commands in the Size group of the Chart Tools Format tab.

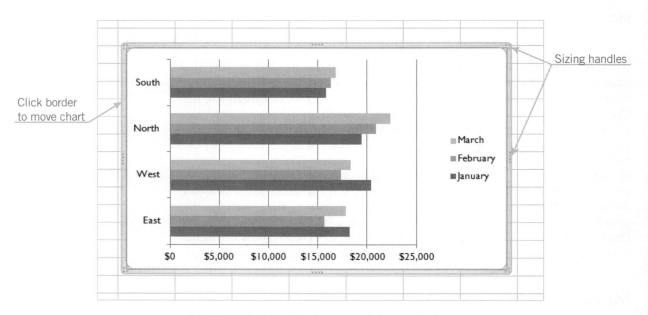

FIGURE EX 4–7   Moving or resizing a chart

Step-by-Step EX 4.2

The First Quarter *XXX* workbook from Step-by-Step EX 4.1 should be open in the Excel program window.

1. Click a blank area of the **chart area** to select the chart. You should see the sizing handles, as shown in Figure EX 4–7.

2. Click the Chart Tools Design tab, if necessary, and in the Type group, click the **Change Chart Type** button to open the Change Chart Type dialog box.

3. Click **Column** in the list of chart categories in the left pane. The Clustered Column subtype is selected by default in the right pane. Click the **OK** button to close the dialog box and change the chart type.

4. On the Chart Tools Design tab, in the Chart Layouts group, click the **More** button ⬇ to open the gallery of chart layouts.

5. Click the **Layout 8 chart layout**, as shown in **Figure EX 4–8**, to change the chart layout.

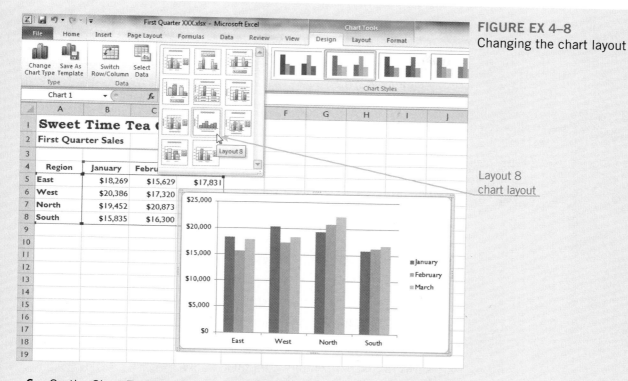

Layout 8
chart layout

6. On the Chart Tools Design tab, in the Chart Styles group, click the **More** button to open the gallery of chart styles.

7. Click the **Style 10 chart style**, as shown in **Figure EX 4–9**, to change the chart style.

Style 10
chart style

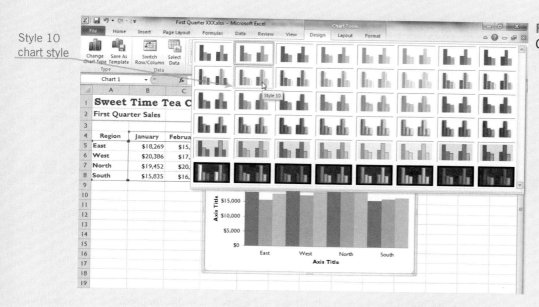

8. Click the **upper-right resizing handle** on the chart. The pointer changes to a double-headed arrow ⤢. Press and hold **Shift** while dragging the sizing handle up and to the right to approximate the chart size shown in **Figure EX 4–10**.

FIGURE EX 4–10
Resizing the chart

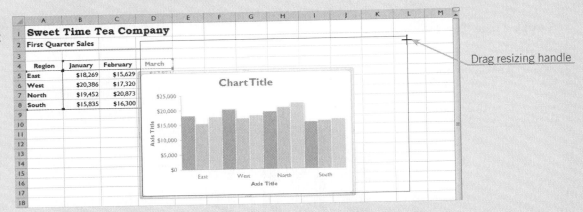

Drag resizing handle

9. Release both the mouse button and Shift to enlarge the chart.

10. On the Chart Tools Design tab, in the Location group, click the **Move Chart** button to open the Move Chart dialog box.

11. Click the **New sheet** option button, and type **1st Q Sales Chart** in the New sheet text box, as shown in **Figure EX 4–11**, and then click the **OK** button to move the chart to a new worksheet named 1st Q Sales Chart in the workbook.

FIGURE EX 4–11
Move Chart dialog box

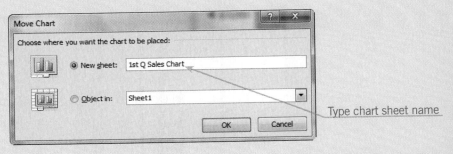

Type chart sheet name

12. Click the **Sheet1** tab to confirm that the chart has been moved from that worksheet.

13. Save the workbook and leave it open for use in the next Step-by-Step.

Modifying Chart Elements

The Chart Tools Layout tab, shown in **Figure EX 4–12**, includes buttons you can use to insert pictures, shapes, and text boxes into the chart; to display, hide, and specify the location of chart elements; to format the axes and plot area; or to change the titles and labels that appear in the chart.

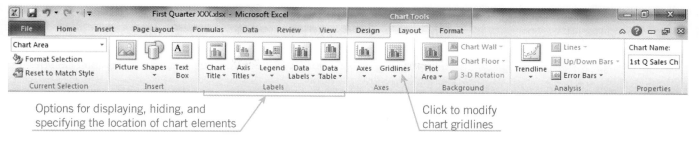

Options for displaying, hiding, and specifying the location of chart elements

Click to modify chart gridlines

FIGURE EX 4–12   Chart Tools Layout tab

To modify a specific element of a chart, you must first select it by positioning the pointer on a chart element until a ScreenTip identifying the element appears, as shown in **Figure EX 4–13**, and then clicking. A selection box surrounds the selected chart element. The currently selected chart element is displayed in the Chart Elements list box in the Current Selection group of the Chart Tools Layout tab. You can also click the Chart Elements list arrow in the Current Selection group and select a different chart element on the menu to activate it for modifying.

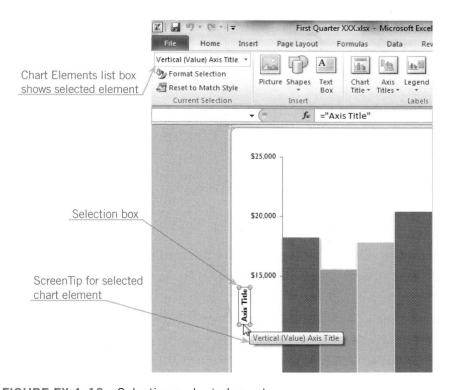

Chart Elements list box shows selected element

Selection box

ScreenTip for selected chart element

FIGURE EX 4–13   Selecting a chart element

You can change the text in a chart title or chart element label by selecting it, typing new text, and pressing the Enter key. To display, hide, or change the location of a chart element, you can click a button in the Labels, Axes, or Background groups on the Chart Tools Layout tab, and then select whether to display the element and where.

To make any chart with axes easier to read, you can choose to display gridlines. You can display horizontal or vertical gridlines across the plot area of the chart by clicking the Gridlines button in the Axes group on the Chart Tools Layout tab.

Step-by-Step EX 4.3

The First Quarter *XXX* workbook from Step-by-Step EX 4.2 should be open in the Excel program window.

1. Click the **1st Q Sales Chart** sheet tab to display the chart sheet.

2. Click the Chart Tools Layout tab, and in the Labels group, click the **Axis Titles** button to open a menu.

3. Point to **Primary Vertical Axis Title,** and then click **None**, as shown in **Figure EX 4–14**, to hide the vertical axis title.

FIGURE EX 4–14
Hiding a chart element

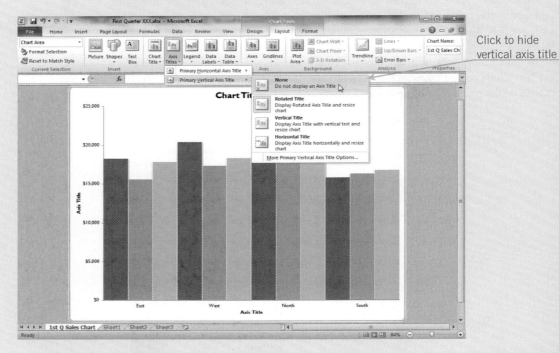

4. On the Chart Tools Layout tab, in the Labels group, click the **Legend** button, and then click **Show Legend at Top** to display the legend beneath the title.

5. On the Chart Tools Layout tab, in the Current Selection group, click the **Chart Elements** list arrow, and then click **Chart Title**, as shown in **Figure EX 4–15**, to select the chart title.

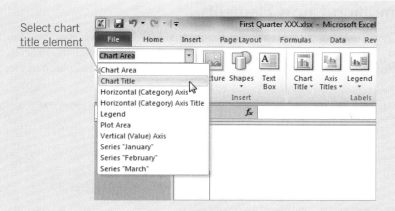

Select chart title element

6. Type **Sales,** and notice the text is displayed in the formula bar. Press **Enter** to change the chart title to *Sales*.

7. Click the horizontal axis title **Axis Title** at the bottom of the chart to select it.

8. Type **Region** and press **Enter** to change the horizontal axis title to *Region*.

9. On the Chart Tools Layout tab, in the Axes group, click the **Chart Gridlines** button, point to **Primary Vertical Gridlines**, and then click **Major Gridlines** to display vertical gridlines between the months. Your workbook window should look similar to **Figure EX 4–16**.

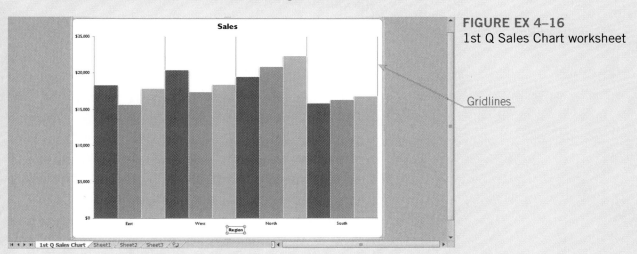

Gridlines

10. Save the workbook and leave it open for use in the next Step-by-Step.

Formatting Chart Elements

The Chart Tools Format tab, shown in **Figure EX 4–17**, includes buttons you can use to format selected elements of the chart, change the shape styles of chart elements, apply WordArt styles to chart labels, arrange the chart on the page, and size a chart precisely.

Chart Elements list box

Shape Styles options

WordArt Styles options

Use to modify chart dimensions

FIGURE EX 4–17   Chart Tools Format tab

You can also click the Format Selection button in the Current Selection group on the Chart Tools Format tab or double-click a chart element to open the Format dialog box and access additional formatting options. The options available depend on which chart element you have selected. For example, if you select Axis Options, the options for formatting an axis are displayed, as shown in **Figure EX 4–18**.

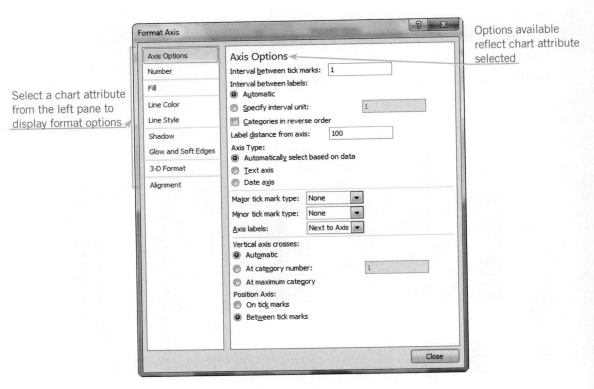

Select a chart attribute from the left pane to display format options

Options available reflect chart attribute selected

FIGURE EX 4–18   Format dialog box

▶ **VOCABULARY**
WordArt

WordArt is a drawing tool that turns words into a graphics object. You can use the WordArt feature to create interesting text effects to enhance charts. WordArt lets you fit text into a variety of shapes, use unusual alignments, and add three-dimensional effects.

Step-by-Step EX 4.4

The First Quarter *XXX* workbook from Step-by-Step EX 4.3 should be open in the Excel program window.

1. Select the chart title, **Sales**.

2. Click the **Chart Tools Format** tab, and in the Shape Styles group, click the **More** button to open a gallery of shape styles.

3. Click the **Light 1 Outline, Colored Fill – Ice Blue, Accent 2** shape style, as shown in **Figure EX 4–19**.

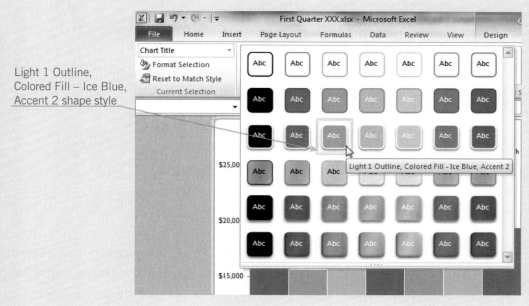

Light 1 Outline, Colored Fill – Ice Blue, Accent 2 shape style

FIGURE EX 4–19
Shape Styles gallery

4. Point to the lower edge of the leftmost column in the chart, and notice the ScreenTip, *Series "January" Point "East" Value: $18,269.* Click to select the column, and notice that the entire January data series in the chart is selected, as shown in **Figure EX 4–20**.

FIGURE EX 4–20
Shape Fill menu

Shape Fill button

Series "January"
Point "East"
Value: $18,269
data marker

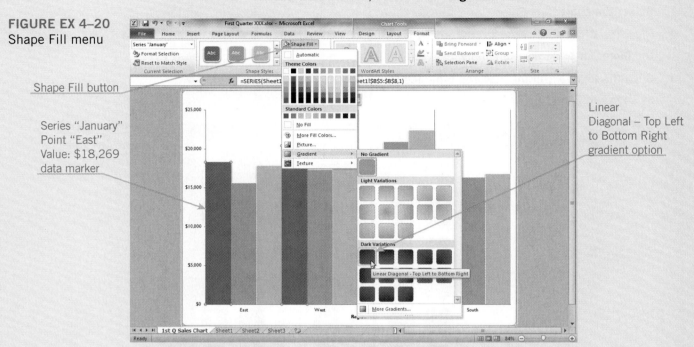

Linear
Diagonal – Top Left
to Bottom Right
gradient option

5. On the Chart Tools Format tab, in the Shape Styles group, click the **Shape Fill** button arrow, point to **Gradient**, and click the **Linear Diagonal – Top Left to Bottom Right** option in the Dark Variations section, as shown in Figure EX 4–20, to fill the data series with a gradient.

6. At the bottom of the chart, click **Region**, the Horizontal (Category) Axis Title.

7. On the Chart Tools Format tab, in the WordArt Styles group, click the **More** button to open the WordArt styles gallery, and click the **Gradient Fill – Blue-Gray, Accent 1** WordArt style, as shown in **Figure EX 4–21**, to apply a WordArt style to the axis title.

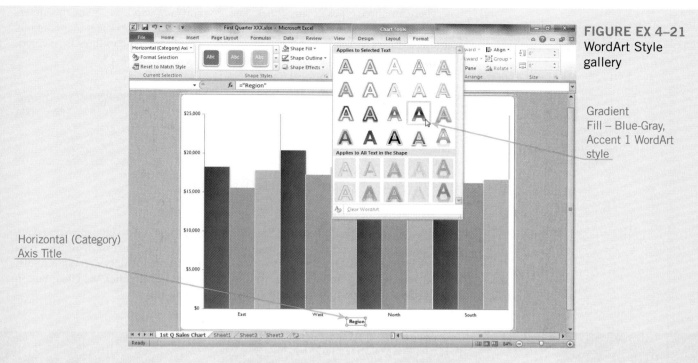

FIGURE EX 4–21
WordArt Style
gallery

Gradient
Fill – Blue-Gray,
Accent 1 WordArt
style

Horizontal (Category)
Axis Title

8.   Save the workbook and leave it open for use in the next Step-by-Step.

Creating and Customizing Sparklines

Sparklines are miniature charts that are embedded in the background of a single cell, as shown in **Figure EX 4–22**. By placing a sparkline near the data it represents, you can display a graphic representation of the data in a small space. This can help you spot patterns or display trends in the data that might otherwise be hard to see.

▶ **VOCABULARY**
sparklines

	A	B	C	D	E
1	**Sweet Time Tea Company**				
2	**First Quarter Sales**				
3					
4	**Region**	**Jan**	**Feb**	**March**	
5	**East**	$18,269	$15,629	$17,831	
6	**West**	$20,386	$17,320	$18,354	
7	**North**	$19,452	$20,873	$22,341	
8	**South**	$15,835	$16,300	$16,769	
9					
10					
11					

Underlying data

Column sparklines

FIGURE EX 4–22   Sparklines in a worksheet

There are three types of sparklines: line, column, and win/loss. When the underlying data changes, so does the sparkline. When you print a worksheet that contains sparklines, the sparklines are printed also. When one or more sparklines is selected, the Sparkline Tools Design tab opens, as shown in **Figure EX 4–23**.

FIGURE EX 4–23   Sparkline Tools Design tab

You can use the buttons on the Sparkline Tools Design tab to edit sparkline data, change the type of sparkline, or format a sparkline. You can also show or hide data markers in a line sparkline, control how a sparkline handles empty cells in a range, or clear selected sparklines. To remove a sparkline from a cell, click the Clear button in the Group group on the Sparkline Tools Design tab.

Step-by-Step EX 4.5

The First Quarter *XXX* workbook from Step-by-Step EX 4.4 should be open in the Excel program window.

1. Click the **Sheet1** sheet tab to display the sales data, and then select cell **E5**.

2. Click the **Insert** tab, and in the Sparklines group, click the **Insert Column Sparkline** button to open the Create Sparklines dialog box.

3. In the Data Range box, type **B5:D5**. The Location Range box should already have cell $E$5 chosen as the cell where you want the sparkline to be placed, as shown in **Figure EX 4–24**.

FIGURE EX 4–24
Create Sparklines dialog box

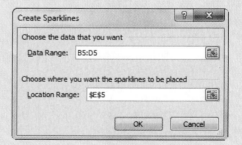

4. Click the **OK** button to insert a column chart within cell E5 and open the Sparkline Tools Design tab.

5. On the Sparkline Tools Design tab, in the Type group, click the **Convert to Line Sparkline** button to change the type of sparkline.

6. In the Show group, click the **Markers** check box to highlight each point of data in the line sparkline.

7. In the Style group, click the **More** button to open a gallery of sparkline styles, and then click the **Sparkline Style Accent 1, (no dark or light)**, as shown in **Figure EX 4–25**.

Sparkline Style Accent 1 (no dark or light)

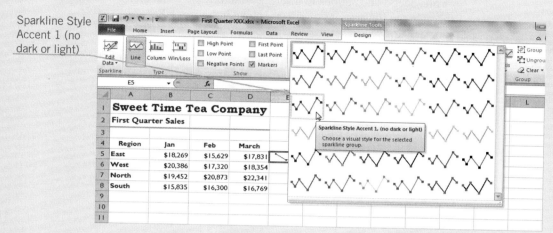

8. In the Style group, click the **Marker Color** button to open a menu, point to **High Point** to open a color palette menu, and then click the **Red standard color**, as shown in **Figure EX 4–26**.

Click to highlight the high point marker in red

9. In cell E5, click the **fill handle,** and drag it to fill cells E6:E8 with sparklines.

10. Select cell **E8**. In the Group group, click the **Clear** button to remove the sparkline from the cell.

11. Save the workbook and leave it open for use in the next Step-by-Step.

Inserting and Modifying Illustrations

Like charts, other types of illustrations such as pictures, clip art, shapes, and SmartArt are also commonly referred to as graphics, which you can use to add visual impact to worksheets. The buttons to insert illustrations are located on the Insert tab on the Ribbon in the Illustrations group, as shown in **Figure EX 4–27**.

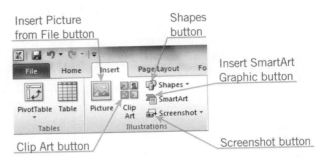

FIGURE EX 4–27   Illustrations group on the Insert tab

▶ VOCABULARY

pictures

clip art

drawing objects

SmartArt graphic

screenshot

The Insert Picture from File button in the Illustrations group can be used to insert *pictures*, which are digital photographs or images, stored on your computer or network. *Clip art* is a collection of predesigned artwork such as drawings or images that can be inserted into worksheets. Clip art can be inserted using the Clip Art button in the Illustrations group on the Insert tab. Excel also provides tools for inserting *drawing objects*, which are shapes, curves, and lines that you create in the worksheet by first selecting the type of shape you want to create, and then clicking and dragging the mouse to create that shape. The Shapes button opens a menu containing lines, basic shapes, block arrows, flowchart elements, callouts, stars, and banners.

Excel also provides a set of SmartArt graphics. A *SmartArt graphic* is a predesigned diagram made up of shapes containing text that illustrates a concept or idea. For example, an organization chart is a diagram that shows the hierarchy of employees in a company. You can insert a SmartArt graphic using the Insert SmartArt Graphic button in the Illustrations group of the Insert tab. The Choose a SmartArt Graphic dialog box that opens contains many types of graphics arranged by category.

After you insert a SmartArt graphic, the SmartArt Tools Design and Format contextual tabs are displayed on the Ribbon with buttons for modifying the SmartArt graphic. SmartArt graphics are inserted with placeholder text that you can replace with your own text by clicking the [Text] placeholder. When you insert a SmartArt graphic, the Text Pane also opens to help simplify the process of entering text. You can click a [Text] placeholder beside a bullet in the Text Pane to enter text in a shape. The Text Pane can be hidden or opened by clicking the Text Pane button on the SmartArt Tools Design tab in the Create Graphic group.

You can include pictures of your screen in a worksheet using the Screenshot button in the Illustrations group on the Insert tab. A *screenshot* is a picture of a computer screen or part of a screen, such as a button. The Screenshot button takes a picture of a nonminimized screen on your computer and inserts it into your worksheet. The Screen Clipping command on the Screenshot menu lets you use the mouse to cut out and insert any part of a screenshot into your document. After you insert a screenshot, you can modify it using the contextual Picture Tools Format tab.

Step-by-Step EX 4.6

The First Quarter *XXX* workbook from Step-by-Step EX 4.5 should be open in the Excel program window.

1. Display the **Sheet1** tab, if necessary.

2. Click the **Insert** tab, and in the Illustrations group, click the **Insert SmartArt Graphic** button to open the Choose a SmartArt Graphic dialog box.

3. In the category list in the left pane, click **Hierarchy,** and then click the **Organization Chart** SmartArt graphic in the center pane, as shown in **Figure EX 4–28**.

Organization Chart SmartArt graphic

Hierarchy category

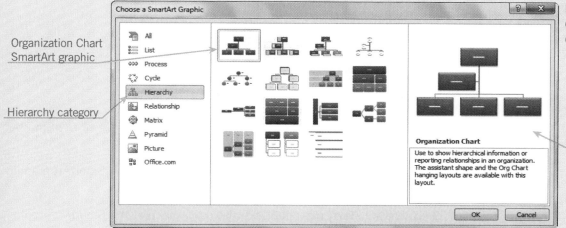

FIGURE EX 4–28
Choose a SmartArt Graphic dialog box

Example and description of the selected SmartArt graphic

4. Click the **OK** button to close the dialog box and insert the SmartArt graphic in the worksheet. The Text Pane opens next to the SmartArt graphic organization chart. (*Note:* If the Text Pane does not open, click the Text Pane button on the SmartArt Tools Design tab in the Create Graphic group to open it.)

5. Click the **[Text]** placeholder in the rectangle at the top of the SmartArt graphic, and type **Regional Sales Director**. Notice that the placeholder text is replaced as you type, and the first bullet in the Text pane now reads *Regional Sales Director*.

6. Double-click to select the second level shape on the SmartArt graphic, as shown in **Figure EX 4–29**, and press **Delete** to remove the box.

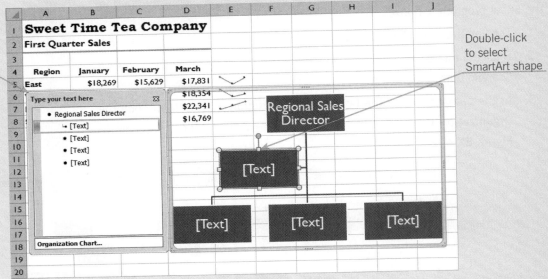

FIGURE EX 4–29
Selecting a
SmartArt shape

7. Click the **[Text]** placeholder in the left rectangle shape of the SmartArt graphic, and type **Karen Friske, East**.

8. Click the **[Text]** placeholder in the center shape of the SmartArt graphic, and type **Marin Bezio, West**.

9. Click the **[Text]** placeholder in the right shape of the SmartArt graphic, and type **Tai Yee, North**.

10. With the insertion point still in the **Tai Yee, North** shape, click the **SmartArt Tools Design** tab on the Ribbon, if necessary. In the Create Graphic group, click the **Add Shape** button arrow, and then click **Add Shape After**, as shown in **Figure EX 4–30**, to insert a new shape.

Click to add
another shape to
the second level

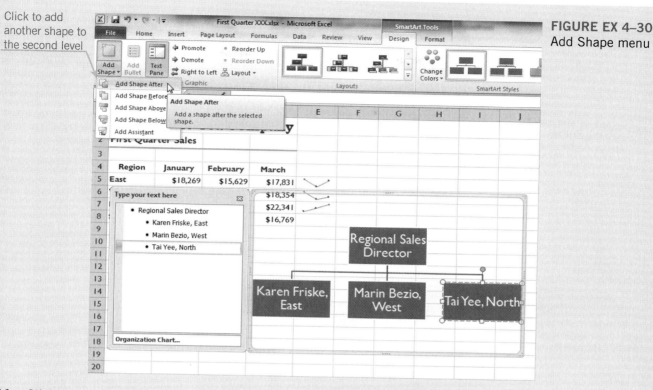

11. Click the last bullet in the Text Pane, and type **Darin Lockert, South**.

Notice that the text is also inserted on the new shape you created.

12. On the SmartArt Tools Design tab, in the SmartArt Styles group, click the **More** button to open a gallery of SmartArt styles, and then click the **Brick Scene** SmartArt style, as shown in **Figure EX 4–31**, to change the style of the SmartArt graphic.

FIGURE EX 4–31
SmartArt Styles gallery

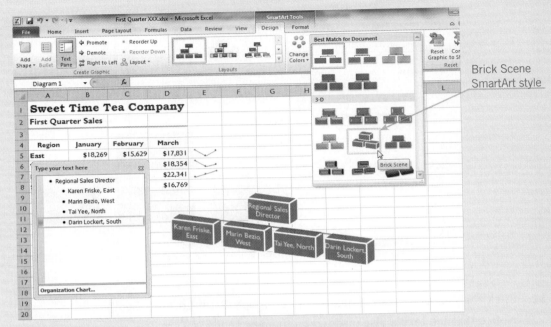

13. Click a blank cell in the workbook to deselect the SmartArt graphic.

14. Save the workbook, close it, and exit Excel.

SUMMARY

In this lesson, you learned:

- About the elements of a chart.
- How to create a chart.
- Ways to modify a chart.

- To create and customize sparklines.
- How to insert and modify illustrations.

■ VOCABULARY REVIEW

Define the following terms:

chart
chart area
chart sheet
clip art
data marker
data series
data source

drawing objects
embedded chart
gridlines
horizontal axis
legend
pictures
plot area

screenshot
SmartArt graphic
sparklines
title
vertical axis
WordArt

■ REVIEW QUESTIONS

MULTIPLE CHOICE

Select the best response for the following statements.

1. A(n) _____ is a dot, a bar, or a symbol used to represent one number from the worksheet.

   A. axis
   B. data marker

   C. data series
   D. legend

2. A _____ chart shows values as a percentage of a whole.

   A. column
   B. line

   C. pie
   D. bar

3. The _____ is the range of cells that contains the data for the chart.

   A. plot area
   B. chart area

   C. data source
   D. data series

4. The Chart Tools _____ tab contains buttons used to change the chart type, chart layout, chart style, or move the chart.

   A. Design
   B. Layout

   C. Format
   D. Data

5. To work with a specific element of a chart, you must first _____.

   A. display the Chart Tools Design tab
   B. move the chart element to a separate chart sheet

   C. resize the chart proportionally
   D. select the chart element

6. When you click the Charts group dialog box launcher on the Insert tab, the _____ dialog box opens.

   A. Insert Chart
   B. Format Chart

   C. Chart Tools
   D. Change Chart Type

7. When a chart is selected, the corresponding data on a worksheet is _____.

   A. hidden
   B. displayed on a separate sheet

   C. color coded
   D. a drawing object

8. Buttons to add pictures, clip art, shapes, and SmartArt to your worksheet are located on the _____ tab on the Ribbon.

   A. Home
   B. Insert

   C. Design
   D. Format

9. _____ is a picture of a computer screen or part of a screen, such as a button.

   A. Clip art   C. A screenshot

   B. A shape   D. SmartArt

10. Which type of illustration would you use to quickly insert an organization chart in your worksheet?

   A. Picture   C. Shapes

   B. Clip art   D. SmartArt

FILL IN THE BLANK

Complete the following sentences by writing the correct word or words in the blanks provided.

1. A(n) _____ is a graphical representation of worksheet data.

2. The _____ identifies the colors or patterns assigned to the various data series in the plot area of a chart.

3. Buttons for the most common chart types are located in the Charts group on the _____ tab.

4. _____ are miniature charts that are embedded in the background of a single cell.

5. By default, a newly created chart is placed in the worksheet as a(n) _____ chart that is a graphic object and is saved as part of the worksheet.

6. To resize a chart proportionally, hold the _____ key while dragging a corner handle.

7. _____ is a drawing tool that turns words into a graphics object.

8. You can use the _____ button to change the location of a chart.

9. Clicking the _____ button in the Illustrations group on the Insert tab opens a menu containing lines, basic shapes, block arrows, flowchart elements, callouts, and stars and banners.

10. A(n) _____ is a predesigned diagram of shapes containing text that illustrates a concept or idea.

■ PROJECTS

PROJECT EX 4–1

1. Open the **Project EX 4-1** workbook from the folder containing the data files for this lesson.

2. Save the workbook as **Sales Projections XXX** (replace *XXX* with your initials).

3. Select the range **A4:G8**, and use it to create a **2-D Clustered Bar** chart.

4. Use the sizing handles to enlarge the chart to approximately twice its current size.

5. In cell B7, change the value to **$42,000**.

6. Select the chart, and change the chart type to **Clustered Column**.

7. Change the chart layout to **Layout 9**.

8. Change the chart style to **Style 7**.

9. Move the chart to a separate chart sheet in the workbook, and name the chart sheet **Sales Projections Chart**.

10. Save the workbook and leave it open for use in the next project.

PROJECT EX 4–2

The Sales Projections *XXX* workbook from Project EX 4-1 should be open in the Excel program window.

1. Save the workbook as **Sales Projections2 *XXX*** (replace *XXX* with your initials).

2. In the Sales Projections Chart sheet, hide the vertical (value) axis title.

3. Change the horizontal (category) axis title to read **Months**.

4. Set the legend to show on the left side of the chart.

5. Change the chart title to **Yearly Sales Projections**.

6. Change the gridlines to display horizontal gridlines for major and minor units.

7. Use the Chart Elements list in the Current Selection group on the Chart Tools Format tab to select the chart area, and then change the shape style to **Colored Fill – Brown, Accent 5** (sixth option on the second row of the gallery).

8. Change the shape fill of the East data series to **Brown, Accent 6**.

9. Change the format of the chart title to the WordArt style **Gradient Fill – Brown, Accent 6, Inner Shadow** (second option on the fourth row of the gallery).

10. Save and close the workbook.

ON YOUR OWN

Open the **Sales Projections2 *XXX*** workbook, and change the shape fill, shape outline, and shape effects of the East, West, North, and South data series to achieve a consistent look of your choice. Save and close the workbook.

PROJECT EX 4–3

1. Open a new blank workbook.

2. Save the workbook as **Tea Types *XXX*** (replace *XXX* with your initials).

3. Insert a **Hierarchy List** SmartArt graphic.

4. Replace the first [Text] bullet placeholder on the left with **Black**.

5. Replace the second [Text] bullet placeholder on the left with **Irish Breakfast**.

6. Replace the third [Text] bullet placeholder on the left with **Earl Grey**.

7. Add another shape after Earl Grey with **Darjeeling** as the text.

8. Continue adding to the SmartArt graphic until it looks like **Figure EX 4–32**.

9. Change the SmartArt style to **Subtle Effect**.

10. Save and close the workbook.

ON YOUR OWN

Open the **Tea Types *XXX*** workbook, and add a Green category to the SmartArt graphic, with Gunpowder, Citron, and Sencha as the tea types. Save and close the workbook.

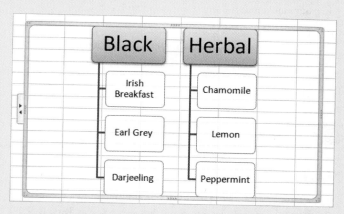

FIGURE EX 4–32   Tea Types *XXX* workbook

PROJECT EX 4–4

1. Open the **Project EX 4-4** workbook from the folder containing the data files for this lesson.

2. Save the workbook as **Blood Pressure XXX** (replace *XXX* with your initials).

3. In cell D18, create a column sparkline using the data in cells D4:D17.

4. Change the sparkline to a line sparkline.

5. Change the sparkline style to **Sparkline Style Colorful #4**.

6. Select the range **B3:D17**, and use it to create a 2-D **Line** chart.

7. Change the chart layout to **Layout 4**.

8. Add a horizontal axis title that reads **Day**.

9. Change the legend to show at the top.

10. Add horizontal gridlines for major units.

11. Change the shape style of the chart area to **Subtle Effect – Orange, Accent 1** (second option on the fourth row of the gallery).

12. Move the chart on the worksheet so the underlying data is visible.

13. Save and close the workbook, and exit Excel.

ON YOUR OWN

Open the **Blood Pressure XXX** workbook. Move the chart to a separate chart sheet, and change the layout, format, and style to best visually represent the data. Compare your chart with a classmate's. Save and close the workbook.

 WEB PROJECT

In the Clip Art task pane, click the Find more at Office.com link. Explore the new images, and browse through the images categories. Find at least one clip art illustration that you might want to use in a workbook and download it.

TEAMWORK PROJECT

With a partner, learn more about the other types of Excel charts that are not listed in Table EX 4–1 from the lesson. What are bubble charts used for? How can you present data in a combination chart? What kind of data can be plotted in a doughnut chart? What types of values do radar charts compare? When is a surface chart useful? Choose one of these types and create a chart. Make a brief presentation to the class about your chart type.

■ CRITICAL THINKING

ACTIVITY EX 4–1

Launch Excel and open **Activity EX 4-1** from the folder containing the data files for this lesson. Save the workbook as **Kayak Sales XXX** (replace *XXX* with your initials). Use the data in cells A4:L5 to create a 2-D Line chart. Use the skills you have learned in this lesson to make the chart look as similar as possible to the one shown in **Figure EX 4–33**. Save and close the workbook.

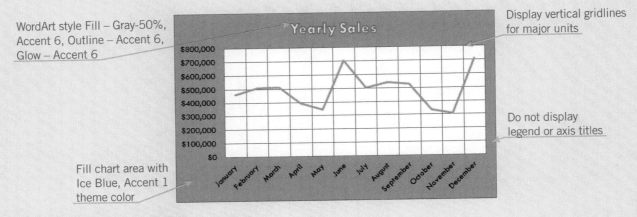

FIGURE EX 4–33   Kayak Sales *XXX* workbook

ACTIVITY EX 4–2

Search for the video in Excel Help titled *Insert sparklines to show data trends,* and watch it. Create a worksheet that shows some kind of data trend (i.e. your grades in this class or the temperature in your city this week) and create sparklines to represent the data. Save the workbook as **Sparklines** *XXX* (replace *XXX* with your initials).

ACTIVITY EX 4–3

Create a worksheet that has a column for your daily activities and a column for the number of hours you spend doing each activity. Create a chart that best represents the data, and format it attractively. Insert at least one illustration. Save the workbook as **Time Chart** *XXX* (replace *XXX* with your initials).

UNIT III REVIEW

Excel

■ REVIEW QUESTIONS

MULTIPLE CHOICE

Select the best response for the following statements.

1. _____ are displayed horizontally and are numbered consecutively down the left side of the worksheet.

   A. Columns   C. Cells

   B. Rows   D. Sheets

2. As you enter data in a cell, the data is displayed in the active cell and in the _____.

   A. Name box   C. formula bar

   B. sheet tab   D. status bar

3. Which workbook view displays the worksheet as it will print so you can make any necessary changes?

   A. Normal   C. Page Break Preview

   B. Page Layout   D. Full Screen

4. Once you have applied formatting to cells, you can use the _____ button to add the same formatting to other cells.

   A. Format Painter   C. Clipboard

   B. Format Cells   D. Conditional Formatting

5. Which of the following is not affected when you apply a theme to a workbook?

   A. Colors   C. Effects

   B. Fonts   D. Number formats

6. A(n) _____ is a set of instructions used to perform calculations on values in a worksheet.

   A. operator   C. formula

   B. constant   D. syntax

7. A(n) _____ reference means the reference to a cell changes in relation to the location of the formula.

   A. absolute   C. mixed

   B. relative   D. cell

8. When you click the _____ button arrow in the Function Library group on the Formulas tab of the Ribbon, a menu of the most common statistical functions opens.

   A. AutoSum   C. Insert Function

   B. Auto Fill   D. Function Arguments

9. A _____ chart displays continuous data over time and shows trends.

   A. column   C. pie

   B. line   D. bar

10. Which graphic element would you use to insert a predesigned diagram made up of shapes containing text that illustrates a concept or idea?

   A. Picture   C. Sparklines

   B. Clip Art   D. SmartArt

FILL IN THE BLANK

Complete the following sentences by writing the correct word or words in the blanks provided.

1. A(n) _____ is the grid with columns and rows where you enter and summarize data.

2. A group of selected cells is called a(n) _____.

3. The _____ tab includes the Font group, which contains options for selecting fonts, font size, font style, underline, and font color.

4. To align text over several columns or rows, you can use the _____ button to join selected cells together into one larger cell.

5. You can adjust the size of all the columns and rows in the worksheet by clicking the _____ button before making changes.

6. An Excel formula must begin with a(n) _____.

7. B$10 is an example of a(n) _____ reference.

8. The range of cells that contains the data for the chart is called the _____.

9. The Chart Tools _____ tab contains buttons you can use to insert pictures, shapes, and text boxes into the chart; to display, hide, and specify the location of chart elements; to format the axes and background; to add lines or bars for analysis; or to change the chart name.

10. You can change the location of a chart by placing it on a(n) _____, which is a separate sheet in the workbook.

■ PROJECTS

PROJECT EX 1

1. Start Excel.

2. Open the file **Project EX 1** from the folder containing the data files for this review, and save it as **Baseball XXX** (replace *XXX* with your initials).

3. Insert a row after row 1.

4. In cell A2, enter the text **Baseball Team Season Stats**.

5. Apply the table style **Table Style Medium 1** to the range A4:J16. (*Note*: Your table has headers.)

6. Convert the table to a normal range so that the filter arrows are not displayed at the top of each column.

7. Clear the contents in cells J5:J16.

8. Replace the text in cell J4 with **Batting Average**, and widen column J to fully display the text.

9. In cell J5, create a formula that divides the number of hits (cell E5) by the number of at bats (D5).

10. Copy the formula in J5 to cells J6:J16, and use the Auto Fill Options button to fill without formatting.

11. Apply a **Number** format displaying three decimal places to cells J5:J16.

12. Save the workbook, and leave it open for use in the next project.

PROJECT EX 2

The Baseball *XXX* workbook from Project EX 1 should be open in the Excel program window.

1. Save the workbook as **Baseball2 *XXX*** (replace *XXX* with your initials).

2. Change the theme to **Apex**.

3. Name the worksheet **Season Stats**.

4. Delete the Sheet2 and Sheet3 worksheets from the workbook.

5. In cell A1, change the cell style to **Title**.

6. In cell A2, change the cell style to **Heading 4**.

7. In cells J5:J16, use the Highlight Cells Rules conditional formatting to format cells that are greater than .300 with **Light Red Fill with Dark Red Text.**

8. Change the width of column J to **9**.

9. Wrap the text in cell J4.

10. Center the text in cells B4:J4.

11. Press **Ctrl+Home** to make cell A1 the active cell.

12. Search for the word *Mu* and replace it with **Mew**.

13. Save and close the workbook.

ON YOUR OWN

Open the **Baseball2 *XXX*** workbook and use functions to determine how many players are on the team, which player played the fewest games, which player had the most hits, the total number of home runs, and the team batting average. Save and close the workbook.

ON YOUR OWN

Open the **Baseball2 *XXX*** workbook and insert a SmartArt graphic below the data using the Equation option in the Relationship category to illustrate the concept that "Effort + Teamwork = Success". Use the SmartArt Tools Design and Format tabs to format the graphic attractively. Save and close the workbook.

PROJECT EX 3

1. Open the file **Project EX 3** from the folder containing the data files for this review, and save it as **Annual Sales *XXX*** (replace *XXX* with your initials).

2. In cell A1, change the font to **Cambria**, **18** point.

3. In cell A2, change the font to **Cambria**, **14** point.

4. Merge and center the contents of the range A1:E1.

5. Merge and center the contents of the range A2:E2.

6. Apply a **Bottom Double Border** to the range A2:E2.

7. In cell A4, apply **bold** formatting to the text, and change the font color to **Dark Blue, Text 2**.

8. Copy the formatting from cell A4 to cells B4:E4.

9. Change the height of row 4 to **20.25 (27 pixels)**.

10. Middle align and center the text in cells A4:E4.

11. Apply the **Currency** format displaying zero decimals to the contents of cells B5:E22.

12. Save the workbook, and leave it open for use in the next project.

PROJECT EX 4

The Annual Sales *XXX* workbook from Project EX 3 should be open in the Excel program window.

1. Save the workbook as **Annual Sales2 XXX** (replace *XXX* with your initials).

2. In cell F5, create a column sparkline that uses the data range B5:E5.

3. Change the sparkline in cell F5 to a line sparkline, and apply the **Style 14** sparkline style.

4. Highlight the highest point of data in the sparkline with the **Black, Text 1** marker color.

5. Copy the sparkline from cell F5 to cells F6:F22. Notice the data pattern that the sparklines illustrate.

6. Copy the contents and formatting in cell A4 to cell A23.

7. Replace the text in A23 with the text **Total**.

8. In cell B23, find the sum of the values in cells B5:B22.

9. Copy the formula from cell B23 to cells C23:E23.

10. Use the data in the range B23:E23 to create a **Clustered Column** chart.

11. Change the chart type to a **Pie** chart.

12. Change the chart layout to **Layout 4** and the chart style to **Style 11**.

13. Move the chart so that all of the worksheet data is visible. Resize the chart if necessary.

14. Save and close the workbook.

ON YOUR OWN

Open the **Annual Sales2 XXX** workbook. Move the chart to a separate sheet in the workbook titled **Sales Chart**. Add a chart title, legend, and data labels. Apply shape styles and WordArt styles to enhance the chart. Save and close the workbook.

PROJECT EX 5

1. Create a new, blank workbook.

2. Save the workbook as **Mileage Log XXX** (replace *XXX* with your initials).

3. Enter the text in the worksheet, as shown in **Figure EX 1**. Widen columns as necessary.

	A	B	C	D	E	F	G	H	I
1	Mileage Log								
2									
3	Employee Name		Rate Per Mile						
4	Vehicle Description		Total Mileage						
5	Authorized By		Total Reimbursement						
6									
7	Date	Starting Location	Destination	Trip Purpose	Odometer Start	Odometer End	Mileage	Reimbursement	
8									
9									
10									

FIGURE EX 1   Mileage Log *XXX* worksheet

4. In cell A8, type today's date, and format it as a **Short Date**.

5. In cell B8, enter the text **Preston Oaks**.

6. In cell C8, enter the text **Buckley Center**.

7. In cell D8, enter the text **Client meeting**.

8. In cell E8, enter the value **23,745**.

9. In cell F8, enter the value **23,792**.

10. In cell D3, enter the value **.79**, and apply the **Currency** format displaying two decimals.

11. In cell G8, create a formula that subtracts the odometer start value (cell E8) from the odometer end value (cell F8).

12. In cell H8, create a formula that multiplies the mileage (cell G8) by the rate per mile (cell D3). Use an absolute reference for the value in D3.

13. If necessary, copy the formatting from cell D3 to cell H8. Adjust the column widths as necessary.

14. Save and close the workbook.

ON YOUR OWN

Open the **Mileage Log *XXX*** workbook, and enter your name in cell B3 and a car description in cell B4. Make at least three more entries. Create a formula in cell D4 to get the total mileage, and create a formula in cell D5 to get the total reimbursement. Save and close the workbook.

ON YOUR OWN

Open the **Mileage Log *XXX*** workbook, and use the skills that you have learned in this unit to format the worksheet attractively. Preview and then print the worksheet. Save and close the workbook.

PROJECT EX 6

1. Open the file **Project EX 6** from the folder containing the data files for this review, and save it as **Salary List *XXX*** (replace *XXX* with your initials).

2. Copy the contents of cell G5 to cells G6:G25.

3. In cell H5, correct the formula to add the salary (cell F5) to the benefits (cell G5).

4. Copy the formula in cell H5 to cells H6:H25.

5. Insert a header that displays the current date in the center header text box.

6. Insert a footer that displays the filename in the left footer text box.

7. View the worksheet in Full Screen view.

8. Return to Page Layout view and then switch to Normal view.

9. Change the page layout to landscape orientation.

10. Replace all occurrences of *Resources* with **Services**.

11. Spell check the worksheet and change *Employe* to **Employee** and change *Deprtment* to **Department**. Ignore all other suggested spelling changes.

12. Freeze panes before column D and above row 5.

13. Switch to Page Break Preview and then back to Normal view.

14. Save and close the workbook.

ON YOUR OWN

Open the **Salary List *XXX*** workbook, and apply a theme. Use functions to find the lowest, highest, and average total salary. Save and close the workbook.

WEB PROJECT

Search Excel Help for the demo titled *Create charts in Excel 2010*, and watch it. Visit a weather Web site, and create a new worksheet that records the high and low temperatures in your city for the past week. Create a chart to visually represent your data, using the chart type that best conveys the information to your audience.

TEAMWORK PROJECT

With a partner, choose a tab on the Ribbon, and review each command that you learned about and how it is used. Choose at least one command on that tab that you did not learn about in this unit, and use Excel Help to research its purpose. Present your findings to the class, and demonstrate how that command would be used in a workbook.

■ CRITICAL THINKING

ACTIVITY EX 1

Create a personal budget worksheet that summarizes your monthly income and expenses. Spend time planning before you begin by making a list of the type of information you will need to include, any formulas you will use for calculations, and make a sketch of how you will structure the rows and columns in the worksheet. Include columns for projected and actual amounts, as well as one for the difference between them. Use at least three formulas or functions in the worksheet. Format the worksheet attractively.

ACTIVITY EX 2

You work for a local organization that helps provide relief for victims of disaster. Use Excel to create a charitable receipt that can be given to those who donate money or other items to help prevent, prepare for, and respond to emergencies in your area. Insert at least one illustration on the worksheet. Preview and print the receipt.

■ PORTFOLIO CHECKLIST

_____	Lesson 1	LostArt2 *XXX*.xlsx
_____	Lesson 1	Test Grades *XXX*.xlsx
_____	Lesson 2	Team Stats *XXX*.xlsx
_____	Lesson 2	Time Sheet2 *XXX*.xlsx
_____	Lesson 3	Open Water2 *XXX*.xlsx
_____	Lesson 3	Trip Budget *XXX*.xlsx
_____	Lesson 4	First Quarter *XXX*.xlsx
_____	Lesson 4	Sales Projections2 *XXX*.xlsx
_____	Unit Review	Annual Sales2 *XXX*.xlsx
_____	Unit Review	Baseball2 *XXX*.xlsx

UNIT IV

MICROSOFT POWERPOINT

LESSON 1   **1 HR.**
Understanding PowerPoint Fundamentals

LESSON 2   **1.5 HRS.**
Formatting and Modifying Presentations

LESSON 3   **2.5 HRS.**
Enhancing Presentations

LESSON 1

Understanding PowerPoint Fundamentals

■ OBJECTIVES

Upon completion of this lesson, you should be able to:

- Examine the PowerPoint program window.
- Start PowerPoint and open an existing presentation.
- Understand slides.
- Navigate a PowerPoint presentation.
- View a presentation.
- Modify slides.
- Save a presentation.
- Preview and print a presentation.
- Close a presentation.

■ DATA FILES

To complete this lesson, you will need these data files:

Step PPT 1-1.pptx

Project PPT 1-1.pptx

Project PPT 1-2.pptx

Project PPT 1-4.pptx

■ VOCABULARY

bullet

collated

drag-and-drop

I-beam

insertion point

layout

masters

Notes pane

Outline tab

placeholders

presentation

presentation software

slide

Slide pane

Slides tab

thumbnails

Introduction

Microsoft PowerPoint 2010 is the presentation program included in the Microsoft Office 2010 suite of software. **Presentation software** lets you prepare a series of slides that are referred to collectively as a presentation. Examples of presentations include employee orientations, sales projections, and business plans.

As in other Office programs, the various tools in PowerPoint are organized on the Ribbon tabs. PowerPoint offers a variety of preformatted designs and backgrounds for slides and graphics that can help you create professional presentations.

Examining the PowerPoint Program Window

A PowerPoint file is called a presentation. A **presentation** is a collection of slides that communicates ideas, facts, suggestions, or other information to an audience. Presentations can be viewed on a computer screen, shown to an audience using projection equipment, distributed as printouts, or published to the Internet for viewing in a browser.

When you start PowerPoint, a blank presentation opens, as shown in **Figure PPT 1–1**. Use this figure to become familiar with the parts of the PowerPoint program window.

VOCABULARY
presentation software

presentation

Slides tab

thumbnails

Outline tab

Slide pane

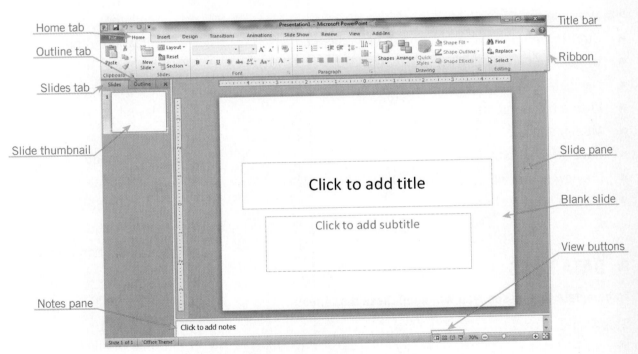

FIGURE PPT 1–1   PowerPoint program window

The default filename of a new presentation is *Presentation1,* and it is displayed at the top of the screen in the title bar. The screen in Normal view is divided into three sections. The Slides tab and Outline tab share the left pane. The **Slides tab** displays **thumbnails**, or miniature pictures, of the slides in the presentation. The **Outline tab** displays the text of each slide in outline form. The **Slide pane** displays the slide currently selected in the Slides tab or Outline tab. You can insert and edit text and graphics in the Slide pane. The **Notes pane** provides an area for you to type speaker notes for the presentation. The four main view buttons—Normal, Slide Sorter, Reading View, and Slide Show—are located on the status bar.

▶ **VOCABULARY**
Notes pane

Starting PowerPoint and Opening an Existing Presentation

To begin using PowerPoint, you first need to open it. You can do this by clicking the Start button on the Windows taskbar, and then clicking the program name in the Microsoft Office program folder on the All Programs menu, or by double-clicking a PowerPoint program icon on the desktop. Once PowerPoint is started, you can begin using it to create a new presentation or to open an existing presentation.

To open an existing presentation, you can search for and then open PowerPoint files using the Open dialog box, as shown in **Figure PPT 1–2**. PowerPoint provides three methods for displaying the Open dialog box. The most common method is to use the Open command found on the File tab in Backstage view. You can also add the Open command as a button to your Quick Access Toolbar or use the Ctrl+O keyboard shortcut.

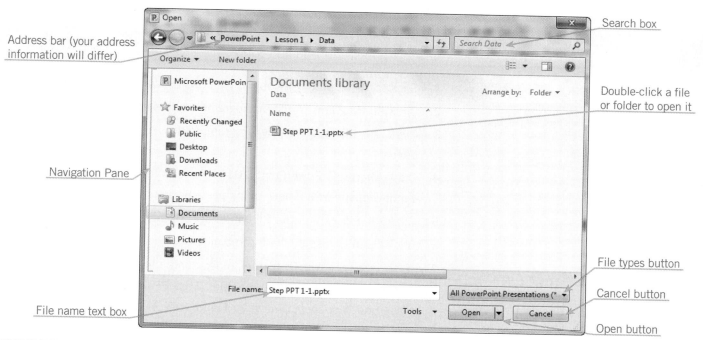

FIGURE PPT 1–2 Open dialog box

You can use the Open dialog box to find and open existing files on your hard drive, CD, or other removable media; on a network drive to which you are connected; on your organization's intranet; or on the Internet.

The following are parts of the Open dialog box:

- The Navigation Pane displays links to folders and libraries that contain documents. You can view a folder's contents or open the folder from the Navigation Pane.

- The Address bar at the top of the dialog box shows the path to the currently selected folder.

- The File types button lists other file types you can choose to open.

- The Open button provides options for opening files, including opening the original file, opening a read-only version (when you want to open a file but keep the original file intact), or opening a copy of the original. If you open a copy or read-only version and edit or change the file, you cannot save changes to the original file. You can, however, use the Save As command to save your revisions with a new filename.

- The Search box allows you to find a file by name, file type, or location.

- The Cancel button closes the dialog box without opening a file.

Step-by-Step PPT 1.1

1. Click the **Start** button ⊕ on the Windows taskbar. The Start menu opens.

2. Click **All Programs**. A list of programs and program folders opens.

3. Click the **Microsoft Office** program folder. A list of Office programs opens.

4. Click **Microsoft PowerPoint 2010**. PowerPoint starts and its program window opens with a new, blank presentation displayed.

5. Click the **File** tab on the Ribbon to access the file-related commands.

6. Click **Open** to display the Open dialog box.

7. If necessary, navigate to the folder containing the data files for this lesson. Double-click the file named **Step PPT 1-1** in the File list. The presentation opens as shown in **Figure PPT 1–3**.

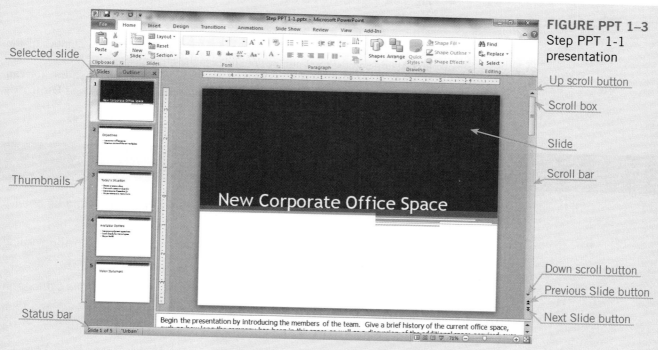

FIGURE PPT 1-3
Step PPT 1-1 presentation

Selected slide

Up scroll button

Scroll box

Slide

Thumbnails

Scroll bar

Down scroll button

Previous Slide button

Status bar

Next Slide button

8. Leave the presentation open for use in the next Step-by-Step.

Understanding Slides

A *slide* is a single image composed of text, graphics, or other content. A presentation is usually made up of many different slides that are presented in order in a slide show. After a slide is displayed as part of a slide show, it is removed from the screen and the next slide in the presentation appears. Slides contain various kinds of content, including text, bullets, pictures, clip art, and charts, in an assortment of combinations and layouts. A slide's *layout* controls how text and other objects are arranged on a slide. For instance, a layout might display a title at the top, text in a column on the left, and a picture with a caption on the right.

PowerPoint contains many built-in design themes from which you can choose to apply a set of coordinated fonts, colors, and backgrounds to slides. You will learn more about these in Lesson 2.

> **VOCABULARY**
> slide
>
> layout

Navigating a PowerPoint Presentation

There are many different ways to move around within a presentation. In Normal view, shown in Figure PPT 1–3, you can click a thumbnail in the Slides tab to select it and display it in the Slide pane. In all but Slide Show view, you can move from slide to slide by doing any of the following:

- Click the Next Slide and Previous Slide buttons on the vertical scroll bar.
- Click the up or down scroll buttons on the vertical scroll bar.
- Drag the scroll box until you see the number and title of the slide you want displayed on a ScreenTip.

■ Press the Page Up or Page Down key.

■ Press the Up arrow or Down arrow key.

As you move through a presentation, the status bar shows the number of the displayed slide and the total number of slides in the presentation.

In Slide Show view, you can click each slide to move through the slides. You can also press Page Down and Page Up to move through the slides, and press Esc to exit a slide show.

Step-by-Step PPT 1.2

The Step PPT 1-1 presentation from Step-by-Step PPT 1.1 should be open in the PowerPoint program window.

1. With slide 1 displayed, click the **Next Slide** button ⬆ on the vertical scroll bar.

2. Drag the scroll box down until you see *Slide: 4 of 5 Available Options* on a ScreenTip next to the scroll bar, as shown in **Figure PPT 1–4**, and then release the mouse button.

FIGURE PPT 1–4
Navigating with
ScreenTips

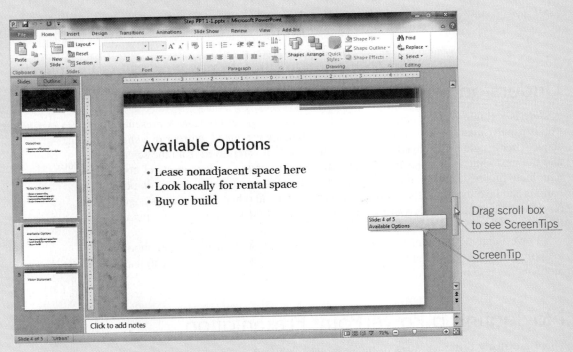

3. Press **Page Up** twice to move to slide 2.

4. Click the **up** scroll button ⬆ to move up to slide 1.

5. Drag the scroll box to the bottom of the vertical scroll bar.

6. Click the **slide 1** thumbnail in the Slides tab to display slide 1 in the Slide pane.

7. Leave the presentation open for use in the next Step-by-Step.

Viewing a Presentation

You can view a PowerPoint presentation many ways. The View tab on the Ribbon contains seven views from which to choose for working with a presentation—four presentation views and three master views. To change the view, use the buttons in the Presentation Views group and the Master Views group on the View tab, as shown in **Figure PPT 1–5**.

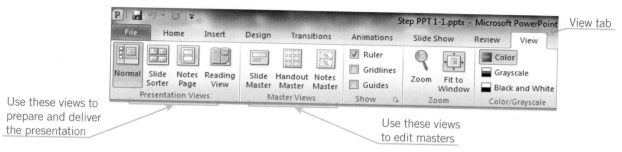

FIGURE PPT 1–5   Presentation Views and Master Views groups on the View tab

Preparing and Delivering a Presentation with Views

The views for preparing and delivering a presentation are Normal view, Slide Sorter view, Notes Page view, and Reading view.

Normal view displays the screen in three sections—the Outline and Slides tabs in the left pane, the Slide pane on the right, and the Notes pane below the Slide pane—so you can work on all parts of your presentation in one view. **Figure PPT 1–6** shows Normal view with the Outline tab displayed; in this view, you can see your entire presentation, enter text and rearrange bullet points and paragraphs, and modify the slide sequence. To adjust the size of the panes in Normal view, click and drag the pane borders.

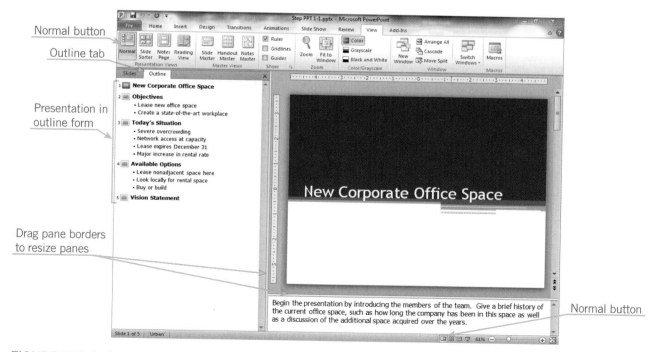

FIGURE PPT 1–6   Outline tab in Normal view

Use Slide Sorter view to display thumbnail versions of all slides in a presentation, as shown in **Figure PPT 1–7**. You can easily reorder slides, add transitions, and set timings using this view.

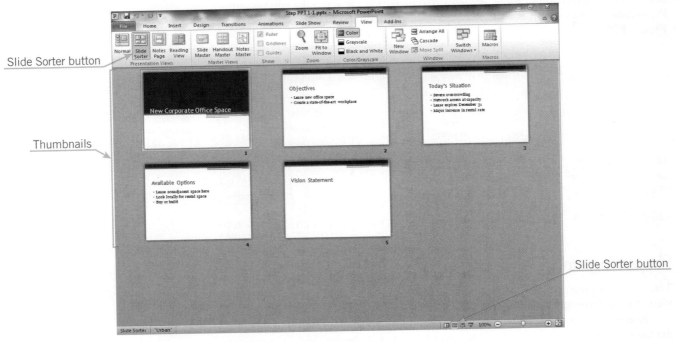

FIGURE PPT 1–7   Slide Sorter view

Notes Page view, shown in **Figure PPT 1–8**, allows you to enter and edit notes on a full screen instead of just in the small Notes pane at the bottom of Normal view. Notes are comments or other information that you can prepare ahead of time and then share with the audience as you deliver a presentation. The audience cannot see notes in a slide show; you print them for your own use during the presentation.

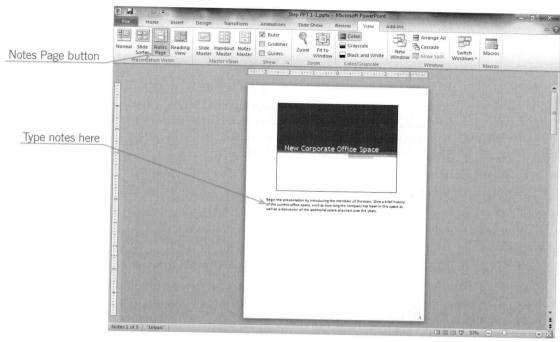

Notes Page button

Type notes here

FIGURE PPT 1–8   Notes Page view

Reading view, shown in **Figure PPT 1–9**, is used to view a presentation within a window on a computer screen rather than having the presentation fill the entire screen. You can adjust the window size of the presentation and use controls at the bottom of the window to advance through the slides.

Previous button

Menu button

Next button

Reading View button

FIGURE PPT 1–9   Reading view

Slide Show view is the primary view for delivering slide shows to an audience. When you run a presentation in Slide Show view, each slide fills the entire screen, and as you advance through the slides, you can see the transitions, animations, and effects that you have added. When you are finished viewing the presentation, you can press Esc to return to the previous view. You can click the Slide Show button on the status bar to get to Slide Show view quickly and start a slide show with the current settings, beginning at the currently selected slide. The Slide Show tab on the Ribbon, however, contains additional commands for delivering a presentation as a slide show to an audience. Buttons for starting a slide show, setting up a slide show, and selecting monitors for delivery are located on the Slide Show tab, as shown in **Figure PPT 1–10**.

FIGURE PPT 1–10   Slide Show tab

Editing Masters with Views

The master views are Slide Master view, Handout Master view, and Notes Master view. These views display *masters*, which are like blueprints that control the layout and design of the slides, handouts, and notes. When you make a change to a master, the change affects every slide in the presentation. For example, in Slide Master view, shown in **Figure PPT 1–11**, you could change the bullet styles that are used on each slide in the presentation by changing the styles on the slide master. In Slide Master view, the left pane displays thumbnails of a slide master at the top and the slide layouts below it. The selected master is displayed on the right. The contextual Slide Master tab is displayed on the Ribbon with additional commands. The Notes Master and Handout Master views also display an additional tab on the Ribbon. You will learn more about masters in Lesson 2.

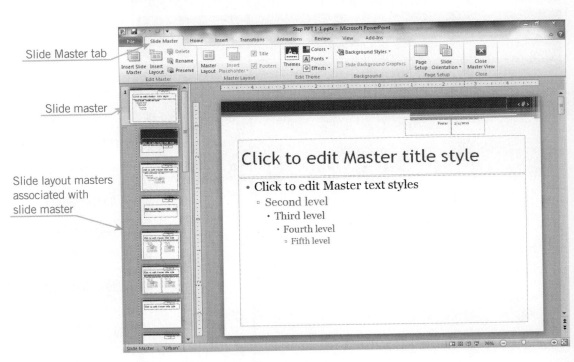

FIGURE PPT 1–11   Slide Master view

Step-by-Step PPT 1.3

The Step PPT 1-1 presentation from Step-by-Step PPT 1.2 should be open in the PowerPoint program window.

1. Click the **Outline** tab to display the presentation in outline form. The outline for the entire presentation is displayed, including for the slide on which you are currently working.

2. Hover your mouse pointer over the view buttons on the status bar until you see the ScreenTip identifying each of the view buttons: Normal, Slide Sorter, Reading View, and Slide Show.

3. Click the **Slide Sorter** button ▦ on the status bar to change the view. You see a thumbnail of each of the slides.

4. Click the **Slide Show** button 🖵 on the status bar. The slide now appears as it would if you were running the slide show. Click your mouse button to advance through the presentation, and then press **Esc** to return to Slide Sorter view when the slide show is over.

5. Click **slide 1**. On the View tab on the Ribbon, in the Presentation Views group, click the **Notes Page** button. In Notes Page view, notice the large area below the slide that contains notes related to the slide.

6. On the View tab, in the Master Views group, click the **Notes Master** button to open Notes Master view. Here you can change the text styles of notes or add headers and footers that would appear on each notes page when printed.

7. On the Notes Master tab, in the Close group, click the **Close Master View** button.

8. On the View tab, in the Master Views group, click the **Slide Master** button to display Slide Master view.

9. On the Slide Master tab, in the Close group, click the **Close Master View** button.

10. On the View tab, in the Presentation Views group, click the **Reading View** button to display Reading view.

11. Click the **Next** button ➡ to advance through the presentation, and then press **Esc** to return to Notes Page view.

12. On the Slide Show tab, in the Start Slide Show group, click the **From Beginning** button to start the slide show from the beginning. Click to advance through the presentation and return to Notes Page view.

13. On the View tab, in the Presentation Views group, click the **Normal** button to display Normal view.

14. Leave the presentation open for use in the next Step-by-Step.

Modifying Slides

As you create and edit a presentation, you may find that you need to make changes to the slides that make up the presentation. These changes might require adding or deleting slides, changing a slide's layout, and entering and editing text.

Selecting Slides

You can select a single slide in Slide Sorter view or in Normal view by clicking it. In later lessons, you will learn to add slide backgrounds or transitions to multiple slides. To make changes to more than one slide at a time, you can select a group of slides by clicking the first slide in the group you want to select, pressing and holding Ctrl, and then clicking each of the slides you want.

    When you need to deselect a slide or a group of selected slides, click in the blank space outside the selection.

Inserting and Deleting Slides

You can add slides, change the layout of slides, and organize slides into sections using the buttons in the Slides group on the Home tab, shown in **Figure PPT 1–12**.

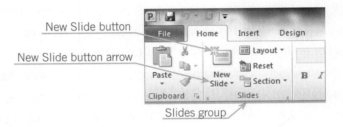

FIGURE PPT 1–12   Slides group on the Home tab

    You can insert a single slide with the default slide layout, Title and Content, by clicking the New Slide button in the Slides group. However, you can select different layout options for a newly inserted slide using the New Slide button arrow. The New Slide button arrow displays a gallery of built-in layouts for the new slide, including options for a title slide, slides showing title and content sections, and other styles of slides that reflect the design theme of your presentation. In addition to the New Slide gallery, the New Slide button arrow includes Duplicate Selected Slides, Slides from Outline, and Reuse Slides commands.

    If a thumbnail in the Slides tab in Normal view is selected, clicking the New Slide button or clicking a layout in the New Slide gallery inserts a new slide after the selected slide. Or, before inserting a slide, you can click in the left pane between thumbnails to display a long, blinking insertion point indicating the location where the new slide will be inserted. To remove one or more selected slides from a presentation, press Delete.

Changing Slide Layout

The Layout button in the Slides group contains the same layout options as the New Slide button arrow, but selecting a layout applies it to the current slide. You can apply a new layout to the current slide (rearranging the placeholders) at any time, and the

 EXTRA FOR EXPERTS

You can insert an exact copy of an existing slide using the Duplicate Selected Slides command. Just select the slide you want to duplicate, click the New Slide button arrow, and then choose Duplicate Selected Slides.

text on the slide will adjust to the new layout. The Reset button in the Slides group changes the slide's layout and formatting back to the default settings.

Step-by-Step PPT 1.4

The Step PPT 1-1 presentation from Step-by-Step PPT 1.3 should be open in the PowerPoint program window.

1. In the Slides tab, click the **slide 5** thumbnail to select it.

2. On the Home tab, in the Slides group, click the **New Slide** button arrow, and then click the **Two Content** layout as shown in **Figure PPT 1–13**. PowerPoint inserts the slide as slide 6.

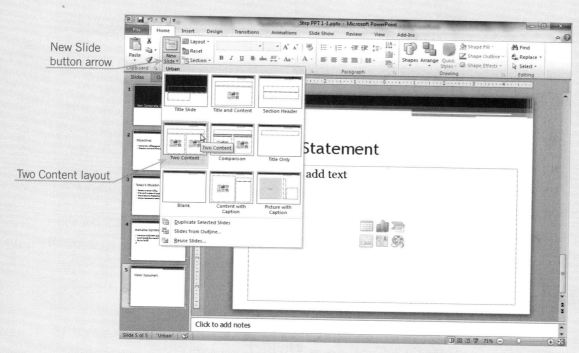

New Slide button arrow

Two Content layout

FIGURE PPT 1–13
New Slide button arrow and gallery

3. On the Home tab, in the Slides group, click the **New Slide** button arrow, and then click the **Title and Content** layout. The new slide is added as slide 7.

4. In the Slides tab, click the **slide 4** thumbnail to select it.

5. On the Home tab, in the Slides group, click the **Layout** button and click the **Two Content** layout. Notice that the text on the current slide adjusted to the new layout.

6. Click the **Layout** button again and click the **Title and Content** layout. The text adjusts to the new layout.

7. In the Slides tab, click the **slide 6** thumbnail to select it, and then press **Delete** to remove the slide from the presentation.

8. On the View tab, in the Presentation Views group, click the **Slide Sorter** button, click **slide 1**, press and hold **Ctrl**, click **slide 3** and **slide 5**, and then release **Ctrl**. Notice that all three slides are surrounded by selection borders, as shown in **Figure PPT 1–14**.

FIGURE PPT 1–14
Selected nonadjacent slides

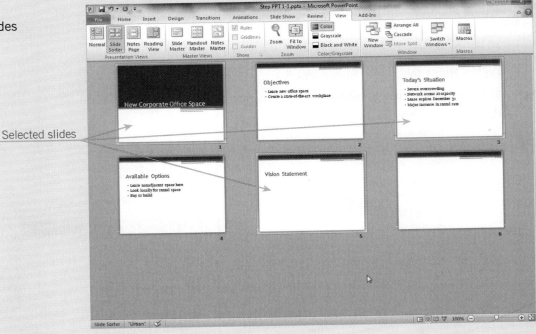

9. Click in the blank space in Slide Sorter view to deselect the slides.

10. On the View tab, in the Presentation Views group, click the **Normal** button.

11. Leave the presentation open for use in the next Step-by-Step.

Entering Text on a Slide

When PowerPoint inserts a new slide in a presentation, the new slide contains *placeholders*; these are specific areas on the slide, indicated by dotted rectangles, where you insert text or other content, such as bulleted lists or graphics. You can move, resize, and rotate a placeholder to customize its position on the slide.

To enter text in a placeholder, click the *I-beam* (which is the shape of the mouse pointer in a text area) anywhere on the placeholder to select it. A blinking cursor, called an *insertion point*, indicates where your entry will appear. Type the text, and then click a blank space on the slide outside the placeholder to deselect it.

Many of PowerPoint's slide layouts contain bulleted lists. A *bullet* is a small symbol that marks the beginning of a list item. When you begin typing, PowerPoint automatically inserts the bullet for the first list item and wraps text for you. Press Tab before typing to indent to a second level in the bulleted list. PowerPoint automatically indents the subordinate bulleted item and may give the entry a different bullet symbol. You can use the Increase List Level and Decrease List Level buttons in the Paragraph group on the Home tab to move a list item up to a higher level or down to a lower level.

▶ **VOCABULARY**
placeholders
I-beam
insertion point
bullet

You can also add text to a slide by typing text in the Outline tab. As you type, the text is entered on the slide. Entering text in the Outline tab is useful for organizing and developing your presentation.

After you enter text in a placeholder, you can easily edit, insert, delete, or copy text from one slide to another. Editing text in a presentation is the same as editing text in Word or other Microsoft Office programs. When you want to insert text in a placeholder that already contains text, you can click the I-beam to position the insertion point, and then type the additional text. New text appears to the left of the insertion point. To delete text in a placeholder, position the insertion point in the text, and then press Backspace to delete characters to the left of the insertion point. Press Delete to delete characters to the right of the insertion point. When deleting more than a few characters, select the text to be deleted and press Delete.

You might need to delete a placeholder to make room for text in another placeholder, or to remove content from a slide. Delete a placeholder by selecting it and pressing Delete. To reverse, or undo, an action, use the Undo button on the Quick Access Toolbar. If you perform an undo action but then decide against the undo, use the Redo button on the Quick Access Toolbar to reverse the undo action.

Step-by-Step PPT 1.5

The Step PPT 1-1 presentation from Step-by-Step PPT 1.4 should be open in the PowerPoint program window.

1. Click the **slide 6** thumbnail in the Slides tab to display it in the Slide pane, if necessary.

2. Click the **Click to add title** placeholder and type **Recommendation** as shown in **Figure PPT 1–15**.

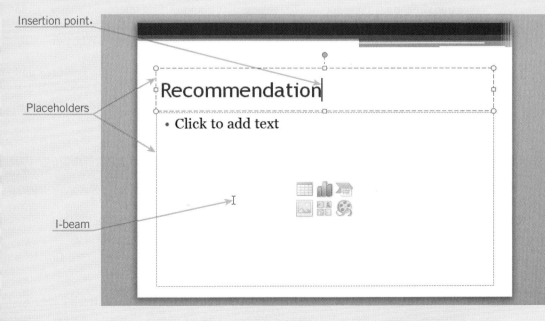

FIGURE PPT 1–15
Text entered in placeholder

3. Click the **Click to add text** placeholder and type **Appoint a Relocation Committee**.

4. Press **Enter** and then press **Tab** to indent to a second level in the bulleted list. Notice the bullet is a different color and style.

5. Type **Determine workplace requirements** and press **Enter** to enter the first subbullet.

6. Type **Visit sites available for sale or rent** and press **Enter** to enter the second subbullet.

7. On the Home tab, in the Paragraph group, click the **Decrease List Level** button ⬛ to return to the first bullet level.

8. Click the **Outline** tab to practice entering text in the outline.

9. In the slide 6 section of the outline, click the blank line under *Visit sites available for sale or rent.*

10. Type **Make recommendations by 9/25** and press **Enter**. Notice that the text is also entered on the slide as you type.

11. Type **Management decision by 10/17**.

12. Click the **Slides** tab.

13. Leave the presentation open for use in the next Step-by-Step.

Copying and Moving Data

You probably have experience moving or copying text in Word or other Office programs using the Cut, Copy, and Paste commands. These commands, located in the Clipboard group on the Home tab in PowerPoint, work the same way to move and copy text within a slide or between slides in a presentation.

▶ **VOCABULARY**
drag-and-drop

You can use *drag-and-drop* to move or copy a selection to a new location on the same slide in the presentation. To move text or graphics, you select and drag with the mouse and then release the mouse button to "drop" the item in its new location. You can also use drag-and-drop to rearrange slides in Slide Sorter view. When dragging and dropping slides in Slide Sorter view, the insertion point is much longer.

To copy instead of move a selection, press and hold Ctrl while you drag and drop. When you copy a selection, you will see a plus sign (+) with the pointer. When you move or copy a selection using drag-and-drop, the selection is not stored on the Clipboard.

Step-by-Step PPT 1.6

The Step PPT 1-1 presentation from Step-by-Step PPT 1.5 should be open in the PowerPoint program window.

1. Display **slide 2**, and then select the second bulleted list item **Create a state-of-the-art workplace**.

2. On the Home tab, in the Clipboard group, click the **Copy** button ▣.

3. Display **slide 5**. Click the **Click to add text** placeholder.

4. On the Home tab, in the Clipboard group, click the **Paste** button to insert the copied text.

5. On the status bar, click the **Slide Sorter** button 🔳 to switch to Slide Sorter view.

6. Click **slide 5** and drag the move pointer 🖱 up and to the left until you see the long insertion bar located on the right of slide 1, as shown in **Figure PPT 1–16**.

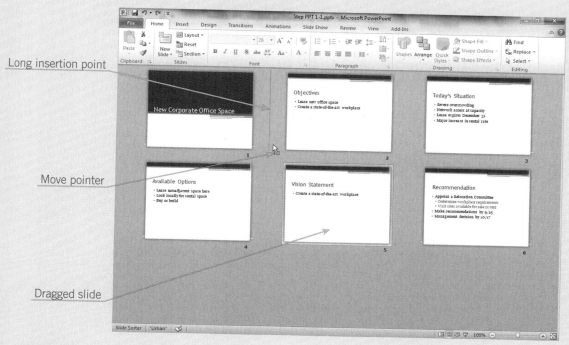

Long insertion point

Move pointer

Dragged slide

FIGURE PPT 1–16
Dragging and dropping to rearrange slides

7. Release the mouse button to drop the slide into its new location.

8. With slide 2 selected, press **Delete** to remove the slide from the presentation.

9. On the status bar, click the **Normal** button 🔳 to switch to Normal view.

10. Leave the presentation open for use in the next Step-by-Step.

Saving a Presentation

The first time you save a presentation, the options for saving include the Save command on the File tab, the Save As command on the File tab, or the Save button on the Quick Access Toolbar. Each of these methods displays the Save As dialog box, as shown in **Figure PPT 1–17**.

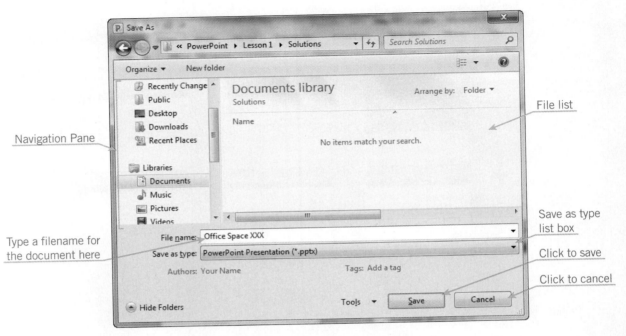

FIGURE PPT 1–17   Save As dialog box

After you save a file the first time, the Save command saves your file with the previously specified name in the location you specified. The Save As command lets you make a copy of the file with a new name, location, or file type. The Save as type list lets you save a presentation in another format or as a template. You will learn more about PowerPoint templates later in this book. You might need to change the format or program and version of a file if you share files with others who use different software. To save a presentation in a specific location, you use the Navigation Pane in the Save As dialog box to navigate to the folder where you want to save the presentation. Once you have saved the file, you can use the Save button on the Quick Access Toolbar or the Save command on the File tab to save your changes.

PowerPoint's AutoRecover feature automatically saves your presentation at regular intervals so that you can recover at least some of your work in case of a power outage or other unexpected shutdown. You can turn this feature on or off and change the setting to save more or less often by opening the PowerPoint Options dialog box using the Options command on the File tab. Click Save in the left pane of the dialog box, and then specify a number in the Save AutoRecover information every *x* minutes box in the right pane. However, you should not rely on this automatic saving feature. Remember to save your work often.

📼 EXTRA FOR EXPERTS

Microsoft PowerPoint 2010 and 2007 files have a .pptx extension and cannot be opened with previous versions of PowerPoint. If you need to share files with someone using an earlier version, you can use the PowerPoint 97-2003 Presentation option in the Save as type list in the Save As dialog box, which saves files with the .ppt extension.

You can use the Save & Send option on the File tab to save a document online in two ways. You can save to Windows Live SkyDrive, which is a free online storage service from Microsoft, to make the presentation accessible from any computer with Internet access. You can also save to an organization's SharePoint site, which provides additional opportunities for collaboration, such as editing documents with multiple people at the same time. Saving online allows you to share and access documents and presentations through an Internet connection and to view and edit them in a Web browser using Microsoft Office Web Apps, which are free online companion programs to Word, Excel, and PowerPoint.

Step-by-Step PPT 1.7

The Step PPT 1-1 presentation from Step-by-Step PPT 1.6 should be open in the PowerPoint program window.

1. Click the **File** tab and then click **Save As** to open the Save As dialog box.

2. Navigate to the location where you save your files.

3. If necessary, select **Step PPT 1-1** in the **File name** text box. Type **Office Space *XXX*** (replace *XXX* with your initials) in the box to rename the file.

4. In the Save as type list, make sure PowerPoint Presentation (*.pptx) is displayed.

5. Click **Save** to save a copy of the presentation with the new name in the specified location.

6. Leave the presentation open for use in the next Step-by-Step.

Previewing and Printing Presentations

Presentations are usually delivered on a computer or projection screen, but there are times when you may need to distribute a printout of the presentation, such as in handouts to accompany a speech or lecture. You can save time and paper by previewing a presentation and adjusting formatting and printing options on the File tab in Backstage view before you click the Print button.

When you choose Print on the File tab, Backstage view displays the Print button and default print settings in the center pane of the window and a preview of the current slide in the right pane, as shown in **Figure PPT 1–18**. To change a print setting in the center pane, click the setting you want to change, and then select a new option from the gallery that opens.

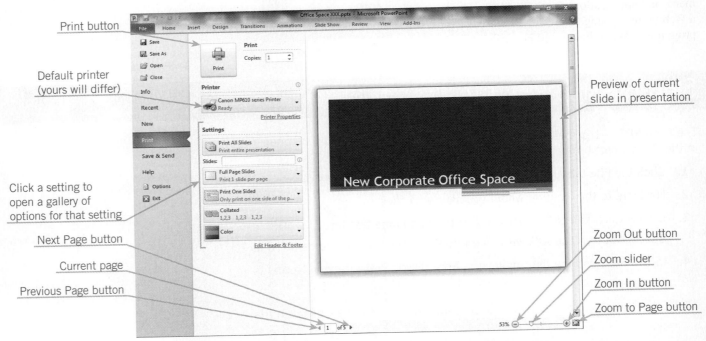

FIGURE PPT 1–18   Printing and previewing options in Backstage view

You can preview any slide in a presentation using the scroll bars or the Next Page and Previous Page buttons at the bottom of the right pane. You can zoom in and out to see different magnifications of a document using the Zoom In and Zoom Out buttons or by moving the Zoom slider. The Zoom to Page button displays the entire page within the preview pane.

The following printing and previewing options are available in Backstage view:

- The Print button prints the presentation with current settings.

- The up and down arrows in the Copies box enable you to indicate the number of copies to print.

- The Printer area displays the default printer. Click the default printer to select a different printer from the gallery of available printers. The Printer Properties link lets you choose paper type, print quality, or color, as well as specify other options for your printer.

- The Settings area lists the current print settings, which vary depending on the capabilities of your printer. Clicking a setting opens a gallery of options that lets you indicate whether to print:

  - All slides, the current slide, or specified slides of a presentation

  - Full-page slides, notes pages, a presentation outline, or handouts showing from 1 to 9 slides per page

- One-sided or on both sides
- Multiple copies of a presentation with pages in order, called *collated*, or uncollated
- Landscape or portrait orientation (this setting is not available when printing full-page slides)
- Color, grayscale, or pure black and white
- The Edit Header & Footer link opens the Header and Footer dialog box where you can decide whether or not to show the date and time, slide number, or footer on the slides, notes, or handouts you are printing.
- The preview pane shows a preview of the slide and allows you to zoom in and out to check for errors. As you make changes to the print settings, the preview is updated to reflect the changes so that you can be sure you are happy with the presentation settings before printing.

▶ **VOCABULARY**
collated

EXTRA FOR EXPERTS

You can add the Quick Print command as a button to the Quick Access Toolbar to print to the default printer with the default settings without opening Backstage view.

Step-by-Step PPT 1.8

The Office Space *XXX* presentation from Step-by-Step PPT 1.7 should be open in the PowerPoint program window.

1. Click the **File** tab to display Backstage view, and then click **Print**.
2. Click the **Next Page** button ▶ at the bottom of the right pane two times to display slide 3.
3. In the center pane under Settings, click the **Full Page Slides** setting, and then in the Handouts section of the gallery, click **3 Slides**. The preview changes to show three slides per page with lines for notes, as shown in **Figure PPT 1–19**.

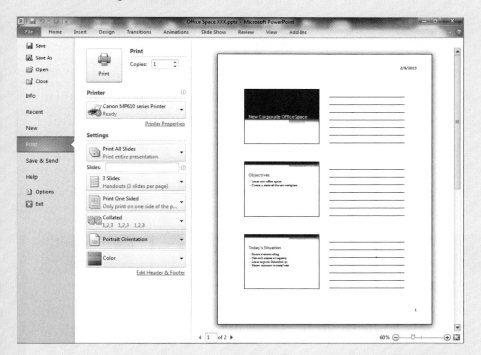

FIGURE PPT 1–19
Handout preview (3 slides per page)

4. Click the **3 Slides** setting, and then click **6 Slides Horizontal** in the gallery. The preview shows all five slides in one handout page.

5. Click the **Portrait Orientation** setting, and then click **Landscape Orientation**.

6. Click the **Color** setting, and then click **Pure Black and White** to change the ink color to be used in the printout.

7. Click the **Print** button to print the handout.

8. Save the presentation and leave it open for use in the next Step-by-Step.

Closing a Presentation

When you are finished with a presentation, you can remove it from your screen using the Close command. To close a presentation without closing PowerPoint, choose the Close command on the File tab. When you only have one presentation open, you can click the Close button on the title bar to close the presentation and exit the PowerPoint program at the same time. The software prompts you to save your work if you made any changes since you last saved.

Step-by-Step PPT 1.9

The Office Space *XXX* presentation from Step-by-Step PPT 1.8 should be open in the PowerPoint program window.

1. In Normal view, display **slide 5** in the Slide pane.

2. In the last bulleted item, change the date from *10/17* to **10/7**.

3. Click the **Close** button [x] on the program title bar. The Microsoft PowerPoint message box is displayed, as shown in **Figure PPT 1–20**.

FIGURE PPT 1–20
Microsoft PowerPoint message box

4. Click **Save** to save and close the presentation and exit PowerPoint.

TECHNOLOGY CAREERS

Corporate trainers may provide job-specific training courses in-house for large companies or they may work as contractors to provide more general professional development training to many different companies. They may present to large audiences or work one-on-one with clients. Video conferencing and online discussion boards may be used to promote participation and collaboration. Corporate trainers often use presentation software such as PowerPoint to deliver dynamic slide shows as part of a training course.

SUMMARY

In this lesson, you learned:

- A presentation is a way of communicating ideas, facts, suggestions, or other information to an audience. PowerPoint is a software program that helps you create presentations.
- How to start PowerPoint and open an existing presentation.
- That to move around a presentation, you can click buttons on the vertical scroll bar, drag the scroll box, press the Page Up or Page Down key, or press the Up arrow or Down arrow.
- The differences between Normal, Slide Sorter, Notes Page, Reading, Slide Master, Handout Master, and Notes Master views in PowerPoint. You can switch to one of these seven views using the View tab. The Slide Show tab contains buttons

for setting up and delivering a presentation to an audience in Slide Show view.
- How to insert, delete, and change slide layouts.
- How to enter text on a slide.
- How to use the Save As command to save a presentation for the first time.
- How to preview presentations in Backstage view before printing slides, handouts, or notes.
- When you close a presentation, PowerPoint prompts you to save your work if you made any changes since you last saved.

VOCABULARY REVIEW

Define the following terms:

bullet
collated
drag-and-drop
I-beam
insertion point
layout

masters
Notes pane
Outline tab
placeholders
presentation

presentation software
slide
Slide pane
Slides tab
thumbnails

REVIEW QUESTIONS

MULTIPLE CHOICE

Select the best response for the following statements.

1. The _____ provides an area for you to type speaker notes for the presentation.
   - A. Notes pane
   - B. Slide pane
   - C. Slides tab
   - D. Outline tab

2. PowerPoint's _____ feature automatically saves your presentation at regular intervals so that you can recover at least some of your work in case of a power outage or other unexpected shutdown.
   - A. Save
   - B. AutoRecover
   - C. Placeholder
   - D. Clipboard

3. A(n) _____ is a small symbol that marks the beginning of a list item.
   - A. placeholder
   - B. I-beam
   - C. slide
   - D. bullet

4. If you perform an undo action but then decide against the undo, use the _____ button to reverse an Undo action.
   - A. Undo
   - B. Redo
   - C. Repeat
   - D. Delete

5. _____ are rectangles with dotted lines around them for inserting text or other content.

   A. Slides   C. Layouts

   B. Clipboards   D. Placeholders

6. _____ view can be used to rearrange the order of slides.

   A. Normal   C. Slide Sorter

   B. Slide Show   D. Notes Page

7. _____ view allows you to make global changes to slides, handouts, or notes that affect the entire presentation.

   A. Normal   C. Slide Sorter

   B. Slide Show   D. Master

8. Press _____ to exit a slide show.

   A. Delete   C. Ctrl

   B. Esc   D. Enter

9. You can use _____ to move or copy a selection to a new location.

   A. drag-and-drop   C. Redo

   B. Undo   D. layout

10. Click the _____ tab to display Backstage view.

   A. File   C. Print

   B. View   D. Slide Show

FILL IN THE BLANK

Complete the following sentences by writing the correct word or words in the blanks provided.

1. A(n) _____ is a way of communicating ideas, facts, suggestions, or other information to an audience.

2. A(n) _____ is a single image composed of text, graphics, or other content.

3. A slide's _____ controls how text and other objects are arranged on a slide.

4. The Slides and Outline tabs are located on the left side of the screen in _____ view.

5. _____ are like blueprints that control the layout and design of the slides, handouts, and notes.

6. You can use the _____ dialog box to find and open existing files on your hard drive, CD, or other removable media.

7. _____ is the shape the mouse pointer takes in a text area.

8. To _____ a placeholder, click the blank space outside the placeholder.

9. Press _____ to start a new bulleted item.

10. When you _____ a presentation, the software prompts you to save your work if you made any changes since you last saved.

■ PROJECTS

PROJECT PPT 1-1

1. Start PowerPoint and open the presentation **Project PPT 1-1** from the folder containing the data files for this lesson.

2. Save the presentation with the filename **Tracking Graduates XXX** (replace *XXX* with your initials).

3. Switch to Slide Show view and advance through the entire presentation.

4. Display slide 1 in Normal view.

5. Change the presenter's name to your name.

6. Display slide 2.

7. Insert a new slide with the Title Only layout.

8. Type **When does tracking begin?** in the title placeholder.

9. Change the layout of the slide to Title and Content.

10. Type **One year after graduation** in the content placeholder.

11. Switch to Slide Sorter view.

12. Move slide 4 to the slide 2 position.

13. Delete slide 2.

14. Save and close the presentation.

PROJECT PPT 1-3

The **Health Challenge XXX** presentation from Project PPT 1–2 should be open in the PowerPoint program window.

1. Save the presentation as **Health Challenge 2 XXX** (replace *XXX* with your initials).

2. Select slide 4 and view it in Notes Page view.

3. Type the following speaker note in the placeholder:

   Discuss the brands and types of equipment that will be available, such as the exercise bikes and treadmills. Remember to ask if there are any questions.

4. Switch to Normal view. In the Outline tab, on slide 6, click after the word *made* in the last bulleted item and press Enter to create a new blank bulleted item. Type the following text:

   Health Challenge committee has been created

5. In the Slide pane, select the new bulleted item, and then use drag-and-drop to move it into position as the first bulleted item on the slide.

6. Preview the presentation in Backstage view, and then print handouts 6 per page (vertical).

7. Save and close the presentation.

ON YOUR OWN

Open **Health Challenge 2 XXX.** Print the one slide that contains notes as a notes page. Close the presentation without saving changes.

PROJECT PPT 1-2

1. Open the presentation **Project PPT 1-2** from the folder containing the data files for this lesson.

2. Save the presentation as **Health Challenge XXX** (replace *XXX* with your initials).

3. On slide 1, replace *Presenter Name* with your name.

4. On slide 2, type **Improve company image** as the fourth bulleted item in the list.

5. Change the layout of slide 3 to Title and Content.

6. Delete slide 4.

7. On slide 6, in the second bulleted item, delete the words *in what areas.*

8. In the fourth bulleted item, delete the word *yet* and type **need**.

9. Increase the indent for the second and third bulleted items to a second level.

10. Display slide 1.

11. Switch to Slide Show view and advance through the entire presentation.

12. Save the presentation and leave it open for use in the next project.

PROJECT PPT 1-4

1. Open the presentation **Office Space XXX** from the folder containing your solution files for this lesson.

2. Display slide 4.

3. Copy the three bulleted items on the slide.

4. Close the file without saving changes.

5. Open the presentation **Project PPT 1-4** from the folder containing the data files for this lesson.

6. Save the presentation as **Office Space Progress XXX** (replace *XXX* with your initials).

7. On slide 2, paste the copied text stored on the Clipboard into the content placeholder.

8. Switch to Slide Sorter view, and then move slide 6 to the slide 5 position.

9. Move slide 7 to the slide 6 position.

10. Use the Slide Show tab to start the presentation in Slide Show view from the beginning. Advance through the entire presentation.

11. Save and close the presentation.

ON YOUR OWN

Open **Office Space Progress XXX.** Add speaker notes to two of the slides and change two slide layouts. Save and close the presentation.

WEB PROJECT

Search the Microsoft Web site (www.microsoft.com) for information about Microsoft Office 2010. Create a presentation consisting of four or five slides that gives basic details about the software, such as features, system requirements, and price. Be prepared to show your presentation to the class.

 ## TEAMWORK PROJECT

With a partner, plan a presentation that encourages students to take some kind of action. For example, you may want them to participate in a new recycling program, attend an event, or participate in a fund-raising activity. Use the Outline tab in Normal view to create the presentation using at least five slides.

 # CRITICAL THINKING

ACTIVITY PPT 1–1

Use PowerPoint Help to find and read the Help article titled, *Tips for creating and delivering an effective presentation*. Which three of the tips do you think are most important and why? Start PowerPoint and use the default *Presentation1* file to create a simple four-slide presentation detailing the three tips that you thought were most important. Use the default title slide, and insert three new slides for the tips. Save the presentation with a meaningful name. Be prepared to share your presentation with the class.

ACTIVITY PPT 1–2

Use PowerPoint Help to learn about reusing slides from another presentation. The Reuse Slides command is located on the New Slide menu. Experiment with the process. Try reusing slide 4 from the Office Space *XXX* file as slide 2 in the Office Space Progress *XXX* file. When you are finished, close each file without saving changes. What are the pros and cons of reusing slides?

ACTIVITY PPT 1–3

Create a five-slide presentation that describes a recent scientific discovery, a favorite person from history, or a recent election. Be prepared to share your presentation with the class.

LESSON 2

Formatting and Modifying Presentations

■ OBJECTIVES

Upon completion of this lesson, you should be able to:

- Create a new blank presentation.
- Use a template to create a new presentation.
- Format text and paragraphs.
- Check spelling.
- Find and replace text.
- Apply themes.
- Customize slide masters.

■ DATA FILES

To complete this lesson, you will need these data files:

Step PPT 2-5.pptx

Project PPT 2-2.pptx

Project PPT 2-4.pptx

■ VOCABULARY

alignment

characters

font

font styles

Format Painter

layout masters

point size

slide master

template

themes

Introduction

Now that you are familiar with PowerPoint basics, you are ready to use PowerPoint's tools to create presentations. In this lesson, you will learn to create a new blank presentation and create a presentation from a template. Like other Microsoft Office programs, PowerPoint lets you format text and paragraphs and use tools such as the spelling checker and the Find and Replace feature. In addition, you will learn how to tailor your presentation by applying themes and customizing slide masters.

Creating a New Blank Presentation

A new blank presentation is a clean canvas. It contains one title slide with two place-holders where you can insert content. Once you've created a new blank presentation, you can build a complete presentation by inserting new slides, choosing the slide layouts that you want, and applying fonts, colors, and formats. You might prefer a plain white background to showcase the data or photos in your presentation, or perhaps a colorful look would better suit your needs. Try to present your information efficiently by minimizing the number of slides in your presentation and limiting the amount of text on each slide.

You can create a new blank presentation by choosing New on the File tab, and then clicking the Create button with the Blank presentation icon selected in Backstage view, as shown in **Figure PPT 2–1**.

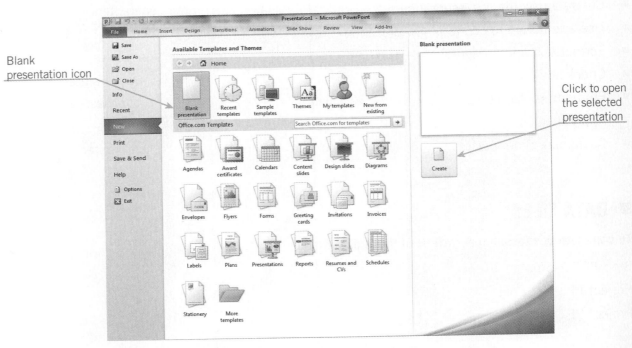

FIGURE PPT 2–1   Options for creating a new presentation

Step-by-Step PPT 2.1

1. Start PowerPoint.

2. Click the **File** tab on the Ribbon, and then click **New**. On the right, options are displayed for creating a new presentation based on available templates and themes. The Blank presentation icon is selected, as shown in Figure PPT 2–1.

3. Click the **Create** button to open a new blank presentation, as shown in **Figure PPT 2–2**.

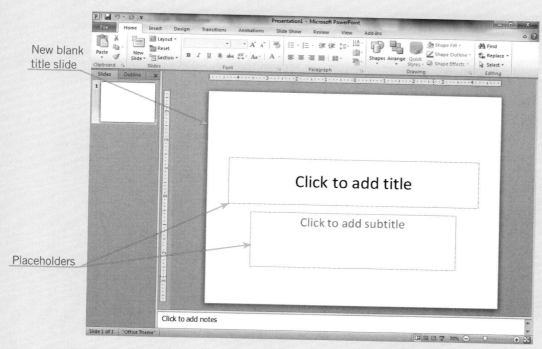

FIGURE PPT 2–2
New blank presentation

4. Click the **Click to add title** placeholder and type **My Favorite Movies**.

5. Click the **Click to add subtitle** placeholder and type your name.

6. Save the presentation as **Favorite Movies XXX** (replace *XXX* with your initials) and close it.

Creating a New Presentation with a Template

One method of creating a well-organized and attractive presentation quickly is to use a template. A **template** is a sample presentation that provides a pattern or model that you can follow to create your own presentation. PowerPoint includes templates for many common types of presentations, including employee orientations, financial performance reports, company handbooks, photo albums, and business plans.

A presentation template contains a group of slides with a common theme and background style, but the added advantage of using a template is that it offers suggestions for content that is standard for a particular type of presentation, giving you an outline of topics to help you get started. For instance, instead of having to create

▶ **VOCABULARY**
template

an employee orientation presentation from scratch, you can use an employee orientation template that contains slides with content or suggestions for content that is typical in such a presentation, such as company background, benefits, policies, work hours, and required paperwork. You can then replace the suggested content on each slide with your own.

PowerPoint includes many templates that come already installed, and you can access them by clicking the File tab, clicking New, and then clicking the Sample templates category in the Available Templates and Themes section of Backstage view, shown in **Figure PPT 2–3**. Many more templates are available online, which you can access by clicking a category in the Office.com Templates section of Backstage view. You can also use the Search Office.com for templates box in the Office.com Templates section to look for an online template using keywords.

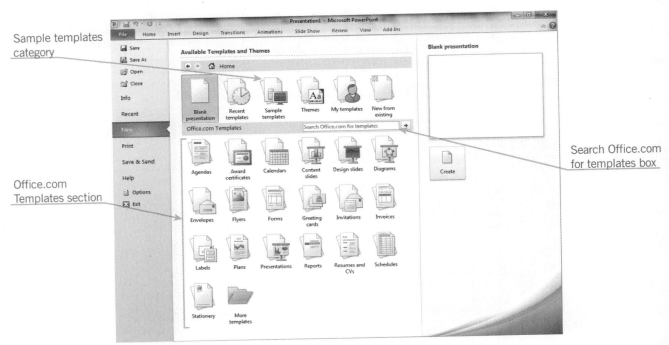

FIGURE PPT 2–3 Available templates and themes in Backstage view

When you have selected the template you want, as shown in **Figure PPT 2–4**, you can click the Create button (if it is an installed template) or the Download button (if it is an online template) to open the template. When you open a template from Backstage view, you are actually opening a copy of the template in presentation format, so the original template file is not altered. Add your own text to a template by clicking a placeholder and then typing to replace the current content with your own. Name and save the new presentation using the Save or Save As command.

Clicking a template selects it and displays a preview on the right

Sample templates

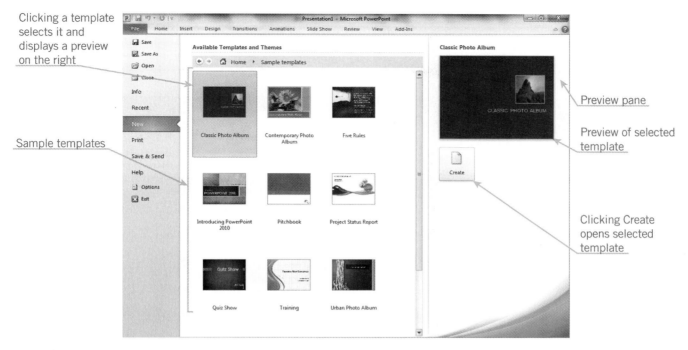

Preview pane

Preview of selected template

Clicking Create opens selected template

FIGURE PPT 2–4   Template selected in the Sample templates category

Step-by-Step PPT 2.2

1. Click the **File** tab on the Ribbon, and then click **New**. On the right, options are displayed for creating a new presentation based on available templates and themes.

2. Click the **Sample templates** category to display the installed templates in the center pane.

3. Click **Classic Photo Album**, if necessary, to select it. Notice the preview in the right pane.

4. Confirm that the Classic Photo Album template is selected, and then under the template preview in the right pane, click the **Create** button. The template opens on your screen as a presentation containing placeholders.

5. Save the presentation as **Nature Portfolio *XXX*** (replace *XXX* with your initials).

6. Click the **Slide Show** button ⊡ on the status bar to switch to Slide Show view, and then click to advance through the entire presentation. Notice the layouts, instructions, and content suggestions throughout.

7. On slide 1 in Normal view, select the **CLASSIC PHOTO ALBUM** title and type **Lostart Photos**.

8. On slide 1, click the **Click to add date and other details** placeholder and type **Nature Photography Portfolio**. Your screen should look similar to **Figure PPT 2–5**.

FIGURE PPT 2–5
Nature Portfolio *XXX* presentation

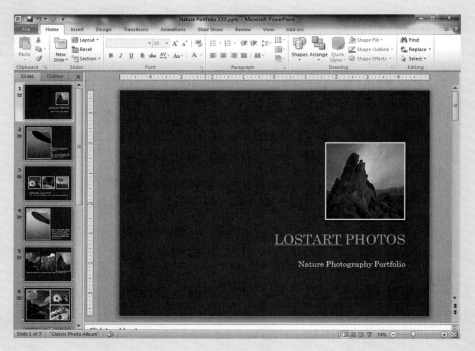

9. On slide 2, select the first paragraph of text that begins *This photo album contains*, and then type **Stock photos**.

10. Select the second paragraph of text that begins *To add your own pages*, and then type **On location photo shoots**.

11. On slide 3, select the **CHOOSE A LAYOUT** title and type **Flowers, Foliage, and Rocks**.

12. Select the second line that begins *...then click the placeholders*, and type **All of nature is beautiful...**

13. On slide 5, select the text that begins *Picture Quick Styles give...*, and then type **For more information on purchasing stock photos or to request a quote for an on-location shoot, call 806-555-0190.**

14. Save the presentation and leave it open for use in the next Step-by-Step.

Formatting Text

Characters are individual letters, numbers, symbols, punctuation marks, and spaces. You can apply one or more formats to a single character or multiple characters. The character formats you can apply are font and font size; font style such as italic and bold; and font effects such as underline, color, and capitalization. The Font group on the Home tab on the Ribbon contains buttons for formatting text, as shown in **Figure PPT 2–6**. In addition to using the Font group to format characters, you can also use the Font dialog box. You access the Font dialog box using the dialog box launcher in the Font group.

Later in this lesson you will learn to copy formats using the Format Painter button in the Clipboard group on the Home tab.

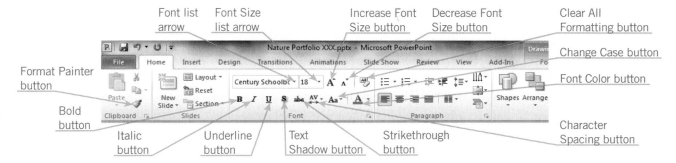

FIGURE PPT 2–6 Home tab

Changing Fonts and Font Sizes

A *font* is the design of a set of letters and numbers. Each set has a name. Below are some examples.

Times New Roman   Arial   **Impact**

For presentations, it is important to choose simple fonts that are readable from a distance. The Font menu, which you access using the Font list arrow in the Font group on the Home tab, displays each font's design. You can also access the Font menu on the Mini toolbar. By default in a new blank presentation, PowerPoint uses the Calibri 44 point font and font size for titles, and Calibri 32 point for text. You change to a different font by selecting text and choosing one of the fonts listed on the Font menu or in the Font dialog box. You can also choose to begin typing text with a new font by selecting the font on the Font menu before typing at the insertion point.

Font sizes are measured in points. *Point size* refers to a measurement for the height of characters. A point is equal to approximately 1/72 inch. A 10-point font is approximately 10/72 inch high. The examples below show what different point sizes look like in the Times New Roman font. Font sizes must be large enough and the slide uncluttered enough for an audience to read the message easily.

18 Point 24 Point 36 Point
To change the font size for existing text, you first select the text and then choose a new size by clicking the Font Size list arrow in the Font group and clicking a size on the Font Size menu, or by choosing a new size in the Size list in the Font dialog box. You can change the size of text you are about to enter by choosing a new size before typing at the insertion point.

The Increase Font Size button in the Font group increases font size one increment on the Font Size menu, which may be one point, two points, or eight points in the larger sizes, and the Decrease Font Size button decreases the size one increment.

▶ **VOCABULARY**
font
point size

▶ **VOCABULARY**
font styles
Format Painter

 EXTRA FOR EXPERTS

You can format text with font styles using shortcut keys: press Ctrl+B to apply bold, Ctrl+I to apply italic, and Ctrl+U to underline text.

Applying Font Styles and Effects

Font styles are variations in the shape or weight of a font's characters. Bold, italic, and underline are common font styles that you can access easily in the Font group.

Additional buttons are available to add effects to text. The Strikethrough button draws a line through the middle of text, the Text Shadow button adds a shadow behind text, and the Character Spacing button lets you adjust the space between characters. The Change Case button provides options for changing the capitalization of text, and the Font Color button and button arrow let you change the text color. You can add more than one effect to text, but make sure the text is still readable for the audience.

Clearing Formatting

To remove formatting from selected text, you perform the same steps you took to apply the formatting, which effectively reverses the formatting. For example, if you want to remove bold formatting that you added to a word, you would click the Bold button again to deselect the button and remove the bold formatting from selected text. Or, you can click the Clear All Formatting button to remove all formatting from selected text. Reversing a font change does not work in the same way; if you want to restore a font you had previously used, you must select the text and use the Font list arrow to change the text back to the original font.

Copying Formats Using the Format Painter

The *Format Painter* can save you time by allowing you to copy multiple formatting characteristics from a section of text and then apply the same formatting to other parts of the presentation.

To copy the formatting of a section of text, you first select the text or paragraph that contains the formatting you want to copy, and then click the Format Painter button in the Clipboard group on the Home tab. The mouse pointer changes to an I-beam with a paintbrush "loaded" with the copied format. Next you can select the text to which you want to apply the formatting, or if you want to apply the formatting to a single word, you can click it.

Double-clicking the Format Painter button allows you to "paint" the copied formatting to more than one selection. When you finish painting formats, click the Format Painter button or press Esc to turn off the Format Painter.

Step-by-Step PPT 2.3

The Nature Portfolio *XXX* presentation from Step-by-Step PPT 2.2 should be open in the PowerPoint program window.

1. On slide 1, select the **LOSTART PHOTOS** title.

2. On the Home tab, in the Font group, click the **Font** list arrow and click **Berlin Sans FB** on the menu, as shown in **Figure PPT 2–7**. If Berlin Sans FB is not available on your computer, select another font.

Font list arrow

Berlin Sans FB

FIGURE PPT 2–7
Font menu

3. Click the **Font Size** list arrow, and then click **40** to increase the font size.

4. Click the **Change Case** button [Aa▾] and click **Capitalize Each Word** to change the case of the text from all uppercase to capitalizing just the first letter of each word.

5. Select the **a** in *Lostart*. Click the **Change Case** button and click **UPPERCASE** to capitalize the letter.

6. Select the **LostArt Photos** title. Click the **Character Spacing** button [AV▾] and click **Loose**.

7. With the title still selected, click the **Bold** button [B]. Click the **Bold** button again to remove the bold formatting.

8. Click the **Increase Font Size** button [A˄] to increase the font size to 44 point.

9. Click the **Font Color** button arrow , and in the Theme Colors section of the palette, click **Black, Background 1**, as shown in **Figure PPT 2–8**.

FIGURE PPT 2–8
Font Color button arrow and palette

10. Click the **Clear All Formatting** button to remove all the applied formatting and return the title to the original font format.

11. Click the **Undo** button to restore the cleared formatting.

12. Select **LostArt Photos** if necessary. In the Clipboard group, click the **Format Painter** button to copy the formatting.

13. In the Slides tab, click slide 3 to display it, drag the paintbrush I-beam across **FLOWERS, FOLIAGE, AND ROCKS**, and then release the mouse button to apply the copied formatting.

14. Save the presentation and leave it open for use in the next Step-by-Step.

Formatting Paragraphs

PowerPoint refers to a paragraph as any amount of text followed by a paragraph mark. Although how paragraphs initially appear on a slide is determined by its design and layout, you can change the format of paragraphs by positioning your insertion point anywhere in the paragraph and then applying formatting. PowerPoint applies paragraph formats to the entire paragraph. You cannot apply paragraph formats to just a selection within a paragraph.

The Paragraph group on the Home tab, shown in **Figure PPT 2–9**, contains buttons for changing paragraph formatting. You can access additional commands in the Paragraph dialog box, which you can display by clicking the dialog box launcher in the Paragraph group.

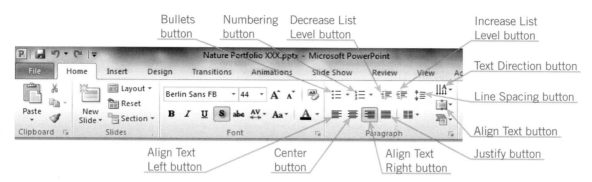

FIGURE PPT 2–9   Paragraph group on the Home tab

Aligning Text Horizontally and Vertically

Alignment is the position of text in relation to the edges of a placeholder on a slide. You can left-align, center, right-align, or justify text horizontally within a placeholder using the alignment buttons—Align Text Left, Center, Align Text Right, and Justify—in the Paragraph group on the Home tab.

The Align Text button provides a menu of options for aligning text vertically within a placeholder. You can align text at the top, middle, or bottom of a placeholder, or click More Options to specify other options such as Top Centered.

Setting Line Spacing

Line spacing determines the vertical distance between lines of text in a paragraph. The Line Spacing button in the Paragraph group lets you choose a common line spacing option, such as 1.0 (single spacing) or 2.0 (double-spacing). You can also click the dialog box launcher in the Paragraph group, or click Line Spacing Options on the Line Spacing menu, to display the Paragraph dialog box, which contains options for creating custom line spacing and for adding spacing before or after a paragraph.

Changing Text Direction

If you want to display text rotated on its side or stacked vertically, use the Text Direction button in the Paragraph group to select an option, such as Rotate all text 90° or Stacked. You can click the More Options command on the Text Direction menu to display the Format Text Effects dialog box, where several different options can be set in one place.

Formatting Lists

Bulleted lists are often used in presentations because they display text in a simple format that audiences can read quickly. Bulleted lists typically use short sentences, phrases, or keywords. The presenter can further discuss each bulleted item as needed. PowerPoint has several different bullet and numbering options. You can select an existing list, and then click the Bullets button or button arrow or the Numbering button or button arrow in the Paragraph group to add or change bullets or numbers.

The Bullets and Numbering command on the Bullets menu and the Numbering menu displays the Bullets and Numbering dialog box, in which you can choose from a gallery of bullet and numbering styles or create custom bullets. You can also use the dialog box to change the color and size of bullets or to import your own picture to further customize the design.

PowerPoint automatically renumbers a numbered list when you insert, move, copy, or delete items. A new bullet or number is added on a blank line when you press Enter at the end of a bulleted or numbered item. You can use the Increase and Decrease List Level buttons in the Paragraph group to promote or demote items to different outline levels in a list.

Step-by-Step PPT 2.4

The Nature Portfolio *XXX* presentation from Step-by-Step PPT 2.3 should be open in the PowerPoint program window.

1. On slide 4, select the text, and then on the Home tab, in the Paragraph group, click the **Align Text Right** button ≡ to right-align the text within the placeholder.

2. In the Paragraph group, click the **Center** button ≡ to center the text.

3. In the Paragraph group, click the **Line Spacing** button and click **2.0** to double-space the lines of text.

4. With the placeholder text selected, type **It all depends on your perspective** to replace it.

5. Select the text and then, in the Paragraph group, click the **Align Text** button and click **Top**, as shown in **Figure PPT 2–10**, to align the text at the top of the placeholder.

FIGURE PPT 2–10
Align Text button and menu

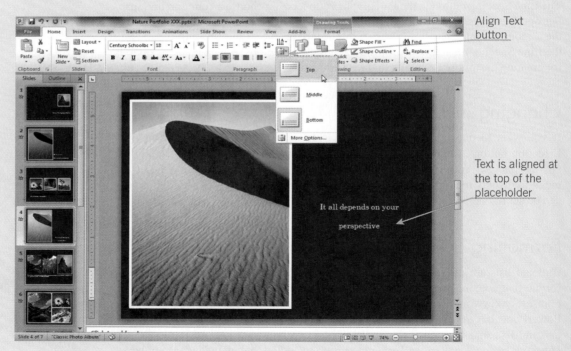

Align Text button

Text is aligned at the top of the placeholder

6. In the Paragraph group, click the **Text Direction** button and click **Rotate all text 270°** to turn the text on its side, as shown in **Figure PPT 2–11**.

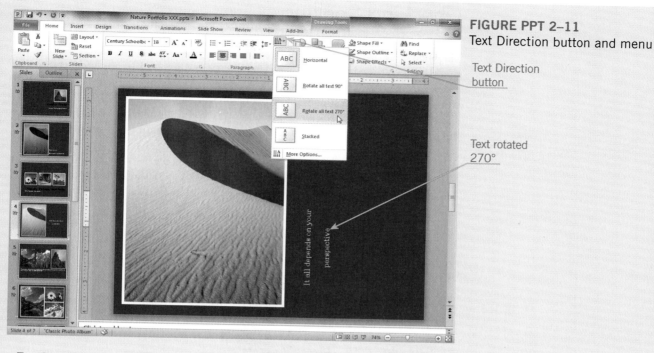

FIGURE PPT 2–11
Text Direction button and menu

Text Direction button

Text rotated 270°

7. On slide 2, select the two lines of text, and then click the **Increase List Level** button.

8. Click the **Bullets** button arrow and click the **Hollow Round Bullets** style, as shown in **Figure PPT 2–12**.

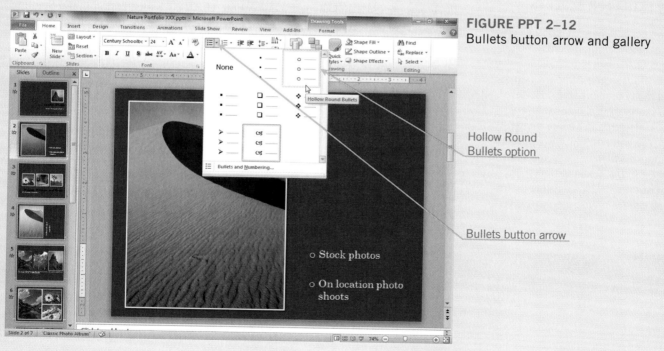

FIGURE PPT 2–12
Bullets button arrow and gallery

Hollow Round Bullets option

Bullets button arrow

9. Save the presentation, and view the presentation from the beginning in Slide Show view.

10. Close the presentation.

Checking Spelling

PowerPoint automatically checks spelling as you type by comparing a document's language to PowerPoint's built-in dictionary. PowerPoint underlines words that might be misspelled with a wavy red line. You can right-click a word that has a wavy red underline and see a shortcut menu with suggestions for corrections. If you don't want to use one of the suggested corrections, you can change the text manually. You should always spell check your presentations. Spelling and grammar mistakes are not only embarrassing, but they can also damage your credibility as a presenter.

You can check the spelling in an entire presentation with a single action using the Spelling button in the Proofing group on the Review tab, as shown in **Figure PPT 2–13**. This approach is useful when you have finished editing a presentation but you want to check it one more time to make sure you didn't miss any mistakes or introduce errors while editing.

FIGURE PPT 2–13   Review tab

The Spelling feature checks the entire presentation from the insertion point forward and then checks from the beginning of the presentation to the insertion point. When a possible error is detected, PowerPoint displays the Spelling dialog box to show you the error and suggest a correction. Use the Change button in the Spelling dialog box to correct an error, or use the Change All button to correct all instances of the same error. If the correct spelling does not appear in the Suggestions list, you can type the correct spelling in the Change to text box and then click the Change button.

The spelling checker will flag many proper nouns and other words as being incorrect. To ignore the word or phrase, or ignore all occurrences of the word or phrase, use the Ignore Once or Ignore All buttons as you use the spelling checker in presentations.

Remember, the Spelling feature does not eliminate the need to proofread a presentation. If a word you misspelled is another English word (for example, you typed *there* instead of *their*), the spelling feature will not detect the error. Although it finds many common errors, the Spelling feature does not always understand the context of the text and might suggest inappropriate corrections. Examine suggestions carefully before you accept them.

EXTRA FOR EXPERTS

PowerPoint's main dictionary contains most common words, including country names, names of many U.S. cities, some company names, and many proper names. However, you probably use words that are not in PowerPoint's main dictionary. You can add those words to a custom dictionary using the Add button in the Spelling dialog box so PowerPoint does not flag them each time you type them.

Step-by-Step PPT 2.5

1. Open the file **Step PPT 2-5** from the folder containing the data files for this lesson, and save it as **Course Rules XXX** (replace **XXX** with your initials).

2. On slide 1, right-click the red underlined letters, *Cours*, to display the shortcut menu.

3. Click **Course**, which is the first option on the menu, as shown in **Figure PPT 2–14**.

Right-click a word with a wavy red underline to display the shortcut menu

Click Course

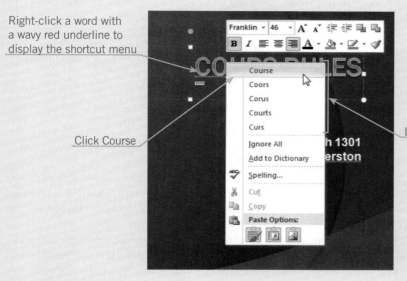

List of suggested words

FIGURE PPT 2–14
Suggested word spellings on the shortcut menu

4. On the Review tab on the Ribbon, in the Proofing group, click the **Spelling** button to open the Spelling dialog box.

5. Click **Ignore** to ignore the suggestions for changing the name, as shown in **Figure PPT 2–15**.

Name not in the dictionary

Click Ignore to make no changes to the name

FIGURE PPT 2–15
Spelling dialog box

6. Click **Change** to accept the correct spelling of *Bring*.

7. Click **Change** to accept the correct spelling of *Know*.

8. Click **Change** to accept the correct spelling of *materials*.

9. The suggested correction for the next error may not be the appropriate word. Click **posted** in the Suggestions list, if necessary, and then click **Change**.

10. Click **OK** to respond to the prompt that the spelling check is complete.

11. Save the presentation and leave it open for use in the next Step-by-Step.

Finding and Replacing Text

The Find and Replace commands are two separate commands that are often used together to find and replace text. The Find and Replace commands are located in the Editing group on the Home tab, as shown in **Figure PPT 2–16**.

Find button

Replace button

FIGURE PPT 2–16   Editing group on the Home tab

You can use the Find command alone to search for a specific word or phrase in a presentation. Click the Find button in the Editing group on the Home tab, and then enter the word or phrase you want to locate in the Find dialog box. You can use the Find Next button to find one search item at a time.

Click the Replace button in the Find dialog box to open the Replace dialog box, where you can use the Find Next and Replace buttons to make just one replacement at a time. The Replace All button in the Replace dialog box replaces all occurrences of a word without confirming each one. But be sure you want to replace every occurrence of the word. For instance, you can run into trouble using Replace All when changing a person's name, such as *Jackson* to *Johnson*. If a company name or city name in the document contains the name *Jackson*, such as *Jacksonville*, Replace All changes it to *Johnsonville*.

Since PowerPoint replaces partial words, you can also run into trouble when changing the word *class* to *course* because it would change the word *classic* to *courseic*. You can designate that PowerPoint find whole words only (words like *work* but not words containing the searched-for word, like *homework*) or match case (find a word with the same uppercase and lowercase combination) when searching for text by clicking the appropriate check box in the Replace dialog box.

EXTRA FOR EXPERTS

You can use the Replace Fonts command on the Replace menu to replace all occurrences of a font such as Arial with a new font, such as Calibri.

Step-by-Step PPT 2.6

The Course Rules *XXX* presentation from Step-by-Step PPT 2.5 should be open in the PowerPoint program window.

1. Display **slide 1**.

2. On the Home tab, in the Editing group, click the **Find** button to display the Find dialog box.

3. Type **Work** in the Find what box, and then click the **Match case** check box, as shown in **Figure PPT 2–17**, to search for the capitalized word.

FIGURE PPT 2–17
Find dialog box

Match case check box

Find whole words only check box

4. Click the **Find Next** button to start the search.

5. Click the **OK** button to respond to the message indicating that the search item wasn't found.

6. Click the **Match case** check box to clear it.

7. Click the **Find Next** button. PowerPoint locates the word *work*. In the Find dialog box, click the **Replace** button. The Find dialog box changes to the Replace dialog box.

8. Type **assignments** in the Replace with box, as shown in **Figure PPT 2–18**, and click the **Replace** button to replace the word *work* with the word *assignments*.

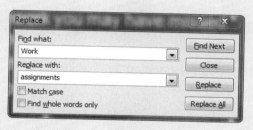

FIGURE PPT 2–18
Replace dialog box

9. PowerPoint moves to the next occurrence and finds the word *coursework*. In the Replace dialog box, click **Find Next** to move to the next search item without making changes.

10. Click the **OK** button to respond to the message indicating that PowerPoint finished searching the presentation.

11. In the Replace dialog box, click the **Find whole words only** check box to select it, and then click **Find Next** to make sure there are no more occurrences of the word *work*.

12. Click the **OK** button to respond to the message indicating that no search item was found.

13. Click the Replace dialog box **Close** button to end the search and close the dialog box.

14. Save the presentation and leave it open for use in the next Step-by-Step.

Applying Themes

PowerPoint provides so many different fonts, sizes, colors, font styles, and effects that it can be difficult to figure out which formatting options you should use together to create a professional-looking presentation. Unless you have an eye for design, it can be tricky to choose one font for titles, a coordinating font for content, and a background color and style that is attractive and readable. To make these decisions easier, PowerPoint includes several different built-in *themes*, which are sets of formatting choices that include colors, fonts, effects, and backgrounds that were predesigned to work well together. The themes are available in other Office programs as well,

▶ **VOCABULARY**
themes

so you can apply the same theme to an Excel spreadsheet, a Word report, and a PowerPoint presentation, resulting in a professionally coordinated package of files.

Each presentation you create is associated with one of PowerPoint's presentation themes, which are accessed through the Themes gallery in the Themes group on the Design tab on the Ribbon. Even a new blank presentation is based on a theme (the Office theme). When you change the theme, you change the entire presentation's color scheme, fonts, and effects to the new design theme. After a theme is applied to a presentation, you can further customize a theme's colors, fonts, and other effects using the buttons in the Themes group. See **Figure PPT 2–19**.

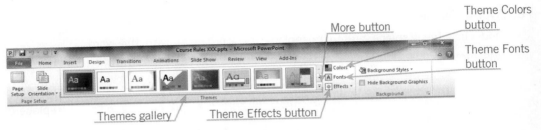

FIGURE PPT 2–19   Themes group on the Design tab

EXTRA FOR EXPERTS

If you want to create a new blank presentation with a theme already applied, you can do so in Backstage view. Just click the Themes category in the Available Templates and Themes section of Backstage view to display the available themes. Click your choice of theme, and then click the Create button to create a new blank presentation with a theme applied.

Additional theme choices are available online and may be accessed in the From Office.com section at the bottom of the Themes gallery, or use the Browse for Themes command below the Themes gallery to locate a presentation that contains a theme you want to apply to the current presentation. After you have customized a theme, you can use the Save Current Theme command below the Themes gallery to name and save it to the Document Themes folder.

When customizing or creating a new theme, aim for high contrast (difference between light and dark) between the background color and the text color to provide maximum readability. For example, white text on a black background is much more readable than white text on a yellow background.

Step-by-Step PPT 2.7

The Course Rules *XXX* presentation from Step-by-Step PPT 2.6 should be open in the PowerPoint program window.

1. Display **slide 1**.

2. On the Design tab on the Ribbon, in the Themes group, click the **More** button ⌄ to display the Themes gallery.

3. Point to several of the theme options to see a Live Preview of the choices available, then scroll down in the gallery and click the **Verve** theme, as shown in **Figure PPT 2–20**. The theme is applied to the presentation.

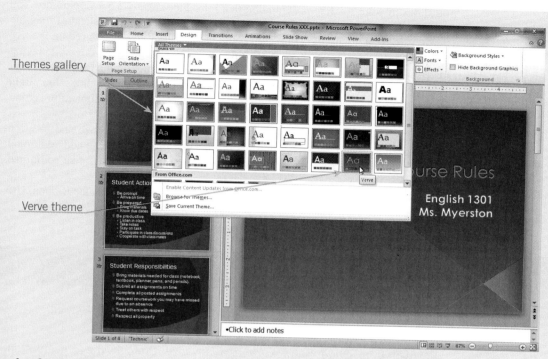

4. On the Design tab, in the Themes group, click the **Theme Colors** button, scroll down, and then click **Origin**. The presentation's theme colors change.

5. In the Themes group, click the **Theme Fonts** button, scroll down, and then click **Solstice**. The presentation's theme fonts change.

6. Save the presentation and leave it open for use in the next Step-by-Step.

Customizing Slide Masters

You have already learned that when you use a theme for a presentation, all the slides are set up with the formatting in that theme. Each theme has its own *slide master* and a set of layout masters. The slide master stores information about the theme (including fonts and background colors) and the layout (position and size of placeholders). When you make a change to the slide master, the change is made to the entire presentation. Slide masters provide a convenient way for you to further customize a presentation, especially one with many slides, with little effort. For example, if you have a 20-slide presentation and you want to change the color of all titles on all slides to match the blue of your company logo, you can open Slide Master view and change the color of the title on the slide master. The change is applied to all titles in the presentation at once—an effect you cannot achieve by changing the theme colors. The alternative would be to open all 20 slides and use the Font Color button to change the title colors one by one—a tedious way to accomplish the same result. In the same way, you can change the bullet styles used for the entire presentation or insert clip art on the slide master that will appear in the same position on every slide.

You can also alter the *layout masters*, which store information about the fonts, colors, effects, and arrangement of each type of slide layout. If no changes are made to the layout masters, the layout masters follow the settings of the slide master and the applied theme. However, you can make changes to individual layout masters and override the slide master settings if you want. For example, you might have five

▶ **VOCABULARY**
slide master

layout masters

title slides in your 20-slide presentation that introduce each of your five points. You decide that you want the titles on the title slides to appear in red instead of the blue you set earlier on the master slide. You could change the font color to red on the five title slides in the presentation, or you could make the change to the title slide layout master in Slide Master view. When you change the font color on the title slide layout master, the change will apply to all five title slides and any new title slides you might insert. The red color setting on the layout master overrides the blue font color setting on the slide master, but only for the title slide layouts.

In addition to changing formatting, you can also change the size and location of the placeholders on the layout masters or the slide master. You can add additional placeholders to the title slide layout master, for example, to accommodate additional text.

In Slide Master view, PowerPoint displays the Slide Master tab on the Ribbon. Use the Close Master View button to close Slide Master view and return to Normal view.

Step-by-Step PPT 2.8

The Course Rules *XXX* presentation from Step-by-Step PPT 2.7 should be open in the PowerPoint program window.

1. Switch to Slide Show view and advance through the presentation. Notice the title font colors and alignments and the bullet styles used in the presentation.

2. On the View tab, in the Master Views group, click the **Slide Master View** button to change to Slide Master view.

3. Click the **slide master** if necessary, which is the top thumbnail in the left pane, as shown in **Figure PPT 2–21**.

FIGURE PPT 2–21
Slide Master view

Slide Master tab

Slide master

Layout masters

Click to close Slide Master view

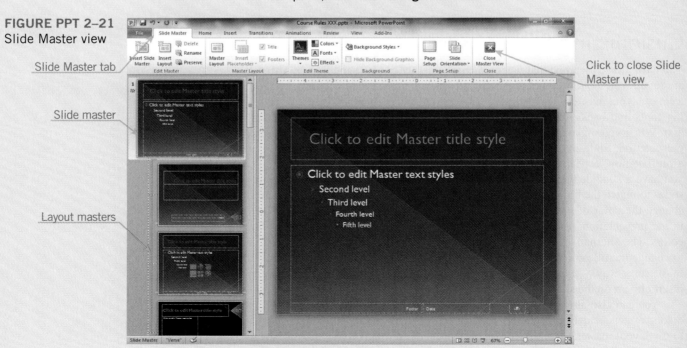

4. In the Slide pane, select the text **Click to edit Master title style** at the top of the slide master.

5. On the Home tab, in the Font group, click the **Font Color** button arrow A ⋅ and click **Blue-Gray**, **Accent 1**, **Lighter 80%**, as shown in **Figure PPT 2–22**, to change the font color of all the titles in the presentation.

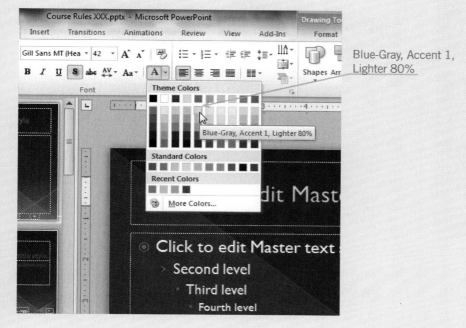

FIGURE PPT 2–22
Modifying the slide master

6. Select the text **Click to edit Master text styles** in the first bullet of the slide master.

7. On the Home tab, in the Paragraph group, click the **Bullets** button arrow and click the **Hollow Square Bullets** style to change the bullet style for all the first-level bullets in the presentation.

8. Click the **Title Slide** layout master, the second thumbnail in the left pane.

9. In the Slide pane, select the text **Click to edit Master title style**, as shown in **Figure PPT 2–23**.

Modifying a
layout master

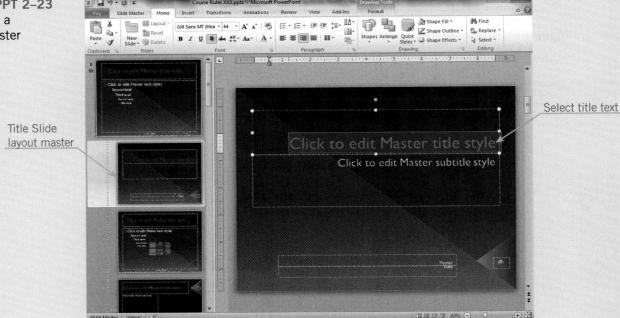

Title Slide
layout master

Select title text

10. On the Home tab, in the Font group, click the **Font Color** button arrow and click **White**, **Text 1** to change the text color to white.

11. In the Font group, click the **Bold** button **B** to change the text style to bold.

12. On the Slide Master tab, in the Close group, click the **Close Master View** button to return to Normal view.

13. On the Slide Show tab, in the Start Slide Show group, click the **From Beginning** button to view the entire presentation. Notice that the title slide has a white, bold title; the remaining slides have gray titles; and slides 2, 3, and 4 now have Hollow Square Bullets for first-level bulleted items.

14. Save and close the presentation.

15. Exit PowerPoint.

SUMMARY

In this lesson, you learned:

- How to create a new blank presentation using Backstage view.
- Well-organized and attractive presentations can be quickly created with templates.
- How to apply character formats including fonts, font sizes, font styles, and font effects using the buttons in the Font group on the Home tab.
- Paragraph formatting, such as alignment and line spacing, can be changed using commands in the Paragraph group on the Home tab.

- How to use the Format Painter button to copy existing formats to other parts of a presentation.
- How spell checking works in PowerPoint.
- How to find a specific word in a presentation and replace it with a new word.
- Themes change the entire presentation's color scheme, fonts, and effects.
- Changes made to slide masters affect the entire presentation.

VOCABULARY REVIEW

Define the following terms:

alignment
characters
font
font styles

Format Painter
layout masters
point size

slide master
template
themes

REVIEW QUESTIONS

MULTIPLE CHOICE

Select the best response for the following statements.

1. A _____ contains a group of slides with a layout, theme, background style, and suggestions for content that are standard for a particular type of presentation.

   A. slide master

   B. template

   C. theme

   D. list

2. A _____ is the design of a set of letters and numbers.

   A. font

   B. font style

   C. point size

   D. template

3. _____ is the position of text in relation to the edge of the placeholder on a slide.

   A. Alignment

   B. Line spacing

   C. Text direction

   D. Point size

4. _____ are often used in presentations because they display text in a simple format that audiences can read quickly.

   A. Bulleted lists

   B. Layout masters

   C. Slide masters

   D. Theme effects

5. The _____ button can rotate or stack text.

   A. Align Text

   B. Align Text Right

   C. Text Direction

   D. Increase List Level

6. The Spelling button is located on the _____ tab.

A. Home   C. Slide Show

B. Insert   D. Review

7. In the Find dialog box, clicking the _____ check box will find the word *work* but not the word *homework*.

A. Match case   C. Find whole words only

B. Replace   D. Find what

8. The _____ button replaces all occurrences of a word at once without confirming each one.

A. Replace   C. Find Next

B. Replace All   D. Find what

9. _____ are sets of formatting choices that include colors, fonts, effects, and backgrounds that were predesigned to work well together.

A. Fonts   C. Templates

B. Slide masters   D. Themes

10. When you make a change to the _____, the change is made to the entire presentation.

A. layout master   C. slide master

B. list   D. paragraph

FILL IN THE BLANK

Complete the following sentences by writing the correct word or words in the blanks provided.

1. To create a new blank presentation, click the File tab on the Ribbon and then click _____.

2. _____ are individual letters, numbers, symbols, punctuation marks, and spaces.

3. Font sizes are measured in _____.

4. _____-clicking the Format Painter button allows you to "paint" the copied format to more than one selection.

5. The _____ _____ button provides options for changing the capitalization of text.

6. _____-click a word that has a wavy red underline to see a shortcut menu with suggestions for corrections.

7. Use the _____ command to search for a specific word or phrase in a presentation.

8. You can use the Theme _____ button to change the preestablished colors for a theme.

9. Each _____ has its own slide master and a set of layout masters.

10. The Slide Master View button is located on the _____ tab.

PROJECTS

PROJECT PPT 2–1

1. Start PowerPoint and create a new presentation using the Introducing PowerPoint 2010 template from the Sample templates category in Backstage view. Save it as **Introduction XXX** (replace *XXX* with your initials).

2. On slide 1, select the *PowerPoint 2010* title, and then change the font to Bauhaus 93 or another font of your choice.

3. Change the color of the title to Orange.

4. Copy the formatting on the title, and then apply it to the *PowerPoint 2010* title on slide 20.

5. On slide 4, select the two paragraphs of text (beginning with *You don't have to...*) in the top text placeholder, change the line spacing of the paragraphs to 1.5, and then justify the paragraphs.

6. Copy the format of the text you changed in step 5 to the text in the placeholder below it.

7. Change the theme of the presentation to Waveform.

8. View the slide show from the beginning.

9. Save and close the presentation.

PROJECT PPT 2–3

The presentation Fitness Challenge *XXX* from Project PPT 2–2 should be open in the PowerPoint program window.

1. Save the presentation as **Fitness Challenge 2 XXX** (replace *XXX* with your initials).

2. In Slide Master view, change the font of the master title style to Franklin Gothic Heavy.

3. In Slide Master view, display the Title and Content layout master, and then change the first-level bullet to the Arrow Bullets style.

4. On the Title and Content layout master, change the line spacing of all bullet levels to 1.5.

5. Close Slide Master view.

6. View the presentation from the beginning.

7. Save and close the presentation.

ON YOUR OWN

Open **Fitness Challenge 2 XXX**. Redesign the first slide using the fonts, font styles, colors, and alignments of your choice. Try to make the slide more attractive, but make sure it is still appropriate for the intended audience. Save and close the presentation.

PROJECT PPT 2–2

1. Open the file **Project PPT 2–2** from the folder containing the data files for this lesson.

2. Save the presentation as **Fitness Challenge XXX** (replace *XXX* with your initials).

3. Find all the occurrences of the phrase *Health Challenge* and replace them with **Fitness Challenge**.

4. Spell check the presentation and correct any misspelled words.

5. Change the theme of the presentation to Adjacency.

6. Change the theme colors to Flow.

7. On slide 1, bold *Company Fitness Challenge*, and then change the color to Turquoise, Accent 3.

8. Save the presentation and leave it open for use in the next project.

PROJECT PPT 2–4

1. Open the file **Project PPT 2–4** from the folder containing the data files for this lesson. Save it as **Job Search *XXX*** (replace *XXX* with your initials).

2. Use the shortcut menu to correct the three misspelled words, indicated by wavy red underlines, in the presentation.

3. Apply the Austin theme to the presentation.

4. Change the theme fonts to Executive.

5. On slide 1, change the *Job Search Strategies* title to 40 point and bold. Add a text shadow.

6. Increase the size of the subtitle, *Steps for Finding Employment*, to 20 point.

7. On slide 2, left-align the list of items.

8. On slide 3, change the case of the title, *Research*, to Capitalize Each Word.

9. On slide 3, decrease the list level on the bulleted items.

10. On slide 4, change the line spacing of the bulleted list to 1.0.

11. On slide 5, change the vertical alignment of the text in the bulleted list to Top.

12. Save and close the presentation.

ON YOUR OWN

Open **Job Search *XXX***. View the presentation in Handout Master view, and then enter **Job Search Strategies** in the left header text box, and **Steps for Finding Employment** in the left footer text box. Preview the handouts, 6 slides per page (horizontal), in Backstage view. Save and close the presentation.

WEB PROJECT

Explore the templates available in the Office.com Templates section of the Available Templates and Themes area of Backstage view. You must be connected to the Internet and have permission to download a presentation. Choose a favorite template to download, and modify it to your specifications.

TEAMWORK PROJECT

With a partner, download and view the Five Rules template from the Sample templates category in Backstage view. Using what you learn from the Five Rules presentation, collaborate with your partner to plan and create a simple 5 to 7 slide presentation that informs your audience about a topic of your choice. For example, you may choose to create a presentation on ways to conserve energy, study tips for college entrance exams, the benefits of playing your favorite sport, or the pros and cons of texting. Be prepared to explain how you incorporated the rules from the Five Rules presentation into your own presentation.

CRITICAL THINKING

ACTIVITY PPT 2–1

Open the **Favorite Movies *XXX*** presentation that you created in Step-by-Step PPT 2.1. Complete the presentation by adding slides and inserting content for about five of your favorite movies. (If you prefer, you may change the topic to another subject, such as favorite books, music, or hobbies.) Include the title, a brief description, and a statement describing the reasons why the movie is a favorite. Experiment with themes. Customize the slide master, and check the spelling. Be prepared to share your presentation with the class and describe the formatting and design options you incorporated.

ACTIVITY PPT 2–3

Open a new, blank presentation and apply a theme. Experiment with the commands in the Background group of the Design tab to answer the following questions, using PowerPoint's Help system if necessary. What is a background style? What options are available? How do you apply background styles to individual slides? How do you apply background styles to all slides? What happens to the background style options when you change the theme? In what situations might you want to hide background graphics? Be prepared to demonstrate the use of background styles.

ACTIVITY PPT 2–2

Create a new theme by customizing one of the themes in the PowerPoint theme gallery. Name and save it. Prepare a brief presentation displaying your theme and explaining the fonts, colors, and other elements used in it. Include ideas for the types of presentations that would demonstrate the appropriate use of your theme.

⊙ **Estimated Time:**
2.5 hours

LESSON 3

Enhancing Presentations

■ OBJECTIVES

Upon completion of this lesson, you should be able to:

- Insert and modify illustrations.
- Create and modify tables.
- Insert text boxes.
- Insert footers.
- Insert special effects.

■ DATA FILES

To complete this lesson, you will need these data files:

Step PPT 3-1.pptx
Project PPT 3-1.pptx
Project PPT 3-2.pptx
Project PPT 3-3.pptx
Project PPT 3-4.pptx
Activity PPT 3-1.pptx

■ VOCABULARY

action button

animation

cell

chart

clip art

crop

drawing objects

footer

header

picture

screenshot

selection handles

SmartArt graphic

table

text box

transition

Introduction

Graphics are visual components that add impact to presentations and help explain the text. Pictures, clip art, shapes, SmartArt, screenshots, and charts are all types of graphics that you can add to and customize in your PowerPoint presentations. Tables provide another way to organize, explain, or supplement text in a presentation. You can add text boxes to position text where there are no placeholders. Special effects such as transitions and animations make your slide show presentation truly professional. In this lesson, you will learn to insert and modify these graphic elements and insert special effects to complete your presentations.

Inserting and Modifying Illustrations

Pictures, clip art, screenshots, shapes, SmartArt, and charts are types of illustrations you can add to your PowerPoint presentations. Many slide layouts contain content placeholders with buttons you can click to insert different types of graphics, as shown in **Figure PPT 3–1**. Inserting a graphic on a slide within a content placeholder makes it easy to arrange the graphic in relation to other elements on the slide. As you recall from Lesson 1, you can always change a slide's layout to better accommodate the graphics and text that you want to include on the slide.

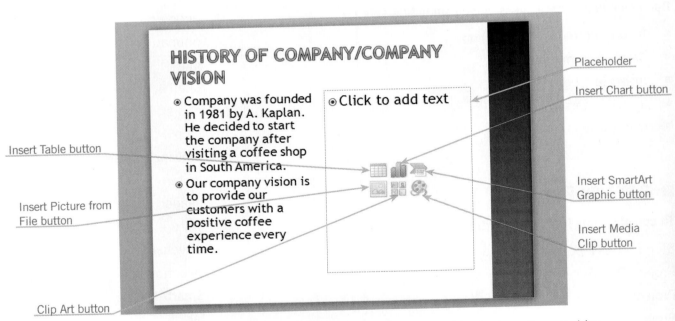

FIGURE PPT 3–1   Slide with placeholder for inserting graphics

You can also use buttons in the Images and Illustrations groups on the Insert tab on the Ribbon, shown in **Figure PPT 3–2**, to insert various types of graphic objects and position them anywhere on a slide.

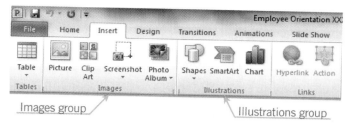

FIGURE PPT 3–2   Insert tab

When you insert a graphic object, you choose the graphic to be inserted using a dialog box, task pane, or menu, depending on the type of image or illustration. After you insert a graphic object, you have many options for modifying it, most of which are the same for each type of graphic.

Inserting and Modifying Pictures

The Insert Picture from File button can be used to insert a *picture*, which is a digital photograph or image that is stored on your computer or network. You can insert pictures of various formats, including .tif, .gif, and .jpg. The Insert Picture from File button opens the Insert Picture dialog box, which you can use to navigate to and insert a picture file from your computer or network.

After you insert a picture and any time the picture is selected, the Picture Tools Format contextual tab is displayed on the Ribbon. This tab contains commands for adjusting the picture, modifying the picture style, arranging the picture on the slide, and resizing the picture precisely.

Before you can modify or size a picture, clip art, or shape, you must select it. To select a graphic within a presentation, click the graphic once. The small circles and squares that appear at the sides and corners of the selected graphic are called *selection handles*. You drag these handles to change the graphic's size. When you want to resize a graphic proportionally, that is, to maintain the original ratio of height to width, you must drag a corner handle. Some types of graphics require that you hold the Shift key while dragging a corner handle in order to resize it proportionally. If you want to distort a graphic horizontally or vertically, drag a middle handle to resize the graphic. You can click the green rotate handle at the top of a graphic to rotate it left or right on its central axis to any position.

When a graphic is selected, you can copy, paste, and delete it the same way you would text using the Cut, Copy, and Paste commands in the Clipboard group on the Home tab. A copy of a graphic is the same size and contains the same formatting as the original graphic. When you paste a copy of a graphic, the new copy might appear on top of or next to the original. Simply drag it to the desired position.

The Color and Artistic Effects buttons in the Adjust group on the Picture Tools Format tab allow you to change the color of a picture or add interesting effects such as paint strokes or blurring. The Change Picture button opens the Insert Picture dialog box so that you can easily replace the current selected picture with a different one. The Picture Styles gallery in the Picture Styles group contains predesigned styles for altering a picture's shape, adding a frame, or changing the perspective. You can use the Rotate button in the Arrange group to rotate or flip an object. The *Crop* button in the Size group lets you crop, or remove, unwanted parts of a picture by dragging cropping handles on the sides and corners of the picture. Using the Shape Height and Shape Width up and down arrows, you can adjust the size of a graphic while maintaining its proportion, or you can type in a number to change the height or width to a specific measurement.

▶ **VOCABULARY**

picture

selection handles

crop

▦ **EXTRA FOR EXPERTS**

When resizing graphics, it can be helpful to display the vertical and horizontal rulers by clicking the Ruler check box in the Show group on the View tab.

▦ **EXTRA FOR EXPERTS**

Large files can take longer to download, and some might be rejected by e-mail servers when sent electronically. Including pictures in presentations increases file size, but you can use the Compress Pictures button in the Adjust group on the Picture Tools Format tab to decrease a picture's file size by reducing the resolution, or the number of pixels, in the picture.

Step-by-Step PPT 3.1

1. Start PowerPoint.

2. Open **Step PPT 3-1** from the folder containing the data files for this lesson, and save the presentation as **Employee Orientation *XXX*** (replace *XXX* with your initials).

3. Display slide 3.

4. In the content placeholder, click the **Insert Picture from File** button to open the Insert Picture dialog box.

5. Navigate to the **Sample Pictures** folder, and then double-click the folder to open it.

6. Click **Desert** (or another picture of your choice) to select the image, and then click the **Insert** button. The picture is inserted on the slide, as shown in **Figure PPT 3–3**.

FIGURE PPT 3–3
Picture inserted into placeholder

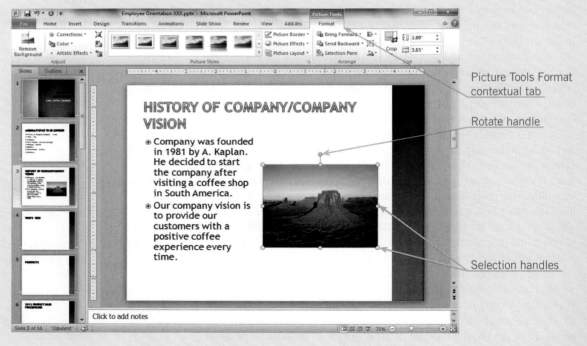

7. On the Picture Tools Format contextual tab, in the Adjust group, click the **Change Picture** button to display the Insert Picture dialog box.

8. In the Sample Pictures folder, double-click **Lighthouse** (or another picture of your choice) to insert the new picture in place of the Desert picture.

9. On the Picture Tools Format tab, in the Size group, click the **Crop** button to display the black cropping handles on the picture.

10. Display the rulers, if necessary. Drag the middle-right cropping handle on the picture to the left about half an inch, as shown in **Figure PPT 3–4**, and then release the mouse button. Click the **Crop** button again to remove the unwanted part of the picture.

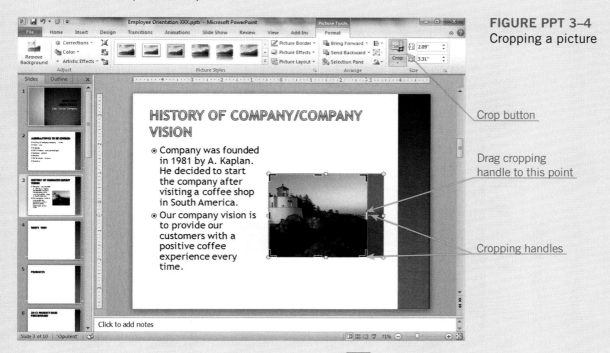

FIGURE PPT 3–4
Cropping a picture

Crop button

Drag cropping handle to this point

Cropping handles

11. In the Arrange group, click the **Rotate** button and click **Flip Horizontal** to flip the image.

12. In the Size group, click the **Shape Height** up arrow button until 3.2" is displayed in the box. Notice that the measurement in the Shape Width box changed to maintain the proportions of the picture.

13. In the Picture Styles group, click the **More** button ⊡ to display the Picture Styles gallery. Point to several different options to see a Live Preview of some of the styles available, and then click the **Rotated, White** option, as shown in **Figure PPT 3–5**, to apply the style to the picture.

FIGURE PPT 3–5
Picture Styles gallery

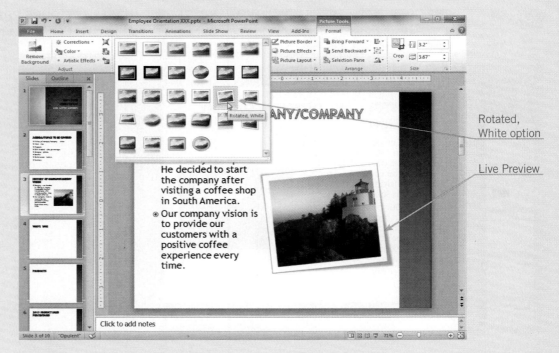

14. Save the presentation and leave it open for use in the next Step-by-Step.

Inserting and Modifying Clip Art

Clip art is ready-made artwork, usually created with a computer, that is used to illustrate documents or presentations. Clip art files may be in formats like .gif, .wmf, or .bmp. Sometimes the term *clip art* refers to any piece of artwork, including pictures, that has been made available on a Web site, on a CD, or with a software program for the purpose of illustrating documents. You can click the Clip Art button in the Images group on the Insert tab or in a content placeholder to display the Clip Art task pane, shown in **Figure PPT 3–6**, which you can use to search for and insert clip art located on your computer, network, or on the Internet. The task pane contains a Search for text box where you can enter a keyword to find related clip art. The Results should be menu lets you choose the type of media file for which you are searching, including illustrations, photos, videos, and audio files.

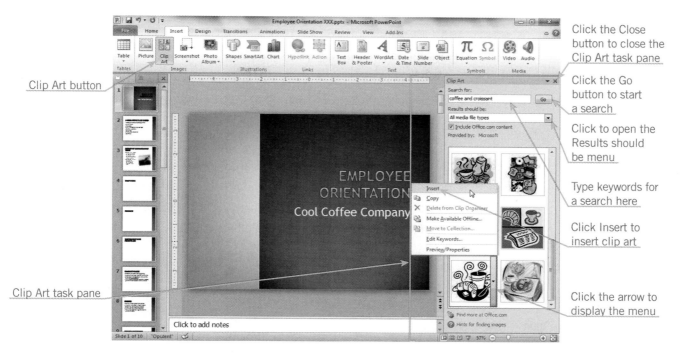

FIGURE PPT 3–6   Clip Art task pane

You can insert clip art simply by clicking an image in the Clip Art task pane. In addition, when you point to a graphic in the Clip Art task pane, an arrow appears next to the graphic that, when clicked, displays a menu containing the Insert command as well as other commands for copying, moving, and previewing the file properties of the selected clip art. Just like with pictures, once you've inserted clip art into a document, the Picture Tools Format contextual tab on the Ribbon enables you to modify the clip art.

Step-by-Step PPT 3.2

The Employee Orientation *XXX* presentation from Step-by-Step PPT 3.1 should be open in the PowerPoint program window.

1. Display slide 1. Notice that there are no empty placeholders on the slide.

2. On the Insert tab, in the Images group, click the **Clip Art** button to display the Clip Art task pane.

3. In the Search for box, type **coffee and croissant**. If necessary, click the **Include Office.com content** check box. Click the **Go** button to start the search.

4. In the Clip Art task pane, scroll down if necessary, and point to the picture of the coffee cup and croissant in the results pane shown in Figure PPT 3–6 (or choose a similar picture). (The clip art might appear in a different location in your Clip Art task pane.)

5. Click the arrow on the right side of the image to display a menu.

6. Click **Insert** to insert the clip art on the slide.

7. On the slide, point to the clip art image to display the move pointer with selection pointer ⁺↖, and then drag the clip art to the lower-left corner of the slide within the gray sidebar.

8. Point to the upper-right corner handle on the image so that the pointer changes to a double-headed arrow resize pointer ↗. Drag the corner handle up and to the right about half an inch to resize the image until the Shape height is approximately 2.4" in the Size group, as shown in **Figure PPT 3–7**. Position the clip art as shown.

FIGURE PPT 3–7
Resizing clip art

Drag selection handle up and to the right to increase the size

Shape height should be approximately 2.4"

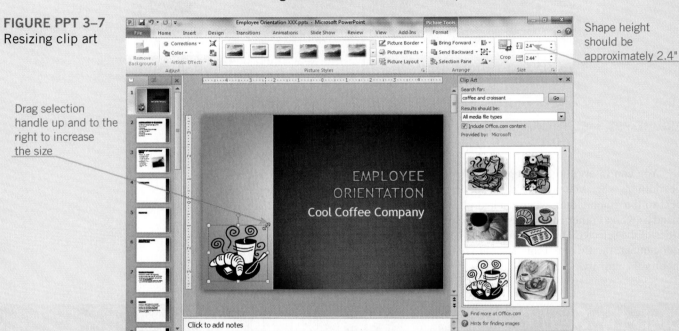

9. On the Picture Tools Format tab, in the Adjust group, click the **Color** button and click **Sepia**, as shown in **Figure PPT 3–8,** to add color to the clip art.

Color button and gallery

10. Click outside the clip art to deselect it.

11. Click the **Close** button ☒ on the Clip Art task pane to close it.

12. Save the presentation and leave it open for use in the next Step-by-Step.

Inserting and Modifying Screenshots

Instructional presentations, such as one teaching an audience to use PowerPoint, would contain illustrations to show what a certain dialog box looks like or what the screen should look like after applying a command. These visuals provide details that would be difficult to describe using words. You can easily include these types of pictures in your own presentations using the *Screenshot* button in the Images group on the Insert tab. A screenshot is a picture of a computer screen or a part of a screen, such as a window or button. The Insert Screenshot button enables you to insert a picture of a nonminimized window on your computer (other than the currently open document window) into your document. The Screen Clipping command on the Screenshot menu lets you use the mouse to cut out and insert any part of a screen into your document. After you insert a screenshot or clipping, you can modify it using the contextual Picture Tools Format tab.

▶ **VOCABULARY**
screenshot

Step-by-Step PPT 3.3

The Employee Orientation *XXX* presentation from Step-by-Step PPT 3.2 should be open in the PowerPoint program window.

1. Display slide 1, if necessary.

2. Create a new blank presentation.

3. On the Insert tab, in the Images group, click the **Screenshot** button, and then click **Screen Clipping**. The new blank presentation is removed from the screen, and the first slide of the Employee Orientation presentation is displayed and dimmed.

4. Click the crosshair pointer at the upper-left corner of the slide, drag down and to the right to the lower-right corner to "cut" out the entire slide, as shown in **Figure PPT 3–9**, and then release the mouse button. The screen clipping is displayed in the blank presentation.

FIGURE PPT 3–9
Creating a
screen clipping

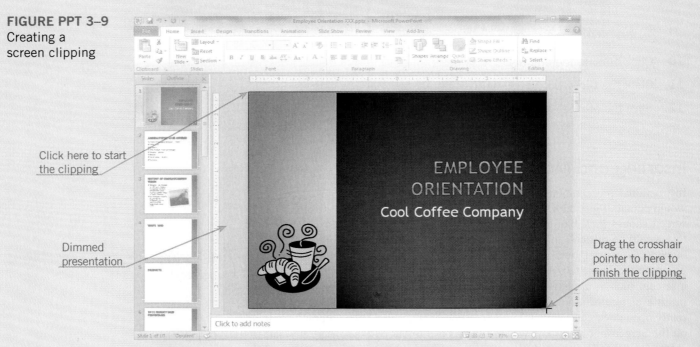

Click here to start the clipping

Dimmed presentation

Drag the crosshair pointer to here to finish the clipping

5. On the Home tab, in the Clipboard group, click the **Cut** button to temporarily move the screen clipping to the Clipboard.

6. Close the blank presentation without saving. The Employee Orientation *XXX* presentation is displayed on your screen.

7. Display slide 10.

8. On the Home tab, in the Clipboard group, click the **Paste** button to insert the screen clipping in the slide.

9. Resize the screen clipping, and then position it on the slide as shown in **Figure PPT 3–10**.

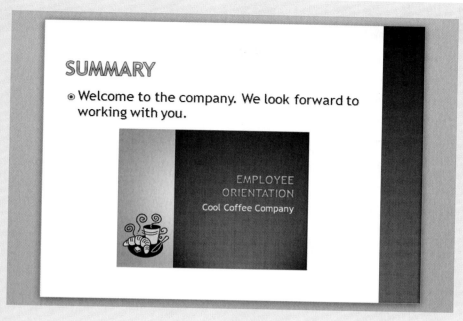

FIGURE PPT 3–10
Inserted screen clipping

10. Save the presentation and leave it open for use in the next Step-by-Step.

Inserting and Modifying Shapes

PowerPoint provides a set of common shapes that you can add to slides with one click and drag of the mouse. The Shapes button on the Insert tab on the Ribbon displays a gallery containing shapes, lines, rectangles, basic shapes, block arrows, equation shapes, flowchart elements, stars and banners, callouts, and action buttons that you can insert anywhere on your slides. To draw a shape, click the shape you want in the gallery, and then position the crosshair pointer in the location on the slide where you want the shape to appear. Drag to draw the shape to the preferred size, or click once to insert the shape in a default size. You can move and resize the shape like any other graphic object.

Shapes, curves, and lines are considered *drawing objects*, which are created with PowerPoint and become part of your presentation, rather than being a separate file. After you insert a shape into a presentation, the Drawing Tools Format contextual tab is displayed on the Ribbon with commands for modifying drawing objects. After inserting a shape, you can delete it using the Delete key while the shape is selected, or by using the Undo button immediately after creating the shape.

An *action button* is a shape that, when clicked, triggers a commonly understood action like going to the next or previous slide or playing a movie or sound. An action button contains a graphic symbol such as an arrow, movie camera, or sound speaker, to indicate the type of action it triggers. When you insert an action button, PowerPoint displays the Action Settings dialog box so you can specify the action to occur when you click or mouse over the action button.

EXTRA FOR EXPERTS

Hold the Shift key when drawing rectangular or oval shapes in order to draw squares or circles.

VOCABULARY
drawing objects
action button

EXTRA FOR EXPERTS

You might want to combine shapes to create a single drawing object, such as several lines and shapes that combine to create a map. You can select multiple shapes simultaneously by holding the Shift key while you click each of the shapes. On the Drawing Tools Format tab, in the Arrange group, click the Group button and click Group to combine the selected shapes into one object that can be moved, formatted, and resized.

Step-by-Step PPT 3.4

The Employee Orientation *XXX* presentation from Step-by-Step PPT 3.3 should be open in the PowerPoint program window.

1. Display slide 10 if necessary.

2. On the Insert tab, in the Illustrations group, click the **Shapes** button to display the gallery.

3. In the Action Buttons category, click the **Action Button: Sound** shape, as shown in **Figure PPT 3–11**. The mouse pointer changes to a cross-hair pointer.

FIGURE PPT 3–11
Shapes button and gallery

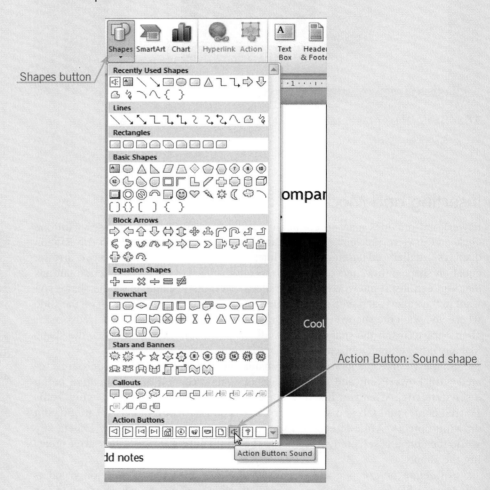

Shapes button

Action Button: Sound shape

4. In the lower-right corner of the slide, drag down and to the right to draw the action button. The Action Settings dialog box opens when you finish drawing the shape.

5. In the Action Settings dialog box, click the **Mouse Over** tab to specify actions that occur when the presenter holds the mouse pointer over the sound action button during the presentation.

6. Click the **Play sound** check box.

7. Click the **Play sound** list arrow and click **Applause**, as shown in **Figure PPT 3–12**.

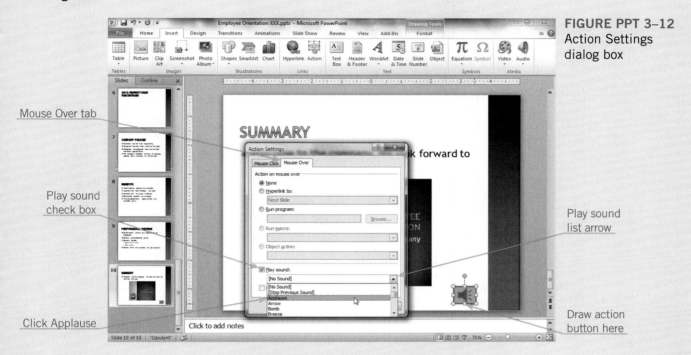

FIGURE PPT 3–12
Action Settings dialog box

Mouse Over tab

Play sound check box

Click Applause

Play sound list arrow

Draw action button here

8. Click the **OK** button to close the Action Settings dialog box.

9. On the Drawing Tools Format tab, in the Shape Styles group, click the **More** button ⏷ to display the Shape Styles gallery. Point to several of the styles to see Live Previews of the button with the styles applied, and then click the **Subtle Effect – Brown, Accent 5** option, as shown in **Figure PPT 3–13**.

FIGURE PPT 3–13
Shape Styles gallery

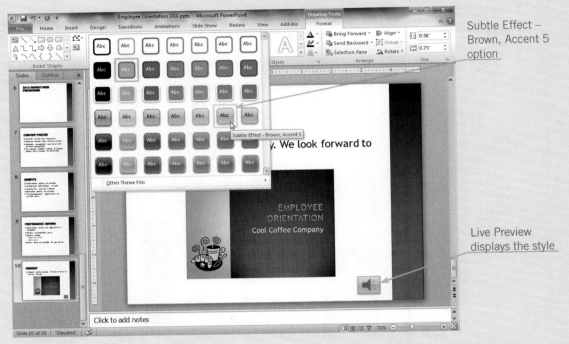

Subtle Effect – Brown, Accent 5 option

Live Preview displays the style

10. Switch to Slide Show view and advance to slide 10, if necessary. Point to the action button you inserted to hear the sound.

11. Return to Normal view.

12. Save the presentation and leave it open for use in the next Step-by-Step.

Inserting and Modifying SmartArt

▶ **VOCABULARY**
SmartArt graphic

Sometimes the best way to convey information is to use a chart or diagram. For example, an organization chart clearly shows a personnel reporting hierarchy, and a flow chart depicts a course of actions. A ***SmartArt graphic*** is a predesigned diagram made up of shapes containing text that illustrates a concept or idea. A hierarchy chart is an example of one type of SmartArt graphic you can create easily in PowerPoint. Other types of SmartArt graphics include lists, processes, cycles, relationships, matrixes, and pyramids.

You insert a SmartArt graphic using the Insert SmartArt Graphic button in the Illustrations group on the Insert tab on the Ribbon, or by clicking the Insert SmartArt Graphic button in a content placeholder. SmartArt graphics are inserted with placeholder text, much like the placeholders used in slides. You can replace the placeholder text with your own text.

After you insert a SmartArt graphic, the SmartArt Tools Design and Format contextual tabs are displayed on the Ribbon and provide access to a range of tools for customizing the graphic.

To add text to a SmartArt graphic, you can type directly into a selected shape. In addition, you can display a Text pane next to the graphic to help simplify the process of entering text. To display or hide the Text pane, click the Text Pane button in the Create Graphic group on the SmartArt Tools Design tab, or click the tab on the left side of the SmartArt graphic. You can click a [Text] placeholder beside a bullet in the Text pane to enter text in a shape.

> **EXTRA FOR EXPERTS**
>
> You can change an existing bulleted list of text into a SmartArt graphic using the Convert to SmartArt Graphic button in the Paragraph group on the Home tab.

Step-by-Step PPT 3.5

The Employee Orientation *XXX* presentation from Step-by-Step PPT 3.4 should be open in the PowerPoint program window.

1. Display slide 4. In the content placeholder, click the **Insert SmartArt Graphic** button to open the Choose a SmartArt Graphic dialog box.

2. Click the **Hierarchy** category, click the **Organization Chart** layout, as shown in **Figure PPT 3–14**, and then click the **OK** button to insert the graphic into the slide. The SmartArt Tools Design and Format tabs are displayed on the Ribbon.

Organization Chart layout

Click a category

Select a layout

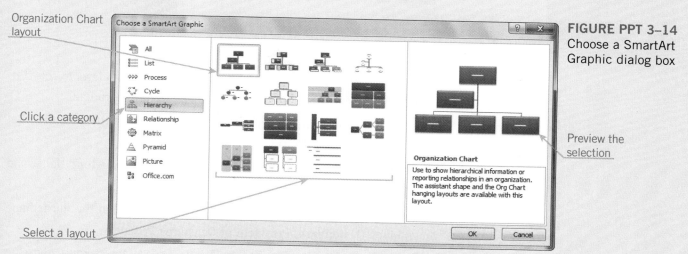

FIGURE PPT 3–14
Choose a SmartArt Graphic dialog box

Preview the selection

3. On the SmartArt Tools Design tab, in the Create Graphic group, click the **Text Pane** button in the Create Graphic group to display the Text pane, if necessary.

4. In the Text pane, type **A. Kaplan, CEO** beside the first-level bullet, as shown in **Figure PPT 3–15**. Notice that the text is entered in the shape, and the text size in the shape automatically adjusts as you type.

FIGURE PPT 3–15
SmartArt Graphic and Text pane

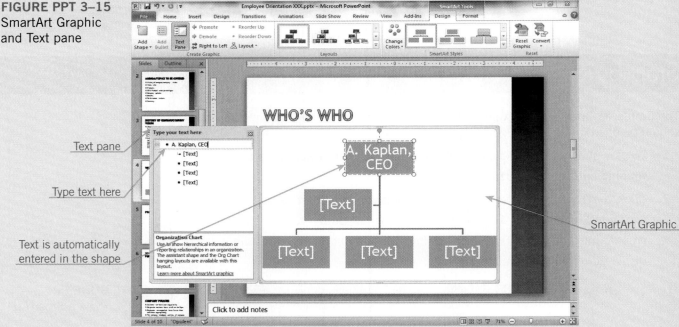

5. In the SmartArt graphic, click the shape on the second level to select it, and then press **Delete** to remove the shape from the graphic.

6. In the Text pane, click the **[Text]** placeholder beside the second bullet and type **M. Jones, President of Operations**.

7. In the Text pane, click the **[Text]** placeholder beside the third bullet and type **B. Petty, President of Procurement**.

8. In the SmartArt graphic, click the **[Text]** placeholder in the third shape and type **O. Donovan, President of Consumer Products**.

9. On the SmartArt Tools Design tab, in the Create Graphic group, click the **Add Shape** button arrow and click **Add Shape After** to insert a new shape on the right side of the second level in the graphic. Type **K. Abii, CFO**.

10. In the Create Graphic group, click the **Text Pane** button to close the Text pane.

11. On the SmartArt Tools Design tab, in the Layouts group, click the **More** button ⊡ to display the Layouts gallery, and then click the **Horizontal Hierarchy** layout, as shown in **Figure PPT 3–16**.

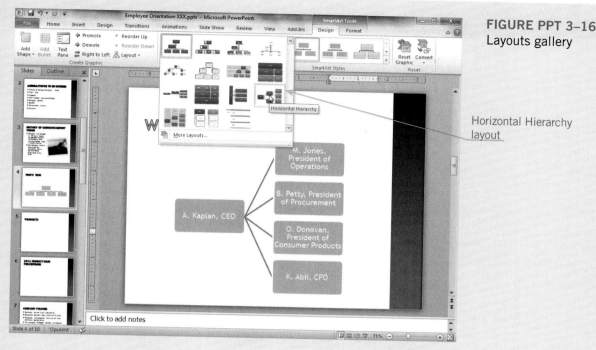

FIGURE PPT 3–16
Layouts gallery

Horizontal Hierarchy
layout

12. In the SmartArt Styles group, click the **Change Colors** button. In the Primary Theme Colors category, click the **Dark 2 Fill** option.

13. In the SmartArt Styles group, click the **More** button to display the SmartArt Styles gallery. In the Best Match for Document category, click the **Moderate Effect** style.

14. Save the presentation and leave it open for use in the next Step-by-Step.

Inserting and Modifying Charts

When you need to illustrate or compare data, such as budget figures, a *chart* is the best tool for the job. A chart is a graphical representation of data that can be inserted into PowerPoint.

The Chart button in the Illustrations group on the Insert tab and the Insert Chart button in a content placeholder provide access to different types of charts, such as bar, line, or pie charts. Using a chart in a PowerPoint presentation differs slightly from using other types of graphics because charts are composed of numerical data. The data that makes up the chart is stored in an Excel worksheet that is included in the PowerPoint file. (*Note*: When you initially create the chart, you enter data in the Excel worksheet; however, you do not need to be familiar with Excel to create a chart.)

As with other types of graphics, after you insert a chart on a slide, PowerPoint displays the Chart Tools Design, Layout, and Format contextual tabs for customizing the chart.

▶ VOCABULARY
chart

Step-by-Step PPT 3.6

The Employee Orientation *XXX* presentation from Step-by-Step PPT 3.5 should be open in the PowerPoint program window.

1. Display slide 6.

2. In the content placeholder, click the **Insert Chart** button to display the Insert Chart dialog box.

3. If necessary, click the **Column** category, and then click the **100% Stacked Column** chart type, as shown in **Figure PPT 3–17**.

FIGURE PPT 3–17
Insert Chart dialog box

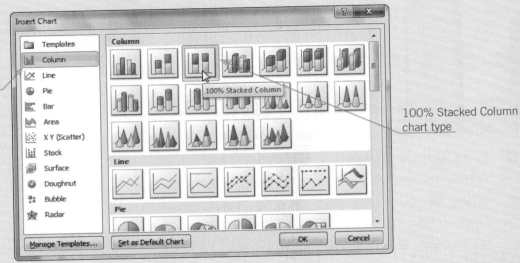

4. Click the **OK** button. An Excel spreadsheet opens in a new window next to your presentation, as shown in **Figure PPT 3–18**, with sample data that you will replace.

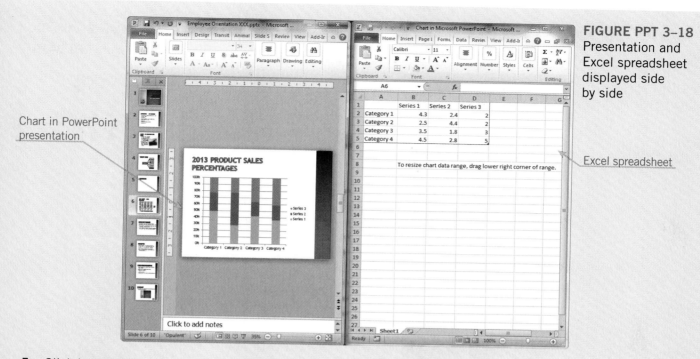

Chart in PowerPoint presentation

Excel spreadsheet

5. Click in cell B1, which contains *Series 1*, and type **Drinks**. Press **Tab**.

6. In cell C1, type **Beans**. Press **Tab** to move to cell D1. Type **Other** and press **Tab**.

7. Enter the remaining data in the spreadsheet as shown below:

	Drinks	Beans	Other
Q1	50	40	10
Q2	55	30	15
Q3	60	25	15
Q4	65	25	10

8. Click the **Close** button ![X] on the Excel program window to close the spreadsheet and view the chart in the slide.

9. On the Chart Tools Design tab, in the Chart Layouts group, click the **More** button ⊽ to display the Layouts gallery, and then click **Layout 4** to change the layout.

10. In the Chart Styles group, click the **More** button ▽ to display the Chart Styles gallery, and then click **Style 38**, as shown in **Figure PPT 3–19**.

FIGURE PPT 3–19
Chart Styles gallery

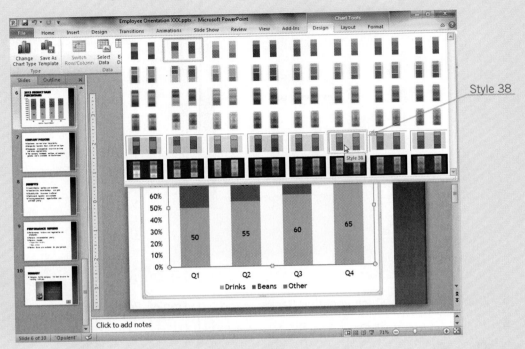

11. Save the presentation and leave it open for use in the next Step-by-Step.

Creating and Modifying Tables

> **VOCABULARY**
> **table**
> **cell**

📇 **EXTRA FOR EXPERTS**

You can use the Excel Spreadsheet command on the Table menu to insert a spreadsheet on a slide that you can use to display and calculate numerical data.

A *table* is a grid of horizontal rows and vertical columns containing numbers or text. Tables are useful for displaying or comparing data in a presentation. A *cell* is the intersection of a row and a column. In a table, you can press Tab to move from cell to cell from left to right and then down to the next row. To move out of a table when you reach the last cell, press the down arrow key or click outside of the table.

You can create a table in a slide using the Insert Table button in a content placeholder, and then enter the desired number of rows and columns in the Insert Table dialog box. You can also use the Table button in the Tables group on the Insert tab to create a table in one of three ways: You can use the Insert Table grid to drag across the desired number of rows and columns; you can use the Insert Table command to open the Insert Table dialog box; or you can use the Draw Table command to draw the desired rows and columns as you would with a pencil.

You can apply various fonts, font styles, and font sizes to table text the same way you apply them to other text in a presentation. To modify the table design with an added row, you can press Tab in the last cell to create a new row and move the insertion point into it. To apply a style or other formatting to a table, you first need to select the table by clicking it.

When you insert a table, the contextual Table Tools Design and Layout tabs are displayed on the Ribbon with options for modifying a table. The Table Styles group on the Table Tools Design tab includes the Table Styles gallery, which you can use to apply predesigned formats to a table. On the Table Tools Layout tab, you can use the buttons in the Rows & Columns group to insert columns and rows and delete cells, columns, rows, and tables. The Merge group contains buttons for merging cells by combining multiple cells into one, and for splitting cells by dividing one cell into multiple cells. The Alignment group contains options for aligning text within cells.

EXTRA FOR EXPERTS

When you want to insert more than one row or column in a table, select the desired number of rows or columns before clicking an Insert button in the Rows & Columns group on the Table Tools Layout tab. PowerPoint inserts that many rows or columns.

Step-by-Step PPT 3.7

The Employee Orientation *XXX* presentation from Step-by-Step PPT 3.6 should be open in the PowerPoint program window.

1. Display slide 5.
2. In the content placeholder, click the **Insert Table** button to display the Insert Table dialog box.
3. In the Number of columns box, type **3** and press **Tab**.
4. In the Number of rows box, type **4**.
5. Click the **OK** button to insert the blank table.
6. Type the following data in the table as shown, pressing **Tab** to move to the next cell and to the next row.

Products		
Coffee Drinks	Coffee Beans	Other
Cold Coffees	Signature Blends	Mugs
Hot Coffees	Decaf Blends	Brewing Equipment

7. Click to the left of the first row to select it (the row should appear a greyish-green color when selected). On the Table Tools Layout tab, in the Merge group, click the **Merge Cells** button to combine the three cells into one.
8. With the first row still selected, in the Rows & Columns group, click the **Delete** button, and then click **Delete Rows** from the menu to delete the first row.
9. Select the new first row. On the Table Tools Layout tab, in the Alignment group, click the **Center** button to center the column headings.

10. Click in the bottom row of the table. On the Table Tools Layout tab, in the Rows & Columns group, click the **Insert Below** button to insert a new blank row at the bottom of the table.

11. Type the following data in the new row.

Herbal Teas	Seasonal Blends	Gift Baskets

12. On the Table Tools Design tab, in the Table Styles group, click the **More** button ⊟ to display the Table Styles gallery.

13. Scroll down if necessary, point to the **Dark Style 1 – Accent 4** option in the Dark category, and then click to apply the style.

14. Save the presentation and leave it open for use in the next Step-by-Step.

Inserting a Text Box

A *text box* is a container for text—similar to a placeholder, but without the suggested text prompts—that allows you to insert and position text anywhere on a slide. Text boxes can be especially useful for adding text to a slide outside of a placeholder, such as for a caption next to a photo.

The Text Box button is located in the Text group on the Insert tab. Text boxes can be moved and resized, and you can apply borders, fills, and effects to text boxes. You can apply custom formatting to text within a text box the same way you would any text in a presentation.

Like a shape, a text box is considered a drawing object, so when you insert a text box, the Drawing Tools Format contextual tab is displayed on the Ribbon. This tab contains tools for modifying text boxes.

▶ **VOCABULARY**
text box

▣ **EXTRA FOR EXPERTS**

You can insert text into a shape without using a text box. Select the shape, and then type to add your text. Once you enter text into a shape, the text attaches to the shape and moves with it.

Step-by-Step PPT 3.8

The Employee Orientation *XXX* presentation from Step-by-Step PPT 3.7 should be open in the PowerPoint program window.

1. Slide 5 should be displayed.

2. On the Insert tab, in the Text group, click the **Text Box** button.

3. Below the table, drag down and to the right to create a box similar to the one shown in **Figure PPT 3–20**.

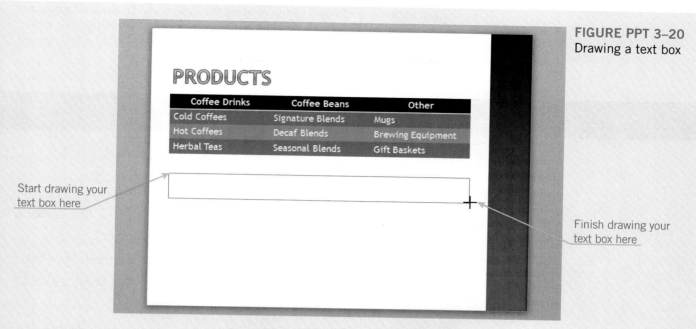

FIGURE PPT 3–20
Drawing a text box

Start drawing your text box here

Finish drawing your text box here

4. Release the mouse button. Notice that the text box borders change to dotted lines.

5. Type **You will learn more about each of these product categories during your individual and group training sessions.** Notice that the words wrap to the next line.

6. On the Drawing Tools Format tab, in the Shape Styles group, click the **More** button ⊡ to display the Shape Styles gallery.

7. Point to several different options to see Live Previews of the text box with the available styles applied. Point to the **Colored Outline – Brown, Accent 4** option in the first row, and then click to apply the style.

8. Select the text inside the text box.

9. On the Home tab, in the Font group, click the **Italic** button *I* to italicize the text.

10. Click in blank space outside the text box to deselect it.

11. Save the presentation and leave it open for use in the next Step-by-Step.

Inserting Footers

A *footer* is text that appears in the bottom margin of a slide, handout, or notes page. A *header* refers to text that appears in the top margin. PowerPoint makes it easy to use footers to include useful information that you would not include as text in the presentation, such as the title of a presentation, slide numbers, or the date.

To insert a footer on a slide, you use the Header & Footer button, located in the Text group on the Insert tab on the Ribbon. This button displays the Header and Footer dialog box, where you can insert footers on slides and headers and footers on notes and handouts.

▶ **VOCABULARY**
footer

header

You cannot add a header to a slide using the Header and Footer dialog box, but you can still add a header by inserting a text box in the top margin of the slide master and typing your text. In addition, if you want a header instead of a footer, you can drag the footer placeholder on the slide master to the top margin.

Step-by-Step PPT 3.9

The Employee Orientation *XXX* presentation from Step-by-Step PPT 3.8 should be open in the PowerPoint program window.

1. Display slide 2.

2. On the Insert tab on the Ribbon, in the Text group, click the **Header & Footer** button to open the Header and Footer dialog box.

3. On the Slide tab in the dialog box, click the **Date and time** check box.

4. Click the **Fixed** option button if necessary, and then type **March 29, 2013** in the Fixed text box.

5. Click the **Slide number** check box.

6. Click the **Footer** check box. In the Footer text box, type **Employee Orientation**.

7. Click the **Don't show on title slide** check box, as shown in **Figure PPT 3–21**, to prevent the footer from being displayed on the presentation's title slide.

FIGURE PPT 3–21
Header and Footer dialog box

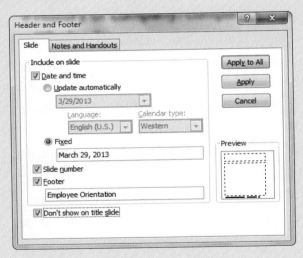

8. Click the **Apply to All** button to apply the settings to all slides and close the dialog box. Scroll through the presentation, and notice the footer was applied to all slides except the title slide.

9. On the View tab, in the Master Views group, click the **Slide Master** button to display Slide Master view.

10. Click the **slide master**, which is the top thumbnail in the left pane.

11. Select **Employee Orientation** in the footer.

12. On the Home tab, in the Paragraph group, click the **Align Text Left** button ▤ to change the footer text alignment from right to left.

13. On the Slide Master tab, in the Close group, click the **Close Master View** button to close Slide Master view. Notice the alignment change was applied to the entire presentation.

14. Save the presentation and leave it open for use in the next Step-by-Step.

Inserting Special Effects

When you deliver a presentation on a computer, you can add special visual, sound, and animation effects to emphasize your points. When adding special effects, you must remember that moderation is very important. The content in your presentation should take center stage. Special effects should not draw attention to themselves.

The Animations and Transitions tabs on the Ribbon contain options for previewing special effects, adding animations, and inserting transitions. After you insert an animation or transition effect, you will see an animation icon—a moving star— beside the thumbnail in Normal view and in Slide Sorter view, indicating a transition or animation is in effect for that slide. Many templates have animations already applied. You can click the star icon next to a thumbnail in the Slides tab to see a preview of the animation in the Slide pane.

Inserting Transitions

A *transition* is an animated effect that controls how one slide is removed from the screen and the next one appears during a slide show. PowerPoint provides a variety of transitions that you can customize by specifying effects, adding sounds, and varying the speed. You can make your presentations more interesting by adding transitions using the Transitions tab, shown in **Figure PPT 3–22**.

▶ **VOCABULARY**
transition

FIGURE PPT 3–22   Transitions tab

The Transitions gallery is located in the Transition to This Slide group on the Transitions tab. It contains transitions in the categories of Subtle, Exciting, and Dynamic Content. After you apply a transition to a slide, you can use the Effect Options button to customize the transition. In the Timing group on the Transitions tab, you can choose Apply To All to apply the transition to every slide in the presentation. You can also add sounds, change the duration of the transition, and set slides to advance automatically after a certain amount of time instead of advancing them with a mouse click.

Use the Preview button in the Preview group on the Transitions tab to preview the transition effect applied to the current slide. Switch to Slide Show view to view the entire presentation, including all transitions.

To remove a transition effect, select the slide or slides, and then click the None style in the Transitions gallery.

Step-by-Step PPT 3.10

The Employee Orientation *XXX* presentation from Step-by-Step PPT 3.9 should be open in the PowerPoint program window.

1. Display slide 1.

2. On the Transitions tab, in the Transition to This Slide group, click the **More** button ⬚ to display the Transitions gallery.

3. In the Exciting category, click **Cube**, as shown in **Figure PPT 3–23**, to apply the transition to the current slide.

FIGURE PPT 3–23
Transitions gallery

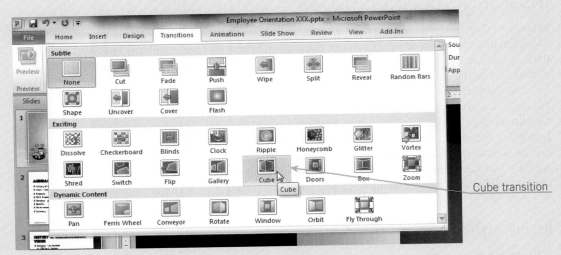

Cube transition

4. In the Transition to This Slide group, click the **Effect Options** button, and then click **From Bottom**. A preview of the transition is shown in the Slide pane.

5. In the Timing group, click the **Sound** list arrow, and then point to several of the sounds to hear what they sound like.

6. Click **Arrow** to apply the sound to the current transition.

7. In the Preview group, click the **Preview** button to see and hear the transition effects applied.

8. In the Timing group, click the **Apply To All** button to apply the transition settings to all the slides in the presentation. Notice that all slide thumbnails in the Slides tab have the star icon beside them.

9. Switch to Slide Show view and view the presentation.

10. Save the presentation and leave it open for use in the next Step-by-Step.

Adding Animations

In addition to transitions, you can add a number of animation effects. An *animation* is a visual or sound effect added to individual text, a picture, a chart, or other object on a slide so you can control the flow of information and add interest to your presentation. Animation options are available on the Animations tab, as shown in **Figure PPT 3–24**.

▶ **VOCABULARY**
animation

FIGURE PPT 3–24   Animations tab

One common animation that you can use in a presentation is to have bulleted items appear one after the other rather than all at once. Titles or bulleted items can fly up from the bottom of the screen, box out from the center, or appear in other ways.

The Animation gallery is located in the Animation group on the Animations tab. It contains effects in the following categories:

- *Entrance* effects bring an object into view on the slide, such as flying in from the top.

- *Emphasis* effects call attention to text or objects by changing the object's color or increasing its size.

- *Exit* effects remove an object from the slide, such as flying out to the bottom.

- *Motion Path* effects make an object move on the screen in a pattern, such as in a circle.

After you apply an animation effect, you can specify additional effects using the Effect Options button in the Animations group on the Animations tab. The Advanced Animation group allows you to add animations to selected objects, set a trigger to start an animation, display the Animation task pane to further customize an animation, or activate the Animation Painter. Like the Format Painter in Word, you can use the Animation Painter to copy animation settings from one object and apply them to other objects.

Use options in the Timing group to designate how an animation starts, the duration of the animation, or to set a delay.

You can also preview your animation effects on the current slide with the Preview button in the Preview group on the Animations tab. Switch to Slide Show view to see the entire presentation with all the applied animations.

Step-by-Step PPT 3.11

The Employee Orientation *XXX* presentation from Step-by-Step PPT 3.10 should be open in the PowerPoint program window.

1. Display slide 3 and select the picture.

2. On the Animations tab, in the Animation group, click the **More** button ⊽ to display the Animations gallery.

3.   Point to several of the animations, and watch the Live Preview of each in the Slide pane.

4.   In the Entrance category, click **Fly In**, as shown in **Figure PPT 3–25**, to apply the animation to the image in the slide.

FIGURE PPT 3–25
Animations gallery

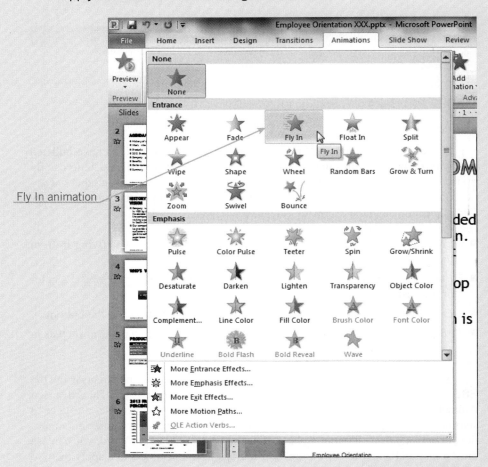

Fly In animation

5.   In the Animation group, click the **Effect Options** button and click **From Top-Right** to change the direction of the applied effect.

6.   On the slide, select the placeholder containing the two bulleted paragraphs.

7.   In the Advanced Animation group, click the **Add Animation** button, and then in the Entrance section, click **Zoom**. Notice that you get a preview of the applied animations in the Slide pane.

8.   In the Advanced Animation group, click the **Animation Pane** button to display the Animation task pane, as shown in **Figure PPT 3–26**.

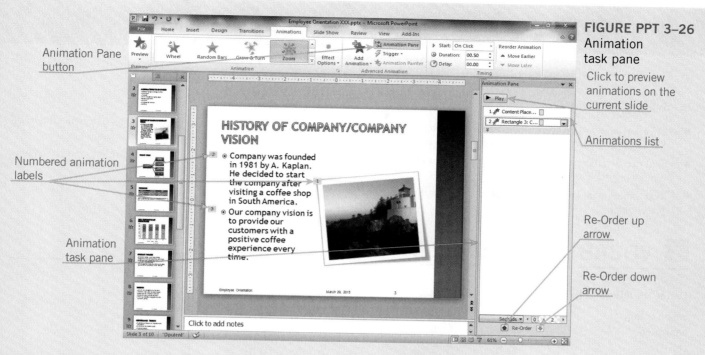

FIGURE PPT 3–26
Animation
task pane

Animation Pane button

Numbered animation labels

Animation task pane

Click to preview animations on the current slide

Animations list

Re-Order up arrow

Re-Order down arrow

9. In the Animation task pane, click the **Play** button to view the animations. Notice that the picture appears on the screen before the paragraphs of text.

10. At the bottom of the task pane, click the **Re-Order** up arrow to change the order of the animations by moving the text animation above the picture animation in the Animation task pane.

11. Click the **Play** button. Notice the picture now appears last on the screen.

12. In the Animation task pane, click the double arrow below the first animation to expand the contents of the list, click the second item in the list, *Our company...*, and then click the arrow next to the item to display a menu of options. Click **Start With Previous** to force the second paragraph of text to appear at the same time as the first paragraph.

13. Click the **Play** button. Notice the paragraphs of text both appear on the screen at the same time.

14. Click the **Close** button on the Animation task pane to close it. On the slide, animation labels appear next to the animation objects, numbered in the order that the animations take place.

15. Save the presentation, run it from the beginning, and then close it.

SUMMARY

In this lesson, you learned:

- To insert and modify pictures, screenshots, shapes, clip art, SmartArt, and charts to add visual impact to presentations.

- Text can be efficiently aligned and presented in rows and columns using tables.

- Text boxes can be used to insert text where there is no placeholder.

- Footers may be used to display the title of a presentation, slide numbers, or the date throughout a presentation.

- How to use special effects such as transitions and animations to add interest to your presentation.

VOCABULARY REVIEW

Define the following terms:

action button	drawing objects	selection handles
animation	footer	SmartArt graphic
cell	header	table
chart	picture	text box
clip art	screenshot	transition
crop		

REVIEW QUESTIONS

MULTIPLE CHOICE

Select the best response for the following statements.

1. The green circle at the top of a graphic is used to _____ a graphic.

   A. insert
   B. crop
   C. resize
   D. rotate

2. Small circles and squares at the sides and corners of a graphic are called _____.

   A. SmartArt
   B. pictures
   C. selection handles
   D. rotate circles

3. Enter a _____ to search for related clip art in the Clip Art task pane.

   A. keyword
   B. text box
   C. picture
   D. placeholder

4. _____ trigger commonly understood actions, such as going to the next or previous slide.

   A. Charts
   B. SmartArt graphics
   C. Text boxes
   D. Action buttons

5. A hierarchy chart is an example of a _____.

   A. table
   B. transition
   C. picture
   D. SmartArt graphic

6. The data that makes up a chart is stored in a(n) _____.

   A. table   C. text box

   B. Excel worksheet   D. Word document

7. The _____ command combines cells so you can center a heading over an entire table.

   A. Merge Cells   C. Insert Table

   B. Properties   D. Group

8. A _____ is a container for text that is similar to a placeholder, but without the suggested text prompts.

   A. chart   C. text box

   B. table   D. transition

9. Slide numbers are usually displayed in the _____.

   A. footer   C. SmartArt graphic

   B. Transitions gallery   D. Animations tab

10. A(n) _____ is a visual or sound effect added to individual text, a picture, a chart, or other object so you can control the flow of information and add interest to your presentation.

   A. style   C. table

   B. animation   D. SmartArt graphic

FILL IN THE BLANK

Complete the following sentences by writing the correct word or words in the blanks provided.

1. A(n) _____ is a digital photograph or image.

2. You can search for pictures, sounds, and movies in the _____ task pane.

3. SmartArt graphics are inserted with _____ text that you can replace with your own text.

4. Bar, line, and pie are types of _____.

5. A(n) _____ is a grid of horizontal rows and vertical columns containing numbers or text.

6. A(n) _____ is the intersection of a row and a column.

7. Shapes and text boxes are considered _____ objects.

8. A(n) _____ is text that appears in the top margin of a slide.

9. The _____ button lets you view the animation or transition effects on the current slide.

10. A(n) _____ is an animated effect that controls how one slide is removed from the screen and the next one appears.

PROJECTS

PROJECT PPT 3-1

1. Open the **Project PPT 3-1** presentation from the folder containing the data files for this lesson, and save it as **Fitness Challenge 2 XXX** (replace *XXX* with your initials).

2. Search for clip art with the keyword **treadmill**, and then insert the black and white clip art image of a businessman on a treadmill (or another picture of your choice) on slide 1.

3. Position the clip art in the lower-right corner on slide 1, and then decrease the size proportionally by about ½". Reposition the image if necessary after resizing so that all of the image is within the lower section of the slide.

4. On slide 5, insert a SmartArt graphic using the Continuous Block Process layout in the Process category.

5. Using the SmartArt Tools Design tab, change the SmartArt style for the graphic to Polished.

6. Enter and format text as shown in **Figure PPT 3-27**. (*Hint*: Enter text into the shapes of the graphic.)

7. In the first shape, select *November* and *December* and change the Text Fill color for each to Turquoise, Accent 3. (*Hint*: Use the SmartArt Tools Format tab.)

8. Change the Text Fill color for *December* in the second shape and *January 1* in the third shape to Turquoise, Accent 3.

9. Change the layout to Continuous Arrow Process.

10. Insert the slide number and the words *Fitness Challenge* in a footer that is not displayed on the title slide.

11. Save and close the presentation.

ON YOUR OWN

Open the **Fitness Challenge2 XXX** presentation, and then add another SmartArt graphic of your choice using the bulleted list on slide 2. (*Hint*: Use the Convert to SmartArt Graphic button in the Paragraph group on the Home tab.) Save and close the presentation.

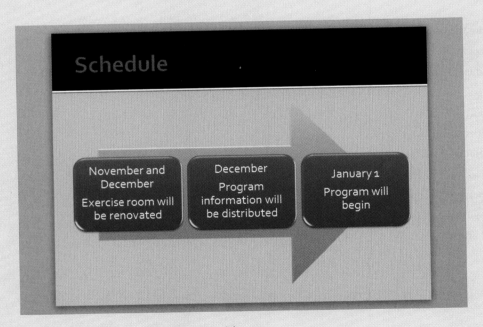

FIGURE PPT 3-27   SmartArt graphic

PROJECT PPT 3–2

1. Open the **Project PPT 3-2** presentation from the folder containing the data files for this lesson, and save it as **Tracking Graduates 2 XXX** (replace *XXX* with your initials).

2. Insert a text box below the clip art on the first slide. Type **Rams Alumni,** and then change the font to Arial Black 20 point.

3. Center the text in the text box, and position it centered under the graphic.

4. On slide 5, insert a pie chart using the following data:

	Graduates
Attending Graduate School	36
Working	40
Searching for Work	14
Unable to locate	10

5. Change the chart layout to Layout 6.

6. Change the chart type to Pie in 3D. (*Hint*: Use the Change Chart Type button in the Type group on the Chart Tools Design tab.)

7. Save and close the presentation.

PROJECT PPT 3–4

1. Open the **Project PPT 3-4** presentation from the folder containing the data files for this lesson, and save it as **Nature Portfolio 2 XXX** (replace *XXX* with your initials).

2. Apply the Fade transition with the Through Black effect option to all slides.

3. Apply the Camera transition sound to all slides.

4. On slide 1, select the photo and add a Random Bars entrance animation with the Vertical effect option.

5. Select the LostArt Photos placeholder, and then add a Fly In entrance animation effect.

6. Reverse the order of animation effects on slide 1.

7. View the entire presentation in Slide Show view.

8. Save and close the presentation.

ON YOUR OWN

Open **Nature Portfolio 2 XXX**. Add an entrance animation effect to the text on slides 2, 3, 4, and 5. Save and close the presentation.

PROJECT PPT 3–3

1. Open the **Project PPT 3-3** presentation from the folder containing the data files for this lesson, and save it as **Course Rules 2 XXX** (replace *XXX* with your initials).

2. On slide 4, insert a table in the content placeholder using the following data:

Grading Scale	
A	90–100
B	80–89
C	70–79
D	65–69
F	0–64

3. Merge the two cells in the first row and center the title.

4. Resize the table. Change the height to 2.4" and the width to 2.5".

5. Apply the Themed Style 2 – Accent 1 table style.

6. Save and close the presentation.

ON YOUR OWN

Open **Course Rules 2 XXX**. Remove all the transitions applied to the presentation. Apply new transitions, and add an animation to the table. Save and close the presentation.

WEB PROJECT

Create a five-slide presentation about your favorite state (or country). Use the Web to research information, such as the date it became a state, the state nickname, state flower, bird, song, motto, and other interesting facts. Use the Find more at Office.com link at the bottom of the Clip Art task pane to search Microsoft Office online for clip art, pictures, or other media to include in your presentation. Include a footer and at least one chart, table, or SmartArt graphic in the presentation. Apply transitions and animations where appropriate. Include an action button that links to a Web site about your state.

 TEAMWORK PROJECT

With a partner, choose any presentation you have worked with in the PowerPoint unit or a presentation from the Internet and critique it. Divide responsibilities and rehearse your presentation. Deliver the slide show to the class as a team, and point out elements you liked about the slide show as well as areas in need of improvement. Remember what you have learned about creating an effective presentation. Comment on the design as well as the use of graphics, transitions, and animations. Be prepared to answer questions from the audience.

CRITICAL THINKING

ACTIVITY PPT 3–1

Open **Activity PPT 3-1** from the folder containing the data files for this lesson. Save it with a meaningful name. Insert graphics, transitions, and animations to make the presentation more interesting. Be prepared to deliver your presentation to the class, explaining the changes you made and why you think they improved the presentation.

ACTIVITY PPT 3–2

In this lesson, you learned how to insert a picture from a file in the Sample Pictures folder. Did you know you can also insert music in the same way? Open a blank presentation, find the Audio from File and Video from File buttons on the Ribbon, and insert a sound or video from a file in the Sample Music or Sample Videos folder that starts either automatically or when clicked. Experiment with the Playback contextual tab. What is looping? In what situations might it be useful to play music or a video on a presentation? How do you remove a sound file from a presentation? How do you trim a video or sound file?

UNIT IV REVIEW

PowerPoint

■ REVIEW QUESTIONS

MULTIPLE CHOICE

Select the best response for the following statements.

1. A(n) _____ is a single image composed of text, graphics, or other content.

   A. header

   B. footer

   C. slide

   D. I-beam

2. Which feature automatically saves your presentation at regular intervals so that you can recover at least some of your work in case of a power outage or other unexpected shutdown?

   A. Quick Access Toolbar

   B. Print Preview

   C. AutoRecover

   D. word wrap

3. When you click the _____ button, the software prompts you to save your work if you made any changes since you last saved.

   A. Margins

   B. Save

   C. Help

   D. Close

4. The _____ button allows you to copy the formatting characteristics of text and then apply the same formatting to other parts of the document.

   A. Paste

   B. Copy

   C. Redo

   D. Format Painter

5. _____ is the vertical distance between lines of text in a paragraph.

   A. Line spacing

   B. Indentation

   C. Alignment

   D. Point size

6. _____ view displays thumbnail versions of all slides in a presentation.

   A. Notes Page

   B. Slide Sorter

   C. Slide Show

   D. Outline

7. _____ are sets of formatting choices that include colors, fonts, effects, and backgrounds that were predesigned to work well together.

    A. Paragraphs   C. Themes

    B. Templates   D. Placeholders

8. You can insert clip art using a _____.

    A. menu   C. window

    B. dialog box   D. task pane

9. A _____ allows you to insert and position text anywhere on a slide.

    A. text box   C. template

    B. theme   D. footer

10. A _____ is an animated effect that controls how one slide is removed from the screen and the next one appears during a slide show.

    A. motion path   C. transition

    B. video clip   D. SmartArt

FILL IN THE BLANK

Complete the following sentences by writing the correct word or words in the blanks provided.

1. The _____ is the blinking vertical bar that signals where any text you type will appear.

2. Applying a new _____ to a slide rearranges the placeholders on the slide, and the text adjusts to the new arrangement.

3. Click the _____ tab to open Backstage view to create a new blank presentation.

4. PowerPoint flags words that might be misspelled with a wavy _____ underline.

5. A(n) _____ is a sample presentation that provides a pattern or model that you can follow to create your own presentation.

6. You can use the _____ command to search for a specific word or phrase in a presentation.

7. Column and line are types of _____.

8. A(n) _____ is a digital photograph or image.

9. Slide numbers are often displayed in the _____.

10. A(n) _____ is a visual or sound effect added to an object on a slide so you can control the flow of information and add interest to your presentation.

■ PROJECTS

PROJECT PPT 1

1. Start PowerPoint and create a new presentation using the **Contemporary Photo Album** template from the Sample templates category in Backstage view. Save it as **Summer Album *XXX*** (replace *XXX* with your initials).

2. On slide 1, replace the title *Contemporary Photo Album* with **Summer Album**.

3. Replace the sideways placeholder text with **2013**.

4. Delete the flower photo from slide 1, and then insert the Chrysanthemum photo (or another photo of your choice) from the Sample Pictures folder.

5. Delete the photo on slide 2, and then insert the Desert photo from the Sample Pictures folder (or another photo of your choice). Type **Desert** to replace the text in the placeholder on slide 2.

6. On slide 3, delete the photos, and then change the slide layout to 2-Up Landscape with Captions.

7. In the left placeholder on slide 3, insert the Koala photo (or another photo of your choice) from the Sample Pictures folder, and then type **Koala** to replace the text in the placeholder below the picture.

8. Insert the Penguins picture (or another photo of your choice) in the right placeholder, and then type **Penguins** to replace the text in the placeholder below it.

9. On slide 4, change the slide layout to **Square with Caption**.

10. Delete the photo on slide 4, and then insert the Jellyfish picture (or another photo of your choice) from the Sample Pictures folder. Type **Jellyfish** to replace the text in the placeholder below it.

11. Delete slides 5 and 6.

12. Add the Metal Frame picture style to the pictures on slides 2, 3, and 4.

13. Add a Camera transition sound to all the slides in the presentation.

14. View the presentation from the beginning in Slide Show view, and then save it and leave it open.

PROJECT PPT 2

The presentation Summer Album *XXX* from Project PPT 1 should be open in the PowerPoint program window.

1. Save the document as **Summer Album 2 *XXX***.

2. On slide 1, change the size of the *2013* text to 80 points and the character spacing to Very Loose.

3. Change the theme to Angles.

4. Change the theme colors to Flow.

5. In Slide Master view, on the slide master, format the Master text styles (the first item in the content placeholder) as 40 point, bold, and with Blue font color.

6. Insert a new slide with a Blank layout after slide 4.

7. In the center of the slide, insert a text box, and then type the words **The End**.

8. Copy the text formatting from the word *Jellyfish* on slide 4 and apply it to the words *The End* on slide 5.

9. Center the text within the placeholder, and position the placeholder centered vertically and horizontally on the slide.

10. View the presentation from the beginning in Slide Show view, and then print 6-slides-per-page (6 Slides Vertical) handouts of the presentation.

11. Save and close the presentation.

ON YOUR OWN

Open the **Summer Album 2 *XXX*** file. Add a new animation effect to an object on each of the slides in the presentation. Save and close the presentation.

PROJECT PPT 3

1. Open the file **Project PPT 3** from the folder containing your data files for this lesson, and save it as **Ways to Go Green *XXX*** (replace *XXX* with your initials).

2. Check the spelling in the presentation and correct any misspellings.

3. Starting at the beginning of the presentation, find the word *power* and replace it with the word ***energy*** when appropriate. (*Hint*: Replace two of the three occurrences.)

4. In Slide Sorter view, move slide 6 before slide 4.

5. Switch to Normal view, and then insert a Title and Content layout slide after slide 8.

6. In the top placeholder, type **Bring your own reusable bags when shopping.**

7. Type **Eight** in the title placeholder at the bottom of the screen.

8. On slide 2, insert the following speaker note: **Mention cell phone chargers.**

9. Change the line spacing of the paragraph in the text placeholder to 1.0 and left-align the text.

10. Change the list format of the text on slide 2 to bulleted and add the following bulleted item:

    Plug computer and television equipment into power strips that you can turn off.

11. Change the font color of the word *Unplug* to white.

12. On slide 3, select the word *Two*. Copy the formatting and apply it to the word *One* on slide 2.

13. On slide 5, cut the speaker note and paste it in the text placeholder as the second bulleted item.

14. Save the presentation and leave it open for use in the next project.

PROJECT PPT 4

The Ways to Go Green *XXX* presentation from Project PPT 3 should be open in the PowerPoint program window.

1. Save the presentation as **Ways to Go Green 2 *XXX***.

2. On slide 8, insert the Basic Process SmartArt graphic.

3. Type ½ **teaspoon olive oil** in the first shape, ¼ **cup vinegar** in the second shape, and **Furniture polish** in the third shape.

4. Apply the Subtle Effect – Tan, Accent 4 shape style to the third shape.

5. On slide 9, insert a Clustered Column chart using the following data. (*Hint*: In the Excel worksheet, delete the data in columns C and D, and resize the chart data range by dragging the lower-right corner of the blue outline to the left to eliminate columns C and D.)

	Billions of Plastic Bags Consumed per Year
US	100
Taiwan	20
Australia	6.9
Ireland	1.2

6. Use the Change Chart Type button in the Type group on the Chart Tools Design tab to change the chart type to Clustered Cylinder, and then apply the Layout 4 layout and the Style 31 chart style to the chart.

7. On slide 2, insert a table with the following data:

Appliance	Stand-by energy costs per year
TV	$10
DVD	$9
Computer in sleep mode	$41

8. Apply the Themed Style 1 - Accent 5 table style. (Adjust the size and/or position of the table to fit attractively on the slide.)

9. On slide 7, resize the clip art to approximately 2 inches square, and then position it in the lower-right corner of the slide.

10. Apply the Fade animation to the clip art on slide 7 and the table on slide 2.

11. Apply the Fade animation with the One by One effect option to the SmartArt graphic on slide 8.

12. Apply the Fade animation with the By Category effect option to the chart on slide 9.

13. Apply the Box transition with the From Top effect option to all slides.

14. View the presentation from the beginning in Slide Show view.

15. Save and close the presentation.

ON YOUR OWN

Open the **Ways to Go Green 2 *XXX*** file. Add a footer displaying the document title. Do not display it on the title page. Switch to Slide Master view and apply formatting options so that the footer is displayed attractively in the presentation. Save and close the presentation.

ON YOUR OWN

Open the **Ways to Go Green 2 *XXX*** file. Insert an appropriate piece of clip art in one of the slides that doesn't contain a graphic. Change the image's color, size, or style to be displayed attractively in the presentation. Save and close the presentation.

 # WEB PROJECT

Visit a job search Web site and conduct a search for jobs that require the use of Microsoft Office PowerPoint. What job titles require experience with PowerPoint? What level of experience is required? What are the other job requirements? What are the salary ranges? Create a presentation that identifies five types of jobs that require experience with PowerPoint and answer these questions. Be prepared to deliver your presentation to the class.

 # TEAMWORK PROJECT

With a partner, research the admission requirements and procedures at your favorite college or university. Create a presentation that would instruct high school students on how to apply for admission. Also include some background information on the school, such as its location, date it was founded, and number of students enrolled. Use at least one chart, table, or SmartArt graphic in your presentation and be sure to include relevant clip art or pictures. Use transitions and animations. Collaborate on the content and design, and be prepared to deliver the presentation to the class.

 # CRITICAL THINKING

ACTIVITY PPT 1

Choose any presentation you have worked with in this unit that contains animations or transitions, and resave it with a meaningful name. Use the commands in the Timing groups on the Transitions and Animations tabs to change the duration of transitions and animations in the presentation. Then, set each slide to advance after a few seconds instead of with a mouse click. Use the Set Up Show command in the Slide Show tab to set the presentation to loop continuously using the timings you set. Be prepared to present your presentation to the class.

ACTIVITY PPT 2

Create a new presentation using the Quiz Show presentation from the Sample templates category in Backstage view. Analyze the presentation by viewing it in Slide Show view and identifying the transitions and animations applied. Replace three of the questions and answers with new ones related to PowerPoint or another Microsoft Office 2010 program. Add at least two new slides with the question format of your choice, and write a question and answer for each so that you have at least five questions in the presentation. Delete the unnecessary slides, and be prepared to deliver your presentation to the class.

■ PORTFOLIO CHECKLIST

_____	Lesson 1	Health Challenge *XXX*.pptx
_____	Lesson 1	Office Space *XXX*.pptx
_____	Lesson 1	Tracking Graduates *XXX*.pptx
_____	Lesson 2	Nature Portfolio *XXX*.pptx
_____	Lesson 2	Job Search *XXX*.pptx
_____	Lesson 2	Course Rules *XXX*.pptx
_____	Lesson 3	Employee Orientation *XXX*.pptx
_____	Lesson 3	Fitness Challenge 2 *XXX*.pptx
_____	Unit Review	Ways to Go Green 2 *XXX*.pptx

UNIT V

MICROSOFT ACCESS

LESSON 1   2.5 HRS.

Understanding Access Fundamentals

LESSON 2   2.5 HRS.

Creating Queries, Forms, and Reports

LESSON 1

Understanding Access Fundamentals

■ OBJECTIVES

Upon completion of this lesson, you should be able to:

- Understand database concepts.
- Recognize the importance of planning and designing a database.
- Identify the elements of the Access program window.
- Start Access and create a new database.
- Create a table in Datasheet view.
- Open an existing database.
- Open tables and navigate records.
- Modify field properties.

■ DATA FILES

To complete this lesson, you will need these data files:

Step AC 1-4.accdb

Project AC 1-1.accdb

Project AC 1-3.accdb

■ VOCABULARY

data type

database

database management
  system (DBMS)

database objects

datasheet

datasheet selector

field

field name

field properties

field value

foreign key

key value

primary key

record

record selector

relational database

tables

Introduction

Microsoft Access 2010 is the database program included in the Microsoft Office 2010 suite of software. A *database* is used to collect and organize information. Any type of list you create to collect information can be considered a database, even a simple list of phone numbers. When you collect more information than can be easily managed on paper, it is helpful to transfer it to a computerized *database management system (DBMS)*, which is software designed to store, organize, and manage large amounts of data. This allows you to keep accurate records and retrieve records quickly.

Although all of the Office programs are designed to work alike using the same basic interface, there are some aspects of Access that are unique. For example, you do not need to use the Save command when you enter or edit information because Access automatically saves the data. You will also notice when you first open a database that the Access program window looks a little different than other Office programs you have used because it has a pane on the left. You will learn more about these differences later in the lesson.

Using Access, you can create database files that are efficient, well organized, and that can help you manage information effectively. Before you discover the power of Access to compile, track, report, and manage related information, you need to learn about the parts of a database and understand basic database concepts. In this lesson, you will learn the importance of planning and designing a database before creating one, as well as techniques for performing fundamental database tasks using Access.

Understanding Database Concepts

Storing information in a database can be compared to using a filing cabinet to collect and organize information. Within the filing cabinet are folders that each contain a different group of related information. These folders are similar to tables in a database. *Tables* are the place in a database where all the data is stored. A database can contain many tables, just as a filing cabinet can contain many folders. Each table in a database stores data related to a different category, such as students or classes in a school database. Within a folder in a filing cabinet are individual pieces of paper, which could correspond to the records in a database table. A *record* is all of the related information about a particular item in the table. For example, all the information about one specific student, such as the student's name, grade level, and phone number would be in one record. A single characteristic or piece of information stored in a table—such as name, grade level, or phone number—is called a *field*.

By default, tables in a database are displayed in a format called a *datasheet*, which has columns and rows similar to an Excel worksheet. Each field in a datasheet is displayed as a column and is identified by its *field name* at the top. Each piece of information in a field is called a *field value*. Each record in a datasheet is displayed as a row and contains the field values that belong to that particular item. **Figure AC 1–1** shows the parts of a datasheet.

FIGURE AC 1–1   Parts of a datasheet

Every table in a database will have a primary key. The ***primary key*** is the field that uniquely identifies each record. Each record in the database must have a ***key value***, shown in Figure AC 1–1, which is a value in the primary key field that makes the record unique. The key value cannot be left blank. By default, Access creates an ID field in every table that can serve as the primary key. Each time you enter a new record, Access assigns a unique number in the ID field as the key value. The primary key is important because it helps set up relationships between tables and tells Access how to associate the data with other tables in the database. When a primary key is included in another table, it is called a ***foreign key*** in the second table.

Access is considered a ***relational database*** because all of the data is stored in separate tables and then connected by establishing relationships between the tables. This is achieved by placing a common field in related tables. For example, you could include a Faculty ID field as the primary key in a Faculty table and also include a Faculty field in a Classes table to relate the two tables. Common fields are not required to have the same name. In Access, you can display the relationships between tables in a database to see how they are connected, as shown in **Figure AC 1–2**.

▶ **VOCABULARY**
primary key
key value
foreign key
relational database
database objects

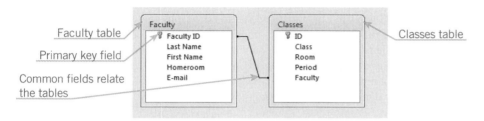

FIGURE AC 1–2   Related tables

There are many advantages to using an electronic filing system like a database, instead of a manual system like filing cabinets. There is more space to store records, and it is much easier to retrieve the records that you need. Plus, a database offers more flexibility in the ways you can work with the information. In addition to the tables that store the information, a database contains other elements that allow you to interact with the data, called ***database objects***. The common database objects are described in **Table AC 1–1**. In this lesson, you will focus on tables, and in the next lesson you will learn more about forms, reports, and queries.

EXTRA FOR EXPERTS

To create, edit, or delete table relationships, you can display the Relationship tab by clicking the Relationships button in the Relationships group on the Database Tools tab.

TABLE AC 1–1   Database objects

OBJECT	ICON	DESCRIPTION
Table		Stores information related to a specific subject; made up of a collection of records and fields
Form		Can be used to enter, edit, maintain, and view records; similar in appearance to a paper form
Report		Summarizes and presents information from one or more tables in an easily readable format that can be printed
Query		Asks a question about the data stored in a database, and then searches for and retrieves specific database information in answer to the question

Planning and Designing a Database

Before you create a new database, it is essential to spend time planning it. You should decide what the purpose of the database is and what you want it to accomplish. You will also need to determine what types of information will be included, so it will be helpful if you can gather together all this information and organize it into categories. Each category will then become a table in the database. For example, if you are planning to create a database for a school administration office, you would need to include tables with information about students, faculty, and classes.

After you have decided what tables should be included in the database, you need to decide what information will be contained in each table. For example, a table of classes might include the name of the class, the days it meets, the times it meets, the room number, the teacher, and a class description. Each of these pieces of information would be a field in the table. When creating tables in a database, keep in mind how the information in each table might be linked together using common fields.

A great starting point when planning a database is to sketch it out on paper, being sure to identify the fields you want to include, and the types of data that each field will contain. This will help you determine the basic format of the database, figure out possible ways to organize the data, and determine how the different types of information are related. The more thorough and accurate you can be when designing the database, the fewer adjustments you will have to make later.

There are established standards and guidelines to help guide you in the process of creating a database. You can always use Access Help if you need assistance designing your database and structuring your tables correctly.

Exploring the Access Program Window

When you create or open an Access database, it is displayed in the Access program window, shown in **Figure AC 1–3**. You will notice that the Access program window is similar to the program windows in other Office programs in some ways, like the Ribbon, the Quick Access Toolbar, and view buttons, but also has some differences, like the Navigation Pane on the left.

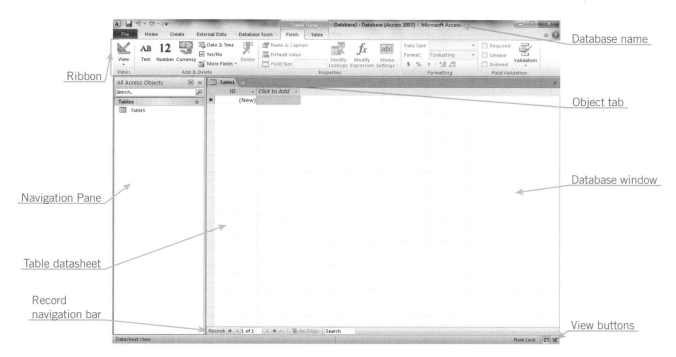

FIGURE AC 1-3   Access program window

The Navigation Pane lists all of the objects in the database. When an object is open, it is displayed in the database window to the right of the Navigation Pane. In this lesson, you will be working in Datasheet view. The other views available depend on which type of database object you are working with, and each view allows you to perform different tasks related to the object. For example, if you display a table in Design view, you can make changes to the design of the table.

Starting Access and Creating a New Database

To begin using Access, you first need to start the program. You can do this by clicking the Start button on the Windows taskbar, and then clicking the program name on the All Programs menu, or by double-clicking an Access program icon on the desktop.

When you start Access, Backstage view, shown in **Figure AC 1–4**, is displayed. In Backstage view you have the option to create a new database using a template, create a new blank database, or open a recently used database.

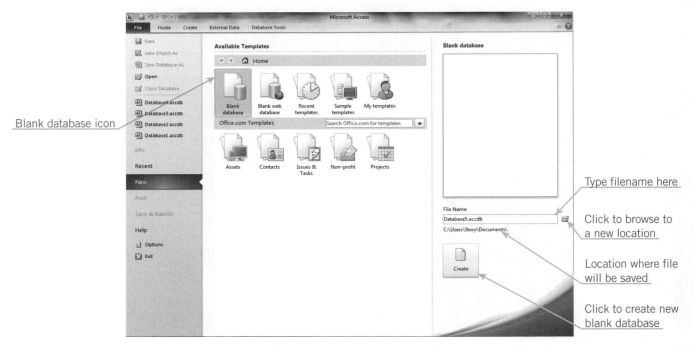

Blank database icon

Type filename here

Click to browse to a new location

Location where file will be saved

Click to create new blank database

FIGURE AC 1–4   Creating a new database in Backstage view

EXTRA FOR EXPERTS

If you do not want to create a database from scratch, you can choose from one of the many templates available. Access templates are predesigned databases—such as a database for event management, inventory, or charitable contributions—that can save you time. You can access installed and online templates in Backstage view.

To create a new blank database, you click the Blank database icon in the center pane. Access suggests a name for the new database in the File Name text box in the right pane, and you can accept it or replace it with your own filename. The location where the database will be saved is shown beneath the File Name text box. If you want to select a new location, you can click the Browse for a new location button—the folder icon next to the File Name text box. This will open the File New Database dialog box, where you can browse for another location to store your database. When you click the Create button, a new blank database is created and opens to a blank table in Datasheet view.

Step-by-Step AC 1.1

1. Click the **Start** button 🏁 on the Windows taskbar. The Start menu opens.
2. Click **All Programs**. A list of programs and program folders opens.
3. Click the **Microsoft Office** program folder. A list of Microsoft Office programs opens.

4. Click **Microsoft Access 2010**. Access 2010 starts and Backstage view is displayed with the **Blank database** icon selected in the center pane.

5. In the right pane, in the File Name text box, click to select the suggested name for the database, and type **Oakville Hills School *XXX*** (replace *XXX* with your initials).

6. Click the **Browse for a location to put your database** icon 📁 to open the File New Database dialog box. Navigate to the location where you save your data files, and then click the **OK** button.

7. Click the **Create** button to create a new blank database. The database opens in the Access program window.

8. Leave the database open for use in the next Step-by-Step.

Creating a Table in Datasheet View

When you create a new database, a new table named Table1 is automatically created for you and displayed in Datasheet view, where you can start to create fields for the table and enter data. You can also create a new, blank table in Datasheet view at any time by clicking the Table button in the Tables group on the Create tab.

Because every table needs a primary key, when you create a new table, Access creates a field named ID by default and sets it as the primary key. The ID field is also assigned the AutoNumber data type, which means Access will automatically enter a unique value each time you enter a record. You can choose to use the default ID field, or change it to suit the design of your database. For example, you could change the primary key to a different field, or you could rename the ID field, and change the data type so you can type your own values instead of letting Access automatically assign them. In that case, you would need to set the field property so that a unique field value is required. You will learn more about field properties later in this lesson.

EXTRA FOR EXPERTS

You can also click the Table Design button in the Tables group on the Create tab to create a table in Design view. Another way to create a table is to import or link to external data by clicking a data source in the Import & Link group on the External Data tab and then following the instructions in the dialog box that opens.

In Datasheet view, the easiest way to create a field is to simply enter data in the Click to Add column in the table. Each field in a table has a *data type* that determines the types of field values you can enter in that field. **Table AC 1–2** explains the different data types available in Access and their purpose.

TABLE AC 1–2   Data types

DATA TYPE	PURPOSE
Text	Stores text and/or numbers up to 255 characters; most common data type
Number	Stores numeric data that can be used in mathematical calculations
Currency	Stores monetary data displayed with dollar sign
Date & Time	Stores dates and/or times
Yes/No	Stores True/False, Yes/No, or On/Off values; used when only two values can be chosen
Lookup & Relationship	Displays a list of values from which a user can choose
Rich Text	Stores rich-formatted text in a Memo field
Memo	Stores text and/or numbers up to 65,535 characters; used for larger amounts of text
Attachment	Stores any supported file type, such as images, documents, and charts
Hyperlink	Stores links such as Web addresses
Calculated Field	Displays a value that is calculated from other data in the same table

You can assign a data type when creating a field by clicking the Click to Add column header and selecting a data type from the menu. If you do not select a data type, Access will automatically assign a data type based on the values that you enter in a field. Once a data type is assigned to a field, you can always change it by clicking the Data Type list arrow in the Formatting group on the Table Tools Fields tab. You can also change the field name by clicking the Name & Caption button in the Properties group on the Table Tools Fields tab and then typing a new field name in the Enter Field Properties dialog box. Other buttons you can use to create and modify fields are also located on the Table Tools Fields tab, shown in **Figure AC 1–5**.

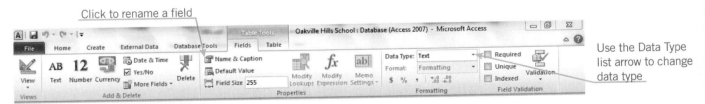

FIGURE AC 1–5   Table Tools Fields tab

Entering Records

As you create a database, you not only need to enter records into tables, but you also need to keep the database up to date by editing and deleting data as well. Access tables are different from Excel worksheets because they exist just to hold the data. You do not format them or change the structure by inserting blank rows or columns. When you want to enter new data, you simply enter it in the last row or column.

To add a new record to a table in Datasheet view, simply click a field in the new blank record, indicated by an asterisk in the box to the left of the row called the *record selector*, and type the information. Then press Enter or Tab to move to the next field and continue entering data until the record is complete. Access automatically saves the information as you enter it. If the column is not wide enough to display the data as you type, simply click the right border of the field name and drag to widen it or double-click the right border of the field name to automatically size the column to fit the header and data. To select an entire field, click the column header that contains the field name.

Step-by-Step AC 1.2

The Oakville Hills School *XXX*.accdb database from Step-by-Step AC 1.1 should be open in the Access program window.

1. Click the field name of the default primary field, the **ID** column header. On the Table Tools Fields Tab, in the Properties group, click the **Name & Caption** button to open the Enter Field Properties dialog box, shown in **Figure AC 1–6**.

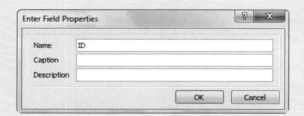

FIGURE AC 1–6
Enter Field Properties dialog box

2. Edit the text in the Name box to read **Student ID,** and click the **OK** button to close the dialog box and rename the field.

3. On the Table Tools Fields tab, in the Formatting group, click the **Data Type** list arrow and then click **Number** to change the data type of the field.

4. On the Table Tools Fields tab, in the Field Validation group, click the **Required** check box to require values in this field. (The **Unique** check box should already be checked, to require values entered in this field to be unique.)

5. In the datasheet, click the **Click to Add** column header and then click **Text** as the data type for the new field, as shown in **Figure AC 1–7**. A new field named *Field1* is added.

FIGURE AC 1–7
Click to Add data type menu

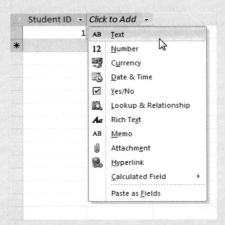

6. With *Field1* selected, type **Last Name**, and then press **Enter** to name the new field. The Click to Add data type menu opens in preparation for creating another field.

7. Click **Text** as the data type, type **First Name**, and then press **Enter** to create a new field and open the Click to Add data type menu again.

8. Click **Number** as the data type, type **Grade,** and then press **Enter** to create a new field.

9. Click anywhere in the datasheet to close the Click to Add data type menu, and then click the **Student ID** field of the first record and type **2618**.

10. Press **Tab** to enter the data and move to the next field in the record, the Last Name field. Notice that a pencil symbol is displayed in the record selector of the record you are creating and that the asterisk in the record selector, indicating a new record ready for data, moves to the next row when you begin to type, as shown in **Figure AC 1–8**.

FIGURE AC 1–8
Entering records

11. In the Last Name field of the first record, type **Ansman-Wolfe**, and then press **Tab** to enter the data.

12. Double-click the **right border** of the Last Name column header, as shown in **Figure AC 1–9,** to automatically widen the column to display all the data.

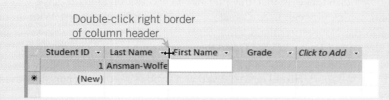

Double-click right border
of column header

FIGURE AC 1–9
Automatically resizing a field in
Datasheet view

13. In the First Name field of the first record, type **Pamela**, and then press **Tab** to enter the data. In the Grade field, type **11**, and then press **Tab** to enter the data and move to the new blank record. Continue entering the rest of the data into the table, shown in **Figure AC 1–10**.

Enter these records

Student ID	Last Name	First Name	Grade	Click to Add
2618	Ansman-Wolfe	Pamela	11	
4943	Berndt	Mattias	12	
1908	Bonifaz	Luis	12	
4607	Bueno	Janaina	10	
6467	Caron	Nicole	11	
4568	Cetinok	Baris	10	
*				

FIGURE AC 1–10
Entering data in a table

14. Leave the database open for use in the next Step-by-Step.

Saving and Closing a Table and Closing a Database

After you have created a table, you can save the design by clicking the Save button on the Quick Access Toolbar to open the Save As dialog box, typing a table name, and clicking the OK button. Changes or additions to data in the table are saved automatically as you enter it, but before you close the table any changes to the table design need to be saved by clicking the Save button on the Quick Access Toolbar.

Before closing a database, all database objects must be saved and closed. You can close a database object by clicking its Close button. If you have not saved an object in the database, you will be prompted to save it before closing. To close a database, you can click the File tab and then click Close Database. Backstage view is then displayed again. To close Access, you click Exit.

Saving Databases and Copying Objects

Some aspects of the saving process in Access are different than in other Office applications. Especially because databases are often shared among multiple users, it is important to be aware of how saving differs. As noted earlier, you do not need to use the Save command when you enter or edit information because Access automatically saves the data. The Save command in Access is used only to save changes that have been made to the design of a database object.

Unlike other applications, when you open a file in Access, the file date is changed—even if you don't edit the database. To keep the file date of the original database unchanged, you would first need to make a copy of the database in the folder window. (For more information on managing files and folders, see Appendix A.) If it is okay for the date on the original database to be changed, you can always save a copy of it using the Save Database As command on the File tab, just as you would use the Save As command in other applications.

Another difference is that the File tab in Access contains a Save Object As command, which you can use to create a copy of a database object. With an object selected in the Navigation Pane, click Save Object As to open the Save As dialog box, as shown in **Figure AC 1–11**, and then choose what you want to save the object as. A table can be saved as a table, query, form, or report; a query can be saved as a query, form, or report; a form can be saved as a form or report; a report, however, can only be saved as a report.

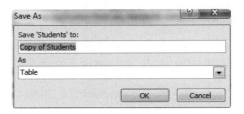

FIGURE AC 1–11   Save As dialog box

Step-by-Step AC 1.3

The Oakville Hills School *XXX*.accdb database from Step-by-Step AC 1.2 should be open in the Access program window.

1. Click the **Save** button 🖫 on the Quick Access Toolbar to open the Save As dialog box.

2. Type **Students** in the Table Name box, and then click the **OK** button to save the table. Notice the new table name is now displayed on the object tab, as shown in **Figure AC 1–12**. Notice the records are rearranged so that the values in the Student ID field are in ascending numeric order.

FIGURE AC 1–12
Saving a table

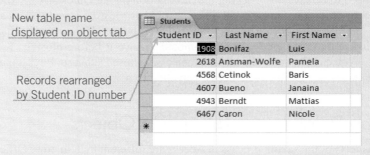

3. In the upper-right corner of the database window, click the **Close** button ⊠ to close the Students table.

4. Click the **Students** table in the Navigation Pane to select it, then click the **File** tab. Click **Save Object As** to open the Save As dialog box.

5. Under As, click the **list arrow** in the text box to see the options, then click **Table**. Click **OK** to create a copy of the table.

6. Click **Home** to see the copy of the table in the Navigation Pane, as shown in **Figure AC 1–13**.

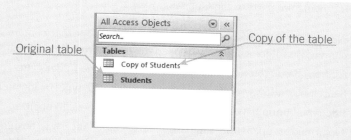

FIGURE AC 1–13
Creating a copy of a table

7. Click the **File** tab and then click **Close Database**. The database closes and Backstage view is displayed.

8. Leave Access open for use in the next Step-by-Step.

Opening an Existing Database

When you click Recent in Backstage view, a list of recently opened databases is displayed. If an existing database that you want to use is not listed, you can click Open to open the Open dialog box shown in **Figure AC 1–14**, and then locate and open the database file. You can also click the Open command on the File tab, add an Open command to your Quick Access Toolbar, or use the keyboard shortcut Ctrl+O.

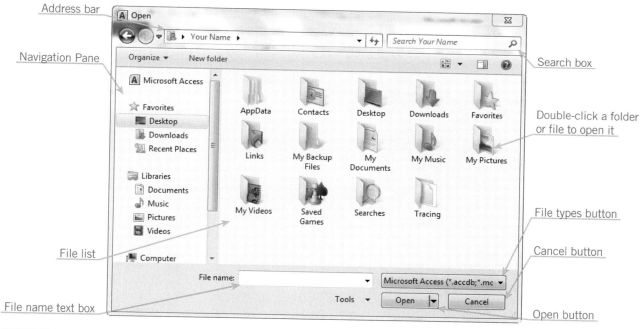

FIGURE AC 1–14   Open dialog box

You can use the Open dialog box to find and open existing files on your hard drive, CD, or other removable media; on a network drive to which you are connected; on your organization's intranet; or on the Internet. Double-clicking on a file in the File list will open the file.

The following are parts of the Open dialog box:

EXTRA FOR EXPERTS

By default, the names of the four most recent files you opened in Access are listed on the File tab. You can click any of these files in the list to open them. You can customize the number of files displayed in the list by clicking Recent in Backstage view and changing the number in the Quickly access this number of Recent Databases box at the bottom of the center pane.

- The Navigation Pane displays favorite links to folders that contain databases. You can view a folder's contents or open the folder from the Navigation Pane.
- The Address bar at the top of the dialog box shows the folder path.
- The Search box allows you to find a file by name, file type, or location.
- The File type button lists other file types you can choose to open.
- The Open button opens the database and, because Access is designed so that multiple users can work on the same database, the Open button list arrow provides options for sharing access with others.
- The Cancel button closes the dialog box without opening a file.

When you open an existing database, a security warning may be displayed in the Message Bar below the Ribbon if Access does not recognize the source as being trustworthy. All the files provided for this book are safe to work with, so you can click the Enable Content button to enable the content.

Step-by-Step AC 1.4

1. On the File tab on the Ribbon, click **Open**.

2. In the Open dialog box, navigate to the folder containing the data files for this lesson. Double-click the file named **Step AC 1-4.accdb** in the File list. The database opens in the Access program window, as shown in **Figure AC 1–15**.

FIGURE AC 1–15
Opening an existing database

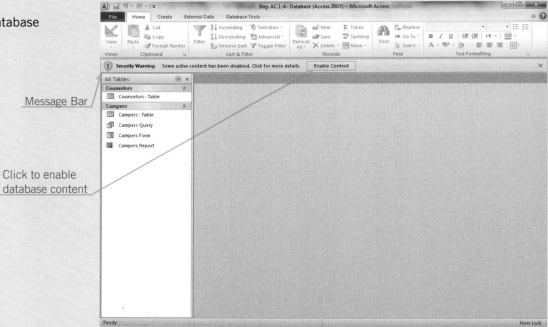

Message Bar

Click to enable database content

3. Click the **File** tab and then click **Save Database As** to open the Save As dialog box.

4. Navigate to the location where you save your files.

5. Click the **File name** text box, and type **Camp Blue Zephyr** *XXX* (replace *XXX* with your initials).

6. Click the **Save** button to save a copy of the database with the new name in the specified location.

7. On the Message Bar, click the **Enable Content** button to remove the Message Bar warning and enable the content of the database.

8. Leave the database open for use in the next Step-by-Step.

Opening Tables and Navigating Records

When you open or create a database, the Navigation Pane is displayed on the left side of the database window and lists all the database objects. The icon to the left of the object name indicates what type of object it is. To open a table, or any database object, you can double-click it in the Navigation Pane. Multiple database objects can be open at the same time. You move between the open objects by clicking the tab with the object name at the top of the database window to display it.

In Datasheet view, you can navigate among the records in a table using the navigation buttons on the record navigation bar or using the keyboard. To use the navigation buttons, shown in **Figure AC 1–16**, click a button to move to the record you want—First, Previous, Next, Last, or New (blank). You can also type the number of the record in the Current Record text box and press Enter to move to a record, or you can type data in the Search text box to move to the next record in the table that matches the search data.

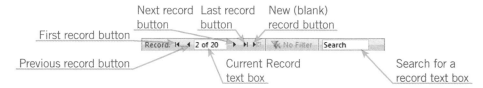

FIGURE AC 1–16   Record navigation bar

Step-by-Step AC 1.5

The Camp Blue Zephyr *XXX*.accdb database from Step-by-Step AC 1.4 should be open in the Access program window.

1.   In the Navigation Pane, double-click the **Counselors: Table** database object to open the table in the database window, as shown in **Figure AC 1–17**.

FIGURE AC 1–17
Table open in
database window

Icons indicate types
of database objects

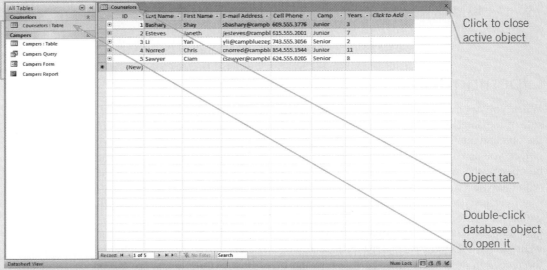

Click to close
active object

Object tab

Double-click
database object
to open it

2.   In the Navigation Pane, double-click the **Campers: Table** database object to open the table. The first record is selected.

3.   Click the **Next record** button at the bottom of the database window to move to record 2 in the Campers table, last name *Bolender*.

4.   Click the **Last record** button to move to record 20 in the database, the record for *Uppal*.

5.   Select the contents of the Current Record text box at the bottom of the database window, type **14**, and press **Enter** to move to record 14, last name *Netz*.

6.   Click the **Counselors** object tab in the database window to display that table.

7.   Click the **Close** button to close the active object, the Counselors table. The Campers table is displayed in the database window.

8.   Leave the database open for use in the next Step-by-Step.

Renaming and Deleting Tables

When you want to rename a table, you can right-click the table name in the Navigation Pane to open the shortcut menu shown in **Figure AC 1–18**, and then click Rename on the shortcut menu. You can then type a new table name and press Enter to rename the table. You can only rename a table when it is closed.

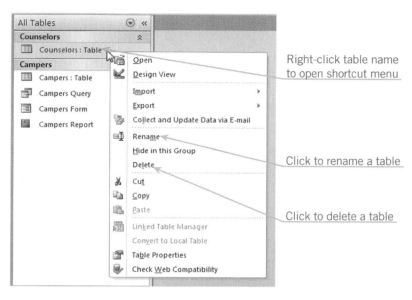

FIGURE AC 1–18   Table shortcut menu

If you need to delete a table, you can right-click the table name in the Navigation Pane and then click Delete on the shortcut menu, shown in Figure AC 1–18. You will be asked to confirm the deletion. Deleting a table is a permanent action and affects any database objects that use the table as a source of data, so be sure you want to delete the table before proceeding.

Editing and Deleting Records

When you want to edit data in a record, select the contents in the field for that record and type new data to replace it. Or click in the field and use the Backspace or Delete key to make changes. If you make a mistake in data entry, you can click the Undo button on the Quick Access Toolbar or press Esc to undo the change before it is entered. When you are editing data in a record, a pencil icon is displayed in the record selector box.

▶ **VOCABULARY**
datasheet selector

To select all records in the database, you can click the ***datasheet selector*** button in the upper-left corner of the datasheet. If you want to select a single record, you can click the record selector box to the left of the row, as shown in **Figure AC 1–19**.

Datasheet selector button

Record selector box

ID	▾	Last Name	▾	First Name	▾	Home State	▾
1		Akers		Kim		California	
2		Bolender		Corinna		Rhode Island	
3		Cook		Cathan		Michigan	
4		Crayton		Terry		Florida	
5		Hagege		Adina		Nebraska	
6		Higa		Sidney		Ohio	
7		Iyer		Raman		Indiana	
8		Koch		Reed		Connecticut	

FIGURE AC 1–19   Selecting records and fields

You can delete an entire record by selecting the record, and then pressing Delete. A message box is displayed asking you to confirm the deletion. Be sure you want to delete a record before you confirm the deletion. Deleting a record is a permanent action and cannot be undone.

Step-by-Step AC 1.6

The Camp Blue Zephyr *XXX*.accdb database from Step-by-Step AC 1.5 should be open in the Access program window.

1. With the Campers table open in the database window, click the **Home State** field for record 4 (*Florida*).

2. Select the word **Florida** and then type **Georgia**. Notice the pencil icon in the record selector box, indicating that the record is being edited, as shown in **Figure AC 1–20**.

FIGURE AC 1–20
Editing a record

Pencil icon indicates
record is being edited

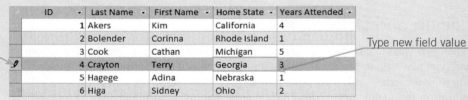

Type new field value

ID	▾	Last Name	▾	First Name	▾	Home State	▾	Years Attended	▾
1		Akers		Kim		California		4	
2		Bolender		Corinna		Rhode Island		1	
3		Cook		Cathan		Michigan		5	
4		Crayton		Terry		Georgia		3	
5		Hagege		Adina		Nebraska		1	
6		Higa		Sidney		Ohio		2	

3. Press **Enter** to save changes to the data.

4. Click the record selector for record 2 to select it and press **Delete**. A message box is displayed, as shown in **Figure AC 1–21**, asking you to confirm you want to delete the selected record.

Record 2 will be deleted

Click to confirm deletion

FIGURE AC 1–21
Deleting a record

5. Click the **Yes** button to confirm the deletion and delete the record.

6. Click the **Close** button to close the Campers table.

7. In the Navigation Pane, right-click the **Counselors: Table** object to open a shortcut menu.

8. Click **Rename** on the menu to select the object name and then type **Staff**, as shown in **Figure AC 1–22**.

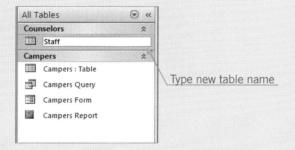

Type new table name

FIGURE AC 1–22
Renaming a table

9. Press **Enter** to rename the table.

10. Click the **File** tab and then click **Close Database**. The database closes and the New options are displayed.

Modifying Field Properties

After you have created the basic structure of a field by naming it and setting the data type, you still may need to make changes to the *field properties* that control the appearance and behavior of the field. You can rename a field, change the data type, and set other basic field properties using the Table Tools Fields tab in Datasheet view. The properties you can set for a field depend on its data type.

You might want to set the Format property of a field to determine how the data you enter will be formatted. For example, you could specify that numbers with decimals be formatted as percent, so that the number 0.63291 would be displayed as 63%. You can set the Unique field property when you want to require that the values in that field are unique for every record, as you did earlier in the lesson when you

▶ **VOCABULARY**
field properties

UNIT V   Microsoft Access

modified the default ID field when you created the Students table in the Oakville Hills School database. You can set the Required field property so that a certain field is required to contain a value in every record.

To rearrange the order of fields in Datasheet view, you can select the field and drag it to a new position. If you decide you do not need a field, you can select the field and press Delete. This action is permanent, and any data in the field will also be deleted, so you will be asked to confirm the deletion before proceeding.

Step-by-Step AC 1.7

Backstage view from Step-by-Step AC 1.6 should be open in the Access program window.

1. On the File tab, click **Recent** to display recently used databases, as shown in **Figure AC 1–23**, then click the **Oakville Hills School XXX.accdb** database that you created earlier in this lesson to open it. If necessary, enable the content of the database.

FIGURE AC 1–23
Opening a recent
database

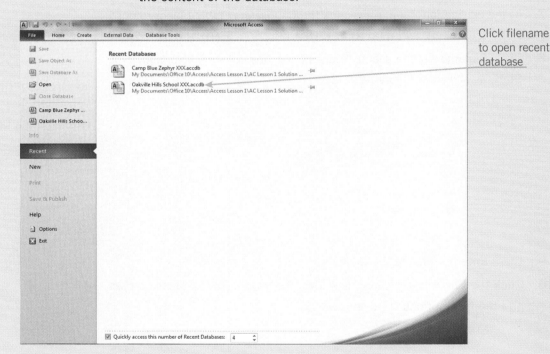

Click filename
to open recent
database

2. In the Navigation Pane, double-click the **Students** database object to open the table.

3. Click the **First Name** column header to select the field.

4. Click the **First Name** column header again, hold the mouse button to display a thick line to the left of the field, and then drag the First Name field column to the left until the line is displayed between the Student ID field column and the Last Name field column, as shown in **Figure AC 1–24**.

Click field column header and drag field to new location

FIGURE AC 1–24
Moving a field

Student ID	Last Name	First Name	Grade	Click to Add
1908	Bonifaz	Luis	12	
2618	Ansman-Wolfe	Pamela	11	
4568	Cetinok	Baris	10	
4607	Bueno	Janaina	10	
4943	Berndt	Mattias	12	
6467	Caron	Nicole	11	

5. Release the mouse button to move the field to its new location.

6. Click the **Last Name** column header to select the field.

7. Click the **Table Tools Fields** tab, and in the Field Validation group, click the **Required** check box to select that option, requiring a value in that field, as shown in **Figure AC 1–25**.

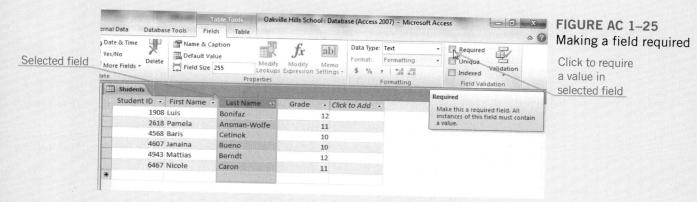

Selected field

FIGURE AC 1–25
Making a field required

Click to require a value in selected field

8. On the Students table datasheet, click the **Click to Add** list arrow and then click **Date & Time** as the data type for the new field type. Type **Date Enrolled** as the field name and press **Enter** to create a new field.

9. Double-click in the Date Enrolled field of the first record, type **9/30/2013** and press **Enter** to enter the date. Widen the column so the entire field name is visible.

10. Click the **Date Enrolled** column header to select the field. On the Table Tools Fields tab, in the Formatting group, click the **Format** text box arrow to display a list of formatting options for Date/Time fields, and then click **Medium Date**, as shown in **Figure AC 1–26**, to change the Date Enrolled field format.

FIGURE AC 1–26
Changing a field's
data type format

Selected field

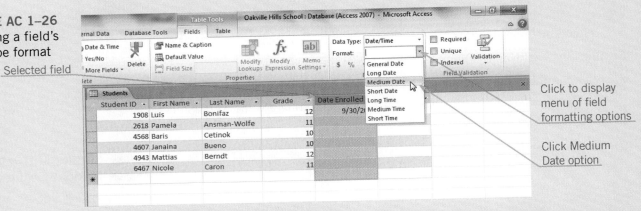

11. Select the Grade field. On the Table Tools Fields tab, in the Add & Delete group, click the **Delete** button. In the message box, click **Yes** to permanently delete the field and all the data it contains.

12. Save the changes you have made to the design of the Students table, and then close the table.

13. Close the database and close Access.

TECHNOLOGY CAREERS

Database administrators are responsible for planning and designing an organization's databases. This can require close coordination with the database users to ensure that the company's databases meet their needs. Database administrators also test and implement the database, making changes and updating it as necessary. In addition, they manage, maintain, and keep the database secure by performing tasks such as backing up, restoring, and encrypting the database with a password.

SUMMARY

In this lesson, you learned:

- Basic database concepts.
- The importance of planning and designing a database.
- To identify elements of the Access program window.
- The process for starting Access and creating a new database.

- How to create tables in Datasheet view.
- Methods for opening an existing database.
- To open tables, navigate records, and edit and delete records.
- Ways to modify field properties.

■ VOCABULARY REVIEW

Define the following terms:

data type
database
database management system (DBMS)
database objects
datasheet
datasheet selector

field
field name
field properties
field value
foreign key
key value

primary key
record
record selector
relational database
tables

■ REVIEW QUESTIONS

MULTIPLE CHOICE

Select the best response for the following statements.

1. Which database object stores and organizes all the data in the database?

   A. Table
   B. Query
   C. Form
   D. Record

2. Each _____ in a datasheet is displayed as a column.

   A. record
   B. field
   C. object
   D. table

3. When a primary key is included in another table, it is called a _____ key.

   A. secondary
   B. related
   C. foreign
   D. dependent

4. What is displayed after you close a database?

   A. Open dialog box
   B. Save dialog box
   C. Backstage view
   D. Navigation Pane

5. By default, tables in a database are displayed in a format called a _____.

   A. form
   B. datasheet
   C. record
   D. report

6. The _____ is the field that uniquely identifies each record.

   A. field name
   B. foreign key
   C. key value
   D. primary key

7. A new record in a table in Datasheet view is indicated by a(n) _____ in the record selector box.

 A. asterisk   C. key icon

 B. pencil icon   D. arrow

8. When you want to rename a table, you can right-click the table name in the _____ to open the shortcut menu.

 A. object tab   C. Navigation Pane

 B. Open dialog box   D. Table Tools Fields tab

9. The _____ data type stores text and/or numbers up to 65,535 characters.

 A. Text   C. Numbers

 B. Memo   D. Currency

10. To select a record in Datasheet view, click the record selector box located _____.

 A. in the record navigation bar C. on the Table Tools Fields tab on the Ribbon

 B. in the upper-left corner of the D. to the left of the record
   datasheet

FILL IN THE BLANK

Complete the following sentences by writing the correct word or words in the blanks provided.

1. When you open or create a database, the _____ is displayed on the left side of the screen and lists all the database objects.

2. When you open a table, it opens by default in _____ view.

3. Access is considered a(n) _____ because all of the data is stored in separate tables and then connected by establishing relationships between the tables through common fields.

4. Each record in the database must have a(n) _____, which is a value in the primary key field that makes the record unique.

5. When you are editing data in a record, a(n) _____ icon is displayed in the record selector box.

6. Each field in a table has a(n) _____ that characterizes the types of values contained in the field.

7. The _____ data type stores monetary data displayed with a dollar sign.

8. Unlike other applications, the File tab in Access contains a _____ command, which you can use to create a copy of a database object.

9. To close a database, you can click the _____ and then click Close Database.

10. When you _____ a table, record, or field, the action is permanent, so you will be asked to confirm before proceeding.

■ PROJECTS

PROJECT AC 1–1

1. Start Access and open the file **Project AC 1-1.accdb** from the folder containing the data files for this lesson and enable the content.

2. Use the Save As command on the File tab to save the workbook with the filename **Contacts XXX** (replace *XXX* with your initials).

3. Open the **Business** table.

4. Click the **Job Title** field of record 1 (*Human Resource Manager*), and edit it to read **Sales Manager**.

5. Widen the Company, E-mail Address, Address, and Web Site field columns so all the data is visible.

6. Select the Country/Region field and delete it.

7. Save and close the Business table.

8. Rename the Personal table as **Friends**.

9. Leave the database open for use in the next project.

PROJECT AC 1–2

The Contacts *XXX*.accdb database from Project AC 1–1 should be open in the Access program window.

1. Open the **Friends** table.
2. Rename the State/Province field as **State**.
3. Rename the ZIP/Postal Code field as **Zip**.
4. Create a new field with the **Text** data type and the field name **Birthday**.
5. In the last field (*Birthday*) of the last record (*6*), enter **Sept 19** as the field value.
6. Make the Last Name field required.
7. Close the Friends table.
8. Close the database.

ON YOUR OWN

Open the **Contacts.accdb** database and create another table named **Family**. Add at least five records with contact information for members of your family. Create fields and modify as needed to fit your data. Save the table and close the database.

PROJECT AC 1–3

1. Open the file **Project AC 1-3.accdb** from the folder containing the data files for this lesson and enable the content.
2. Use the Save As command on the File tab to save the workbook with the filename **Vehicle Records *XXX*** (replace *XXX* with your initials).
3. Open the **Vehicle** table.
4. Enter the data shown below as a new record. (*Note*: Access will automatically add the number in the ID field.)

   Vehicle: **Nissan**

   Make: **Altima**

   Model: **2.5 S**

   Color: **Metallic Jade**

   Year Made: **2009**

   Date Purchased: **4/30/2009**

   Purchase Price: **$26,165**

   License Plate: **VLS-429**

5. Add a new field to the database with the Memo data type and the field name **Notes**.
6. Click the **Notes** field of the first record and type **7-yr warranty.**
7. Change the format of the Date Purchased field to **Medium Date**.
8. Make the Vehicle field required.
9. Close the Vehicle table.
10. Leave the database open for use in the next project.

PROJECT AC 1–4

The Vehicle Records *XXX*.accdb database from Project AC 1–3 should be open in the Access program window.

1. Click the **Create** tab, and in the Tables group, click the **Table** button to create a new table.
2. Enter the following data as a new record. Assign the data types and change the field names as you create the fields. Note that the ID field is created automatically.

   Vehicle (Text): **Jeep**

   Service Description (Memo): **oil change**

   Service Date (Date & Time): **6/12/2013**

   Mileage (Number): **58034**

   Cost (Currency): **$39.95**

   Shop (Text): **Joe's Quick Change**

   Invoice # (Number): **102449**

3. Widen any fields as necessary to display the field names or data.

4. Save the table as **Expenses** and close it.
5. Close the database and close Access.

ON YOUR OWN

Open the **Vehicle Records *XXX*.accdb** database and open the **Vehicle** table. Create a field named **Online Info** with a **Hyperlink** data type. Search online to find the official Web site for each make of car in the table and enter the Web site address in the new Hyperlink field. Save the table and close the database.

ON YOUR OWN

Use Access Help to learn more about relating tables. Open the **Vehicle Records *XXX*.accdb** database and make any changes necessary to relate the tables. Be prepared to explain to the class how you related them and demonstrate how to create a relationship between tables. Close the database.

TEAMWORK PROJECT

Search for the article in Access Help titled *Database design basics* and read it. With a partner, plan a database that will contain information about all of the scholarships that are available locally to graduating seniors. Consider all of the data that might be stored and design the tables and fields accordingly. Compare your design with other teams. How were the plans similar or different? Incorporate all of the best ideas in the class into a single database plan.

 WEB PROJECT

Visit a Web site with information about upcoming events in your area. Use the information you found to plan, design, and then create a new blank database that includes a table named Events. Create whatever fields you need to store the data and modify the table fields to suit your needs. Enter at least 10 records about events that you would be interested in attending.

CRITICAL THINKING

ACTIVITY AC 1–1

You want to create a database about a collection you own (or would like to own). Decide what type of information the database will contain and how it will be organized, then sketch a rough draft on paper, being sure to identify the fields and data types. Use Access to create the database using the skills you learned in this lesson. Compare the database to your original design. Did you need to make any adjustments? Enter at least 10 records in your database.

ACTIVITY AC 1–3

You want to create a database to help you manage your school assignments and projects. Use Access to create a new blank database and create a table within that database named Assignments. Spend some time deciding what type of information the Assignments table will contain and how it will be designed, then sketch a rough draft on paper, being sure to identify the fields and data types. Enter at least six class assignments as records in the table.

ACTIVITY AC 1–2

Search for the video in Access Help titled *Ten quick tips to help work more efficiently in Access 2010* and watch it. What are some ways that Access 2010 is designed to help you work easier, faster, and more efficiently? Practice at least one new skill you have learned.

**Estimated Time:
2.5 hours**

LESSON 2

Creating Queries, Forms, and Reports

■ OBJECTIVES

Upon completion of this lesson, you should be able to:

- Create queries.
- Create and use forms.
- Modify the form's design.
- Create reports.
- Modify and print reports.
- Sort and filter records.

■ DATA FILES

To complete this lesson, you will need these data files:

Step AC 2-1.accdb
CVA logo.jpg
Project AC 2-1.accdb
Project AC 2-4.accdb
Math logo.jpg

■ VOCABULARY

filter

form

Form Wizard

query

Query Wizard

record source

report

Report Wizard

run

select query

simple form

sort

theme

VOCABULARY

record source

query

select query

Query Wizard

run

Introduction

Once you have created a database with tables, you can work with the data in the database to create other database objects. In this lesson, you will learn about creating and using the other database objects—queries, forms, and reports—to manipulate, display, and present data in a database.

When you create a query, form, or report, it is based on an existing object in the database. The underlying data that is used to create queries, forms, and reports is called the *record source*. In this lesson, you will use a table as the record source. The buttons you use to create database objects are located on the Create tab, as shown in **Figure AC 2–1**.

FIGURE AC 2–1   Create tab on Ribbon

Creating Queries

A *query* is a database object that is based upon a specific question you ask about the data in the database. Access displays the exact records that answer your question. For example, if you want to know which apartment unit would be available on a specific date, then you would create a query in which Access would locate the records in the database that meet that criteria. Queries are powerful tools that can extract data from one or more tables and that can be saved to use again.

You can create several different types of queries using the Query Wizard, including a simple select query. A *select query* simply retrieves specific data out of a record source for you to use. For example, you might want to view all of the supporters who have donated to your organization. The *Query Wizard* is an Access tool that guides you through the process of creating a query. You can start the Query Wizard by clicking the Query Wizard button in the Queries group on the Create tab. When you finish, the query is displayed in Datasheet view.

When you save a query, you are actually saving the design of the query, not the query results. You can save the query design the same way as other database objects—by clicking the Save button on the Quick Access Toolbar to display the Save As dialog box. When you click the Close Query button in the database window, if you have not already saved the query, you will be prompted to save it before closing. If you create a query using the Query Wizard, it is saved automatically when you complete the wizard.

Databases are continually updated, and in order to see the results of a query with the latest data, you must run the query. When you *run* a query, you perform the query with the most recent data, and give instructions to display the records and fields in your original query design. To run a query at any time, double-click it in the Navigation Pane. The records that are displayed are based on the most current information in the database.

You can display a query in different views. The most commonly used views are Datasheet view and Design view. You can use Datasheet view to see the results of a query, and Design view to create a query from scratch or modify the design of an existing query. To change views, click the View button arrow in the Views group on the Home tab to display a menu. You can also change views using the view buttons in the lower-right corner of the Access program window.

EXTRA FOR EXPERTS

If the queries you can create using the Query Wizard do not suit your needs, you can always create a query in Design view by clicking the Query Design button in the Queries group on the Create tab. In Design view, you can create more advanced action queries that perform tasks on the data, such as adding, updating, or deleting.

Step-by-Step AC 2.1

1. Start Access.

2. Open **Step AC 2-1.accdb** from the folder containing the data files for this lesson.

3. Use the **Save Database As** command on the File tab to save the database with the filename **Caprock View Apartments XXX** (replace XXX with your initials). On the Message Bar, click **Enable Content** to remove the warning and enable the content of the database.

4. Double-click the **Units** table in the Navigation Pane to open it in the database window, as shown in **Figure AC 2–2**. Notice the table contains data about apartment units. Click the **Close** button to close the table.

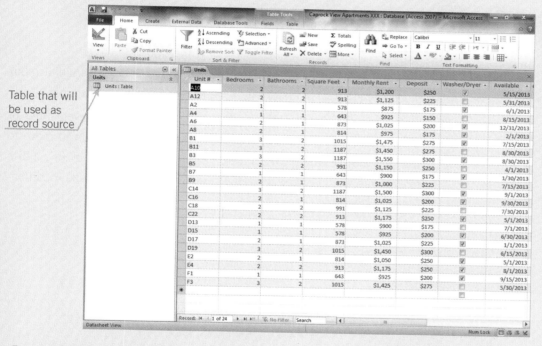

Table that will be used as record source

FIGURE AC 2–2
Units table to be used as a record source

5. If necessary, click the **Units** table in the Navigation Pane to select it. Click the **Create** tab, and in the Queries group, click the **Query Wizard** button to open the New Query dialog box.

6. Make sure **Simple Query Wizard** is selected in the list. Click the **OK** button to start the Query Wizard to create a simple select query.

7. In the first Simple Query Wizard dialog box, in the Available Fields list box, click **Unit #** to select it, and then click the **Add field** button ▷ to move it to the Selected Fields list box.

8. Repeat Step 2 to move the **Bedrooms**, **Bathrooms**, and **Available** fields to the Selected Fields list box. The Simple Query Wizard dialog box should look similar to **Figure AC 2–3**.

FIGURE AC 2–3
First Simple Query
Wizard dialog box

Selected record source

Add Field button

Fields selected for query

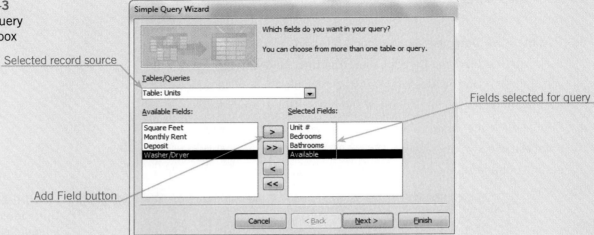

9. Click the **Next** button to move to the next Simple Query Wizard dialog box to specify the type of query results you want—detailed or summary.

10. Make sure the **Detail** option button is selected so that every field of every record will be shown, and then click the **Next** button to move to the next Simple Query Wizard dialog box in which you can specify a title for the query, and either preview the query or choose to make modifications to its design.

11. In the What title do you want for your query? text box, type **Unit Availability**. Make sure the **Open the query to view information** option button is selected, and then click the **Finish** button to create the query and display its results in Datasheet view, as shown in **Figure AC 2–4**.

Fields requested
by query

New query listed
in Navigation Pane

Name of query
on Object tab

Query displayed in
Datasheet view

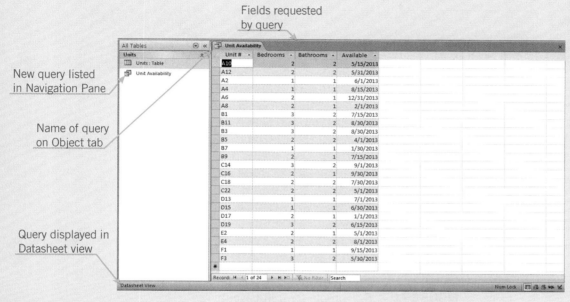

FIGURE AC 2–4
Creating a query using the Query Wizard

12. Click the **Close** button to close the query. There is no need to save the query as it was already saved when you created it using the Query Wizard.

13. Leave the database open for use in the next Step-by-Step.

Creating and Using Forms

An Access *form* is an object that you use to enter new records into the database or to edit data in existing records. Although you can enter new records directly into a table datasheet, using a form is an easier way to view, enter, and edit records. Forms allow you to focus on one record at a time. Forms can also be used to control what types of information can be viewed, changed, or entered by certain users as they work with an established database. Often a database is used by multiple people, and forms can help prevent errors or unwanted changes to the database records or structure. For example, you can create a form that only includes certain fields or only allows certain tasks to be performed.

Access offers a variety of tools for creating different types of forms. You can design your own forms in Design view; use the Form Wizard, which is an Access tool that walks you through creating a form; or you can use the Form tool to create a simple form with a single mouse click. These options are all accessible in the Forms group on the Create tab.

Creating a Simple Form Using the Form Tool

You can use the Form tool to create a *simple form* that includes all the fields from the selected record source. When you select the table in the Navigation Pane that you want to use as the record source for the form and then click the Form button in the

▶ **VOCABULARY**
form
simple form

Forms group on the Create tab, a simple form is created that includes all the fields from that table, as shown in **Figure AC 2–5**.

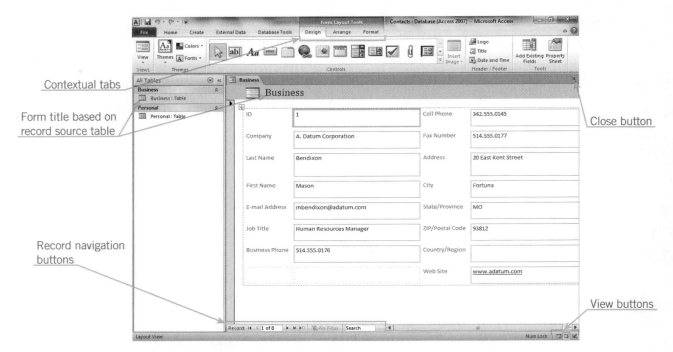

FIGURE AC 2–5   Simple form in Layout view

The form has a simple format and its title reflects the name of the record source table. Every field from the table is on the form, and the information from the first record is displayed.

When you create a simple form, it is initially displayed in Layout view. Layout view allows you to make modifications to the design of the form while the form displays data, allowing you to see the effect of your changes right away. You can make these types of design changes using the options on the Form Layout Tools Design, Arrange, and Format contextual tabs that are open on the Ribbon when a form is displayed in Layout view. The views available when working with form objects are summarized in **Table AC 2–1**. To change views, click the View button arrow in the Views group on the Form Layout Tools Design tab or on the Home tab.

TABLE AC 2–1   Views available for forms

VIEW NAME	ICON	DESCRIPTION
Form view		Allows you to view, enter, or edit data; you cannot alter the layout or design of the form in this view
Layout view		Allows you to make design changes to the form while it is displaying data; useful for performing tasks that affect the visual appearance and usability of a form; Form Layout Tools contextual tabs are available in this view
Design view		Gives a detailed view of the structure of the form; you cannot see the underlying data, but you have more control over the design of the form; Form Design Tools contextual tabs are available in this view

You can use the form to enter new data into the table or edit existing records by switching to Form view. The navigation buttons at the bottom of the Access program window can be used to move among records in a form just as you used the navigation buttons to move between records in a table. Click a button to move to the record you want—First, Previous, Next, Last—or click the New (blank) button to create a new record. You can enter or edit data by typing or changing it in the text boxes next to the field name. A pencil icon is displayed in the upper-left corner of the form when a record is being edited.

Saving Forms

Forms can be saved the same way as other database objects—by clicking the Save button on the Quick Access Toolbar to display the Save As dialog box. When you click a form's Close button, if you have not already saved it, you will be prompted to save it before closing.

Step-by-Step AC 2.2

The Caprock View Apartments *XXX*.accdb database from Step-by-Step AC 2.1 should be open in the Access program window.

1. Click the **Units** table in the Navigation Pane to select it. On the Create tab, in the Forms group, click the **Form** button to create a simple form based on the Units table, as shown in **Figure AC 2–6**.

Simple form has same name as its record source

All fields from the table are included

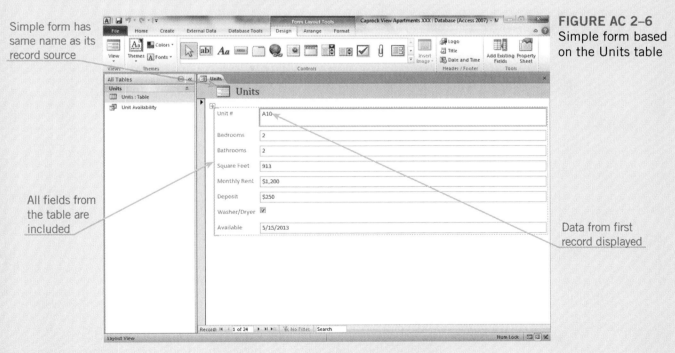

FIGURE AC 2–6
Simple form based on the Units table

Data from first record displayed

2. Click the **Save** button on the Quick Access Toolbar to open the Save As dialog box.

3. Access displays *Units* in the Form Name box as the suggested name for the simple form. Click the **OK** button to save the form with the suggested name.

4. Click the **Next record** button ▶ at the bottom of the form window to display the next record, for Unit A12.

5. In the Views group on the Form Layout Tools Design tab, click the **View** button arrow, and then click **Form View** on the menu. The form switches to Form view so that you can enter a new record.

6. Click the **New (blank) record** button ▶꙾ to create a new blank record.

7. Type the data shown in **Figure AC 2–7** in the new blank record. As you start entering data in the record, notice a pencil icon appears in the upper-left corner of the form, indicating the record is being edited. Press **Tab** to move to the next field. If you had more records to enter, you could press Enter after typing the last field value to display a new blank record.

FIGURE AC 2–7
New record
to enter

Pencil icon
indicates
record is
being edited

Units

Unit #	F5
Bedrooms	2
Bathrooms	1
Square Feet	873
Monthly Rent	$1,050
Deposit	$225
Washer/Dryer	☐
Available	12/1/2013

Record: I◀ ◀ 25 of 25 ▶ ▶I ▶꙾   No Filter   Search

8. Click the **Close** button to close the form.

9. Open the Units table and notice that the data you entered using the form has been recorded and appears as the last record in the datasheet.

10. Close the Units table and leave the database open for use in the next Step-by-Step.

Using the Form Wizard

If you want to select which fields are included on a form and also choose the form layout and style, then you can use the Form Wizard. The *Form Wizard* is an Access tool that guides you through the process of creating a form. You can start the Form Wizard by clicking the Form Wizard button in the Forms group on the Create tab.

Depending on the options that you choose, the resulting forms can vary. If the form is not what you expected, you can always modify it, or just delete it and start over. You can delete a form by right-clicking it in the Navigation Pane, and then clicking Delete on the shortcut menu.

> **VOCABULARY**
> **Form Wizard**

Step-by-Step AC 2.3

The Caprock View Apartments *XXX*.accdb database from Step-by-Step AC 2.2 should be open in the Access program window.

1. If necessary, click the Units table in the Navigation Pane to select it.

2. Click the **Create** tab, and in the Forms group, click the **Form Wizard** button to start the Form Wizard and open the first dialog box of the wizard. In this first dialog box, you select the data source to be used to create the form, and you select the fields to be included on the form.

3. If necessary, click **Unit #** in the Available Fields list box to select it, and then click the **Add field** button to move it to the Selected Fields list box.

4. Repeat Step 3 to move the **Monthly Rent** and **Deposit** fields to the Selected Fields list box. The Form Wizard dialog box should look similar to **Figure AC 2–8**.

> **EXTRA FOR EXPERTS**
>
> There are other tools that you can use to create different types of forms using the buttons in the Forms group on the Create tab. You can use Access Help to learn more about the purpose of these other types of forms.

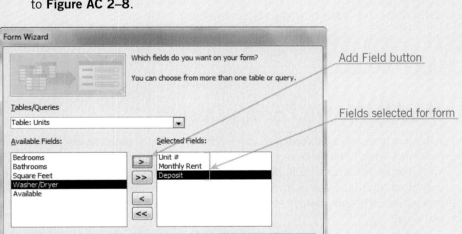

Add Field button

Fields selected for form

FIGURE AC 2–8
Selecting fields in the Form Wizard

5. Click the **Next** button to move to the next Form Wizard dialog box, which provides layout options for the form.

6. Click the **Tabular** option button to select a form layout similar to a spreadsheet. A sample of the tabular layout is displayed on the left.

7. Click the **Next** button to move to the next Form Wizard dialog box, in which you name the form and decide what you want to do next: open the form or continue to work on it by modifying its design. Usually it is best to view the finished form before making design changes to it.

8. In the What title do you want for your form? text box, type **Unit Cost**.

9. Click the **Finish** button to create the form and display it in Form view in the database window, as shown in **Figure AC 2–9**.

FIGURE AC 2–9
Form created using the Form Wizard

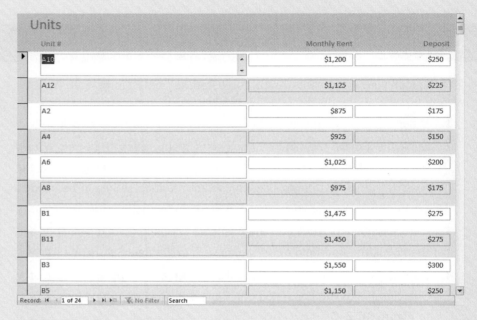

10. Click the **Close** button to close the form.

11. Leave the database open for use in the next Step-by-Step.

Modifying the Form's Design

After you have created a form, you can modify it to fit your needs using Layout view or Design view. In this lesson, you will use Layout view. When the form is in Layout view, the Form Layout Tools Design, Arrange, and Format contextual tabs are displayed on the Ribbon so you can modify the layout of the form. Using the buttons in the Header/Footer group on the Design tab, you can add a logo, a title, or the date and time.

An easy way to change the appearance of a form is to use a theme. A *theme* is a set of predesigned formatting elements—including colors and fonts—that can be applied to quickly give your forms a professional and consistent look. Themes are available in the Themes group on the Form Layout Tools Design tab. You can click the Themes button to open a gallery of options, or you can change only one element by clicking the Theme Colors or the Theme Fonts buttons.

▶ **VOCABULARY**
theme

You can also modify a form by moving, adding, or resizing fields. To move a field, use the Move Up or Move Down buttons in the Move group on the Form Layout Tools Arrange tab. To add a field, click the Add Existing Fields button in the Tools group of the Form Layout Tools Design tab to display the Fields List pane, then click the field and drag it to the form. To resize a field, click the field name to select it, which is indicated by an orange border. Point to the right border of the selected field to display a two-headed arrow pointer, and then click and drag to resize the field.

Step-by-Step AC 2.4

The Caprock View Apartments *XXX*.accdb database from Step-by-Step AC 2.3 should be open in the Access program window.

1. Double-click the **Units** form in the Navigation Pane to open it.

2. On the Home tab, in the Views group, click the **View** button arrow, and then click **Layout View** on the menu. The form switches to Layout view, and the Form Layout Tools Design contextual tab is displayed on the Ribbon.

3. On the Form Layout Tools Design tab, in the Header/Footer group, click the **Title** button to select the title for editing, and then type **Apartments**, as shown in **Figure AC 2–10**. Press **Enter** to change the form title.

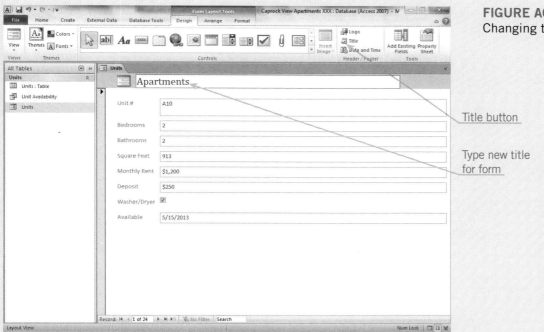

FIGURE AC 2–10
Changing the form title

4. In the Header/Footer group, click the **Logo** button to open the Insert Picture dialog box.

5. Navigate to the location where you store your data files for this lesson, select the **CVA logo.jpg** file, and then click **OK** to insert the logo onto the form.

6. In the Themes group, click the **Themes** button to open the Themes gallery, and then click the **Civic** theme, as shown in **Figure AC 2–11**, to apply a theme.

FIGURE AC 2–11
Applying a theme

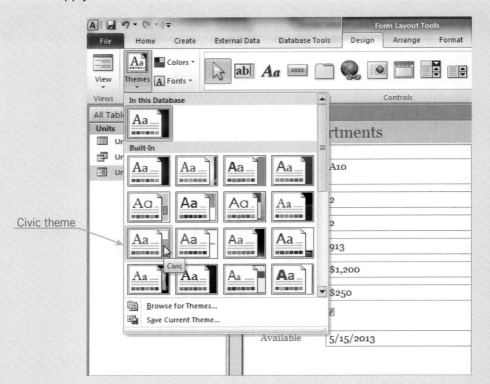

7. On the form, click the **Available** field name to select it, then press and hold **Shift** while clicking the **text box** next to it with the data *5/15/2013*, so that both the field name and the text box are surrounded by orange borders.

8. Click the **Form Layout Tools Arrange** tab, and then in the Move group, click the **Move Up** button six times until the selected boxes are displayed between the Unit # and Bedroom fields, as shown in **Figure AC 2–12**.

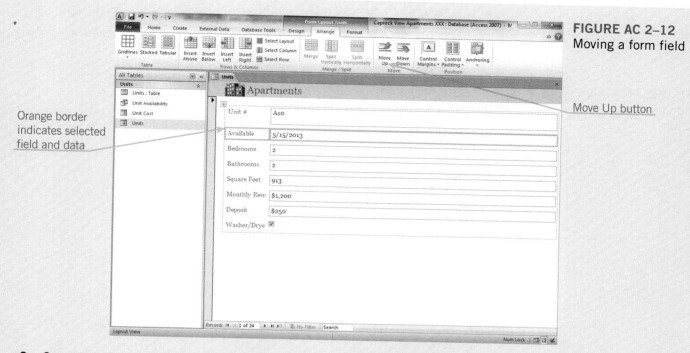

FIGURE AC 2–12
Moving a form field

Orange border
indicates selected
field and data

Move Up button

9. Save and close the Units form, and then open the **Unit Cost** form and switch to Layout view.

10. Click the **Unit #** field name to select it (if the title box becomes selected instead, press Tab to move the selection to the Unit # field name) and display it with an orange border. Press **Shift** and click the top **Unit #** field to select the column. Point to the left border to display a two-headed arrow pointer, click and drag to the right to make the field smaller, as shown in **Figure AC 2–13**, and then release the mouse button.

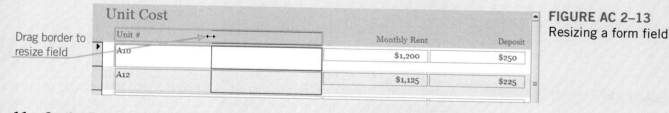

Drag border to
resize field

FIGURE AC 2–13
Resizing a form field

11. On the Form Layout Tools Design tab, in the Tools group, click the **Add Existing Fields** button to open the Field List pane.

12. Click the **Available** field in the Field List pane, drag it to the form before the Unit # field, as shown in **Figure AC 2–14**, then release the mouse button to add the field to the form.

FIGURE AC 2–14
Adding a field to a form

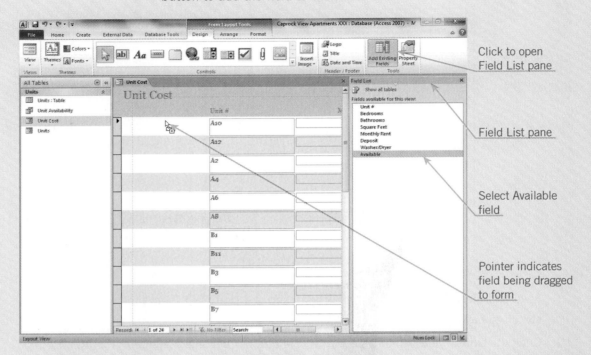

13. Click the **Available** field name to select it (and to deselect the fields), and drag it down to align with the other field names.

14. Click the **Close** button on the Field List pane to close it. Save and close the Unit Cost form, and leave the database open for use in the next Step-by-Step.

Creating Reports

▶ **VOCABULARY**
report

Another type of database object is a report. A ***report*** is a formatted display or print-out of the contents of one or more tables in a database. For example, you can use reports to create a formatted list of the records in a table. A report can also be generated from query results. When generated from a query, reports enable you to display a particular aspect of the data, such as how many items were sold last month or which cities had the most rainfall, or even to create mailing labels of clients from a specific ZIP code. After you have created a report, you can run it at any time by double-clicking it in the Navigation Pane to open it. Each time you run a report, it pulls the current data from the database, so it is always up to date. You can make adjustments to the design of a report so it presents the data you want to include in an attractive and readable format.

When you create a report, it is based on underlying data contained in a database object, just like a form. In this lesson, you will use a table as the record source. Access offers a variety of tools for creating different types of reports in the Reports group of the Create tab.

Using the Report Button

You can use the Report button to quickly create a simple report that includes all the fields from the underlying table. When you select the table in the Navigation Pane on which you want to base the report and then click the Report button in the Reports group on the Create tab, a report with a basic columnar format is displayed in Layout view, as shown in **Figure AC 2–15**.

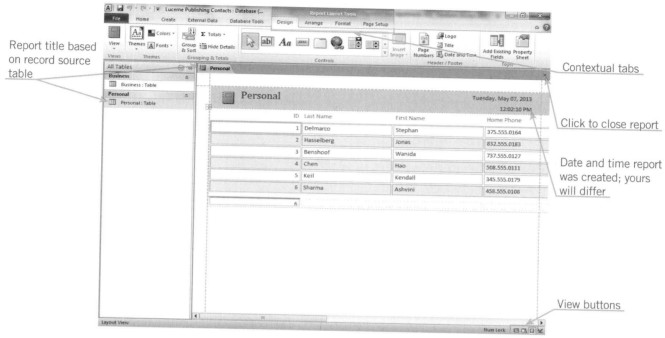

FIGURE AC 2–15   Simple report in Layout view

The report in Figure AC 2–15 has a simple format and has the same title as the title of the record source table. Every field from the table is on the report, as well as the date and time the report was created. The Record Layout Tools Design, Arrange, Format, and Page Setup contextual tabs are displayed on the Ribbon, providing tools you can use to modify the report.

You can display a report in different views. To change views, click the View button arrow in the Views group on the Home tab. Layout view and Design view can be used to modify the report. Or, you can switch to Report view to view the report, although you cannot make changes to the report in Report view. To see how a report will look when printed, you can display it in Print Preview.

Saving Reports

Reports can be saved the same way as other database objects—by clicking the Save button on the Quick Access Toolbar to open the Save As dialog box. When you click a report's Close button, if you have not saved it, you will be prompted to save it before closing.

Step-by-Step AC 2.5

The Caprock View Apartments *XXX*.accdb database from Step-by-Step AC 2.4 should be open in the Access program window.

1. Click the **Units** table in the Navigation Pane to select it.

2. Click the **Create** tab, and in the Reports group, click the **Report** button to create a simple report based on the Units table, as shown in **Figure AC 2–16**.

FIGURE AC 2–16
Simple report based on Units table

All fields from table included

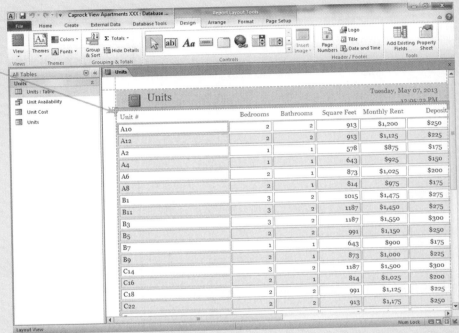

3. Click the **Save** button on the Quick Access Toolbar to open the Save As dialog box.

4. Type **All Units** in the Report Name text box, and then click the **OK** button to save the report.

5. In the Views group, click the **View** button arrow, and then click **Report View** to display the report in Report view.

6. Click the **Close** button to close the report.

7. Leave the database open for use in the next Step-by-Step.

Using the Report Wizard

If you want to select which fields are included on a report, how information is grouped or sorted, and also choose the report layout, orientation, and style, then you can use the Report Wizard. The ***Report Wizard*** is an Access tool that guides you through the process of creating a report. You start the Report Wizard by clicking the Report Wizard button in the Reports group on the Create tab.

▶ **VOCABULARY**
Report Wizard

Depending on the options that you choose, the resulting reports can vary. If the report is not what you expected, you can always modify it or just delete it and start over. You can delete a report by right-clicking it in the Navigation Pane and clicking Delete on the shortcut menu.

Step-by-Step AC 2.6

The Caprock View Apartments *XXX*.accdb database from Step-by-Step AC 2.5 should be open in the Access program window.

1. Click the **Create** tab, and in the Reports group, click the **Report Wizard** button to start the Report Wizard. In the first Report Wizard dialog box, you need to select the data source you want to use for generating the report, and you need to select the fields to be included in the report.

2. In the Tables/Queries box, be sure **Table: Units** is selected. In the Available Fields list box, click **Unit #** to select it if necessary, and then click the **Add Field** button to move it to the Selected Fields list box.

3. Repeat Step 2 to move the **Bedrooms**, **Bathrooms**, **Monthly Rent**, and **Available** fields to the Selected Fields list box, as shown in **Figure AC 2–17**.

FIGURE AC 2–17
Selecting fields in the Report Wizard

4. Click the **Next** button to move to the next Report Wizard dialog box, which displays options for selecting grouping levels by choosing which field(s) to use to organize the data in the report.

5. Click **Monthly Rent** in the list box on the left, and then click the **Add Field** button to organize the report information according to how much the monthly rent costs.

6. Click the **Next** button to move to the next Report Wizard dialog box, which displays options for sorting and summarizing detail records.

7. You do not want to sort the records or calculate summary values, so click the **Next** button to move to the next Report Wizard dialog box, which provides options for selecting various layouts for the report.

8. Click the **Outline** option button in the Layout section of the dialog box to have the report appear as an outline, as shown in the Preview in the dialog box. The Portrait option should be selected in the Orientation section.

9. Click the **Next** button to move to the next Report Wizard dialog box in which you name the form and decide what you want to do next: preview the report or modify its design. Usually it is best to view the finished report before making design changes to it.

10. In the What title do you want for your report? text box, enter **Units by Price**.

11. Click the **Finish** button to create the report and display it in the Print Preview window, as shown in **Figure AC 2–18**.

FIGURE AC 2–18
Completing a report using the Report Wizard

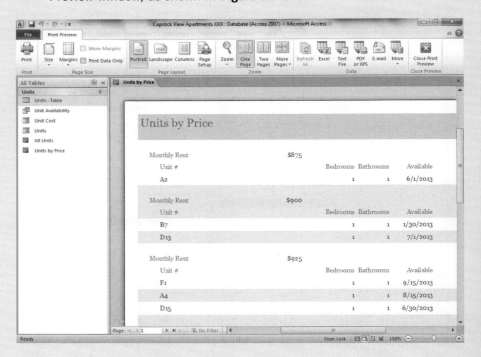

12. Click the **Close** button to close the report.

13. Leave the database open for use in the next Step-by-Step.

Modifying and Printing Reports

After you have created a report, you can modify it to fit your needs using Layout view. When the report is in Layout view, the Report Layout Tools Design, Arrange, Format and Page Setup contextual tabs are displayed so you can modify the layout of the report. You can use Layout view to modify the format or appearance of a report while still viewing the underlying data. Just as you did with forms, you can easily change the appearance of a report by using a theme, available on the Report Layout Tools Design tab in the Themes group.

You can also modify a report by moving, adding, deleting, resizing, or renaming fields. To move a field, click the field name to select it, as indicated by an orange border. Point to the field to display a four-headed arrow pointer, then click and drag the field to a new location on the report. To add a field, you can click the Add Existing Fields button on the Report Layout Tools Design tab in the Tools group to open the Fields List pane, then click the field and drag it onto the report. To delete a field in a simple report, select the field name, click the Select Column button in the Rows & Columns group on the Report Layout Tools Arrange tab, and then press Delete. If you decide you don't want to delete the field, just click the Undo button on the Quick Access Toolbar. To resize a field, click the field name to select it, as indicated by an orange border. Point to the right border of a selected field to display a two-headed arrow pointer, then click and drag to resize the field. You can rename a field by double-clicking the field name, then editing the name or selecting the name and typing a new one.

After you are satisfied with the report, you can print it. Reports can be printed from any view or even while closed. Before printing a report, you should preview it in the Print Preview window to make sure it looks the way you want. The commands on the Print Preview tab can be used to make changes to page layout and setup or to zoom to display the report differently. Click the Close Print Preview button to close the Print Preview window.

Step-by-Step AC 2.7

The Caprock View Apartments *XXX*.accdb database from Step-by-Step AC 2.6 should be open in the Access program window.

1. Double-click the **All Units** report in the Navigation Pane to open it.

2. On the Home tab, in the Views group, click the **View** button arrow, and then click **Layout View** on the menu to switch to Layout view and display the Report Layout Tools contextual tabs.

3. Click the **Unit #** field name to select it and display it with an orange border, point to the right border to display a two-headed arrow pointer, then click and drag to the left to make the field smaller (approximately the same size as the Bedrooms field).

4. Click the **Washer/Dryer** field name to select it. Click the **Report Layout Tools Arrange** tab, and in the Rows & Columns group, click the **Select Column** button to select all the data in the field as well, then press **Delete**.

5. Click the **Report Layout Tools Design** tab, and in the Themes group, click the **Themes** button to open the Themes gallery. Scroll down and click the **Solstice** theme, as shown in **Figure AC 2–19**, to apply the theme.

FIGURE AC 2–19
Applying a theme to a report

Solstice theme

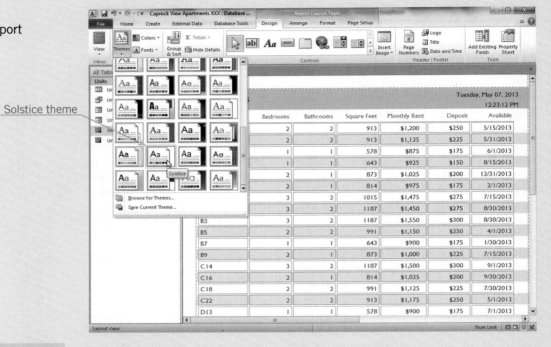

6. On the Design tab, in the Views group, click the **View** button arrow, and then click **Print Preview** on the menu to switch to Print Preview.

7. On the Print Preview tab, in the Zoom group, click the **Zoom** button arrow, and then click **Fit to Window** to preview entire report, as shown in **Figure AC 2–20**.

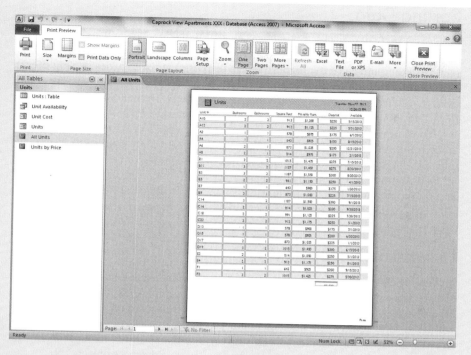

FIGURE AC 2–20
Viewing a report in Print Preview

8. On the Print Preview tab, in the Print group, click the **Print** button to open the Print dialog box.

9. Click the **Cancel** button to close the Print dialog box.

10. On the Print Preview tab, in the Close Preview group, click the **Close Print Preview** button to close Print Preview.

11. Save and close the All Units report.

12. Leave the database open for use in the next Step-by-Step.

Sorting and Filtering Records

Once you have created a database object—whether it is a table, query, form, or report—you can organize the data so that it is easier to work with and analyze by sorting or filtering the records. The commands to sort and filter data are located on the Home tab in the Sort & Filter group, as shown in **Figure AC 2–21**.

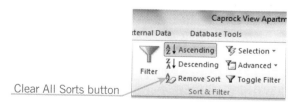

FIGURE AC 2–21   Sort & Filter group on Home tab

Sorting Data

When you *sort* data, Access rearranges selected data alphabetically, numerically, or chronologically. You can specify whether you want the lowest values displayed at the top (ascending order) or the highest values displayed at the top (descending order). When you choose ascending order, text is sorted from A to Z, numbers are sorted from 0 to 9, and dates are sorted from earliest to latest. Descending order sorts text from Z to A, numbers from 9 to 0, and dates from latest to earliest.

You can sort data in a form in Form view, a report in Layout view, or a query or table in Datasheet view. To sort by a field, you can select any field value in the column by which you want to sort and then click the Ascending or Descending button in the Sort & Filter group on the Home tab. Access will rearrange the records to match the sort order you choose. To remove the sort, you can click the Remove Sort (Clear All Sorts) button in the Sort & Filter group on the Home tab.

Using AutoFilter

A *filter* is helpful when you want to find and work with data that meets certain criteria or a specific set of conditions. For example, you might want to display only the records for employees in a certain department. The data in the database object you want to see will be visible, and the rest is hidden until you remove the filter. A filter is different from a query because a filter temporarily displays certain records without changing the design of the database object, while a query is saved as a database object.

If you need to specify complex conditions, you can click the Advanced Filter Options button in the Sort & Filter group on the Home tab to open a menu with more advanced commands. But for most purposes, using AutoFilter is the quickest and easiest way to display the data you need. When you click a field header and then click the Filter button in the Sort & Filter group on the Home tab, an AutoFilter menu opens with options that are specific to the type of data in that field, as shown in **Figure AC 2–22**.

Date filters for Available field

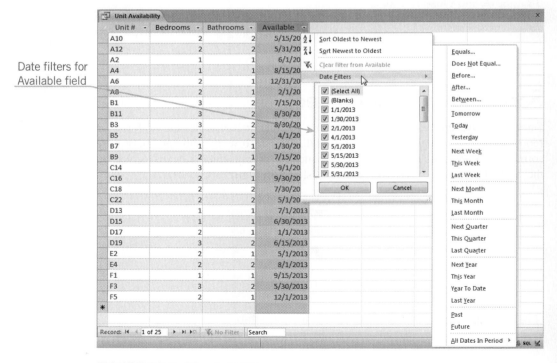

FIGURE AC 2–22   AutoFilter menu

On the AutoFilter menu, you can choose to filter from a list of values by selecting or clearing the check boxes. You can also filter by common criteria using the options on the Date Filters submenu (or Text Filters or Number Filters, depending on the field's data type). To remove a filter, you click the Toggle Filter button in the Sort & Filter group on the Home tab.

Step-by-Step AC 2.8

The Caprock View Apartments *XXX*.accdb database from Step-by-Step AC 2.7 should be open in the Access program window.

1. Double-click the **All Units** report in the Navigation Pane to open it.

2. On the Home tab, in the Views group, click the **View** button arrow, and then click **Layout View** to display the report in Layout view.

3. Click the **Square Feet** field header to select this field.

4. Click the **Home** tab, and in the Sort & Filter group, click the **Descending** button to sort the records in descending order by square footage, as shown in **Figure AC 2–23**.

FIGURE AC 2–23
Sorting a report

Field sorted in descending order

Unit #	Bedrooms	Bathrooms	Square Feet	Monthly Rent	Deposit	Available
C14	3	2	1187	$1,500	$300	9/1/2013
B11	3	2	1187	$1,450	$275	8/30/2013
B3	3	2	1187	$1,550	$300	8/30/2013
D19	3	2	1015	$1,450	$300	6/15/2013
B1	3	2	1015	$1,475	$275	7/15/2013
F3	3	2	1015	$1,425	$275	5/30/2013
C18	2	2	991	$1,125	$225	7/30/2013
B5	2	2	991	$1,150	$250	4/1/2013
A12	2	2	913	$1,125	$225	5/31/2013
E4	2	2	913	$1,175	$250	8/1/2013
C22	2	2	913	$1,175	$250	5/1/2013
A10	2	2	913	$1,200	$250	5/15/2013
A6	2	1	873	$1,025	$200	12/31/2013
B9	2	1	873	$1,000	$225	7/15/2013
D17	2	1	873	$1,025	$225	1/1/2013
C16	2	1	814	$1,025	$200	9/30/2013

Units — Tuesday, May 07, 2013 12:31:20 PM

5. On the Home tab, in the Sort & Filter group, click the **Clear All Sorts** (Remove Sort) button to clear the sort.

6. Close the All Units report without saving the design changes.

7. Double-click the **Unit Cost** form in the Navigation Pane to open it, and then switch to Layout view.

8. Select a value in the **Monthly Rent** field.

9. Click the **Home** tab, and in the Sort & Filter group, click the **Filter** button to open the AutoFilter menu for that field.

10. Point to **Number Filters** and then click **Less Than**, as shown in **Figure AC 2–24**, to open the Custom Filter dialog box.

FIGURE AC 2–24
Filtering a form

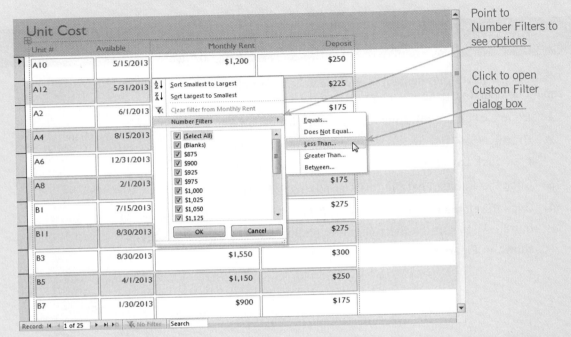

11. In the Monthly rent is less than or equal to text box, type **1000**, and then click the **OK** button to display only the records where the monthly rent is less than or equal to $1,000.

12. On the Home tab, in the Sort & Filter group, click the **Toggle Filter** button to remove the filter.

13. Close the Unit Cost form without saving the changes.

14. Close the database and close Access.

SUMMARY

In this lesson, you learned:

- The process of creating a query.
- Ways to create and use different forms.
- How to modify a form's design.

- Ways to create reports.
- How to modify and print reports.
- To sort and filter records.

■ VOCABULARY REVIEW

Define the following terms:

filter	record source	select query
form	report	simple form
Form Wizard	Report Wizard	sort
query	run	theme
Query Wizard		

■ REVIEW QUESTIONS

MULTIPLE CHOICE

Select the best response for the following statements.

1. The underlying data in a database that is used to create forms, reports, and queries is called the _____.

   A. table source   C. field source

   B. record source   D. data source

2. You can use the Form tool to create a _____ that includes all the fields from the selected record source.

   A. simple form   C. multiple items form

   B. split form   D. form in Design view

3. You can use _____ view to enter or edit data in a form.

   A. Form   C. Design

   B. Layout   D. Datasheet

4. To select a table to use as the record source for a report, select it in the _____.

   A. Open dialog box   C. Record Wizard

   B. Create tab   D. Navigation Pane

5. You can print a report from _____ view.

   A. Report   C. Layout

   B. Print Preview   D. any of the above

6. A _____ is a database object that is based upon a specific question you ask about the data in the database.

   A. table   C. form

   B. query   D. report

7. When you use the Query Wizard to create a simple select query, it is initially displayed in _____ view.

   A. Datasheet   C. Design

   B. Layout   D. Query

8. When you click the Add Existing Fields button in the Tools group on the Form Layout Tools Design tab, the _____ opens.

   A. Add Fields pane   C. Fields List pane

   B. Add Fields dialog box D. Fields List dialog box

9. When you _____ data, Access rearranges selected data alphabetically, numerically, or chronologically.

   A.   sort   C.   query
   B.   filter   D.   save

10. To remove an active filter, you can click the _____ button in the Sort & Filter group on the Home tab.

   A.   Delete Filter   C.   Undo Filter
   B.   Toggle Filter   D.   Clear Filter

FILL IN THE BLANK

Complete the following sentences by writing the correct word or words in the blanks provided.

1. When you use the Form button to create a form that includes all fields from that table, it is displayed in _____ view.

2. To delete a field from a report in Layout view, click the field name to select and display it with a(n) _____ border, then press Delete.

3. The _____ is an Access tool that guides you through the process of creating a form.

4. A(n) _____ is a database object used to present a summary of data in a table that is often printed out.

5. To see how a report will look when printed, you can display it in _____.

6. You can start the Report Wizard by clicking the Report Wizard button in the Reports group on the _____ tab.

7. A(n) _____ is a set of predesigned formatting elements—including colors and fonts—that can be applied to quickly give your form a professional and consistent look.

8. A(n) _____ query retrieves specific data out of a record source.

9. _____ order sorts text from Z to A, numbers from 9 to 0, and dates from latest to earliest.

10. A(n) _____ is different from a query because it temporarily displays certain records without changing the design of the database object, while a query is saved as a database object.

■ PROJECTS

PROJECT AC 2–1

1. Open the file **Project AC 2-1** from the folder containing the data files for this lesson, and enable the database content. Save the database as **Contributions XXX** (replace XXX with your initials).

2. Open the **Donations** table to view the data, and then close it.

3. Create a simple form based on the Donations table.

4. Navigate through all the records.

5. Save the form with the default name **Donations**.

6. Move the Payment Method field up so it appears between the Amount and Payment Date fields.

7. Switch to Form view. Create a new record with the following information (data in the ID field will be entered automatically):

   Contributor: **Consolidated Messenger**

   Amount: **$125**

   Payment Method: **cash**

   Payment Date: **12/16/2013**

8. Save and close the Donations form.

9. Open the Donations table, and see that the new data was added.

10. Close the Donations table, and leave the database open for use in the next project.

ON YOUR OWN

Open the **Contributions XXX** database, and use the Form Wizard to create a form based on the Contributors table using all the fields except the ID field, with a Columnar layout, and name it **Company Contributors**.

PROJECT AC 2–2

The **Contributions** *XXX* database from Project AC 2–1 should be open in the Access program window.

1. Create a simple report based on the Donations table.
2. Save the report with the default name **Donations**.
3. Apply the Median theme to the report.
4. Sort the Payment Date column in Descending order.
5. Clear the sort order.
6. Sort the Amount column in Ascending order.
7. Select the ID field and all the data in the column, and delete it.
8. Select the Payment Method column, and size it to fit the data.
9. Switch to Print Preview view and print the report.
10. Save and close the Donations report. Leave the database open for use in the next project.

ON YOUR OWN

In the **Contributions** *XXX* database, use the Report Wizard to create a report based on the Contributors table using the Company, Contact Last Name, and Business Phone fields. Experiment with the options until you create a report that you like. Modify and format it as needed, and then print it.

PROJECT AC 2–3

The **Contributions** *XXX* database from Project AC 2–2 should be open in the Access program window.

1. Create a simple query based on the Donations table that includes the Contributor, Amount, and Payment Date fields; that shows the details; and uses the default name **Donations Query**.
2. Filter the query to only show donations where the amount is greater than or equal to $275.
3. Remove the filter.
4. Filter the query to only show donations made by the Graphic Design Institute.
5. Remove the filter.
6. Sort the query by the Amount field in Descending order.
7. Save and close the query.
8. Close the database.

PROJECT AC 2–4

1. Open the file **Project AC 2-4** from the folder containing the data files for this lesson and enable the content. Save the database as **Math Department** *XXX* (replace *XXX* with your initials).
2. Select the **Faculty** table in the Navigation Pane.
3. Use the Form Wizard to create a form that includes all fields except the Faculty ID field. Use a Justified layout and title it **Faculty**.
4. Switch to Layout view, and apply the Technic theme.
5. View the form in Form view. Navigate to the last record, and change the Homeroom field value from 219 to 109.
6. Close the form.
7. Use the Report Wizard to create a report based on the Classes table that includes the Period, Room, and Teacher fields; grouped by period; with no sort order; with Stepped layout; and title it **Classes by Periods**.
8. Print the report and close it.
9. Create a simple form based on the Classes table.
10. Change the title of the form to **Math Classes**.
11. Insert the logo file **Math logo.jpg** from the location where you store your data files for this lesson.
12. Save the form as **Classes**.
13. Close the database.

 TEAMWORK PROJECT

Open the **Caprock View Apartments** *XXX* database that you worked with in this lesson. With a partner, take turns providing requirements for an apartment you might want to rent. For example, you might want to rent a two-bedroom apartment that has a washer and dryer. Or, you might want to rent something for less than $1,100 per month. Take turns with your partner to create a query to determine which apartments meet the other's requirements.

WEB PROJECT

Many businesses and organizations use databases to provide information online—for example, genealogy sites offer ancestral information and car dealerships show which cars are in stock. Search the Internet for other examples of how databases are used online. Visit the Web site of a local library that has an online database of available books. On a piece of paper, sketch a database table that would contain information about books the library has that you have read or want to check out. In Access, create the database table that you sketched and enter at least five records. Create a simple report based on the information and format it attractively.

 CRITICAL THINKING

ACTIVITY AC 2–1

Open a database that you worked with in Access Lesson 1, and create a form that you can use to enter data into one of the tables. Which type of form did you create and why? View the form in Layout view, and use the buttons on the Format Layout Tools Format, Design, and Arrange tabs to modify the design of the form to your liking.

ACTIVITY AC 2–2

Open a database that you worked with in Access Lesson 1, and create a report based on one of the tables. Which tool did you use to create the report and why? View the report in Layout view, and use the buttons on the Report Layout Tools contextual tabs to modify the design of the form to your liking. Preview the report and then print it.

UNIT V REVIEW

Access

REVIEW QUESTIONS

MULTIPLE CHOICE

Select the best response for the following statements.

1. All the information about one specific student in a table, such as the student's name, grade level, and phone number, would be stored in one _____.

   A. field   C. datasheet

   B. record   D. field value

2. Each field in a datasheet is displayed as a column and is identified by its _____ on the column header.

   A. foreign key   C. field value

   B. primary key   D. field name

3. Each record in the database must have a _____, which is the value in the primary key field that makes the record unique.

   A. field value   C. foreign key

   B. key value   D. record selector box

4. Access is considered a _____ because all of the data is stored in separate tables and then connected by establishing relationships between the tables.

   A. primary database   C. relational database

   B. key database   D. table database

5. Which database object summarizes and presents information in an easily readable format suitable for printing?

   A. Table   C. Form

   B. Query   D. Report

6. The _____ on the left side of the Access program window lists all of the objects in the database.

   A. Ribbon   C. Blank Database pane

   B. Navigation Pane   D. File tab

7. When you create a simple form, it is initially displayed in _____ view.

   A. Form   C. Datasheet

   B. Layout   D. Design

8. You can start the Form Wizard by clicking the Form Wizard button in the Forms group on the _____ tab.

   A. Home   C. Database Tools

   B. Create   D. Form Layout Tools Design

9. Each field in a table has a _____ that determines the types of field values you can enter in that field.

   A. key value   C. data type

   B. field value   D. field name

10. A _____ is helpful when you want to find and work with data that meets certain criteria or a specific set of conditions.

   A. key value   C. record source

   B. filter   D. sort

FILL IN THE BLANK

Complete the following sentences by writing the correct word or words in the blanks provided.

1. The _____ is an Access tool that guides you through the process of creating a query.

2. When you start Access, _____ view is displayed.

3. One difference from other applications is that the File tab in Access contains a(n) _____ command, which you can use to create a copy of a database object.

4. A single characteristic or piece of information stored in a table—like name, grade level, or phone number—is called a(n) _____.

5. The database object that you use to enter new records into the database, or to edit existing records is the _____.

6. When you create a new table, Access creates an ID field by default, sets it as the primary key, and assigns it _____ data type.

7. A(n) _____ is a database object that is based upon a specific question you ask about the data in the database.

8. After you have created a report, you can run it at any time by double-clicking it in the _____ to open it.

9. To see how a report will look when printed, you can display it in _____.

10. To remove a sort from a database object, you can click the _____ button in the Sort & Filter group on the Home tab.

■ PROJECTS

PROJECT AC 1

1. Start Access.

2. Open the **Project AC 1** database from the folder containing the data files for this review, and save it as *Voting XXX* (replace *XXX* with your initials). Enable the database content.

3. Rename the Location table as **Polling Places**.

4. Open the Polling Places table.

5. Widen the fields so all field names and data are visible.

6. Add a new field named **Early Voting,** and assign a Yes/No data type.

7. Place check marks in the Early Voting field check boxes for records 2 and 5.

8. Edit the location in record 1 to read **Aurora City Hall**.

9. Create a field named **Notes,** and assign it the Memo data type.

10. In the Notes field of record 3, type **not wheelchair accessible**, and widen the column so the data is fully visible.

11. Save and close the Polling Places table.

12. Open the Election Judges table to verify that it does not contain any data, then close the table and delete it.

13. Close the database.

PROJECT AC 2

1. Create a new, blank database named **Swim Meets XXX** (replace *XXX* with your initials).

2. Rename the default ID field as **Event ID**, change the data type to Text, and make the field values required and unique.

3. Add the following fields with corresponding data type:

   Event—Text data type

   Location—Text data type

   Event Date—Date & Time data type

4. Enter the data into the table, as shown in **Figure AC–1**. Widen fields as necessary to fully display data.

Event ID	Event	Location	Event Date	Click to Add
MAC-S1	Time Trials	Massey Aquatic Center	9/30/2013	
LRC-S2	Lorenzo Relays	Lorenzo Rec Center	10/15/2013	
GSD-SD1	Early Bird Invitational	Greenville Swim Deck	10/25/2013	
MAC-SD2	Northwest Invitational	Massey Aquatic Center	11/14/2013	
FAC-SD3	Franklin Invitational	Franklin Athletic Complex	12/2/2013	
GSD-SD4	Regional Championship	Greenville Swim Deck	1/9/2014	
PMP-SD5	State Championship	Pierre Municipal Pool	1/17/2014	

FIGURE AC–1   Swim Meets new table data

5. Save the table as **Events**.

6. In the Events table, move the Event Date field between the Event and Location fields.

7. Change the format of the Event Date field to Medium Date.

8. Make the Event field required.

9. Save and close the table.

10. Leave the database open for use in the next project.

PROJECT AC 3

The Swim Meets *XXX*.accdb database from Project AC 2 should be open in the Access program window.

1. Create a simple report based on the Events table, and save it as **Events Schedule**.

2. Apply the Flow theme to the report.

3. View the report in Print Preview.

4. Save and close the report.

5. Create a simple form based on the Events table.

6. Save the form as **Events Form**, and switch to Form view.

7. Use the form to create a new record with the following information:

   Event ID: **AWD-SD6**

   Event: **Award Ceremony**

   Location: **Massey Aquatic Center**

   Event Date: **January 30, 2014**

8. Switch to Layout view.

9. Change the title of the form to **Swimming and Diving**.

10. Insert a logo on the form using the **Swim Logo.jpg** file from the folder containing the data files for this review.

11. In the Events Form object, delete the Event ID field.

12. Save and close the form, and close the database.

PROJECT AC 4

1. Open the **Project AC 4** database from the folder containing the data files for this review. Save the database as **Film Festival** *XXX* (replace *XXX* with your initials), and enable the database content.

2. Create a simple query based on the Competition Shorts table that includes the Title, Director Last Name, and Director First Name fields. Title the query **Shorts Directors**.

3. Sort the query results by director last name in ascending order.

4. Save and close the query.

5. Use the Form Wizard to create a form based on the Competition Shorts table that includes the ID, Title, Minutes, and Seconds fields. Use the Columnar form, and title it **Shorts Times**.

6. Navigate to record 5.

7. Capitalize the *i* in *is,* and close the form.

8. Use the Report Wizard to create a report based on the Staff table that includes the Last Name and Title fields. Do not include any grouping or sort order. Use the Tabular layout, and title it with the default name **Staff**.

9. View the report in Print Preview, and then print it.

10. Save the report and close it. Close the database.

ON YOUR OWN

Open the **Film Festival** *XXX* database. Create a simple query, report, and form based on the Fundraisers table. Sort or filter the data and modify the format of each database object using the tools available on the contextual tabs. Close the database.

 # WEB PROJECT

You want to create a database that has information about your favorite restaurants. Plan the data that you want to include—such as restaurant name, location, phone number, type of food, or favorite dish—and sketch it out on paper. In Access, create a table that includes the fields you designed. Visit the Web sites for at least five restaurants in your city, and gather the information you need. Enter at least five records into your table. Create a report based on the table, format it to suit the data, and then print it.

 # TEAMWORK PROJECT

As a member of the school council, you have been asked to create a database of schoolwide activities for the school year. With a partner, discuss the tables you will need to create to contain this information, what fields will be used, and what data types will be assigned to each field. Sketch a rough draft on paper, and then use Access to create the database. Create a form, and use it to enter at least 20 records. What kind of database object would you create to find out all the activities going on next month? What are some practical ways your database could be used?

■ CRITICAL THINKING

ACTIVITY AC 1

Open the **Activity AC 1** database from the folder containing the data files for this review. Save the database as **Class Assignments *XXX*** (replace *XXX* with your initials), and enable the content. Open each of the tables, and add at least two records to each. Use actual assignments or make them up. Create a report for each table, modify it to suit you, and then print each report.

ACTIVITY AC 2

Use Access Help to search for the video titled *Introduction to the Access 2010 user interface* and watch it. Open the **Film Festival *XXX*** database that you used in Project AC 4, and view the information about it in Backstage view. How would you pin it to the Recent Datasebases list?

ACTIVITY AC 3

You want to create a database for all of your music CDs. Think about what kind of information the database will contain—for example, album, artist, year released, or genre of music. Spend some time deciding how it will be designed, and sketch a rough draft on paper. After planning your database, use Access to create it. Create a simple form, and use it to enter at least 10 records. Create a report that groups the records by some category—for example the most recent CDs or all CDs by one artist—and then print it.

■ PORTFOLIO CHECKLIST

_____	Lesson 1	Contacts *XXX*.accdb
_____	Lesson 1	Vehicle Records *XXX*.accdb
_____	Lesson 2	Caprock View Apartments *XXX*.accdb
_____	Lesson 2	Math Department *XXX*.accdb
_____	Unit Review	Voting *XXX*.accdb
_____	Unit Review	Swim Meets *XXX*.accdb

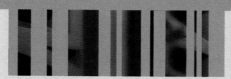

UNIT VI

MICROSOFT PUBLISHER

LESSON 1   **1.5 HRS.**

Understanding Publisher Fundamentals

LESSON 1

Understanding Publisher Fundamentals

■ OBJECTIVES

Upon completion of this lesson, you should be able to:

- Examine the Publisher program window.
- Start Publisher and open an existing publication.
- Navigate a publication.
- Use a template to create a new publication.
- Enter text.
- Format text and paragraphs.
- Save a publication.
- Modify the design of a publication.
- Insert graphics.
- Preview and print a publication.
- Close a publication.

■ DATA FILES

Step PB 1-1

■ VOCABULARY

alignment

building blocks

bullets

business information set

clip art

color scheme

crop

desktop publishing software

font

font scheme

font styles

Format Painter

I-beam

insertion point

line spacing

paragraph

pictures

placeholders

point size

publication

scratch area

selection handles

Smart Tag button

story

template

text boxes

thumbnails

Introduction

Microsoft Publisher 2010 is a desktop publishing program included in the Microsoft Office 2010 suite of software. ***Desktop publishing software*** is used to combine text and graphics to produce high-quality marketing and communications documents for print on a personal desktop printer or by a commercial printer.

Publisher offers a variety of publication templates and designs that you can combine and customize to create professional publications, or you can start from scratch with a blank page. In this lesson, you will learn to create publications using templates and customize them with text, graphics, and predefined designs. You will also learn how to save, print, and close publications.

Examining the Publisher Program Window

A Publisher file is called a publication. A ***publication*** is a document that is created to market a product or communicate a message to an audience, such as a newsletter, brochure, business card, or greeting card.

Like other Microsoft Office 2010 programs, Publisher organizes commands on tabs on the Ribbon, as shown in **Figure PB 1–1**. Use this figure to become familiar with the parts of the Publisher program window.

> **VOCABULARY**
> **desktop publishing software**
> **publication**

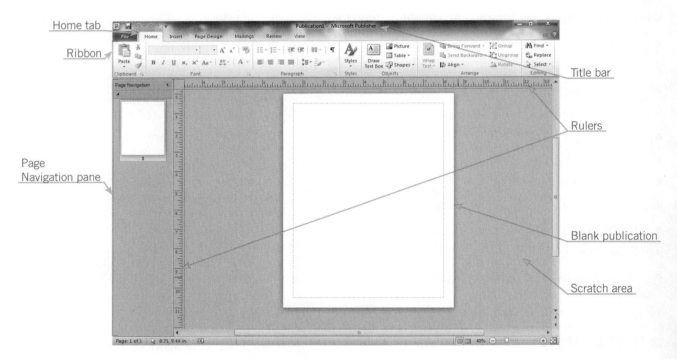

FIGURE PB 1–1   Publisher program window

The default file name of a new publication is Publication1; the filename is displayed at the top of the screen in the title bar, as shown in Figure PB 1–1. The Page Navigation pane is located on the left side of the screen and is used to navigate the pages of the publication. Publisher also displays horizontal and vertical rulers. The blank area around the publication is called the *scratch area*, which is a workspace that you can use to store or work with graphics or text boxes. Items on the scratch area are visible while you work on any page in your publication. For example, you can move a graphic from page 1 to the scratch area, continue working, and then display page 5 and drag the graphic from the scratch area onto the page where you want it.

▶ **VOCABULARY**
scratch area

Starting Publisher and Opening an Existing Publication

To begin using Publisher, you first need to open it. You can do this by clicking the Start button on the Windows taskbar, and then clicking the program name in the Microsoft Office program folder on the All Programs menu, or by double-clicking a Publisher program icon on the desktop. Once Publisher is started, you can begin using it to create a new publication or open an existing publication. When you start Publisher, the Available Templates section of Backstage view is displayed, as shown in **Figure PB 1–2**, where you can create a publication based on a template, create a blank publication, or open an existing publication.

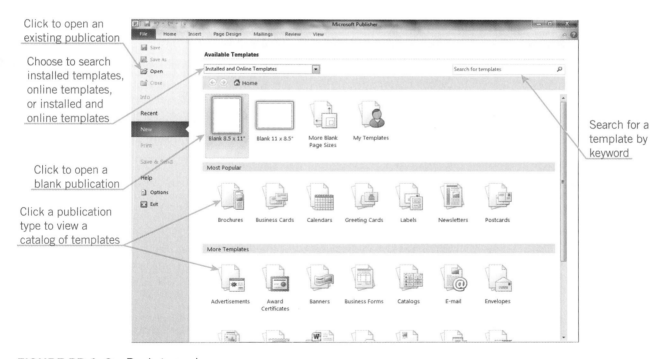

FIGURE PB 1–2   Backstage view

If you want to open an existing publication, click Open on the File tab to display the Open Publication dialog box, shown in **Figure PB 1–3**, where you can navigate to and open the publication you want, just like you do in other Office programs.

Address bar (your address information will be different)

Double-click to open a file

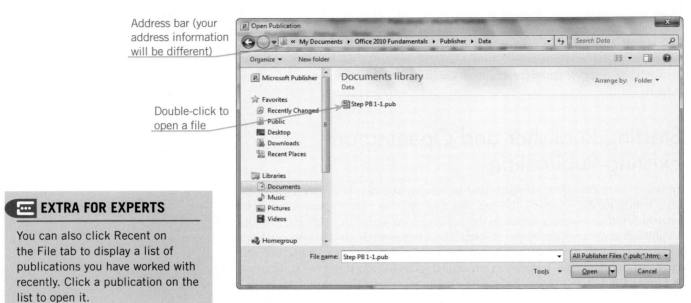

FIGURE PB 1–3   Open Publication dialog box

Step-by-Step PB 1.1

1. Click the **Start** button 🏁 on the Windows taskbar. The Start menu opens.

2. Click **All Programs**. A list of programs and program folders opens.

3. Scroll down if necessary and click the **Microsoft Office** program folder. A list of Office programs opens.

4. Click **Microsoft Publisher 2010**. Publisher starts and the Available Templates section of Backstage view is displayed.

5. On the File tab, click **Open** to display the Open Publication dialog box.

6. If necessary, navigate to the folder containing the data files for this lesson. Double-click the file named **Step PB 1.1** in the File list. The publication opens, as shown in **Figure PB 1–4**.

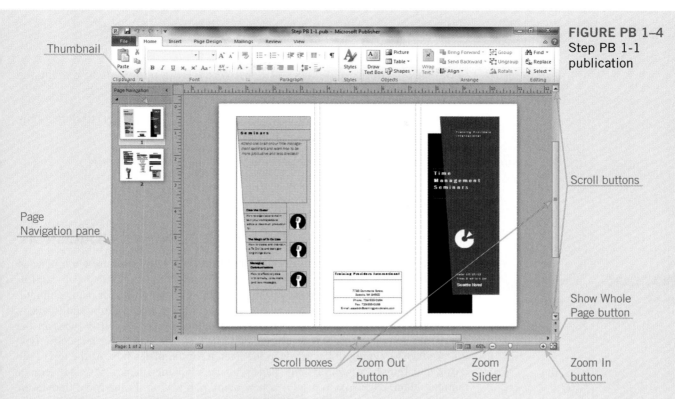

FIGURE PB 1–4
Step PB 1-1 publication

7.   Leave the publication open for use in the next Step-by-Step.

Navigating the Publication

When working with a publication, it is important to know how to move from page to page and to zoom in and out. You navigate a publication in Publisher similarly to the way you get around in other programs. Use the vertical and horizontal scroll buttons and scroll boxes, shown in Figure PB 1–4, to display parts of a page. The Page Navigation pane on the left side of the screen contains small pictures of pages, called *thumbnails*, that you can click to move from page to page. When you need to zoom in or out to work on a particular area of a publication, use the Zoom In or Zoom Out buttons on the status bar or move the Zoom slider left or right to the desired magnification. You can also use the buttons in the Zoom group on the View tab on the Ribbon to adjust the magnification.

▶ **VOCABULARY**
thumbnails

Step-by-Step PB 1.2

The publication from Step-by-Step PB 1.1 should be open in the Publisher program window.

1.   In the Page Navigation pane, click the page **2** thumbnail to display page 2 in the right pane.

2.   On the status bar, click the **Zoom In** button ⊕ three times.

3. Drag the vertical scroll box to the bottom of the scroll bar.

4. On the status bar, click the **Zoom Out** button ⊖ three times.

5. On the status bar, click the **Show Whole Page** button ⊞ to display the entire page on the screen.

6. In the Page Navigation pane, click the page **1** thumbnail to display the first page on the screen.

7. Leave the publication open for use in the next Step-by-Step.

Using a Template to Create a New Publication

▶ **VOCABULARY**
template

One method of creating a well-designed publication quickly is to use a template. A *template* is a sample publication that provides a pattern or model that you can follow to create your own publication. Publisher includes templates for many common types of publications, including newsletters, brochures, greeting cards, and flyers.

Publisher's templates are organized in categories of publication types in the Available Templates section of Backstage view. You can search for a specific type of template by typing in keywords in the Search for templates box. At the top of the Available Templates section home page, you can click the Blank 8.5" × 11" icon or another blank page size to display a new blank publication. In the Most Popular or More Templates areas on the Available Templates section home page, you can click a category, such as Brochures, to view the available templates in that category.

When you open a template, you are actually creating a new publication based on the template, so the original template is not altered as you customize the publication. A publication template contains a color scheme, font scheme, clip art or other graphics, text boxes, and placeholders for text. You can name and save a new publication using the Save or Save As command on the File tab.

Step-by-Step PB 1.3

The publication from Step-by-Step PB 1.2 should be open in the Publisher program window.

1. Click the **File** tab to display file-related commands.

2. On the File tab, click **New** to display the Available Templates section of Backstage view.

3. In the More Templates area, click the **Flyers** category to display a catalog of flyer templates.

4. In the Marketing area, click the **All Marketing** folder to display additional templates.

5. Scroll down to the Installed Templates area, and then click the **Bounce** template under *Informational*, as shown in **Figure PB 1–5**. Notice that a preview appears in the right pane, along with customizable design elements that you can change now or later.

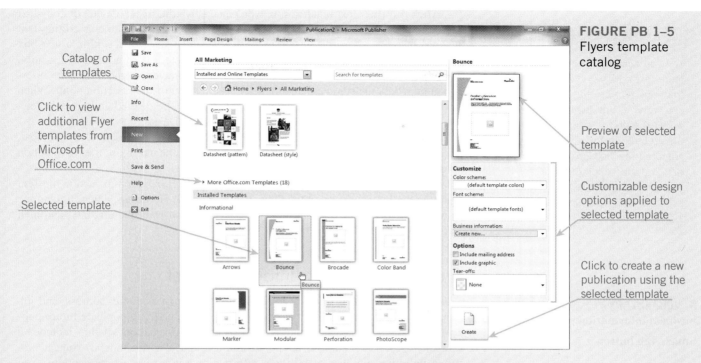

Catalog of templates

Click to view additional Flyer templates from Microsoft Office.com

Selected template

FIGURE PB 1–5
Flyers template catalog

Preview of selected template

Customizable design options applied to selected template

Click to create a new publication using the selected template

6. Click the **Create** button to create a new publication based on the template. Notice that the publication Step PB 1.1 from the previous exercise is closed (without having to be saved since you made no changes) and was replaced with the new publication.

7. Leave the publication open for use in the next Step-by-Step.

Entering Text

Unlike Word, where you type on the page and the text flows from margin to margin and from page to page, a Publisher publication is made up of an arrangement of several different text boxes. *Text boxes* are containers for text. All text in a publication is stored within text boxes. All the text within a single text box is called a *story*, and you can select a story by pressing Ctrl+A. Text boxes are objects within Publisher, so you can click them once to select them. The small circles at the sides and corners of the text box are *selection handles*. You drag these handles to change the size of an object. A green rotate handle at the top of the box allows you to rotate the text box. When a text box is selected, you can add borders, fills, and effects. *Placeholders* are text boxes in templates that contain suggestions for content that is standard for a particular type of publication. You can click the placeholder text to select it and begin typing to replace the content provided with your own.

> **VOCABULARY**
> **text boxes**
> **story**
> **selection handles**
> **placeholders**
> **I-beam**
> **insertion point**

Entering Text in a Text Box

To enter text in a text box, click the *I-beam* (the shape of the mouse pointer in a text box) anywhere in the text box. A blinking cursor, called an *insertion point*, indicates where your entry will appear. When you click placeholder text, all the text is selected, and you can begin typing to replace the text. Click a blank space on a publication to deselect.

EXTRA FOR EXPERTS

You can connect, or link, two or more text boxes so that text flows from one text box to the other as one story. To link two text boxes, select the first text box, click the Create Link button in the Linking group on the Text Box Tools Format tab, and then click the text box you want to link to (when linking text boxes, the pointer changes to a pitcher icon).

▶ VOCABULARY

business information set

Smart Tag button

After you enter text in a text box, you can easily edit, insert, delete, or copy text from one text box to another. Editing text in a text box is the same as editing text in Word or other Microsoft Office programs. You can select text within a text box by dragging or using keyboard combinations. To delete text in a text box, position the insertion point and press Backspace to delete characters to the left of the insertion point. Press Delete to delete characters to the right of the insertion point. When deleting more than a few characters, select the text to be deleted and press Delete. You can delete a text box by selecting it and pressing Delete.

To reverse, or undo, an action, use the Undo button on the Quick Access Toolbar. If you perform an undo action but then decide against the undo, use the Redo button to reverse the undo action.

You can draw a new text box using the Draw Text Box button located in the Text group on the Insert tab and in the Objects group on the Home tab. After clicking the Draw Text Box button, click in the location where you want the text box, and then drag to draw the text box the size that you want.

Creating a Business Information Set

A *business information set* is a collection of data, such as name, address, and job title, that can be saved together as a set and used repeatedly to populate future publications. For example, you can create a business information set that includes a company logo, name, address, telephone number, and Web site address. You can create an unlimited number of business information sets to use in publications. You may have one for your organization and a different one for personal use. Business information sets can be edited, changed, and updated any time using the Business Information button in the Text group on the Insert tab, or you can click a Smart Tag button to display a shortcut menu for editing, saving, or updating information. A *Smart Tag button* is a circle icon with an *i* in the center that appears when you point to or click on data that is part of a business information set. If no business information set is saved in Publisher, you can create a new one by clicking the Business Information button or the Smart Tag button and then clicking Edit Business Information Set to open the Create New Business Information Set dialog box.

If a business information set already exists, clicking Edit Business Information Set opens the Business Information dialog box with the current business information set data listed. This dialog box contains buttons for editing or deleting the selected business information set and a New button you can click to create a new business information set. After you have created more than one business information set, you can choose the one you want from the Select a Business Information set list in the Business Information dialog box.

Step-by-Step PB 1.4

The publication from Step-by-Step PB 1.3 should be open in the Publisher program window.

1. Click the **Product/Service Information** placeholder text to select it, as shown in **Figure PB 1–6**.

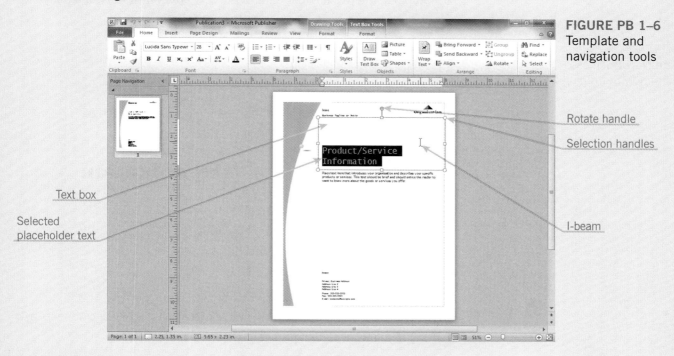

FIGURE PB 1–6
Template and navigation tools

Rotate handle

Selection handles

Text box

Selected placeholder text

I-beam

2. Type **Scuba Diving Lessons** as the title of the publication.

3. Zoom in so that you can read the text.

4. Click the placeholder text in the text box below the title that begins with *Place text here...* and type the following text:

   Whether you dream of swimming with colorful fish, brushing past a sea turtle, or investigating jellyfish, exploring the ocean is a very rewarding experience. Our goal is to train you to be a safe, confident diver. We offer a professional educational experience that will also be great fun. Contact us for a personal consultation.

5. Position the pointer over the word *Microsoft* in blue text near the bottom of the page until you see the Smart Tag button ⓘ appear. (*Note*: If no one has set up a business information set on your computer before, *home* or *Business Name* might be displayed as a placeholder instead of *Microsoft*. If a business information set has been created, the previously entered information will be displayed.)

6. Point to the **Smart Tag** button to display the **Smart Tag** button arrow ⓘ ▾, and then click it to display the shortcut menu.

7. Click **Edit Business Information** to display the Create New Business Information Set dialog box (*Note*: If a business information set already exists, click the **New** button to display the Create New Business Information Set dialog box.)

8. Type **Jacque Blue** in the Individual name box and press **Tab**.

9. Replace the placeholder data in the text boxes with the remaining business information, as shown in **Figure PB 1–7**.

FIGURE PB 1–7
Create New Business
Information Set dialog box

10. Below the logo (if one is shown), click **Remove**. A message appears asking if you want to remove the logo. Click **Yes**.

11. Type **Azul Scuba Diving** in the Business Information set name box.

12. Click the **Save** button to save the business information set.

13. In the Business Information dialog box, click the **Update Publication** button to populate the publication. Notice that the publication now reflects the business set data.

14. Leave the publication open for use in the next Step-by-Step.

Formatting Text and Paragraphs

▶ **VOCABULARY**
font

A *font* is a design of a set of letters and numbers. Each font has a name, such as Arial or Times New Roman. The characteristics of text that you can change are font and font size, font style such as italic and bold, and font effects such as underline, color, and capitalization. The Font group on the Home tab on the Ribbon contains buttons for formatting text, as shown in **Figure PB 1–8**. These commands are also available in the Font group on the contextual Text Box Tools tab.

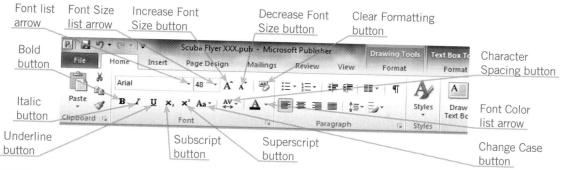

FIGURE PB 1–8 Font group on the Home tab

The Font menu on the Home tab displays each font's design before you make a choice. You change to a different font by selecting text and choosing one of the fonts listed on the Font menu.

Font sizes are measured in points. *Point size* refers to a measurement for the height of characters. To change the font size for existing text, you first select the text and then choose a new size on the Font Size menu in the Font group on the Home tab.

The Increase Font Size button increases font size one increment on the Font Size menu, which may be one point, two points, or eight points in the larger sizes, and the Decrease Font Size button decreases the size one increment.

Font styles are variations in the shape or weight of a font's characters. Bold, italic, and underline are common font styles that you can access easily in the Font group. The Font Color button arrow in the Font group lets you change the text color.

Formatting Paragraphs

The alignment, spacing, and indentation of text in a publication depend on the formatting you apply to *paragraphs*. Publisher refers to any amount of text or other items followed by a paragraph mark as a paragraph. You may have one or more paragraphs within a text box, and each can be formatted independently.

To apply paragraph formatting, position your insertion point anywhere in a paragraph. Publisher will apply the paragraph formats you select to the entire paragraph. You cannot apply paragraph formatting to only a selection of the paragraph.

The Paragraph group on the Home tab, shown in **Figure PB 1–9**, contains buttons for changing paragraph formatting. You can access additional commands in the Paragraph dialog box, which you can display by clicking the dialog box launcher in the Paragraph group.

> **VOCABULARY**
> **point size**
> **font styles**
> **paragraph**

EXTRA FOR EXPERTS

You can use shortcut keys to apply font styles: Press Ctrl+B to apply bold, Ctrl+I to apply italic, and Ctrl+U to underline text.

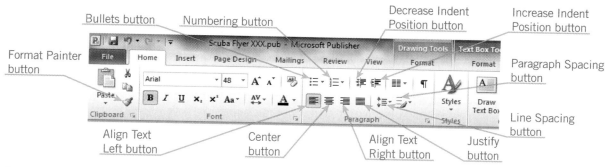

FIGURE PB 1–9 Paragraph group on the Home tab

▶ **VOCABULARY**

alignment

line spacing

bullets

Format Painter

> ### ▤ EXTRA FOR EXPERTS
>
> Another way to change fonts, font sizes, font styles, and font effects is to click the dialog box launcher in the Font group to display the Font dialog box, where you can make several changes in one place.

> ### ▤ EXTRA FOR EXPERTS
>
> You can use shortcut keys to align text: Press Ctrl+L to align text left, Ctrl+R to align text right, Ctrl+E to center text, and Ctrl+J to justify text.

Alignment is the position of text in relation to the edges of a text box. You can left-align, center, right-align, or justify a paragraph horizontally within a text box using the alignment buttons—Align Text Left, Center, Align Text Right, and Justify—in the Paragraph group on the Home tab.

Line spacing determines the vertical distance between lines of text in a paragraph. The Line Spacing button in the Paragraph group lets you choose a common line spacing option, such as 1.0 (single spacing) or 2.0 (double-spacing). You can also click Line Spacing Options on the Line Spacing menu to display the Paragraph dialog box, which contains options for creating custom line spacing and for adding spacing before or after a paragraph. To add or remove space between paragraphs using a button in the Paragraph group, you can use the Paragraph Spacing button.

Formatting Lists

Bullets are small symbols that mark the beginning of each item in a list. You can select an existing list and then click the Bullets button or the Numbering button in the Paragraph group to add bullets or numbers. The Bullets and Numbering command, located at the bottom of the Bullets menu and Numbering menu, displays the Bullets and Numbering dialog box, where you can choose bullet symbols and numbering formats.

Use the Increase Indent Position and Decrease Indent Position buttons in the Paragraph group to move a list item to a higher level or down to a lower level in the list.

Publisher automatically renumbers a numbered list when you insert, move, copy, or delete items from the list. Similarly, a new bullet is added on a blank line when you press Enter at the end of a bulleted item.

Copying Formats Using the Format Painter

The *Format Painter* can save you time and helps ensure consistency by allowing you to copy multiple formatting characteristics from selected text and then apply the same formatting to other parts of the publication.

To copy the formatting of a section of text, you first select the text or paragraph that contains the formatting you want to copy, and then click the Format Painter button in the Clipboard group on the Home tab. When you click the Format Painter button, the mouse pointer changes to an I-beam with a paintbrush "loaded" with the copied format. Next, you can click in the text box where you want to apply the formatting and the formatting is applied to the entire text box.

Step-by-Step PB 1.5

The publication from Step-by-Step PB 1.4 should be open in the Publisher program window.

1. Select the text **Scuba Diving Lessons**.

2. On the Home tab, in the Font group, click the **Font** list arrow 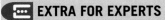, scroll up, and click **Arial** to change the font.

3. In the Font group, click the **Font Size** list arrow , scroll down if necessary, and click **48** to increase the size of the text.

4. In the Font group, click the **Bold** button **B** to apply bold to the text.

5. In the Paragraph group, click the **Center** ☰ button to center the title horizontally within the text box.

6. Select the text that begins *Whether you dream....* On the Home tab, in the Paragraph group, click the **Line Spacing** button 🔳 and click **2.0**.

7. At the top of the page, select **Azul Scuba School**. On the Home tab, in the Font group, click the **Font Color** list arrow 🅰️⁃, and click **Blue** under Standard Colors.

8. Make sure the text is still selected. On the Home tab, in the Clipboard group, click the **Format Painter** button 🖌️. The pointer changes to an I-beam with a paintbrush.

9. Scroll near the bottom of the page, and then drag across **Azul Scuba School** to apply the copied formatting.

10. Leave the publication open for use in the next Step-by-Step.

Saving a Publication

The first time you save a publication, the options for saving include the Save button on the Quick Access Toolbar or the Save and Save As commands on the File tab. Each of these methods displays the Save As dialog box, as shown in **Figure PB 1–10**.

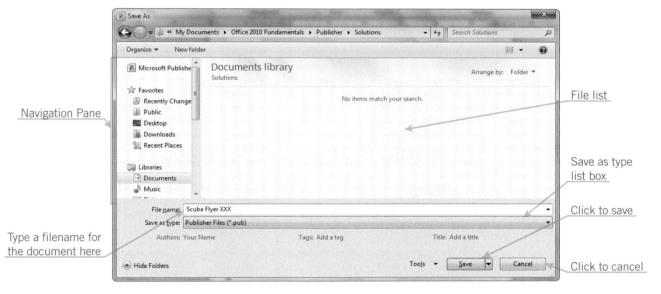

FIGURE PB 1–10   Save As dialog box

EXTRA FOR EXPERTS

Publisher files are saved with the extension .pub. If you want to save a publication as a template, choose the Publisher Template option from the Save as type list in the Save As dialog box. You can save a publication in the .pdf format by clicking Save & Send on the File tab, and then clicking Create PDF/XPS Document.

After you save a file the first time, the Save command saves your file with the previously specified name in the location you specified. The Save As command opens the Save As dialog box to let you make a copy of the file with a new name, location, or file type. The Save as type list in the Save As dialog box lets you save a publication in another format or as a template. To save a publication in a specific location, you use the Navigation Pane to navigate to the folder in which you want to save the publication. Once you have saved the file, you can use the Save button on the Quick Access Toolbar, the Save command on the File tab, or press Ctrl+S to save your changes.

Publisher's AutoRecover feature automatically saves your publication at regular intervals so that you can recover at least some of your work in case of a power outage or other unexpected shutdown. You can turn this feature on or off and change the setting to save more or less often by opening the Options dialog box using the Options command on the File tab. On the Save tab in the Options dialog box, specify a number in the Save AutoRecover information every *x* minutes box. However, you should not rely on this automatic saving feature. Remember to save your work often.

Step-by-Step PB 1.6

The publication from Step-by-Step PB 1.5 should be open in the Publisher program window.

1. Click the **File** tab and then click **Save As** to open the Save As dialog box.

2. Navigate to the location where you will save your files.

3. If necessary, select **Publication2.pub** in the File name text box, and then type **Scuba Flyer *XXX*** (replace *XXX* with your initials) in the box to rename the file.

4. Click **Save** to save a copy of the publication with the new name in the specified location.

5. Leave the publication open for use in the next Step-by-Step.

Modify the Design of a Publication

Publisher provides many options for modifying the look of your publication. The Page Design tab, shown in **Figure PB 1–11**, contains several types of options, including commands for changing the template and modifying the color scheme.

Change Template button

Color Schemes gallery

Scheme Fonts button

FIGURE PB 1–11   Page Design tab

The Template group on the Page Design tab contains options for changing the template for the open publication. The Change Template button opens the Change Template dialog box, which allows you to create a new publication based on a different template using your current data, or to apply a different template to your current publication. If you change to a different type of template, the new template might not have placeholders for all of the data; for example, changing from a newsletter to a business card template will leave some of the newsletter content without an equivalent location in the new template. In this case, extra data is moved into the Extra Content task pane on the right side of the publication window. You can add the extra content to your publication from the task pane, delete it, or save it for use it in another publication.

The Schemes group on the Page Design tab provides options for changing the colors and fonts associated with a publication. Unless you have an eye for design, it can be difficult to coordinate colors and choose appropriate fonts for headings and text. Publisher has done it for you by creating schemes of colors and fonts that work well together. The Schemes gallery has options for choosing a predesigned set of coordinated colors, or *color scheme*, for your publication. The Scheme Fonts button lets you choose a new *font scheme*, which is a set of fonts in styles and sizes that complement each other.

WARNING

If you change templates and use the Apply template to the current publication option without saving the file first, the original publication will be lost.

▶ **VOCABULARY**
color scheme

font scheme

Step-by-Step PB 1.7

The Scuba Flyer *XXX* publication from Step-by-Step PB 1.6 should be open in the Publisher program window.

1. On the Page Design tab, in the Schemes group, click the **More** button ⏷ to open the Schemes gallery.

2. Click the **Marine** option to apply the new color scheme, as shown in **Figure PB 1–12**.

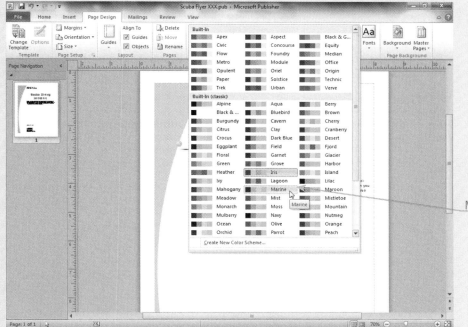

FIGURE PB 1–12
Color Schemes gallery

3. In the Schemes group, click the **Scheme Fonts** button.

4. Scroll down and click the **Breve** option to apply the new font scheme.

5. In the Template group, click the **Change Template** button to display the Change Template dialog box.

6. In the Marketing area, click the **All Marketing** folder to see additional options.

7. Scroll down to the More Installed Templates area, and then click **Waves**, as shown in **Figure PB 1–13**.

FIGURE PB 1–13
Change Template dialog box

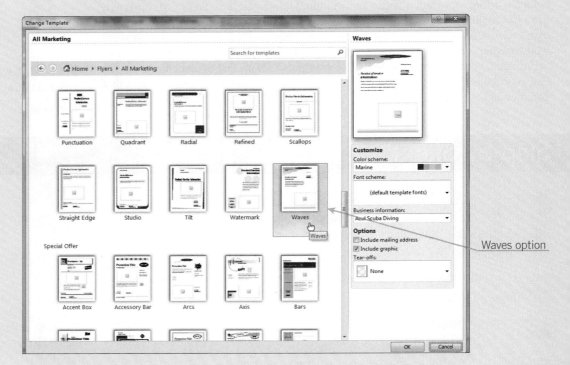

8. Click **OK** to display a different Change Template dialog box, in which you indicate whether to apply a template to the current publication or create a new publication.

9. Click the **Apply template to the current publication** option button, and then click **OK** to apply the new template.

10. Click the **Save** button on the Quick Access Toolbar to save the changes. Leave the publication open for use in the next Step-by-Step.

Inserting Graphics

Pictures, clip art, and other graphic objects add visual interest to a publication. The Insert tab, shown in **Figure PB 1–14**, contains commands for inserting various types of objects and information. The Illustrations group contains buttons for inserting graphic objects such as pictures, clip art, shapes, and picture placeholders. The Building Blocks group lets you insert reusable objects that you can modify to fit your publication. The Text group contains buttons for drawing text boxes and inserting business information.

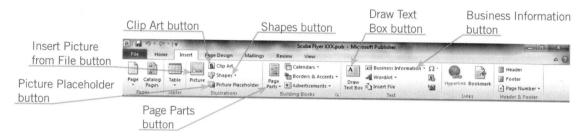

FIGURE PB 1–14   Insert tab

When you click a button on the Insert tab, you can choose the object to be inserted from a dialog box, task pane, or menu; the access method varies by object. You can modify the object after you insert it.

Inserting Building Blocks

Building blocks are design objects that you can use in your publications. Building blocks include page parts, which are page elements such as pull quotes and sidebars; calendars to add to planning documents; graphic borders and accents, such as bars and frames; and advertisements, such as coupons and attention getters for sales materials. The Building Blocks group on the Insert tab contains buttons for inserting each type of building block. You can click the Page Parts button, Calendars button, Borders & Accents button, or Advertisements button, and then select an option from the gallery that opens to insert the building block in your publication. After a building block is inserted, its size, shape, and content can be modified to fit your needs.

▶ **VOCABULARY**
building blocks

Step-by-Step PB 1.8

The Scuba Flyer *XXX* publication from Step-by-Step PB 1.7 should be open in the Publisher program window.

1. On the Insert tab, in the Building Blocks group, click the **Page Parts** button to open the Page Parts gallery.

2. In the Pull Quotes section, click the **Brackets** pull quote, as shown in **Figure PB 1–15**, to insert it. The pull quote contains placeholder text.

FIGURE PB 1–15
Page Parts gallery

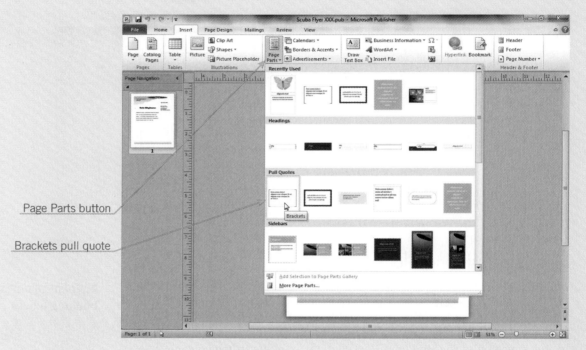

Page Parts button

Brackets pull quote

3. Drag the pull quote into position beside the text box, as shown in **Figure PB 1–16**.

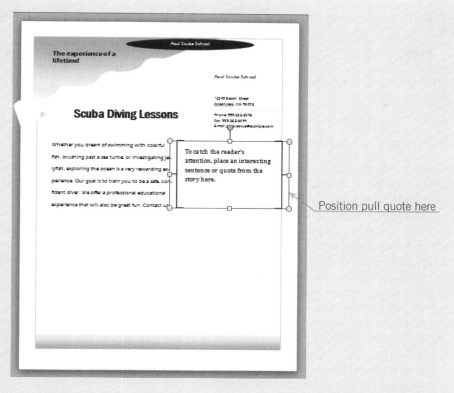

FIGURE PB 1–16
Pull quote

4. Zoom the publication to 100% or a readable size, click the pull quote placeholder text, and type **"The Azul Scuba School is great! The instructors are very knowledgeable and professional."**

5. Press **Enter** and type **Anneleise Marc.**

6. Drag the lower-left corner handle down and to the right, as shown in **Figure PB 1–17**, to resize the text box.

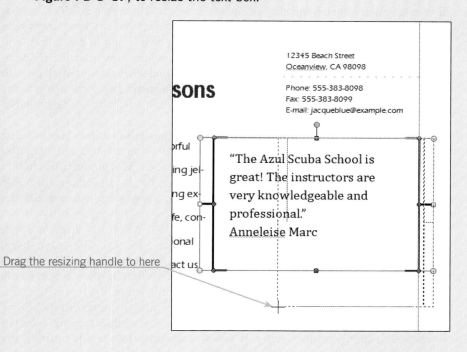

FIGURE PB 1–17
Resizing a text box

7. On the Drawing Tools Format tab, in the Shape Styles group, click the **More** button ⬇ to display the Shape Styles gallery, and then click the **Linear Up Gradient – Accent 3** style.

8. Save and leave the publication open for use in the next Step-by-Step.

Inserting and Modifying Illustrations

Pictures, clip art, shapes, and picture placeholders are types of illustrations you can add to your publications. The Illustrations group on the Insert tab contains buttons for inserting these types of objects.

Pictures, or digital photographs or images, may be stored on your computer or network. The Insert Picture from File button in the Illustrations group displays the Insert Picture dialog box that lets you navigate to and insert a picture file from your computer or network. You can insert pictures of various formats, including .tif, .gif, and .jpeg. Any time a picture is selected, the Picture Tools Format tab is displayed. This tab contains commands for modifying the picture, such as adjusting the brightness or contrast, applying a picture style, recoloring it, adding effects, arranging the picture on the page, and adjusting the size of a picture. The crop button is a common command used to *crop*, or remove, unwanted areas of a picture. You can also replace a selected picture with a new picture by clicking the Change Picture button in the Adjust group on the Picture Tools Format tab, and then selecting a new picture.

Clip art is ready-made artwork, usually created with a computer, that is used to illustrate publications. The Clip Art button in the Illustrations group displays the Clip Art task pane, where you can search for and insert clip art located on your computer, network, or on the Internet. The task pane contains a Search for text box where you can enter a keyword to find related clip art. The Results should be menu lets you choose the type of media file you are searching for, including illustrations, photographs, videos, and audio.

Publisher provides a set of common shapes that you can add to publications with one click and drag of the mouse. The Shapes button in the Illustrations group displays a gallery containing shapes, lines, rectangles, basic shapes, block arrows, flowchart elements, stars and banners, and callouts that you can insert anywhere in your publication. To draw a shape, click the shape you want in the gallery, and then position the crosshair pointer in the location where you want the shape to appear on the slide. Drag to draw the shape to the preferred size, or click once to insert the shape in a default size. After you insert a shape into a publication, the Drawing Tools Format contextual tab is displayed on the Ribbon with commands for modifying the shape.

The Picture Placeholder button in the Illustrations group allows you to insert an empty picture frame to reserve space for a picture you want to add later. You can adjust the size of the frame to fit the desired space. The picture placeholder contains a Picture button that you can click to open the Insert Picture from File dialog box and find the picture you want to insert. Many templates contain picture placeholders.

After you insert a graphic, you might want to change its size, location, shape, or color. But, before you can modify or resize a picture, clip art, or shape, you must select it. To select a graphic within a publication and display its selection handles, click the graphic once. You drag the selection handles to change the graphic's size. When you want to resize a graphic proportionally, that is, to maintain the original ratio of height to width, you must drag a corner handle. Some types of graphics require that you hold the Shift key while dragging a corner handle when sizing proportionally. If you want to distort a graphic horizontally

▶ VOCABULARY
pictures

crop

clip art

📇 EXTRA FOR EXPERTS

Large files can take longer to download, and some may be rejected by e-mail servers. Including pictures in publications increases file size, but you can use the Compress Pictures button in the Adjust group on the Picture Tools Format tab to decrease a picture's file size by reducing the resolution, or the number of pixels in a picture.

⚠ WARNING

You can use the images, sounds, and movies Microsoft provides with Publisher, or for free on its Web site, in any advertising, promotional and marketing materials, or product or service created with Publisher, as long as the material, product, or service is for noncommercial purposes. You may not sell any promotional and marketing materials or any products or services containing the images.

or vertically, drag a middle handle to resize the graphic. You can click the green rotate handle at the top of a graphic to rotate it on its central axis left or right to any position.

When a graphic is selected, you can copy, paste, and delete it the same way you would with any text using the Cut, Copy, and Paste commands in the Clipboard group on the Home tab.

Step-by-Step PB 1.9

The Scuba Flyer *XXX* publication from Step-by-Step PB 1.8 should be open in the Publisher program window.

1. Position the mouse pointer in the lower-right portion of the page. Notice that a picture placeholder is displayed.

2. Click the **Picture** button ⊞ inside the placeholder to open the Insert Picture dialog box.

3. Navigate to the Sample Pictures folder in the Pictures library, and then double-click the **Penguins** picture to insert it into the publication.

4. On the Picture Tools Format tab, in the Adjust group, click the **Change Picture** button ⊞ and click **Change Picture** to display the Insert Picture dialog box.

5. In the Sample Pictures folder, double-click the **Jellyfish** picture to insert it.

6. On the Picture Tools Format tab, in the Picture Styles group, click the **More** button ⊞ and click **Picture Style 5** to apply the style to the picture. Click on a blank area of the screen to deselect the picture.

7. On the Insert tab, in the Illustrations group, click the **Clip Art** button to display the Clip Art task pane.

8. Type **scuba diving** in the Search for box. Make sure *All media file types* is displayed in the Results should be box. If necessary, click the **Include Office.com content** check box, and then click the **Go** button to start the search for clip art.

9. In the Clip Art task pane, scroll down if necessary, and click the picture of the **diver with the shark overhead**, as shown in **Figure PB 1–18,** to insert it.

FIGURE PB 1–18
Clip Art task pane

Type keywords
for a search here

Click Go button
to start a search

Click the Close button to
close the Clip Art task pane

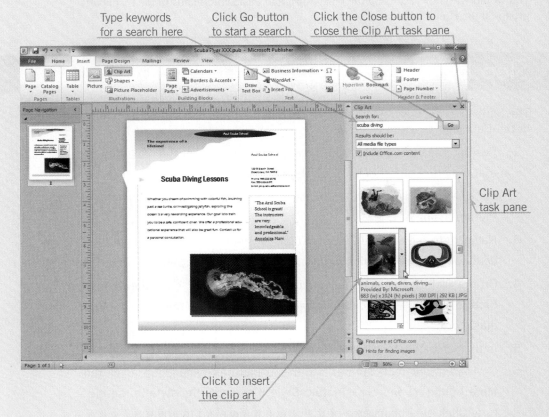

Clip Art
task pane

Click to insert
the clip art

10. Drag the diver photo to the left to position it in the lower corner of the page, with its lower edge in line with the lower edge of the jellyfish picture. Zoom in or out if necessary.

11. With the photo selected, click the **Picture Tools Format** tab, and then in the Crop group, click the **Crop** button to display black cropping handles around the photo.

12. Drag the upper-middle cropping handle down to just below the shark, as shown in **Figure PB 1–19**, to remove the unwanted portion of the picture.

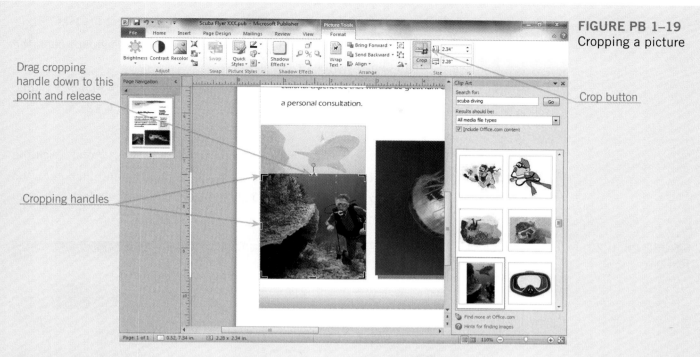

FIGURE PB 1–19
Cropping a picture

Drag cropping handle down to this point and release

Cropping handles

Crop button

13. Click the **Crop** button again to remove the unwanted part of the picture, and then click the **Close** button ⊠ on the Clip Art task pane to close it.

14. Save and leave the publication open for use in the next Step-by-Step.

Inserting and Modifying Text Boxes

The Text group on the Insert tab contains options for adding objects like text boxes, WordArt, business information, and text files to your publications. Since all text in a publication is contained within text boxes, you'll probably be using them often. You can add a text box anywhere on the page. When you click the Draw Text Box button, the pointer changes to a crosshair pointer that you can click and drag to draw a text box any size you want. After you've inserted the text box, you can move and resize it like other drawing objects. You can also use the contextual Drawing Tools Format tab to modify the text box and the Text Box Tools Format tab to change the format, effects, and alignment of the text inside.

Step-by-Step PB 1.10

The Scuba Flyer *XXX* publication from Step-by-Step PB 1.9 should be open in the Publisher program window.

1. On the Insert tab, in the Text group, click the **Draw Text Box** button.

2. Position the crosshair on the left side of the bottom of the publication. Click near the bottom margin and draw a text box that is approximately 3/4" tall and 6" wide.

3. Type **Free Consultation!** in the text box, and then select the text.

4. On the Text Box Tools Format tab, in the Alignment group, click the **Align Center** button 🔲.

5. In the Font group, click the **Font** list arrow and click **Franklin Gothic Heavy**, and then click the **Font Size** list arrow and click **36**.

6. Select the text box.

7. On the Drawing Tools Format tab, in the Shape Styles group, click the **More** button ▾ to display the Shape Styles gallery, and then click the **Linear Up Gradient – Accent 3** style. Your text box should look similar to the one in **Figure PB 1–20**.

FIGURE PB 1–20
Text box

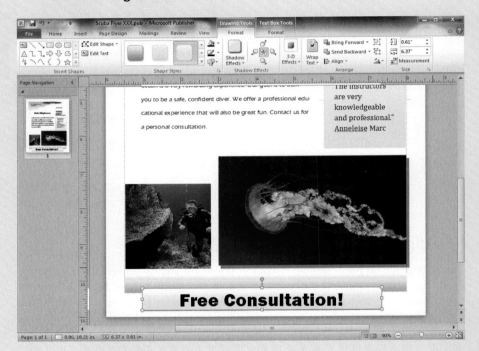

8. Save and leave the publication open for use in the next Step-by-Step.

Previewing and Printing a Publication

Publications are usually printed either at a commercial printer or on a desktop printer. When printing your own publications, you can save time, ink, and paper by reviewing your choices before you print. You can preview a publication and change formatting and printing options on the File tab in Backstage view before you click the Print button.

When you choose Print on the File tab, Backstage view displays the Print button and default print settings in the center pane of the window and a preview of the current page in the right pane, as shown in **Figure PB 1–21**. To change a print setting in the center pane, click the setting you want to change, and then select a new option from the gallery that opens. You can preview any page in a multipage publication using the scroll bars or the Next Sheet and Previous Sheet buttons in the lower-left corner of the right pane. When you move the mouse pointer over the preview, the pointer changes to a magnifying glass that you can click to zoom in and out. You can also zoom in and out to see different magnifications of a publication using the Zoom In and Zoom Out buttons or by moving the Zoom slider below the preview. The Fit to Sheet button displays the entire page within the preview pane.

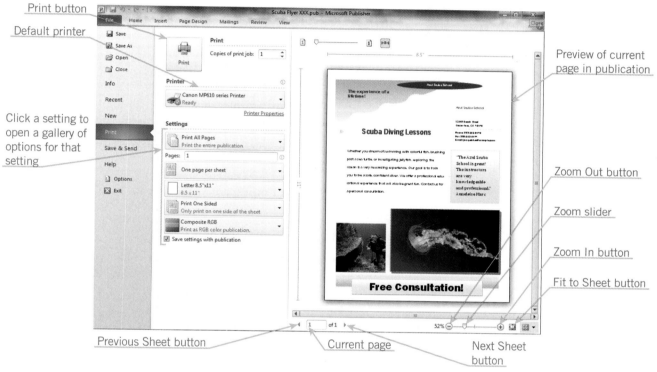

FIGURE PB 1–21   Printing and previewing options in Backstage view

The following printing and previewing options are available in Backstage view:

- The Print button prints the document with current settings.
- Use the up and down arrows in the Copies of print job box to indicate the quantity of copies to print.
- The Printer area displays the default printer. Click the default printer to select a different printer from the gallery of available printers. The Printer Properties link lets you choose paper type, print quality, and color, as well as specify other options for your printer.
- The Settings area lists the current print settings, which vary depending on the capability of your printer. Clicking a setting opens a gallery of options that lets you indicate whether to print:
  - All pages, selected pages, the current page, or specified pages of a document.
  - One page per sheet, tiled, multiple copies per sheet, or side-folded options.

EXTRA FOR EXPERTS

You can add the Quick Print button to the Quick Access Toolbar to print to the default printer with the default settings without opening Backstage view.

- Letter size or another paper size.
- One sided, or on both sides.
- As an RGB color publication or as a grayscale publication.

- The preview pane shows a preview of the document and allows you to zoom in and out to check for errors. As you make changes to the print settings, the preview is updated to reflect the changes so that you can be sure you are happy with the publication settings before printing.

Step-by-Step PB 1.11

The Scuba Flyer *XXX* publication from Step-by-Step PB 1.10 should be open in the Publisher program window.

1. Click the **File** tab to display Backstage view, and then click **Print**.
2. Click the **Zoom In** button ⊕ below the document preview.
3. Click the **Composite RGB** setting, and then click **Composite Grayscale** to display the page in grayscale.
4. Click the **Composite Grayscale** setting, and then click **Composite RGB** to display the page in color.
5. Click the **Fit to Sheet** button 🔲 below the preview to return to the previous magnification.
6. Click the **Print** button to print the publication.
7. Save the publication and leave it open for use in the next Step-by-Step.

Deleting a Business Information Set

If you share your computer with other students or other classes, the business information sets you save will remain with the computer until they are deleted. Therefore, another person will be able to view and use the business information sets you created. For the purposes of this book, you will delete the business information sets you create. In a business setting or at home, this might not be necessary. However, it is always a good idea to keep your personal contact information private.

You can delete a business information set by displaying the set in the Business Information dialog box, and then clicking the Delete button.

Step-by-Step PB 1.12

The Scuba Flyer *XXX* publication from Step-by-Step PB 1.11 should be open in the Publisher program window.

1. On the Insert Tab, in the Text group, click the **Business Information** button, and then click **Edit Business Information** on the menu to display the Business Information dialog box as shown in **Figure PB 1–22**.

Business Information dialog box

2. Make sure the Azul Scuba Diving business information set is displayed in the Select a Business Information set list box. (*Note*: If a different business information set is displayed, click the **Select a Business Information set** list arrow, and then click **Azul Scuba Diving**.)

3. Click the **Delete** button to delete the business information set. A message box appears asking if you are sure you want to delete the business information set. Click **Yes**.

4. Click the **Close** button.

5. Save the publication and leave it open for use in the next Step-by-Step.

Closing a Publication

When you are finished with a publication, you can remove it from your screen using the Close command. To close a publication without closing Publisher, choose the Close command on the File tab. When you only have one publication open, you can click the Close button on the title bar or choose the Exit command on the File tab to close the publication and exit Publisher at the same time. The program prompts you to save your work if you made any changes since you last saved the file.

Step-by-Step PB 1.13

The Scuba Flyer *XXX* publication from Step-by-Step PB 1.12 should be open in the Publisher program window.

1. Click the **File** tab and click **Close**. The publication closes and Backstage view is displayed.

2. Click the **Close** button ![X] on the program title bar to exit the program.

TECHNOLOGY CAREERS

Graphic Designer

A graphic designer is often involved in planning, designing, creating, and maintaining a client's Web site. Projects can range from a single Web page to complex sites that include e-commerce capabilities and other advanced interactive features. When creating a Web site, a graphic designer incorporates design principles, typography, graphics manipulation, and technology using publishing software such as Microsoft Publisher to create a positive user experience.

SUMMARY

In this lesson, you learned:

- That like other Office 2010 programs, Publisher organizes commands on tabs on the Ribbon.
- To start Publisher and open an existing document.
- That templates are one method of creating a well-designed publication quickly.
- That it is often necessary to use zoom in and zoom out commands to work with a publication.
- To enter and format text within text boxes.

- The Page Design tab contains options for modifying the look of a publication and changing the template.
- To insert pictures, clip art, building blocks, and text boxes.
- To use the Save As command to save a publication for the first time.
- To preview publications before printing.
- That when you close a publication, Publisher prompts you to save your work if you made any changes since you last saved.

■ VOCABULARY REVIEW

Define the following terms:

alignment	font scheme	point size
building blocks	font styles	publication
bullets	Format Painter	scratch area
business information set	I-beam	selection handles
clip art	insertion point	Smart Tag button
color scheme	line spacing	story
crop	paragraph	template
desktop publishing software	pictures	text boxes
font	placeholders	thumbnails

■ REVIEW QUESTIONS

MULTIPLE CHOICE

Select the best response for the following statements.

1. The _____ is positioned vertically on the left side of the screen and contains thumbnails of publication pages.
   A. Ribbon
   B. Clip Art task pane
   C. Page Navigation pane
   D. File tab

2. The blank area around the publication is called the _____.
   A. placeholder
   B. text box
   C. desktop
   D. scratch area

3. All text in a publication is stored within _____.
   A. text boxes
   B. I-beams
   C. placeholders
   D. selection handles

4. A _____ appears when you point to business information text.
   A. rotate handle
   B. Smart Tag button
   C. magnifier pointer
   D. bullet

5. Arial and Times New Roman are examples of _____.
   A. fonts
   B. font styles
   C. bullets
   D. objects

6. The _____ button is used to apply a new template design.
   A. Font Schemes
   B. Color Schemes
   C. Design Gallery
   D. Change Template

7. To resize a graphic proportionally, drag a _____ handle.
   A. corner
   B. middle
   C. green
   D. square

8. When you click the Format Painter button, your mouse pointer changes to a(n) _____.
   A. magnifying glass
   B. double-sided arrow
   C. crosshair
   D. I-beam with a paintbrush

9. The _____ button removes unwanted parts of a picture.
   A. Compress Pictures
   B. Crop
   C. Undo
   D. More Brightness

10. When you have one publication open, you can click the _____ to close the publication and exit Publisher at the same time.
    A. Print button
    B. Close command on the File menu
    C. Close button on the title bar
    D. Exit button on the title bar

FILL IN THE BLANK

Complete the following sentences by writing the correct word or words in the blanks provided.

1. A Publisher file is called a(n) _____.

2. When you first start Publisher, the _____ _____ section of Backstage view is displayed.

3. One method of creating a well-designed publication quickly is to use a(n) _____.

4. _____ is the position of text in relation to the edges of a text box.

5. _____ _____ are design objects that you can use in your publications.

6. The green _____ handle is located at the top of a graphic or text box.

7. You can search for clip art, pictures, sounds, and movies in the _____ task pane.

8. To remove a text box, select it and press _____.

9. The Print command is on the _____ tab.

10. When you _____ a publication, the program prompts you to save your work if you made any changes since you last saved.

■ PROJECTS

PROJECT PB 1–1

1. Start Publisher, and then in the Available Templates section of Backstage view, open the Award Certificates category. Create a new award certificate using the Employee of the Month template in the Award Certificates category, and save it as **Employee Award XXX** (replace *XXX* with your initials).

2. Create a new business information set (remove the logo if necessary) using the following data:

   Eli Parker

   Head Chef

   Eli's Catering

   9876 Main St.

   Kansas City, MO 64188

   Phone: 555-816-9876

   Tagline or motto: **We cater to you!**

   Business Information set name: **Eli's Catering**

3. Update the publication with the new business information set.

4. Change the color scheme to Concourse.

5. Change the font scheme to Archival.

6. Change the font size of the Employee of the Month text to 26 and apply bold.

7. Replace the *Name of Recipient* placeholder text with **Mac Wilmon**, and change the font color to Accent 2.

8. Replace the *Month and Year* placeholder text with **June 2013**.

9. Save the publication and leave it open for use in the next project.

PROJECT PB 1–2

The **Employee Award XXX** publication from Project PB 1–1 should be open in the Publisher program window.

1. Save the publication with the filename **Employee Award 2 XXX** (replace *XXX* with your initials).

2. Insert the Shadowed Slant building block from the Attention Getters area of the Advertisements gallery.

3. Replace the Free Offer text with **Eli's Catering**.

4. Position the logo in the lower-right corner of the certificate, below the second Date text box.

5. Change the font size of the first instance of *Signature* to 10 point and italics.

6. Use the Format Painter button to copy the format and apply it to the second instance of *Signature* and both instances of *Date*.

7. Save and close the publication.

ON YOUR OWN

Open the **Employee Award 2 XXX** publication. Insert an appropriate piece of clip art and position it anywhere on the publication. Save and close the publication.

PROJECT PB 1–3

1. Create business cards using the Color Band business card template, and save the publication as **Business Cards XXX** (replace *XXX* with your initials). Use the business information for Eli's Catering on the business cards.

2. Change the color scheme to Concourse and the font scheme to Archival.

3. Delete the empty picture placeholder in the lower-left corner.

4. Apply bold to *Eli's Catering*.

5. Change the template to the Arrows design by applying the template to the current publication.

6. Use the Text Box button to draw a new text box on the scratch area to the right of the business card. The new text box should be approximately 1" × 1".

7. Type the following list of items, using Georgia font and 6 point font size, pressing Enter after each item:

   Meetings

   Events

   Weddings

8. Select the list and add bullets using the Bullets button in the Paragraph group on the Home tab (choose Small Bullets). Change the line spacing to 1.0. Use the Paragraph Spacing button in the Paragraph group to change the paragraph spacing to None.

9. Drag the text box from the scratch area onto the business card below *Eli's Catering*. Decrease the height of the phone number text box so that the phone number appears on one line under the list.

10. Search the Clip Art task pane for clip art related to the keyword **catering**.

11. Insert the clip art of the cartoon waiter character with a blue suit and red bowtie.

12. Resize the clip art and position it as shown in **Figure PB 1–23**. (If necessary, adjust the position of the bulleted list text box as shown.)

13. View the publication in Backstage view before printing one page.

14. Delete the Eli's Catering Business Information set.

15. Save and close the publication.

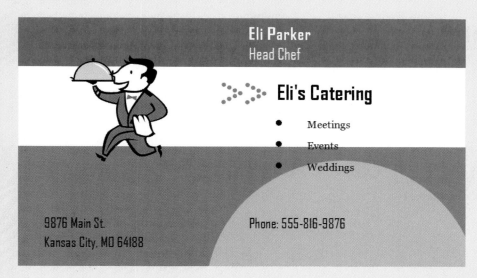

FIGURE PB 1–23 Business card

PROJECT PB 1–4

1. Create a current monthly calendar using the Photo Album template in the Calendars category, and save it as **Calendar XXX** (replace *XXX* with your initials).

2. Replace the photo with the Desert picure from the Sample Pictures folder.

3. Change the color scheme to Black and White.

4. Change the font scheme to Online.

5. Apply picture style 19 to the photo.

6. Save and close the publication.

WEB PROJECT

Visit your city's Web site (or a city near you) and find a calendar or list of upcoming events. Choose an event, such as a special meeting, citywide celebration, or library event and create an invitation that could be sent to citizens. Use the templates in Publisher, and be sure to include all necessary details, such as the date, time, and place. Add appropriate building blocks and graphics. Save the publication and then close it.

CRITICAL THINKING

ACTIVITY PB 1–1

In Backstage view, open the **Scuba Flyer XXX** file from the Recent Publications list. Change the template to a gift certificate template of your choice, creating a new publication using your text and graphics. Insert the jellyfish picture from the Extra Content task pane by clicking the arrow next to the image, and then clicking Insert. Resize and position the picture as necessary to enhance the certificate. Save the publication with a new name, print multiple copies per sheet, and close it. Do not save the data in the Extra Content task pane.

ON YOUR OWN

Open the **Calendar XXX** publication. Change the template to a new calendar template of your choice, creating a new publication. Apply new fonts, colors, clip art, or pictures of your choice. Save the publication with a new name, and then close it. Do not save the contents of the Extra Content task pane, if any.

TEAMWORK PROJECT

With a partner, use an advertisement template to create an ad for the Azul Scuba School that is consistent in design with the flyer you created in this lesson. Work together to create the design and to write any necessary text for the advertisement. Be prepared to present your advertisement to the class.

ACTIVITY PB 1–2

Choose a letterhead template to use for personal stationery for yourself. Create a new business information set with your information. Insert building blocks, pictures, and/or clip art of your choice. Apply the font scheme and color scheme of your choice. Print one copy. Save the publication.

Estimated Time for Unit:
1.5 hours

UNIT VII

INTEGRATION

LESSON 1   1.5 HRS.

Understanding Integration Fundamentals

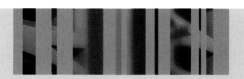

LESSON 1

Understanding Integration Fundamentals

■ OBJECTIVES

Upon completion of this lesson, you should be able to:

- Explain methods for sharing information between Office programs.
- Link an Excel table to a Word document.
- Embed an Excel table in a PowerPoint presentation.
- Create a PowerPoint presentation from a Word outline.
- Create a mail merge document.
- Import Excel data into an Access table.
- Export data from an Access query to a Word document.

■ DATA FILES

To complete this lesson, you will need these data files:

Step INT 1-1.docx   Project INT 1-1.docx

Step INT 1-1.xlsx   Project INT 1-2.docx

Step INT 1-3.pptx   Bank Customers.accdb

Step INT 1-4.docx   Project INT 1-3.docx

Step INT 1-5.docx   Project INT 1-3.xlsx

Honors Band.accdb   Project INT 1-4.xlsx

Step INT 1-6.xlsx   Project INT 1-5.accdb

Step INT 1-6.accdb   Project INT 1-5.xlsx

■ VOCABULARY

destination file

destination program

embed

exporting

importing

integration

link

mail merge

merge fields

object

object linking and embedding (OLE)

source file

source program

Introduction

Office programs are designed to let you easily share information between programs through integration. *Integration* is the process of using information in a file created in one program and incorporating it into a file created in another program. When you integrate information between programs, the information being shared is referred to as an *object*. The program used to create the object is called the *source program*, and the originating file is called the *source file*. The *destination program* is the program used to create the *destination file* into which the object is inserted. For instance, you can insert an Excel chart into a PowerPoint slide, create a presentation from a Word outline, or create a table in Access using data from an Excel worksheet.

In this lesson, you will learn more about how to share information between programs by linking, embedding, importing, and exporting information.

Methods for Sharing Information Between Office Programs

There are a variety of ways to share information between files created in the different Office programs. Each integration method provides unique options for working with the shared information.

You are already familiar with using the Office Clipboard to copy and paste data within a document, worksheet, or presentation. You can also use the Office Clipboard to copy and paste between two files created in different Office programs. This method is best when you need to share information between programs once and you do not need to work with the two programs together again, and the commands and tools in the program into which the information has been copied are sufficient for any changes you might need to make to it.

Object linking and embedding (OLE) is an integration technology in Office that allows you to share information between Office programs. OLE is used to make content that is created in the source program available and fully editable in the destination program. You will learn more about OLE and using the Paste Special command in the Office programs to embed and link data later in this lesson.

Importing and exporting data is an integration method in which you convert information from the source program into a format supported by the destination program, so it can be fully manipulated in the destination program. *Importing* refers to converting data from a source program's format to the format of the destination program, while working in the destination program. *Exporting* refers to converting data from a source program's format to the format of the destination program, while working in the source program. Office includes specialized importing and exporting tools, such as Mail Merge, that you will work with later in this lesson.

Linking and Embedding

OLE allows you to either link or embed an object in a destination file. The main difference between linking and embedding has to do with where the information is stored and edited. When you *link* an object, the object remains in the source file and you place a link to the object in the destination file. The object is updated in the destination file when changes are made in the source file. When you *embed* an object, you place a copy of the object in the destination file that is no longer connected to the original object in the source file. In this way, embedding is similar to copying and pasting an object. However, the difference between simply pasting an object and embedding it is that the embedded object can be edited using the source program's commands and features.

Linking an Excel Table to a Word Document

Linking data is useful when the information in a file needs to continually be kept up to date using data that is maintained separately. Linking is also a good choice if file size and efficient use of disk storage space is important, because the source file is not resaved in the destination file. It may take longer, however, for Office to open files with links.

To link objects between files created in different programs, you must have access to both programs when working with the destination file, and the source and destination files must be stored on the same computer or network. A destination file cannot display linked data without being able to access the source file.

When linking between two Office programs, you should have both programs open and save any open files before you begin linking. You should also check your computer's clock to be sure it is set with the correct time and date because links use the date of the source file for the most recent information.

To link an Excel object such as a table to a Word document, you can copy the Excel table, switch to Word, and use the Paste Special command to insert the table as a linked object.

Step-by-Step INT 1.1

1. Start Word, and then open the **Step INT 1-1.docx** file from the folder containing the data files for this lesson.

2. Save the document as **Fundraiser Letter *XXX*.docx** (replace *XXX* with your initials).

3. Start Excel and then open the **Step INT 1-1.xlsx** workbook from the folder containing the data files for this lesson.

4. Save the workbook as **Band Fundraiser *XXX*.xlsx** (replace *XXX* with your initials).

5. Select the table in range **A1:D6** in the Band Fundraiser *XXX*.xlxs workbook.

6. On the Home tab, in the Clipboard group, click the **Copy** button to copy the table object.

7. Switch to the Fundraiser Letter *XXX*.docx document in Word, and place the insertion point in the blank line after the last line of the letter and before *Sincerely*.

8. On the Home tab, in the Clipboard group, click the **Paste** button arrow, and then click **Paste Special** to open the Paste Special dialog box.

9. Click the **Paste link** option, and then click **Microsoft Excel Worksheet Object** in the As list box, as shown in **Figure INT 1–1**.

FIGURE INT 1–1
Linking using the Paste Special dialog box

Click to specify an Excel worksheet object

Paste the object as a link

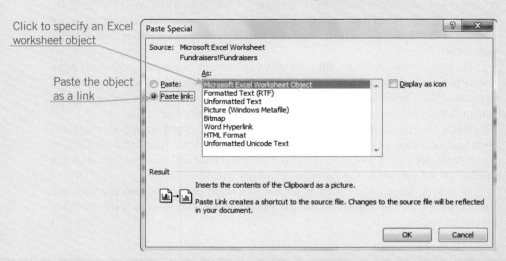

10. Click the **OK** button to paste the Excel table as a linked object in the document. Your document window should look similar to **Figure INT 1–2**.

FIGURE INT 1–2
Inserting a linked object

Linked object inserted from Excel file

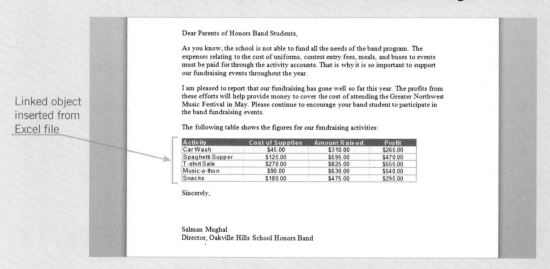

11. Save the Fundraiser Letter *XXX*.docx document, close it, and exit Word.
12. Leave the Band Fundraiser *XXX*.xlsx workbook open in the Excel program window for use in the next Step-by-Step.

Updating and Breaking Links

If the destination file containing a linked object is open when you make a change to the original object in the source file, the object in the destination file is changed at the same time. If the destination file containing the linked object is not open when you make changes to the object in the source file, the next time you open the destination file, you will see a message indicating the file is linked to source data and asking if you want to update the data.

If you decide you no longer want an object linked between the source and destination files, you can break the link between the source file and the destination file; the object in the destination file will become just a static copy of the original object. To view or edit links in the destination file, you can click the File tab, click Info, and then click Edit Links to Files, as shown in **Figure INT 1–3**, to open the Links dialog box.

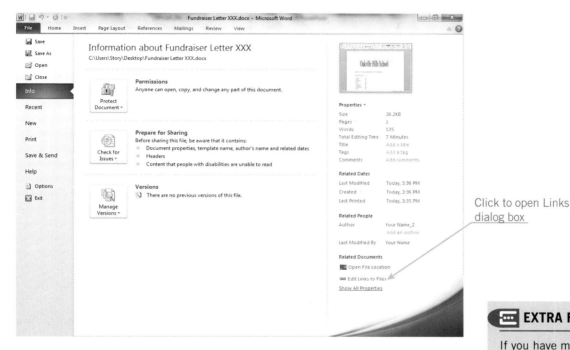

Click to open Links dialog box

FIGURE INT 1–3   Editing links to files

To break a link, you can select the link in the Links dialog box, and then click the Break Link button. When you rename or move a source file, you must redirect the link so the destination file looks for the correct filename and the correct location of the file to update the link. You can redirect the link using the Change Source button in the Links dialog box. To lock a link, temporarily preventing it from being updated, you can use the Locked option in the Links dialog box.

EXTRA FOR EXPERTS

If you have many links in a document and it is taking too long to update each time you open the document, if you want to control when the links are updated, or if you only want to update certain links, you can select the Manual update option in the Links dialog box to update links manually.

Step-by-Step INT 1.2

The Band Fundraiser *XXX*.xlsx workbook from Step-by-Step INT 1.1 should be open in the Excel program window.

1. Click cell **A6**.

2. Edit the content of the cell to replace *Snacks* with **Concession Stand** and press **Enter**.

3. Start Word and open the **Fundraiser Letter *XXX*.docx** file. A message is displayed asking if you want to update the document with data from the linked file. Click the **Yes** button, and notice that the linked Excel table has been updated to reflect the change you just made to the source object in Excel.

4. In the Fundraiser Letter *XXX*.docx file in the Word window, click the **File** tab, and then click **Edit Links to Files** at the bottom of the right pane to open the Links dialog box with the link selected, as shown in **Figure INT 1–4**.

FIGURE INT 1–4
Links dialog box

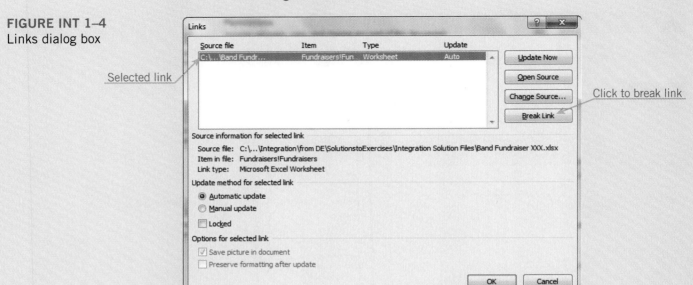

5. Click the **Break Link** button to break the link, and then click the **Yes** button to confirm the action. The link is broken, and the Excel table becomes just a table in the Word document, without any connection to the source program.

6. Save and close the Fundraiser Letter *XXX*.docx document and exit Word.

7. Save the Band Fundraiser *XXX*.xlsx workbook and leave it open for use in the next Step-by-Step.

Embedding an Excel Table in a PowerPoint Presentation

When you embed an object from a source file into a destination file, you are copying and pasting the object itself, as well as a connection to the source program. This allows you to work with the embedded object to format or edit it using the source program's commands and features, while within the destination file. You simply double-click the embedded object in the destination file to open the object's source program and make your changes—without leaving the destination file. When you click outside the object to deselect it, the source program is closed, and you return to the object in the destination program. Embedding is useful when the object you are integrating requires tools and features not normally supported by the destination program.

Because the source file is duplicated in the destination file and increases the size of the file, use embedding if the size of the file is not important.

Step-by-Step INT 1.3

The Band Fundraiser *XXX*.xlsx workbook from Step-by-Step INT 1.2 should be open in the Excel program window.

1. Select the table in range **A1:D6**.

2. On the Home tab, in the Clipboard group, click the **Copy** button to copy the table.

3. Start PowerPoint and open the **Step INT 1-3.pptx** presentation from the folder containing the data files for this lesson. Save the presentation as **Band Trip Presentation *XXX*.pptx** (replace *XXX* with your initials).

4. On the Home tab, in the Slides group, click the **New Slide** button arrow, and then click **Title Only** to insert a new slide.

5. In the slide pane, click the **Click to add title** placeholder, type **Fundraisers**, and then click a blank area of the slide.

6. On the Home tab, in the Clipboard group, click the **Paste** button arrow, and then click **Paste Special** to open the Paste Special dialog box, shown in **Figure INT 1–5**.

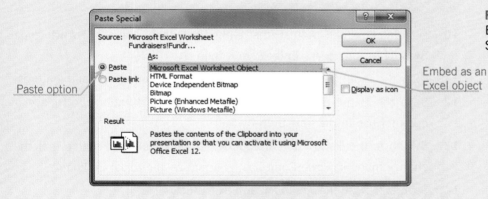

FIGURE INT 1–5
Embedding using the Paste Special dialog box

7. Make sure the Paste option is selected, and that Microsoft Excel Worksheet Object is selected in the As list box, and then click the **OK** button to close the dialog box and paste the Excel table as an embedded object on the slide.

8. Drag a corner of the object to make it larger, and then drag the object to center it on the slide, if necessary.

9. Double-click the embedded table to display Excel's commands and features for editing. Your slide should look similar to **Figure INT 1–6**.

FIGURE INT 1–6
Slide with embedded Excel table selected for editing

Excel commands and features on the Ribbon in PowerPoint

Table selected for editing and displaying an Excel program window

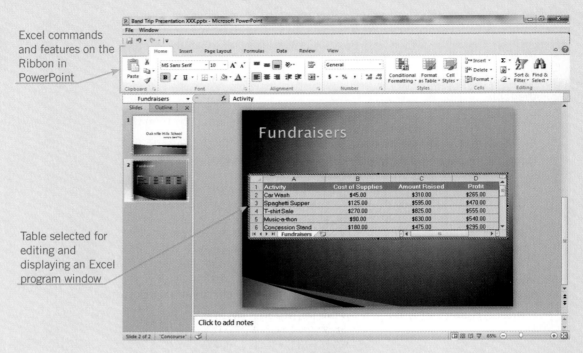

10. Double-click cell **A4** of the embedded table, select **T-shirt**, type **Sweatshirt**, and press **Enter** to edit the text.

11. Click the slide outside the table to close Excel's commands and features.

12. Save the Band Trip Presentation *XXX*.pptx presentation, and leave it open for use in the next Step-by-Step.

13. Switch to the Band Fundraiser *XXX*.xlsx workbook, and notice that the change made in PowerPoint has no effect on the Excel workbook.

14. Save and close the workbook and exit Excel.

Creating a PowerPoint Presentation from a Word Outline

If you have a file that contains outline text created in another program that supports heading styles, you can use it to create the basic structure of a PowerPoint presentation. For example, you may have an existing report in Word that you want to present. When you use an outline from Word, PowerPoint converts the heading levels in the outline into titles and bulleted lists on slides. Although you may have to make some minor adjustments, this is a quick way to convert text from a word-processing program into a slide presentation.

To use an existing outline, you start PowerPoint and on the Home tab in the Slides group, click the New Slide button arrow, and then click Slides from Outline to open the Insert Outline dialog box. When you select the file that contains the outline and click Insert, the slides are created based on the outline text.

Step-by-Step INT 1.4

The Band Trip Presentation *XXX*.pptx presentation from Step-by-Step INT 1.3 should be open in the PowerPoint program window.

1. Start Word and open the **Step INT 1-4.docx** file from the folder containing the data files for this lesson. Notice the document is displayed in Outline view. This is the text that will be converted to slides.

2. Save the document as **Band Trip Outline *XXX*.docx** (replace *XXX* with your initials).

3. Close the document and exit Word.

4. In PowerPoint, click the **slide 1** thumbnail in the Slides tab in the left pane to select it.

5. On the Home tab, in the Slides group, click the **New Slide** button arrow, and then click **Slides from Outline** from the menu to open the Insert Outline dialog box.

6. Navigate to the folder containing the data files for this lesson, select the **Band Trip Outline *XXX*.docx** file, and then click the **Insert** button to create slides based on the outline text. Display slide 2, as shown in **Figure INT 1–7**.

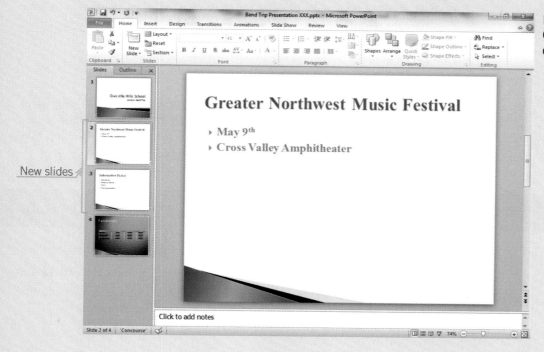

FIGURE INT 1–7
Creating slides from a Word outline

7. Click the **Slide Show** tab, and in the Start Slide Show group, click the **From Beginning** button to view the presentation as a slide show. Advance through all the slides, and exit the slide show.

8. Save and close the Band Trip Presentation *XXX*.pptx presentation and exit PowerPoint.

Creating a Mail Merge Document

If you have a lot of form letters, cards, e-mail messages, or envelopes to send, you can simplify the process by using the information in an Access table or Excel worksheet as a data source for a mail merge using the Word Mail Merge Wizard. A *mail merge* is used to create a set of documents that are identical except for custom or personalized information in specific areas. For example, you could create a set of form letters with the same message, but personalized for each client using name and address information from the data source.

Each mail merge follows the same process:

1. Set up the main document that contains the static information.

2. Connect to the data source that contains the variable information.

3. Select the list of recipients.

4. Add placeholders—called *merge fields*—to the main document that indicate where the information from the data source will go.

5. Preview the documents.

6. Complete the merge.

You can set up the mail merge yourself, or use the Mail Merge Wizard, which leads you through this process, by clicking the Start Mail Merge button on the Mailings tab in the Start Mail Merge group and then clicking Step by Step Mail Merge Wizard to open the Mail Merge Wizard task pane.

Step-by-Step INT 1.5

1. Start Word and open the **Step INT 1-5.docx** file from the folder containing the data files for this lesson, and save the document as **Band Trip Letter Main *XXX*.docx** (replace *XXX* with your initials). You will use this document as the main document for the mail merge.

2. Click the **Mailings** tab, and in the Start Mail Merge group click the **Start Mail Merge** button, and then click **Step by Step Mail Merge Wizard** to open the Mail Merge Wizard task pane, Step 1 of 6. The Letters option should be selected in the Select document type section, as shown in **Figure INT 1–8**.

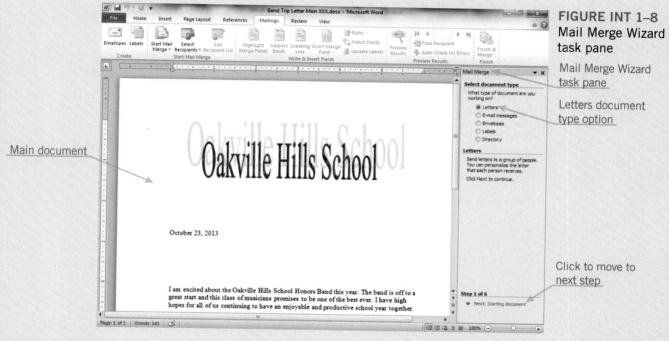

FIGURE INT 1–8
Mail Merge Wizard task pane

3. In the Mail Merge Wizard task pane, click **Next: Starting document** to move to Step 2 of the Mail Merge Wizard.

4. Make sure the **Use the current document** option is selected in the Select starting document section. Click **Next: Select recipients** to move to Step 3 of the Mail Merge Wizard.

5. Make sure the **Use an existing list** option is selected in the Select recipients section, and in the Use an existing list section click **Browse** to open the Select Data Source dialog box. Navigate to the folder containing the data files for this lesson, select the **Honors Band.accdb** database file, and then click the **Open** button.

6. Click the **Band Members** table in the Select Table dialog box, and then click the **OK** button to open the Mail Merge Recipients dialog box, shown in **Figure INT 1–9**. Click the **OK** button to use the list of recipients in the list without making any changes, and close the Mail Merge Recipients dialog box.

FIGURE INT 1–9
Mail Merge Recipients dialog box

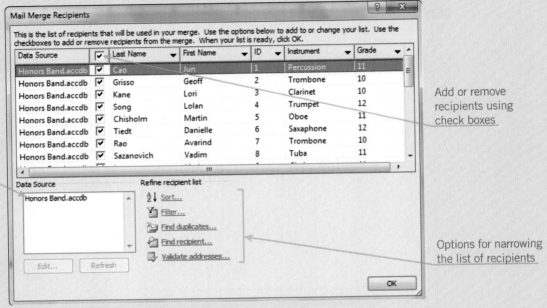

File(s) being used as data source

Add or remove recipients using check boxes

Options for narrowing the list of recipients

7. In the Mail Merge Wizard task pane, click **Next: Write your letter** to move to Step 4 of the Mail Merge Wizard. In the document window, place the insertion point in the blank line above the first paragraph. In the Mail Merge Wizard task pane, click **Greeting line...** to open the Insert Greeting Line dialog box, shown in **Figure INT 1–10**.

FIGURE INT 1–10
Insert Greeting Line dialog box

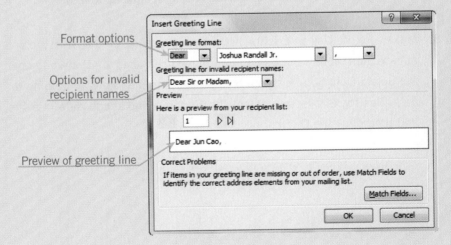

Format options

Options for invalid recipient names

Preview of greeting line

8. Click the **OK** button to insert the <<GreetingLine>> merge field in the document. In the Mail Merge Wizard task pane, click **Next: Preview your letters** to move to Step 5 of the Mail Merge Wizard and preview one of the letters in the document window, the one for Jun Cao.

9. In the Preview your letters section of the Mail Merge Wizard task pane, click the **Next Record** button to preview the letter for the second recipient. Continue clicking the **Next Record** button until you get to Recipient 23, Belinda Newman, and notice how the name in the greeting line changes each time.

10. In the Mail Merge Wizard task pane, click **Next: Complete the merge** to move to Step 6 of the Mail Merge Wizard. In the Merge section, click **Print** to open the Merge to Printer dialog box.

11. Click the **Current record** option, click the **OK** button to open the Print dialog box, and then click the **OK** button to print the letter for Belinda Newman.

12. In the Mail Merge Wizard task pane, click **Edit individual letters** to open the Merge to New Document dialog box.

13. Click the **All** option and then click the **OK** button to merge all 23 letters to a new document. Scroll through the document to see that each letter is on a separate page. Save the document as **Band Trip Letter Merge** **_XXX_.docx** (replace _XXX_ with your initials) and close it.

14. Save and close the main document, Band Trip Letter Main _XXX_.docx, and exit Word. If you open the main document again in the future, you will get a message asking if you want to maintain the connection to the external data source.

Importing and Exporting Data

You can also share information between programs by importing or exporting. For example, you could import the data in an Access table into Excel so you could perform calculations on it in a worksheet, or you could export the data in an Access query to a Word document to use in a report. Importing and exporting are one-time operations—there is no connection established between the data in the two programs, and the data in the source file is not altered.

Importing Excel Data into an Access Table

When you import from Excel into Access, a copy of the data is brought into Access and stored in a new or existing table. To import data, you can use the Import Wizard in the destination program to guide you through the process and make decisions such as whether to change data types or add headers. In Access, on the External Data tab, in the Import & Link group, you can click the Import Excel spreadsheet

EXTRA FOR EXPERTS

When you are finished importing or exporting data in Access, you can save the steps of the process so that they can easily be repeated again in the future without using the wizard.

button to start importing data. The Excel workbook, the source file, should be closed before you begin importing data from it. Formulas will not be imported from Excel to Access, only the results of the formulas.

Step-by-Step INT 1.6

1. Start Excel, open the **Step INT 1-6.xlsx** workbook from the folder containing the data files for this lesson, view the data, and then close the file and exit Excel.

2. Start Access and open the **Step INT 1-6.accdb** database from the folder containing the data files for this lesson. Save the database as **Honors Band XXX.accdb** (replace *XXX* with your initials), and enable the content, if necessary.

3. Click the External Data tab, and in the Import & Link group, click the **Import Excel spreadsheet** button to open the Get External Data – Excel Spreadsheet dialog box, shown in **Figure INT 1–11**.

FIGURE INT 1–11
Get External
Data – Excel
Spreadsheet
dialog box

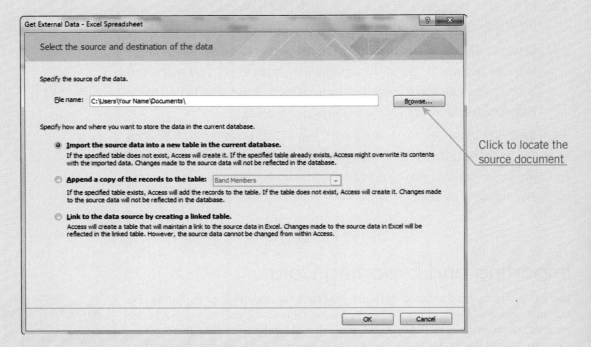

Click to locate the source document

4. Click the **Browse** button to open the File Open dialog box.

5. Navigate to the folder containing the data files for this lesson, click the **Step INT 1-6.xlsx** file, then click the **Open** button to return to the Get External Data – Excel Spreadsheet dialog box. The Step INT 1-6.xlsx file is displayed as the data source in the File name text box.

6. Click the **OK** button to open the Import Spreadsheet Wizard, shown in **Figure INT 1–12**. The first step in the wizard requires you to specify the worksheet or range containing the data to be imported.

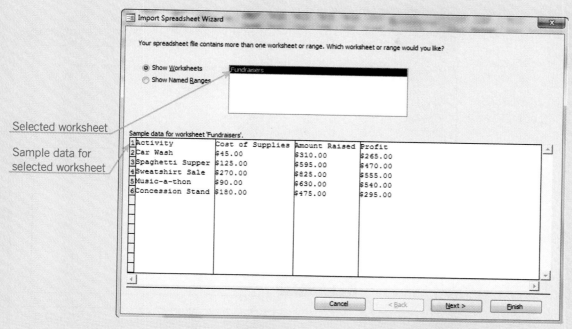

Selected worksheet

Sample data for selected worksheet

FIGURE INT 1–12
First step in the Import Spreadsheet Wizard

7. Make sure the Fundraisers worksheet is selected in the list box, and then click the **Next** button to display the next step in the wizard, where you specify what should be used for field names in the table.

8. To use column headings as field names, make sure the **First Row Contains Column Headings** check box is selected, and then click the **Next** button to display the next step in the wizard to specify information about the fields to be imported; for example, the Activity field has a Text data type.

9. Click the **Cost of Supplies** field heading, and notice that the data type is already set to *Currency*, as shown in **Figure INT 1–13**. Click the **Next** button to display the next step in the wizard, where you specify the primary key for the table.

FIGURE INT 1–13
Fields to be imported

Data type for
selected field

Name of
selected field

Click heading to
select field

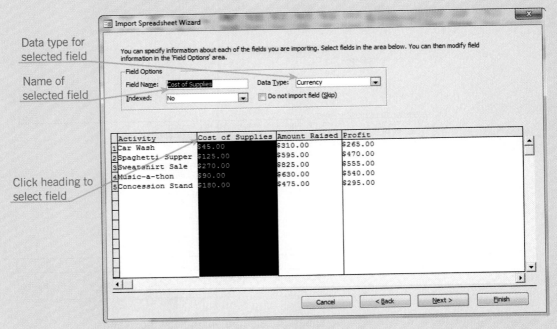

10. Make sure the **Let Access add primary key** option is selected, and then click the **Next** button to display the last step in the wizard, where you can name the table. In this case, *Fundraisers* is displayed in the Import to Table text box.

11. Click the **Finish** button to accept the name Fundraisers and open the Get External Data – Excel Spreadsheet dialog box.

12. Click the **Close** button to close the dialog box and create the table without saving the import steps.

13. Double-click the **Fundraisers** table in the Navigation Pane to display the table in the database window, as shown in **Figure INT 1–14**.

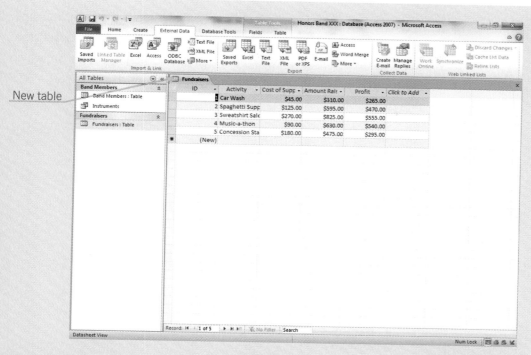

FIGURE INT 1–14
Importing data to a
new table

14. Close the Fundraisers table, and leave the Honors Band *XXX*.accdb database open for use in the next Step-by-Step.

Exporting an Access Query to Word

You can export a table, query, form, or report from Access to a variety of Office programs, including an Excel worksheet, another Access database, a Word document, or a text file. No matter to what program you are exporting the Access object, the process is similar.

For example, to export data from an Access query to a Word document, you select the query in the Navigation Pane in Access. On the External Data tab, in the Export group, click the More button, and then click Word to use the Export Wizard. When you export from Access to Word, the data is always displayed in a new document. You do not have the option of adding the data to an existing document.

Step-by-Step INT 1.7

The Honors Band *XXX*.accdb database from Step-by-Step INT 1.6 should be open in the Access program window.

1. Select the **Instruments** query in the Navigation Pane.

2. On the External Data tab, in the Export group, click the **More** button and then click **Word** to open the Export – RTF File dialog box.

3. Click the **Browse** button to open the File Save dialog box.

4. Navigate to the folder where you save your files. Notice the filename, *Instruments.rtf*, already appears in the File name text box, and that Rich Text Format is already listed as the format type, as shown in **Figure INT 1–15**. Click the **Save** button to return to the Export – RTF File dialog box.

FIGURE INT 1–15
File Save dialog box

File name and format type are already selected

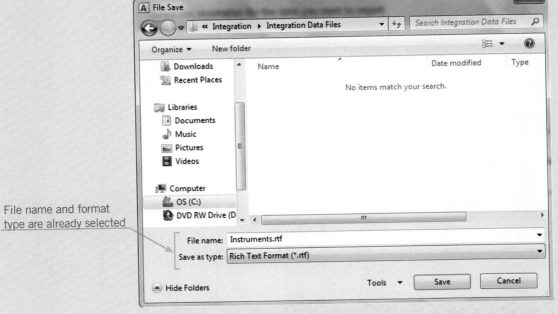

5. Click the **Open the destination file after the export operation is complete** check box to select this option.

6. Click the **OK** button to export the query data and display it as a table in a new Word document, as shown in **Figure INT 1–16**. Notice the Table Tools contextual tabs appear on the Ribbon in Word.

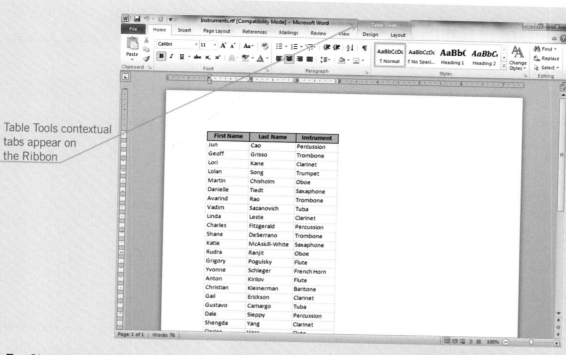

FIGURE INT 1–16
Access query
exported as a
table to a Word
document

Table Tools contextual
tabs appear on
the Ribbon

7. Close the Instruments.rtf document and exit Word.

8. In Access, click the **Close** button in the Export – RTF File dialog box to close it without saving the export steps.

9. Close the database and exit Access.

SUMMARY

In this lesson, you learned:

- The methods for sharing information between Office programs.
- To link an Excel table to a Word document.
- How to embed an Excel table in a PowerPoint presentation.
- How to create a PowerPoint presentation from a Word outline.

- The process for creating a mail merge document.
- The steps to import Excel data into an Access table.
- The steps to export data from an Access query to a Word document.

■ VOCABULARY REVIEW

Define the following terms:

destination file
destination program
embed
exporting
importing

integration
link
mail merge
merge fields

object
object linking and embedding (OLE)
source file
source program

■ REVIEW QUESTIONS

MULTIPLE CHOICE

Select the best response for the following statements.

1. Which of the following is an example of integration?

   A. Inserting an Excel chart into a PowerPoint slide

   B. Creating a presentation from a Word outline

   C. Creating an Access table using Excel data

   D. All of the above

2. You can set up a mail merge yourself, or use the Mail Merge _____ which leads you through the process.

   A. dialog box

   B. group

   C. Wizard

   D. tab

3. In a mail merge, the _____ contains the static information.

   A. main document

   B. data source

   C. placeholder

   D. list of recipients

4. When you _____ an object, the object remains in the source file and you place a connection to the object in the destination file.

   A. link

   B. embed

   C. import

   D. export

5. When you _____ an object, you place a copy of the object in the destination file that it is no longer connected to the source file but is a separate object.

   A. link

   B. embed

   C. import

   D. export

6. You can use the _____ command to insert a range as a linked object.

   A. Insert

   B. Link

   C. Paste

   D. Paste Special

7. If the destination file with a linked object is open when you make a change in the source file, changes are made in the destination file _____.

   A. at the same time

   B. when you close the file

   C. the next time you open the file

   D. when you click the Update button

8. _____ refers to converting data from a source program's format to the format of the destination program while working in the destination program.

   A. Linking

   B. Embedding

   C. Importing

   D. Exporting

9. _____ refers to converting data from a source program's format to the format of the destination program while working in the source program.

   A. Linking

   B. Embedding

   C. Importing

   D. Exporting

10. In Access, on the _____ tab, in the Import & Links group, you can click the Excel button to start importing data.

   A. Home

   B. Create

   C. External Data

   D. Database Tools

FILL IN THE BLANK

Complete the following sentences by writing the correct word or words in the blanks provided.

1. _____ is taking a file or object from one program and incorporating it into a file in another program.

2. When you integrate information between programs, the _____ is used to create the original information.

3. When you integrate information between programs, the _____ is used to create the destination file.

4. To import an outline into PowerPoint, on the Home tab in the Slides group, click the _____ button arrow, and then click Slides from Outline to open the Insert Outline dialog box.

5. A(n) _____ is used to create a set of documents that are identical except for custom or personalized information in specific areas.

6. When you integrate information between two files, a(n) _____ is shared information.

7. You can break the link between the source file and the destination file in the _____ dialog box.

8. _____ are placeholders in the main document of a mail merge that indicate where the information from the data source will go.

9. A destination file cannot display linked data without being able to access the _____.

10. To export data from an Access query to a Word document, first select the query in the _____.

◼ PROJECTS

PROJECT INT 1–1

1. Start Word and open **Project INT 1-1.docx** from the folder containing the data files for this lesson.

2. Save the document as **Card Safety XXX.docx** (replace *XXX* with your initials).

3. View the outline text, close the document, and exit Word.

4. Start PowerPoint and open a new, blank presentation.

5. On Slide 1, type **ATM/Debit Card Safety** as the title and **Tips for Secure Transactions** as the subtitle.

6. Use the **Card Safety XXX.docx** file to create slides based on the outlined text.

7. Apply the Foundry theme to the presentation.

8. Save the presentation as **Security Tips XXX.pptx** (replace *XXX* with your initials).

9. View the presentation as a slideshow from the beginning.

10. Close the presentation and exit PowerPoint.

PROJECT INT 1–2

1. Start Word and open **Project INT 1-2.docx** from the folder containing the data files for this lesson.

2. Save the document as **Overdraft Service Main XXX.docx** (replace *XXX* with your initials) to use as the main document for the mail merge.

3. Start the Mail Merge Wizard, and select **Letters** as the document type.

4. Move to the next step in the Mail Merge Wizard task pane where the current document should be selected as the starting document.

5. Move to the next step of the Mail Merge Wizard task pane, and browse to select the **Bank Customers.accdb** database file as the data source.

6. In the Mail Merge Recipients dialog box, use the list of recipients in the list without making any changes.

7. Move to the next step of the Mail Merge Wizard task pane, and insert a <<GreetingLine>> merge field in the document between the date and the first paragraph.

8. Move to the next step to preview your letters. Preview each of the 20 letters.

9. Move to the last step in the Mail Merge Wizard task pane to complete the merge. Merge the letters to the printer, and then print the letter for Eugene Kogan, the last recipient.

10. Merge all the records to a new document. Scroll through the document to see that each letter is on a separate page, save it as **Overdraft Service Merge XXX.docx**, and close it.

11. Save and close the Overdraft Service Main *XXX*.docx document. Leave Word open for the next project.

ON YOUR OWN

Open the **Overdraft Service Main** *XXX***.docx**, and add an address merge field to the document that will insert the customer's address between the date and the greeting line. Preview the letters, then merge the letters and print the first letter. Save the merged document as **Overdraft Service Merge2** *XXX***.docx** (replace *XXX* with your initials) and close the document. Save and close the main document.

PROJECT INT 1–3

1. In Word, open **Project INT 1-3.docx** from the folder containing the data files for this lesson.

2. Save the document as **Best Sellers** *XXX***.docx** (replace *XXX* with your initials).

3. Start Excel and open **Project INT 1-3.xlsx** from the folder containing the data files for this lesson.

4. Save the workbook as **Sweet Time Best** *XXX***.xlsx** (replace *XXX* with your initials).

5. Select the table in the range A1:G7 and copy it.

6. Switch to Word and place the insertion point below the *Best Sellers* subtitle, and then paste the Excel table as a linked object.

7. Save the Best Sellers *XXX*.docx document and close it.

8. In the Excel worksheet, enter **Blends** in cell G5, **Organic** in cell G6, and **Herbal** in cell G7.

9. In Word, open the **Best Sellers** *XXX***.docx** linked document and choose to update the data. Notice that the data has been updated with the change you just made in Excel.

10. From the File tab, open the Links dialog box and break the link.

11. Save and close the Best Sellers *XXX*.docx document and exit Word.

12. Save the Sweet Time Best *XXX*.xlsx workbook and close it.

PROJECT INT 1–5

1. Start Access and open **Project INT 1-5.accdb** from the folder containing the data files for this lesson. Save the database as **Bank Customers** *XXX* (replace *XXX* with your initials), and enable the database content.

2. Open the Get External Data – Excel Spreadsheet dialog box.

3. Browse to and select the **Project INT 1-5.xlsx** file from the folder containing the data files for this lesson as the source of the data.

4. Choose to import the source data into a new table in the current database, and then open the Import Spreadsheet Wizard.

5. Choose to use column headings from the first row as field names in the table.

PROJECT INT 1–4

1. In Excel, open the **Project INT 1-4.xlsx** file from the folder containing the data files for this lesson.

2. Select the table in the range B3:C9 and copy the information.

3. Open PowerPoint, open the **Security Tips** *XXX***.pptx** presentation that you created in Project INT 1-1, and save it as **Security Tips2** *XXX***.pptx**.

4. Insert a new Title Only slide at the end of the presentation.

5. Type **Contact Information** as the title.

6. Embed the copied range onto the slide.

7. Increase the font size of the pasted information to 20 point, widen column B and resize the embedded object to display all the data, and place the object attractively on the slide. Click anywhere outside the embedded object.

8. Save and close the Security Tips2 *XXX*.pptx presentation and exit PowerPoint.

9. Close the Project INT 1-4.xlsx workbook without saving it and exit Excel.

6. Move to the next step in the wizard, and do not change any information about the fields you are importing.

7. Move to the next step in the wizard, and if necessary, select the option for Access to define a primary key.

8. Move to the last step of the wizard, accept the table name **New Customers**, then finish the wizard and return to the Get External Data – Excel Spreadsheet dialog box.

9. Close the dialog box without saving the import steps.

10. Open the New Customers table in the database window, and widen the Address field to display all the data.

11. Save and close the New Customers table, and leave the database open for the next project.

PROJECT INT 1–6

The Bank Customers *XXX*.accdb database from Project INT 1-5 should be open in the Access program window.

1. Select the New Customers table in the Navigation Pane.

2. Open the Export – RTF File dialog box.

3. Browse to select the folder with your solutions, and save the New Customers.rtf.

4. Select the check box to open the destination file after the export operation is complete.

5. Export the table data with the default name, and display it in a new Word document named **New Customers.rtf**.

6. Change the orientation of the document to Landscape.

7. Save and close the New Customers.rtf document and exit Word.

8. In Access, close the Export – RTF File dialog box without saving the export steps.

9. Close the Bank Customers *XXX*.accdb database and exit Access.

 WEB PROJECT

Search the Web for information about a place you would like to visit. To create a presentation about your findings, in Word create an outline that lists pertinent information about this place, such as weather, things to do, and places to eat. Include enough headings and bullet points for at least three slides. Create a presentation by importing the outline into PowerPoint. Enhance the presentation however you like, and run your presentation for the class.

 TEAMWORK PROJECT

With a partner, create a mail merge letter that gives information about an upcoming event at school, a class assignment, or a new school policy. Work together to create the main document in Word and to create a data source in Access that contains information about your recipients. Try to include more than one merge field placeholder in the main document. Merge the information and print the letters.

 CRITICAL THINKING

ACTIVITY INT 1–1

In this lesson, you have learned just a few of the ways to integrate Office programs. There are other ways you can share information using different combinations of programs. For example, you can import a plain Word document into Publisher to work with it in a desktop publishing program. In Word, write a short thank-you note to someone and save the document. Open Publisher and choose one of the greeting card Thank You templates. Use the Insert File command in the Text group on the Insert tab to import your thank-you note into Publisher. Format the publication, then save, preview, and print it. Use Publisher Help if you need assistance.

ACTIVITY INT 1–2

Search for the Excel Help article titled *Exchange data between Excel and Access* and read it. How can you connect to Access data from Excel instead of importing it? What is the main benefit of this? As an extra challenge, try putting the information you just learned into practice using Excel and Access together.

APPENDIX A

Understanding Windows 7 Fundamentals

■ OBJECTIVES

Upon completion of this lesson, you should be able to:

- Start Windows 7.
- Identify parts of the Windows 7 desktop.
- Customize Windows 7.
- Manage files and folders.
- Access the Windows Help and Support system.
- Shut down Windows 7.

■ DATA FILES

You do not need data files to complete this appendix.

■ VOCABULARY

Control Panel

desktop

folder

gadgets

icons

Live Taskbar Preview

notification area

operating system

password

personal folder

Recycle Bin

screen saver

shortcut

taskbar

user account

user name

wallpaper

APPENDIX A

Introduction

Microsoft Windows 7 is an operating system that can help enhance your experience using Microsoft Office 2010. An *operating system* is the program that manages and controls the basic operations of your computer. In this appendix, you will become familiar with the parts of the Windows 7 desktop, customize your Windows 7 environment, manage files and folders, and learn how to get help.

Starting Windows 7

If Windows 7 is already installed, it will start automatically when you turn on the computer. The first screen you will see is the Welcome screen, which you will use to log on to Windows. The Welcome screen displays all of the user accounts on the computer. A *user account* is a collection of information about a specific person who is a regular user of the computer—including unique settings and preferences, and which files and programs that user can access. If you are the only one using the computer, there may be only one user account. If there are multiple users, each person can have a separate account so that you can all share the same computer while maintaining individual settings and files. Each user account on the computer has a *user name* that identifies it. For security purposes, you may also have a password associated with your user account. A *password* is a secret set of characters that a user types to log on to a computer or account. On the Welcome screen, you can choose which user account you want to access and then type the password, if necessary.

There are different versions of Windows 7, so not all features may be available, and your screens may look different than those in this appendix.

Identifying Parts of the Windows 7 Desktop

The basic Windows 7 desktop is shown in **Figure WIN–1**. The *desktop* is the main area of the screen that is displayed when you turn on the computer and log on to Windows with your user name and password. Use this figure to become familiar with the parts of the Windows 7 desktop.

▶ VOCABULARY
operating system
user account
user name
password
desktop

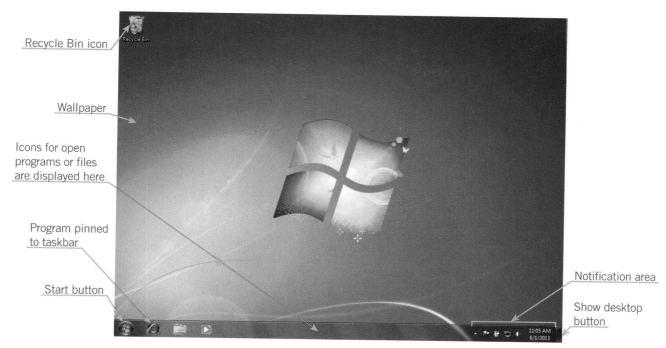

Recycle Bin icon

Wallpaper

Icons for open
programs or files
are displayed here

Program pinned
to taskbar

Start button

Notification area

Show desktop
button

FIGURE WIN–1   Windows 7 desktop

Your desktop includes *icons*—small pictures that represent programs, folders, files, and other objects, such as the Recycle Bin. The *Recycle Bin* contains the files and folders you have deleted. You can point to an icon or object on the desktop to see a ScreenTip with its description.

A horizontal bar, called the *taskbar*, is displayed at the bottom of the desktop. The taskbar contains the Start button to open the Start menu, a section that shows which files or folders you have open and that allows you to switch between them, and a *notification area* with the time and icons that provide information about programs and computer settings.

You can create a shortcut on the taskbar for a program you use regularly. A *shortcut* is an icon that points to a program to provide easy access; to open the program, double-click the shortcut. To create a shortcut on the taskbar, right-click a program icon on the taskbar (or desktop), and then click Pin this program to taskbar (or Pin to Taskbar) on the shortcut menu. Pinned icons are displayed on the left of the taskbar. To unpin an icon from the taskbar, you can right-click it and then click Unpin this program from taskbar. You can also pin program icons to the Start menu, as you will learn later in this appendix.

When you are working in a maximized program window, the desktop is not visible, but you can always display it without closing the program window you are working in by clicking the Show desktop button on the right side of the taskbar.

When you have multiple programs, documents, or browser windows open, you can manage them easily using Live Taskbar Preview. The *Live Taskbar Preview* feature allows you to display thumbnail and full-screen previews of all open windows.

▶ **VOCABULARY**

icons

Recycle Bin

taskbar

notification area

shortcut

Live Taskbar Preview

APPENDIX A

Hover your mouse over an icon on the taskbar to see a thumbnail version of the window, as shown in **Figure WIN–2**, then point to the thumbnail image to see a full-screen preview. You can click the full-screen image to begin working with it, or you can close the window by clicking the Close button on the thumbnail image.

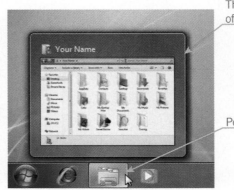

Thumbnail image of window

Point to taskbar icon

FIGURE WIN–2 Live Taskbar Preview thumbnail image

There are many ways to control what you see on the desktop, so yours may not look exactly the same as the figures in this appendix.

Step-by-Step WIN 1

1. Turn on your computer and the monitor, if necessary, to start Windows 7.
2. On the Welcome screen, click your **user name** and type your **password**, if prompted, to display the desktop.
3. Point to any icons on your desktop or taskbar, including shortcuts if there are any, and read the ScreenTip descriptions.
4. Leave the computer on with the Windows 7 desktop displayed for use in the next Step-by-Step.

Customizing Windows 7

You can customize many aspects of your Windows 7 environment by modifying properties and settings or personalizing aspects of the desktop's appearance and sounds. Many of these options can be accessed in the Appearance and Personalization window in the Control Panel, shown in **Figure WIN–3**. The *Control Panel* is used to change the settings for Windows, including how it looks and works. The Appearance and Personalization setting in the Control Panel can be displayed by clicking the Start button, clicking Control Panel, and then clicking Appearance and Personalization. There are many ways to change how you work using Windows 7—if it isn't covered in this appendix, you can explore the various options on your own.

▶ **VOCABULARY**
Control Panel

APPENDIX A

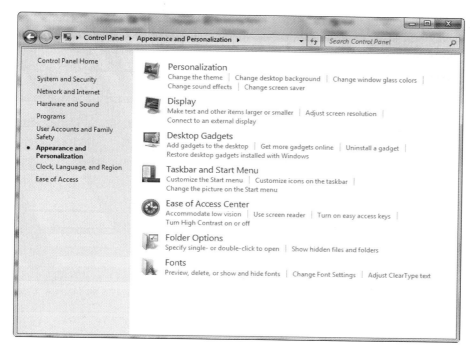

FIGURE WIN-3   Control Panel Appearance and Personalization options

Customizing the Taskbar and the Start Menu

As stated earlier, the taskbar displays the Start button and a notification area containing icons that provide information about programs and your connection status to a network or the Internet. For example, you can click the time on the right of the taskbar to view or change the time and date settings. To change which icons and notifications appear on the taskbar, click the Show hidden icons button on the taskbar, and then click the Customize link, as shown in **Figure WIN-4**. This will open the Notification Area Icons window of the Control Panel where you can choose which icons and notifications to show or hide.

Link to customize the notification area

Show hidden icons button

Customize...

12:06 PM
5/27/2010

FIGURE WIN-4   Customize the notification area

APPENDIX A

You can customize the taskbar by right-clicking it and clicking Properties to open the Taskbar tab of the Taskbar and Start Menu Properties dialog box, shown in **Figure WIN–5**. For more information on customizing the taskbar, you can click the *How do I customize the taskbar?* link at the bottom of the dialog box. Other tabs in the dialog box provide other customization options.

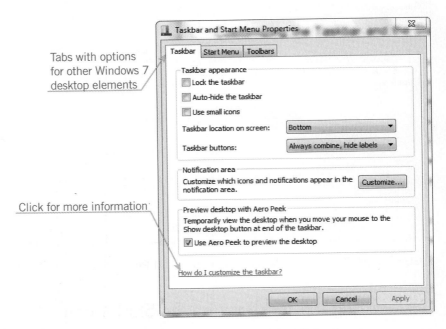

FIGURE WIN–5   Taskbar and Start Menu Properties dialog box

Clicking the Start button on the taskbar opens the Start menu. The Start menu is used for many common tasks, such as starting programs, accessing common folders, searching for files, getting help, switching to a different user account, or turning off the computer. The Start menu is divided into two panes. The left pane shows recently used programs. If there is an arrow next to the program name, you can point to it to open a list of recently used files. You can create a shortcut on the Start menu to a program you use regularly by right-clicking a program icon on the Start menu or desktop and then clicking Pin to Start Menu on the shortcut menu. Pinned icons are displayed above the bar in the left pane. To unpin an icon from the Start menu, you can right-click it and then click Unpin from Start Menu. The right pane of the Start menu displays links to the parts of Windows that you are likely to use frequently, such as your personal folders and the Control Panel.

Each user account has a picture associated with it, and this picture appears on the top of the right pane of the Start menu and on the Welcome screen when you start Windows 7. If you want to change the picture associated with your user account, click the picture at the top of the right pane of the Start menu to open the User Accounts window, click Change your picture, choose a new picture, and then click the Change Picture button at the bottom.

Step-by-Step WIN 2

1. Click the **Start** button ⊚ on the taskbar. The Start menu opens, as shown in **Figure WIN–6**. Your settings will differ.

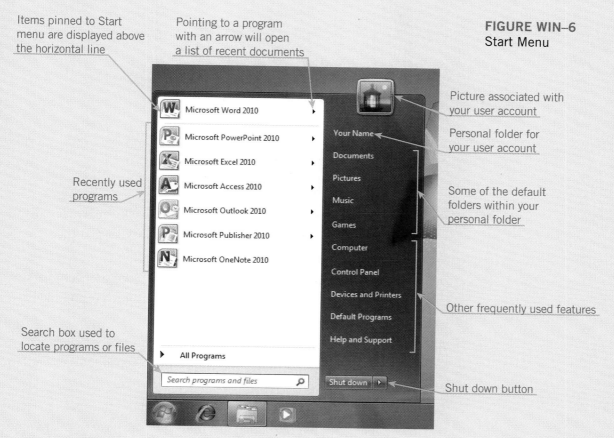

Items pinned to Start menu are displayed above the horizontal line

Pointing to a program with an arrow will open a list of recent documents

Recently used programs

Search box used to locate programs or files

FIGURE WIN–6
Start Menu

Picture associated with your user account

Personal folder for your user account

Some of the default folders within your personal folder

Other frequently used features

Shut down button

2. In the left pane, right-click a program you use frequently, and then click **Pin to Start Menu** on the shortcut menu to move it to above the bar in the left pane; this program icon will now always be displayed on the Start menu.

3. Right-click the program icon that you just pinned above the bar in the left pane of the Start menu, and then click **Unpin from Start Menu** on the shortcut menu to remove the icon.

4. If there is an arrow next to any program name on the Start menu, point to the program name to see a list of recent documents. Click a blank area of the desktop to close the Start menu.

5. Click the **date and time** button in the notification area of the taskbar to open the date and time settings window, as shown in **Figure WIN–7**.

FIGURE WIN–7
Date and time settings window

Click to open settings window

6. Right-click a blank area of the taskbar, and click **Properties** on the shortcut menu to open the Taskbar tab of the Taskbar and Start Menu Properties dialog box.

7. Click the **Auto-hide the taskbar** check box to place a check mark in it, and then click the **OK** button to close the dialog box and hide the taskbar.

8. Point to the bottom of the desktop to display the taskbar, right-click a blank area of the taskbar, and click **Properties** to open the Taskbar tab of the Taskbar and Start Menu Properties dialog box.

9. Click the **Auto-hide the taskbar** check box to remove the check mark in it, and then click the **OK** button to close the dialog box and display the taskbar again.

10. Leave the computer on with the Windows 7 desktop displayed for use in the next Step-by-Step.

Personalizing Appearance and Sound

You can change various aspects of the desktop's appearance and sounds for your computer using the Personalization window in the Control Panel. For example, you can change the background picture on your desktop, called *wallpaper*, or choose a different *screen saver*, which is the moving picture or pattern that is displayed on the screen when the computer has been inactive for a certain amount of time. You can also pick which sounds are emitted for different actions, apply another theme, or adjust the display settings. You can access these options by clicking the Start button, and then clicking Control Panel. In the Control Panel, click the Appearance and Personalization link, and then click the Personalization link to view the options for changing visuals and sounds on your computer. A shortcut to accessing these options is to right-click a blank area of the desktop and then click Personalize.

You can also add miniprograms and tools, called *gadgets*, to the desktop that can help make your computer time more enjoyable and more productive. For example, you can display updated weather, view a calendar, or track the news. You can add gadgets to the desktop by right-clicking a blank area of the desktop, clicking Gadgets to open the Gadget Gallery, and then double-clicking a gadget. You can download a gadget by clicking the Get more gadgets online link in the Gadget Gallery.

When you point to a gadget on the desktop, as shown in **Figure WIN–8**, a Close button is displayed that you can click to remove it. If the gadget can be enlarged, a Larger size button is displayed. If the gadget has settings that can be changed, an Options button is also displayed that you can use to customize it. You can click the Drag gadget button to drag the gadget to another location on the desktop. Other controls may be displayed for a particular gadget. For example, when you point to the Slideshow gadget (as shown in Figure WIN–8), the Previous, Pause, Next, and View buttons are displayed.

> **VOCABULARY**
> **wallpaper**
> **screen saver**
> **gadgets**

FIGURE WIN–8 Gadget on the desktop

Step-by-Step WIN 3

1. Right-click a blank area of the desktop, and then click **Personalize** on the shortcut menu to open the Personalization window.

2. Click the **Desktop Background** link at the bottom of the window to open the Desktop Background window, shown in **Figure WIN–9**. Depending on your settings, your screen may differ.

FIGURE WIN–9
Desktop Background window

Click a picture

Choose a position

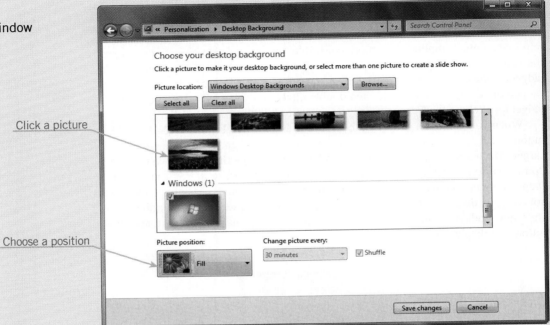

3. Scroll through the pictures available for use as a desktop background, and then click the **Cancel** button to close the dialog box without changing the desktop background.

4. In the Personalization window, click the **Screen Saver** link to open the Screen Saver Setting dialog box, shown in **Figure WIN–10**.

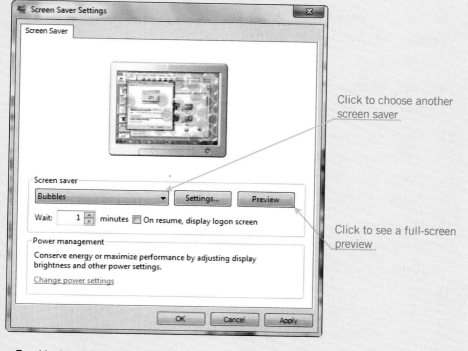

5. Under Screen saver, click the **list** arrow, click **Bubbles**, and then click the **Preview** button to see a full-screen preview of the screen saver.

6. Move the mouse or press a key to return to the dialog box, and then click the **Cancel** button to close the dialog box without changing the screen saver.

7. Click the **Close** button ![X] to close the Personalization window.

8. Right-click a blank area of the desktop, and then click **Gadgets** on the shortcut menu to open the Gadget Gallery, as shown in **Figure WIN–11**.

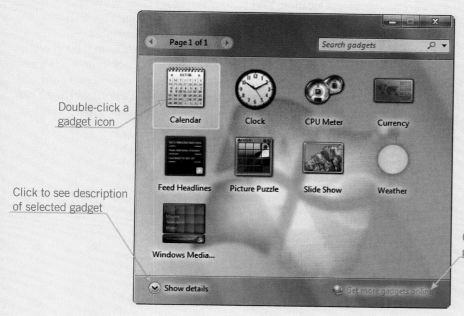

FIGURE WIN–11
Gadget Gallery

9. Click the **Show details** button 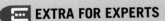, and then click the **Currency** gadget icon and read the description of this gadget at the bottom of the Gadget Gallery.

10. Click the **Show desktop** button on the right of the taskbar to reduce the Gadget Gallery window to an icon on the taskbar.

11. Hover the mouse over the Gadget Gallery icon on the taskbar to display a thumbnail image, point to the thumbnail image to display a full-size image, then click the full-size image to resume working with the Gadget Gallery window.

12. Double-click the **Calendar** gadget icon to add it to the desktop. Point to the gadget on the desktop to display its Close button, and then click the **Close** button to remove the gadget from the desktop.

13. In the Gadget Gallery, click the **Hide details** button to hide the gadget details, and then click the **Close** button on the Gadget Gallery to close it.

14. Leave the computer on with the Windows 7 desktop displayed for use in the next Step-by-Step.

Managing Files and Folders

In the lessons for individual Office programs, you learn to open, close, and save files. At times, you may need to move, rename, or delete a file as well. To manage your files, you also need to know how to use folders. A *folder* is a container for storing and organizing files, and it can also contain subfolders. Each user account has a *personal folder*, labeled with your user name that stores your frequently used folders in one convenient location. Within your personal folder, Windows 7 provides default folders that you can use as a starting point for organizing your files—such as Documents, Downloads, Music, and Pictures—or you can create your own.

Some of these common folders are located on the Start menu in the top section of the right pane, or you can click the Start button and then click your user name at the top of the Start menu's right pane to display a folder window showing the contents of the personal folder for your user account, as shown in **Figure WIN–12**. Use this figure and **Table WIN–1** to become familiar with the parts of a folder window.

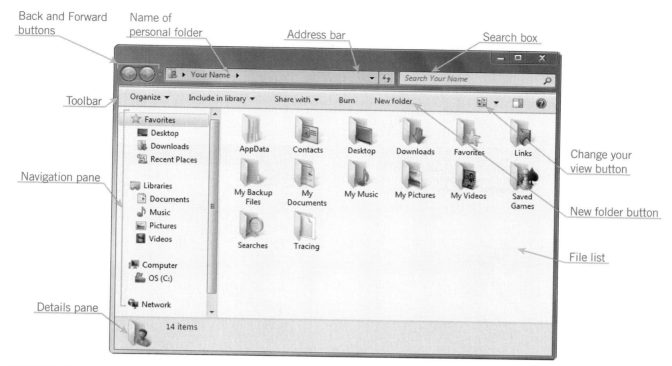

FIGURE WIN–12 Folder window

TABLE WIN–1 Elements of a folder window

ELEMENT	USED TO
Navigation pane	Access common folders; quickly navigate to any folder on the computer
Back and Forward buttons	Return to the previously viewed folder in either direction
Address bar	Display your current location; navigate to another folder
Search box	Look for a file or folder in the current folder that contains the search word or phrase
Toolbar	Perform common tasks related to the folder that is displayed
Details pane	View information about the file such as the author, size, or date created
File list	Access the files and folders located in the current folder
Column headings	Change how the files are organized by sorting, grouping, or stacking; only visible in Details view
New folder button	Create a new empty folder
Change your view button	Change the types of information about a file or the icon size displayed in the folder window

APPENDIX A

Changing Views

You might want to see different kinds of information about the files in a folder, or you might prefer the icons be a different size. You can change how files are displayed in the folder window by clicking the Change your view button repeatedly to toggle through the view options. You can also click the Change your view button arrow on the toolbar, and then drag the slider or click another view, as shown in **Figure WIN–13**.

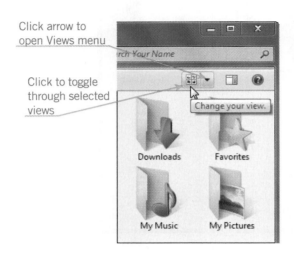
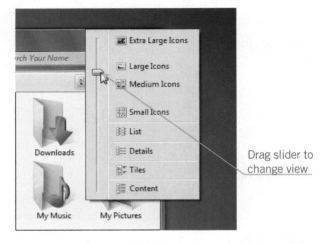

FIGURE WIN–13   Change your view button and Views menu

Create, Rename, and Delete Files and Folders

You can manage your files and folders by clicking the Organize button on the toolbar in the folder window. On the menu that is displayed, you can use the commands to cut, copy, rename, or delete a file or folder.

Deleting unneeded files or folders saves space and reduces clutter on your computer. When you delete a file or folder, a message will be displayed asking you to confirm the deletion, and then the file or folder will be temporarily stored in the Recycle Bin. This allows you to retrieve a file or folder if you deleted it accidentally. The Recycle Bin is similar to a trash can—you can throw something away, but it is not permanently gone. However, occasionally you should free up space by emptying the Recycle Bin. This will permanently delete all the files and folders that were temporarily stored there.

Copying and Moving Files and Folders

If you want to change where files and folders are stored on your computer or copy them to a different location, the easiest way is to use the drag-and-drop method. Click the file or folder you want to move or copy, drag it to another location, and drop it. If the folders are located on the same hard drive, the item will be moved so that you don't have multiple copies. If the folders are located on different hard drives, such as a network or CD, the item will be copied so that you don't lose the original.

Step-by-Step WIN 4

1. Click the **Start** button on the taskbar, and then click your **user name** in the top of the right pane to open the folder window displaying the contents of the personal folder belonging to your user account.

2. Click the **Downloads** folder to select it, and notice the folder information displayed in the Details pane.

3. Click the **New folder** button on the toolbar to create a new empty folder, and then type **Receipts** and press **Enter** to name the new folder.

4. On the toolbar, click the **Organize** button to display the menu, as shown in **Figure WIN–14**.

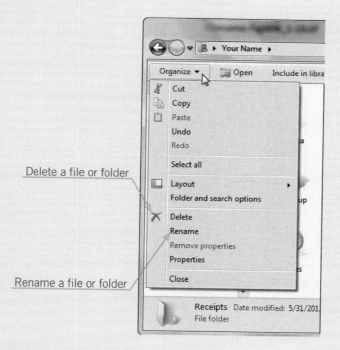

FIGURE WIN–14
Organize menu

5. Click **Rename** to select the folder name.

6. Type **Invoices** and then press **Enter** to rename the folder.

7. On the toolbar, click the **Change your view** button arrow to display the menu, notice what the current setting is, and then drag the slider to the **Details** setting to change the view. Notice the size of the icons in the folder window changes as you drag the slider.

8. On the toolbar, click the **Change your view** button arrow, and move the slider to reset the view to its previous setting.

9. Select the **Invoices** folder you created. Be sure the My Documents folder is visible within the folder window.

10. Drag the Invoices folder to the My Documents folder, as shown in **Figure WIN–15**, and drop it in its new location.

FIGURE WIN–15
Moving a folder

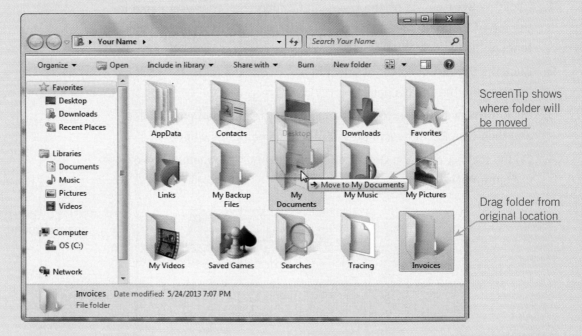

ScreenTip shows where folder will be moved

Drag folder from original location

11. Double-click the My **Documents** folder to open it, and select the **Invoices** folder you moved there.

12. Click the **Organize** button on the toolbar, and then click **Delete**. Click the **Yes** button to confirm the deletion and delete the folder.

13. Click the **Close** button on the folder window to close it.

14. Leave the computer on with the Windows 7 desktop displayed for use in the next Step-by-Step.

Getting Help

If you need more information about Windows features, the Windows Help and Support system, shown in **Figure WIN–16**, can answer questions, troubleshoot problems, and give instructions. You can access it by clicking the Start button and then clicking Help and Support.

Help and Support home button

Search Help box

Ask button

Browse Help button

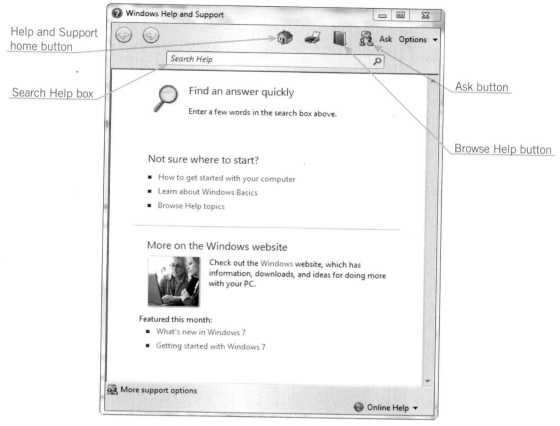

FIGURE WIN–16 Windows Help and Support

You can type a word or phrase in the Search box, browse the topics by clicking the Browse Help button, or get customer support options for your computer by clicking the Ask button. In the Not sure where to start? section, you can click a suggested help link. Because there are many different types of help you can access, it is a good idea to explore Windows Help to familiarize yourself with the various options.

Step-by-Step WIN 5

1. Click the **Start** button, then click **Help and Support** to open the Windows Help and Support window.

2. Click the **Browse Help** button on the toolbar to display a list of help categories.

3. In the Search Help box, type **Windows desktop** and press **Enter** to display a list of results.

4. In the list of results, click the **What's new with the Windows desktop?** link, and then read the article, shown in **Figure WIN–17**.

Windows Help and Support article

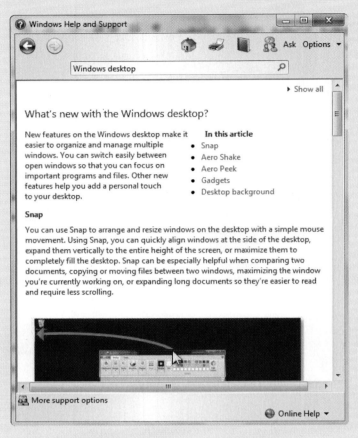

5. Click the **Help and Support home** button on the toolbar to return to the home page.

6. Click the **Ask** button on the toolbar to display the More support options window.

7. Click the **Show desktop** button on the right of the taskbar to reduce the Windows Help and Support window to an icon on the taskbar.

8. Hover the mouse over the Help icon on the taskbar to display a thumbnail image, point to the thumbnail image to display a full-size image, then click the thumbnail image to restore the Windows Help and Support window to the screen.

9. Click the **Close** button to close Windows Help and Support.

10. Leave the computer on with the Windows 7 desktop displayed for use in the next Step-by-Step.

Shutting Down Windows 7

When you are finished working on the computer, you can close your Windows 7 session and shut down the computer by clicking the Start button and then clicking the Shut down button. This action closes all programs and files and turns off the computer—it is the best option if you won't be using your computer for several days or longer.

If you point to the arrow next to the Shut down button, a menu opens, as shown in **Figure WIN–18**.

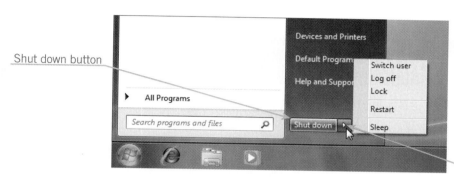

FIGURE WIN–18 Shut down button menu

The Shut down menu also provides other options, which are described in **Table WIN–2**.

TABLE WIN–2 Shut down menu options

OPTION	DESCRIPTION
Switch user	Changes users on a computer without closing programs and files first
Log off	Closes all the open programs, but does not turn off the computer
Lock	Displays the Welcome screen to prevent other people from accessing or viewing your work; useful when you will be away from the computer for short periods of time in a public place
Restart	Shuts down the computer and then starts it back up
Sleep	Power-saving mode that saves all files and programs to computer memory and allows you to quickly resume working

Not all computers are the same, so some of these options may not be available or they may operate differently. For example, the Sleep option may not be supported by your computer. On most computers, you can resume working by pressing the power button, but you may be able to press a key or use the mouse button to wake the computer. If you have questions about your computer, check the documentation or the manufacturer's Web site.

Step-by-Step WIN 6

1. Click the **Start** button and point to the arrow next to the Shut down button to open the menu and view the options.

2. Click the **Shut down** button to close Windows 7 and turn off the computer.

SUMMARY

In this appendix, you learned:

- How to start Windows 7 and log into your account.
- To identify parts of the Windows 7 desktop and their functions.
- Ways to customize Windows 7 by modifying properties and settings or personalizing aspects of the desktop's appearance and sounds.
- Methods for moving, renaming, or deleting files and folders.

- The ways to get information about Windows features; answer questions; or troubleshoot problems using the Windows Help and Support sytem.
- How to shut down Windows 7 and the purpose of the other Shut down menu options.

APPENDIX B

Understanding Outlook Fundamentals

■ **OBJECTIVES**

Upon completion of this appendix, you should be able to:

■ Start Outlook and view the folders.

■ Send and receive e-mail.

■ Enter contacts.

■ Create and manage tasks.

■ Enter appointments in the Calendar.

■ Preview and print Outlook items.

■ Exit Outlook.

■ **DATA FILES**

You do not need data files to complete this appendix.

■ **VOCABULARY**

appointment

contact

Date Navigator

e-mail

event

forward

mail server

personal information manager
    software

signature

task

To-Do List

APPENDIX B

Introduction

Microsoft Outlook 2010 is the e-mail and personal information manager (PIM) program included in the Microsoft Office 2010 suite of software. ***Personal information manager software*** is software that helps you communicate and organize business and personal information. Using Outlook, you can send and receive e-mail, add contacts to your address book, manage tasks, and enter appointments and reminders in the calendar.

Starting Outlook and Changing Views

You open Outlook by clicking the Start button on the Windows taskbar, and then clicking the program name in the Microsoft Office folder on the All Programs menu, or by double-clicking an Outlook program icon on the desktop. Once Outlook is started, you can begin using it to organize your tasks and information.

Outlook has different windows for its various functions. You access the e-mail, task, contact, and calendar windows of the program using the appropriate buttons in the Navigation Pane. Like other Office programs, Outlook organizes commands for working within each Outlook function on tabs on the Ribbon.

You can see a summary of your day in one window, including calendar events, tasks, and unread messages, by displaying Outlook Today, as shown in **Figure OL–1**. You can access this window by clicking your e-mail address (or it may be named Personal Folders, depending on how it was set up) in the Navigation Pane. Almost every part of the Outlook window can be rearranged, hidden, or customized to your specifications, so your screen may look different.

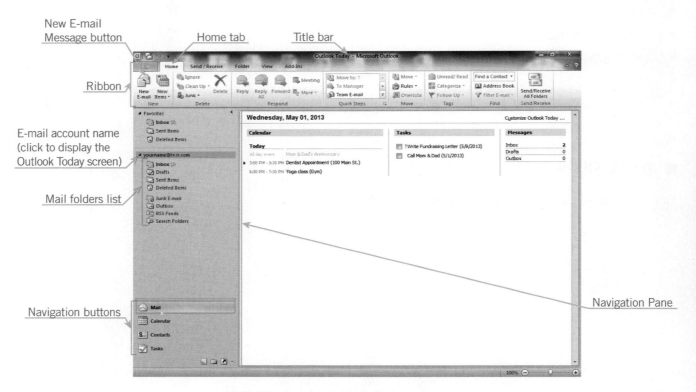

FIGURE OL–1   Outlook Today

The Navigation Pane contains buttons you can use to access the different features of Outlook:

- Mail—Displays the folders, message lists, and commands necessary for sending and receiving e-mail
- Calendar—Contains a planner you can use to record and organize appointments, meetings, holidays, and events
- Contacts—Contains names, addresses, e-mail addresses, and other information about people you contact regularly
- Tasks—Lets you create lists of tasks to be completed and assign due dates for each task

Step-by-Step OL 1

1. Click the **Start** button ⊕ on the Windows taskbar. The Start menu opens.
2. Click **All Programs**. A list of programs and program folders opens.
3. Scroll down if necessary, and click the **Microsoft Office** program folder. A list of Office programs opens.
4. Click **Microsoft Outlook 2010**. Outlook starts and the Outlook 2010 Mail window opens on the desktop. (*Note*: If you get a message that Outlook is not your default mail program, check with your instructor about whether you should set Outlook as the default mail program on your system.)
5. In the Navigation Pane, click your e-mail address (or Personal Folders) to display Outlook Today.
6. In the Navigation Pane, click the **Inbox** folder to return to the Mail window.
7. In the Navigation Pane, click the **Calendar** button to display the Calendar.
8. In the Navigation Pane, click the **Contacts** button to display the Contacts.
9. In the Navigation Pane, click the **Tasks** button to display the To-Do List.
10. In the Navigation Pane, click the **Mail** button to display the Mail window again.
11. Leave the Outlook window open for use in the next Step-by-Step.

Sending and Receiving E-Mail

When you click the Mail button in the Navigation Pane, the Mail window is displayed with the Inbox folder open. The Mail folders list, located in the Navigation Pane, contains folders you can use to organize your Outlook e-mail messages. When you click a Mail folder, the contents are displayed in the center pane.

Your list might include different categories of folders. The folders you need to become familiar with include the following:

- Inbox—Contains all the e-mail messages you have received.
- Drafts—Contains drafts of messages you have created and saved but have not yet sent.
- Sent Items—Contains a copy of each message you have sent.
- Deleted Items—Contains messages you have deleted. Messages are not permanently deleted until you empty this folder. You can configure Outlook to empty it automatically, or you can empty it manually.
- Junk E-mail—Contains the e-mail messages that you received that were considered spam or junk. Before you empty this folder, it is a good idea to review the items first to make sure you don't delete a legitimate message that was incorrectly sent to the Junk E-mail folder.
- Outbox—Contains the e-mail messages that you have written but that the computer has not yet sent.

The To-Do Bar, which summarizes the appointments and tasks for the day, may be displayed on the right side of any of the Outlook windows. On the View tab on the Ribbon, in the Layout group, you can use the To-Do Bar button to display the To-Do Bar, minimize it, or turn it off in the current view.

Creating a New E-Mail Message

Mail is probably the most used feature of Outlook. **E-mail**, short for electronic mail, is a way to send and receive messages over the Internet or any other network. Sending e-mail is as simple as entering an e-mail address, a subject, and a message, and then clicking the Send button. You open a blank e-mail message by clicking the New E-mail button on the Home tab on the Ribbon. The Untitled – Message window opens, as shown in **Figure OL–2**.

EXTRA FOR EXPERTS

You can create new folders in which to file your e-mail messages. In addition, you can create a wide variety of rules that will move e-mail you receive from a particular person or of a particular type to a specific folder as soon as it arrives in your Inbox.

▶ **VOCABULARY**

e-mail

EXTRA FOR EXPERTS

It's a good idea to check your spelling before sending a message. Use the buttons in the Proofing group on the Review tab in the message window to check spelling and grammar, use the thesaurus, or look up a word in the dictionary.

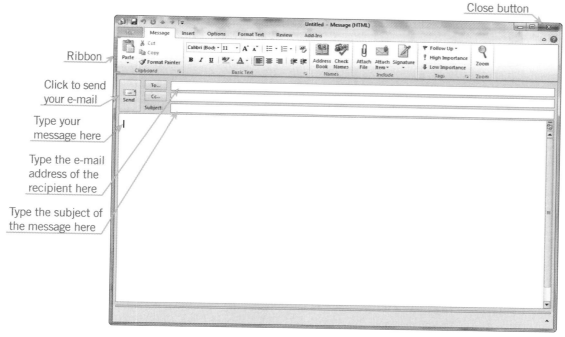

FIGURE OL–2 Untitled – Message window

If you want to use formatting options such as bullets, alignment, or colored text in your message, you can do so as long as your mail format is set to the default HTML format. You can select the text you want to format and use the buttons on the Ribbon in the message window to apply the formatting of your choice. If you want to change to a different format in your e-mail, such as Plain Text or Rich Text, you can do so using a button in the Format group on the Format Text tab. These other formats might not provide as many formatting options, though.

Many people like to include a signature with their e-mail messages. A *signature* is text and/or a graphic, such as a picture, that is added automatically to the end of a message. You can use the Signature button in the Include group on the Message tab in the message window to create one signature or as many as you like.

▶ **VOCABULARY**
signature

⚡ **WARNING**

To send and receive e-mail, your computer and Outlook software must be configured to communicate with an Internet service provider (ISP), and an e-mail account must be established. If your computer is set up to handle e-mail, you can easily send and receive e-mail using Outlook. If you need help setting up an e-mail account, research the options using Outlook Help.

Step-by-Step OL 2

The Mail window should be displayed from Step-by-Step OL 1.

1. In the Navigation Pane, click the **Inbox** folder, if necessary, to display the Inbox messages in the center pane.

2. On the Home tab, in the New group, click the **New E-mail** button to display the Untitled – Message window.

3. In the To box, type your own e-mail address.

4. In the Subject box, type **Outlook**.

5. In the message area, type **Mail is probably the most popular feature of Outlook.**

6. Select the word **Mail**. On the Message tab in the message window, in the Basic Text group, click the **Bold** button **B**.

7. Select the entire sentence. In the Basic Text group, click the **Font Color** button **A** to apply the color Red.

8. Click the **Send** button to send the message to yourself and remove the message from the screen.

9. Leave Outlook open for use in the next Step-by-Step.

EXTRA FOR EXPERTS

You can sort messages in the Inbox quickly by selecting an option in the Arrangement group on the View tab. For example, you can display all messages from Microsoft by clicking a message from Microsoft in the center pane, and then clicking the From option in the Arrangement group on the View tab.

Receiving and Replying to E-Mail

In **Figure OL–3**, the word Inbox is in bold, indicating that the Inbox folder contains unread messages. Next to the Inbox, the number 1 that is blue and in parentheses (**1**) indicates that there is one unread message in the Inbox. When the Inbox folder is selected, the messages received in the Inbox appear in the center pane of the figure. In the center pane, each message's sender, subject, and date received are displayed. The Reading pane to the right of the Inbox displays a preview of the message selected in the center pane. You can turn the Reading pane on or off or move it using the Reading pane button on the View tab.

When you reply to or forward an e-mail message, Outlook includes the original message at the bottom of your new reply or forwarded message. You can use the Options command on the Tools menu to change this setting.

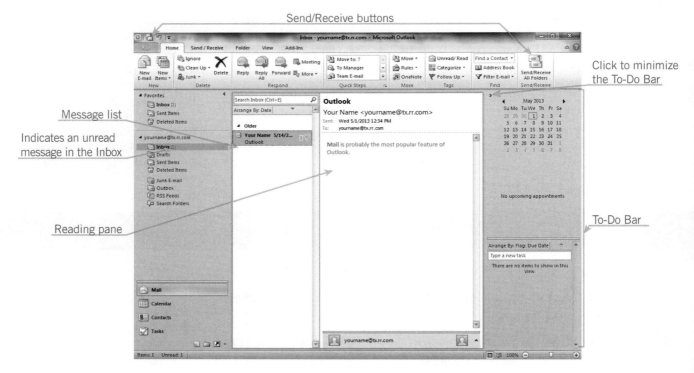

FIGURE OL–3   Inbox

You double-click a message to open it in a new window. The Message tab on the Ribbon within the message window has buttons for working with an e-mail message. In the Respond group, the Reply button lets you reply to the sender of the message you received. The Reply to All button lets you reply to all the addresses on the message. The *Forward* button lets you send the message along to someone else. The Message tab in the message window also contains buttons for moving the message to a folder, deleting it, or flagging it for follow-up.

By default, Outlook is configured to send a message as soon as you click the Send button. If you are not connected to the Internet, the message will be stored in the Outbox folder until you are connected again. Outlook is set to automatically perform a send/receive action every 30 minutes, meaning Outlook will send any messages in the Outbox folder and retrieve messages from the *mail server*, a computer at your Internet service provider (ISP) that transfers messages from one computer to another. You can change these settings in the Advanced section of the Outlook Options dialog box, which you open by clicking the Options command on the File tab. You can also click the Send/Receive All Folders button in the Send/Receive group on the Home tab or on the Quick Access Toolbar to prompt Outlook to perform a send/receive action at any time.

▶ **VOCABULARY**
forward
mail server
contact

Step-by-Step OL 3

The Mail window should be displayed from Step-by-Step OL 2.

1. On the Quick Access Toolbar, click the **Send/Receive** button, if necessary, to prompt Outlook to retrieve messages.

2. In the Inbox message list, double-click the **Outlook** message you just received from yourself to open the e-mail message in a new window.

3. On the Message tab in the message window, in the Respond group, click the **Reply** button to open a reply e-mail with RE: Outlook as the subject.

4. Type **It is important to reply to e-mails in a timely manner and to keep your messages brief.**

5. Click the **Send** button.

6. Click the **Close** button ⊠ to close the original Outlook message window.

Entering Contacts

Because Contacts stores all contact information within Outlook, Contacts is Outlook's second-most popular feature. A *contact* is the information you have about one person, such as their name, title, address, telephone and fax numbers, and e-mail address. All contacts are stored in the Address Book. You can create separate contacts lists for work, family, and friends that are separate folders within the Address Book. Adding contacts to the Address Book makes it easy for you to access that information when you want to e-mail, call, fax, or write to a contact. In fact, after you enter contacts, you can click the To button in a new e-mail message to easily access your Address Book and click the contact to whom you want to send the e-mail, so you don't have to type in the address from memory.

APPENDIX B

When you click the Contacts button in the Navigation Pane, the Contacts list is displayed in the center pane, as shown in **Figure OL–4**. The default Contacts view is Business Card, which shows the information about each contact in the contacts list organized similarly to a business card. You can click the Change View button on the View tab and then click an option on the Change View menu to view contacts in Card, Phone, or List view.

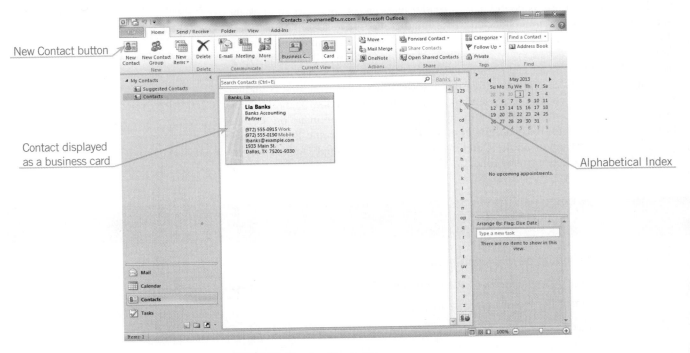

New Contact button

Contact displayed as a business card

Alphabetical Index

FIGURE OL–4   Contacts

In the Contacts window, you can use the commands on the Home tab to create a new contact, delete contacts, flag a contact for follow-up, communicate and share contacts, categorize contacts, and find contacts. Click a letter in the alphabetical index on the right side of the center pane to display contacts by the first letter of each contact's last name.

You can add new contacts easily using the New Contact button in the New group on the Home tab. Just type the contact information into the Untitled – Contact window and save it when you are finished. When creating a new contact, enter as much or as little information about a contact as you want. If you have only a person's name and e-mail address, just enter those. You can always double-click a contact to open and edit the contact to add other information.

The Save & Close button in the contact window saves the contact information (or edits to it) and closes the window. If you want to enter another contact, click the Save & New button instead, to close the current window and open a new blank contact window. You can assign the contact to a category with the Categorize button on the Contact tab in the contact window, or on the Home tab in the Contacts window. For example, you might want to categorize all work-related contacts with a green color and personal contacts with blue, so that you can distinguish them easily.

Select a contact and then click the Delete button on the Contact tab in the contact window or on the Home tab in the Contacts window to remove a contact from your contacts list.

Step-by-Step OL 4

The Mail window should be displayed from Step-by-Step OL 3.

1. In the Navigation Pane, click the **Contacts** navigation button to display the Contacts list.

2. On the Home tab, in the New group, click the **New Contact** button to display the Untitled – Contact window.

3. Enter the data for the contact, as shown in **Figure OL–5**. (Don't worry about adding underlines, parentheses, or other formatting; Outlook will add it for you. In addition, Outlook fills in the File as and Display as fields automatically.)

Save & Close button

FIGURE OL–5
Contact window

Business card

4. Click the **Save & Close** button to save the contact and close the contact window. Lia Banks' contact information now appears in the Contacts list displayed as a business card.

5. Leave Outlook open for use in the next Step-by-Step.

APPENDIX B

Creating and Managing Tasks

▶ **VOCABULARY**
task
To-Do List

A *task* is a job or duty that you must complete. Outlook's *To-Do List* is similar to a handwritten to-do list that displays all your tasks. However, in Outlook you can set reminders and due dates so that Outlook can help you stay on top of your work. A task that repeats on a regular basis, such as creating a weekly report each Friday, can be set to recur every week in your task list.

The To-Do List, shown in **Figure OL–6**, displays all your tasks and lets you arrange them in different ways, such as by due date, start date, or category. Icons beside a task in the To-Do List let you know at a glance the priority, follow-up, whether a reminder is set, and category. The Current View options in the Navigation Pane provide you with alternate ways to display tasks, such as displaying only overdue tasks or completed tasks.

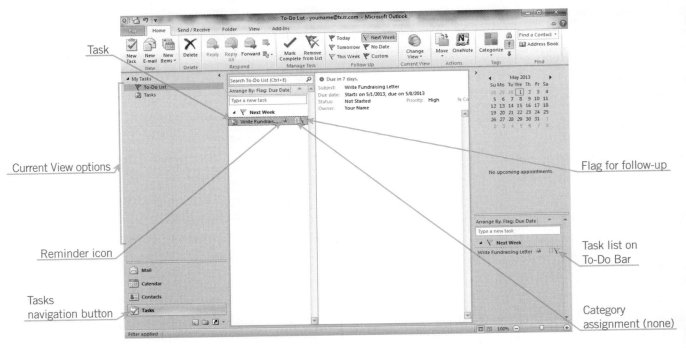

FIGURE OL–6   To-Do List

You can create a new task by clicking the New Task button in the New group on the Home tab. In the Untitled - Task window, type a subject as well as start and due dates. To set a reminder, click the Reminder check box and choose a date from the calendar that appears when you click the Reminder list arrow. On the task's due date, Outlook plays a sound and displays a notification window reminding you of the task, at which time you can respond by opening the item to change or delete the reminder, snoozing the reminder (like pressing the snooze button on an alarm clock) for 5 minutes to a week, or dismissing the reminder. You can also click the Complete check box to mark the item as completed and then dismiss the reminder.

To help you rank the importance of tasks, you can prioritize them by assigning each one a high, normal, or low priority. After you save a task, it appears in the To-Do List and in the To-Do Bar. When you complete a task, you can open the task and adjust the % Complete box to 100%, or you can right-click the flag in the To-Do List and click Mark Complete on the shortcut menu. If the completion of a task is past due, the task appears red in the To-Do List.

📠 **EXTRA FOR EXPERTS**

After you create a task, you can assign it to someone else using the Assign Task button in the Manage Task group on the Task tab in the task window. That person will receive the task by e-mail, and then he or she has the choice of accepting, declining, or assigning the task to someone else.

Step-by-Step OL 5

The Contacts window should be displayed from Step-by-Step OL 4.

1. In the Navigation Pane, click the **Tasks** button to display the To-Do List.

2. On the Home tab, in the New group, click the **New Task** button to display the Untitled – Task window.

3. Type **Write Fundraising Letter** in the Subject box.

4. Click the **Start date** list arrow to display a Calendar, and click today's date.

5. Click the **Due date** list arrow to display a calendar, and click the day that is one week from today.

6. Click the **Reminder** check box, and then click the Reminder list arrow beside it to display the calendar. Click tomorrow's date to set a reminder that will play a sound and display a Reminder dialog box tomorrow.

7. Click the **Priority** list arrow, and then click **High** to specify that the task is in the high-priority category. Your screen should look similar to **Figure OL–7**.

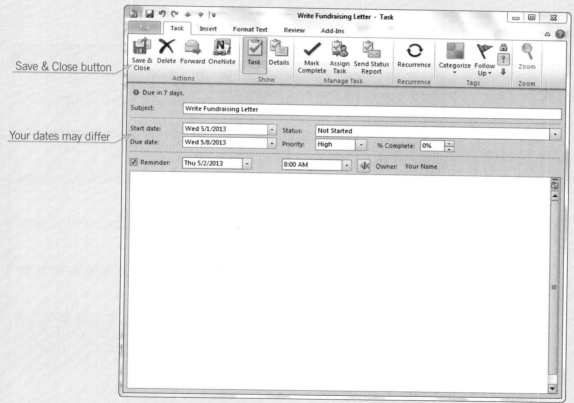

Save & Close button

Your dates may differ

FIGURE OL–7
Task window

8. On the Task tab in the task window, in the Actions group, click the **Save & Close** button to save the task and close the task window.

9. Notice that the task you created appears in the To-Do List and in the To-Do Bar, if displayed.

10. Leave Outlook open for use in the next Step-by-Step.

Entering Appointments and Events in the Calendar

The Outlook Calendar can help you keep track of appointments, meetings, events, and holidays in your schedule, just as you can on a paper calendar. But as you've learned with tasks, the Outlook Calendar can do more, such as schedule recurring appointments or events such as a birthday. You can enter the birthday information once and then set Outlook to display that event every year on the same day. You can also set up a reminder to notify you a few days in advance.

There are various ways to view the Outlook Calendar, shown in **Figure OL–8**. Click a date on the **Date Navigator**, which is the small monthly calendar at the top of the Calendar Navigation Pane, and then use the buttons on the Ribbon to display the calendar by Day, Work Week, Week, or Month.

▶ **VOCABULARY**

Date Navigator

appointment

event

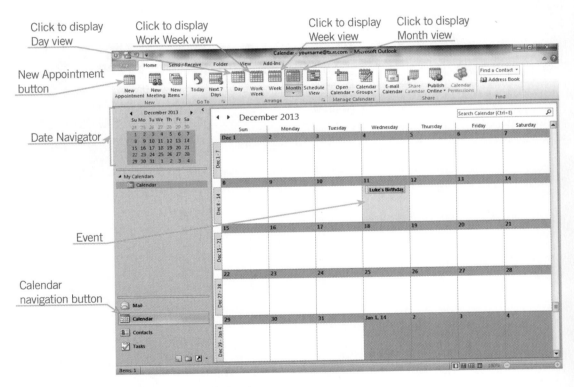

FIGURE OL–8 Calendar

To enter a new appointment or an all-day event, you click the New Appointment button in the New group on the Home tab in the Calendar window. An *appointment*, such as a dentist's appointment, has a beginning and ending time and occupies that amount of time on your calendar. An *event*, such as a birthday, lasts all day and is displayed on your calendar as a banner but does not occupy all the time in your schedule. You might have a friend's birthday entered in your calendar, but you can still schedule a dentist's appointment in your calendar for an hour on that day.

You can also schedule a meeting by clicking the New Meeting button in the New group. Outlook will send e-mail invitations to the attendees that you specify. Recipients using Outlook will have the option of accepting or declining the meeting request or proposing a new meeting time. If a recipient accepts the meeting request, a meeting entry will be added to his or her Outlook calendar.

When scheduling a recurring event, such as a class, use the Recurrence button to specify the recurrence pattern. Reminders can be set in increments of minutes, hours, or days. For a meeting, you might want to set a reminder for 30 minutes in advance; for a birthday, you might want to be reminded a few days before the event.

You can double-click an event or appointment in the calendar to open it and edit it. If it is a recurring event, you might see a message asking if you want to edit the entire series of events or just this one occurrence.

EXTRA FOR EXPERTS

Instead of requiring you to enter each holiday in the calendar, Outlook has compiled the major holidays for various countries/regions and religions into groups. To add the holiday group of your choice, choose the Options command on the File tab and click Calendar in the Outlook Options dialog box. In the Calendar options section, click the Add Holidays button to select a location whose holidays you want added to your calendar.

Step-by-Step OL 6

The To-Do List should be displayed from Step-by-Step OL 5.

1. In the Navigation Pane, click the **Calendar** button to display the Calendar.

2. In the Date Navigator, click tomorrow's date to display it in daily view.

3. On the Home tab, in the Arrange group, click the **Week** button to display the weekly view.

4. In the Arrange group, click the **Month** button to display the monthly view.

5. On the Home tab, in the New group, click the **New Appointment** button to display the Untitled – Appointment window.

6. Type **Luke's Birthday** in the Subject box.

7. Click the Start time list arrow. Use the arrows on the calendar to move to **December** of the current (or coming) year. Click day **11** on the calendar. You do not need to set the time in the hour boxes.

8. Click the **All day event** check box. Notice the End time is changed automatically to match the start date and time and the hour boxes are dimmed. Your screen should look similar to **Figure OL–9**.

FIGURE OL–9
Event window

Click to display a calendar

All day event check box

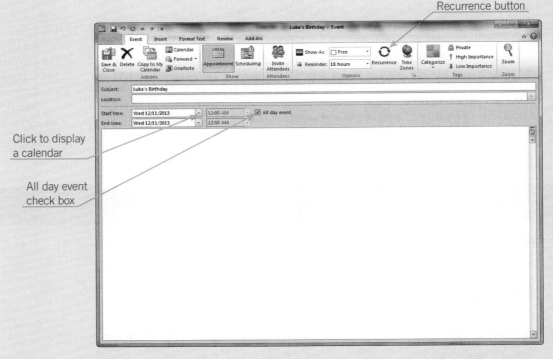

9. On the Event tab in the appointment window, in the Options group, click the **Recurrence** button to display the Appointment Recurrence dialog box.

10. In the Recurrence pattern area, click the **Yearly** option button, as shown in **Figure OL–10**, and then click **OK** to set Luke's birthday as a yearly event.

FIGURE OL–10
Appointment Recurrence dialog box

Yearly option button

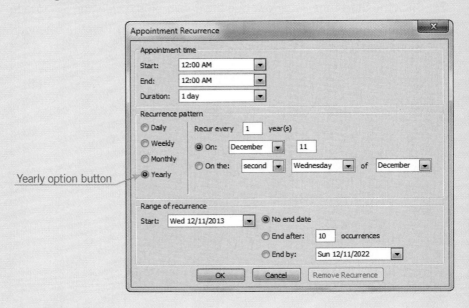

11. On the Recurring Event tab in the appointment window, in the Actions group, click the **Save & Close** button to save the event and close the window.

12. In the Calendar, click the arrows in the Date Navigator to go to the month of December to see the event on the calendar.

13. Leave Outlook open for use in the next Step-by-Step.

Previewing and Printing Outlook Items

You can print individual calendars, e-mail messages, contacts, and tasks. You can preview how your item will look when printed and change formatting and printing options in Backstage view before you click the Print button.

When you choose Print on the File tab, Backstage view displays the Print button and default print settings in the center pane of the window and a preview of the currently selected item (such as calendar month, task, e-mail message, or contact list) in the right pane.

To change a print setting in the center pane, click the setting you want to change, and then select a new option from the gallery that opens. You can preview any page in a multipage item, such as a contacts list or detailed e-mail message, using the scroll bars or the Next Page and Previous Page buttons in the lower-left corner of the right pane. When you move the mouse pointer over the preview, the pointer changes to a magnifying glass that you can click to zoom in and out. You can click the One Page button in the lower-right corner of the right pane to display the entire page within the preview pane.

The settings and options available in Backstage view will differ according to the printer you are using and the item you are printing.

Step-by-Step OL 7

The Calendar should be displayed from Step-by-Step OL 6.

1. Click the **File** tab, and then click **Print** to display Backstage view.

2. If necessary, click **Monthly Style** in the Settings area, as shown in **Figure OL–11**.

FIGURE OL–11
Printing options in Backstage view

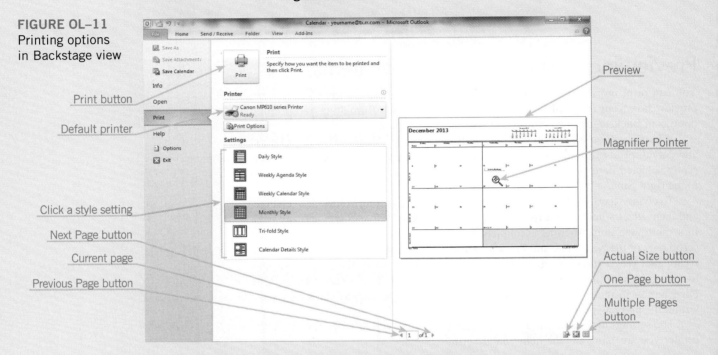

Print button

Default printer

Click a style setting

Next Page button

Current page

Previous Page button

Preview

Magnifier Pointer

Actual Size button

One Page button

Multiple Pages button

3. On the preview, click the magnifying glass pointer on the *Luke's Birthday* event to zoom in.

4. In the lower-right corner, click the **One Page** button to view the entire calendar month on the screen.

5. In the Settings area, click the **Calendar Details** style to preview that style in the right pane.

6. In the Settings area, click the **Monthly Style** setting.

7. Click the **Print** button to print the page. (*Note*: If you have been instructed not to print, do not click the Print button.)

8. Leave Outlook open for use in the next Step-by-Step.

Exiting Outlook

When you are working at your computer, you may find that you leave Outlook open most of the day and check your e-mail periodically along with updating tasks and adding appointments. When you are finished working in Outlook, you can close it using the Exit command on the File tab or by clicking the Close button on the title bar.

COMPUTER ETHICS

E-mail has many advantages—it is easy to compose and can be rapidly sent. But some advantages can tempt misuse, including being able to send the same message to many people at once. Sending unsolicited bulk e-mail is called spamming. Spamming generates unwanted junk e-mail, wastes time as people sort through it, and violates basic e-mail ethics. Outlook has a Junk E-mail Filter you can use to identify and manage junk mail.

Step-by-Step OL 8

The Calendar should be displayed from Step-by-Step OL 7.

1. Click the **File** tab, and then click **Exit** to quit the program.

SUMMARY

In this appendix, you learned:

- Personal information manager software helps you organize and communicate information.

- The Navigation Pane buttons let you access the mail, calendar, contacts, and task features of Outlook.

- Sending e-mail requires entering an e-mail address, a subject, and a message, and then clicking the Send button.

- The Reading pane lets you view a message without opening it in a new window.

- Adding contacts to the Contacts list makes it easy for you to access that information when you want to e-mail, call, fax, or write to a contact.

- The Outlook To-Do List lets you set reminders and due dates to help you organize and accomplish your tasks.

- The Outlook Calendar can help you schedule appointments, meetings, holidays, and other important events.

- You can preview and print calendars, e-mail messages, contacts, and tasks in Backstage view using the Print command on the File tab.

GLOSSARY

A

absolute reference   In Excel, a permanent reference to a cell, which does not change in relation to the location of the formula.

action button   A shape in PowerPoint that, when clicked, triggers a commonly understood action like going to the next or previous slide or playing a movie or sound.

active cell   The currently selected cell in an Excel worksheet.

alignment   The position of text in relation to the margins in a document or the edges of a text box, cell, or placeholder.

animation   Visual or sound effect added to individual text, a picture, a chart, or other object on a slide and used to control the flow of information and add interest to a PowerPoint presentation.

appointment   An entry in the Outlook Calendar that has a beginning and end time.

argument   The text, number, or cell references on which an Excel function is to be performed.

arithmetic operator   The element of a formula that performs basic mathematical operations to produce numeric results in an Excel formula.

Auto Fill   A feature in Excel that automatically fills in adjacent worksheet cells with data in any direction.

B

Backstage view   A feature in Microsoft 2010 programs which allows access to file-related commands, such as those used to open, save, and close documents.

badge   A small label with a number or letter that appears on each command on the Ribbon when you activate KeyTips.

building blocks   Predesigned, reusable document parts or design objects.

bullets   Symbols that mark the beginning of each entry in a list.

business information set   A collection of data in Publisher, such as name, address, and job title, that can be saved together as a set and used repeatedly to populate future publications.

C

cell   The rectangle where a column and row intersect in an Excel worksheet or Word table.

cell reference   The column letter heading followed by the row number heading that identifies a worksheet cell, such as B5.

cell style   A defined combination of cell formatting characteristics in Excel, such as number, alignment, font, border, and fill.

characters   Individual letters, numbers, symbols, punctuation marks, and spaces.

chart   A graphical representation of numeric data.

chart area   In Excel, the complete chart and all its elements, including the plot area, titles, axes, legend, and any other objects.

chart sheet   A separate worksheet in an Excel workbook that contains a chart.

clip art   Predefined set of ready-made artwork, usually created with a computer, that comes with Microsoft Office programs.

Clipboard   An area of memory that temporarily stores a cut or copied selection.

collate   To print the pages in a document or file in a specific order.

color scheme   A predesigned set of coordinated colors for a publication.

column   The cells that display vertically in an Excel worksheet or other table. In Excel, cells are labeled with headings from left to right across the top of the worksheet, beginning with A through Z, then AA through AZ, and so on.

columns   A way to format text where it flows from the bottom of one vertical section to the top of the next.

comparison operator   A sign or symbol in an Excel formula used to compare two values to obtain a logical value (either TRUE or FALSE).

conditional formatting   A feature in Excel that enables you to apply specific formatting to cells that meet specific conditions.

constant   A number entered directly into an Excel formula that does not change.

contact   In Outlook, the set of information about one person, such as name, title, address, telephone and fax numbers, and e-mail address.

content control   A small program within a placeholder that saves the content entered in the placeholder and displays it automatically in all locations in the document using that same placeholder.

contextual tabs   The tabs on the Ribbon that appear only when you have selected a specific object or you are completing a specific task, and provide commands that relate to the selected object or the task that you are performing.

Control Panel   A Windows 7 tool providing options for selecting and changing the settings for Windows, including how it looks and works.

copy   To duplicate a selection so you can paste it into another position without deleting it from its original location.

cover page   The first page of a Word document that provides introductory information about the document, such as the title, author, and date.

crop   To remove unwanted parts of a picture or object.

cut   To remove a selection from a position in a file so you can paste it into another position; in Excel, to remove the contents (data and formatting) from a cell or range so they can be pasted elsewhere.

D

data marker   A dot, bar, or symbol used to represent one number from an Excel worksheet in a chart.

data series   A series of related values from an Excel worksheet graphically represented by a unique color or pattern in the plot area of a chart.

data source   A range of cells in an Excel worksheet that contain the data for a chart.

data type   The property of an Access field that determines the kind of values (such as text or number) contained in that field.

database   A tool used to collect and organize information.

database management system (DBMS)   A program designed to store, organize, and manage large amounts of data.

database objects   Elements that allow you to interact with the data in Access.

datasheet   In Access, a table with columns and rows similar to a spreadsheet.

datasheet selector   The button in the upper-left corner of an Access datasheet that selects all the records in the datasheet.

Date Navigator   A small monthly calendar in Outlook from which you can choose a date to view.

desktop   The main area of the computer screen that is displayed when you turn the computer on and log on to Windows 7 with your user name and password.

desktop publishing software   The software used to combine text and graphics to produce high quality marketing and communications documents for print on a personal desktop printer or by a commercial printer.

destination file   The file into which an object is inserted when integrating between Office programs.

destination program   The program used to create the destination file in the process of integration.

dialog box launcher   A small arrow in the lower-right corner of a group on the Ribbon that you click to open a dialog box or task pane with more options for executing related commands.

document   Written information printed on paper or distributed electronically.

drag   To move the mouse pointer over an object, press and hold the mouse button, and then move the mouse, bringing the selected object with it.

drag-and-drop method   To use the mouse to move or copy a selection by dragging a selection and dropping it in a new location.

drawing objects   Shapes, curves, and lines that become part of a document, worksheet, or presentation, rather than being a separate file.

drop cap   A large initial capital letter or a large first word used to add visual interest to text.

E

e-mail   Short for electronic mail; a way to send and receive messages over the Internet or another network.

embed   To place a copy of an object in the destination file that is no longer connected to the original object in the source file.

embedded chart   A chart that is a graphic object saved as part of the Excel worksheet in which the data source resides.

error value   In Excel, an indication that a formula has resulted in an error.

event   An entry in the Outlook Calendar that lasts all day, or 24 hours; it is displayed as a banner on the calendar but does not occupy all the time in the schedule.

export   To convert data from a source program's format to the format of the destination program while working in the source program.

F

field   A single characteristic or piece of information in an Access database table.

field name   Identifies a field in an Access database.

field properties   Characteristics that control the appearance and behavior of a field in an Access database.

field value   A piece of information stored in a field in a database table.

fill handle   A little black square in the lower-right corner of the selected cell in an Excel worksheet; it is used to fill a range cells with data based on contents of the selected cells.

filter   To display data that meets certain criteria or a specific set of conditions in an Excel worksheet or an Access datasheet.

first-line indent   Indenting only the first line of a paragraph in a document.

floating object   An object that is not connected to the text in a document; text can wrap around and flow in front of or behind it.

folder   A container for storing and organizing files in Windows 7.

font   The design of a set of letters and numbers.

font scheme   A set of fonts in styles and sizes that complement each other, for use in a publication.

font styles   Variations in the shape or weight of a font's characters.

footer   Text or graphics that appears in the bottom margin of each page in a document, presentation, or worksheet.

foreign key   The primary key from one Access database table as it appears in another related table.

form   An Access database object that provides a way to enter new records into the database or to edit data in existing records.

Form Wizard   A tool in Access that walks you through the process of creating a form.

Format Painter   A tool that copies multiple formatting characteristics from selected text and then applies the same formatting to other parts of the presentation, document, publication, or worksheet.

formula   A set of instructions used to perform calculations on values in an Excel worksheet.

formula bar   Located next to the Name box in the Excel program window and displays the value or formula of the active cell.

forward   To send a message to a different e-mail address in Outlook.

freeze panes   To lock specified rows or columns into place in the Excel worksheet window.

function   A built-in shortcut for entering formulas in Excel.

G

gadgets   Mini programs and tools located in the Windows 7 desktop that can help make your computer time more enjoyable and productive.

gallery   A set of options on the Ribbon that shows you a sample end result.

gridlines   Lines extending from the vertical or horizontal axes across the plot area of a chart.

groups   A logical set of related commands on a Ribbon tab.

H

hanging indent   Indenting all the lines in a paragraph from the left except the first line.

header   Text or graphics that appears in the top margin of each page in a document, presentation, or worksheet.

horizontal axis   A line on a chart used for showing categories, also called the X-axis.

I

I-beam   The shape of the mouse pointer when it is positioned in a text area.

icon   A small picture that represents a program, folder, file, or other objects and can appear on the desktop, the Ribbon, a menu, the taskbar, etc.

import   To convert data from a source program's format to the format of the destination program, while working in the destination program.

indent   The space between text and the margin.

inline object   An object that appears on the same line as text and moves with the text around it.

insertion point   A blinking vertical bar that signals where any newly typed text will appear.

integration   The process of using information in a file created in one program and incorporating it into a file created in another program.

interface   A uniform set of commands and elements that create an environment and means for interacting with a computer program.

K

key value   The value in the primary key field that makes the record unique in a database.

KeyTip   A label that appears on each button, menu, or command on the Ribbon when you press the ALT key and allows you to use the keyboard instead of the mouse to execute the command.

L

landscape   Horizontal page orientation.

launch   To start a program.

layout   The arrangement of text and other objects on a PowerPoint slide.

layout masters   Master slides in a presentation that store information about the fonts, colors, effects, and arrangement of each type of slide layout.

leader   A dotted, dashed, or solid line used to fill the empty space before a tab stop.

legend   A list that identifies the patterns or colors of the data series or categories in a chart.

line spacing   A setting that determines the vertical distance between lines of text in a paragraph.

link   In the integration technique of object linking and embedding (OLE), the connection between an object in the source file and an object in the destination file, or the process of creating that connection.

list   A series of related words, numbers, or phrases, with each item in the list starting with a bullet or number.

Live Preview   An Office 2010 feature that applies the editing or formatting change to your document as you point to a gallery option.

Live Taskbar Preview   A Windows 7 feature that allows you to display thumbnail and full-screen previews of all open windows.

M

mail merge   The creation of a set of Word documents that are identical except for custom or personalized information in specific areas; the personalized information is integrated into the Word document from another data source such as a Word table or Excel spreadsheet.

mail server   A computer at an Internet Service Provider (ISP) that transfers messages from one computer to another.

margins   The areas of white space that border the text on the edges of a page.

masters   Blueprints that control the layout and design of the slides, handouts, and notes in a PowerPoint presentation.

merge fields   Placeholders in the main document of a mail merge that indicate where the information from the data source will go.

Microsoft Office 2010   A group of computer programs that provide different tools for completing certain tasks.

Mini toolbar   A small toolbar of common formatting commands that becomes available when you select text.

mixed reference   A cell reference in Excel that contains both absolute and relative cell references.

N

Name box   In Excel, a box located below the Ribbon that displays the cell reference of the active cell.

negative indent   An indent that extends into the left margin.

nonprinting symbols   Spaces, paragraph marks, tabs, and other symbols within a document that affect the appearance of a document but are not printed.

Notes pane   An area in the PowerPoint program window in which you can type speaker notes for the active presentation.

notification area   The section of the Windows 7 taskbar with the time and icons that provide information about programs and computer settings.

O

object   In object linking and embedding (OLE), the information from the source file that is displayed in the destination file.

object linking and embedding (OLE)   An integration technology in Office that allows you to share information between Office programs.

Office   See *Microsoft Office 2010*.

operating system   The program that manages and controls the basic operations of a computer.

operator   A sign or symbol that indicates what calculation is to be performed in a formula in Excel.

order of operation   A specific sequence used to calculate the value of a formula in Excel.

orphan   A single line that appears at the bottom of a page in a document.

Outline tab   In PowerPoint, a tab that displays the title and text of each slide in a presentation in outline form.

P

page borders   Decorative lines that frame the page in a Word document.

page break   A command that ends a page and starts a new one in a Word document.

paragraph   Any amount of text or other items followed by a paragraph mark.

password   A secret set of characters that a user types to log on to a computer or account.

paste   To insert copied or moved contents in another location.

personal folder   A location on the computer labeled with the user name that stores frequently used folders for that account.

personal information manager software   Software that helps you communicate and organize business and personal information.

picture   Digital photograph or image.

placeholder   Within an Office program, a box that appears in a specific location in a file and that indicates the type of text or object to be inserted in the box.

plot area   The area in an Excel chart where the values from the data series are displayed graphically.

point size   A measurement for the height of characters.

portrait   Vertical page orientation.

presentation   A collection of slides that communicate ideas, facts, suggestions, or other information to an audience.

presentation software   Software that lets you prepare a series of slides that are referred to collectively as a presentation.

primary key   A field that uniquely identifies each record in an Access table.

publication   A document that is created to market a product or communicate a message to an audience.

pull quote   In Word or Publisher, an enlarged quotation that is placed on the page for emphasis.

Q

query   An Access database object that allows you to answer specific questions about the data in a database.

Query Wizard   A tool in Access that guides you through the process of creating a query.

Quick Access Toolbar   A toolbar located on the left side of a program window's title bar; it can be customized with commands used most frequently.

Quick Part   In Word, a type of building block made up of an image and/or text that you can create, save, and reuse.

R

range   A group of select adjacent cells.

record   All of the related information about a particular item in an Access table.

record selector   The box to the left of a row that selects a single record in an Access table.

record source   The underlying data in an Access database used to create forms, reports, and queries.

Recycle Bin   A storage location on the computer for the files and folders you have deleted.

relational database   Information stored in separate tables that are connected through common fields.

relative reference   In Excel, a reference to a cell that changes in relation to the location of the formula in the worksheet.

report An Access database object that is a formatted display or printout of the contents of one or more tables in a database.

Report Wizard A tool in Access that guides you through the process of creating a report.

Ribbon An element of the program window that displays and organizes the commands and tools for a program into tabs and groups for easy access.

row The cells that display horizontally and are numbered consecutively down the left side of an Excel worksheet.

run To perform an Access query with the most recent data, and to give instructions to display the records and fields in the original query design.

S

scratch area In Publisher, a workspace that you can use to store or work with graphics or text boxes.

screen saver A moving picture or pattern that is displayed on the screen when the computer has been inactive for a certain amount of time.

screenshot A picture of a computer screen or part of a screen.

ScreenTip A box that appears when you rest the mouse pointer on a button and that displays the name of the button, a keyboard shortcut if available, and a description of the button's function.

select To highlight text, an object, a cell, or a range of cells.

select query A query in Access that retrieves specific data out of a record source for you to use.

selection handles Small circles that are displayed at the sides and corners of a selected text box or graphic and are used to resize the object.

sheet See *worksheet*.

sheet tab Displays the name of each sheet in the workbook.

shortcut An icon that points to a program or document to provide easy access; to open a program or document you double-click the icon.

signature Text or a graphic, such as a picture, that is added automatically to the end of an e-mail message.

simple form An Access form that includes all of the fields from the selected record source.

slide A single image in a PowerPoint presentation composed of text, graphics, or other content.

slide master The slide in a presentation that stores information about the theme (including fonts and background colors), and the layout (position and size of placeholders).

Slide pane In PowerPoint, an area of the screen that displays the slide selected in the Slides tab or Outline tab.

Slides tab In PowerPoint, a tab that displays thumbnails of the slides in a presentation.

Smart Tag button In Publisher, a circle icon with an i in the center that appears when you point to or click on data that is part of a business information set; clicking on it displays a shortcut menu for editing, saving, or updating business information sets in Publisher.

SmartArt graphic A predesigned diagram made up of shapes that contains text and illustrates a concept or idea.

sort To rearrange selected data alphabetically, numerically, or chronologically.

source file The file containing the original information when transferring data between programs.

source program In integration, the program used to create the source file.

sparkline In Excel, a miniature chart embedded in the background of a single cell.

spreadsheet software A program used to electronically calculate, analyze, and visually represent numerical data.

story All the text within a single text box or linked text boxes.

style A reusable set of character or paragraph formats stored with a name.

suite A combination of Office programs packaged together.

syntax A set of established rules that specifies how a function must be entered in Excel.

T

tab Category of commands on the Ribbon that relate to a particular activity. In Word, a stop used to align or position text in a document.

table A grid of horizontal rows and vertical columns of numbers, text, or graphics. In Access, a database object that stores information related to a specific subject, made up of a collection of records and fields.

task A job or duty that you must complete and can be tracked in Outlook.

Glossary

taskbar A horizontal strip at the bottom of the Windows 7 desktop containing the Start button, a section showing which files or folders you have open and allowing you to switch between them, and a notification area.

template A sample file included with an Office program that provides a pattern or model for a new document, worksheet, presentation, or publication.

text box A container for text that can be positioned like a graphic.

text wrapping The flow of text around the edges of an object.

themes Sets of formatting choices that include colors, fonts, and effects that were predesigned to work well together in a Word document, PowerPoint presentation, Excel worksheet, or Access database.

thumbnails Miniature pictures of pages in a Word document or Publisher publication or of slides in a PowerPoint presentation.

title In Excel, the descriptive name that identifies the chart, or the chart's axes.

To-Do List A list that displays all your tasks in Outlook.

transition An animated effect in PowerPoint that controls how one slide is removed from the screen and the next one appears during a slide show.

U

user account A collection of information that contains unique settings and preferences and tells Windows which files and programs on a computer a specific user may access.

user name A word or phrase that identifies a person's account on the computer.

V

vertical axis The line on chart used for plotting values, also called the Y-axis.

W

wallpaper The background picture on the computer desktop.

watermark Text or a graphic that appears behind text in a document.

widow A single line that appears at the top of a page in a document.

word-processing software A program that lets you insert and manipulate text and graphics to create all kinds of professional-looking documents.

word wrap A feature that automatically continues text to the next line within a paragraph when you enter new text.

WordArt A drawing tool that turns text characters into a graphic object.

workbook An Excel file that consists of a worksheet or a collection of related worksheets.

workbook window The area of the Excel program window where the active worksheet is displayed.

worksheet In Excel, a grid with columns and rows where you enter and summarize data.

INDEX

Index

Index